GARDNER'S
ART
through the
AGES

THE WESTERN PERSPECTIVE

THIRTEENTH EDITION

BACKPACK EDITION
Modern Europe and America

FRED S. KLEINER

WADSWORTH
CENGAGE Learning™

Australia • Brazil • Japan • Korea • Mexico • Singapore • Spain • United Kingdom • United States

Gardner's Art through the Ages: The Western Perspective, Thirteenth Edition, Modern Europe and America, Book D
Fred S. Kleiner

Publisher: Clark Baxter

Senior Development Editor: Sharon Adams Poore

Assistant Editor: Kimberly Apfelbaum

Editorial Assistant: Nell Pepper

Senior Media Editor: Wendy Constantine

Senior Marketing Manager: Diane Wenckebach

Marketing Communications Manager: Heather Baxley

Senior Project Manager, Editorial Production: Lianne Ames

Senior Art Director: Cate Rickard Barr

Senior Print Buyer: Judy Inouye

Production Service/Layout: Joan Keyes,
    Dovetail Publishing Services

Text Designer: tani hasegawa

Photo Researchers: Sarah Evertson, Stephen Forsling

Cover Designer: tani hasegawa

Cover Image: HENRY MOORE working on the plaster for
Three Piece Sculpture: Vertebrae 1968–1969. Detail.
(LH 580), Perry Green, ca. 1969. © Keystone/Getty
Images. Reproduced with permission of the Henry Moore
Foundation.

Compositor: Thompson Type

For product information and technology assistance, contact us at
Cengage Learning Academic Resource Center,
1-800-423-0563
For permission to use material from this text or product, submit all
requests online at **www.cengage.com/permissions.**
Further permissions questions can be emailed to
permissionrequest@cengage.com

Library of Congress Control Number: 2008938884

ISBN-13: 978-0-495-79462-2
ISBN-10: 0-495-79462-7

Wadsworth
25 Thomson Place
Boston, MA 02210-1202
USA

Cengage Learning products are represented in Canada by Nelson
Education, Ltd.

For your course and learning solutions, visit **academic.cengage.com**

Purchase any of our products at your local college store or at our
preferred online store **www.ichapters.com**

Printed in the United States of America
1 2 3 4 5 6 7 13 12 11 10 09

About the Cover Art

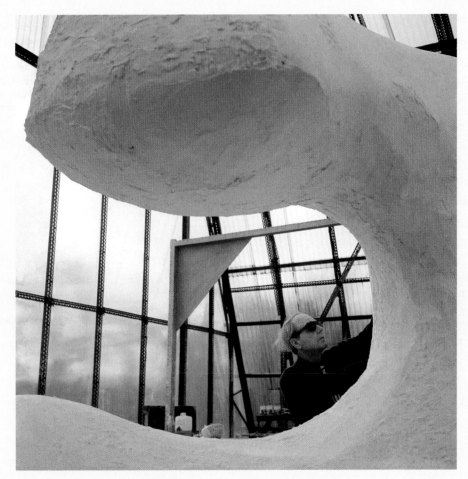

HENRY MOORE working on the plaster for *Three Piece Sculpture: Vertebrae 1968–1969*. Detail. (LH 580), Perry Green, England, ca. 1969.

Known for his large organically shaped sculptures, HENRY MOORE (1898–1986) often worked on a grand scale, and although the forms in his bronze *Three Piece Sculpture: Vertebrae 1968–1969* are organic, the vertebrae were enlarged to such an extent that the work appears abstract. Size is important not only in scaling a work to its surroundings, but also in managing the logistics of creating, transporting, and displaying large works of modern sculpture. Moore intended his large sculptures to be placed in expansive landscapes so they could be appreciated from all angles under various lighting conditions, like those the change of seasons provides. He believed that the barriers between art and viewers were arrogant and pretentious, which is why visitors to Perry Green are meant to touch and even lean against the large works on display there.

Moore often created a model, a plaster maquette, small enough to be held in the palm of his hand before making an intermediary working model made of plaster on which he could make changes, as we see him doing here. For a bronze piece such as this one, once he was satisfied with the plaster it was prepared for casting and sent to a bronze foundry where the ancient lost-wax method of casting produced the version of the sculpture exhibited at Perry Green.

In contrast to the modern notion of the artist as a solitary genius, most artists before the 14th century toiled in anonymity in the service of their patrons, whether Egyptian pharaohs, Roman emperors, or medieval bishops. *Art through the Ages* surveys the art of all periods from prehistory to the present and examines how artworks of all kinds, anonymous or signed, have always reflected the historical contexts in which they were created.

CONTENTS

PREFACE   vii
BEFORE 1300   xi

CHAPTER 21
EUROPE AND AMERICA, 1700 TO 1800   583

Rococo   583

The Enlightenment   589

Neoclassicism   598

▌ WRITTEN SOURCES: Femmes Savantes and Salon Culture   585

▌ WRITTEN SOURCES: Diderot on Chardin   592

▌ ART AND SOCIETY: The Grand Tour and Veduta Painting   597

▌ ART AND SOCIETY: The Excavations of Herculaneum and Pompeii   598

▌ ARTISTS ON ART: David on Greek Style and Public Art   600

THE BIG PICTURE   607

CHAPTER 22
EUROPE AND AMERICA, 1800 TO 1870   609

Art under Napoleon   609

Romanticism   616

Realism   630

Architecture   642

Photography   647

▌ ART AND SOCIETY: The Romantic Spirit in Art, Music, and Literature   622

▌ ARTISTS ON ART: Delacroix in Morocco   624

▌ ARTISTS ON ART: Courbet on Realism   631

▌ MATERIALS AND TECHNIQUES: Lithography   633

▌ MATERIALS AND TECHNIQUES: Daguerreotype, Calotype, and Wet-Plate Photography   646

THE BIG PICTURE   651

CHAPTER 23
EUROPE AND AMERICA, 1870 TO 1900   653

Impressionism   654

Post-Impressionism   663

Symbolism   670

Sculpture   675

Architecture and Decorative Arts   678

▌ ART AND SOCIETY: Academic Salons and Independent Art Exhibitions   655

▌ ARTISTS ON ART: Renoir on the Art of Painting   659

▌ ART AND SOCIETY: Japonisme   661

▌ MATERIALS AND TECHNIQUES: 19th-Century Color Theory   664

▌ ARTISTS ON ART: The Letters of Vincent van Gogh   666

▌ ARTISTS ON ART: Rodin on Movement in Art and Photography   677

THE BIG PICTURE   683

CHAPTER 24
EUROPE AND AMERICA, 1900 TO 1945   685

Europe, 1900 to 1920   686

America, 1900 to 1930   708

Europe, 1920 to 1945   716

America, 1930 to 1945   729

Architecture   736

▌ ARTISTS ON ART: Matisse on Color 688

▌ ART AND SOCIETY: Science and Art in the Early
20th Century 691

▌ ART AND SOCIETY: Gertrude and Leo Stein
and the Avant-Garde 694

▌ ART AND SOCIETY: Primitivism and Colonialism 696

▌ ARTISTS ON ART: Picasso on Cubism 700

▌ ARTISTS ON ART: Futurist Manifestos 703

▌ ART AND SOCIETY: Art "Matronage" in America 709

▌ ART AND SOCIETY: The Armory Show 710

▌ ART AND SOCIETY: Degenerate Art 721

▌ ARTISTS ON ART: Brancusi, Hepworth, and Moore
on Abstract Sculpture 727

▌ ART AND SOCIETY: The Museum of Modern Art
and the Avant-Garde 730

▌ ARTISTS ON ART: Rivera on Art for the People 735

THE BIG PICTURE 743

CHAPTER 25
EUROPE AND AMERICA
AFTER 1945 745

Painting and Sculpture, 1945 to 1970 746

Painting and Sculpture since 1970 763

Architecture and Site-Specific Art 778

Performance and Conceptual Art and New Media 793

▌ ARTISTS ON ART: Jackson Pollock on Easel
and Mural Painting 749

▌ ARTISTS ON ART: Helen Frankenthaler on Color-Field
Painting 753

▌ ARTISTS ON ART: David Smith on Outdoor Sculpture 754

▌ ARTISTS ON ART: Donald Judd on Sculpture and
Industrial Materials 755

▌ ARTISTS ON ART: Roy Lichtenstein on Pop Art 759

▌ ARTISTS ON ART: Chuck Close on Portrait Painting
and Photography 762

▌ ARTISTS ON ART: Judy Chicago on The Dinner Party 766

▌ ART AND SOCIETY: Public Funding of Controversial Art 772

▌ ART AND SOCIETY: Maya Lin's Vietnam Veterans
Memorial 783

▌ ARTISTS ON ART: Philip Johnson on Postmodern
Architecture 785

▌ ARTISTS ON ART: Frank Gehry on Architectural Design
and Materials 788

▌ ART AND SOCIETY: Richard Serra's Tilted Arc 792

▌ ARTISTS ON ART: Carolee Schneemann on Painting,
Performance Art, and Art History 794

THE BIG PICTURE 801

NOTES 802

GLOSSARY 804

BIBLIOGRAPHY 812

CREDITS 817

INDEX 819

PREFACE

When Helen Gardner published the first edition of *Art through the Ages* in 1926, she could not have imagined that more than 80 years later instructors all over the world would still be using her textbook in their classrooms. Indeed, if she were alive today, she would not recognize the book that long ago became—and remains—the most widely read introduction to the history of art and architecture in the English language. During the past half century, successive authors have constantly reinvented Helen Gardner's groundbreaking survey, always keeping it fresh and current, and setting an ever-higher standard in both content and publication quality with each new edition. I hope both professors and students will agree that this 13th edition lives up to that venerable tradition.

Certainly, this latest edition offers much that is fresh and new (enumerated below), but some things have not changed, including the fundamental belief that guided Helen Gardner—namely, that the primary goal of an introductory art history textbook should be to foster an appreciation and understanding of historically significant works of art of all kinds from all periods. Because of the longevity and diversity of the history of art, it is tempting to assign responsibility for telling its story to a large team of specialists. The Gardner publishers themselves took this approach for the first edition they produced after Helen Gardner's death, and it has now become the norm for introductory art history surveys. But students overwhelmingly say that the very complexity of the history of art makes it all the more important for the story to be told with a consistent voice if they are to master so much diverse material. I think Helen Gardner would be pleased to know that this new edition of *Art through the Ages* once again has a single storyteller.

Along with the late Richard Tansey and my more recent collaborator, Christin Mamiya, with whom I had the honor and pleasure of working on the 10th, 11th, and 12th editions, I continue to believe that the most effective way to tell the story of art through the ages, especially to someone studying art history for the first time, is to organize the vast array of artistic monuments according to the civilizations that produced them and to consider each work in roughly chronological order. This approach has not merely stood the test of time. It is the most appropriate way to narrate the *history* of art. The principle that underlies my approach to every period of art history is that the enormous variation in the form and meaning of the paintings, sculptures, buildings, and other artworks men and women have produced over the past 30,000 years is largely the result of the constantly changing contexts in which artists and architects worked. A historically based narrative is therefore best suited for a comprehensive history of art because it permits the author to situate each work discussed in its historical, social, economic, religious, and cultural context. That is, after all, what distinguishes art history from art appreciation.

In the first (1926) edition of *Art through the Ages*, Helen Gardner discussed Henri Matisse and Pablo Picasso in a chapter entitled "Contemporary Art in Europe and America." Since then many other artists have emerged on the international scene, and the story of art through the ages has grown longer and even more complex. More important, perhaps, the discipline of art history has changed markedly in recent decades, and so too has Helen Gardner's book. The 13th edition fully reflects the latest art historical research emphases while maintaining the traditional strengths that have made previous editions of *Art through the Ages* so popular. While sustaining attention to style, chronology, iconography, and technique, I also ensure that issues of patronage, function, and context loom large in every chapter. I treat artworks not as isolated objects in sterile 21st-century museum settings but with a view toward their purpose and meaning in the society that produced them at the time they were produced. I examine not only the role of the artist or architect in the creation of a work of art or a building, but also the role of the individuals or groups who paid the artists and influenced the shape the monuments took. Further, I devote more space than previously to the role of women and women artists in diverse societies over time. In every chapter, I have tried to choose artworks and buildings that reflect the increasingly wide range of interests of scholars today, while not rejecting the traditional list of "great" works or the very notion of a "canon." Consequently, the selection of works in this edition encompasses every artistic medium and almost every era and culture in the Western world, and includes many works that until recently art historians would not have considered to be "art" at all.

The 12th edition of *Art through the Ages* was the number-one choice for art history survey courses and the best-selling version of the book in its long history, and for this 13th edition I have retained all of the features that made its predecessor so successful. Once again, this edition, which contains 25 chapters on the Western tradition and its roots in the ancient Near East and Egypt, plus a chapter on Islamic art and architecture, boasts roughly 1,100 photographs, plans, and drawings, virtually all in color and reproduced according to the highest standards of clarity and color fidelity. The 13th edition, however, also features hundreds of new or upgraded photos by a host of new photographers as well as redesigned maps and plans and an extraordinary new set of architectural drawings prepared exclusively for *Art through the Ages* by John Burge.

The captions to the illustrations in this edition of *Art through the Ages*, as before, contain a wealth of information, including the name of the artist or architect, if known; the formal title (printed in italics), if assigned, description of the work, or name of the building; the provenance or place of production of the object or location of the building; the date; the material(s) used; the size; and the current location if the work is in a museum or private collection. As in previous editions, scales accompany all plans, but for the first time scales now also appear next to each photograph of a painting, statue, or other artwork. The works illustrated vary enormously in size, from colossal sculptures carved into mountain cliffs and paintings that cover entire walls or ceilings to tiny figurines, coins, and jewelry that one can hold in the hand. Although the captions contain the pertinent dimensions, it is hard for students who have never seen the paintings or statues in person to translate those dimensions into an appreciation of the real size of the objects. The new scales provide an effective and direct way to visualize how big or how small a given artwork is and its relative size compared with other objects in the same chapter and throughout the book.

Also new to this edition are the Quick-Review Captions that students found so useful when these were introduced in 2006 in the first edition of *Art through the Ages: A Concise History*. These brief synopses of the most significant aspects of each artwork or building illustrated accompany the captions to all images in the book. They have proved invaluable to students preparing for examinations in one-semester art history survey courses, and I am confident they will be equally useful to students enrolled in yearlong courses. In the 13th edition, however, I have provided two additional tools to aid students in reviewing and mastering the material. Each chapter now ends with a full-page feature called The Big Picture, which sets forth in bullet-point format the most important characteristics of each period or artistic movement discussed in the chapter. Small illustrations of characteristic works discussed accompany the summary of major points. Finally, I have attempted to tie all of the chapters together by providing with each copy of *Art through the Ages* a poster-size Global Timeline. This too features illustrations of key monuments of each age and geographical area as well as a brief enumeration of the most important art historical developments during that period. The timeline is global in scope to permit students in Western art courses to place developments in Europe and America in a worldwide context. The poster has four major horizontal bands corresponding to Europe, the Americas, Asia, and Africa, and 34 vertical columns for the successive chronological periods from 30,000 BCE to the present.

Another pedagogical tool not found in any other introductory art history textbook is the *Before 1300* section that appears at the beginning of Books C and D. Because many students taking the second half of a yearlong survey course will not have access to Books A and B, I have provided a special set of concise primers on religion and mythology and on architectural terminology and construction methods in the ancient and medieval worlds—information that is essential for understanding the history of Western art after 1300. The subjects of these special boxes are The Gods and Goddesses of Mount Olympus; The Life of Jesus in Art; Greco-Roman Temple Design and the Classical Orders; Arches and Vaults; and Medieval Church Design.

Boxed essays once again appear throughout the book as well. This popular feature first appeared in the 11th edition of *Art through the Ages*, which won both the Texty and McGuffey Prizes of the Text and Academic Authors Association for the best college textbook of 2001 in the humanities and social sciences. In this edition the essays are more closely tied to the main text than ever before. Consistent with that greater integration, most boxes now incorporate photographs of important artworks discussed in the text proper that also illustrate the theme treated in the boxed essays. These essays fall under six broad categories, one of which is new to the 13th edition.

Architectural Basics boxes provide students with a sound foundation for the understanding of architecture. These discussions are concise explanations, with drawings and diagrams, of the major aspects of design and construction. The information included is essential to an understanding of architectural technology and terminology. The boxes address questions of how and why various forms developed, the problems architects confronted, and the solutions they used to resolve them. Topics discussed include how the Egyptians built the pyramids, the orders of classical architecture, Roman concrete construction, and the design and terminology of mosques and Gothic cathedrals.

Materials and Techniques essays explain the various media artists employed from prehistoric to modern times. Since materials and techniques often influence the character of artworks, these discussions contain essential information on why many monuments appear as they do. Hollow-casting bronze statues; fresco painting; Islamic tile work; embroidery and tapestry; perspective; engraving, etching, and lithography; and daguerreotype and calotype photography are among the many subjects treated.

Religion and Mythology boxes introduce students to the principal elements of great religions, past and present, and to the representation of religious and mythological themes in painting and sculpture of all periods and places. These discussions of belief systems and iconography give readers a richer understanding of some of the greatest artworks ever created. The topics include the gods and goddesses of Egypt, Mesopotamia, Greece, and Rome; the life of Jesus in art; and Muhammad and Islam.

Art and Society essays treat the historical, social, political, cultural, and religious context of art and architecture. In some instances, specific monuments are the basis for a discussion of broader themes, as when the Hegeso stele serves as the springboard for an exploration of the role of women in ancient Greek society. Another essay discusses how people's evaluation today of artworks can differ from those of the society that produced them by examining the problems created by the contemporary market for undocumented archaeological finds. Other subjects include Egyptian mummification, Etruscan women, Byzantine icons and iconoclasm, artistic training in Renaissance Italy, 19th-century academic salons and independent art exhibitions, and public funding of controversial art.

Written Sources present and discuss key historical documents illuminating important monuments of art and architecture throughout the Western world. The passages quoted permit voices from the past to speak directly to the reader, providing vivid and unique insights into the creation of artworks in all media. Examples include Bernard of Clairvaux's treatise on sculpture in medieval churches, Giovanni Pietro Bellori's biographies of Annibale Carracci and Caravaggio, Jean François Marmontel's account of 18th-century salon culture, as well as texts that bring the past to life, such as eyewitness accounts of the volcanic eruption that buried Roman Pompeii and of the fire that destroyed Canterbury Cathedral in medieval England.

A new category is *Artists on Art* in which artists and architects throughout history discuss both their theories and individual works. Examples include Sinan the Great discussing the mosque he designed for Selim II, Leonardo da Vinci and Michelangelo debating the relative merits of painting and sculpture, Artemisia Gentileschi talking about the special problems she confronted as a woman artist, Jacques-Louis David on Neoclassicism, Gustave Courbet on Realism, Henri

Matisse on color, Pablo Picasso on Cubism, Diego Rivera on art for the people, and Judy Chicago on her seminal work *The Dinner Party*.

Instructors familiar with previous editions of *Art through the Ages* will also find that many of the chapters in the 13th edition have been reorganized, especially in volume two. For example, the treatment of European 17th-century art now appears in two discrete chapters, one devoted to Baroque Italy and Spain, the other to Northern Europe. A single chapter is devoted to the 18th century, another to the period from 1800 to 1870, and a third to 1870 to 1900. In addition, in recognition that different instructors at different colleges and universities end the first semester and begin the second semester at different points, for the first time *two* volumes of *Art through the Ages* include Chapter 14 on Italian art from 1200 to 1400. And *The Western Perspective* is now also available in this special backpack edition consisting of four, rather than the traditional two, paperback volumes: Book A (Antiquity: Chapters 1–7), Book B (The Middle Ages: Chapters 8–14), Book C (Renaissance and Baroque: Chapters 14–20), and Book D (Modern Europe and America: Chapters 21–25). These books can also be purchased separately.

Rounding out the features in the book itself is a Glossary containing definitions of all terms introduced in the text in italics and a Bibliography of books in English, including both general works and a chapter-by-chapter list of more focused studies. In this edition I have also taken care to italicize and define in the text all Glossary terms that appear in Books C and D even if they have been used and defined in Books A and B, because many students enrolled in the second semester of a yearlong course will not have taken the first semester and will not be familiar with those terms.

The 13th edition of *Art through the Ages* is not, however, a standalone text, but one element of a complete package of learning tools. In addition to the Global Timeline, every new copy of the book comes with a password to *ArtStudy Online,* a web site with access to a host of multimedia resources that students can employ throughout the entire course, including image flashcards, tutorial quizzes, podcasts, vocabulary, and more. Instructors have access to a host of teaching materials, including digital images with zoom capabilities, video, and Google™ Earth coordinates.

A work as extensive as this history of art could not be undertaken or completed without the counsel of experts in all areas of Western art. As with previous editions, the publisher has enlisted more than a hundred art historians to review every chapter in order to ensure that the text lived up to the Gardner reputation for accuracy as well as readability. I take great pleasure in acknowledging here the invaluable contributions to the 13th edition of *Art through the Ages: The Western Perspective* made by the following for their critiques of various chapters: Charles M. Adelman, University of Northern Iowa; Kirk Ambrose, University of Colorado–Boulder; Susan Ashbrook, Art Institute of Boston; Zainab Bahrani, Columbia University; Susan Bakewell, University of Texas–Austin; James J. Bloom, Florida State University; Suzaan Boettger, Bergen Community College; Colleen Bolton, Mohawk Valley Community College; Angi Elsea Bourgeois, Mississippi State University; Kimberly Bowes, Fordham University; Elizabeth Bredrup, St. Christopher's School; Lawrence E. Butler, George Mason University; Alexandra Carpino, Northern Arizona University; Jane Carroll, Dartmouth College; Hipolito Rafael Chacon, The University of Montana; Catherine M. Chastain, North Georgia College & State University; Violaine Chauvet, Johns Hopkins University; Daniel Connolly, Augustana College; Michael A. Coronel, University of Northern Colorado; Nicole Cox, Rochester Institute of Technology; Jodi Cranston, Boston University; Giovanna De Appolonia, Boston University; Marion de Koning, Grossmont College; John J. Dobbins, University of Virginia; Erika Doss, University of Colorado–Boulder; B. Underwood DuRette, Thomas Nelson Community College; Lisa Farber, Pace University; James Farmer, Virginia Commonwealth University; Sheila ffolliott, George Mason University; Ferdinanda Florence, Solano Community College; William B. Folkestad, Central Washington University; Jeffery Fontana, Austin College; Mitchell Frank, Carleton University; Sara L. French, Wells College; Norman P. Gambill, South Dakota State University; Elise Goodman, University of Cincinnati; Kim T. Grant, University of Southern Maine; Elizabeth ten Grotenhuis, Silk Road Project; Sandra C. Haynes, Pasadena City College; Valerie Hedquist, The University of Montana; Susan Hellman, Northern Virginia Community College; Marian J. Hollinger, Fairmont State University; Cheryl Hughes, Alta High School; Heidrun Hultgren, Kent State University; Joseph M. Hutchinson, Texas A&M University; Julie M. Johnson, Utah State University; Sandra L. Johnson, Citrus College; Deborah Kahn, Boston University; Fusae Kanda, Harvard University; Catherine Karkov, Miami University; Wendy Katz, University of Nebraska–Lincoln; Nita Kehoe-Gadway, Central Wyoming College; Nancy L. Kelker, Middle Tennessee State University; Cathie Kelly, University of Nevada–Las Vegas; Katie Kempton, Ohio University; John F. Kenfield, Rutgers University; Herbert L. Kessler, Johns Hopkins University; Monica Kjellman-Chapin, Emporia State University; Ellen Konowitz, State University of New York–New Paltz; Kathryn E. Kramer, State University of New York–Cortland; Carol Krinsky, New York University; Lydia Lehr, Atlantic Cape Community College; Krist Lien, Shelton State Community College; Ellen Longsworth, Merrimack College; David A. Ludley, Clayton State University; Henry Luttikhuizen, Calvin College; Christina Maranci, University of Wisconsin–Milwaukee; Dominic Marner, University of Guelph; Jack Brent Maxwell, Blinn College; Anne McClanan, Portland State University; Brian McConnell, Florida Atlantic University; Heather McPherson, University of Alabama–Birmingham; Cynthia Millis, Houston Community College–Southwest; Cynthia Taylor Mills, Brookhaven College; Keith N. Morgan, Boston University; Johanna D. Movassat, San Jose State University; Helen Nagy, University of Puget Sound; Heidi Nickisher, Rochester Institute of Technology; Bonnie Noble, University of North Carolina–Charlotte; Abigail Noonan, Rochester Institute of Technology; Marjorie Och, University of Mary Washington; Karen Michelle O'Day, University of Wisconsin–Eau Claire; Edward J. Olszewski, Case Western Reserve University; Allison Lee Palmer, University of Oklahoma; Martin Patrick, Illinois State University; Glenn Peers, University of Texas–Austin; Jane Peters, University of Kentucky; Julie Anne Plax, University of Arizona; Frances Pohl, Pomona College; Virginia C. Raguin, College of the Holy Cross; Donna Karen Reid, Chemeketa Community College; Albert W. Reischuch, Kent State University; Jonathan Ribner, Boston University; Cynthea Riesenberg, Washington Latin School; James G. Rogers Jr., Florida Southern College; Carey Rote, Texas A&M University–Corpus Christi; David J. Roxburgh, Harvard University; Conrad Rudolph, University of California–Riverside; Catherine B. Scallen, Case Western Reserve University; Denise Schmandt-Besserat, University of Texas–Austin; Natasha Seaman, Berklee College of Music; Malia E. Serrano, Grossmont College; Laura Sommer, Daemen College; Natasha Staller, Amherst College; Nancy Steele-Hamme, Midwestern State University; Andrew Stewart, University of California–Berkeley; Francesca Tronchin, Ohio State University; Frances Van Keuren, University of Georgia; Kelly Wacker, University of Montevallo; Carolynne Whitefeather, Utica College; Nancy L. Wicker, University of Mississippi; Alastair Wright, Princeton University; John G. Younger, University of Kansas; Michael Zell, Boston University.

I am also happy to have this opportunity to express my gratitude to the extraordinary group of people at Wadsworth involved with the editing, production, and distribution of *Art through the Ages.* Some of them I have now worked with on various projects for more than a decade and feel privileged to count among my friends. The success of the Gardner series in all of its various permutations depends in no small part on the expertise and unflagging commitment of these dedicated professionals: Sean Wakely, executive vice president, Cengage Arts and Sciences; P. J. Boardman, vice president, editor-in-chief of Cengage Learning Arts and Sciences; Clark Baxter, publisher; Sharon Adams Poore, senior development editor; Helen Triller-Yambert, development editor; Lianne Ames, senior content project manager; Wendy Constantine, senior media editor; Kimberly Apfelbaum, assistant editor; Nell Pepper, editorial assistant; Cate Rikard Barr, senior art director; Scott Stewart, vice president managing director sales; Diane Wenckebach, senior marketing manager; as well as Kim Adams, Heather Baxley, William Christy, Doug Easton, tani hasegawa, Cara Murphy, Ellen Pettengell, Kathryn Stewart, and Joy Westberg.

I am also deeply grateful to the following for their significant contributions to the 13th edition of *Art through the Ages:* Joan Keyes, Dovetail Publishing Services; Ida May Norton, copy editor; Sarah Evertson and Stephen Forsling, photo researchers; Pete Shanks and Jon Peck, accuracy readers; Pat Lewis, proofreader; John Pierce, Thompson Type; Rick Stanley, Digital Media Inc., U.S.A; Don Larson, Mapping Specialists; Anne Draus, Scratchgravel; Cindy Geiss, Graphic World; and, of course, John Burge, for his superb architectural drawings. I also wish to acknowledge my debt to Edward Tufte for an illuminating afternoon spent discussing publication design and production issues and for his invaluable contribution to the creation of the scales that accompany all reproductions of paintings, sculptures, and other artworks in this edition.

Finally, I owe thanks to my colleagues at Boston University and to the thousands of students and the scores of teaching fellows in my art history courses during the past three decades. From them I have learned much that has helped determine the form and content of *Art through the Ages* and made it a much better book than it otherwise might have been.

Fred S. Kleiner

About the Author

FRED S. KLEINER (Ph.D., Columbia University) is the co-author of the 10th, 11th, and 12th editions of *Art through the Ages* and more than a hundred publications on Greek and Roman art and architecture, including *A History of Roman Art,* also published by Wadsworth. He has taught the art history survey course for more than three decades, first at the University of Virginia and, since 1978, at Boston University, where he is currently Professor of Art History and Archaeology and Chair of the Art History Department. Long recognized for his inspiring lectures and devotion to students, Professor Kleiner won Boston University's Metcalf Award for Excellence in Teaching as well as the College Prize for Undergraduate Advising in the Humanities in 2002 and is a two-time winner of the Distinguished Teaching Prize in the College of Arts and Sciences Honors Program. He was Editor-in-Chief of the *American Journal of Archaeology* from 1985 to 1998.

A History of Roman Art (Wadsworth 2007; ISBN 0534638465)

Gardner's Art through the Ages: Non-Western Perspectives, Thirteenth Edition (Wadsworth 2010; ISBN 0495573671)

BEFORE 1300

Sculptors at work, detail of the south wall of the main hall of the funerary chapel of Rekhmire, Thebes, Egypt, 18th Dynasty, ca. 1425 BCE.

RUFILLUS, Initial R, folio 244 recto of a Passional, from Weissenau, Germany, ca. 1170–1200. Bibliotheca Bodmeriana, Geneva.

BEFORE 1300
Contents

▌ RELIGION AND MYTHOLOGY

The Gods and Goddesses of Mount Olympus   xiii

The Life of Jesus in Art   xiv

▌ ARCHITECTURAL BASICS

Greco-Roman Temple Design and the Classical Orders   xvi

Arches and Vaults   xviii

Medieval Church Design   xx

The Gods and Goddesses of Mount Olympus

The chief deities of the Greeks ruled the world from their home on Mount Olympus, Greece's highest peak. They figure prominently not only in Greek, Etruscan, and Roman art but also in art from the Renaissance to the present.

The 12 Olympian gods (and their Roman equivalents) were

▌ *Zeus* (*Jupiter*) King of the gods, Zeus ruled the sky and allotted the sea to his brother Poseidon and the Underworld to his other brother Hades. His weapon was the thunderbolt. Jupiter was also the chief god of the Romans.

▌ *Hera* (*Juno*) Wife and sister of Zeus, Hera was the goddess of marriage.

▌ *Poseidon* (*Neptune*) Poseidon was lord of the sea. He controlled waves, storms, and earthquakes with his three-pronged pitchfork (*trident*).

▌ *Hestia* (*Vesta*) Sister of Zeus, Poseidon, and Hera, Hestia was goddess of the hearth.

▌ *Demeter* (*Ceres*) Third sister of Zeus, Demeter was the goddess of grain and agriculture.

▌ *Ares* (*Mars*) God of war, Ares was the son of Zeus and Hera and the lover of Aphrodite, and the father of the twin founders of Rome, Romulus and Remus.

▌ *Athena* (*Minerva*) Goddess of wisdom and warfare, Athena was a virgin born from the head of Zeus.

▌ *Hephaistos* (*Vulcan*) God of fire and of metalworking, Hephaistos was the son of Zeus and Hera. Born lame and, uncharacteristically for a god, ugly, he married Aphrodite, who was unfaithful to him.

▌ *Apollo* (*Apollo*) God of light and music and son of Zeus, the young, beautiful Apollo was sometimes identified with the sun (*Helios/Sol*).

▌ *Artemis* (*Diana*) Sister of Apollo, Artemis was goddess of the hunt. She was occasionally equated with the moon (*Selene/Luna*).

▌ *Aphrodite* (*Venus*) Daughter of Zeus and a *nymph* (goddess of springs and woods), Aphrodite was the goddess of love and beauty.

▌ *Hermes* (*Mercury*) Son of Zeus and another nymph, Hermes was the fleet-footed messenger of the gods. He carried the *caduceus*, a magical herald's rod.

Other important Greek gods and goddesses were

▌ *Hades* (*Pluto*), lord of the Underworld and god of the dead. Although the brother of Zeus and Poseidon, Hades never resided on Mount Olympus.

▌ *Dionysos* (*Bacchus*), god of wine.

▌ *Eros* (*Amor* or *Cupid*), the winged child-god of love, son of Aphrodite and Ares.

▌ *Asklepios* (*Aesculapius*), god of healing. His serpent-entwined staff is the emblem of modern medicine.

Zeus, from Cape Artemision, ca. 460–450 BCE

Athena, by Phidias, ca. 438 BCE

Aphrodite, by Praxiteles, ca. 350–340 BCE

Hermes and infant Dionysos, by Praxiteles, ca. 340 BCE

The Life of Jesus in Art

Christians believe that Jesus of Nazareth is the son of God, the *Messiah* (Savior, Christ) of the Jews prophesied in the Old Testament. His life—his miraculous birth from the womb of a virgin mother, his preaching and miracle working, his execution by the Romans and subsequent ascent to Heaven—has been the subject of countless artworks from Roman times through the present day.

INCARNATION AND CHILDHOOD

The first "cycle" of the life of Jesus consists of the events of his conception (Incarnation), birth, infancy, and childhood.

▌ *Annunciation to Mary* The archangel Gabriel announces to the Virgin Mary that she will miraculously conceive and give birth to God's son Jesus.

▌ *Visitation* The pregnant Mary visits her cousin Elizabeth, who is pregnant with John the Baptist. Elizabeth is the first to recognize that Mary is bearing the Son of God.

▌ *Nativity*, *Annunciation to the Shepherds*, and *Adoration of the Shepherds* Jesus is born at night in Bethlehem and placed in a basket. Mary and her husband Joseph marvel at the newborn, while an angel announces the birth of the Savior to shepherds in the field, who rush to adore the child.

▌ *Adoration of the Magi* A bright star alerts three wise men (*magi*) in the East that the King of the Jews has been born. They travel 12 days to present precious gifts to the infant Jesus.

▌ *Presentation in the Temple* In accordance with Jewish tradition, Mary and Joseph bring their firstborn son to the temple in Jerusalem, where the aged Simeon recognizes Jesus as the prophesied Savior of humankind.

▌ *Massacre of the Innocents* and *Flight into Egypt* King Herod, fearful that a rival king has been born, orders the massacre of all infants, but the Holy Family escapes to Egypt.

▌ *Dispute in the Temple* Joseph and Mary travel to Jerusalem for the feast of Passover. Jesus, only a boy, debates the astonished Jewish scholars in the temple, foretelling his ministry.

PUBLIC MINISTRY

The public-ministry cycle comprises the teachings of Jesus and the miracles he performed.

▌ *Baptism* The beginning of Jesus' public ministry is marked by his baptism at age 30 by John the Baptist in the Jordan River. God's voice is heard proclaiming Jesus as his son.

▌ *Calling of Matthew* Jesus summons Matthew, a tax collector, to follow him, and Matthew becomes one of his 12 disciples, or *apostles* (from the Greek for "messenger").

▌ *Miracles* Jesus performs many miracles, revealing his divine nature. These include acts of healing and raising the dead, turning water into wine, walking on water and calming storms, and creating wondrous quantities of food.

▌ *Delivery of the Keys to Peter* Jesus chooses the fisherman Peter (whose name means "rock") as his successor. He declares that Peter is the rock on which his church will be built and symbolically delivers to Peter the keys to the kingdom of Heaven.

▌ *Transfiguration* Jesus scales a mountain and, in the presence of Peter and two other disciples, is transformed into radiant light. God announces from a cloud that Jesus is his son.

▌ *Cleansing of the Temple* Jesus returns to Jerusalem, where he finds money changers and merchants conducting business in the temple. He rebukes them and drives them out.

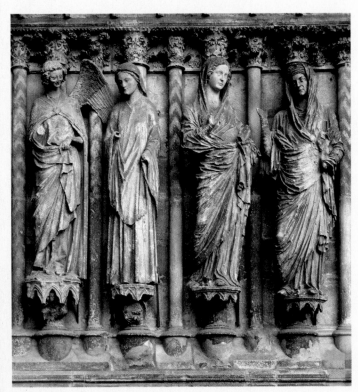

Annunciation and Visitation, Reims Cathedral, ca. 1230

Annunciation to the Shepherds, *Lectionary of Henry II*, 1002–1014

PASSION

The Passion (Latin *passio,* "suffering") cycle includes the events leading to Jesus' death, Resurrection, and ascent to Heaven.

▌ *Entry into Jerusalem* On the Sunday before his Crucifixion (Palm Sunday), Jesus rides into Jerusalem on a donkey.

▌ *Last Supper* In Jerusalem, Jesus celebrates Passover with his disciples. During this Last Supper, Jesus foretells his imminent betrayal, arrest, and death and invites the disciples to remember him when they eat bread (symbol of his body) and drink wine (his blood). This ritual became the celebration of *Mass* (*Eucharist*).

▌ *Agony in the Garden* Jesus goes to the Mount of Olives in the Garden of Gethsemane, where he struggles to overcome his human fear of death by praying for divine strength.

▌ *Betrayal* and *Arrest* The disciple Judas Iscariot betrays Jesus to the Jewish authorities for 30 pieces of silver. Judas identifies Jesus to the soldiers by kissing him, and Jesus is arrested.

▌ *Trials of Jesus* Jesus is brought before Caiaphas, the Jewish high priest, who interrogates Jesus about his claim to be the Messiah. Jesus is then brought before the Roman governor of Judaea, Pontius Pilate, on the charge of treason because he had proclaimed himself King of the Jews. Pilate asks the crowd to choose between freeing Jesus or Barabbas, a murderer. The people choose Barabbas, and the judge condemns Jesus to death.

▌ *Flagellation* The Roman soldiers who hold Jesus captive whip (flagellate) him and mock him by dressing him as King of the Jews and placing a crown of thorns on his head.

▌ *Carrying of the Cross, Raising of the Cross*, and *Crucifixion* The Romans force Jesus to carry the cross on which he will be crucified from Jerusalem to Mount Calvary. Soldiers erect the cross and nail Jesus' hands and feet to it. Jesus' mother, John the Evangelist, and Mary Magdalene mourn at the foot of the cross, while soldiers torment Jesus. One of them stabs Jesus in the side with a spear. After suffering great pain, Jesus dies on Good Friday.

▌ *Deposition, Lamentation,* and *Entombment* Two disciples, Joseph of Arimathea and Nicodemus, remove Jesus' body from the cross (Deposition) and take him to his tomb. Joseph, Nicodemus, the Virgin Mary, Saint John the Evangelist, and Mary Magdalene mourn over the dead Jesus (Lamentation). (When in art the isolated figure of the Virgin Mary cradles her dead son in her lap, it is called a *Pietà*—Italian for "pity.") Then his followers lower Jesus into a sarcophagus in the tomb (Entombment).

▌ *Descent into Limbo* During the three days he spends in the tomb, Jesus (after death, Christ) descends into Hell, or Limbo, and frees the souls of the righteous, including Adam, Eve, Moses, David, Solomon, and John the Baptist.

▌ *Resurrection* and *Three Marys at the Tomb* On the third day (Easter Sunday), Christ rises from the dead and leaves the tomb. The Virgin Mary, Mary Magdalene, and Mary, the mother of James, visit the tomb, find it empty, and learn from an angel that Christ has been resurrected.

▌ *Noli Me Tangere, Supper at Emmaus,* and *Doubting of Thomas* During the 40 days between Christ's Resurrection and his ascent to Heaven, he appears on several occasions to his followers. Christ warns Mary Magdalene, weeping at his tomb, with the words "Don't touch me" (*Noli me tangere* in Latin). At Emmaus he eats supper with two astonished disciples. Later, Thomas, who cannot believe that Christ has risen, touches the wound in his side inflicted at the Crucifixion.

▌ *Ascension* On the 40th day, on the Mount of Olives, with his mother and apostles as witnesses, Christ gloriously ascends to Heaven in a cloud.

Crucifixion, Church of the Dormition, Daphni, ca. 1090–1100

Ascension, *Rabbula Gospels*, 586

Greco-Roman Temple Design and the Classical Orders

The gable-roofed columnar stone temples of the Greeks and Romans have had more influence on the later history of architecture in the Western world than any other building type ever devised. Many of the elements of classical temple architecture are present in buildings from the Renaissance to the present day. The basic design principles of Greek and Roman temples and the most important components of the classical orders can be summarized as follows.

▎ *Temple design* The core of a Greco-Roman temple was the *cella*, a room with no windows that usually housed the statue of the god or goddess to whom the shrine was dedicated. Generally, only the priests, priestesses, and chosen few would enter the cella. Worshipers gathered in front of the building, where sacrifices occurred at open-air altars. In most Greek temples, for example, the second temple erected in honor of Hera at Paestum, a *colonnade* was erected all around the cella to form a *peristyle*. In contrast, Roman temples, for example, the Temple of Portunus in Rome, usually have freestanding columns only in a porch at the front of the building. Sometimes, as in the Portunus temple, *engaged* (attached) half-columns adorn three sides of the cella to give the building the appearance of a *peripteral* temple. Architectural historians call this a *pseudoperipteral* design.

▎ *Classical orders* The Greeks developed two basic architectural orders, or design systems: the *Doric* and the *Ionic*. The forms of the columns and *entablature* (superstructure) generally differentiate the orders. Classical columns have two or three parts, depending on the order: the shaft, which is usually marked with vertical channels (*flutes*); the *capital*; and, in the Ionic order, the *base*. The Doric capital consists of a round *echinus* beneath a square abacus block. Spiral *volutes* constitute the distinctive feature of the Ionic capital. Classical entablatures have three parts: the *architrave,* the *frieze,* and the triangular *pediment* of the gabled roof, framed by the *cornice.* In the Doric order, the frieze is subdivided into *triglyphs* and *metopes,* whereas in the Ionic, the frieze is left open.

The *Corinthian capital,* a later Greek invention very popular in Roman times, is more ornate than either the Doric or Ionic. It consists of a double row of acanthus leaves, from which tendrils and flowers emerge. Although this capital often is cited as the distinguishing element of the Corinthian order, in strict terms no Corinthian order exists. Architects simply substituted the new capital type for the volute capital in the Ionic order, as in the *tholos* (round temple) at Epidauros.

Sculpture played a major role on the exterior of classical temples, partly to embellish the deity's shrine and partly to tell something about the deity to those gathered outside. Sculptural ornament was concentrated on the upper part of the building, in the pediment and frieze.

DORIC ORDER

IONIC ORDER

Doric and Ionic orders

Greek Doric peripteral temple (Temple of Hera II, Paestum, Italy, ca. 460 BCE)

Roman Ionic pseudoperipteral temple
(Temple of Portunus, Rome, ca. 75 BCE)

Corinthian capital (Tholos, Epidauros, Greece, ca. 350 BCE)

Arches and Vaults

Although earlier architects used both arches and vaults, the Romans employed them more extensively and effectively than any other ancient civilization. The Roman forms became staples of architectural design from the Middle Ages until today.

▌ *Arch* The arch is one of several ways of spanning a passageway. The Romans preferred it to the *post-and-lintel* (column-and-architrave) system used in the Greek orders. Builders construct arches using wedge-shaped stone blocks called *voussoirs.* The central voussoir is the arch's *keystone.*

▌ *Barrel vault* Also called the *tunnel vault,* the barrel vault is an extension of a simple arch, creating a semicylindrical ceiling over parallel walls.

▌ *Groin vault* The groin vault, or *cross vault,* is formed by the intersection at right angles of two barrel vaults of equal size. When a series of groin vaults covers an interior hall, the open lateral arches of the vaults function as windows admitting light to the building.

▌ *Dome* The hemispherical dome may be described as a round arch rotated around the full circumference of a circle, usually resting on a cylindrical *drum.* The Romans normally constructed domes using *concrete,* a mix of lime mortar, volcanic sand, water, and small stones, instead of with large stone blocks. Concrete dries to form a solid mass of great strength, which allowed the Romans to puncture the apex of a concrete dome with an *oculus* (eye), so that much-needed light could reach the interior of the building.

Barrel vaults, as noted, resemble tunnels, and groin vaults are usually found in a series covering a similar *longitudinally* oriented interior space. Domes, in contrast, crown *centrally* planned buildings, so named because the structure's parts are of equal or almost equal dimensions around the center.

Arch

Barrel vault

Groin vault

Hemispherical dome with oculus

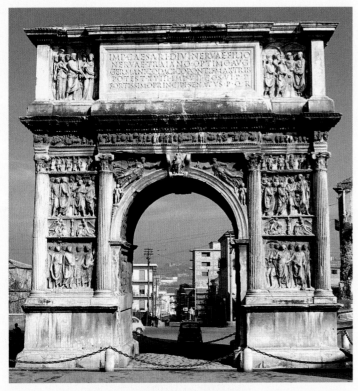

Roman arch (Arch of Trajan, Benevento, Italy, ca. 114–118)

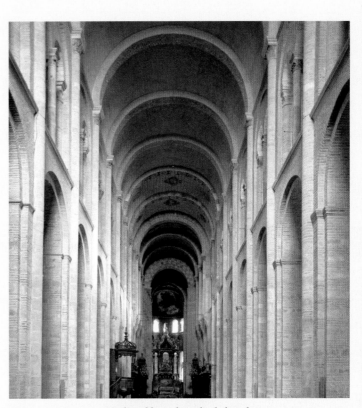

Medieval barrel-vaulted church
(Saint-Sernin, Toulouse, France, ca. 1070–1120)

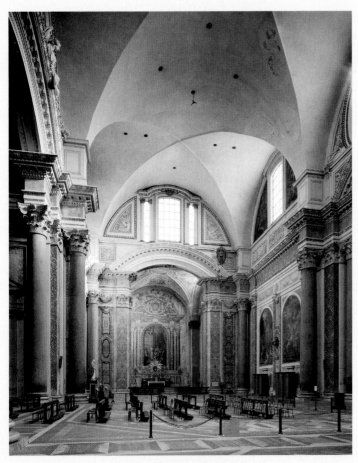

Roman hall with groin vaults
(Baths of Diocletian [Santa Maria degli Angeli],
Rome, Italy, ca. 298–306)

Roman dome with oculus (Pantheon, Rome, Italy, 118–125)

Medieval Church Design

Church design during the Middle Ages set the stage for ecclesiastical architecture from the Renaissance to the present. Both the longitudinal- and central-plan building types of antiquity had a long postclassical history.

■ *Basilican churches* In Western Christendom, the typical medieval church had a *basilican* plan, which evolved from the Roman columnar hall, or basilica. The great European cathedrals of the Gothic age, which were the immediate predecessors of the churches of the Renaissance and Baroque eras, shared many elements with the earliest basilican churches constructed during the fourth century, including a wide central *nave* flanked by *aisles* and ending in an *apse.* Some basilican churches also have a *transept,* an area perpendicular to the nave. The nave and transept intersect at the *crossing.* Gothic

churches, however, have many additional features. The key components of Gothic design are labeled in the drawing of a typical French Gothic cathedral and the plan of Chartres Cathedral.

Gothic architects frequently extended the aisles around the apse to form an *ambulatory,* onto which opened *radiating chapels* housing sacred relics. Groin vaults formed the ceiling of the nave, aisles, ambulatory, and transept alike, replacing the timber roof of the typical Early Christian basilica. These vaults rested on *diagonal* and *transverse ribs* in the form of pointed arches. On the exterior, *flying buttresses* held the nave vaults in place. These masonry struts transferred the thrust of the nave vaults across the roofs of the aisles to tall piers frequently capped by pointed ornamental *pinnacles.* This structural system made it possible to open up the walls above the *nave arcade* with huge *stained-glass* windows in the nave *clerestory.*

Plan of Chartres Cathedral, Chartres, France, rebuilt after 1194

Left: Cutaway view of a typical French Gothic cathedral
(1) pinnacle, (2) flying buttress, (3) vaulting web,
(4) diagonal rib, (5) transverse rib, (6) springing,
(7) clerestory, (8) oculus, (9) lancet, (10) triforium,
(11) nave arcade, (12) compound pier with responds

Central-plan churches The domed central plan of classical antiquity dominated the architecture of the Byzantine Empire but with important modifications. Because the dome covered the crossing of a Byzantine church, architects had to find a way to erect domes on square bases instead of on the circular bases (cylindrical drums) of Roman buildings. The solution was *pendentive* construction in which the dome rests on what is in effect a second, larger dome. The top portion and four segments around the rim of the larger dome are omitted, creating four curved triangles, or pendentives. The pendentives join to form a ring and four arches whose planes bound a square. The first use of pendentives on a grand scale occurred in the sixth-century church of Hagia Sophia (Holy Wisdom) in Constantinople.

The interiors of Byzantine churches differed from those of basilican churches in the West not only in plan and the use of domes but also in the manner in which they were adorned. The original mosaic decoration of Hagia Sophia is lost, but at Saint Mark's in Venice, some 40,000 square feet of mosaics cover all the walls, arches, vaults, and domes.

Hagia Sophia, Constantinople (Istanbul), Turkey, 532–537

Saint Mark's, Venice, Italy, begun 1063

Pendentives

Dome on pendentives

21-1 JEAN-HONORÉ FRAGONARD, *The Swing*, 1766. Oil on canvas, 2′ 8 $\frac{5}{8}$″ × 2′ 2″. Wallace Collection, London.

In this painting epitomizing Rococo style, pastel colors and soft light complement a sensuous scene in which a young lady flirtatiously kicks off her shoe at a statue of Cupid while her lover watches.

1 in.

EUROPE
AND AMERICA,
1700 TO 1800

In 1700, Louis XIV still ruled as the Sun King of France, presiding over his realm and French culture from his palatial residence at Versailles (FIG. 20-32). By 1800, revolutions had overthrown the monarchy in France and achieved independence for the British colonies in America (MAP 21-1). The 18th century also gave birth to a revolution of a different kind—the Industrial Revolution, which began in England and soon transformed the economies of continental Europe and North America and eventually the world. Against this backdrop of revolutionary change, social as well as political, economic, and technological, came major transformations in the arts. Indeed, *Pilgrimage to Cythera* (FIG. 21-6), painted in 1717 and set in a lush landscape, celebrates the romantic dalliances of the moneyed elite. In contrast, the 1784 *Oath of the Horatii* (FIG. 21-23) takes place in an austere Doric hall and glorifies the civic virtue and heroism of an ancient Roman family. The two works have little in common other than that both are French oil paintings. In the 18th century, shifts in style and subject matter were both rapid and significant.

ROCOCO

The death of Louis XIV in 1715 brought many changes in French high society. The elite quickly abandoned the court of Versailles for the pleasures of town life. Although French citizens still owed allegiance to a monarch, the early 18th century brought a resurgence of aristocratic social, political, and economic power. Members of the nobility not only exercised their traditional privileges (for example, exemption from certain taxes and from forced labor on public works) but also sought to expand their power. In the cultural realm, aristocrats reestablished their predominance as art patrons. The *hôtels* (town houses) of Paris soon became the centers of a new, softer style called *Rococo*. Associated with the regency (1715–1723) that followed the death of Louis XIV and with the reign of Louis XV (r. 1723–1774), the Rococo style in art and architecture was the perfect expression of the sparkling gaiety the wealthy cultivated in their elegant homes (see "Femmes Savantes and Salon Culture," page 585).

MAP 21-1 The United States in 1800.

Architecture

Rococo appeared in France in about 1700, primarily as a style of interior design. The French Rococo exterior was most often simple, or even plain, but Rococo exuberance took over the interior. The term derived from the French word *rocaille* (literally, "pebble"), but it referred especially to the small stones and shells used to decorate grotto interiors. Shells or shell forms were the principal motifs in Rococo ornament.

SALON DE LA PRINCESSE A typical French Rococo room is the Salon de la Princesse (FIG. 21-2) in the Hôtel de Soubise in Paris, designed by GERMAIN BOFFRAND (1667–1754). Parisian salons of this sort were the center of Rococo social life. They usurped the role that Louis XIV's Versailles palace (FIG. 20-32) played in the 17th century, when the Sun King set the tone for French culture. In the early 18th century, the centralized and grandiose palace-based culture of Baroque France gave way to a much more intimate and decentralized culture based in private homes. The new architectural style mirrored this social and cultural shift. A comparison between the Salon de la Princesse and the Galerie des Glaces (FIG. 20-33) at Versailles reveals how Boffrand softened the strong architectural lines and panels of the earlier style into flexible, sinuous curves luxuriantly multiplied in mirror reflections. The walls melt into the vault. Irregular painted shapes, surmounted by sculpture and separated by the typical rocaille shells, replace the hall's cornices. Painting, architecture, and sculpture combine to form a single ensemble. The profusion of curving tendrils and sprays of foliage blends with the shell forms to give an effect of freely growing nature, suggesting that the designer permanently decked the Rococo room for a festival.

French Rococo interiors were lively total works of art. Exquisitely wrought furniture, enchanting small sculptures, ornamented mirror frames, delightful ceramics and silver, small paintings, and decorative *tapestries* complemented the architecture, relief sculptures, and mural paintings. The Salon de la Princesse no longer has most of the movable furnishings and decor that once contributed so much to its total ambience. Visitors can imagine, however, how this and similar Rococo rooms—with their alternating gilded moldings, vivacious relief sculptures, luxurious furniture, and daintily colored ornamentation of flowers and garlands—must have harmonized with the chamber music played in them, with the elaborate costumes of satin and brocade, and with the equally elegant etiquette and sparkling wit of the people who graced them.

AMALIENBURG The French Rococo style quickly spread beyond Paris. The Amalienburg, a small lodge the French architect FRANÇOIS DE CUVILLIÉS (1695–1768) built in the park of the Nymphenburg Palace in Munich, is a prime example of Germany's adoption of the Parisian style. The most spectacular room in the lodge is the circular Hall of Mirrors (FIG. 21-3), a silver-and-blue ensemble of architecture, stucco relief, silvered bronze mirrors, and crystal that represents the Rococo style at its zenith. The hall dazzles the eye with myriad scintillating motifs, forms, and figurations the designer borrowed from the full Rococo ornamental repertoire. Silvery light, reflected and amplified by windows and mirrors, bathes the room and creates shapes and contours that weave rhythmically around the upper walls and the ceiling coves. Everything seems organic, growing, and in motion, an ultimate refinement of illusion that the architect, artists, and artisans, all magically in command of their varied media, created with virtuoso flourishes.

21-2 GERMAIN BOFFRAND, Salon de la Princesse, with painting by CHARLES-JOSEPH NATOIRE and sculpture by J. B. LEMOINE, Hôtel de Soubise, Paris, France, 1737–1740.

Elegant Rococo rooms such as this salon, featuring sinuous curves, gilded moldings and mirrors, small sculptures and paintings, and floral ornament, were the center of Parisian social and intellectual life.

Femmes Savantes and Salon Culture

The feminine look of the Rococo style suggests that the taste and social initiative of women dominated the age—and, to a large extent, they did. Women—for example, Madame de Pompadour (1721–1764), mistress of Louis XV of France; Maria Theresa (1717–1780), archduchess of Austria and queen of Hungary and Bohemia; and Empresses Elizabeth (r. 1741–1762) and Catherine the Great (r. 1762–1796) of Russia—held some of the most influential positions in Europe. Female taste also had an impact in numerous smaller courts as well as in the private sphere.

In the early 18th century, Paris was the social capital of Europe, and the Rococo salon (FIG. 21-2) was the center of Parisian society. Wealthy, ambitious, and clever society hostesses competed to attract the most famous and the most accomplished people to their salons, whether in Paris or elsewhere in Europe (FIG. 21-3). The medium of social intercourse was conversation spiced with wit, repartee as quick and deft as a fencing match. Artifice reigned supreme, and participants considered enthusiasm or sincerity in bad taste.

The women who hosted these salons referred to themselves as *femmes savantes,* or learned women. Among them was Julie de Lespinasse (1732–1776), one of the most articulate, urbane, and intelligent French women of the time. She held daily salons from five o'clock until nine in the evening. The book *Memoirs of Marmontel* documented the liveliness of these gatherings and the remarkable nature of this hostess.

The circle was formed of persons who were not bound together. She had taken them here and there in society, but so well assorted were they that once there they fell into harmony like the strings of an instrument touched by an able hand. Following out that comparison, I may say that she played the instrument with an art that came of genius; she seemed to know what tone each string would yield before she touched it; I mean to say that our minds and our natures were so well known to her that in order to bring them into play she had but to say a word. Nowhere was conversation more lively, more brilliant, or better regulated than at her house. It was a rare phenomenon indeed, the degree of tempered, equable heat which she knew so well how to maintain, sometimes by moderating it, sometimes by quickening it. The continual activity of her soul was communicated to our souls, but measurably; her imagination was the mainspring, her reason the regulator. Remark that the brains she stirred at will were neither feeble nor frivolous. . . . Her talent for casting out a thought and giving it for discussion to men of that class, her own talent in discussing it with precision, sometimes with eloquence, her talent for bringing forward new ideas and varying the topic—always with the facility and ease of a fairy . . . these talents, I say, were not those of an ordinary woman. It was not with the follies of fashion and vanity that daily, during four hours of conversation, without languor and without vacuum, she knew how to make herself interesting to a wide circle of strong minds.*

* Jean François Marmontel, *Memoirs of Marmontel,* translated by Brigit Patmore (London: Routledge, 1930), 270.

21-3 FRANÇOIS DE CUVILLIÉS, Hall of Mirrors, the Amalienburg, Nymphenburg Palace park, Munich, Germany, early 18th century.

Designed by a French architect, this circular hall in a German lodge displays the Rococo architectural style at its zenith, dazzling the eye with the organic interplay of mirrors, crystal, and stucco relief.

designed. The interior (FIG. 21-4, *top*) exhibits a vivacious play of architectural fantasy that retains the dynamic energy of Italian Baroque architecture (see Chapter 19) but not its drama. Numerous large windows in the richly decorated but continuous walls of Vierzehnheiligen flood the interior with an even, bright, and cheerful light. The feeling is one of lightness and delicacy.

Vierzehnheiligen's plan (FIG. 21-4, *bottom*) reveals the influence of Borromini (FIGS. 19-10 and 19-13) but is even more complex. Neumann seems deliberately to have banished all straight lines. The composition, made up of tangent ovals and circles, achieves a quite different interior effect within the essential outlines of a traditional rectilinear basilican church with a nave, transept, and apse. Undulating space is in continuous motion, creating unlimited vistas bewildering in their variety and surprise effects. The structural features pulse, flow, and commingle as if they were ceaselessly in the process of being molded. The design's fluidity of line, the floating and hovering surfaces, the interwoven spaces, and the dematerialized masses combine to suggest a "frozen" counterpart to the intricacy of voices in a Bach fugue. The church is a brilliant ensemble of architecture, painting, sculpture, and music that dissolves the boundaries of the arts in a visionary unity.

Painting and Sculpture

ANTOINE WATTEAU The painter whom scholars most associate with French Rococo is ANTOINE WATTEAU (1684–1721). The differences between the Baroque age in France and the Rococo age can be

21-4 BALTHASAR NEUMANN, interior (*top*) and plan (*bottom*) of the pilgrimage church of Vierzehnheiligen, near Staffelstein, Germany, 1743–1772.

The Rococo style also appeared in ecclesiastical architecture. Vierzehnheiligen's interior is light and delicate. Its plan features undulating lines and a dynamic interplay of ovals and circles.

VIERZEHNHEILIGEN Rococo style was not exclusively a domestic phenomenon, however. One of the most splendid examples of Rococo ecclesiastical architecture is the pilgrimage church of Vierzehnheiligen (Fourteen Saints; FIG. 21-4) near Staffelstein (MAP 20-1), which the German architect BALTHASAR NEUMANN (1687–1753)

21-5 ANTOINE WATTEAU, *L'Indifférent*, ca. 1716. Oil on canvas, 10″ × 7″. Louvre, Paris.

This small Rococo painting of a languid, gliding dancer exhibits lightness and delicacy in both color and tone. It contrasts sharply with Rigaud's majestic portrait (FIG. 20-30) of the pompous Louis XIV.

21-6 ANTOINE WATTEAU, *Pilgrimage to Cythera*, 1717. Oil on canvas, 4′ 3″ × 6′ 4½″. Louvre, Paris.

Watteau's *fête galante* paintings depict the outdoor amusements of French upper-class society. The haze of color, subtly modeled shapes, gliding motion, and air of suave gentility match Rococo taste.

seen clearly by contrasting Rigaud's portrait of Louis XIV (FIG. 20-30) with one of Watteau's paintings, *L'Indifférent* (*The Indifferent One;* FIG. 21-5). Rigaud portrayed pompous majesty in supreme glory, as if the French monarch were reviewing throngs of bowing courtiers at Versailles. Watteau's painting, in contrast, is more delicate and lighter in both color and tone. The artist presented a languid, gliding dancer whose stilted minuet could be a parody of the monarch's solemnity if the paintings were hung together. In Rigaud's portrait, stout architecture, bannerlike curtains, flowing ermine, and fleur-de-lis exalt the king. In Watteau's painting, the dancer moves in a rainbow shimmer of color, emerging onto the stage of the intimate comic opera to the silken sounds of strings. As in architecture, this contrast of paintings also highlights the different patronage of the eras. Whereas royal patronage, particularly that of Louis XIV, dominated the French Baroque period, Rococo was the culture of a wider aristocracy in which private patrons dictated taste.

PILGRIMAGE TO CYTHERA Watteau was largely responsible for creating a specific type of Rococo painting, called a *fête galante* (amorous festival) painting. These works depicted the outdoor entertainment or amusements of French high society. An example of a fête galante painting is Watteau's masterpiece (painted in two versions), *Pilgrimage to Cythera* (FIG. 21-6). The painting was the artist's entry for admission to the French Royal Academy of Painting and Sculpture (see "Academic Salons," Chapter 23, page 655). In 1717 the fête galante

was not an acceptable category for submission, but rather than reject Watteau's candidacy, the academy created a new category to accommodate his entry. At the turn of the century, two competing doctrines sharply divided the membership of the French academy. Many members followed Nicolas Poussin in teaching that form was the most important element in painting, whereas "colors in painting are as allurements for persuading the eyes"—additions for effect and not really essential.[1] The other group took Peter Paul Rubens as its model and proclaimed the natural supremacy of color and the coloristic style as the artist's proper guide. Depending on which doctrine they supported, academy members were either *Poussinistes* or *Rubénistes*. Watteau was Flemish, and Rubens's coloristic style heavily influenced his work. With Watteau in their ranks, the Rubénistes carried the day, establishing Rococo painting as the preferred style of the early 18th century.

Watteau's *Pilgrimage to Cythera* (FIG. 21-6) portrays luxuriously costumed lovers who have made a "pilgrimage" to Cythera, the island of eternal youth and love, sacred to Aphrodite. The elegant figures move gracefully from the protective shade of a woodland park filled with amorous cupids and voluptuous statuary. Watteau's figural poses blend elegance and sweetness. He composed his generally quite small paintings from albums of superb drawings in which he sought to capture slow movement from difficult and unusual angles, obviously intending to find the smoothest, most poised, and most refined attitudes. As he experimented with nuances of posture and movement, Watteau also strove for the most exquisite shades of

1 ft.

21-7 FRANÇOIS BOUCHER, *Cupid a Captive*, 1754. Oil on canvas, 5′ 6″ × 2′ 10″. Wallace Collection, London.

In this Rococo canvas, François Boucher, painter for Madame de Pompadour, portrayed a rosy pyramid of infant and female flesh and fluttering draperies set off against a cool, leafy background.

21-8 GIAMBATTISTA TIEPOLO, *Apotheosis of the Pisani Family*, ceiling fresco in the Villa Pisani, Stra, Italy, 1761–1762. Fresco, 77′ 1″ × 44′ 3″.

A master of illusionistic ceiling painting in the Baroque tradition, Tiepolo adopted the bright, cheerful colors and weightless figures of Rococo easel paintings for huge frescoes.

color difference, defining in a single stroke the shimmer of silk at a bent knee or the iridescence that touches a glossy surface as it emerges from shadow. The haze of color, the subtly modeled shapes, the gliding motion, and the air of suave gentility appealed greatly to the Rococo artist's wealthy patrons.

FRANÇOIS BOUCHER After Watteau's early death at 37, his follower, FRANÇOIS BOUCHER (1703–1770), rose to dominance in French painting, in large part because of Madame de Pompadour's patronage. Although he was an excellent portraitist, Boucher's fame rested primarily on his graceful canvases depicting Arcadian shep-

herds, nymphs, and goddesses cavorting in shady glens engulfed in pink and sky-blue light. *Cupid a Captive* (FIG. 21-7) presents a rosy pyramid of infant and female flesh set off against a cool, leafy background, with fluttering draperies both hiding and revealing the nudity of the figures. Boucher used the full range of Italian and French Baroque devices—the dynamic play of crisscrossing diagonals, curvilinear forms, and slanting recessions—to create his masterly composition. But in his work he dissected powerful Baroque curves into a multiplicity of decorative flourishes, dissipating Baroque drama into sensual playfulness. Lively and lighthearted, Boucher's artful Rococo fantasies became mirrors for his patrons, the wealthy French, to behold the ornamental reflections of their cherished pastimes.

JEAN-HONORÉ FRAGONARD Boucher's greatest student, JEAN-HONORÉ FRAGONARD (1732–1806), was an outstanding colorist whose decorative skill almost surpassed his master's. An example of his manner can stand as characteristic not only of his work but also of the later Rococo style in general. In *The Swing* (FIG. 21-1), a young gentleman has managed an arrangement whereby an unsuspecting old bishop swings the young man's pretty sweetheart higher

21-9 CLODION, *Satyr Crowning a Bacchante*, 1770. Terracotta, 1′ $\frac{5}{8}$″ high. Louvre, Paris.

1 in.

The erotic playfulness of Boucher's and Fragonard's paintings is evident in Clodion's tabletop terracotta sculptures representing sensuous fantasies often involving satyrs and bacchantes, the followers of Bacchus.

and higher, while her lover (and the work's patron), in the lower left corner, stretches out to admire her ardently from a strategic position on the ground. The young lady flirtatiously and boldly kicks off her shoe toward the little statue of Cupid. The infant love god holds his finger to his lips. The landscape setting is out of Watteau—a luxuriant perfumed bower in a park that very much resembles a stage scene for comic opera. The glowing pastel colors and soft light convey, almost by themselves, the theme's sensuality.

GIAMBATTISTA TIEPOLO *The Swing* is less than three feet in height, and Watteau's *L'Indifférent* (FIG. 21-5) barely 10 inches tall. But the intimate Rococo style could also be adopted for paintings of huge size, as the work of GIAMBATTISTA TIEPOLO (1696–1770) demonstrates. Of Venetian origin, Tiepolo worked for patrons in Austria, Germany, and Spain as well as in Italy. A master of illusionistic ceiling decoration in the Baroque tradition, Tiepolo favored the bright, cheerful colors and relaxed compositions of Rococo easel paintings. *Apotheosis of the Pisani Family* (FIG. 21-8), a ceiling fresco in the Villa Pisani at Stra in northern Italy (MAP 20-1), shows airy figures fluttering through vast sunlit skies and fleecy clouds, their forms casting dark accents against the brilliant light of high noon. Tiepolo here elevated the Pisani family members to the rank of gods in a heavenly scene that recalls the ceiling paintings of POZZO (FIG. 19-24). But while retaining 17th-century illusionism, Tiepolo softened the rhetoric and created pictorial schemes of great elegance and grace, unsurpassed for their sheer effectiveness as decor.

CLODION Rococo was nonetheless a style best suited for small-scale works that projected a mood of sensual intimacy in elegant salons. Artists such as Claude Michel, called CLODION (1738–1814), specialized in small, lively sculptures representing sensuous Rococo

fantasies. Clodion lived in Rome for several years, and his work incorporates echoes of Italian Mannerist sculpture. His small group *Satyr Crowning a Bacchante* (FIG. 21-9) depicts two mythological followers of Bacchus, the Roman god of wine. The languorous bacchante being crowned by the satyr with a floral wreath is reminiscent of the nude female personification in Benvenuto Cellini's *Saltcellar of Francis I* (FIG. 17-51). The erotic playfulness of Boucher's and Fragonard's paintings is also evident in Clodion's sculpture. He captured the sensual exhilaration of the Rococo style in diminutive scale and inexpensive terracotta. As is true of so many Rococo artifacts, the artist designed this group for a tabletop.

THE ENLIGHTENMENT

The aristocratic culture celebrated in Rococo art did not go unchallenged during the 18th century. Indeed, the feudal system that served as the foundation of social and economic life in Europe dissolved, and the rigid social hierarchies that provided the basis for Rococo art and patronage relaxed. By the end of the 18th century, revolutions had erupted in France and America. A major factor in these political, social, and economic changes was the Enlightenment.

Philosophy and Science

The *Enlightenment* was in essence a new way of thinking critically about the world and about humankind, independently of religion, myth, or tradition. The basis of Enlightenment thought was empirical evidence. Enlightenment thinkers promoted the scientific questioning of all assertions and rejected unfounded beliefs about the nature of humankind and of the world. Thus, the Enlightenment encouraged and stimulated the habit and application of mind known as the scientific method.

This new approach to the acquisition of knowledge had its roots in the 17th century, with the mathematical and scientific achievements of René Descartes (1596–1650), Blaise Pascal (1623–1662), Isaac Newton (1642–1727), and Gottfried Wilhelm von Leibniz (1646–1716). England and France were the principal centers of the Enlightenment, though its dictums influenced the thinking of intellectuals throughout Europe and in the American colonies. Benjamin Franklin (1706–1790), Thomas Jefferson (1743–1826), and other American notables embraced its principles.

NEWTON AND LOCKE Of particular importance for Enlightenment thought was the work of Great Britain's Isaac Newton and John Locke (1632–1704). In his scientific studies, Newton insisted on empirical proof of his theories and encouraged others to avoid metaphysics and the supernatural—realms that extended beyond the natural physical world. This emphasis on both tangible data and concrete experience became a cornerstone of Enlightenment thought. In addition, Newton's experiments revealed a rationality in the physical world, and Enlightenment thinkers transferred that concept to the sociopolitical world by promoting a rationally organized society. Locke, whose works acquired the status of Enlightenment gospel, developed these ideas further. According to Locke's "doctrine of empiricism," knowledge comes to people through their sense perception of the material world. From these perceptions alone people form ideas. Locke asserted that human beings are born good, not cursed by Original Sin. The laws of Nature grant them the natural rights of life, liberty, and property as well as the right to freedom of conscience. Government is by contract, and its purpose is to protect these rights. If and when government abuses these rights, the citizenry has the further natural right of revolution. Locke's ideas empowered people to take control of their own destinies.

PHILOSOPHES The work of Newton and Locke also inspired many French intellectuals, or *philosophes*. These thinkers conceived of individuals and societies at large as parts of physical nature. They shared the conviction that the ills of humanity could be remedied by applying reason and common sense to human problems. They criticized the powers of church and state as irrational limits placed on political and intellectual freedom. They believed that by the accumulation and propagation of knowledge, humanity could advance by degrees to a happier state than it had ever known. This conviction matured into the "doctrine of progress" and its corollary doctrine of the "perfectibility of humankind." Previous societies, for the most part, perceived the future as inevitable—the cycle of life and death. Religious beliefs determined fate. The notion of progress—the systematic and planned improvement of society—first developed during the 18th century and continues to influence 21st-century thought.

DIDEROT Animated by their belief in human progress and perfectibility, the philosophes took on the task of gathering knowledge and making it accessible to all who could read. Their program was, in effect, the democratization of knowledge. Denis Diderot (1713–1784) greatly influenced the Enlightenment's rationalistic and materialistic thinking. He became editor of the pioneering *Encyclopédie*, a compilation of articles written by more than a hundred contributors, including all the leading philosophes. The *Encyclopédie* was truly comprehensive (its formal title was *Systematic Dictionary of the Sciences, Arts, and Crafts*) and included all available knowledge—historical, scientific, and technical as well as religious and moral—and political theory. The first volume appeared in 1751 and the last of the 35 volumes of text and illustrations in 1780. Other Enlightenment authors produced different compilations of knowledge. Diderot's contemporary, Comte de Buffon (1707–1788), undertook a kind of encyclopedia of the natural sciences. His *Natural History*, a monumental work of 44 volumes, was especially valuable for its zoological study. Buffon's contemporary, the Swedish botanist Carolus Linnaeus (1707–1778), established a system of plant classification.

The political, economic, and social consequences of this increase in knowledge and the doctrine of progress were explosive. It is no coincidence that the French Revolution, the American Revolution, and the Industrial Revolution in England all occurred during this period. These upheavals precipitated yet other major changes, including the growth of cities, the emergence of an urban working class, and the expansion of colonialism as the demand for cheap labor and raw materials increased. This enthusiasm for growth gave birth to the doctrine of Manifest Destiny—the ideological justification for continued territorial expansion. Thus, the Age of Enlightenment ushered in a new way of thinking and affected historical developments worldwide.

VOLTAIRE François Marie Arouet, better known as Voltaire (1694–1778), became, and still is, the most representative figure—almost the personification—of the Enlightenment spirit. Voltaire was instrumental in introducing Newton and Locke to the French intelligentsia. He hated, and attacked through his writings, the arbitrary despotic rule of kings, the selfish privileges of the nobility and the church, religious intolerance, and, above all, the injustice of the *ancien régime* (the "old order"). In his numerous books and pamphlets, which the authorities regularly condemned and burned, he protested against government persecution of the freedoms of thought and religion. Voltaire believed humankind could never be happy until an enlightened society removed the traditional obstructions to the progress of the human mind. His personal and public involvement in the struggle against established political and religious authority gave authenticity to his ideas. It converted a whole generation to the conviction that fundamental changes were necessary. This conviction paved the way for a revolution in France that Voltaire never intended, and he probably would never have approved of it. He was not convinced that "all men are created equal," the credo of Jean-Jacques Rousseau, Thomas Jefferson, and the American Declaration of Independence.

21-10 JOSEPH WRIGHT OF DERBY, *A Philosopher Giving a Lecture at the Orrery*, ca. 1763–1765. Oil on canvas, 4′ 10″ × 6′ 8″. Derby Museums and Art Gallery, Derby.

Wright's celebration of the inventions of the Industrial Revolution was in tune with the Enlightenment doctrine of progress. In this dramatically lit scene, the wonders of science mesmerize everyone present.

1 ft.

INDUSTRIAL REVOLUTION The Enlightenment's emphasis on scientific investigation and technological invention opened up new possibilities for human understanding of the world and for control of its material forces. Research into the phenomena of electricity and combustion, along with the discovery of oxygen and the power of steam, had enormous consequences. Steam power as an adjunct to, or replacement for, human labor began a new era in world history, beginning with the Industrial Revolution in England. These technological advances, coupled with the celebration of "progress," gave rise to industrialization. Most scholars mark the beginning of the Industrial Revolution with the invention of steam engines in England for industrial production and, later, their use for transportation in the 1740s. By 1850, England had a manufacturing economy—a revolutionary development because for the first time in history, societies were capable of producing a seemingly limitless supply of goods and services. Within a century, the harnessed power of steam, coal, oil, iron, steel, and electricity working in concert transformed Europe. These scientific and technological developments also affected the arts, particularly the use of new materials for constructing buildings (FIG. 21-11) and the invention of photography (see Chapter 22).

JOSEPH WRIGHT Technological advance fueled a new enthusiasm for mechanical explanations about the wonders of the universe. The fascination science held for ordinary people as well as for the learned is the subject of *A Philosopher Giving a Lecture at the Orrery* (FIG. 21-10) by the English painter JOSEPH WRIGHT OF DERBY (1734–1797). Wright specialized in painting dramatic candlelit and moonlit scenes. He loved subjects such as the orrery demonstration, which could be illuminated by a single light from within the picture. In the painting, a scholar demonstrates a mechanical model of the solar system called an *orrery,* in which each planet (represented by a metal orb) revolves around the sun (a lamp) at the correct relative velocity. Light from the lamp pours forth from in front of the boy silhouetted in the foreground to create dramatic light and shadows that heighten the drama of the scene. Awed children crowd close to the tiny orbs that represent the planets within the arcing bands that symbolize their orbits. An earnest listener makes notes, while the lone woman seated at the left and the two gentlemen at the right

look on with rapt attention. The wonders of scientific knowledge mesmerize everyone in Wright's painting. The artist visually reinforced the fascination with the orrery by composing his image in a circular fashion, echoing the device's orbital design. The postures and gazes of all the participants and observers focus attention on the cosmic model. Wright scrupulously rendered with careful accuracy every detail of the figures, the mechanisms of the orrery, and even the books and curtain in the shadowy background.

Wright's realism appealed to the great industrialists of his day. Scientific-industrial innovators, such as Josiah Wedgwood, who pioneered many techniques of mass-produced pottery, and Sir Richard Arkwright, whose spinning frame revolutionized the textile industry, often purchased works such as *Orrery*. To them, Wright's elevation of the theories and inventions of the Industrial Revolution to the plane of history painting was exciting and appropriately in tune with the future.

COALBROOKDALE BRIDGE Advances in engineering and the development of new industrial materials during the 18th century had a profound impact on the history of architecture, leading eventually to the steel-and-glass skyscrapers of cities all over the world today. The first use of iron in bridge design was in the cast-iron bridge (FIG. 21-11) built over the Severn River, near Coalbrookdale in England (MAP 22-1), where ABRAHAM DARBY III (1750–1789), one of the bridge's two designers, ran his family's cast-iron business. The Darby family had spearheaded the evolution of the iron industry in England, and they vigorously supported the investigation of new uses for the material. The fabrication of cast-iron rails and bridge elements inspired Darby to work with architect THOMAS F. PRITCHARD (1723–1777) in designing the Coalbrookdale Bridge. The cast-iron armature that supports the roadbed springs from stone pier to stone pier until it leaps the final 100 feet across the Severn River gorge. The style of the graceful center arc echoes the grand arches of Roman aqueducts (FIG. 7-33). At the same time, the exposed structure of the bridge's cast-iron parts prefigured the skeletal use of iron and steel in the 19th century. Visible structural armatures became expressive factors in the design of buildings such as the Crystal Palace (FIG. 22-48) in England and the Eiffel Tower (FIG. 23-1) in France.

21-11 ABRAHAM DARBY III and THOMAS F. PRITCHARD, iron bridge, Coalbrookdale, England, 1776–1779.

The first use of iron in bridge design was in this bridge over the Severn River. The Industrial Revolution brought engineering advances and new materials that revolutionized architectural construction.

Diderot on Chardin and Naturalism

Denis Diderot was a pioneer in the field of art criticism as well as in the encyclopedic compilation of human knowledge. Between 1759 and 1781 he contributed reviews of the biennial Salon of the French Royal Academy of Painting and Sculpture (see "Academic Salons," Chapter 23, page 655) to the Parisian journal *Correspondence littéraire*. In his review of the 1763 Salon, Diderot, a great admirer of Jean-Baptiste-Siméon Chardin (FIG. **21-12**), had the following praise for that painter's still lifes and for naturalism in painting.

> There are many small pictures by Chardin at the Salon, almost all of them depicting fruit with the accoutrements for a meal. This is nature itself. The objects stand out from the canvas and they are so real that my eyes are fooled by them. . . . In order to look at other people's paintings, I feel as though I need different eyes; but to look at Chardin's, I need only keep the ones nature gave me and use them properly. If I had painting in mind as a career for my child, I'd buy this one [and have him copy it]. . . . Yet nature itself may be no more difficult to copy. . . . O Chardin, it's not white, red or black pigment that you grind on your palette but rather the very substance of objects; it's real air and light that you take onto the tip of your brush and transfer onto the canvas. . . . It's magic, one can't understand how it's done: thick layers of colour, applied one on top of the other, each one filtering through from underneath to create the effect. . . . Close up, everything blurs, goes flat and disappears. From a distance, everything comes back to life and reappears.*

* Translated by Kate Tunstall, in Charles Harrison, Paul Wood, and Jason Gaiger, eds., *Art in Theory 1648–1815: An Anthology of Changing Ideas* (Oxford: Blackwell, 2000), 604.

21-12 Jean-Baptiste-Siméon Chardin, *Saying Grace*, 1740. Oil on canvas, 1′ 7″ × 1′ 3″. Louvre, Paris.

Chardin embraced naturalism and celebrated the simple goodness of ordinary people, especially mothers and children, who lived in a world far from the frivolous Rococo salons of Paris.

"Natural" Art

ROUSSEAU The second key figure of the French Enlightenment, who was also instrumental in preparing the way ideologically for the French Revolution, was Jean-Jacques Rousseau (1712–1778). Voltaire believed the salvation of humanity was in the advancement of science and in the rational improvement of society. In contrast, Rousseau declared that the arts, sciences, society, and civilization in general had corrupted "natural man"—people in their primitive state—and that humanity's only salvation lay in a return to something like "the ignorance, innocence and happiness" of its original condition. According to Rousseau, human capacity for feeling, sensibility, and emotions came before reason: "To exist is to feel; our feeling is undoubtedly earlier than our intelligence, and we had feelings before we had ideas." Nature alone must be the guide: "All our natural inclinations are right." Fundamental to Rousseau's thinking was the notion that "Man by nature is good . . . he is depraved and perverted by society." He rejected the idea of progress, insisting that "Our minds have been corrupted in proportion as the arts and sciences have improved."[2] Rousseau's elevation of feelings above reason as the most primitive—and hence the most "natural"—of human expressions led him to exalt as the ideal the peasant's simple life, with its honest and unsullied emotions.

CHARDIN Rousseau's views, popular and widely read, were largely responsible for the turning away from the Rococo sensibility and the formation of a taste for the "natural," as opposed to the artificial and frivolous. Reflecting Rousseau's values, Jean-Baptiste-Siméon Chardin (1699–1779) painted quiet scenes of domestic life, which offered the opportunity to praise the simple goodness of ordinary people, especially mothers and young children, who in spirit, occupation, and environment lived far from corrupt society. In *Saying Grace* (FIG. **21-12**), Chardin ushers the viewer into a modest room where a mother and her small daughters are about to dine. The mood of quiet attention is at one with the hushed lighting and mellow color and with the closely studied still-life accessories whose worn surfaces tell their own humble domestic history. The viewer witnesses a moment of social instruction, when mother and older sister supervise the younger sister in the simple, pious ritual of giving thanks to God before a meal. The simplicity of the composition reinforces the subdued charm of this scene, with the three figures highlighted against the dark background. Chardin was the poet of the commonplace and the master of its nuances. A gentle sentiment prevails in all his pictures, an emotion not contrived and artificial but born of the painter's honesty, insight, and sympathy. Chardin's paintings had wide appeal, even in unexpected places. Louis XV, the royal personification of the Rococo in his life and tastes, once owned *Saying Grace*. The painter was also a favorite of Diderot, the leading art critic of the day as well as the editor of the *Encylopédie* (see "Diderot on Chardin and Naturalism," above).

Greuze was a master of sentimental narrative, which appealed to a new audience that admired "natural" virtue. Here, in an unadorned room, a father blesses his daughter and her husband-to-be.

JEAN-BAPTISTE GREUZE

The sentimental narrative in art became the specialty of French artist Jean-Baptiste Greuze (1725–1805), whose most popular work, *Village Bride* (FIG. 21-13), sums up the characteristics of the genre. The setting is an unadorned room in a rustic dwelling. In a notary's presence, the elderly father has passed his daughter's dowry to her youthful husband-to-be and blesses the pair, who gently take each other's arms. The old mother tearfully gives her daughter's arm a farewell caress, while the youngest sister melts in tears on the shoulder of the demure bride. An envious older sister broods behind her father's chair. Rosy-faced, healthy children play around the scene. The picture's story is simple—the happy climax of a rural romance. The painting's moral is just as clear—happiness is the reward of "natural" virtue.

Greuze produced this work at a time when the audience for art was expanding. The strict social hierarchy that provided the foundation for Rococo art and patronage gave way to a bourgeois economic and social system. Members of this bourgeois class increasingly embraced art, and paintings such as *Village Bride* particularly appealed to them. They carefully analyzed each gesture and each nuance of sentiment and reacted enthusiastically. At the 1761 Salon of the Royal Academy, Greuze's picture received enormous attention. Diderot, who reviewed the exhibition for *Correspondence littéraire*, declared that it was difficult to get near it because of the throngs of admirers.

VIGÉE-LEBRUN *Self-Portrait* (FIG. 21-14) by Élisabeth Louise Vigée-Lebrun (1755–1842) is another variation of the "naturalistic" impulse in 18th-century French art. In this new mode of portraiture, Vigée-Lebrun looks directly at viewers and pauses in her work to return their gaze. Although her mood is lighthearted and her costume's details echo the serpentine curve Rococo artists and wealthy patrons loved, nothing about Vigée-Lebrun's pose or her mood speaks of Rococo frivolity. Hers is the self-confident stance of a woman whose art has won her an independent role in her society. She portrayed herself in a close-up, intimate view at work on one of the portraits that won her renown, that of Queen Marie Antoinette (1755–1793). Like many of her contemporaries, Vigée-Lebrun lived a life of extraordinary personal and economic independence, working for the nobility throughout Europe. She was famous for the force and grace of her portraits, especially those of highborn ladies and royalty. She was successful during the age of the late monarchy in France and was one of the few women admitted to the Royal Academy. After the French

21-14 Élisabeth Louise Vigée-Lebrun, *Self-Portrait*, 1790. Oil on canvas, $8' 4'' \times 6' 9''$. Galleria degli Uffizi, Florence.

Vigée-Lebrun was one of the few women admitted to France's Royal Academy of Painting and Sculpture. In this self-portrait, she depicted herself confidently painting the likeness of Queen Marie Antoinette.

21-15 WILLIAM HOGARTH, *Breakfast Scene,* from *Marriage à la Mode,* ca. 1745. Oil on canvas, 2′ 4″ × 3′. National Gallery, London.

Hogarth won fame for his paintings and prints satirizing 18th-century English life with comic zest. This is one of a series of six paintings in which he chronicled the marital immoralities of the moneyed class.

1 ft.

Revolution, however, the Academy rescinded her membership, because women were no longer welcome, but she enjoyed continued success owing to her talent, wit, and ability to forge connections with those in power in the postrevolutionary period.

WILLIAM HOGARTH Across the Channel, a truly English style of painting emerged with WILLIAM HOGARTH (1697–1764), who satirized the lifestyle of the newly prosperous middle class with comic zest. Traditionally, the British imported painters from the Continent—Holbein, Rubens, and Van Dyck among them. Hogarth waged a lively campaign throughout his career against the English feeling of dependence on, and inferiority to, these artists. Although Hogarth would have been the last to admit it, his own painting owed much to the work of his contemporaries in France, the Rococo artists. Yet his subject matter, frequently moral in tone, was distinctively English. It was the great age of English satirical writing, and Hogarth—who knew and admired this genre and included Henry Fielding (1701–1754), the author of *Tom Jones,* among his closest friends—clearly saw himself as translating satire into the visual arts.

Hogarth's favorite device was to make a series of narrative paintings and prints, in a sequence like chapters in a book or scenes in a play, following a character or group of characters in their encounters with some social evil. *Breakfast Scene* (FIG. **21-15**), from *Marriage à la Mode,* is one in a sequence of six paintings that satirize the marital immoralities of the moneyed classes in England. In it, the marriage of a young viscount is just beginning to founder. The husband and wife are tired after a long night spent in separate pursuits. While the wife stayed home for an evening of cards and music-making, her young husband had been away from the house for a night of suspicious business. He thrusts his hands deep into the empty money-pockets of his breeches, while his wife's small dog sniffs inquiringly at a woman's lacy cap protruding from his coat pocket. A steward, his hands full of unpaid bills, raises his eyes to Heaven in despair at the actions of his no-

ble master and mistress. The house is palatial, but Hogarth filled it with witty clues to the dubious taste of its occupants. For example, the row of pious religious paintings on the upper wall of the distant room concludes with a curtain-shielded work that undoubtedly depicts an erotic subject. According to the custom of the day, ladies could not view this discretely hidden painting, but at the pull of a cord, the master and his male guests could gaze at the cavorting figures. In *Breakfast Scene,* as in all his work, Hogarth proceeded as a novelist might, elaborating on his subject with carefully chosen detail, whose discovery heightens the comedy.

Hogarth designed the marriage series to be published as a set of engravings. The prints of this and his other moral narratives were so popular that unscrupulous entrepreneurs produced unauthorized versions almost as fast as the artist created his originals. The popularity of these prints speaks not only to the appeal of their subjects but also to the democratization of knowledge and culture the Enlightenment fostered and to the exploitation of new printing technologies that produced a more affordable and widely disseminated visual culture.

THOMAS GAINSBOROUGH A contrasting blend of "naturalistic" representation and Rococo setting is found in the portrait *Mrs. Richard Brinsley Sheridan* (FIG. **21-16**) by the British painter THOMAS GAINSBOROUGH (1727–1788). This painting shows a lovely woman, dressed informally, seated in a rustic landscape faintly reminiscent of Watteau (FIG. 21-6) in its soft-hued light and feathery brushwork. Gainsborough intended to match the natural, unspoiled beauty of the landscape with that of his sitter. Mrs. Sheridan's dark brown hair blows freely in the slight wind, and her clear "English" complexion and air of ingenuous sweetness contrast sharply with the pert sophistication of those that Continental Rococo artists portrayed. Gainsborough originally had planned to give the picture a more pastoral air by adding several sheep, but he did not live long enough to paint them. Even without this element, the painting

21-16 Thomas Gainsborough, *Mrs. Richard Brinsley Sheridan,* 1787. Oil on canvas, 7′ 2⅝″ × 5′ ⅝″. National Gallery of Art, Washington, D.C. (Andrew W. Mellon Collection).

In this life-size portrait, Gainsborough sought to match the natural beauty of Mrs. Sheridan with that of the landscape. The rustic setting, soft-hued light, and feathery brushwork recall Rococo painting.

clearly expresses the artist's deep interest in the landscape setting. Although he won greater fame in his time for his portraits, he had begun as a landscape painter and always preferred painting scenes of nature to depicting human likenesses.

JOSHUA REYNOLDS Morality of a more heroic tone than that found in the work of Greuze, yet in harmony with "naturalness," included the virtues of honor, valor, and love of country. According to 18th-century Western thought, these virtues produced great people and exemplary deeds. The concept of "nobility," especially as discussed by Rousseau, referred to character, not to aristocratic birth. As the century progressed and people felt the tremors of coming revolutions, these virtues of courage and resolution, patriotism, and self-sacrifice assumed greater importance. Having risen from humble origins, the modern military hero, not the decadent aristocrat, brought the tumult of war into the company of the "natural" emotions.

Sir Joshua Reynolds (1723–1792) specialized in what became known as *Grand Manner portraiture* and often depicted contemporaries who participated in the great events of the latter part of the 18th century. Although clearly showing individualized people, Grand Manner portraiture also elevated the sitter by conveying refinement and elegance. Painters communicated a person's grace and class through

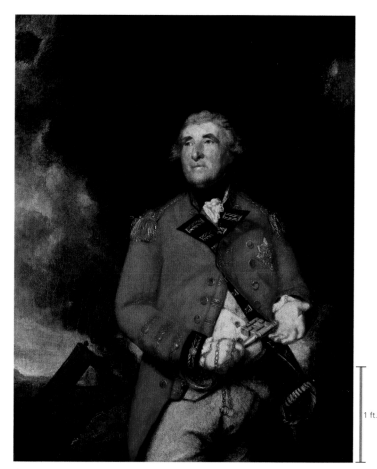

21-17 Sir Joshua Reynolds, *Lord Heathfield,* 1787. Oil on canvas, 4′ 8″ × 3′ 9″. National Gallery, London.

In this Grand Manner portrait, Reynolds depicted the English commander who defended Gibraltar. Typical of this genre, Heathfield is large in relation to the canvas size and stands in a dramatic pose.

certain standardized conventions, such as the large scale of the figure relative to the canvas, the controlled pose, the landscape setting, and the low horizon line. Reynolds painted his portrait of *Lord Heathfield* (FIG. **21-17**) in 1787. This burly, ruddy English officer, commandant of the fortress at Gibraltar, was a perfect subject for a Grand Manner portrait. Heathfield had doggedly defended the British fortress against the Spanish and the French, and later received the honorary title Baron Heathfield of Gibraltar. Here, he holds the huge key to the fortress, the symbol of his victory. He stands in front of a curtain of dark smoke rising from the battleground, flanked by one cannon that points ineffectively downward and another whose tilted barrel indicates that it lies uselessly on its back. Reynolds portrayed the features of the general's heavy, honest face and his uniform with unidealized realism. But Lord Heathfield's posture and the setting dramatically suggest the heroic themes of battle and refer to the revolutions (American and French) then taking shape in deadly earnest, as the old regimes faded into the past.

BENJAMIN WEST Some American artists also became well known in England. Benjamin West (1738–1820), born in Pennsylvania on what was then the colonial frontier, traveled to Europe early in life to study art and then went to England, where he met with almost immediate success. A cofounder of the Royal Academy of Arts, West succeeded Reynolds as its president. He became official painter to King George III (r. 1760–1801) and retained that position during the strained period of the American Revolution.

21-18 BENJAMIN WEST, *Death of General Wolfe,* 1771. Oil on canvas, 4′ 11½″ × 7′. National Gallery of Canada, Ottawa (gift of the Duke of Westminster, 1918).

West's great innovation was to blend contemporary subject matter and costumes with the grand tradition of history painting. Here, West likened General Wolfe's death to that of a martyred saint.

In *Death of General Wolfe* (FIG. 21-18), West depicted the mortally wounded young English commander just after his defeat of the French in the decisive battle of Quebec in 1759, which gave Canada to Great Britain. In portraying a contemporary historical subject, he put his characters in contemporary costume (although the military uniforms are not completely accurate in all details). However, West blended this realism of detail with the grand tradition of history painting by arranging his figures in a complex, theatrically ordered composition. His modern hero dies among grieving officers on the field of victorious battle in a way that suggests the death of a great saint. West wanted to present this hero's death in the service of the state as a martyrdom charged with religious emotions. His innovative combination of the conventions of traditional heroic painting with a look of modern realism was so effective that it won viewers' hearts in his own day and continued to influence history painting well into the 19th century.

JOHN SINGLETON COPLEY American artist JOHN SINGLETON COPLEY (1738–1815) matured as a painter in the Massachusetts Bay Colony. Like West, Copley later emigrated to England, where he absorbed the fashionable English portrait style. But unlike Grand Manner portraiture, Copley's *Portrait of Paul Revere* (FIG. 21-19), painted before Copley left Boston, conveys a sense of directness and faithfulness to visual fact that marked the taste for honesty and plainness many visitors to America noticed during the 18th and 19th centuries. When Copley painted his portrait, Revere was not yet the familiar hero of the American Revolution. In the picture, he is working at his profession of silversmithing. The setting is plain, the lighting clear and revealing. Revere sits in his shirtsleeves, bent over a teapot in progress. He pauses and turns his head to look the observer straight in the eye. Copley treated the reflections in the polished wood of the tabletop with as much care as Revere's figure, his tools, and the teapot resting on its leather graver's pillow. Copley gave special prominence to Revere's eyes by reflecting intense reddish light onto the darkened side of his face and hands. The informality and the sense of the moment link this

21-19 JOHN SINGLETON COPLEY, *Portrait of Paul Revere,* ca. 1768–1770. Oil on canvas, 2′ 11⅛″ × 2′ 4″. Museum of Fine Arts, Boston (gift of Joseph W., William B., and Edward H. R. Revere).

In contrast to Grand Manner portraiture, Copley's *Paul Revere* emphasizes his subject's down-to-earth character, differentiating this American work from its European counterparts.

The Grand Tour and Veduta Painting

Although travel throughout Europe was commonplace in the 18th century, Italy became a particularly popular destination. This "pilgrimage" of aristocrats, the wealthy, politicians, and diplomats from France, England, Germany, Flanders, Sweden, the United States, Russia, Poland, and Hungary came to be known as the Grand Tour. Italy's allure fueled the revival of classicism, and the popularity of Neoclassical art drove this fascination with Italy. One British observer noted: "All our religion, all our arts, almost all that sets us above savages, has come from the shores of the Mediterranean."*

The Grand Tour was not simply leisure travel. The education available in Italy to the inquisitive mind made the trip an indispensable experience for anyone who wished to make a mark in society. The Enlightenment had made knowledge of ancient Rome and Greece imperative, and a steady stream of Europeans and Americans traveled to Italy in the late 18th and early 19th centuries. These tourists aimed to increase their knowledge of literature, the visual arts, architecture, theater, music, history, customs, and folklore. Given this extensive agenda, it is not surprising that a Grand Tour could take a number of years to complete, and most travelers moved from location to location, following an established itinerary.

The British were the most avid travelers, and they conceived the initial "tour code," including important destinations and required itineraries. Although they designated Rome early on as the primary destination, visitors traveled as far north as Venice and as far south as Naples. Eventually, Paestum, Sicily, Florence, Genoa, Milan, Siena, Pisa, Bologna, and Parma (MAP 20-1) all appeared in guidebooks and in paintings. Joseph Wright of Derby (FIG. 21-10) and Joseph Mallord William Turner (FIG. 22-23) were among the many British artists to undertake a Grand Tour.

Many of those who completed a Grand Tour returned home with a painting by Antonio Canaletto, the leading painter of scenic views (*vedute*) of Venice. It must have been very cheering on a gray winter afternoon in England to look up and see a sunny, panoramic view such as that in Canaletto's *Riva degli Schiavoni, Venice* (FIG. 21-20), with its cloud-studded sky, picturesque water traffic, and well-known Venetian landmarks (the Doge's Palace, FIG. 14-21, is at the left in *Riva degli Schiavoni*) painted in scrupulous perspective and minute detail. Canaletto usually made drawings "on location" to take back to his studio and use as sources for paintings. To help make the on-site draw-

21-20 Antonio Canaletto, *Riva degli Schiavoni, Venice,* ca. 1735–1740. Oil on canvas, $1' 6\frac{1}{2}'' \times 2' 7\frac{7}{8}''$. Toledo Museum of Art, Toledo.

Canaletto was the leading painter of Venetian *vedute,* which were treasured souvenirs for 18th-century travelers visiting Italy on a Grand Tour. He used a camera obscura for his on-site drawings.

ings true to life, he often used a camera obscura, as Vermeer (FIGS. 20-1 and 20-19) did before him. These instruments were darkened chambers (some of them virtually portable closets) with optical lenses fitted into a hole in one wall through which light entered to project an inverted image of the subject onto the chamber's opposite wall. The artist could trace the main details from this image for later reworking and refinement. The camera obscura allowed artists to create visually convincing paintings that included variable focus of objects at different distances. Canaletto's paintings give the impression of capturing every detail, with no omissions. In fact, he presented each site within Renaissance perspectival rules and exercised great selectivity about which details to include and which to omit to make a coherent and engagingly attractive veduta.

---

* Cesare de Seta, "Grand Tour: The Lure of Italy in the Eighteenth Century," in Andrew Wilton and Ilaria Bignamini, eds., *Grand Tour: The Lure of Italy in the Eighteenth Century* (London: Tate Gallery, 1996), 13.

---

painting to contemporaneous English and European portraits. But the spare style and the emphasis on the sitter's down-to-earth character differentiate this American work from its European counterparts.

THE GRAND TOUR The 18th-century public also sought "naturalness" in artists' depictions of landscapes. Documentation of particular places became popular, in part due to growing travel opportunities and expanding colonialism. These depictions of geographic settings also served the needs of the many scientific expeditions mounted during the century and satisfied the desires of genteel tourists for mementos of their journeys. By this time, a "Grand Tour" of the major

sites of Europe was an essential part of every well-bred person's education (see "The Grand Tour," above). Naturally, those on tour wished to return with items that would help them remember their experiences and impress those at home with the wonders they had seen. The English were especially eager collectors of pictorial souvenirs. Certain artists in Venice specialized in painting the most characteristic scenes, or *vedute* (views), of that city to sell to British visitors. Chief among the Venetian painters was Antonio Canaletto (1697–1768), whose works, for example *Riva degli Schiavoni, Venice* (FIG. 21-20), English tourists avidly acquired as evidence of their visit to the city of the Grand Canal.

The Excavations of Herculaneum and Pompeii

Among the events that fueled the European fascination with classical antiquity were the excavations of two ancient Roman cities on the Bay of Naples—Herculaneum and Pompeii. The violent eruption of Mount Vesuvius in August 79 CE had buried both cities under volcanic ash and mud (see "An Eyewitness Account of the Eruption of Mount Vesuvius," Chapter 7, page 165). Although each city was "rediscovered" at various times during the ensuing centuries, systematic exploration of both sites did not begin until the mid-1700s. Because Vesuvius buried these cities under volcanic ash and lava, the excavations produced unusually rich evidence for reconstructing Roman art and life. The 18th-century excavators uncovered paintings, sculptures, furniture, vases, and silverware in addition to buildings. As a result, European interest in ancient Rome expanded tremendously. European collectors acquired many of the newly discovered objects. For example, Sir William Hamilton, British consul in Naples from 1764 to 1800, purchased numerous vases and small objects, which he sold to the British Museum in 1772. The finds at Pompeii and Herculaneum, therefore, quickly became available to a wide public.

"Pompeian" style soon became all the rage in England, as evident in the interior designs of Robert Adam, which were inspired by the slim, straight-lined, elegant frescoes of the Third and early Fourth Styles of Roman mural painting (FIGS. 7-21 and 7-22). The new Neoclassical style almost entirely displaced the curvilinear Rococo (FIGS. 21-2 and 21-3) after midcentury. In the Etruscan Room (FIG. 21-21) at Osterley Park House, Adam took decorative motifs (medallions, urns, vine scrolls, sphinxes, and tripods) from Roman art and arranged them sparsely within broad, neutral spaces and slender margins, as in his ancient models. Adam was an archaeologist as well, and he had explored and written accounts of the ruins of Diocletian's palace (FIG. 7-74) at Split. Kedleston House in Derbyshire, Adelphi Terrace in London, and a great many other structures he designed show the influence of the Split palace on his work.

21-21 ROBERT ADAM, Etruscan Room, from Osterley Park House, Middlesex, England, begun 1761. Victoria & Albert Museum, London.

Inspired by the recent discoveries at Herculaneum and Pompeii, Adam incorporated classical decorative motifs into his Etruscan Room, which he based on Roman mural painting.

The archaeological finds from Herculaneum and Pompeii also affected garden and landscape design, fashion, and tableware. Clothing based on classical garb became popular, and Emma Hamilton, wife of Sir William Hamilton, often gave lavish parties dressed in floating and delicate Greek-style drapery. Neoclassical taste also determined the pottery designs of John Flaxman (1755–1826) and Josiah Wedgwood (1730–1795). Wedgwood established his reputation in the 1760s with his creamware inspired by ancient art. He eventually produced vases based on what were thought to be Etruscan designs (actually Greek vases found in Etruscan tombs) and expanded his business by producing small busts of classical figures as well as cameos and medallions adorned with copies of antique reliefs and statues.

NEOCLASSICISM

One of the defining characteristics of the late 18th century was a renewed admiration for classical antiquity, which the Grand Tour was instrumental in fueling. This interest gave rise to the artistic movement known as *Neoclassicism,* which incorporated the subjects and styles of ancient art. Painting, sculpture, and architecture, however, were only the most prominent manifestations of Neoclassicism. Fascination with Greek and Roman culture was widespread and extended to the public culture of fashion and home decor. The Enlightenment's emphasis on rationality in part explains this classical focus, because the geometric harmony of classical art and architecture embodied Enlightenment ideals. In addition, classical cultures represented the pinnacle of civilized society, and Greece and Rome served as models of enlightened political organization. These cultures, with their traditions of liberty, civic virtue, morality, and sacrifice, were ideal models during a period of great political upheaval. Given these traditional associations, it is not coincidental that Neoclassicism was particularly appealing during the French and American Revolutions. Further whetting the public appetite for classicism were the excavations of Herculaneum (begun in 1738) and Pompeii (1748), which the volcanic eruption of Mount Vesuvius had buried (see "The Excavations of Herculaneum and Pompeii," page 598). Soon, murals based on artwork unearthed in the excavations began to appear on the walls of rooms in European town houses, such as the "Etruscan Room" (FIG. 21-21) by ROBERT ADAM (1728–1792) in Osterley Park House in Middlesex, begun in 1761.

WINCKELMANN The enthusiasm for classical antiquity also permeated much of the scholarship of the time. In the late 18th century, the ancient world increasingly became the focus of scholarly attention. A visit to Rome stimulated Edward Gibbon (1737–1794) to begin his monumental *Decline and Fall of the Roman Empire,* which appeared between 1776 and 1788. Earlier, in 1755, Johann Joachim Winckelmann (1717–1768), the first modern art historian, published *Reflections on the Imitation of Greek Works in Painting and Sculpture,* uncompromisingly designating Greek art as the most perfect to come from human hands—and far preferable to "natural" art.

> Good taste, which is becoming more prevalent throughout the world, had its origins under the skies of Greece. . . . The only way for us to become great . . . is to imitate the ancients. . . . In the masterpieces of Greek art, connoisseurs and imitators find not only nature at its most beautiful but also something beyond nature, namely certain ideal forms of its beauty. . . . A person enlightened enough to penetrate the innermost secrets of art will find beauties hitherto seldom revealed when he compares the total structure of Greek figures with most modern ones, especially those modelled more on nature than on Greek taste.[3]

In his *History of Ancient Art* (1764), Winckelmann described each monument and positioned it within a huge inventory of works organized by subject matter, style, and period. Before Winckelmann, art historians had focused on biography, as did Giorgio Vasari and

Giovanni Pietro Bellori in the 16th and 17th centuries. Winckelmann thus initiated one modern art historical method thoroughly in accord with Enlightenment ideas of ordering knowledge—a system of description and classification that provided a pioneering model for the understanding of stylistic evolution. His familiarity with classical art derived predominantly (as was the norm) from Roman works and Roman copies of Greek art in Italy. Yet he was instrumental in bringing to scholarly attention the distinctions between Greek and Roman art. Thus, he paved the way for more thorough study of the distinct characteristics of the art and architecture of these two cultures. Winckelmann's writings also laid a theoretical and historical foundation for the enormously widespread taste for Neoclassicism that lasted well into the 19th century.

Painting

ANGELICA KAUFFMANN One of the pioneers of Neoclassical painting was ANGELICA KAUFFMANN (1741–1807). Born in Switzerland and trained in Italy, Kauffmann spent many of her productive years in England. A student of Reynolds, and an interior decorator of many houses built by Adam, she was a founding member of the British Royal Academy of Arts and enjoyed an enviable reputation. Her *Cornelia Presenting Her Children as Her Treasures,* or *Mother of the Gracchi* (FIG. 21-22), is an *exemplum virtutis* (example or model of virtue) drawn from Greek and Roman history and literature. The moralizing pictures of Greuze (FIG. 21-13) and Hogarth (FIG. 21-15) already had marked a change in taste, but Kauffmann replaced the modern setting and character of their works. She clothed her actors in ancient Roman garb and posed them in statuesque attitudes within Roman interiors. The theme in this painting is the virtue of Cornelia, mother of the future political leaders Tiberius and Gaius Gracchus, who, in the second century BCE, attempted to reform the Roman Republic. Cornelia reveals her character in this scene, which takes place after the seated visitor showed off her fine jewelry and then insisted haughtily that Cornelia show hers. Instead of rushing to get her own precious adornments, Cornelia brought her sons forward, presenting them as her jewels. The architectural setting is severely Roman, with no Rococo motif in evidence, and the composition and drawing have the simplicity and firmness of low-relief carving.

1 ft.

21-22 ANGELICA KAUFFMANN, *Cornelia Presenting Her Children as Her Treasures,* or *Mother of the Gracchi,* ca. 1785. Oil on canvas, 3′ 4″ × 4′ 2″. Virginia Museum of Fine Arts, Richmond (the Adolph D. and Wilkins C. Williams Fund).

Kauffmann's painting of a virtuous Roman mother who presented her children to a visitor as her jewels exemplifies the Enlightenment fascination with classical antiquity and with classical art.

David on Greek Style and Public Art

Jacques-Louis David was the leading Neoclassical painter in France at the end of the 18th century. He championed a return to Greek style and the painting of inspiring heroic and patriotic subjects. In 1796 he made the following statement to his pupils:

> I want to work in a pure Greek style. I feed my eyes on antique statues, I even have the intention of imitating some of them. The Greeks had no scruples about copying a composition, a gesture, a type that had already been accepted and used. They put all their attention and all their art on perfecting an idea that had been already conceived. They thought, and they were right, that in the arts the way in which an idea is rendered, and the manner in which it is expressed, is much more important than the idea itself. To give a body and a perfect form to one's thought, this—and only this—is to be an artist.*

David also strongly believed that paintings depicting noble events in ancient history, such as *Oath of the Horatii* (FIG. 21-23),

would instill patriotism and civic virtue in the public at large in postrevolutionary France. In November 1793 he wrote:

> [The arts] should help to spread the progress of the human spirit, and to propagate and transmit to posterity the striking examples of the efforts of a tremendous people who, guided by reason and philosophy, are bringing back to earth the reign of liberty, equality, and law. The arts must therefore contribute forcefully to the education of the public. . . . The arts are the imitation of nature in her most beautiful and perfect form. . . . [T]hose marks of heroism and civic virtue offered the eyes of the people [will] electrify the soul, and plant the seeds of glory and devotion to the fatherland.†

* Translated by Robert Goldwater and Marco Treves, eds., *Artists on Art*, 3d ed. (New York: Pantheon Books, 1958), 206.
† Ibid., 205.

21-23 JACQUES-LOUIS DAVID, *Oath of the Horatii*, 1784. Oil on canvas, 10′ 10″ × 13′ 11″. Louvre, Paris.

David was the Neoclassical painter-ideologist of the French Revolution. This huge canvas celebrating ancient Roman patriotism and sacrifice features statuesque figures and classical architecture.

1 ft.

JACQUES-LOUIS DAVID The Enlightenment idea of a participatory and knowledgeable citizenry lay behind the revolt against the French monarchy in 1789, but the immediate causes of the French Revolution were the country's economic crisis and the clash between the Third Estate (bourgeoisie, peasantry, and urban and rural workers) and the First and Second Estates (the clergy and nobility, respectively). They fought over the issue of representation in the legislative body, the Estates-General, which had been convened to discuss taxation as a possible solution to the economic problem. However, the ensuing revolution revealed the instability of the monarchy and of French society's traditional structure and resulted in a succession of republics and empires as France struggled to find a way to adjust to these decisive changes.

JACQUES-LOUIS DAVID (1748–1825) became the Neoclassical painter-ideologist of the French Revolution. A distant relative of Boucher, he followed the Rococo painter's style until a period of study in Rome won the younger man over to the classical art tradition. David favored the academic teachings about using the art of the ancients and of the great Renaissance masters as models. He rebelled against Rococo style as an "artificial taste" and exalted the "perfect form" of Greek art (see "David on Greek Style and Public Art," page 600).

OATH OF THE HORATII David concurred with the Enlightenment belief that subject matter should have a moral and should be presented so that noble deeds in the past could inspire virtue in the present. A milestone painting in David's career, *Oath of the Horatii* (FIG. 21-23), depicts a story from pre-Republican Rome, the heroic phase of Roman history. The topic was not too arcane for David's audience. Pierre Corneille (1606–1684) had retold this story of conflict between love and patriotism, first recounted by the ancient Roman historian Livy, in a play performed in Paris several years earlier, making it familiar to David's viewing public. According to the story, the leaders of the warring cities of Rome and Alba decided to resolve their conflicts in a series of encounters waged by three representatives from each side. The Romans chose as their champions the three Horatius brothers, who had to face the three sons of the Curatius family from Alba. A sister of the Horatii, Camilla, was the bride-to-be of one of the Curatius sons, and the wife of the youngest Horatius was the sister of the Curatii.

David's painting shows the Horatii as they swear on their swords, held high by their father, to win or die for Rome, oblivious to the anguish and sorrow of their female relatives. In its form, *Oath of the Horatii* is a paragon of the Neoclassical style. Not only does the subject matter deal with a narrative of patriotism and sacrifice excerpted from Roman history, but the painter presented the image with force and clarity. David depicted the scene in a shallow space much like a stage setting, defined by a severely simple architectural framework. He deployed his statuesque and carefully modeled figures across the space, close to the foreground, in a manner reminiscent of ancient relief sculpture. The rigid, angular, and virile forms of the men on the left effectively contrast with the soft curvilinear shapes of the distraught women on the right. This pattern visually pits virtues the Enlightenment leaders ascribed to men (such as courage, patriotism, and unwavering loyalty to a cause) against the emotions of love, sorrow, and despair that the women in the painting express. The French viewing audience perceived such emotionalism as characteristic of the female nature. The message was clear and of a type readily identifiable to the prerevolutionary French public. The picture created a sensation at its first exhibition in Paris in 1785, and although David had painted it under royal patronage and did not intend the painting as a revolutionary statement, the Neoclassical style of *Oath of the Horatii* soon became the semiofficial voice of the French Revolution. David may have painted in the academic tradition, but he brought new impetus to it. He created a program for arousing his audience to patriotic zeal.

DEATH OF MARAT When the French Revolution broke out in 1789, David threw in his lot with the Jacobins, the radical and militant revolutionary faction. He accepted the role of de facto minister of propaganda, organizing political pageants and ceremonies that included floats, costumes, and sculptural props. David believed that art could play an important role in educating the public and that dramatic paintings emphasizing patriotism and civic virtue would prove

21-24 JACQUES-LOUIS DAVID, *Death of Marat*, 1793. Oil on canvas, 5′ 5″ × 4′ 2½″. Musées Royaux des Beaux-Arts de Belgique, Brussels.

David depicted the revolutionary Marat as a tragic martyr, stabbed to death in his bath. Although the painting displays severe Neoclassical spareness, its convincing realism conveys pain and outrage.

effective as rallying calls. However, rather than continuing to create artworks focused on scenes from antiquity, David began to portray scenes from the French Revolution itself. He intended *Death of Marat* (FIG. 21-24) not only to serve as a record of an important event in the struggle to overthrow the monarchy but also to provide inspiration and encouragement to the revolutionary forces. Jean-Paul Marat (1743–1793), a writer and David's friend, was tragically assassinated in 1793. David depicted the martyred revolutionary after Charlotte Corday (1768–1793), a member of a rival political faction, stabbed him to death in his medicinal bath. (Marat suffered from a painful skin disease.) David presented the scene with directness and clarity. The cold neutral space above Marat's figure slumped in the tub produces a chilling oppressiveness. The painter vividly placed narrative details—the knife, the wound, the blood, the letter with which the young woman gained entrance—to sharpen the sense of pain and outrage and to confront viewers with the scene itself. *Death of Marat* is convincingly real, yet David masterfully composed the painting to present Marat as a tragic martyr who died in the service of the revolution. David based the figure of Marat on Christ in Michelangelo's *Pietà* (FIG. 17-12) in Saint Peter's in Rome. The reference to Christ's martyrdom made the painting a kind of "altarpiece" for the new civic "religion," inspiring the French people with the saintly dedication of their slain leader.

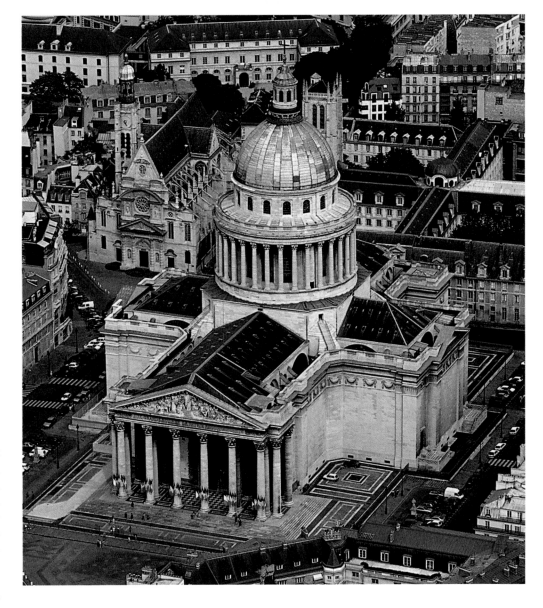

21-25 JACQUES-GERMAIN SOUFFLOT, Panthéon (Sainte-Geneviève), Paris, France, 1755–1792.

Soufflot's Panthéon is a testament to the Enlightenment admiration for Greece and Rome. It combines a portico based on an ancient Roman temple with a colonnaded dome and a Greek-cross plan.

Architecture and Sculpture

Architecture in the Enlightenment era also exhibits a dependence on classical models. Early in the 18th century, architects began to turn away from the theatricality and ostentation of Baroque and Rococo design and embraced a more streamlined antique look.

PANTHÉON The portico of the Parisian church of Sainte-Geneviève, now the Panthéon (FIG. **21-25**), by JACQUES-GERMAIN SOUFFLOT (1713–1780), stands as testament to the revived interest in Greek and Roman cultures. The Roman ruins at Baalbek in Lebanon, especially the titanic colonnade of the temple of Jupiter, provided much of the inspiration for Soufflot's design. The columns, reproduced with studied archaeological precision, stand out from walls that are severely blank, except for a repeated garland motif near the top. The colonnaded dome, a Neoclassical version of the domes of Saint Peter's (FIGS. 19-3 and 19-4) in Rome, the Église du Dôme (FIG. 20-36) in Paris, and Saint Paul's (FIG. 20-38) in London, rises above a Greek-cross plan. Both the dome and the vaults rest on an interior grid of splendid freestanding Corinthian columns, as if the portico's colonnade continued within. Although the overall effect, inside and out, is Roman, the structural principles employed are essentially Gothic. Soufflot was one of the first 18th-century builders to suggest that the logical engineering of Gothic cathedrals (see "The Gothic Cathedral," Chapter 13, page 347) could be applied to modern buildings. In his work, the curious, but not unreasonable, conjunction of Gothic and classical has a structural integration that laid the foundation for the 19th-century admiration of Gothic building principles.

CHISWICK HOUSE The appeal of classical antiquity extended well beyond French borders. The popularity of Greek and Roman cultures was due not only to their association with morality, rationality, and integrity but also to their connection to political systems ranging from Athenian democracy to Roman imperial rule. Thus, parliamentary England joined revolutionary France in embracing Neoclassicism. In England, Neoclassicism's appeal also was due to its clarity and simplicity. These characteristics provided a stark contrast to the complexity and opulence of Baroque art, then associated with the flamboyant rule of absolute monarchy. In English architecture, the preference for a simple style derived indirectly from the authority of the classical Roman architect Vitruvius, through Andrea Palladio's work (FIGS. 17-29 to 17-32), and on through that of Inigo Jones (FIG. 20-37).

RICHARD BOYLE (1695–1753), earl of Burlington, strongly restated Jones's Palladian doctrine in a new style in Chiswick House (FIG. **21-26**), which he built on London's outskirts with the help of WILLIAM KENT (ca. 1686–1748). The way had been paved for this shift in style by, among other things, the publication of Colin Campbell's *Vitruvius Britannicus* (1715), three volumes of engravings of ancient buildings, prefaced by a denunciation of Italian Baroque and high praise for Palladio and Jones. Chiswick House is a free variation on the theme of Palladio's Villa Rotonda (FIG. 17-29). The exterior design provided a clear alternative to the colorful splendors of Versailles (FIG. 20-32). In its simple symmetry, unadorned planes, right

21-26 RICHARD BOYLE and WILLIAM KENT, Chiswick House, near London, England, begun 1725.

For this British villa, Boyle and Kent emulated the simple symmetry and unadorned planes of the Palladian architectural style. Chiswick House is a free variation on the Villa Rotonda (FIG. 17-29).

21-27 JAMES STUART, Doric portico, Hagley Park, Worcestershire, England, 1758.

Most Neoclassical architects used Roman buildings in Italy and France as models. Stuart, who spent four years in Greece, based his Doric portico on a fifth-century BCE temple in Athens.

angles, and precise proportions, Chiswick looks very classical and "rational." But the Palladian-style villa's setting within informal gardens, where a charming irregularity of layout and freely growing uncropped foliage dominate the scene, mitigates the classical severity and rationality. Just as the owners of English villas cultivated irregularity in the landscaping surrounding their homes, they sometimes preferred interiors ornamented in a style more closely related to Rococo decoration. At Chiswick, the interior design creates a luxurious Baroque foil to the stern symmetry of the exterior and the plan. Palladian classicism prevailed in English architecture until about 1760, when it began to evolve into Neoclassicism.

STUART AND REVETT British painters and architects JAMES STUART (1713–1788) and NICHOLAS REVETT (1720–1804) introduced to Europe the splendor and originality of Greek art in their enormously influential *Antiquities of Athens,* the first volume of which appeared in 1762. These volumes firmly distinguished Greek art from the "derivative" Roman style that had served as the model for classicism since the Renaissance. Stuart and Revett fostered a new preference for Greek art and architecture over Roman antiquities, despite the fact that in the 18th century, familiarity with Greek art continued to be based primarily on Roman copies of Greek originals. Notwithstanding the popularity of the Grand Tour (see "The Grand Tour," page 597), travel to Greece was hazardous, making firsthand inspection of Greek monuments difficult. Stuart and Revett spent four years visiting Greece in the early 1750s, where they formed their preference for Greek art. When Stuart received the commission to design a portico (FIG. 21-27) for Hagley Park in Worcestershire, he used as his model the fifth-century BCE Doric temple in Athens known as the Theseion. His Doric portico is consequently much more severe (and authentic) than any contemporaneous Neoclassical building in Europe based on Roman or Renaissance designs.

21-28 Thomas Jefferson, Monticello, Charlottesville, Virginia, 1770–1806.

Jefferson led the movement to adopt Neoclassicism as the architectural style of the United States. Although built of local materials, his Palladian Virginia home recalls Chiswick House (FIG. 21-26).

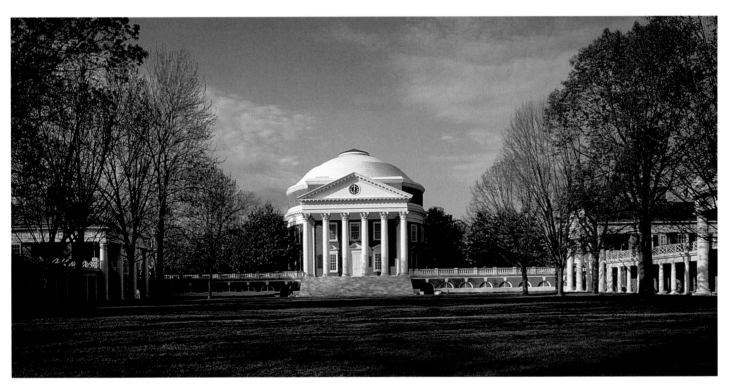

21-29 Thomas Jefferson, Rotunda and Lawn, University of Virginia, Charlottesville, Virginia, 1819–1826.

Modeled on the Pantheon (FIG. 7-49), Jefferson's Rotunda, like a temple in a Roman forum, sits on an elevated platform overlooking the colonnaded Lawn of the University of Virginia.

THOMAS JEFFERSON Part of the appeal of Neoclassicism was due to the values with which it was connected—morality, idealism, patriotism, and civic virtue. Thus, it is not surprising that in the new American republic (MAP 21-1), THOMAS JEFFERSON (1743–1826)— scholar, economist, educational theorist, statesman, and gifted amateur architect—spearheaded a movement to adopt Neoclassicism as the national architectural style. Jefferson admired Palladio immensely and read carefully the Italian architect's *Four Books of Architecture.* Later, while minister to France, he studied French 18th-century classical architecture and city planning and visited the Maison Carrée (FIG. 7-32), a Roman temple at Nîmes. After his European trip, Jefferson completely remodeled his own home, Monticello (FIG. 21-28), near Charlottesville, Virginia, which he first had designed in a different style. The final version of Monticello is somewhat reminiscent of Palladio's Villa Rotonda (FIG. 17-29) and of Chiswick House (FIG. 21-26), but its materials are the local wood and brick used in Virginia.

UNIVERSITY OF VIRGINIA Jefferson's Neoclassicism was an extension of the Enlightenment belief in the perfectibility of human beings and in the power of art to help achieve that perfection. When he became president, he selected Benjamin Latrobe (1764–1820) to build the United States Capitol in Washington, D.C., specifying that Latrobe use a Roman style. Jefferson's choice in part reflected his admiration for the beauty of the Roman buildings he had seen in Europe and in part his association of those buildings with an idealized Roman republican government and, through that, with the democracy of ancient Greece.

In his own designs for public buildings, Jefferson also looked to Rome for models. He modeled the State Capitol in Richmond, Virginia, on the Maison Carrée (FIG. 7-32). For the University of Virginia, which he founded, Jefferson turned to the Pantheon (FIG. 7-49). The Rotunda (FIG. 21-29) is the centerpiece of Jefferson's "academical village" in Charlottesville. It sits on an elevated platform at one end of a grassy quadrangle ("the Lawn"), framed by Neoclassical pavilions and colonnades—just as temples in Roman forums (FIGS. 7-12 and 7-43) stood at one short end of a colonnaded square. Each of the ten pavilions (five on each side) resembles a small classical temple. No two are exactly alike. Jefferson experimented with variations of all the different classical orders in their designs. Jefferson was no mere copyist. He had absorbed all the principles of classical architecture and clearly delighted in borrowing from major buildings in his own designs, which were nonetheless highly original—and, in turn, frequently emulated.

JEAN-ANTOINE HOUDON Neoclassicism also became the preferred style for public sculptural commissions in the new American republic. When the Virginia legislature wanted to erect a life-size marble statue of Virginia-born George Washington, the commission turned to the leading French Neoclassical sculptor of the late 18th century, JEAN-ANTOINE HOUDON (1741–1828). Houdon had already carved a bust portrait of Benjamin Franklin when he was U.S. ambassador to France. His portrait of Washington (FIG. 21-30) is the sculptural equivalent of a painted Grand Manner portrait (FIG. 21-18). But although both Washington and West's General Wolfe (FIG. 21-18) wear contemporary garb, the Houdon statue makes overt reference to the Roman Republic. The "column" on which Washington leans is a bundle of rods with an ax attached—the ancient Roman *fasces,* an emblem of authority (used much later as the emblem of Mussolini's Fascist—the term derives from "fasces"—government in 20th-century Italy). The 13 rods symbolize the 13 original states. The plow behind Washington and the fasces alludes to Cincinnatus, a patrician of the early Roman Republic who was elected dictator during a time of war and resigned his position as soon as victory had been achieved in order to return to his farm. Washington wears the badge of the Society of the Cincinnati (visible beneath the bottom of his waistcoat), an association founded in 1783 for officers in the revolutionary army who had resumed their peacetime roles. Tellingly, Washington no longer holds his sword in Houdon's statue.

1 ft.

21-30 JEAN-ANTOINE HOUDON, *George Washington,* 1788–1792. Marble, 6′ 2″ high. State Capitol, Richmond.

Houdon portrayed Washington in contemporary garb, but he incorporated the Roman *fasces* and Cincinnatus's plow in the statue, because Washington had returned to his farm after his war service.

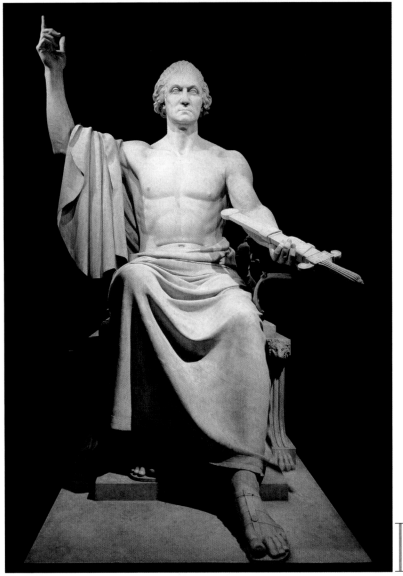

21-31 HORATIO GREENOUGH, *George Washington*, 1840. Marble, 11′ 4″ high. Smithsonian American Art Museum, Washington, D.C.

In this posthumous portrait, Greenough likened Washington to a god by depicting him seminude and enthroned in the manner of Phidias's Olympian statue of Zeus, king of the Greek gods.

1 ft.

HORATIO GREENOUGH After his death, Washington gradually acquired almost godlike stature as the "father of his country." In 1840 the United States Congress commissioned the American sculptor HORATIO GREENOUGH (1805–1852) to make a statue (FIG. 21-31) of the country's first president for the Capitol. Greenough used Houdon's portrait as his model for the head, but he portrayed Washington as seminude and enthroned, like the famous lost statue of Zeus that Phidias made for the god's temple at Olympia in ancient Greece. The statue, which epitomizes the Neoclassical style, did not, however, win favor with either the Congress that commissioned it or the public. Although no one ever threw Greenough's statue into the Potomac River, as one congressman suggested, the legislators never placed it in its intended site beneath the Capitol dome. In fact, by 1840 the Neoclassical style itself was no longer in vogue. The leading artists of Europe and America had embraced a new style, Romanticism, examined in the next chapter.

EUROPE AND AMERICA, 1700 TO 1800

ROCOCO

▌ In the early 18th century, the centralized and grandiose palace-based culture of Baroque France gave way to the much more intimate Rococo culture based in the town houses of Paris. There, aristocrats and intellectuals gathered for witty conversation in salons featuring delicate colors, sinuous lines, gilded mirrors, elegant furniture, and small paintings and sculptures.

▌ The leading Rococo painter was Antoine Watteau, whose usually small canvases feature light colors and elegant figures in ornate costumes moving gracefully through lush landscapes. His *fête galante* paintings depict the outdoor amusements of French high society.

▌ Watteau's successors included François Boucher and Jean-Honoré Fragonard, who carried on the Rococo style late into the 18th century. In Italy, Giambattista Tiepolo adapted the Rococo manner to huge ceiling frescoes in the Baroque tradition.

Watteau, *Pilgrimage to Cythera*, 1717

THE ENLIGHTENMENT

▌ By the end of the 18th century, revolutions had overthrown the monarchy in France and achieved independence for the British colonies in America. A major factor was the Enlightenment, a new way of thinking critically about the world independently of religion and tradition.

▌ The Enlightenment promoted scientific questioning of all assertions and embraced the doctrine of progress. The first modern encyclopedias appeared during the 18th century. The Industrial Revolution began in England in the 1740s. Engineers and architects developed new building materials. Iron was first used in bridge construction at Coalbrookdale, England, in 1776.

▌ The Enlightenment also made knowledge of ancient Rome imperative for the cultured elite, and Europeans and Americans in large numbers undertook a Grand Tour of Italy. Among the most popular souvenirs of the Grand Tour were Antonio Canaletto's *vedute* of Venice rendered in precise Renaissance perspective with the aid of a camera obscura.

▌ Rejecting the idea of progress, Rousseau, one of the leading French *philosophes,* argued for a return to natural values and exalted the simple, honest life of peasants. His ideas had a profound impact on artists such as Jean-Baptiste-Siméon Chardin and Jean-Baptiste Greuze, who painted sentimental narratives about rural families.

▌ The taste for naturalism also led to the popularity of portrait paintings set against landscape backgrounds, a specialty of Thomas Gainsborough, among others, and to a reawakening of an interest in realism. Benjamin West represented the protagonists in his history paintings wearing contemporary costumes.

Canaletto, *Riva degli Schiavoni, Venice*, ca. 1735–1740

Greuze, *Village Bride*, 1761

NEOCLASSICISM

▌ The Enlightenment revival of interest in Greece and Rome, which spurred systematic excavations at Herculaneum and Pompeii, also gave rise in the late 18th century to the artistic movement known as Neoclassicism, which incorporated the subjects and styles of ancient art.

▌ One pioneer of the new style was Angelica Kauffmann, who often chose subjects drawn from Roman history for her paintings. Jacques-Louis David, who exalted classical art as "the imitation of nature in her most beautiful and perfect form," also favored ancient Roman themes. Painted on the eve of the French Revolution, *Oath of the Horatii,* set in a severe classical hall, served as an example of patriotism and sacrifice.

▌ The Neoclassical style also became the rage in interior decoration, fashion, and architecture. Roman and Italian Renaissance structures inspired Jacques-Germain Sofflot's Panthéon in Paris and Richard Boyle's Chiswick House near London. A Greek temple in Athens was the model for James Stuart's Doric portico in Worcestershire.

▌ In the United States, Thomas Jefferson adopted the Neoclassical style in his designs for Monticello, the Virginia Capitol, and the University of Virginia. He championed Neoclassicism as the official architectural style of the new American republic because it represented for him idealism, patriotism, and civic virtue.

David, *Oath of the Horatii*, 1784

Jefferson, Monticello, Charlottesville, 1770–1806

1 in.

22-1 Nadar, *Eugène Delacroix*, ca. 1855. Modern print, $8\frac{1}{2}'' \times 6\frac{2}{3}''$, from the original negative. Bibliothèque Nationale, Paris.

Eugène Delacroix, the great Romantic painter, was one of many 19th-century artists intrigued by how photography presented reality. Here, he sat for Nadar, one of the earliest portrait photographers.

22

EUROPE
AND AMERICA,
1800 TO 1870

The revolution of 1789 initiated a new era in France, but the overthrow of the monarchy also opened the door for Corsican-born Napoleon Bonaparte (1769–1821) to exploit the resulting disarray and establish a different kind of monarchy with himself at its head. In 1799, after serving in various French army commands, including leading major campaigns in Italy and Egypt, Napoleon became first consul of the French Republic, a title with clear and intentional links to the ancient Roman Republic (see Chapter 7). During the next 15 years, the ambitious general gained control of almost all of continental Europe in name or through alliances (MAP **22-1**). In May 1804, for example, he became king of Italy. Later that year, the pope journeyed to Paris for Napoleon's coronation as Emperor of the French (FIG. **22-2**). But in 1812, Napoleon launched a disastrous invasion of Russia that ended in retreat, and in 1815 he suffered a devastating loss at the hands of the British at Waterloo in present-day Belgium. Forced to abdicate the imperial throne, Napoleon went into exile on the island of Saint Helena in the South Atlantic, dying there six years later.

Following Napoleon's exile, the political geography of Europe changed dramatically (MAP **22-2**), but in many ways the more significant changes during the first half of the 19th century were technological and economic. The Industrial Revolution caused a population boom in European cities, and railroads spread to many parts of the Continent, facilitating the transportation of both goods and people. During this period, the arts also underwent important changes. The century opened with Neoclassicism still supreme, but by 1870 Romanticism and Realism in turn had captured the imagination of artists and public alike. New construction techniques had a major impact on architectural design, and the invention of photography revolutionized picture making of all kinds.

ART UNDER NAPOLEON

At the fall of the French revolutionary Maximilien Robespierre (1758–1794) and his party in 1794, Jacques-Louis David, who had aligned himself personally and through his work with the revolutionary forces (see Chapter 21), barely escaped with his life. He stood trial and went to prison. After his release in

MAP 22-1
The Napoleonic
Empire in 1815.

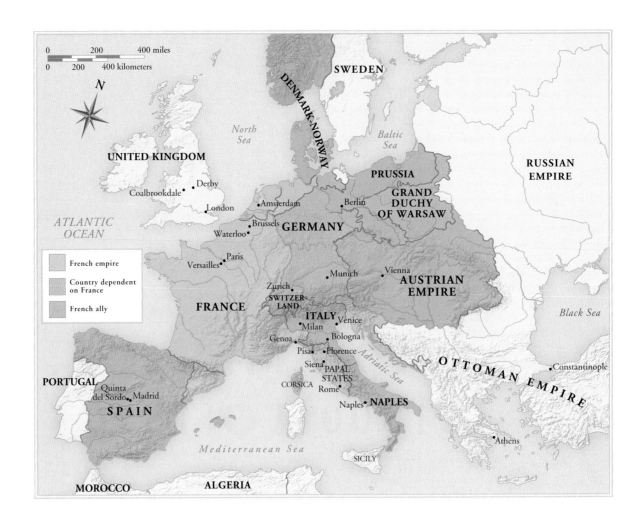

MAP 22-2
Europe around 1850.

22-2 JACQUES-LOUIS DAVID, *Coronation of Napoleon,* 1805–1808. Oil on canvas, 20′ 4½″ × 32′ 1¾″. Louvre, Paris.

As First Painter of the Empire, David recorded Napoleon at his December 1804 coronation crowning his wife with the pope as witness, thus underscoring the authority of the state over the church.

1795, he worked hard to resurrect his career. When Napoleon Bonaparte approached David in 1804 and offered him the position of First Painter of the Empire, David seized the opportunity. It was not just the artist's personal skill but Neoclassicism in general that appealed to Napoleon. The emperor embraced all links with the classical past as symbolic sources of authority. Classical associations, particularly connections to the Roman Empire, served Napoleon well, since he aspired to rule an empire that might one day rival ancient Rome's.

CORONATION OF NAPOLEON One of the major paintings David produced for Napoleon was *Coronation of Napoleon* (FIG. 22-2), a monumental painting (20 by 32 feet) that documented the pomp and pageantry of the new emperor's coronation in December 1804. Napoleon was well aware of the power of art for constructing a public image and of David's ability to produce inspiring patriotic images. To a large extent, David adhered to historical fact regarding the coronation, duly recording the appearance of the interior of Paris's Notre-Dame Cathedral as Napoleon's architects, Charles Percier (1764–1838) and Pierre-François-Léonard Fontaine (1762–1853), had decorated it for the occasion. David also faithfully portrayed those in attendance. In addition to Napoleon, his wife Josephine (1763–1814; kneeling to receive her crown), and Pope Pius VII (r. 1800–1823; seated behind Napoleon), others present at the occasion and in the painting included Joseph (1768–1814) and Louis (1778–1846) Bonaparte, Napoleon's ministers, the retinues of the emperor and empress, and a representative group of the clergy, as well as David himself, seated among the rows of spectators in the balconies. Despite the

artist's apparent fidelity to historical fact, preliminary studies and drawings reveal that David made changes at Napoleon's request. For example, Napoleon insisted that the painter depict the pope with his hand raised in blessing. Further, Napoleon's mother appears prominently in the center background, yet she had refused to attend the coronation.

Although David had to incorporate numerous figures and lavish pageantry in his painting, he retained the structured composition central to the Neoclassical style. As in his *Oath of the Horatii* (FIG. 21-23), David presented the action as if on a theater stage—which in this instance was literally the case, even if the stage Percier and Fontaine constructed was inside a church. In addition, as he did in his arrangement of the men and women in *Oath of the Horatii,* David conceptually divided the painting to reveal polarities. The pope, prelates, and priests representing the Catholic Church appear on the right, contrasting with members of Napoleon's imperial court on the left. The relationship between church and state was one of this period's most contentious issues. Napoleon's decision to crown himself, rather than to allow the pope to perform the coronation, as was traditional, reflected Napoleon's concern about the power relationship between church and state. For the painting commemorating the occasion, the emperor insisted that David depict the moment when, having already crowned himself, Napoleon places a crown on his wife's head, further underscoring his authority. Thus, although this painting represents an important visual document in the tradition of history painting, it is also a more complex statement about the changing politics in Napoleonic France.

Art under Napoleon **611**

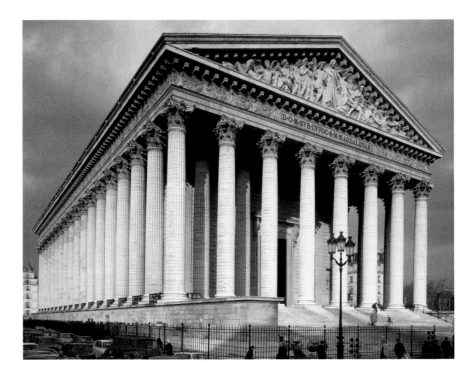

22-3 Pierre Vignon, La Madeleine, Paris, France, 1807–1842.

Napoleon constructed La Madeleine as a "temple of glory" for his armies. Based on ancient temples (FIG. 7-32) and Neoclassical in style, Vignon's design linked the Napoleonic and Roman empires.

LA MADELEINE Napoleon also embraced Neoclassical architecture as an ideal vehicle for expressing his imperial authority. For example, the emperor resumed construction of the church of La Madeleine (FIG. 22-3) in Paris, which had begun in 1764 but ceased in 1790. However, he converted the building to a "temple of glory" for France's imperial armies. The structure reverted again to a church after Napoleon's defeat and long before its completion in 1842. Designed by Pierre Vignon (1763–1828), the grandiose Napoleonic temple includes a high podium and broad flight of stairs leading to a deep porch in the front. These architectural features, coupled with the Corinthian columns, recall Roman temples in France, such as the Maison Carrée (FIG. 7-32) at Nîmes, making La Madeleine a symbolic link between the Napoleonic and Roman empires. Curiously, the building's classical shell surrounds an interior covered by a sequence of three domes, a feature found in Byzantine and Romanesque churches. It is as though Vignon clothed a traditional church in the costume of pagan Rome.

ANTONIO CANOVA Neoclassical sculpture also was in vogue under Napoleon. His favorite sculptor was Antonio Canova (1757–1822), who somewhat reluctantly left a successful career in Italy to settle in Paris and serve the emperor. Once in France, Canova became Napoleon's admirer and made numerous portraits, all in the Neoclassical style, of the emperor and his family. Perhaps the best known of these works is the marble portrait (FIG. 22-4) of Napoleon's sister, Pauline Borghese, as Venus. Initially, Canova had suggested depicting Borghese as Diana, goddess of the hunt. Pauline, however, demanded to be shown as Venus, the goddess of love. Thus, she appears reclining on a divan and gracefully holding the golden apple, the symbol of the goddess's triumph in the judgment of Paris. Canova clearly based his work on Greek statuary—the sensuous pose and seminude body recall Hellenistic works such as *Venus de Milo* (FIG. 5-83)—and the reclining figure has parallels on Roman sarcophagus lids (FIG. 7-61; compare FIG. 6-5).

22-4 Antonio Canova, *Pauline Borghese as Venus*, 1808. Marble, 6′ 7″ long. Galleria Borghese, Rome.

Canova was Napoleon's favorite sculptor. Here, the artist depicted the emperor's sister nude—at her request—as the Roman goddess of love in a marble statue inspired by classical models.

The French public never got to admire Canova's portrait, however. Napoleon had arranged the marriage of his sister to an heir of the noble Roman Borghese family. Once Pauline was in Rome, her behavior was less than dignified, and the public gossiped extensively about her affairs. Her insistence on being portrayed as the goddess of love reflected her self-perception. Due to his wife's questionable reputation, Prince Camillo Borghese (1775–1832), the work's official patron, kept the sculpture sequestered in the Villa Borghese in Rome, where it remains today. Borghese allowed relatively few people to see it (and then only by torchlight). Still, knowledge of the existence of the sculpture was widespread and increased the notoriety of both artist and subject.

22-5

ANTOINE-JEAN
GROS, *Napoleon at
the Pesthouse at
Jaffa,* 1804. Oil on
canvas, 17′ 5″ ×
23′ 7″. Louvre,
Paris.

Gros's huge
painting glorifies
Napoleon as pos-
sessing the mirac-
ulous power to
heal and reflects
David's composi-
tional principles,
but Gros's fasci-
nation with the
exotic Near East
presaged
Romanticism.

1 ft.

DAVID'S STUDENTS Given Jacques-Louis David's stature and prominence as an artist in Napoleonic France, along with the popularity of Neoclassicism, it is not surprising that he attracted numerous students and developed an active and flourishing teaching studio. David gave practical instruction to and deeply influenced many important artists of the period. So strong was David's commitment to classicism that he encouraged all his students to learn Latin, the better to immerse themselves in and understand classical culture. David even initially demanded that his pupils select their subjects from Plutarch, the ancient author of *Lives of the Great Greeks and Romans* and a principal source of Neoclassical subject matter. Due to this thorough classical foundation, David's students produced work that at its core retains Neoclassical elements. Yet David was open-minded and far from authoritarian in his teaching, and he encouraged his students to find their own artistic identities. The work of three of David's pupils—Antoine-Jean Gros, Anne-Louis Girodet-Trioson, and Jean-Auguste-Dominique Ingres—represents a departure from the structured confines of Neoclassicism. These artists laid the foundation for the Romantic movement, discussed in detail later. They explored the realm of the exotic and the erotic, and often turned to fictional narratives for the subjects of their paintings, as Romantic artists also did.

GROS Like his teacher David, ANTOINE-JEAN GROS (1771–1835) was aware of the benefits that could accrue to artists whom the powerful favored. Following David's lead, Gros produced several paintings that contributed to the growing mythic status of Napoleon Bonaparte in the early 1800s. In *Napoleon at the Pesthouse at Jaffa* (FIG. 22-5), the artist, at Napoleon's request, recorded an incident during an outbreak of the bubonic plague that erupted in the course of the Near

Eastern campaigns of 1799. This fearsome disease struck Muslim and French forces alike, and in March 1799, Napoleon himself visited the pesthouse at Jaffa to quell the growing panic and hysteria. Gros depicted Napoleon's staff officers covering their noses against the stench of the place, whereas Napoleon, amid the dead and dying, is fearless and in control. He comforts those still alive, who are clearly awed by his presence and authority. Indeed, by depicting the French leader touching the sores of a plague victim, Gros implied that Napoleon possessed the miraculous power to heal. This exaltation of the French leader was necessary to counteract the negative publicity he was subject to at the time. Apparently, two months after his visit to the pesthouse, Napoleon ordered all plague-stricken French soldiers poisoned so as to relieve him of having to return them to Cairo or abandon them to the Turks. Some of the soldiers survived, and from their accounts highly critical stories about Napoleon began to circulate. Gros's painting was an attempt at damage control—to resurrect the event and rehabilitate Napoleon's compromised public image.

Gros structured his composition in a manner reminiscent of David's major paintings, with the horseshoe arches and Moorish arcades of the mosque courtyard providing a backdrop for the unfolding action. In addition, Gros's placement of Muslim doctors ministering to plague-stricken Muslims on the left contrasts them with Napoleon and his soldiers on the right, bathed in radiant light. David had used this polarized compositional scheme to great effect in works such as *Oath of the Horatii* (FIG. 21-23). However, Gros's fascination with the exoticism of the Near East, as is evident in his attention to the unique architecture, attire, and terrain, represented a departure from Neoclassicism. This interest in the exotic, along with the artist's emphasis on death, suffering, and an emotional rendering of the scene, foreshadowed prominent aspects of Romanticism.

22-6 ANNE-LOUIS GIRODET-TRIOSON, *Burial of Atala*, 1808. Oil on canvas, 6′ 11″ × 8′ 9″. Louvre, Paris.

Girodet's depiction of Native American lovers in the Louisiana wilderness appealed to the French public's fascination with what it perceived as the passion and primitivism of tribal life in the New World.

GIRODET-TRIOSON Another of David's students, ANNE-LOUIS GIRODET-TRIOSON (1767–1824), also produced paintings that conjured images of exotic locales and cultures. He moved further into the domain of Romanticism with *Burial of Atala* (FIG. **22-6**), based on *The Genius of Christianity,* a novel by French writer François René de Chateaubriand (1768–1848). The section of the novel dealing with Atala appeared as an excerpt a year before the publication of the entire book in 1802. Both the excerpt and the novel were enormously successful, and as a result, Atala became almost a cult figure. The exoticism and eroticism integral to the narrative accounted in large part for the public's interest in *The Genius of Christianity.* Set in Louisiana, Chateaubriand's work focuses on two young Native Americans, Atala and Chactas. The two, from different tribes, fall in love and run away together through the wilderness. Erotic passion permeates the story, and Atala, sworn to lifelong virginity, finally commits suicide rather than break her oath. Girodet's painting depicts this tragedy. Atala's grief-stricken lover, Chactas, buries the heroine in the shadow of a cross. Assisting in the burial is a cloaked priest, whose presence is appropriate given Chateaubriand's emphasis on the revival of Christianity (and the Christianization of the New World) in his novel. Like Gros's depiction of the foreign Muslim world, Girodet's representation of American Indian lovers in the Louisiana wilderness appealed to the public's fascination (whetted by the Louisiana Purchase in 1803) with what it perceived as the passion and primitivism of Native American tribal life. *Burial of Atala* speaks here to emotions, rather than inviting philosophical meditation or revealing some grand order of nature and form. Unlike David's appeal in *Oath of the Horatii* (FIG. **21-23**) to feelings that manifest themselves in public action, the appeal here is to the viewer's private world of fantasy and emotion.

INGRES JEAN-AUGUSTE-DOMINIQUE INGRES (1780–1867) arrived at David's studio in the late 1790s after Girodet-Trioson had left to establish an independent career. Ingres's study there was to be short-

22-7 JEAN-AUGUSTE-DOMINIQUE INGRES, *Apotheosis of Homer*, 1827. Oil on canvas, 12′ 8″ × 16′ 10¾″. Louvre, Paris.

Inspired by *School of Athens* (FIG. **17-9**) by Ingres's favorite painter, Raphael, this monumental canvas is a Neoclassical celebration of Homer and other ancient worthies, Dante, and select French authors.

22-8 Jean-Auguste-Dominique Ingres, *Grande Odalisque*, 1814. Oil on canvas, 2′ 11⅞″ × 5′ 4″. Louvre, Paris.

The reclining female nude was a Greco-Roman subject, but Ingres converted his Neoclassical figure into an odalisque in a Turkish harem, consistent with the new Romantic taste for the exotic.

1 ft.

lived, however, as he soon broke with David on matters of style. This difference of opinion involved Ingres's embrace of what he believed to be a truer and purer Greek style than what David employed. The younger artist adopted flat and linear forms approximating those found in Greek vase painting (see Chapter 5). In many of his works, Ingres placed the figure in the foreground, much like a piece of low-relief sculpture.

Ingres exhibited his huge composition *Apotheosis of Homer* (FIG. 22-7) at the Salon of 1827 (see "Academic Salons," Chapter 23, page 655). The painting presented in a single statement the doctrines of ideal form and of Neoclassical taste, and generations of academic painters remained loyal to that style. Raphael's *School of Athens* (FIG. 17-9) served as the inspiration for *Apotheosis of Homer*. Enthroned before an Ionic temple, the epic poet Homer receives a crown from Fame or Victory. At the poet's feet are two statuesque women, who personify the *Iliad* and the *Odyssey,* the offspring of his imagination. Symmetrically grouped about him is a company of the "sovereign geniuses"—as Ingres called them—who expressed humanity's highest ideals in philosophy, poetry, music, and art. To Homer's left are the Greek poet Anacreon with his lyre, Phidias with his sculptor's hammer, the philosophers Plato and Socrates, and other ancient worthies. To his far right are the Roman poets Horace and Vergil, and two Italian greats: Dante and, conspicuously, Raphael, the painter Ingres most admired. Among the forward group on the painting's left side are Poussin (pointing) and Shakespeare (half concealed), and at the right are French writers Jean Baptiste Racine, Molière, Voltaire, and François de Salignac de la Mothe Fénelon. Ingres had planned a much larger and more inclusive group, but he never completed the project. For years he agonized over whom to choose for this select company of heroes in various humanistic disciplines.

GRANDE ODALISQUE As a true Neoclassical painter, Ingres condemned "modern" styles such as Romanticism. But despite his commitment to ideal form and careful compositional structure, Ingres also produced works that, like those of Gros and Girodet, his contemporaries saw as departures from Neoclassicism. One of those paintings was *Grande Odalisque* (FIG. 22-8). Ingres's subject, the reclining nude figure, followed the tradition of Giorgione and Titian (FIG. 17-40). The work also shows Ingres's admiration for Raphael in his borrowing of that master's type of female head (FIGS. 17-7 and 17-8). The figure's languid pose, small head and elongated limbs, and the generally cool color scheme reveal his debt to Parmigianino (FIG. 17-43) and the Italian Mannerists. However, by converting the figure to an *odalisque* (woman in a Turkish harem), the artist made a strong concession to the contemporary Romantic taste for the exotic.

This rather strange mixture of artistic allegiances—the combination of precise classical form and Romantic themes—prompted confusion, and when Ingres first exhibited *Grande Odalisque* in 1814, the painting drew acid criticism. Critics initially saw Ingres as a rebel in terms of both the form and content of his works. They did not cease their attacks until the mid-1820s, when another enemy of the official style, Eugène Delacroix, appeared on the scene. Then they suddenly perceived that Ingres's art, despite its innovations and deviations, still contained many elements that adhered to the official Neoclassicism—the taste for the ideal. Ingres soon led the academic forces in their battle against the "barbarism" of Delacroix, Théodore Géricault, and the Romantic movement. Gradually, Ingres warmed to the role his critics had cast for him, and he came to see himself as the conservator of good and true art, a protector of its principles against its would-be destroyers.

1 ft.

22-9 HENRY FUSELI, *The Nightmare,* 1781. Oil on canvas, 3′ 3¾″ × 4′ 1½″. Detroit Institute of the Arts (Founders Society Purchase with funds from Mr. and Mrs. Bert L. Smokler and Mr. and Mrs. Lawrence A. Fleishman).

The transition from Neoclassicism to Romanticism marked a shift in emphasis from reason to feeling. Fuseli was among the first painters to depict the dark terrain of the human subconscious.

ROMANTICISM

Whereas Neoclassicism's rationality reinforced Enlightenment thought (see Chapter 21), particularly Voltaire's views, Rousseau's ideas contributed to the rise of *Romanticism*. Rousseau's exclamation "Man is born free, but is everywhere in chains!"—the opening line of his *Social Contract* (1762)—summarizes a fundamental Romantic premise. Romanticism emerged from a desire for freedom—not only political freedom but also freedom of thought, of feeling, of action, of worship, of speech, and of taste. Romantics asserted that freedom was the right and property of all. They believed the path to freedom was through imagination rather than reason and functioned through feeling rather than through thinking.

The allure of the Romantic spirit grew dramatically during the late 18th century. The term originated toward the end of that century among German literary critics, who aimed to distinguish peculiarly "modern" traits from the Neoclassical traits that already had displaced Baroque and Rococo design elements. Consequently, many scholars refer to Romanticism as a phenomenon that began around 1750 and ended about 1850, but most use the term more narrowly to denote a movement that flourished from about 1800 to 1840, between Neoclassicism and Realism.

Roots of Romanticism

The transition from Neoclassicism to Romanticism represented a shift in emphasis from reason to feeling, from calculation to intuition, and from objective nature to subjective emotion. Among Romanticism's manifestations were the interests in the medieval period and in the sublime. For people living in the 18th century, the Middle Ages were the "dark ages," a time of barbarism, superstition, dark mystery, and miracle. The Romantic imagination stretched its perception of the Middle Ages into all the worlds of fantasy open to it, including the ghoulish, the infernal, the terrible, the nightmarish, the grotesque, the sadistic, and all the imagery that emerges from the chamber of horrors when reason sleeps. Related to the imaginative sensibility was the period's notion of the sublime. Among the individuals most involved in studying the sublime was the British politician and philosopher Edmund Burke (1729–1797). In his 1757 publication *A Philosophical Enquiry into the Origins of Our Ideas of the Sublime and Beautiful,* Burke articulated his definition of the sublime—feelings of awe mixed with terror. Burke observed that pain or fear evoked the most intense human emotions and that these emotions could also be thrilling. Thus, raging rivers and great storms at sea could be sublime to their viewers. Accompanying this taste for

22-10 William Blake, *Ancient of Days*, frontispiece of *Europe: A Prophecy*, 1794. Metal relief etching, hand colored, $9\frac{1}{2}'' \times 6\frac{3}{4}''$. Pierpont Morgan Library, New York.

Although art historians classify Blake as a Romantic artist, he incorporated classical references in his works. Here, ideal classical anatomy merges with the inner dark dreams of Romanticism.

1 in.

to depict the dark terrain of the human subconscious that became fertile ground for later artists to sow.

WILLIAM BLAKE In their images of the sublime and the terrible, Romantic artists often combined Baroque dynamism with naturalistic details in their quest for grippingly moving visions. These preferences became the mainstay of Romantic art and contrasted with the more intellectual, rational Neoclassical themes and presentations. The two were not mutually exclusive, however. Gros, Girodet-Trioson, and Ingres effectively integrated elements of Neoclassicism with Romanticism. So too did the visionary English poet, painter, and engraver WILLIAM BLAKE (1757–1827). Blake greatly admired ancient Greek art because it exemplified for him the mathematical and thus the eternal, and his work often incorporated classical references. Yet Blake did not align himself with prominent Enlightenment figures. Like many other Romantic artists, he also found the art of the Middle Ages appealing. Blake derived the inspiration for many of his paintings and poems from his dreams. The importance he attached to these nocturnal experiences led him to believe that the rationalist search for material explanations of the world stifled the spiritual side of human nature. He also believed that the stringent rules of behavior imposed by orthodox religions killed the individual's creative impulse.

Blake's vision of the Almighty in *Ancient of Days* (FIG. 22-10) combines his ideas and interests in a highly individual way. For Blake, this figure united the concept of the Creator with that of wisdom as a part of God. He chose *Ancient of Days* as the frontispiece for his book *Europe: A Prophecy*, and juxtaposed it with a quotation ("When he set a compass upon the face of the deep") from Proverbs 8:27 in the Old Testament. The speaker in that Bible chapter is Wisdom, who tells the reader how she was with the Lord through all the time of the Creation (Prov. 8:22–23, 27–30). Energy fills Blake's composition. The Almighty leans forward from a fiery orb, peering toward earth and unleashing power through his outstretched left arm into twin rays of light. These emerge between his spread fingers as might an architect's measuring instrument. A strong wind surges through his thick hair and beard. Only the strength of his Michelangelesque physique keeps him firmly planted on his heavenly perch. Here, ideal classical anatomy merges with the inner dark dreams of Romanticism.

the sublime was the taste for the fantastic, the occult, and the macabre—for the adventures of the soul voyaging into the dangerous reaches of consciousness.

HENRY FUSELI The concept of the nightmare is the subject of a 1781 painting (FIG. 22-9) by HENRY FUSELI (1741–1825). Swiss by birth, Fuseli settled in England and eventually became a member of the Royal Academy and an instructor there. Largely self-taught, he contrived a distinctive manner to express the fantasies of his vivid imagination. Fuseli specialized in night moods of horror and in dark fantasies—in the demonic, in the macabre, and often in the sadistic. In *The Nightmare*, a beautiful young woman lies asleep, draped across the bed with her limp arm dangling over the side. An *incubus*, a demon believed in medieval times to prey, often sexually, on sleeping women, squats ominously on her body. In the background, a ghostly horse with flaming eyes bursts into the scene from beyond the curtain. Despite the temptation to see the painting's title as a pun because of this horse, the word "nightmare" actually derives from "night" and "Mara." Mara was a spirit in Northern European mythology that people thought tormented and suffocated sleepers. Fuseli was among the first to attempt

Spain and France

From its roots in the work of Fuseli, Blake, and other late-18th-century artists, Romanticism gradually displaced Neoclassicism as the dominant painting style of the first half of the 19th century. Romantic artists, including Francisco Goya in Spain and Théodore Géricault and Eugène Delacroix in France, explored the exotic, erotic, and fantastic in their paintings.

FRANCISCO GOYA The Spaniard FRANCISCO JOSÉ DE GOYA Y LUCIENTES (1746–1828) was David's contemporary, but their work has little in common. Goya did not arrive at his general dismissal of Neoclassicism without considerable thought about the Enlightenment and the Neoclassical penchant for rationality and order. This reflection emerges in such works as *The Sleep of Reason Produces Monsters* (FIG. 22-11) from a series titled *Los Caprichos* (*The Caprices*). In this print, Goya depicted himself asleep, slumped onto a table or writing stand, while threatening creatures converge on him. Seemingly poised to attack the artist are owls (symbols of folly) and bats (symbols of ignorance). The viewer might read this as a portrayal of what emerges when reason is suppressed and, therefore, as an espousal of Enlightenment ideals. However, it also can be interpreted as Goya's commitment to the creative process and the Romantic spirit—the unleashing of imagination, emotions, and even nightmares.

FAMILY OF CHARLES IV The emotional art Goya produced during his long career stands as testimony not only to the allure of the Romantic vision but also to the turmoil in Spain and to the conflicts in Goya's life. His art is multifaceted in character, however, and many of his works deal with traditional religious subjects. Others are royal portraits painted after 1786, when Goya became Pintor del Rey (Painter to the King). Charles IV (r. 1788–1808) promoted him to First Court Painter in 1799. In his official capacity, Goya produced paintings very different in character from his *Caprichos*, such as *Family of Charles IV* (FIG. 22-12). Goya greatly admired the achievements of his predecessor Diego Velázquez, and Velázquez's *Las Meninas* (FIG. 19-30) was the inspiration for this image of the king and his queen, Maria Luisa, surrounded by their children. As in *Las Meninas*, the royal family appears facing the viewer in an interior space while the artist included himself on the left, dimly visible, in the act of painting on a large canvas. Goya's portrait of the royal family has been subjected to intense scholarly scrutiny, resulting in a variety of interpretations. Some scholars see this painting as a naturalistic depiction of Spanish royalty. Others believe it to be a pointed commentary in a time of Spanish turmoil. It is clear that his patrons authorized the painting's basic elements—the king and his family, their attire, and Goya's inclusion. Little evidence exists as to how the royal family reacted to this painting. Although some scholars have argued that they disliked the portrait, others have suggested that the painting confirmed the Spanish monarchy's continuing presence and strength and thus elicited a positive response from the patrons.

As dissatisfaction with the rule of Charles IV and Maria Luisa increased, the political situation grew more tenuous. The Spanish people eventually threw their support behind Ferdinand VII, son of the royal couple, in the hope that he would initiate reform. To overthrow his father and mother, Ferdinand VII enlisted the aid of Napoleon Bonaparte, who possessed uncontested authority and military expertise at that time. Napoleon had designs on the Spanish throne and thus willingly sent French troops to Spain. Not surprisingly, as soon as he ousted Charles IV, Napoleon revealed his plan to rule Spain himself by installing his brother Joseph Bonaparte (r. 1808–1813) on the Spanish throne.

22-11 FRANCISCO GOYA, *The Sleep of Reason Produces Monsters,* from *Los Caprichos,* ca. 1798. Etching and aquatint, $8\frac{1}{2}'' \times 5\frac{7}{8}''$. Metropolitan Museum of Art, New York (gift of M. Knoedler & Co., 1918).

In this print, Goya depicted himself asleep while threatening creatures converge on him, revealing his commitment to the Romantic spirit—the unleashing of imagination, emotions, and nightmares.

THIRD OF MAY, 1808 The Spanish people, finally recognizing the French as invaders, sought a way to expel the foreign troops. On May 2, 1808, in frustration, the Spanish attacked Napoleon's soldiers in a chaotic and violent clash. In retaliation and as a show of force, the French responded the next day by executing numerous Spanish citizens. This tragic event is the subject of Goya's most famous painting, *Third of May, 1808* (FIG. 22-13). In emotional fashion, Goya depicted the anonymous murderous wall of French soldiers ruthlessly executing the unarmed and terrified Spanish peasants. The artist encouraged empathy for the Spanish by portraying horrified expressions and anguish on their faces, endowing them with a humanity absent from the firing squad. Moreover, the peasant about to be shot throws his arms out in a cruciform gesture reminiscent of Christ's position on the cross. Goya enhanced the emotional drama of this tragic event through his stark use of darks and lights and by extending the time frame depicted. Although Goya captured the specific moment when one man is about to be executed, he also

22-12 Francisco Goya, *Family of Charles IV,* 1800. Oil on canvas, 9′ 2″ × 11′. Museo del Prado, Madrid.

Goya painted the family of the Spanish king Charles IV while serving as Pintor del Rey. Goya's model for the portrait was Velázquez's *Las Meninas* (FIG. **19-30**), which also included the artist in the painting.

1 ft.

22-13 Francisco Goya, *Third of May, 1808,* 1814–1815. Oil on canvas, 8′ 9″ × 13′ 4″. Museo del Prado, Madrid.

Goya encouraged empathy for the massacred Spanish peasants by portraying horrified expressions and anguish on their faces, endowing them with a humanity lacking in the French firing squad.

1 ft.

depicted the bloody bodies of others already lying dead on the ground. Still others have been herded together to be shot in a few moments. Its depiction of the resistance and patriotism of the Spanish people notwithstanding, *Third of May, 1808*, was a royal commission, painted in 1814 for Ferdinand VII (r. 1813–1833), who had reclaimed the throne after the ouster of the French.

SATURN Over time, Goya became increasingly disillusioned and pessimistic, and his declining health only contributed to this state of mind. Among his later works are the Black Paintings, frescoes he painted on the walls of his farmhouse in Quinta del Sordo, outside Madrid. Because Goya created these works solely on his terms and for his private viewing, they provide great insight into the artist's outlook, which is terrifying and disturbing. *Saturn Devouring One of His Children* (FIG. **22-14**) depicts the raw carnage and violence of Saturn (the Greek god Kronos; see "The Gods and Goddesses of Mount Olympus," Chapter 5, page 87, or in the "Before 1300" section), wild-eyed and monstrous, as he consumes one of his children. Because of the similarity of Kronos and *khronos* (Greek for "time"), Saturn has come to be associated with time. This has led some scholars to interpret Goya's painting as an expression of the artist's despair over the passage of time. Despite the simplicity of the image, it conveys a wildness, boldness, and brutality that cannot help but evoke an elemental response from any viewer. Goya's work, rooted both in personal and national history, presents darkly emotional images well in keeping with Romanticism.

THÉODORE GÉRICAULT In France one of the artists most closely associated with the Romantic movement was THÉODORE GÉRICAULT (1791–1824), who studied with an admirer of David, P. N. Guérin (1774–1833). Although Géricault retained an interest in the heroic and the epic and was well trained in classical drawing, he chafed at the rigidity of the Neoclassical style, instead producing works that captivate the viewer with their drama, visual complexity, and emotional force.

Géricault's most ambitious project was a gigantic canvas (approximately 16 by 23 feet) titled *Raft of the Medusa* (FIG. **22-15**). In this depiction of a historical event, the artist abandoned the idealism of Neoclassicism and instead invoked the theatricality of Romanticism. The painting's subject is a shipwreck that occurred in 1816 off the African coast. The French frigate *Medusa* ran aground on a reef due to the incompetence of the captain, a political appointee. In an attempt to survive, 150 remaining passengers built a makeshift raft from pieces of the disintegrating ship. The raft drifted for 12 days, and the number of survivors dwindled to 15. Finally, a ship spotted the raft and rescued the emaciated survivors. This horrendous event was political dynamite once it became public knowledge.

In *Raft of the Medusa*, which Géricault took eight months to complete, the artist sought to capture the horror, chaos, and emotion of the tragedy yet invoke the grandeur and impact of large-scale history painting. Géricault went to great lengths to ensure the accuracy of his representation. He visited hospitals and morgues to examine corpses, interviewed the survivors, and had a model of the raft constructed in his studio. In the painting, the few despairing survivors summon what little strength they have left to flag down the passing ship far on the horizon. Géricault departed from the straightforward organization of Neoclassical compositions and instead presented a jumble of writhing bodies. He arranged the survivors and several corpses in a powerful **X**-shaped composition, and piled one body on another in every attitude of suffering, despair, and death (recalling the plague-stricken bodies in Gros's *Napoleon at Jaffa*, FIG. **22-5**). One light-filled diagonal axis stretches from bodies

22-14 FRANCISCO GOYA, *Saturn Devouring One of His Children*, 1819–1823. Detached fresco mounted on canvas, 4' 9$\frac{1}{8}$" × 2' 8$\frac{5}{8}$". Museo del Prado, Madrid.

This disturbing fresco in Goya's farmhouse uses a mythological tale perhaps to express the aging artist's despair over the passage of time. Saturn's Greek name Kronos is similar to the Greek word for time.

1 ft.

at the lower left up to the black man raised on his comrades' shoulders and waving a piece of cloth toward the horizon. The cross axis descends from the storm clouds and the dark, billowing sail at the upper left to the shadowed upper torso of the body trailing in the open sea. Géricault's decision to place the raft at a diagonal so that a corner juts outward further compels viewers' participation in this scene. Indeed, it seems as though some of the corpses are sliding off the raft into the viewing space. The subdued palette and prominent shadows lend an ominous pall to the scene.

Géricault also took this opportunity to insert a comment on the practice of slavery. The artist was a member of an abolitionist group that sought ways to end the slave trade in the colonies. Given his

1 ft.

22-15 THÉODORE GÉRICAULT, *Raft of the Medusa*, 1818–1819. Oil on canvas, 16′ 1″ × 23′ 6″. Louvre, Paris.

In this gigantic history painting, Géricault rejected Neoclassical compositional principles and, in the Romantic spirit, presented a jumble of writhing bodies in every attitude of suffering, despair, and death.

antipathy to slavery, it is appropriate that Géricault placed Jean Charles, a black soldier and one of the few survivors, at the top of the pyramidal heap of bodies.

INSANE WOMAN Mental aberration and irrational states of mind could not fail to interest the rebels against Enlightenment rationality. Géricault, like many of his contemporaries, examined the influence of mental states on the human face and believed, as others did, that a face accurately revealed character, especially in madness and at the moment of death. He made many studies of the inmates of hospitals and institutions for the criminally insane, and he studied the severed heads of guillotine victims. Scientific and artistic curiosity often accompanied the morbidity of the Romantic interest in derangement and death. Géricault's *Insane Woman* (FIG. **22-16**)— her mouth tense, her eyes red-rimmed with suffering—is one of several of his portraits of the insane that have a peculiar hypnotic power. These portraits present the psychic facts with astonishing authenticity, especially in contrast to earlier idealized commissioned portraiture.

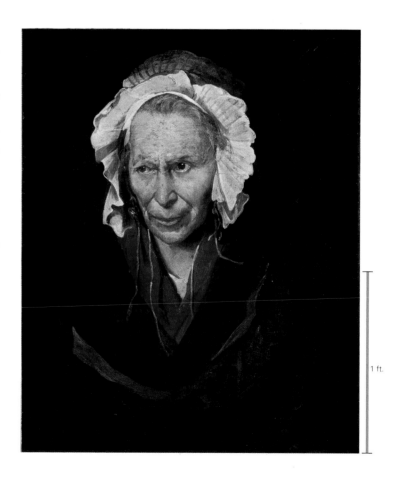

1 ft.

22-16 THÉODORE GÉRICAULT, *Insane Woman*, 1822–1823. Oil on canvas, 2′ 4″ × 1′ 9″. Musée des Beaux-Arts, Lyons.

The insane and the influence of aberrant states of mind on the appearance of the human face fascinated Géricault and other Romantic artists, who rebelled against Enlightenment rationality.

The Romantic Spirit in Art, Music, and Literature

The appeal of Romanticism, with its emphasis on freedom and feeling, extended well beyond the realm of the visual arts. The imagination and vision that characterized Romantic paintings and sculptures were equally moving and riveting in musical or written form. In European music, literature, and poetry, the Romantic spirit was a dominant presence during the late 18th and early 19th centuries. These artistic endeavors rejected classicism's structured order in favor of the emotive and expressive. In music, the compositions of Franz Schubert (1797–1828), Franz Liszt (1811–1886), Frédéric Chopin (1810–1849), and Johannes Brahms (1833–1897) all emphasized the melodic or lyrical. For these composers, music had the power to express the unspeakable and to communicate the subtlest and most powerful human emotions.

In literature, Romantic poets such as John Keats (1795–1821), William Wordsworth (1770–1850), and Samuel Taylor Coleridge (1772–1834) published volumes of poetry that serve as manifestations of the Romantic interest in lyrical drama. *Ozymandias*, by Percy Bysshe Shelley (1792–1822), speaks of faraway, exotic locales. The setting of Lord Byron's *Sardanapalus* is the ancient Assyrian Empire (see Chapter 2). Byron's poem conjures images of eroticism and fury unleashed—images that appear in Delacroix's painting *Death of Sardanapalus* (FIG. 22-17). One of the best examples of the Romantic spirit is the engrossing novel *Frankenstein*, written in 1818 by Shelley's wife, Mary Wollstonecraft Shelley (1797–1851). This tale of a monstrous creature run amok remains popular to the present day. As was true of many Romantic artworks, the novel not only embraced the emotional but also rejected the rationalism that underlay Enlightenment thought. Dr. Frankenstein's monster was a product of science, and the novel is an indictment of the tenacious belief in science that Enlightenment thinkers such as Voltaire promoted. *Frankenstein* served as a cautionary tale of the havoc that could result from unrestrained scientific experimentation and from the arrogance of scientists like Dr. Frankenstein.

22-17 EUGÈNE DELACROIX, *Death of Sardanapalus*, 1827. Oil on canvas, 12′ 1½″ × 16′ 2⅞″. Louvre, Paris.

Inspired by Byron's 1821 poem, Delacroix painted the Romantic spectacle of an Assyrian king on his funeral pyre. The richly colored and emotionally charged canvas is filled with exotic figures.

1 ft.

EUGÈNE DELACROIX Art historians often present the history of painting during the first half of the 19th century as a contest between two major artists—Ingres, the Neoclassical draftsman, and EUGÈNE DELACROIX (1798–1863), the Romantic colorist. Their dialogue recalls the quarrel between the Poussinistes and the Rubénistes at the end of the 17th century and into the 18th (see Chapter 21). The Poussinistes were conservative defenders of academism who regarded drawing as superior to color, whereas the Rubénistes proclaimed the importance of color over line (line quality being more intellectual and thus more restrictive than color). Delacroix's works were products of his view that the artist's powers of imagination would in turn capture and inflame the viewer's imagination. Literature of imaginative power served Delacroix (and many of his contemporaries) as a useful source of subject matter. Théophile Gautier (1811–1872), the prominent Romantic critic and novelist, recalled:

> In those days painting and poetry fraternized. The artists read the poets, and the poets visited the artists. We found Shakespeare, Dante, Goethe, Lord Byron and Walter Scott in the studio as well as in the study. There were as many splashes of color as there were blots of ink in the margins of those beautiful books which we endlessly perused. Imagination, already excited, was further fired by reading those foreign works, so rich in color, so free and powerful in fantasy.[1]

DEATH OF SARDANAPALUS Delacroix's *Death of Sardanapalus* (FIG. 22-17) is grand Romantic pictorial drama. Although inspired by the 1821 narrative poem *Sardanapalus* by Lord Byron (1788–1824), the painting does not illustrate that text (see "The Romantic Spirit in Art, Music, and Literature," page 622). Instead, Delacroix depicted the last hour of the Assyrian king (who had just received news of his armies' defeat and the enemies' entry into his city) in a much more tempestuous and crowded setting than Byron described. Here, orgiastic destruction replaces the sacrificial suicide found in the poem. In the painting, the king reclines on his funeral pyre, soon to be set alight, and gloomily watches the destruction of all of his most precious possessions—his women, slaves, horses, and treasure. Sardanapalus's favorite concubine throws herself on the bed, determined to go up in flames with her master. The king presides like a genius of evil over the tragic scene. Most conspicuous are the tortured and dying bodies of the harem women. In the foreground, a muscular slave plunges his knife into the neck of one woman. Delacroix filled this awful spectacle of suffering and death with the most daringly difficult and tortuous poses, and chose the richest intensities of hue. With its exotic and erotic overtones, *Death of Sardanapalus* tapped into the Romantic fantasies of 19th-century viewers.

LIBERTY LEADING THE PEOPLE Although *Death of Sardanapalus* is a seventh-century BCE drama, Delacroix, like Géricault, also turned to current events, particularly tragic or sensational ones, for his subject matter. For example, he produced several images based on the Greek war for independence (1821–1829). Certainly, the French perception of the Greeks locked in a brutal struggle for freedom from the cruel and exotic Ottoman Turks generated great interest in Romantic circles. Closer to home, Delacroix captured the passion and energy of the 1830 revolution in France in his painting *Liberty Leading the People* (FIG. 22-18). Based on the Parisian uprising against Charles X (r. 1824–1830) at the end of July 1830, it depicts the allegorical personification of Liberty defiantly thrusting forth the republic's tricolor banner as she urges the masses to fight on. The scarlet Phrygian cap (the symbol of a freed slave in antiquity) she wears reinforces the urgency of this struggle. Arrayed around Liberty are bold Parisian types—the street boy brandishing his pistols, the menacing worker with a cutlass, and the intellectual dandy in top hat with sawed-off musket. As in Géricault's *Raft of the Medusa* (FIG. 22-15), dead bodies lie all around. In the background, the towers of Notre-Dame rise through the smoke and haze. The painter's inclusion of this recognizable Parisian landmark announces the specificity of locale and event, balancing contemporary historical fact with poetic allegory.

22-18 EUGÈNE DELACROIX, *Liberty Leading the People*, 1830. Oil on canvas, 8′ 6″ × 10′ 8″. Louvre, Paris.

Balancing contemporaneous historical fact with poetic allegory, Delacroix captured the passion and energy of the 1830 revolution in this painting of Liberty leading the Parisian uprising against Charles X.

1 ft.

Delacroix in Morocco

Romantic painters often depicted exotic faraway places they had never seen, but Eugène Delacroix journeyed to Morocco in 1832 and discovered in the sun-drenched landscape—and in the hardy and colorful Moroccans dressed in robes reminiscent of the Roman toga—new insights into a culture built on proud virtues. He found there a culture more classical than anything European Neo-classicism could conceive. In a letter to his friend Fréderic Villot dated February 29, 1832, he wrote:

> This place is made for painters. . . . [B]eauty abounds here; not the over-praised beauty of fashionable paintings. The heroes of David and Co. with their rose-pink limbs would cut a sorry figure beside these children of the sun, who moreover wear the dress of classical antiquity with a nobler air, I dare assert.*

In a second letter, written June 4, 1832, he reported to Auguste Jal:

> You have seen Algiers and you can imagine what the natives of these regions are like. Here there is something even simpler and more primitive; there is less of the Turkish alloy; I have Romans and Greeks on my doorstep: it makes me laugh heartily at David's Greeks, apart, of course, from his sublime skill as a painter. I know now what they were really like; . . . If painting schools persist in [depicting classical subjects], I am convinced, and you will agree with me, that they would gain far more from being shipped off as cabin boys on the first boat bound for the Barbary coast than from

spending any more time wearing out the classical soil of Rome. Rome is no longer to be found in Rome.†

The gallantry, valor, and fierce love of liberty of the Moroccans made them, in Delacroix's eyes, unspoiled heroes uncontaminated by European decadence. The Moroccan journey renewed Delacroix's Romantic conviction that beauty exists in the fierceness of nature, natural processes, and natural beings, especially animals. After Morocco, more and more of Delacroix's subjects involved combats between beasts and between beasts and men. He painted snarling tangles of lions and tigers, battles between horses, and clashes of Muslims with great cats in swirling hunting scenes using compositions reminiscent of those of Rubens (FIG. I-13), as in his 1854 painting *Tiger Hunt* (FIG. 22-19), which clearly speaks to the Romantic interest in faraway lands and exotic cultures.

* Translated by Jean Stewart, in Charles Harrison, Paul Wood, and Jason Gaiger, eds., *Art in Theory 1815–1900: An Anthology of Changing Ideas* (Oxford: Blackwell, 1998), 87.
† Ibid., 88.

22-19 EUGÈNE DELACROIX, *Tiger Hunt*, 1854. Oil on canvas, 2′ 5″ × 3′. Musée d'Orsay, Paris.

Tiger Hunt reflects Delacroix's 1832 trip to Morocco, which had a lasting impact on his art. His paintings of men battling ferocious beasts are consistent with the Romantic interest in exotic places.

1 ft.

TIGER HUNT An enormously influential event in Delacroix's life that affected his art in both subject and form was his visit to North Africa in 1832 (see "Delacroix in Morocco," above). Things he saw there shocked his imagination with fresh impressions that lasted throughout his life and resulted in paintings such as *Tiger Hunt* (FIG. 22-19), which he completed more than two decades after his trip.

Delacroix's African experience also further heightened his already considerable awareness of the expressive power of color and light. What Delacroix knew about color he passed on to later painters of the 19th century, particularly the Impressionists (see Chapter 23). He observed that pure colors are as rare in nature as lines and that color appears only in an infinitely varied scale of different tones, shadings, and reflections, which he tried to re-create in his paintings. He recorded his observations in his journal, which became for later painters and scholars a veritable handbook of pre-Impressionist color theory. Delacroix anticipated the later development of Impressionist color science. But that art-science had to await the discoveries by Michel Eugène Chevreul (1786–1889) and Hermann von Helmholtz (1821–1894) of the laws of light decomposition and the properties of complementary colors before the problems of color perception and juxtaposition in painting could be properly formulated (see "19th-Century Color Theory," Chapter 23, page 664). Nevertheless, Delacroix's observations were significant, and he advised other artists not to fuse their brush strokes, as those strokes would appear to fuse naturally from a distance.

No other painter of the time explored the domain of Romantic subject and mood as thoroughly and definitively as Delacroix. His technique was impetuous, improvisational, and instinctive, rather than deliberate, studious, and cold. It epitomized Romantic colorist painting, catching the impression quickly and developing it in the execution process. His contemporaries commented on how furiously Delacroix worked once he had an idea, keeping the whole painting progressing at once. The fury of his attack matched the fury of his imagination and his subjects.

22-20 FRANÇOIS RUDE, *Departure of the Volunteers of 1792* (*La Marseillaise*), Arc de Triomphe, Paris, France, 1833–1836. Limestone, 41′ 8″ high.

In this historical-allegorical sculpture, the figures wear classical costumes, but the violent motion, jagged contours, and densely packed masses relate more closely to the compositions of Romantic paintings.

FRANÇOIS RUDE The Romantic spirit pervaded all media during the early 19th century. Many sculptors, like the painters of the period, produced work that incorporated both Neoclassical and Romantic elements. The colossal sculptural group *Departure of the Volunteers of 1792* (FIG. **22-20**), also called *La Marseillaise*, is one example. The limestone relief by FRANÇOIS RUDE (1784–1855) decorates one of the gigantic piers of the Arc de Triomphe in Paris. This French landmark was commissioned by Napoleon in 1806 and designed by Jean François Thérèse Chalgrin (1739–1811) on the model of the triumphal arches of ancient Rome (FIGS. **7-39, 7-47,** and **7-75**). Work on the arch stopped after Napoleon's defeat but resumed in 1833. Three years later, workers inserted Rude's group (and three similar ones by other sculptors) into the completed arch. The sculpture depicts the volunteers of 1792 departing to defend France's borders against the foreign enemies of the revolution. The Roman goddess of war, Bellona (who here personifies Liberty as well as the "Marseillaise," the revolutionary hymn that is now France's national anthem), soars above patriots of all ages, exhorting them forward with her thundering battle cry. The figures recall David's classically armored (FIG. **21-23**) or nude heroes, as do the rhetorical gestures of the wide-flung arms and the striding poses. Yet the violent motion, the jagged contours, and the densely packed, overlapping masses relate more closely to the compositional method of dramatic Romanticism, as found in Géricault (FIG. **22-15**) and Delacroix (FIG. **22-18**), whose Liberty is the spiritual sister of the allegorical figure in *La Marseillaise*. Rude's stone figure shares the same Phrygian cap, the badge of liberty, with Delacroix's earlier painted figure, but Rude's soldiers wear classical costumes or are heroically nude, whereas those in Delacroix's painting appear in modern Parisian dress. Both works are allegorical, but one looks to the past and the other to the present.

Landscape Painting

Landscape painting came into its own in the 19th century as a fully independent and respected genre. Briefly eclipsed at the century's beginning by the taste for ideal form, which favored figural composition and history, landscape painting flourished as leading painters made it their profession. Increasing tourism, which came courtesy of improved and expanded railway systems both in Europe (MAP **22-2**) and America, contributed to the popularity of landscape painting.

The notion of the picturesque became particularly resonant in the Romantic era. Already in the 18th century, artists had regarded the pleasurable, aesthetic mood that natural landscape inspired as making the landscape itself "picturesque"—that is, worthy of being painted. Rather than simply describe nature, Romantic poets and artists often used nature as allegory. In this manner, artists commented on spiritual, moral, historical, or philosophical issues. Landscape painting was a particularly effective vehicle for such commentary.

In the early 19th century, most Northern European (especially German) landscape painting to some degree expressed the Romantic view (first extolled by Rousseau) of nature as a "being" that included the totality of existence in organic unity and harmony. In nature—"the living garment of God," as German poet and dramatist Johann Wolfgang von Goethe (1749–1832) called it—artists found an ideal subject to express the Romantic theme of the soul unified with the natural world. As all nature was mysteriously permeated by "being," landscape artists had the task of interpreting the signs, symbols, and emblems of universal spirit disguised within visible material things. Artists no longer merely beheld a landscape but rather participated in its spirit, becoming translators of nature's transcendent meanings.

22-21 Caspar David Friedrich, *Abbey in the Oak Forest*, 1810. Oil on canvas, 3' 7½" × 5' 7¼". Nationalgalerie, Staatliche Museen zu Berlin, Berlin.

Friedrich was a master of the Romantic transcendental landscape. The reverential mood of this winter scene with the ruins of a Gothic church and cemetery demands the silence appropriate to sacred places.

1 ft.

CASPAR DAVID FRIEDRICH Among the first Northern European artists to depict the Romantic transcendental landscape was CASPAR DAVID FRIEDRICH (1774–1840). For Friedrich, landscapes were temples and his paintings were altarpieces. The reverential mood of his works demands from the viewer the silence appropriate to sacred places filled with a divine presence. *Abbey in the Oak Forest* (FIG. 22-21) serves as a solemn requiem. Under a winter sky, through the leafless oaks of a snow-covered cemetery, a funeral procession bears a coffin into the ruins of a Gothic church that Friedrich based on the remains of Eldana Abbey in Greifswald. The emblems of death are everywhere—the season's desolation, the leaning crosses and tombstones, the black of mourning that the grieving wear, the skeletal trees, the destruction time has wrought on the church. The painting is a meditation on human mortality. As Friedrich himself remarked: "Why, it has often occurred to me to ask myself, do I so frequently choose death, transience, and the grave as subjects for my paintings? One must submit oneself many times to death in order some day to attain life everlasting."[2] The artist's sharp-focused rendering of details demonstrates his keen perception of everything in the physical environment relevant to his message. Friedrich's work balances inner and outer experience. "The artist," he wrote, "should not only paint what he sees before him, but also what he sees within him. If he does not see anything within him, he should give up painting what he sees before him."[3] Although Friedrich's works may not have the theatrical energy of the paintings of Géricault or Delacroix, a resonant and deep emotion pervades them.

JOHN CONSTABLE One of the most momentous developments in Western history—the Industrial Revolution—influenced the evolution of Romantic landscape painting in England. Although discussion of the Industrial Revolution invariably focuses on technological advances, factory development, and growth of urban centers, its effect on the countryside and the land itself was no less severe. The detrimental economic impact industrialization had on the prices for agrarian products produced significant unrest in the English countryside. In particular, increasing numbers of displaced farmers could no longer afford to farm their small land plots.

JOHN CONSTABLE (1776–1837) addressed the agrarian situation in his landscape paintings. *The Haywain* (FIG. 22-22) is representative of Constable's art and reveals much about his outlook. A small cottage sits on the left of this placid, picturesque scene of the countryside, and in the center foreground a man leads a horse and wagon across the stream. Billowy clouds float lazily across the sky. The muted greens and golds and the delicacy of Constable's brush strokes augment the scene's tranquility. The artist portrayed the oneness with nature that the Romantic poets sought. The relaxed figures are not observers but participants in the landscape's being.

Constable made countless studies from nature for each of his canvases, which helped him produce in his paintings the convincing sense of reality that won so much praise from his contemporaries. In his quest for the authentic landscape, Constable studied it as a meteorologist (which he was by avocation). His special gift was for capturing the texture that the atmosphere (the climate and the weather, which delicately veil what is seen) gave to landscape. Constable's use of tiny dabs of local color, stippled with white, created a sparkling shimmer of light and hue across the canvas surface—the vibration itself suggestive of movement and process.

The Haywain is also significant for precisely what it does not show—the civil unrest of the agrarian working class and the outbreaks of violence and arson that resulted. The people who populate Constable's landscapes blend into the scenes and are at one with nature. Rarely does the viewer see workers engaged in tedious labor. Indeed, this painting has a nostalgic, wistful air to it, and reflects Constable's memories of a disappearing rural pastoralism. The artist's father was a rural landowner of considerable wealth, and many of the scenes Constable painted (*The Haywain* included) depict his family's property near East Bergholt in Suffolk, East Anglia. This nostalgia, presented in such naturalistic terms, renders Constable's works Romantic in tone. That Constable felt a kindred spirit with the Romantic artists is revealed by his comment "painting is but another word for feeling."[4]

J.M.W. TURNER Constable's contemporary in the English school of landscape painting, JOSEPH MALLORD WILLIAM TURNER (1775–1851), produced work that also responded to encroaching in-

22-22 JOHN CONSTABLE, *The Haywain,* 1821. Oil on canvas, 4′ 3″ × 6′ 2″. National Gallery, London.

The Haywain is a nostalgic view of the disappearing English country-side during the Industrial Revolution. Constable had a special gift for capturing the texture that climate and weather give to landscape.

1 ft.

dustrialization. However, where Constable's paintings are serene and precisely painted, Turner's feature turbulent swirls of frothy pigment. The passion and energy of Turner's works reveal the Romantic sensibility that was the foundation for his art and also clearly illustrate Edmund Burke's concept of the sublime—awe mixed with terror.

Among Turner's most notable works is *The Slave Ship* (FIG. 22-23). Its subject is a 1783 incident reported in an extensively read book titled *The History of the Abolition of the Slave Trade,* by Thomas Clarkson. Because the book had just been reprinted in

1839, Clarkson's account probably prompted Turner's choice of subject for this 1840 painting. The incident involved the captain of a slave ship who, on realizing that his insurance company would reimburse him only for slaves lost at sea but not for those who died en route, ordered the sick and dying slaves thrown overboard. Appropriately, the painting's full title is *The Slave Ship* (*Slavers Throwing Overboard the Dead and Dying, Typhoon Coming On*). Turner's frenzied emotional depiction of this act matches its barbaric nature. The artist transformed the sun into an incandescent comet amid flying

22-23 JOSEPH MALLORD WILLIAM TURNER, *The Slave Ship* (*Slavers Throwing Overboard the Dead and Dying, Typhoon Coming On*), 1840. Oil on canvas, 2′ 11$\frac{11}{16}$″ × 4′ $\frac{5}{16}$″. Museum of Fine Arts, Boston (Henry Lillie Pierce Fund).

The essence of Turner's innovative style is the emotive power of color. He released color from any defining outlines to express both the forces of nature and the painter's emotional response to them.

1 ft.

22-24 THOMAS COLE, *The Oxbow* (*View from Mount Holyoke, Northampton, Massachusetts, after a Thunderstorm*), 1836. Oil on canvas, 4′ 3½″ × 6′ 4″. Metropolitan Museum of Art, New York (gift of Mrs. Russell Sage, 1908).

Cole divided his canvas into dark wilderness on the left and sunlit civilization on the right. The minuscule painter at the bottom center seems to be asking for advice about America's future course.

scarlet clouds. The slave ship moves into the distance, leaving in its wake a turbulent sea choked with the bodies of slaves sinking to their deaths. The relative scale of the minuscule human forms compared with the vast sea and overarching sky reinforces the sense of the sublime, especially the immense power of nature over humans. Almost lost in the boiling colors are the event's particulars, but on close inspection, the viewer can discern the iron shackles and manacles around the wrists and ankles of the drowning slaves, cruelly denying them any chance of saving themselves.

A key ingredient of Turner's highly personal style is the emotive power of pure color. The haziness of the painter's forms and the indistinctness of his compositions intensify the colors and energetic brush strokes. Turner's innovation in works such as *The Slave Ship* was to release color from any defining outlines so as to express both the forces of nature and the painter's emotional response to them. In his paintings, the reality of color is at one with the reality of feeling. Turner's methods had an incalculable effect on the later development of painting. His discovery of the aesthetic and emotive power of pure color and his pushing of the medium's fluidity to a point where the paint itself is almost the subject were important steps toward 20th-century abstract art, which dispensed with shape and form altogether (see Chapter 25).

THOMAS COLE In America, landscape painting was the specialty of a group of artists known as the Hudson River School, so named because its members drew their subjects primarily from the uncultivated regions of New York State's Hudson River Valley, although many of these painters depicted scenes from across the country. Like the early-19th-century landscape painters in Germany and England, the artists of the Hudson River School not only presented Romantic panoramic landscape views but also participated in the ongoing exploration of the individual's and the country's relationship to the land. American landscape painters frequently focused on identifying qualities that made America unique. One American painter of

English birth, THOMAS COLE (1801–1848), often referred to as the leader of the Hudson River School, articulated this idea:

> Whether he [an American] beholds the Hudson mingling waters with the Atlantic—explores the central wilds of this vast continent, or stands on the margin of the distant Oregon, he is still in the midst of American scenery—it is his own land; its beauty, its magnificence, its sublimity—all are his; and how undeserving of such a birthright, if he can turn towards it an unobserving eye, an unaffected heart![5]

Another issue that surfaced frequently in Hudson River School paintings was the moral question of America's direction as a civilization. Cole addressed this question in *The Oxbow* (*View from Mount Holyoke, Northampton, Massachusetts, after a Thunderstorm;* FIG. **22-24**). A splendid scene opens before the viewer, dominated by the lazy oxbow-shaped curve of the Connecticut River. Cole divided the composition in two, with the dark, stormy wilderness on the left and the more developed civilization on the right. The minuscule artist in the bottom center of the painting (wearing a top hat), dwarfed by the landscape's scale, turns to the viewer as if to ask for input in deciding the country's future course. Cole's depictions of expansive wilderness incorporated reflections and moods romantically appealing to the public.

ALBERT BIERSTADT Other Hudson River artists used the landscape genre as an allegorical vehicle to address moral and spiritual concerns. ALBERT BIERSTADT (1830–1902) traveled west in 1858 and produced many paintings depicting the Rocky Mountains, Yosemite Valley, and other dramatic sites. His works, such as *Among the Sierra Nevada Mountains, California* (FIG. **22-25**), present breathtaking scenery and natural beauty. This panoramic view (the painting is 10 feet wide) is awe-inspiring. Deer and waterfowl appear at the edge of a placid lake, and steep and rugged mountains soar skyward on the left and in the distance. A stand of trees, uncultivated and wild, frames the lake on the right. To underscore the almost transcendental nature of this scene, Bierstadt depicted the sun's rays

22-25 ALBERT BIERSTADT, *Among the Sierra Nevada Mountains, California*, 1868. Oil on canvas, 6′ × 10′. National Museum of American Art, Smithsonian Institution, Washington, D.C.

Bierstadt's panoramic landscape presents the breathtaking natural beauty of the American West. His paintings reinforced the 19th-century doctrine of Manifest Destiny, which justified western expansion.

breaking through the clouds overhead, which suggests a heavenly consecration of the land. That Bierstadt focused attention on the West is not insignificant. By calling national attention to the splendor and uniqueness of the regions beyond the Rocky Mountains, Bierstadt's paintings reinforced the idea of Manifest Destiny. This popular 19th-century doctrine held that westward expansion across the continent was the logical destiny of the United States. As John L. O'Sullivan (1813–1895) expounded in the earliest known use of the term in 1845, "Our manifest destiny [is] to overspread the continent allotted by Providence for the free development of our yearly multiplying millions."[6] Paintings of the scenic splendor of the American West helped to mute growing concerns about the realities of conquest, the displacement of the Native Americans, and the exploitation of the environment. It should come as no surprise that among those most eager to purchase Bierstadt's work were mail-service magnates and railroad builders—the very entrepreneurs and financiers involved in westward expansion.

FREDERIC CHURCH Another painter usually associated with the Hudson River School was FREDERIC EDWIN CHURCH (1826–1900), but his interest in landscape scenes extended beyond America. During his life he traveled to South America, Mexico, Europe, the Middle East, Newfoundland, and Labrador. Church's paintings are firmly in the idiom of the Romantic sublime, yet they also reveal contradictions and conflicts in the constructed mythology of American providence and character. *Twilight in the Wilderness* (FIG. **22-26**) presents a panoramic view of the sun setting over the majestic landscape. Beyond Church's precise depiction of the awe-inspiring spectacle of nature, the painting is remarkable for what it does not depict. Like Constable, Church and the other Hudson River

22-26 FREDERIC EDWIN CHURCH, *Twilight in the Wilderness*, 1860s. Oil on canvas, 3′ 4″ × 5′ 4″. Cleveland Museum of Art, Cleveland (Mr. and Mrs. William H. Marlatt Fund, 1965.233).

Church's paintings eloquently express the Romantic notion of the sublime. Painted during the Civil War, this wilderness landscape presents an idealistic view of America free of conflict.

Romanticism **629**

School painters worked in a time of great upheaval. *Twilight in the Wilderness* dates to the 1860s, when the Civil War was tearing apart the country. Yet this painting does not display evidence of turbulence or discord. Indeed, it does not include even a trace of humanity. By constructing such an idealistic and comforting view, Church contributed to the national mythology of righteousness and divine providence—a mythology that had become increasingly difficult to maintain in the face of conflict.

Landscape painting was immensely popular in the late 18th and early 19th centuries, in large part because it provided viewers with breathtaking and sublime spectacles of nature. Artists also could allegorize nature, and it was rare for a landscape painting not to touch on spiritual, moral, historical, or philosophical issues. Landscape painting became the perfect vehicle for artists (and the viewing public) to "naturalize" conditions, rendering debate about contentious issues moot and eliminating any hint of conflict.

REALISM

Realism was a movement that developed in France around midcentury against the backdrop of an increasing emphasis on science. Advances in industrial technology during the early 19th century reinforced the Enlightenment's foundation of rationalism. The connection between science and progress seemed obvious to many, both in intellectual circles and among the general public, and people increasingly embraced *empiricism* (the search for knowledge based on observation and direct experience). Indicative of the widespread faith in science was the influence of *positivism,* a Western philosophical model developed by the French philosopher Auguste Comte (1798–1857). Positivists promoted science as the mind's highest achievement and advocated a purely empirical approach to nature and society. Comte believed that scientific laws governed the environment and human activity and could be revealed through careful recording and analysis of observable data. Like the empiricists and positivists, Realist artists argued that only the things of one's own time—what people could see for themselves—were "real." Accordingly, Realists focused their attention on the experiences and sights of everyday contemporary life and disapproved of historical and fictional subjects on the grounds that they were neither real and visible nor of the present.

France

GUSTAVE COURBET The leading figure of the Realist movement in 19th-century art was GUSTAVE COURBET (1819–1877). In fact, Courbet used the term *Realism* when exhibiting his works, even though he shunned labels (see "Courbet on Realism," page 631). The Realists' sincerity about scrutinizing their environment led them to portray objects and images that in recent centuries artists had deemed unworthy of depiction—the mundane and trivial, working-class laborers and peasants, and so forth. Moreover, the Realists depicted these scenes on a scale and with an earnestness and seriousness previously reserved for grand history painting.

STONE BREAKERS Courbet presented a glimpse into the life of rural menial laborers in *The Stone Breakers* (FIG. 22-27), capturing on canvas in a straightforward manner two men—one about 70, the other quite young—in the act of breaking stones, traditionally the lot of the lowest in French society. By juxtaposing youth and age, Courbet suggested that those born to poverty remain poor their entire lives. The artist neither romanticized nor idealized the men's work but depicted their thankless toil with directness and accuracy. Courbet's palette of dirty browns and grays conveys the dreary and dismal nature of the task, while the angular positioning of the older stone breaker's limbs suggests a mechanical monotony.

This interest in the working poor as subject matter had special meaning for the mid-19th-century French audience. In 1848 laborers rebelled against the bourgeois leaders of the newly formed Second Republic and against the rest of the nation, demanding better working conditions and a redistribution of property. The army quelled the revolution in three days, but not without long-lasting trauma and significant loss of life. That uprising thus raised the issue of labor as a national concern and placed workers center stage, both literally and symbolically. Courbet's depiction of stone breakers in 1849 was very timely and populist.

BURIAL AT ORNANS Also representative of Courbet's work is *Burial at Ornans* (FIG. 22-28), which depicts a funeral set in a bleak provincial landscape outside his home town. Attending the funeral are the types of ordinary people Honoré de Balzac (1799–1850) and Gustave Flaubert (1821–1880) presented in their novels. While an officious clergyman reads the Office of the Dead, those attending

22-27 GUSTAVE COURBET, *The Stone Breakers,* 1849. Oil on canvas, 5′ 3″ × 8′ 6″. Formerly Gemäldegalerie, Dresden (destroyed in 1945).

Courbet was the leading figure in the Realist movement. Using a palette of dirty browns and grays, he conveyed the dreary and dismal nature of menial labor in mid-19th-century France.

1 ft.

Courbet on Realism

The Parisian academic jury selecting work for the 1855 Salon (part of the Exposition Universelle in that year) rejected two paintings by Gustave Courbet on the grounds that his subjects and figures were too coarse (so much so as to be plainly "socialistic") and too large (*Burial at Ornans*, FIG. **22-28**, is almost 22 feet long). In response, Courbet withdrew all of his works and set up his own exhibition outside the grounds, calling it the Pavilion of Realism. Courbet was the first artist ever to stage a private exhibition of his own work. His pavilion and the statement he issued to explain the paintings shown there amounted to the new movement's manifestos. Although Courbet maintained that he founded no school and was of no school, he did, as the name of his pavilion suggests, accept the term *Realism* as descriptive of his art. The statement Courbet distributed at his pavilion reads in part:

> The title of "realist" has been imposed upon me . . . . Titles have never given a just idea of things; were it otherwise, the work would be superfluous. . . . I have studied the art of the moderns, avoiding any preconceived system and without prejudice. I have no more wanted to imitate the former than to copy the latter; nor have I thought of achieving the idle aim of "art for art's sake." No! I have simply wanted to draw from a thorough knowledge of tradition the reasoned and free sense of my own individuality. . . . To be able to translate the customs, ideas, and appearances of my time as I see them—in a word, to create a living art—this has been my aim.*

Six years later, on Christmas Day, 1861, Courbet wrote an open letter, published a few days later in the *Courier du dimanche,* addressed to prospective students. In the letter, the painter reflected on the nature of his art.

> [An artist must apply] his personal faculties to the ideas and the events of the times in which he lives. . . . [A]rt in painting should consist only of the representation of things that are visible and tangible to the artist. Every age should be represented only by its own artists, that is to say, by the artists who have lived in it. I also maintain that painting is an essentially concrete art form and can consist only of the representation of both real and existing things. . . . An abstract object, not visible, nonexistent, is not within the domain of painting.†

Courbet's most famous statement, however, is his blunt dismissal of academic painting, in which he concisely summed up the core principle of Realist painting:

> I have never seen an angel. Show me an angel, and I'll paint one.‡

* Translated by Robert Goldwater and Marco Treves, eds., *Artists on Art from the XIV to the XX Century,* 3rd ed. (New York: Pantheon, 1958), 295.
† Translated by Petra ten-Doesschate Chu, *Letters of Gustave Courbet* (Chicago: University of Chicago Press, 1992), 203–204.
‡ Quoted by Vincent van Gogh in a July 1885 letter to his brother Theo. Ronald de Leeuw, *The Letters of Vincent van Gogh* (New York: Penguin, 1996), 302.

1 ft.

22-28 GUSTAVE COURBET, *Burial at Ornans,* 1849. Oil on canvas, 10′ 3½″ × 21′ 9½″. Musée d'Orsay, Paris.

Although as monumental in scale as a traditional history painting, *Burial at Ornans* horrified critics because of the ordinary nature of the subject and Courbet's starkly antiheroic composition.

cluster around the excavated grave site, their faces registering all degrees of response to the situation. Although the painting has the monumental scale of a traditional history painting, the subject's ordinariness and the starkly antiheroic composition horrified contem-poraneous critics. Arranged in a wavering line extending across the broad horizontal width of the canvas are three groups—the somberly clad women at the back right, a semicircle of similarly clad men by the open grave, and assorted churchmen at the left. This wall of

22-29 JEAN-FRANÇOIS MILLET, *The Gleaners*, 1857. Oil on canvas, 2′ 9″ × 3′ 8″. Musée d'Orsay, Paris.

Millet and the Barbizon School painters specialized in depictions of French country life. Here, Millet portrayed three impoverished women gathering the remainders left in the field after a harvest.

1 ft.

figures, seen at eye level in person, blocks any view into deep space. The faces are portraits. Some of the models were Courbet's sisters (three of the women in the front row, toward the right) and friends. Behind and above the figures are bands of overcast sky and barren cliffs. The dark pit of the grave opens into the viewer's space in the center foreground. Despite the unposed look of the figures, Courbet controlled the composition in a masterful way by his sparing use of bright color. In place of the heroic, the sublime, and the dramatic, Courbet aggressively presents the viewer with the mundane realities of daily life and death. In 1857, Jules-François-Félix Husson Champfleury (1821–1889), one of the first critics to recognize and appreciate Courbet's work, wrote of *Burial at Ornans*, "[I]t represents a small-town funeral and yet reproduces the funerals of *all* small towns."[7] Unlike the theatricality of Romanticism, Realism captured the ordinary rhythms of daily existence.

Of great importance for the later history of art, Realism also involved a reconsideration of the painter's primary goals and departed from the established priority on illusionism. Accordingly, Realists called attention to painting as a pictorial construction by the ways they applied pigment or manipulated composition. Courbet's intentionally simple and direct methods of expression in composition and technique seemed unbearably crude to many of his more traditional contemporaries, who called him a primitive. Although his bold, somber palette was essentially traditional, Courbet often used the *palette knife* for quickly placing and unifying large daubs of paint, producing a roughly wrought surface. His example inspired the young artists who worked for him (and later Impressionists such as Claude Monet and Auguste Renoir; see Chapter 23), but the public accused him of carelessness and critics wrote of his "brutalities."

JEAN-FRANÇOIS MILLET Like Courbet, JEAN-FRANÇOIS MILLET (1814–1878) found his subjects in the people and occupations of the everyday world. Millet was one of a group of French painters of country life who, to be close to their rural subjects, settled near the village of Barbizon in the forest of Fontainebleau. This Barbizon School specialized in detailed pictures of forest and countryside. Millet, perhaps their most prominent member, was of peasant stock and identified with the hard lot of the country poor. In *The Gleaners* (FIG. **22-29**), he depicted three peasant women performing the backbreaking task of gleaning the last wheat scraps. These impoverished women were members of the lowest level of peasant society. Landowning nobles traditionally permitted them to glean— to pick up the remainders left in the field after the harvest. Millet characteristically placed his monumental figures in the foreground, against a broad sky. Although the field stretches back to a rim of haystacks, cottages, trees, and distant workers and a flat horizon, the gleaners quietly doing their tedious and time-consuming work dominate the canvas.

Although Millet's works have a sentimentality absent from those of Courbet, the French public still reacted to his paintings with disdain and suspicion. In the aftermath of the 1848 revolution, for Millet to invest the poor with solemn grandeur did not meet with the approval of the prosperous classes. In particular, middle-class landowners resisted granting gleaning rights, and thus Millet's relatively dignified depiction of gleaning did not gain their favor. The middle class also linked the poor with the dangerous, newly defined working class, which was finding outspoken champions in men such as Karl Marx (1818–1883), Friedrich Engels (1820–1895), and the novelists Émile Zola (1840–1902) and Charles Dickens (1812–1870).

Lithography

In 1798 the German printmaker Alois Senefelder (1771–1834) created the first prints using stone instead of metal plates or wooden blocks. In contrast to earlier printing techniques (see "Woodcuts, Engravings, and Etchings," Chapter 15, page 415) in which the artist applied ink to either a raised or incised surface, in *lithography* (Greek, "stone writing") the printing and nonprinting areas of the plate are on the same plane.

The chemical phenomenon fundamental to lithography is the repellence of oil and water. The lithographer uses a greasy, oil-based crayon to draw directly on a stone plate and then wipes water onto the stone, which clings only to the areas the drawing does not cover. Next, the artist rolls oil-based ink onto the stone, which adheres to the drawing but is repelled by the water. When the artist presses the stone against paper, only the inked areas—the drawing—transfer to the paper. Color lithography requires multiple plates, one for each color, and the printmaker must take special care to make sure that each impression lines up perfectly with the previous one so that each color prints in its proper place.

One of the earliest masters of this new printmaking process was Honoré Daumier (FIG. 22-30), whose politically biting lithographs published in a widely read French journal reached an audience of unprecedented size.

1 in.

22-30 Honoré Daumier, *Rue Transnonain*, 1834. Lithograph, $1' \times 1' 5\frac{1}{2}''$. Philadelphia Museum of Art, Philadelphia (bequest of Fiske and Marie Kimball).

Daumier used the recent invention of lithography to reach a wide audience for his social criticism and political protest. This print records the horrific 1834 massacre in a workers' housing block.

Socialism was a growing movement, and both its views on property and its call for social justice, even economic equality, frightened the bourgeoisie. In Millet's sympathetic portrayal of the poor, many saw a political manifesto.

HONORÉ DAUMIER Because people widely recognized the power of art to serve political means, the political and social agitation accompanying the violent revolutions in France and the rest of Europe in the later 18th and early 19th centuries prompted the French people to suspect artists of subversive intention. A person could be jailed for too bold a statement in the press, in literature, in art—even in music and drama. Realist artist Honoré Daumier (1808–1879) was a defender of the urban working classes, and in his art he boldly confronted authority with social criticism and political protest. In response, the authorities imprisoned the artist. A painter, sculptor, and, like Dürer, Rembrandt, and Goya, one of the world's great printmakers, Daumier produced *lithographs* (see "Lithography," above) that allowed him to create an unprecedented number of prints, thereby reaching a broader audience. In addition to producing individual lithographs for sale, Daumier also contributed satirical lithographs to the widely read, liberal French Republican journal *Caricature*. In these prints, he mercilessly lampooned the foibles and misbehavior of politicians, lawyers, doctors, and the rich bourgeoisie in general. His in-depth knowledge of the acute political and social unrest in Paris during the revolutions of 1830 and 1848 endowed his work with truthfulness and, therefore, with power.

RUE TRANSNONAIN Daumier's lithograph *Rue Transnonain* (FIG. 22-30) depicts an atrocity with the same shocking impact as Goya's *Third of May, 1808* (FIG. 22-13). The title refers to a street in Paris where an unknown sniper killed a civil guard, part of a government force trying to repress a worker demonstration. Because the fatal shot had come from a workers' housing block, the remaining guards immediately stormed the building and massacred all of its inhabitants. With Goya's power, Daumier created a view of the slaughter from a sharp, realistic angle of vision. He depicted not the dramatic moment of execution but the terrible, quiet aftermath. The broken, scattered forms lie amid violent disorder, as if newly found. The print's significance lies in its factualness. It is an example of the period's increasing artistic bias toward using facts as subject, and not always illusionistically. Daumier's pictorial manner is rough and spontaneous. How it carries expressive exaggeration is part of its remarkable force. Daumier's work is true to life in content, but his style is uniquely personal.

22-31 HONORÉ DAUMIER, *Third-Class Carriage*, ca. 1862. Oil on canvas, 2' 1¾" × 2' 11½". Metropolitan Museum of Art, New York (H. O. Havemeyer Collection, bequest of Mrs. H. O. Havemeyer, 1929).

Daumier frequently depicted the plight of the disinherited masses of 19th-century industrialism. Here, he portrayed the anonymous poor cramped together in a grimy third-class railway carriage.

1 ft.

THIRD-CLASS CARRIAGE Daumier brought the same convictions exhibited in his graphic work to his paintings as well, especially after 1848. His unfinished *Third-Class Carriage* (FIG. 22-31) provides a glimpse into the cramped and grimy railway carriage of the 1860s. The riders are poor and can afford only third-class tickets. While first- and second-class carriages had closed compartments, third-class passengers were crammed together on hard benches that filled the carriage. The disinherited masses of 19th-century industrialism were Daumier's indignant concern, and he made them his subject repeatedly. He showed them in the unposed attitudes and unplanned arrangements of the millions thronging the modern cities—anonymous, insignificant, dumbly patient with a lot they could not change. Daumier saw people as they ordinarily appeared, their faces vague, impersonal, and blank—unprepared for any observers. He tried to achieve the real by isolating a random collection of the unrehearsed details of human existence from the continuum of ordinary life. Daumier's vision anticipated the spontaneity and candor of scenes captured with the camera by the end of the century.

1 ft.

22-32 ROSA BONHEUR, *The Horse Fair*, 1853–1855. Oil on canvas, 8' ¼" × 16' 7½". Metropolitan Museum of Art, New York (gift of Cornelius Vanderbilt, 1887).

Bonheur was the most celebrated woman artist of the 19th century. A Realist, she went to great lengths to record accurately the anatomy of living horses, even studying carcasses in slaughterhouses.

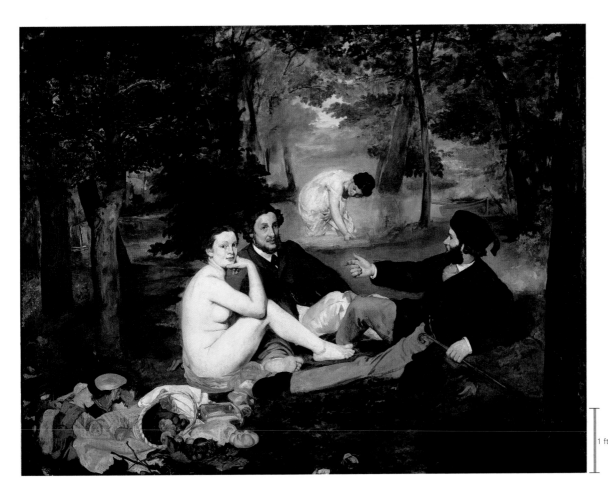

1 ft.

ROSA BONHEUR The most celebrated woman artist of the 19th century was Marie-Rosalie (Rosa) Bonheur (1822–1899). The winner of the gold medal at the Salon of 1848, Bonheur became in 1894 the first woman officer in the French Legion of Honor. Bonheur received her artistic training from her father, who was a proponent of *Saint-Simonianism,* an early-19th-century utopian socialist movement that championed the education and enfranchisement of women. As a result of her father's influence, Bonheur launched her career believing that as a woman and an artist, she had a special role to play in creating a new and perfect society. A Realist passion for accuracy in painting drove Bonheur, but she resisted depicting the problematic social and political situations seen in the work of Courbet, Millet, Daumier, and other Realists. Rather, she turned to the animal world—not, however, to the exotic wild animals that so fascinated Delacroix (FIG. 22-19), but to animals common in the French countryside, especially horses, but also rabbits, cows, and sheep. She went to great lengths to observe the anatomy of living horses at the great Parisian horse fair and spent long hours studying the anatomy of carcasses in the Paris slaughterhouses. For her best-known work, *The Horse Fair* (FIG. 22-32), she adopted a panoramic composition similar to that in Courbet's *Burial at Ornans* (FIG. 22-28). Bonheur filled her broad canvas with the sturdy farm Percherons and their grooms seen on parade at the annual Parisian horse sale. Some horses, not quite broken, rear up. Others plod or trot, guided on foot or ridden by their keepers. Bonheur recorded the Percherons' uneven line of march, their thunderous pounding, and their seemingly overwhelming power based on her close observation of living animals, even though she acknowledged some inspiration from the Parthenon frieze (FIG. 5-50, *top*). The dramatic lighting, loose brushwork, and rolling sky also reveal her admiration of the style of Géricault (FIG. 22-15). The equine drama in *The Horse Fair* captivated viewers, who eagerly bought engraved reproductions of Bonheur's painting, making it one of the best-known artworks of the century.

ÉDOUARD MANET Like Gustave Courbet, Édouard Manet (1832–1883) was a pivotal artist during the 19th century. Not only was his work critical for the articulation of Realist principles, but his art also played an important role in the development of Impressionism in the 1870s (see Chapter 23). Manet's masterpiece, *Le Déjeuner sur l'Herbe* (*Luncheon on the Grass;* FIG. 22-33), depicts two women, one nude, and two clothed men enjoying a picnic of sorts. Consistent with Realist principles, Manet based all of the foreground figures on living people. The seated nude is Victorine Meurend (Manet's favorite model at the time), and the gentlemen are his brother Eugène (with cane) and probably the sculptor Ferdinand Leenhof, although scholars have suggested other identifications. The two men wear fashionable Parisian attire of the 1860s, and the foreground nude not only is a distressingly unidealized figure type but also seems disturbingly unabashed and at ease, gazing directly at the viewer without shame or flirtatiousness.

This audacious painting outraged the public—rather than a traditional pastoral scene, like the Renaissance *Pastoral Symphony* (FIG. 17-35), which featured anonymous idealized figures in an idyllic setting, *Le Déjeuner* seemed merely to represent ordinary men and promiscuous women in a Parisian park. One hostile critic, no doubt voicing public opinion, said: "A commonplace woman of the demimonde, as naked as can be, shamelessly lolls between two dandies dressed to the teeth. These latter look like schoolboys on a holiday, perpetrating an outrage to play the man. . . . This is a young man's practical joke—a shameful, open sore."[8] Manet surely anticipated criticism of his painting, but shocking the public was not his primary aim. His goal was more complex and involved a reassessment of the entire range of

22-34 ÉDOUARD MANET, *Olympia,* 1863. Oil on canvas, 4′ 3″ × 6′ 2¼″. Musée d'Orsay, Paris.

Manet scandalized the public with this painting of a nude prostitute and her black maid carrying a bouquet from a client. Critics also faulted him for using rough brush strokes and abruptly shifting tonality.

art. *Le Déjeuner* contains sophisticated references and allusions to many painting genres—history painting, portraiture, pastoral scenes, nudes, and even religious scenes. What *Le Déjeuner* thus represents is an impressive synthesis and critique of the history of painting.

The negative response to this painting by public and critics alike extended beyond subject matter. Manet's manner of presenting his figures also prompted severe criticism. He rendered them in soft focus and broadly painted the landscape, including the pool in which the second woman bathes. The loose manner of painting contrasts with the clear forms of the harshly lit foreground trio and the pile of discarded female attire and picnic foods at the lower left. The lighting creates strong contrasts between darks and highlighted areas. In the main figures, many values are summed up in one or two lights or darks. The effect is both to flatten the forms and to give them a hard snapping presence. Form, rather than a matter of line, is only a function of paint and light. Manet himself declared that the chief actor in the painting is the light. Manet used art to call attention to art. In other words, he was moving away from illusionism and toward open acknowledgment of painting's properties, such as the flatness of the painting surface, which would become a core principle of many later 19th- and 20th-century painters. The public, however, saw only a crude sketch without the customary finish. The style of the painting, coupled with the unorthodox subject matter, made this work exceptionally controversial.

OLYMPIA Even more scandalous to the French viewing public was Manet's 1863 painting *Olympia* (FIG. **22-34**). This work depicts

a young white prostitute (Olympia was a common "professional" name for prostitutes in the 19th century) reclining on a bed that extends across the foreground. Entirely nude except for a thin black ribbon tied around her neck, a bracelet on her arm, an orchid in her hair, and fashionable mule slippers on her feet, Olympia meets the viewer's eyes with a look of cool indifference. Behind her appears a black maid, who presents her a bouquet of flowers from a client.

Olympia horrified public and critics alike. Although images of prostitutes were not unheard of during this period, the shamelessness of Olympia and her look that verges on defiance shocked viewers. The depiction of a black woman was also not new to painting, but the viewing public perceived Manet's inclusion of both a black maid and a nude prostitute as evoking moral depravity, inferiority, and animalistic sexuality. The contrast of the black servant with the fair-skinned courtesan also made reference to racial divisions. One critic described Olympia as "a courtesan with dirty hands and wrinkled feet . . . her body has the livid tint of a cadaver displayed in the morgue; her outlines are drawn in charcoal and her greenish, bloodshot eyes appear to be provoking the public, protected all the while by a hideous Negress."[9] From this statement, it is clear that viewers were responding not just to the subject matter but to Manet's artistic style as well. Manet's brush strokes are rougher and the shifts in tonality are more abrupt than those found in traditional academic painting. This departure from accepted practice exacerbated the audacity of the subject matter.

ADOLPHE-WILLIAM BOUGUEREAU To understand better the public's reaction to Manet's radically new painting style, it is in-empiricism and positivism appealed to artists in many European countries and in the United States.

WILHELM LEIBL *Three Women in a Village Church* (FIG. 22-36) by WILHELM LEIBL (1844–1900) demonstrates the German artist's commitment to Realist principles and his mastery of the quaint and quiet details of country life. His painting records a sacred moment—the moment of prayer—in the life of three country women of different generations. Dressed in rustic costume, their Sunday best, they pursue their devotions unself-consciously, their prayer books held in large hands roughened by work. Their manners and dress reflect their unaffected nature, untouched by the refinements of urban life. Leibl highlighted their natural virtues: simplicity, honesty, steadfastness, patience.

Leibl spent three years working on this image of peasants in their village church, often under impossible conditions of lighting and temperature. Despite the meticulous application of paint and sharpness of focus, *Three Women* is a moving expression of the German artist's compassionate view of his subjects, a reading of character without sentimentality.

22-35 ADOLPHE-WILLIAM BOUGUEREAU, *Nymphs and a Satyr,* 1873. Oil on canvas, 9′ $\frac{3}{8}$″ × 5′ $10\frac{7}{8}$″. Sterling and Francine Clark Art Institute, Williamstown.

More renowned than Manet in his own day, Bouguereau was an artist in the French academic tradition who specialized in depicting subjects from classical mythology with polished naturalism.

structive to compare *Olympia* with a work by a highly acclaimed French academic artist of the time, ADOLPHE-WILLIAM BOUGUEREAU (1825–1905). In *Nymphs and a Satyr* (FIG. 22-35), Bouguereau characteristically depicted a classical mythological subject with polished illusionism. The flirtatious and ideally beautiful nymphs strike graceful poses yet seem based as closely on nature as are the details of their leafy surroundings. They playfully pull in different directions the *satyr*, the mythical Greek beast-man, with a goat's hindquarters and horns, a horse's ears and tail, and a man's upper body. Although Bouguereau arguably depicted this scene in a very naturalistic manner, it is emphatically not Realist. His choice of a fictional theme and adherence to established painting conventions were staunchly traditional. In contrast to the daring and pioneering—and underappreciated—Manet, Bouguereau was immensely popular during the later 19th century, enjoying the favor of state patronage throughout his career.

Germany and the United States

Although French artists took the lead in promoting Realism and the notion that artists should depict the realities of modern life, this movement was not exclusively French. The Realist foundation in

22-36 WILHELM LEIBL, *Three Women in a Village Church,* 1878–1882. Oil on canvas, 2′ 5″ × 2′ 1″. Kunsthalle, Hamburg.

French Realism spread quickly to Germany, where Leibl painted this moving depiction of simple peasant women of different generations holding their prayer books in hands roughened by work.

22-37 WINSLOW HOMER, *Veteran in a New Field*, 1865. Oil on canvas, $2' \frac{1}{8}'' \times 3' 2\frac{1}{8}''$. Metropolitan Museum of Art, New York (bequest of Miss Adelaide Milton de Groot, 1967).

This veteran's productive work implies a smooth transition to peace after the Civil War, but Homer placed a single-bladed scythe in his hands, a symbol of the deaths of soldiers and of Abraham Lincoln.

1 ft.

WINSLOW HOMER Realism received an especially warm reception in the United States. One of the leading American Realist painters was WINSLOW HOMER (1836–1910) of Boston. Homer experienced at first hand the most momentous event of his lifetime—the Civil War. In 1860 he joined the Union campaign as an artist-reporter for *Harper's Weekly*. At the end of the war, he painted *Veteran in a New Field* (FIG. 22-37). Although it is fairly simple and direct, this painting provides significant commentary on the effects and aftermath of America's catastrophic national conflict. The painting depicts a man with his back to the viewer, harvesting wheat. Homer identified him as a veteran by the uniform and canteen carelessly thrown on the ground in the lower right corner, but the man's current occupation is as a farmer, and he has cast aside his former role as a soldier. The veteran's involvement in meaningful, productive work implies a smooth transition from war to peace. This postwar transition to work and the fate of disbanded soldiers were national concerns. Echoing the sentiments that lay behind Houdon's portrayal of George Washington as the new Cincinnatus (FIG. 21-30), the *New York Weekly Tribune* commented: "Rome took her great man from the plow, and made him a dictator—we must now take our soldiers from the camp and make them farmers."[10] America's ability to effect a smooth transition was seen as evidence of its national strength. "The peaceful and harmonious disbanding of the armies in the summer of 1865," poet Walt Whitman wrote, was one of the "immortal proofs of democracy, unequall'd in all the history of the past."[11] Homer's painting thus reinforced the perception of the country's greatness.

Veteran in a New Field also comments symbolically about death. By the 1860s, farmers used cradled scythes to harvest wheat. In this instance, however, Homer rejected realism in favor of symbolism. He painted a single-bladed scythe, thereby transforming the veteran into a symbol of Death—the Grim Reaper himself—and the painting into an elegy to the thousands of soldiers who died in the Civil War and into a lamentation on the death of recently assassinated President Abraham Lincoln.

THOMAS EAKINS Even more resolutely a Realist than Homer was Philadelphia-born THOMAS EAKINS (1844–1916), who possessed a dedicated appetite for showing the realities of the human experience. Eakins studied both painting and medical anatomy in Philadelphia before undertaking further study under French artist Jean-Léon Gérôme (1824–1904). Eakins aimed to paint things as he saw them rather than as the public might wish them portrayed. This attitude was very much in tune with 19th-century American taste, combining an admiration for accurate depiction with a hunger for truth.

The too-brutal Realism of Eakins's early masterpiece, *Gross Clinic* (FIG. 22-38), prompted the art jury to reject it for the Philadelphia exhibition that celebrated the American independence centennial in 1876. The work presents the renowned surgeon Dr. Samuel Gross in the operating amphitheater of the Jefferson Medical

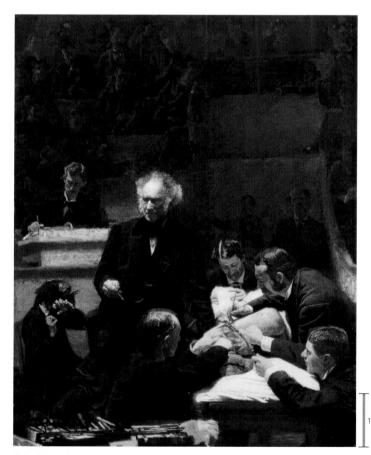

1 ft.

22-38 THOMAS EAKINS, *The Gross Clinic*, 1875. Oil on canvas, $8' \times 6' 6''$. Philadelphia Museum of Art, Philadelphia.

The too-brutal realism of Eakins's unsparing depiction of a medical college operating amphitheater caused rejection of this painting from the Philadelphia exhibition celebrating America's centennial.

College in Philadelphia, where the painting hung until its sale in 2006. That Eakins chose to depict this event testifies to the public's increasing faith in scientific and medical progress. Dr. Gross, with bloody fingers and scalpel, lectures about his surgery on a young man's leg. The patient suffered from osteomyelitis, a bone infection. Watching the surgeon, acclaimed for his skill in this particular operation, are several colleagues, all of whom historians have identified, and the patient's mother, who covers her face. Indicative of the contemporaneity of this scene is the anesthetist in the background holding the cloth over the patient's face. Anesthetics had been introduced in 1846, and their development eliminated a major obstacle to extensive surgery. The painting is an unsparing description of an unfolding event, with a good deal more reality than many viewers could endure. "It is a picture," one critic said, "that even strong men find difficult to look at long, if they can look at it at all."[12]

Eakins believed that knowledge—and where relevant, scientific knowledge—was a prerequisite to his art. As a scientist (in his anatomical studies), Eakins preferred a slow, deliberate method of careful invention based on his observations of the perspective, the anatomy, and the details of his subject. This insistence on scientific fact corresponded to the dominance of empiricism during the latter half of the 19th century. Eakins's concern for anatomical correctness led him to investigate the human form and humans in motion, both with regular photographic apparatuses and with a special camera devised by the French kinesiologist (a person who studies the physiology of body movement) Étienne-Jules Marey (1830–1904). Eakins's later collaboration with Eadweard Muybridge (FIG. 22-54) in the photographic study of animal and human action of all types anticipated the motion picture.

JOHN SINGER SARGENT The expatriate American artist JOHN SINGER SARGENT (1856–1925), born in Florence, Italy, was a younger contemporary of Eakins. Sargent developed a looser, more dashing Realist portrait style, in contrast to Eakins's carefully rendered details. Sargent studied art in Paris before settling in London, where he won renown both as a cultivated and cosmopolitan gentleman and as a facile and fashionable portrait painter. He learned his adept brushing of paint in thin layers and his effortless achievement of quick and lively illusion from his study of Velázquez, whose masterpiece, *Las Meninas* (FIG. 19-30), may have influenced Sargent's portrait *The Daughters of Edward Darley Boit* (FIG. 22-39). The four girls (the children of one of Sargent's close friends) appear in a hall and small drawing room in their Paris home. The informal, eccentric arrangement of their slight figures suggests how much at ease they are within this familiar space and with objects such as the monumental Japanese vases, the red screen, and the fringed rug, whose scale subtly emphasizes the children's diminutive stature. Sargent must have known the Boit daughters well and liked them. Relaxed and trustful, they gave the artist an opportunity to record a gradation of young innocence. He sensitively captured the naive, wondering openness of the little girl in the foreground, the grave artlessness of the 10-year-old child, and the slightly self-conscious poise of the adolescents. Sargent's casual positioning of the figures and seemingly random choice of the setting communicate a sense of spontaneity. The children seem to be attending momentarily to an adult who has asked them to interrupt their activity. The painting embodies the Realist belief that the artist's business is to record modern people in modern contexts.

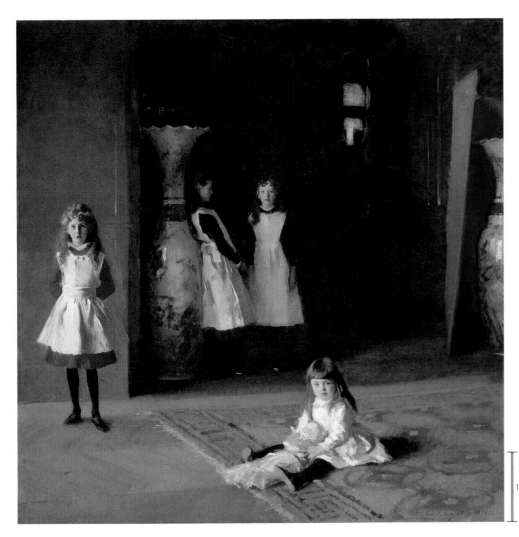

22-39 JOHN SINGER SARGENT, *The Daughters of Edward Darley Boit*, 1882. Oil on canvas, 7′ 3⅜″ × 7′ 3⅝″. Museum of Fine Arts, Boston (gift of Mary Louisa Boit, Florence D. Boit, Jane Hubbard Boit, and Julia Overing Boit, in memory of their father, Edward Darley Boit).

Sargent's casual positioning of the Boit sisters creates a sense of the momentary and spontaneous, consistent with Realist painters' interest in recording modern people in modern contexts.

1 ft.

22-40 Henry Ossawa Tanner, *The Thankful Poor*, 1894. Oil on canvas, 2′ 11½″ × 3′ 8¼″. Collection of William H. and Camille Cosby.

Tanner combined the Realists' belief in careful study from nature with a desire to portray with dignity the life of African American families. Expressive lighting reinforces the painting's reverent spirit.

HENRY OSSAWA TANNER Typical of the Realist painter's desire to depict the lives of ordinary people is the early work of the American artist HENRY OSSAWA TANNER (1859–1937). Tanner studied art with Eakins before moving to Paris. There he combined Eakins's belief in careful study from nature with a desire to portray with dignity the life of the ordinary people he had been raised among as the son of an African American minister in Pennsylvania. The mood in *The Thankful Poor* (FIG. **22-40**) is one of quiet devotion not far removed from the Realism of Millet (FIG. **22-29**). Tanner painted the grandfather, grandchild, and main objects in the room with the greatest detail, while everything else dissolves into loose strokes of color and light. Expressive lighting reinforces the painting's reverent spirit, with deep shadows intensifying the man's devout concentration and golden light pouring in the window to illuminate the quiet expression of thanksgiving on the younger face. The deep sense of sanctity expressed here in terms of everyday experience became increasingly important for Tanner. Within a few years of completing *The Thankful Poor,* he began painting biblical subjects grounded in direct study from nature and in the love of Rembrandt that had inspired him from his days as a Philadelphia art student.

EDMONIA LEWIS About 15 years older than Tanner, the sculptor EDMONIA LEWIS (ca. 1845–after 1909) produced work that was stylistically indebted to Neoclassicism but depicted contemporary Realist themes. *Forever Free* (FIG. **22-41**) is a marble sculpture

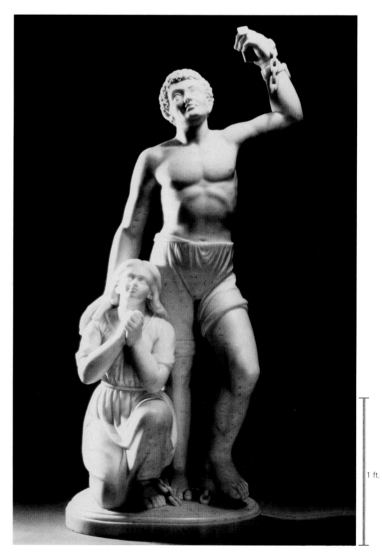

22-41 Edmonia Lewis, *Forever Free,* 1867. Marble, 3′ 5¼″ high. James A. Porter Gallery of Afro-American Art, Howard University, Washington, D.C.

Lewis was a sculptor whose work owes a stylistic debt to Neoclassicism but depicts contemporary Realist themes. She carved *Forever Free* four years after Lincoln's Emancipation Proclamation.

Lewis carved while living in Rome, surrounded by examples of both classical and Renaissance art. It represents two freed African American slaves. The man stands heroically in a contrapposto stance reminiscent of classical statues. His right hand rests on the shoulder of the kneeling woman, and his left hand holds aloft a broken manacle and chain as literal and symbolic references to his former servitude. Produced four years after President Lincoln's issuance of the Emancipation Proclamation, *Forever Free* (originally titled *The Morning of Liberty*) was widely perceived as an abolitionist statement. However, other factors caution against an overly simplistic reading. Because Lewis was female, African American, and Native American (she was the daughter of a Chippewa mother and African American father), scholars have debated the degree to which the sculptor attempted to inject a statement about African American gender relationships into this statue. For example, does the kneeling position of the woman represent Lewis's acceptance of female subordination?

Lewis's accomplishments as a sculptor speak to the increasing access to training that was available to women in the 19th century. Educated at Oberlin College (the first American college to grant degrees to women), Lewis financed her trip to Rome with the sale of medallions and marble busts. Her success in a field dominated by white male artists is a testament to both her skill and her determination.

Pre-Raphaelite Brotherhood

Realism did not appeal to all artists, however. In England a group of painters who called themselves the Pre-Raphaelite Brotherhood refused to be limited to the contemporary scenes strict Realists portrayed. These artists chose instead to represent fictional, historical, and fanciful subjects but with a significant degree of convincing illusion.

JOHN EVERETT MILLAIS One of the founders of the Pre-Raphaelite Brotherhood was JOHN EVERETT MILLAIS (1829–1896). So painstakingly careful was Millais in his study of visual facts closely observed from nature that Charles Baudelaire (1821–1867) called him "the poet of meticulous detail." The Pre-Raphaelite Brotherhood, organized in 1848, wished to create fresh and sincere art, free from what its members considered the tired and artificial manner propagated in the academies by the successors of Raphael. Influenced by the well-known critic, artist, and writer John Ruskin (1819–1900), the Pre-Raphaelites agreed with his distaste for the materialism and ugliness of the contemporary industrializing world. They also expressed appreciation for the spirituality and idealism (as well as the art and artisanship) of past times, especially the Middle Ages and the Early Renaissance.

Millais's *Ophelia* (FIG. **22-42**) garnered enthusiastic praise when he exhibited it in the Exposition Universelle in Paris in 1855, where Courbet set up his Pavilion of Realism. The subject, from Shakespeare's *Hamlet* (4.7.176–179), is the drowning of Ophelia, who, in her madness, is unaware of her plight:

> *Her clothes spread wide,*
> *And mermaidlike awhile they bore her up—*
> *Which time she chanted snatches of old tunes,*
> *As one incapable of her own distress.*

To make the pathos of the scene visible, Millais became a faithful and feeling witness of its every detail, reconstructing it with a lyricism worthy of the original poetry. Although the scene is fictitious, Millais worked diligently to present it with unswerving fidelity to visual fact. He painted the background on-site at a spot along the Hogsmill River in Surrey. For the figure of Ophelia, Millais had a friend lie in a heated bathtub full of water for hours at a stretch.

DANTE GABRIEL ROSSETTI Another founder of the Pre-Raphaelite Brotherhood was DANTE GABRIEL ROSSETTI (1828–1882), who established an enviable reputation as both a painter and poet. Like other members of the group, Rossetti focused on literary and biblical themes in his art. He also produced numerous portraits of

22-42 JOHN EVERETT MILLAIS, *Ophelia,* 1852. Oil on canvas, 2′ 6″ × 3′ 8″. Tate Gallery, London.

Millet was a founder of the Pre-Raphaelite Brotherhood, whose members refused to be limited to the contemporary scenes strict Realists portrayed. The drowning of Ophelia is a Shakespearean subject.

1 ft.

22-43 Dante Gabriel Rossetti, *Beata Beatrix*, ca. 1863. Oil on canvas, 2′ 10″ × 2′ 2″. Tate Gallery, London.

This painting of a beautiful and sensuous woman is ostensibly a literary portrait of Dante's Beatrice, but the work also served as a memorial to Rossetti's wife, who died of an opium overdose.

women that projected an image of ethereal beauty and melded apparent opposites—a Victorian prettiness with sensual allure. His *Beata Beatrix* (FIG. 22-43) is ostensibly a portrait of a literary figure—Beatrice, from Dante's *Vita Nuova*—as she overlooks Florence in a trance after being mystically transported to Heaven. Yet the portrait also had personal resonance for Rossetti. It served as a memorial to his wife, Elizabeth Siddal (the model for Millais's *Ophelia*), who had died shortly before Rossetti began this painting in 1862. In the image, the woman (Siddal-Beatrice) sits in a trancelike state, while a red dove (a messenger of both love and death) deposits a poppy (symbolic of sleep and death) in her hands. Because Siddal died of an opium overdose, the presence of the poppy assumes greater significance.

ARCHITECTURE

As 19th-century scholars gathered the documentary materials of European history in extensive historiographic enterprises, each nation came to value its past as evidence of the validity of its ambitions and claims to greatness. Intellectuals appreciated the art of the remote past as a product of cultural and national genius. Italy, of course, had its Roman ruins, which had long inspired later architects. In France, Napoleon had co-opted the classical tradition, but even at the height of his power a reawakening of interest in Gothic architecture also surfaced. In 1802 the eminent French writer François-René de Chateaubriand (1768–1848) published his influential *Genius of Christianity,* which defended religion on the grounds of its beauty and mystery rather than on the grounds of truth. Gothic cathedrals, according to Chateaubriand, were translations of the sacred groves of the ancient Gauls into stone and should be cherished as manifestations of France's holy history. One result of this new nationalistic respect for the Gothic style was that Eugène Emmanuel Viollet-le-Duc (1814–1879) received a commission in 1845 to restore the inte-

22-44 Charles Barry and A.W.N. Pugin, Houses of Parliament, London, England, designed 1835.

The 19th century brought the revival of many architectural styles, often reflecting nationalistic pride. The Houses of Parliament have an exterior veneer and towers that recall late English Gothic style.

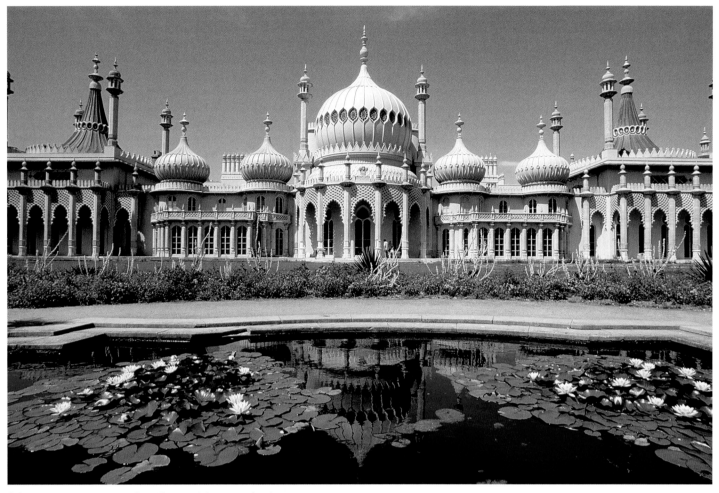

22-45 John Nash, Royal Pavilion, Brighton, England, 1815–1818.

British territorial expansion brought a familiarity with many exotic styles. This palatial "Indian Gothic" seaside pavilion is a conglomeration of Islamic domes, minarets, and screens.

rior of Paris's Notre-Dame to its Gothic splendor after removing the Baroque and Napoleonic (FIG. 22-2) alterations.

HOUSES OF PARLIAMENT England also celebrated its medieval heritage with *Neo-Gothic* buildings. In London, after the old Houses of Parliament burned in 1834, the Parliamentary Commission decreed that designs for the new building be either Gothic or Elizabethan. CHARLES BARRY (1795–1860), with the assistance of A.W.N. PUGIN (1812–1852), submitted the winning design (FIG. 22-44) in 1835. By this time, style had become a matter of selection from the historical past. Barry had traveled widely in Europe, Greece, Turkey, Egypt, and Palestine, studying the architecture of each place. He preferred the classical Renaissance styles, but he had designed some earlier Neo-Gothic buildings, and Pugin successfully influenced him in the direction of English Late Gothic. Pugin was one of a group of English artists and critics who saw moral purity and spiritual authenticity in the religious architecture of the Middle Ages. They also glorified the careful medieval artisans who built the great cathedrals. The Industrial Revolution was flooding the market with cheaply made and ill-designed commodities, and machine work was replacing handicraft. Many, such as Pugin, believed in the necessity of restoring the old artisanship, which had honesty and quality. The design of the Houses of Parliament, however, is not genuinely Gothic, despite its picturesque tower groupings (the Clock Tower, containing Big Ben, at one end, and the Victoria Tower at the other). The building has a formal axial plan and a kind of Pal-

ladian regularity beneath its Neo-Gothic detail. Pugin himself said of it, "All Grecian, Sir. Tudor [late English Gothic] details on a classical body."[13]

ROYAL PAVILION Although the Neoclassical and Neo-Gothic styles dominated early-19th-century architecture, exotic new styles of all types soon began to appear, due in part to European imperialism and in part to the Romantic spirit that permeated all the arts. Great Britain's forays throughout the world, particularly India, had exposed English culture to a broad range of non-Western artistic styles. The Royal Pavilion (FIG. 22-45), designed by JOHN NASH (1752–1835), exhibits a wide variety of these styles. Nash was an established architect, known for Neoclassical buildings in London, when he was asked to design a royal pleasure palace in the seaside resort of Brighton for the prince regent (later King George IV). The structure's fantastic exterior is a conglomeration of Islamic domes, minarets, and screens that historians have called "Indian Gothic," and sources ranging from Greece and Egypt to China influenced the interior decor. Underlying the exotic facade is a cast-iron skeleton, an early (if hidden) use of this material in noncommercial building. Nash also put this metal to fanciful use, creating life-size palm-tree columns in cast iron to support the Royal Pavilion's kitchen ceiling. The building, an appropriate enough backdrop for gala throngs pursuing pleasure by the seaside, served as the prototype for numerous playful architectural exaggerations still found in European and American resorts.

22-46 CHARLES GARNIER, the Opéra, Paris, France, 1861–1874.

For Paris's opera house, Garnier chose a festive and spectacularly theatrical Neo-Baroque facade well suited to a gathering place for fashionable audiences in an age of conspicuous wealth.

PARIS OPÉRA The Baroque style also found favor in 19th-century architecture because it was well suited to conveying a grandeur worthy of the riches the European elite acquired during this age of expansion. The Paris Opéra (FIG. **22-46**), designed by CHARLES GARNIER (1825–1898), mirrored the opulence that permeated the lives of these privileged few. The opera house has a festive and spectacularly theatrical Neo-Baroque front and two wings resembling Baroque domed central-plan churches. Inside, intricate arrangements of corridors, vestibules, stairways, balconies, alcoves, entrances, and exits facilitate easy passage throughout the building and provide space for entertainment and socializing at intermissions. The Baroque grandeur of the layout and of the building's ornamental appointments is characteristic of an architectural style called *Beaux-Arts*, which flourished in the late 19th and early 20th centuries in France. Based on ideas taught at the dominant École des Beaux-Arts (School of Fine Arts) in Paris, the Beaux-Arts style incorporated classical principles (such as symmetry in design, including interior spaces that extended radially from a central core or axis) and included extensive exterior ornamentation. As an example of a Beaux-Arts building, Garnier's Opéra proclaims, through its majesty and lavishness, its function as a gathering place for fashionable audiences in an era of conspicuous wealth. The style was so attractive to the moneyed classes who supported the arts that theaters and opera houses continued to reflect the Paris Opéra's design until World War I transformed society.

CAST-IRON CONSTRUCTION Work on Garnier's Opéra began in 1861, but by the middle of the 19th century, many architects had already abandoned sentimental and Romantic designs from the past. They turned to honest expressions of a building's purpose. Since the 18th century, bridges had been built of cast iron (FIG. 21-11), and most other utilitarian architecture—factories, warehouses, dockyard structures, mills, and the like—long had been built

simply and without historical ornamentation. Iron, along with other industrial materials, permitted engineering advancements in the construction of larger, stronger, and more fire-resistant structures than before. The tensile strength of iron (and especially of steel, available after 1860) permitted architects to create new designs involving vast enclosed spaces, as in the great train sheds of railroad stations and in exposition halls.

SAINTE-GENEVIÈVE LIBRARY The Bibliothèque Sainte-Geneviève (1843–1850), built by HENRI LABROUSTE (1801–1875), is an interesting mix of Renaissance revival style and modern cast-iron construction. Its two-story facade with arched windows recalls Renaissance palazzo designs, but Labrouste exposed the structure's metal skeleton on the interior. The lower story of the library housed the book stacks. The upper floor featured a spacious reading room (FIG. **22-47**) consisting essentially of two barrel-vaulted halls, roofed in terracotta and separated by a row of slender cast-iron columns on concrete pedestals. The columns, recognizably Corinthian, support the iron roof arches pierced with intricate vine-scroll ornament out of the Renaissance architectural vocabulary. Labrouste's design highlights how the peculiarities of the new structural material aesthetically altered the forms of traditional masonry architecture. But it also makes clear how reluctant the 19th-century architect was to surrender traditional forms, even when fully aware of new possibilities for design and construction. Architects scoffed at "engineers' architecture" for many years and continued to clothe their steel-and-concrete structures in the Romantic "drapery" of a historical style.

CRYSTAL PALACE Completely "undraped" construction first became popular in the conservatories (greenhouses) of English country estates. JOSEPH PAXTON (1801–1865) built several such structures for his patron, the duke of Devonshire. In the largest—

300 feet long—he used an experimental system of glass-and-metal roof construction. Encouraged by the success of this system, Paxton submitted a winning glass-and-iron building plan to the design competition for the hall to house the Great Exhibition of 1851, organized to present "works of industry of all nations" in London. Paxton constructed the exhibition building, the Crystal Palace (FIG. 22-48), with prefabricated parts. This allowed the vast structure to be erected in the then-unheard-of time of six months and dismantled at the exhibition's closing to avoid permanent obstruction of the park. The plan borrowed much from ancient Roman and Christian basilicas, with a central flat-roofed "nave" and a barrel-vaulted crossing "transept." The design provided ample interior space to contain displays of huge machines as well as to accommodate decorative touches in the form of large working fountains and giant trees. The public admired the building so much that the workers who dismantled it erected an enlarged version of the Crystal Palace at a new location on the outskirts of London at Sydenham, where it remained until fire destroyed it in 1936. A few old black-and-white photographs and several color lithographs (FIG. 22-48) preserve a record of the Crystal Palace's appearance.

22-48 Joseph Paxton, Crystal Palace, London, England, 1850–1851; enlarged and relocated at Sydenham, England, 1852–1854. Detail of a color lithograph by Achille-Louis Martinet, ca. 1862. Private collection.

The tensile strength of iron permitted Paxton to experiment with a new system of glass-and-metal roof construction. Built with prefabricated parts, the vast Crystal Palace required only six months to erect.

Daguerreotype, Calotype, and Wet-Plate Photography

The earliest photographic processes were the *daguerreotype,* named after L.J.M. Daguerre (FIG. 22-50), and the *calotype.* Daguerre was an architect and theatrical set painter and designer. This background led Daguerre and a partner to open a popular entertainment called the Diorama. Audiences witnessed performances of "living paintings" created by changing the lighting effects on a "sandwich" composed of a painted backdrop and several layers of painted translucent front curtains. Daguerre used a camera obscura for the Diorama, but he wanted to find a more efficient and effective procedure. Through a mutual acquaintance, he met Joseph Nicéphore Niépce (1765–1833), who in 1826 had successfully made a permanent picture of the cityscape outside his upper-story window by exposing, in a camera obscura, a metal plate covered with a light-sensitive coating. Niépce's process, however, had the significant drawback that it required an eight-hour exposure time. After Niépce died in 1833, Daguerre continued his work, making two important discoveries. Latent development—that is, bringing out the image through treatment in chemical solutions—considerably shortened the length of time needed for exposure. Daguerre also discovered a better way to "fix" the image by chemically stopping the action of light on the photographic plate, which otherwise would continue to darken until the image turned solid black.

The daguerreotype reigned supreme in photography until the 1850s, but the second major photographic invention, the ancestor of the modern negative-print system, eventually replaced it. On January 31, 1839, less than three weeks after Daguerre unveiled his method in Paris, William Henry Fox Talbot presented a paper on his "photogenic drawings" to the Royal Institution in London. As early as 1835, Talbot made "negative" images by placing objects on sensitized paper and exposing the arrangement to light. This created a design of light-colored silhouettes recording the places where opaque or translucent objects had blocked light from darkening the paper's emulsion. In his experiments, Talbot next exposed sensitized papers inside simple cameras and, with a second sheet, created "positive" images. He further improved the process with more light-sensitive chemicals and a chemical development of the negative image. This technique allowed multiple prints. However, in Talbot's process, which he named the calotype (from the Greek word *kalos,* "beautiful"), the photographic images incorporated the texture of the paper. This produced a slightly blurred, grainy effect very different from the crisp detail and wide tonal range available with the daguerreotype. Also discouraging widespread adoption of the calotype were the stiff licensing and equipment fees charged for many years after Talbot patented his new process in 1841.

An early master of an improved kind of calotype photography was the multitalented Frenchman known as Nadar. He used glass negatives and albumen printing paper (prepared with egg white), which could record finer detail and a wider range of light and shadow than Talbot's calotype process. The new *wet-plate* technology (so named because the photographic plate was exposed, developed, and fixed while wet) almost at once became the universal way of making negatives until 1880. However, wet-plate photography had drawbacks. The plates had to be prepared and processed on the spot. Working outdoors

NADAR. élevant la Photographie à la hauteur de l'Art

22-49 HONORÉ DAUMIER, *Nadar Raising Photography to the Height of Art,* 1862. Lithograph, $10\frac{3}{4}'' \times 8\frac{3}{4}''$. **Museum of Fine Arts, Boston.**

Daumier's lithograph commemorates a court decision acknowledging photography as an art form protected by copyright law. Nadar (FIG. 22-1) was one of photography's early masters.

meant taking along a portable darkroom of some sort—a wagon, tent, or box with light-tight sleeves for the photographer's arms.

Nadar achieved so much fame for his wet-plate photographic portraits (FIG. 22-1) that he became the subject of a Daumier lithograph (FIG. 22-49) that provides incisive and amusing commentary about the struggle of photography to be recognized as a fine art. Daumier made his print in response to an 1862 court decision acknowledging that photography was indeed an art and therefore entitled to protection under copyright law. In the lithograph, Nadar energetically takes pictures with his camera as his balloon rises over Parisian rooftops—Daumier's literal representation of the elevation of photography's status that the court decision reaffirmed. The image also refers to the fact that Nadar was a staunch advocate of balloon transportation and aerial reconnaissance. He produced the first aerial photographs of Paris in 1858 from his balloon Le Géant (The Giant).

PHOTOGRAPHY

A technological device of immense consequence for the modern experience was invented shortly before the mid-19th century: the camera, with its attendant art of photography. Ever since Frenchman LOUIS-JACQUES-MANDÉ DAGUERRE (1789–1851) and Briton William Henry Fox Talbot (1800–1877) announced the first practical photographic processes in 1839, people have celebrated photography as a revelation of visible things. The relative ease of the process, even in its earliest and most primitive form, seemed a dream come true for 19th-century scientists and artists, who for centuries had grappled with less satisfying methods of capturing accurate images of their subjects. Photography also perfectly suited an age that saw artistic patronage continue to shift away from the elite few toward a broader base of support. The growing and increasingly powerful middle class embraced both the comprehensible images of the new medium and its lower cost.

For the traditional artist, photography suggested new answers to the great debate about what was real and how to represent the real in art. It also challenged the place of traditional modes of pictorial representation originating in the Renaissance. Artists as diverse as Delacroix, Ingres, Courbet, and the Impressionist Edgar Degas (see Chapter 23) welcomed photography as a helpful auxiliary to painting. In a memorable lithograph (FIG. 22-49), Daumier celebrated the new medium as a genuine art form, and many artists marveled at the ability of photography to translate three-dimensional objects onto a two-dimensional surface. Other artists, however, saw photography as a mechanism capable of displacing the painstaking work of skilled painters dedicated to representing the optical truth of chosen subjects. Photography's challenge to painting, both historically and technologically, seemed to some artists an expropriation of the realistic image, until then the exclusive property of painting. But just as some painters looked to the new medium of photography for an-swers on how best to render an image in paint, so too some photographers looked to painting for suggestions about ways to imbue the photographic image with qualities beyond simple reproduction.

Artists themselves were instrumental in the development of this new technology. The camera obscura was familiar to 18th-century artists. In 1807 the invention of the *camera lucida* (lighted room) replaced the enclosed chamber of the camera obscura. Now the photographer aimed a small prism lens, hung on a stand, downward at an object. The lens projected the image of the object onto a sheet of paper. Artists using either of these devices found the process long and arduous, no matter how accurate the resulting work. All yearned for a more direct way to capture a subject's image. Two very different scientific inventions that accomplished this—the *daguerreotype* (FIG. 22-50) and the *calotype* (see "Daguerreotype, Calotype, and Wet-Plate Photography," page 646)—were announced almost simultaneously in France and England in 1839.

DAGUERREOTYPES The French government presented the new daguerreotype process at the Academy of Science in Paris on January 7, 1839, with the understanding that its details would be made available to all interested parties without charge (although the inventor received a large annuity in appreciation). Soon, people worldwide began taking pictures with the daguerreotype "camera" (a name shortened from camera obscura) in a process almost immediately christened "photography," from the Greek *photos* ("light") and *graphos* ("writing"). From the start, the possibilities of the process as a new art medium intrigued painters. Paul Delaroche (1797–1856), a leading academic painter of the day, wrote in an official report to the French government:

> Daguerre's process completely satisfies all the demands of art, carrying certain essential principles of art to such perfection that it must become a subject of observation and study even to the most

22-50 LOUIS-JACQUES-MANDÉ DAGUERRE, *Still Life in Studio*, 1837. Daguerreotype, $6\frac{1}{4}'' \times 8\frac{1}{4}''$. Société Française de Photographie, Paris.

One of the first plates Daguerre produced after perfecting his new photographic process was this still life, in which he was able to capture amazing detail and finely graduated tones from black to white.

1 in.

22-51 Josiah Johnson Hawes and Albert Sands Southworth, *Early Operation under Ether, Massachusetts General Hospital*, ca. 1847. Daguerreotype, $6\frac{1}{2}'' \times 8\frac{1}{2}''$. Massachusetts General Hospital Archives and Special Collections, Boston.

In this early daguerreotype, which predates Eakins's *Gross Clinic* FIG. 22-38) by almost 30 years, Hawes and Southworth demonstrated the documentary power of the new medium of photography.

1 in.

accomplished painters. The pictures obtained by this method are as remarkable for the perfection of the details as for the richness and harmony of the general effect. Nature is reproduced in them not only with truth, but also with art.[14]

Each daguerreotype is a unique work with amazing detail and finely graduated tones from black to white. *Still Life in Studio* (FIG. 22-50) is one of the first successful plates Daguerre produced after perfecting his method. The process captured every detail—the subtle forms, the varied textures, the diverse tones of light and shadow—in Daguerre's carefully constructed tableau. The three-dimensional forms of the sculptures, the basket, and the bits of cloth spring into high relief and are convincingly represented. The inspiration for the composition came from 17th-century Dutch vanitas still lifes, such as those of Claesz (FIG. 20-21). Like Claesz, Daguerre arranged his objects to reveal their textures and shapes clearly. Unlike a painter, Daguerre could not alter anything within his arrangement to effect a stronger image. However, he could suggest a symbolic meaning through his choice of objects. Like the skull and timepiece in Claesz's painting, Daguerre's sculptural and architectural fragments and the framed print of an embrace suggest that even art is vanitas and will not endure forever.

HAWES AND SOUTHWORTH In the United States, photographers began to make daguerreotypes within two months of Daguerre's presentation in Paris. Two particularly avid and resourceful advocates of the new medium were Josiah Johnson Hawes (1808–1901), a painter, and Albert Sands Southworth (1811–1894), a pharmacist and teacher. Together, they ran a daguerreotype studio in Boston that specialized in portraiture, then popular due to the shortened exposure time required for the process (although it was still long enough to require head braces to help subjects remain motionless while photographers recorded their images).

The partners also took their equipment outside the studio to record places and events of particular interest to them. One resultant image is *Early Operation under Ether, Massachusetts General Hospital* (FIG. 22-51). This daguerreotype, taken from the gallery of a hospital operating room, put the viewer in the position of medical students looking down on a lecture-demonstration typical throughout the 19th century. An image of historical record, this early daguerreotype, which predates Eakins's *Gross Clinic* (FIG. 22-38) by almost three decades, gives the viewer a glimpse into the whole of Western medical practice. The focus of attention in *Early Operation* is the white-draped patient surrounded by a circle of darkly clad doctors. The details of the figures and the room's furnishings are in sharp focus, but the slight blurring of several of the figures betrays motion during the exposure. The elevated viewpoint flattens the spatial perspective and emphasizes the relationships of the figures in ways that the Impressionists, especially Degas, found intriguing.

NADAR Portraiture was one of the first photography genres to use a technology that improved the calotype. Making portraits was an important economic opportunity for most photographers, as Southworth and Hawes proved, but the greatest of the early portrait photographers was undoubtedly Gaspar-Félix Tournachon, known simply as Nadar (1828–1910), a French novelist, journalist, enthusiastic balloonist, caricaturist, and, later, photographer (see "Daguerreotype," page 646). Photographic studies for his caricatures led Nadar to open a portrait studio. So talented was he at capturing the essence of his subjects that the most important people in France, including Delacroix, Daumier, Courbet, and Manet, flocked to his studio to have their portraits made. Nadar said he sought in his work "that instant of understanding that puts you in touch with the model—helps you sum him up, guides you to his habits, his ideas, presence. Even in half-length, his gesture and expression create a mood that seems to reveal much about him. Perhaps Delacroix responded to Nadar's famous gift for putting his clients at ease by assuming the pose that best expressed his personality. The new photographic materials made possible the rich range of tones in Nadar's images.

JULIA MARGARET CAMERON Among the most famous portrait photographers in 19th-century England was JULIA MARGARET CAMERON (1815–1879), who did not take up photography seriously until age 48. Although she produced images of many well-known men of the period, including Charles Darwin, Alfred Tennyson, and Thomas Carlyle, she photographed more women than men, as was true of many women photographers. *Ophelia, Study No. 2* (FIG. **22-52**) typifies her portrait style. Cameron often depicted her female subjects as characters in literary or biblical narratives. The slightly blurred focus also became a distinctive feature of her work—the byproduct of photographing with a lens having a short focal length, which allowed only a small area of sharp focus. The blurriness adds an ethereal, dreamlike tone to the photographs, appropriate for Cameron's fictional "characters." Her photograph of Ophelia has a mysterious, fragile quality reminiscent of Pre-Raphaelite paintings (FIG. **22-43**) of literary heroines.

TIMOTHY O'SULLIVAN Photographers were quick to realize the documentary power of their new medium. Thus began the story of photography's influence on modern life and of the immense changes it brought to communication and information management. Historical events could be recorded in permanent form on the spot for the first time. The photographs taken of the Crimean War (1856) by Roger Fenton (1819–1869) and of the American Civil War by Mathew B. Brady (1823–1896), Alexander Gardner (1821–1882), and TIMOTHY O'SULLIVAN (1840–1882) remain unsurpassed as incisive accounts of military life, unsparing in their truthful detail and poignant as expressions of human experience.

Of the Civil War photographs, the most moving are the inhumanly objective records of combat deaths. Perhaps the most reproduced of these photographs is O'Sullivan's *A Harvest of Death, Gettysburg, Pennsylvania, July 1863* (FIG. **22-53**). Although viewers

22-52 JULIA MARGARET CAMERON, *Ophelia, Study No. 2*, 1867. Albumen print, 1′ 1″ × 10⅔″. George Eastman House, Rochester (gift of Eastman Kodak Company; formerly Gabriel Cromer Collection).

Cameron was a prominent 19th-century photographer who often depicted her female subjects as characters in literary or biblical narratives. The slightly blurred focus is a distinctive feature of her work.

and character and enables you to produce . . . a really convincing and sympathetic likeness, an intimate portrait."[15]

Nadar's *Eugène Delacroix* (FIG. **22-1**) shows the painter at the height of his career. In this photograph, the artist imparts remarkable

22-53 TIMOTHY O'SULLIVAN, *A Harvest of Death, Gettysburg, Pennsylvania, July 1863*, 1863. Negative by Timothy O'Sullivan. Albumen print by ALEXANDER GARDNER, 6¾″ × 8¾″. New York Public Library (Astor, Lenox and Tilden Foundations, Rare Books and Manuscript Division), New York.

Wet-plate technology enabled photographers to record historical events on the spot— and to comment on the high price of war, as in this photograph of dead Union soldiers at Gettysburg in 1863.

22-54 EADWEARD MUYBRIDGE, *Horse Galloping,* 1878. Calotype print, 9″ × 12″. George Eastman House, Rochester.

Muybridge specialized in photographic studies of the successive stages in human and animal motion—details too quick for the human eye to capture. Modern cinema owes a great deal to his work.

1 in.

could regard this image as simple news reportage, it also functions to impress on people the high price of the Civil War. Corpses litter the battlefield as far as the eye can see. O'Sullivan presented a scene stretching far to the horizon. As the photograph modulates from the precise clarity of the bodies of Union soldiers in the foreground, boots stolen and pockets picked, to the almost indistinguishable corpses in the distance, the suggestion of innumerable other dead soldiers is unavoidable. This "harvest" is far more sobering and depressing than that in Winslow Homer's Civil War painting, *Veteran in a New Field* (FIG. 22-37). Though it would be many years before photolithography could reproduce photographs like this in newspapers, photographers exhibited them publicly. They made an impression that newsprint engravings never could.

EADWEARD MUYBRIDGE The Realist photographer and scientist EADWEARD MUYBRIDGE (1830–1904) came to the United States from England in the 1850s and settled in San Francisco, where he established a prominent international reputation for his photographs of the western United States. In 1872 the governor of California, Leland Stanford (1824–1893), sought Muybridge's assistance in settling a bet about whether, at any point in a stride, all four feet of a horse galloping at top speed were off the ground. Through his sequential photography, as seen in *Horse Galloping* (FIG. 22-54), Muybridge proved they were. This experience was the beginning of Muybridge's photographic studies of the successive stages in human

and animal motion—details too quick for the human eye to capture. These investigations culminated in 1885 at the University of Pennsylvania with a series of multiple-camera motion studies that recorded separate photographs of progressive moments in a single action. Muybridge's discoveries received extensive publicity through the book *Animal Locomotion* (1887), and his motion photographs earned him a place in the history of science as well as art. These sequential motion studies, along with those of Eakins and Marey, influenced many other artists, including their contemporary, the painter and sculptor Edgar Degas (FIG. 23-10), and 20th-century artists such as Marcel Duchamp (FIG. 24-1).

Muybridge presented his work to scientists and general audiences with a device called the *zoopraxiscope*, which he invented to project his sequences of images (mounted on special glass plates) onto a screen. The result was so lifelike that one viewer said it "threw upon the screen apparently the living, moving animals. Nothing was wanting but the clatter of hoofs upon the turf."[16] The illusion of motion here was the result of an aspect of human eyesight called "persistence of vision." Stated simply, it means that the brain retains whatever the eye sees for a fraction of a second after the eye stops seeing it. Thus, viewers saw a rapid succession of different images merging one into the next, producing the illusion of continuous change. This illusion lies at the heart of the motion-picture industry that debuted in the 20th century, and thus was born cinema as a new art form.

EUROPE AND AMERICA, 1800 TO 1870

ART UNDER NAPOLEON

▮ As Emperor of the French from 1804 to 1815, Napoleon embraced the Neoclassical style in order to associate his regime with the empire of ancient Rome. Napoleon chose Jacques-Louis David as First Painter of the Empire. Roman temples were the models for La Madeleine in Paris, which Pierre Vignon built as a temple of glory for France's imperial armies.

▮ Napoleon's favorite sculptor was Antonio Canova, who carved marble Neoclassical portraits of the imperial family, including Napoleon's sister, Pauline Borghese, in the guise of Venus.

▮ The beginning of a break from Neoclassicism can already be seen in the work of some of David's students, including Gros, Girodet-Trioson, and Ingres, all of whom painted some exotic subjects that reflect Romantic taste.

Canova, Pauline Borghese as Venus, 1808

ROMANTICISM

▮ The roots of Romanticism are in the 18th century, but usually the term more narrowly denotes the artistic movement that flourished from 1800 to 1840, between Neoclassicism and Realism. Romantic artists gave precedence to feeling and imagination over Enlightenment reason. Romantic painters explored the exotic, erotic, and fantastic in their art. In Spain, Francisco Goya's *Caprichos* series celebrated the unleashing of imagination, emotions, and even nightmares.

▮ In France, Eugène Delacroix led the way in depicting Romantic narratives set in faraway places and distant times. He set his colorful *Death of Sardanapalus* in ancient Assyria.

▮ Romantic painters often chose landscapes as an ideal subject to express the Romantic theme of the soul unified with the natural world. Masters of the transcendental landscape include Friedrich in Germany, Constable and Turner in England, and Cole, Bierstadt, and Church in the United States.

Delacroix, Death of Sardanapalus, 1827

REALISM

▮ Realism developed as an artistic movement in mid-19th-century France. Its leading proponent was Gustave Courbet, whose paintings of menial labor and ordinary people exemplify his belief that painters should depict only their own time and place. Honoré Daumier boldly confronted authority with his satirical lithographs commenting on the plight of the working classes. Édouard Manet shocked the public with his paintings featuring promiscuous women and rough brush strokes, which emphasized the flatness of the painting surface, paving the way for modern abstract art.

▮ American Realists include Winslow Homer, Thomas Eakins, and John Singer Sargent. Eakins's painting of surgery in progress was too brutally realistic for the Philadelphia art jury that rejected it.

Courbet, The Stone Breakers, 1849

ARCHITECTURE

▮ Territorial expansion, the Romantic interest in exotic locales and earlier eras, and nationalistic pride led to the revival in the 19th century of older architectural styles, especially the Gothic.

▮ By the middle of the century, many architects had already abandoned sentimental and Romantic designs from the past in favor of exploring the possibilities of cast-iron construction, as in Henri Labrouste's Sainte-Geneviève Library in Paris and Joseph Paxton's Crystal Palace in London.

Labrouste, Bibliothèque Sainte-Geneviève, Paris, 1843–1850

PHOTOGRAPHY

▮ In 1839, Daguerre in Paris and Talbot in London invented the first practical photographic processes. In 1862, a French court formally recognized photography as an art form subject to copyright protection. Many of the earliest photographers, including Nadar and Cameron, specialized in portrait photography, but others, including Hawes, Southworth, and O'Sullivan in the United States, quickly realized the documentary power of the new medium. Muybridge's sequential photos of human and animal motion were the forerunners of the modern cinema.

O'Sullivan, A Harvest of Death, 1863

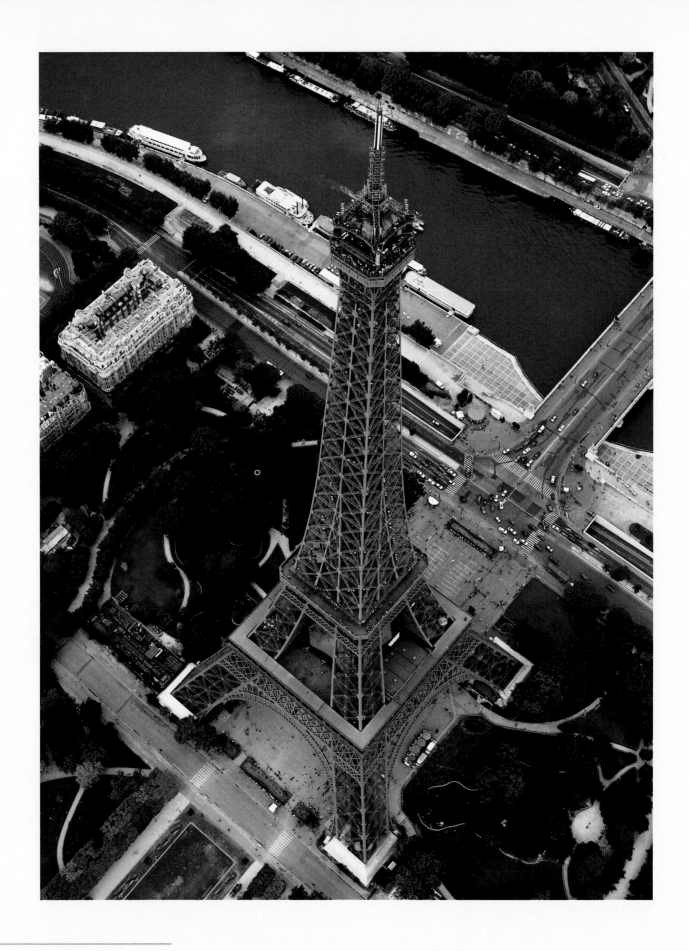

23-1 ALEXANDRE-GUSTAVE EIFFEL, Eiffel Tower, Paris, France, 1889.

New materials and technologies and the modernist aesthetic fueled radically new architectural designs in the late 19th century. Eiffel jolted the world with the exposed iron skeleton of his tower.

23

EUROPE
AND AMERICA,
1870 TO 1900

The momentous Western developments of the early 19th century—industrialization, urbanization, and increased economic and political interaction worldwide—matured quickly during the latter half of the century. The Industrial Revolution in England spread to France (MAP **23-1**) and the rest of Europe and to the United States. Because of this dramatic expansion, historians often refer to the third quarter of the 19th century as the second Industrial Revolution. Whereas the first Industrial Revolution centered on textiles, steam, and iron, the second focused on steel, electricity, chemicals, and oil. The discoveries in these fields provided the foundation for developments in plastics, machinery, building construction, and automobile manufacturing and paved the way for the invention of the radio, electric light, telephone, and electric streetcar.

One of the most significant consequences of industrialization was urbanization. The number and size of Western cities grew dramatically during the later 19th century, largely due to migration from rural regions. Rural dwellers relocated to urban centers because expanded agricultural enterprises squeezed the smaller property owners from the land. The widely available work opportunities in the cities, especially in the factories, were also a major factor in this migration. In addition, improving health and living conditions in the cities contributed to their explosive growth.

MARXISM AND DARWINISM The rise of the urban working class was fundamental to the ideas of Karl Marx (1818–1883), one of the era's dominant figures. Born in Trier, Marx received a doctorate in philosophy from the University of Berlin. After moving to Paris, he met fellow German Friedrich Engels (1820–1895), who became his lifelong collaborator. Together they wrote *The Communist Manifesto* (1848), which called for the working class to overthrow the capitalist system. Like other 19th-century empiricists, Marx believed that scientific, rational law governed nature and, indeed, all human history. For Marx, economic forces based on class struggle induced historical change. Throughout history, insisted Marx, those who controlled the means of production conflicted with those whose labor they exploited for their own enrichment. This constant opposition—a dynamic he called "dialectical materialism"—generated change. Marxism's ultimate goal was to create a socialist state in which the working class seized power and destroyed capitalism. Marxism held great appeal for the oppressed as well as many intellectuals.

Equally influential was the English naturalist Charles Darwin (1809–1882), whose theory of natural selection did much to increase interest in science. Darwin and his compatriot Alfred Russel Wallace (1823–1913), working independently, proposed a model for the process of evolution based on mechanistic laws, rather than attributing evolution to random chance or God's plan. They postulated a competitive system in which only the fittest survived. Darwin's controversial ideas, as presented in *On the Origin of Species by Means of Natural Selection* (1859), sharply contrasted with the biblical narrative of creation. By challenging traditional Christian beliefs, Darwinism contributed to a growing secular attitude.

Other theorists and social thinkers, most notably British philosopher Herbert Spencer (1820–1903), applied Darwin's principles to the rapidly changing socioeconomic realm. As in the biological world, they asserted, industrialization's intense competition led to the survival of the most economically fit companies, enterprises, and countries. The social Darwinists provided Western leaders with justification for the colonization of peoples and cultures that they deemed less advanced. By 1900 the major economic and political powers had divided up much of the world. The French had colonized most of North Africa and Indochina, while the British occupied India, Australia, and large areas of Africa, including Nigeria, Egypt, Sudan, Rhodesia, and the Union of South Africa. The Dutch were a major presence in the Pacific, and the Germans, Portuguese, Spanish, and Italians all established themselves in various areas of Africa.

Map 23-1 France around 1870.

MODERNISM The combination of extensive technological changes and increased exposure to other cultures, coupled with the rapidity of these changes, led to an acute sense in Western cultures of the world's impermanence. Darwin's ideas of evolution and Marx's emphasis on a continuing sequence of economic conflicts reinforced this awareness of a constantly shifting reality. These societal changes in turn fostered a new and multifaceted artistic approach that historians call *modernism*. Modernist artists seek to capture the images and sensibilities of their age, but modernism transcends the simple present to involve the artist's critical examination of or reflection on the premises of art itself. Modernism thus implies certain concerns about art and aesthetics that are internal to art production, regardless of whether the artist is producing scenes from contemporary social life. Clement Greenberg (1909–1994), an influential American art critic, explained:

> The essence of Modernism lies . . . in the use of the characteristic methods of a discipline to criticize the discipline itself—not in order to subvert it, but to entrench it more firmly in its area of competence. . . . Realistic, illusionist art had dissembled the medium, using art to conceal art. Modernism used art to call attention to art. The limitations that constitute the medium of painting—the flat surface, the shape of the support, the properties of pigment—were treated by the Old Masters as negative factors that could be acknowledged only implicitly or indirectly. Modernist painting has come to regard these same limitations as positive factors that are to be acknowledged openly.[1]

The work of Gustave Courbet and the Realists (see Chapter 22) already expressed this modernist viewpoint, but modernism emerged even more forcefully in the late-19th-century movements that art historians call Impressionism, Post-Impressionism, and Symbolism.

IMPRESSIONISM

Impressionism, both in content and in style, was an art of industrialized, urbanized Paris, a reaction to the sometimes brutal and chaotic transformation of French life that occurred during the latter half of the 19th century. The rapidity of these changes made the world seem unstable and insubstantial. As the poet and critic Charles Baudelaire (1821–1867) observed in 1860 in his essay "The Painter of Modern Life": "[M]odernity is the transitory, the fugitive, the contingent."[2] Accordingly, Impressionist works represent an attempt to capture a fleeting moment—not in the absolutely fixed, precise sense of a Realist painting but by conveying the elusiveness and impermanence of images and conditions.

CLAUDE MONET A hostile critic applied the term "Impressionism" in response to the painting *Impression: Sunrise* (FIG. 23-2) that CLAUDE MONET (1840–1926) exhibited in the first Impressionist show in 1874 (see "Academic Salons and Independent Art Exhibitions," page 655). Although the critic intended the label to be derogatory, by the third Impressionist show in 1878 the artists had embraced it and were calling themselves Impressionists. Artists and

Academic Salons and Independent Art Exhibitions

For both artists and art historians, modernist art stands in marked contrast—indeed in forceful opposition—to academic art, that is, to the art the established art schools such as the Royal Academy of Painting and Sculpture in France (founded 1648) and the Royal Academy of Arts in Britain (founded 1768) promoted. These academies provided instruction for art students and sponsored exhibitions, exerting tight control over the art scene. The annual exhibitions, called "Salons" in France, were highly competitive, as was membership in these academies. Subsidized by the government, the French Royal Academy supported a limited range of artistic expression, focusing on traditional subjects and highly polished technique. Because of the challenges modernist art presented to established artistic conventions, the juries for the Salons and other exhibitions often rejected the works more adventurous artists wished to display. As noted in the previous chapter, Gustave Courbet's reaction to the rejection of some of his paintings was to set up his own Pavilion of Realism in 1855 (see "Courbet on Realism," Chapter 22, page 631). Years later, he wrote:

> [I]t is high time that someone have the courage to be an honest man and that he say that the Academy is a harmful, all-consuming institution, incapable of fulfilling the goal of its so-called mission.[*]

Growing dissatisfaction with the decisions of the French Academy's jurors prompted Napoleon III (r. 1852–1870) in 1863 to establish the Salon des Refusés (Salon of the Rejected) to show all of the works not accepted for exhibition in the regular Salon. Manet's *Le Déjeuner sur l'Herbe* (FIG. 22-33) was among them. The public greeted it and the entire exhibition with derision. One reviewer of the rejected works summed up the prevailing attitude:

This exhibition, at once sad and grotesque, . . . offers abundant proof . . . that the jury always displays an unbelievable leniency. Save for one or two questionable exceptions there is not a painting which deserves the honor of the official galleries . . . . There is even something cruel about this exhibition; people laugh as they do at a farce.[†]

In 1867, after further rejections, Manet, following Courbet, mounted a private exhibition of 50 of his paintings outside the Paris World's Fair. Six years later, the Impressionists (FIG. 23-2) formed their own society and began mounting shows of their works in Paris. This decision gave the Impressionists much more freedom, for they did not have to contend with the Academy's authoritative and confining viewpoint, and thereafter they held exhibitions at one- or two-year intervals from 1874 until 1886.

Another group of artists unhappy with the Salon's conservative nature adopted the same renegade approach. In 1884 these artists formed the Société des Artistes Indépendants (Society of Independent Artists) and held annual Salons des Indépendants. Georges Seurat's *A Sunday on La Grande Jatte* (FIG. 23-15) was one of the paintings in the Independents' 1886 Salon.

As the art market expanded, venues for the exhibition of art increased. Art circles and societies sponsored private shows in which both amateurs and professionals participated. Dealers became more aggressive in promoting the artists they represented by mounting exhibitions in a variety of spaces, some fairly intimate and small, others large and grandiose. All of these proliferating opportunities for exhibition gave artists alternatives to the traditional constraints of the Salon and provided fertile breeding ground for the development of radically new art forms and styles.

[*] Letter to Jules-Antoine Castagnary, October 17, 1868. Translated by Petra ten-Doesschate Chu, *Letters of Gustave Courbet* (Chicago: University of Chicago Press, 1992), 346.
[†] Maxime du Camp, in *Revue des deux mondes*, 1863, quoted in George Heard Hamilton, *Manet and His Critics* (New Haven: Yale University Press, 1986), 42–43.

1 in.

23-2 CLAUDE MONET, *Impression: Sunrise*, 1872. Oil on canvas, $1' 7\frac{1}{2}'' \times 2' 1\frac{1}{2}''$. Musée Marmottan, Paris.

A hostile critic applied the derogatory term "Impressionism" to this painting because of its sketchy quality and clearly evident brush strokes. Monet and his circle embraced the label for their movement.

critics had used the term before, but only in relation to sketches. Impressionist paintings do incorporate the qualities of sketches—abbreviation, speed, and spontaneity. This is apparent in *Impression: Sunrise*, in which Monet made no attempt to disguise the brush strokes or blend the pigment to create smooth tonal gradations and an optically accurate scene. This concern with acknowledging the paint and the canvas surface continued the modernist exploration that the Realists began. Beyond this connection to the sketch, Impressionism operated at the intersection of what the artists saw and what they felt. In other words, the "impressions" these artists recorded in their paintings were neither purely objective descriptions of the exterior world nor solely subjective responses but the interaction between the two. They were sensations—the artists' subjective and personal responses to nature.

In sharp contrast to traditional studio artists, Monet painted outdoors, which sharpened his focus on the roles light and color play in capturing an instantaneous representation of atmosphere and climate. Monet carried the systematic investigation of light and color further than any other Impressionist, but all of them recognized the importance of carefully observing and understanding how light and color operate. This thorough study permitted the Impressionists to present images that truly conveyed a sense of the momentary and transitory. Lila Cabot Perry (1848–1933), a student of Monet's late in his career, gave this description of Monet's approach:

> I remember his once saying to me: "When you go out to paint, try to forget what objects you have before you—a tree, a house, a field, or whatever. Merely think, here is a little square of blue, here an oblong of pink, here a streak of yellow, and paint it just as it looks to you, the exact color and shape, until it gives your own naïve impression of the scene before you."[3]

Scientific studies of light and the invention of chemically synthesized pigments increased artists' sensitivity to the multiplicity of colors in nature and gave them new colors for their work. After scrutinizing the effects of light and color on forms, the Impressionists concluded that *local color*—an object's true color in white light—becomes modified by the quality of the light shining on it, by reflections from other objects, and by the effects juxtaposed colors produce. Shadows do not appear gray or black, as many earlier painters thought, but are composed of colors modified by reflections or other conditions. If artists use complementary colors (see "19th-Century Color Theory," page 664) side by side over large enough areas, the colors intensify each other, unlike the effect of small quantities of adjoining mixed pigments, which blend into neutral tones. Furthermore, the "mixing" of colors by juxtaposing them on a canvas produces a more intense hue than the same colors mixed on the palette. It is not strictly true that the Impressionists used only primary hues, placing them side by side to create secondary colors (blue and yellow, for example, to create green). But they did achieve remarkably brilliant effects with their characteristically short, choppy brush strokes, which so accurately caught the vibrating quality of light. The fact that their canvas surfaces look incomprehensible at close range and their forms and objects appear only when the eye fuses the strokes at a certain distance accounts for much of the early adverse criticism leveled at their work. Some critics even accused the Impressionists of firing their paint at the canvas with pistols.

ROUEN CATHEDRAL Monet's intensive study of the phenomena of light and color is especially evident in several series of paintings he made of the same subject. In one series he painted some 40 views of Rouen Cathedral, northwest of Paris (MAP 23-1). For each canvas in the series, Monet observed the cathedral from nearly

23-3 CLAUDE MONET, *Rouen Cathedral: The Portal* (*in Sun*), 1894. Oil on canvas, 3′ 3¼″ × 2′ 1⅞″. Metropolitan Museum of Art, New York (Theodore M. Davis Collection, bequest of Theodore M. Davis, 1915).

Monet painted some 40 views of Rouen Cathedral at different times of day and under various climatic conditions. The real subject of this painting is not the building but the sunlight shining on it.

the same viewpoint but at different times of the day or under various climatic conditions. In the painting illustrated here (FIG. 23-3), Monet depicted the church bathed in bright light. With scientific precision, he created an unparalleled record of the passing of time as seen in the movement of light over identical forms. In fact, the real subject of Monet's painting—as the title *Rouen Cathedral: The Portal* (*in Sun*) implies—is not the cathedral, which he shows only in part, but the sunlight on the building's main portal. Later critics accused Monet and his companions of destroying form and order for fleeting atmospheric effects, but Monet focused on light and color precisely to reach a greater understanding of the appearance of form.

SAINT-LAZARE Most of the Impressionists depicted scenes in and around Paris, the heart of modern life in France. Monet's *Saint-Lazare Train Station* (FIG. 23-4) shows a dominant aspect of the contemporary urban scene. The expanding railway network had made travel more convenient, bringing throngs of people into Paris. In this painting, Monet captured the energy and vitality of Paris's modern transportation hub. The train, emerging from the steam

23-4 CLAUDE MONET, *Saint-Lazare Train Station*, 1877. Oil on canvas, $2' 5\frac{3}{4}'' \times 3' 5''$. Musée d'Orsay, Paris.

Impressionist canvas surfaces are incomprehensible at close range, but the eye fuses the brush strokes at a distance. Monet's agitated application of paint contributes to the sense of energy in this urban scene.

smoke, which lashes the glass roof of the main hall. . . . We see the vast and manic movements at the station where the ground shakes with every turn of the wheel. The platforms are sticky with soot, and the air is full of that bitter scent exuded by burning coal. As we look at this magnificent picture, we are overcome by the same feelings as if we were really there, and these feelings are perhaps even more powerful, because in the picture the artist has conveyed his own feelings as well.[4]

and smoke it emits, rumbles into the station. In the background haze are the tall buildings that were becoming a major component of the Parisian landscape. Monet's agitated paint application contributes to the sense of energy and conveys the atmosphere of urban life.

Georges Rivière (1855–1943), a critic and friend of some of the Impressionists, saw this painting in the third Impressionist exhibition and recorded the essence of what Monet had tried to achieve:

> Like a fiery steed, stimulated rather than exhausted by the long trek that it has only just finished, [the locomotive] tosses its mane of

GUSTAVE CAILLEBOTTE Other Impressionists also represented facets of city life, although not always using Monet's impressionistic brush strokes. The setting of *Paris: A Rainy Day* (FIG. **23-5**) by GUSTAVE CAILLEBOTTE (1849–1893) is a junction of spacious boulevards that resulted from the redesigning of Paris that began in 1852. The city's population had reached nearly 1.5 million by midcentury. To accommodate this congregation of humanity—and to facilitate the movement of troops in the event of another revolution—Napoleon III ordered Paris rebuilt. The emperor named Baron Georges Haussmann (1809–1891), a city superintendent, to oversee the entire project. In addition to new water and sewer systems, street lighting, and new residential and commercial buildings, a major component of the new Paris was the creation of the wide, open boulevards seen in Caillebotte's painting. These great avenues, whose construction caused the demolition of thousands of old buildings and streets, transformed medieval Paris into the present modern city, with its superb vistas and wide uninterrupted arteries for the flow of vehicular and pedestrian traffic. Caillebotte chose to focus on these markers of the city's rapid urbanization.

23-5 GUSTAVE CAILLEBOTTE, *Paris: A Rainy Day*, 1877. Oil on canvas, $6' 9'' \times 9' 9''$. Art Institute of Chicago, Chicago (Worcester Fund).

Although Caillebotte did not use Impressionistic broken brush strokes, the seemingly randomly placed figures and the arbitrary cropping of the vista suggest the transitory nature of modern life.

Impressionism **657**

23-6 CAMILLE PISSARRO, *La Place du Théâtre Français*, 1898. Oil on canvas, 2′ 4½″ × 3′ ½″. Los Angeles County Museum of Art, Los Angeles (Mr. and Mrs. George Gard De Sylva Collection).

This Impressionist view of a crowded Paris square seen from several stories above street level has much in common with photographs, especially the flattening spatial effect resulting from the high viewpoint.

1 ft.

Although Caillebotte did not dissolve his image into the broken color and brushwork characteristic of Impressionism, he did use an informal and asymmetrical composition. The figures seem randomly placed, with the frame cropping them arbitrarily, suggesting the transitory nature of the street scene. Well-dressed Parisians of the leisure class share the viewer's space. Despite the sharp focus of *Paris: A Rainy Day*, the picture captures the artist's "impression" of urban life.

CAMILLE PISSARRO Other Impressionists also found the spacious boulevards and avenues that were the product of "Haussmannization" attractive subjects for paintings. *La Place du Théâtre Français* (FIG. **23-6**) is one of many panoramic scenes of Paris that CAMILLE PISSARRO (1830–1903) painted. The artist recorded the blurred dark accents against a light ground that constituted his visual sensations of a crowded Paris square viewed from several stories above street level. The moment Pissarro captured in this painting is not so much of fugitive light effects as it is of the street life, achieved through a deliberate casualness in the arrangement of figures. To accomplish this sense of spontaneity, Pissarro, like many of his fellow Impressionists, sometimes used photography to record the places he wished to paint. Scholars have been quick to point out the visual parallels between Impressionist paintings and photographs. These parallels include, here, the arbitrary cutting off of figures at the frame's edge and the curious flattening spatial effect produced by the high viewpoint.

BERTHE MORISOT Many Impressionist paintings depict scenes from resort areas on the seashore or along the Seine River, such as Argenteuil, Bougival, and Chatou. The railway line that carried people to and from Saint-Lazare Station connected Argenteuil to Paris, so transportation was not an obstacle. Parisians often would take the train out to these resort areas for a day of sailing, picnicking, and strolling along the Seine. BERTHE MORISOT (1841–1895), Édouard Manet's sister-in-law, regularly exhibited with the Impres-

23-7 BERTHE MORISOT, *Villa at the Seaside*, 1874. Oil on canvas, 1′ 7¾″ × 2′ ⅛″. Norton Simon Art Foundation, Los Angeles.

In this informal view of a woman and child enjoying their leisure time at a fashionable seashore resort, Berthe Morisot used swift, sketchy strokes of light colors to convey a feeling of airiness.

1 in.

Renoir on the Art of Painting

Many 19th-century artists were concerned with the theoretical basis of picture making. One of the most cogent statements on this subject is Pierre-Auguste Renoir's concise summary of how he, as an Impressionist, painted pictures (for example, FIG. 23-8) and what he hoped to achieve as an artist.

> I arrange my subject as I want it, then I go ahead and paint it, like a child. I want a red to be sonorous, to sound like a bell; if it doesn't turn out that way, I add more reds and other colors until I get it. I am no cleverer than that. I have no rules and no methods; . . . I have no secrets. I look at a nude; there are myriads of tiny tints. I must find the ones that will make the flesh on my canvas live and quiver. . . .
>
> [If viewers] could explain a picture, it wouldn't be art. Shall I tell you what I think are the two qualities of art? It must be indescribable and it must be inimitable. . . . The work of art must seize upon you, wrap you up in itself, carry you away. It is the means by which the artist conveys his passions. . . . I want people to feel that neither the setting nor the figures are dull and lifeless.*

* Quoted in Eric Protter, ed., *Painters on Painting* (New York: Grosset & Dunlap, 1971), 145.

1 ft.

23-8 PIERRE-AUGUSTE RENOIR, *Le Moulin de la Galette,* 1876. Oil on canvas, 4′ 3″ × 5′ 8″. Musée d'Orsay, Paris.

Renoir's painting of this popular Parisian dance hall is dappled by sunlight and shade, artfully blurred into the figures to produce the effect of floating and fleeting light that the Impressionists cultivated.

sionists. Most of her paintings focus on domestic subjects, the one realm of Parisian life where society allowed an upper-class woman such as Morisot free access, but she also produced many outdoor scenes. Morisot's considerable skills are evident in *Villa at the Seaside* (FIG. 23-7). Both the subject and style correlate well with Impressionist concerns. The setting is the shaded veranda of a summer hotel at a fashionable seashore resort. A woman elegantly but not ostentatiously dressed sits gazing out across the railing to a sunlit beach with its umbrellas and bathing cabins. Her child, its discarded toy boat a splash of red, is attentive to the passing sails on the placid sea. The mood is of relaxed leisure. Morisot used the open brushwork and the *plein air* (outdoor) lighting characteristic of Impressionism. Sketchy brush strokes record her quick perceptions. Nowhere did Morisot linger on contours or enclosed details. She presented the scene in a slightly filmy soft focus that conveys a feeling of airiness. The composition also recalls the work of other Impressionists. The figures fall informally into place, as someone who shared their intimate space would perceive them. Morisot was both immensely ambitious and talented, as her ability to catch the pictorial moment demonstrates. She escaped the hostile criticism directed at most of the other Impressionists. People praised her work for its sensibility, grace, and delicacy.

PIERRE-AUGUSTE RENOIR Another facet of the new industrialized Paris that drew the Impressionists' attention was the leisure activities of its inhabitants. Scenes of dining, dancing, the café-concerts, the opera, the ballet, and other forms of urban recreation were mainstays of Impressionism. Although seemingly unrelated, industrialization facilitated these pursuits. With the advent of set working hours, people's schedules became more regimented, allowing them to plan their favorite pastimes. *Le Moulin de la Galette* (FIG. 23-8) by PIERRE-AUGUSTE RENOIR (1841–1919) depicts throngs of people gathered in a popular Parisian dance hall. Some crowd the tables and chatter, while others dance energetically. So lively is the atmosphere that the viewer can virtually hear the sounds of music, laughter, and tinkling glasses. The painter dappled the whole scene with sunlight and shade, artfully blurred into the figures to produce just the effect of floating and fleeting light the Impressionists so cultivated. Renoir's casual, unposed placement of the figures and the suggested continuity of space, spreading in all directions and only accidentally limited by the frame, position the viewer as a participant rather than as an outsider. Whereas classical art sought to express universal and timeless qualities, Impressionism attempted to depict just the opposite—the incidental, momentary, and passing aspects of reality (see "Renoir on the Art of Painting," above).

23-9 Édouard Manet, *Bar at the Folies-Bergère*, 1882. Oil on canvas, 3′ 1″ × 4′ 3″. Courtauld Institute of Art Gallery, London.

In this painting set in a Parisian café, Manet called attention to the canvas surface by creating spatial inconsistencies, such as the relationship between the barmaid and her apparent reflection in a mirror.

1 ft.

ÉDOUARD MANET Another artist who depicted Parisian nightlife was Édouard Manet, whose career bridged Realism (see Chapter 22) and Impressionism. One of his later paintings in the Impressionist mode is *Bar at the Folies-Bergère* (FIG. **23-9**). The Folies-Bergère was a popular café with music-hall performances, one of the fashionable gathering places for Parisian revelers that many Impressionists frequented. In Manet's 1882 painting, a barmaid, centrally placed, looks out from the canvas but seems disinterested or lost in thought, divorced from her patrons as well as from the viewer. Manet blurred and roughly applied the brush strokes, particularly those in the background, and the effects of modeling and perspective are minimal. This painting method further calls attention to the surface by forcing the viewer to scrutinize the work to make sense of the scene. On such scrutiny, visual discrepancies emerge. For example, what initially seems easily recognizable as a mirror behind the barmaid creates confusion throughout the rest of the painting. Is the woman on the right the barmaid's reflection? If so, it is impossible to reconcile the spatial relationship among the barmaid, the mirror, the bar's frontal horizontality, and the barmaid's seemingly displaced reflection. These visual contradictions reveal Manet's insistence on calling attention to the pictorial structure of his painting, in keeping with his modernist interest in examining the basic premises of the medium.

EDGAR DEGAS Impressionists also depicted more formal leisure activities. The fascination EDGAR DEGAS (1834–1917) had with patterns of motion brought him to the Paris Opéra (FIG. **22-46**) and its ballet school. There, his great observational power took in the formalized movements of classical ballet, one of his favorite subjects. In *The Rehearsal* (FIG. **23-10**), Degas used several devices to bring the observer into the pictorial space. The frame cuts off the spiral stair, the windows in the background, and the group of figures in the right foreground. The figures are not at the center of a classically balanced composition. Instead, Degas arranged them in a seemingly random manner. The prominent diagonals of the wall bases and floorboards carry the viewer into and along the directional lines of the dancers. Finally, as is customary in Degas's ballet pictures, a large, off-center, empty space creates the illusion of a continuous floor that connects the observer with the pictured figures.

The often arbitrarily cut-off figures, the patterns of light splotches, and the blurriness of the images in this and other Degas works indicate the artist's interest in reproducing single moments. Further, they reveal his fascination with photography. Degas not only studied the photography of others but also used the camera to make preliminary studies for his works, particularly photographing figures in interiors. Japanese woodblock prints (see "Japonisme," page 661) were another inspirational source for paintings such as *The Rehearsal*. The cunning spatial projections in Degas's paintings probably derived in part from Japanese prints, such as those by Suzuki Harunobu. Japanese artists used diverging lines not only to

23-10 EDGAR DEGAS, *The Rehearsal*, 1874. Oil on canvas, 1′ 11″ × 2′ 9″. Glasgow Art Galleries and Museum, Glasgow (Burrell Collection).

The arbitrarily cut-off figures, the patterns of light splotches, and the blurry images in this work reveal Degas's interest in reproducing fleeting moments, as well as his fascination with photography.

1 ft.

Japonisme

Despite Europe's and America's extensive colonization during the 19th century, Japan avoided Western intrusion until 1853–1854, when Commodore Matthew Perry (1794–1858) and American naval forces exacted trading and diplomatic privileges from Japan. From the increased contact, Westerners became familiar with Japanese culture. So intrigued were the French with Japanese art and culture that they introduced a specific label—*Japonisme*—to describe the Japanese aesthetic, which, because of both its beauty and exoticism, greatly appealed to the fashionable segment of Parisian society. In 1867 at the Exposition Universelle in Paris, the Japanese pavilion garnered more attention than any other. Soon, Japanese kimonos, fans, lacquer cabinets, tea caddies, folding screens, tea services, and jewelry flooded Paris. Japanese-themed novels and travel books were immensely popular as well. As demand for Japanese merchandise grew in the West, the Japanese began to develop import-export businesses, and the foreign currency that flowed into Japan helped to finance much of its industrialization.

Artists in particular were great admirers of Japanese art. Among those the Japanese aesthetic influenced were the Impressionists and Post-Impressionists, especially Édouard Manet, Edgar Degas, Mary Cassatt, James Abbott McNeill Whistler, Henri de Toulouse-Lautrec, Vincent van Gogh, and Paul Gauguin. For the most part, the Japanese presentation of space in woodblock prints, which were more readily available in the West than any other art form, intrigued these artists. Because of the simplicity of the woodblock printing process, these prints feature broad areas of flat color with a limited amount of modulation or gradation. This flatness interested modernist painters, who sought ways to call attention to the picture surface. The right side of Degas's *The Tub* (FIG. 23-11, *left*), for example, has this two-dimensional quality. Degas, in fact, owned a print by Japanese artist TORII KIYONAGA (1752–1815) depicting eight women at a bath in various poses and states of undress. That print inspired Degas's painting. A comparison between Degas's bather and a detail (FIG. 23-11, *right*) of a bather from another of Kiyonaga's prints is striking, although Degas did not closely copy any of the Japanese artist's figures. Instead, he absorbed the essence of Japanese compositional style and the distinctive angles employed in representing human figures, and he translated them into the Impressionist mode.

The decorative quality of Japanese images also appealed to the artists associated with the Arts and Crafts movement in England. Artists such as William Morris (FIG. 23-34) and Charles Rennie Mackintosh (FIG. 23-35) found Japanese prints attractive because those artworks intersected nicely with two fundamental Arts and Crafts principles: Art should be available to the masses, and functional objects should be artistically designed.

1 ft.

1 in.

23-11 *Left:* EDGAR DEGAS, *The Tub*, 1886. Pastel, 1' 11½" × 2' 8⅜". Musée d'Orsay, Paris. *Right:* TORII KIYONAGA, detail of *Two Women at the Bath*, ca. 1780. Color woodblock, full print 10½" × 7½", detail 3¾" × 3½". Musée Guimet, Paris.

The Tub reveals the influence of Japanese prints, especially the distinctive angles artists such as Torii Kiyonaga used in representing figures. Degas translated his Japanese model into the Impressionist mode.

organize the flat shapes of figures but also to direct the viewer's attention into the picture space. The Impressionists, acquainted with these prints as early as the 1860s, greatly admired their spatial organization, familiar and intimate themes, and flat unmodeled color areas, and drew much instruction from them.

THE TUB Although color and light were major components of the Impressionist quest to capture fleeting sensations, these artists considered other formal elements as well. Degas, for example, became a superb master of line, so much so that his works often differ significantly from those of Monet and Renoir. Degas specialized in studies of figures in rapid and informal action, recording the quick impression of arrested motion, as is evident in *The Rehearsal* (FIG. 23-10). He often employed lines to convey this sense of movement. In *The Tub* (FIG. 23-11, *left*), inspired by a Japanese print similar to the one illustrated here (FIG. 23-11, *right*), a young woman crouches in a washing tub. The artist outlined the major objects in the painting—the woman, tub, and pitchers—and covered all surfaces with linear

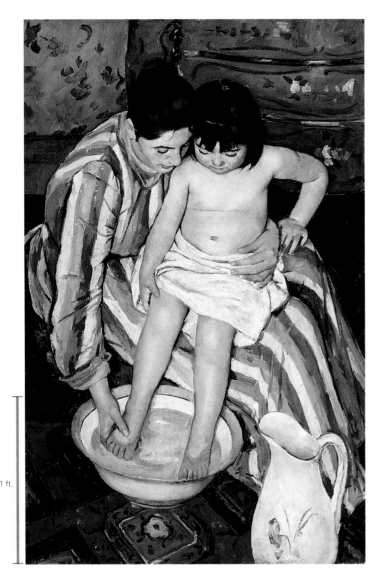

23-12 MARY CASSATT, *The Bath*, ca. 1892. Oil on canvas, 3′ 3″ × 2′ 2″. Art Institute of Chicago, Chicago (Robert A. Walker Fund).

Cassatt's style owed much to the compositional devices of Degas and of Japanese prints, but her subjects differed from those of most Impressionists, in part because, as a woman, she could not frequent cafés.

1 ft.

daughter of a Philadelphia banker. Degas befriended and influenced Cassatt, who exhibited regularly with the Impressionists. She had trained as a painter before moving to Europe to study masterworks in France and Italy. As a woman, she could not easily frequent the cafés with her male artist friends, and she had the responsibility of caring for her aging parents, who had moved to Paris to join her. Because of these restrictions, Cassatt's subjects, like Morisot's (FIG. 23-7), were principally women and children, whom she presented with a combination of objectivity and genuine sentiment. Works such as *The Bath* (FIG. 23-12) show the tender relationship between a mother and child. As in Degas's *The Tub*, the visual solidity of the mother and child contrasts with the flattened patterning of the wallpaper and rug. Cassatt's style in this work owed much to the compositional devices of Degas and of Japanese prints, but the painting's design has an originality and strength all its own.

JAMES WHISTLER Another American expatriate artist in Europe was JAMES ABBOTT MCNEILL WHISTLER (1834–1903), who spent time in Paris before settling finally in London. He met many of the French Impressionists, and his art is a unique combination of some of their concerns and his own. Whistler shared the Impressionists' interests in the subject of contemporary life and the sensations color produces on the eye. To these influences he added his own desire to create harmonies paralleling those achieved in music.

1 in.

23-13 JAMES ABBOTT MCNEILL WHISTLER, *Nocturne in Black and Gold* (*The Falling Rocket*), ca. 1875. Oil on panel, 1′ 11⅝″ × 1′ 6½″. Detroit Institute of Arts, Detroit (gift of Dexter M. Ferry Jr.).

In this painting, Whistler displayed an Impressionist's interest in conveying the atmospheric effects of fireworks at night, but he also emphasized the abstract arrangement of shapes and colors.

hatch marks. Degas achieved this leaner quality with *pastels*, his favorite medium. Using these dry sticks of powdered pigment, Degas drew directly on the paper, as one would with a piece of chalk, thus accounting for the linear basis of his work. Although the applied pastel is subject to smudging, the colors tend to retain their autonomy, so they appear fresh and bright.

The Tub also reveals how Degas's work, like that of the other Impressionists, continued the modernist exploration of the premises of painting by acknowledging the artwork's surface. Although the viewer clearly perceives the woman as a depiction of a three-dimensional form in space, the tabletop or shelf on the right of the image appears so severely tilted that it seems to parallel the picture plane. The two pitchers on the table complicate this visual conflict between the table's flatness and the illusion of the bathing woman's three-dimensional volume. The limited foreshortening of the pitchers and their shared edge, in conjunction with the rest of the image, create a visual perplexity for the viewer.

MARY CASSATT In the Salon of 1874, Degas admired a painting by a young American artist, MARY CASSATT (1844–1926), the

Nature contains the elements, in color and form, of all pictures, as the keyboard contains the notes of all music. But the artist is born to pick, and choose, and group with science, these elements, that the result may be beautiful—as the musician gathers his notes, and forms his chords, until he brings forth from chaos glorious harmony.[5]

To underscore his artistic intentions, Whistler began calling his paintings "arrangements" or "nocturnes." *Nocturne in Black and Gold*, or *The Falling Rocket* (FIG. **23-13**), is a daring painting with gold flecks and splatters that represent the exploded firework punctuating the darkness of the night sky. More interested in conveying the atmospheric effects than in providing details of the scene, Whistler emphasized creating a harmonious arrangement of shapes and colors on the rectangle of his canvas, an approach that appealed to many 20th-century artists. These works angered many 19th-century viewers, however. The British critic John Ruskin (1819–1900) responded to this painting with a scathing review accusing Whistler of "flinging a pot of paint in the public's face" with his style. In reply, Whistler sued Ruskin for libel. During the trial, Ruskin's attorney asked Whistler about the subject of *Nocturne:*

> What is your definition of a Nocturne?
>
> It is an arrangement of line, form, and colour first; . . . Among my works are some night pieces; and I have chosen the word Nocturne because it generalizes and amplifies the whole set of them. . . . The nocturne in black and gold is a night piece and represents the fireworks at Cremorne [Gardens in London].
>
> Not a view of Cremorne?
>
> If it were a view of Cremorne, it would certainly bring about nothing but disappointment on the part of the beholders. It is an artistic arrangement.[6]

The court transcript notes that the spectators in the courtroom laughed at that response, but Whistler won the case. However, his victory had sadly ironic consequences for him. The judge in the case, showing where his—and the public's—sympathies lay, awarded the artist only one farthing (less than a penny) in damages and required him to pay all of the court costs, which ruined him financially.

POST-IMPRESSIONISM

By 1886 most critics and a large segment of the public accepted the Impressionists as serious artists. Just when their images of contemporary life no longer seemed crude and unfinished, however, some of these painters and a group of younger followers came to feel that the Impressionists were neglecting too many of the traditional elements of picture making in their attempts to capture momentary sensations of light and color on canvas. In a conversation with the influential art dealer Ambroise Vollard (1866–1939) in about 1883, Renoir commented: "I had wrung impressionism dry, and I finally came to the conclusion that I knew neither how to paint nor how to draw. In a word, impressionism was a blind alley, as far as I was concerned."[7] By the 1880s, some artists were more systematically examining the properties and the expressive qualities of line, pattern, form, and color. Among them were Dutch-born Vincent van Gogh and the French painter Paul Gauguin, who focused their artistic efforts on exploring the expressive capabilities of formal elements, and Georges Seurat and Paul Cézanne, also from France, who were more analytical in orientation. Because their art had its roots in Impressionist precepts and methods, but is not stylistically homogeneous, these artists and others have become known as the *Post-Impressionists.*

HENRI DE TOULOUSE-LAUTREC Closest to the Impressionists in many ways was the French artist HENRI DE TOULOUSE-LAUTREC (1864–1901), who deeply admired Degas and shared the Impressionists' interest in capturing the sensibility of modern life. His work, however, has an added satirical edge to it and often borders on caricature. Genetic defects that stunted his growth and in part crippled him led to Toulouse-Lautrec's self-exile from the high society his ancient aristocratic name entitled him to enter. He became a denizen of the night world of Paris, consorting with a tawdry population of entertainers, prostitutes, and other social outcasts. He reveled in the energy of cheap music halls, cafés, and bordellos. *At the Moulin Rouge* (FIG. **23-14**) reveals the influences of Degas, of the Japanese print, and of photography in the oblique and asymmetrical composition, the spatial diagonals, and the strong line patterns with added dissonant colors. But although Toulouse-Lautrec closely studied such scenes in real life and they were already familiar to viewers in the work of the earlier Impressionists, he so emphasized or exaggerated each element that

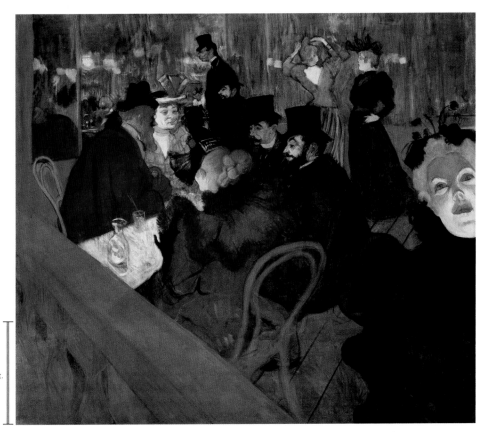

23-14 HENRI DE TOULOUSE-LAUTREC, *At the Moulin Rouge,* 1892–1895. Oil on canvas, 4′ × 4′ 7″. Art Institute of Chicago, Chicago (Helen Birch Bartlett Memorial Collection).

The influences of Degas, Japanese prints, and photography show in this painting's oblique composition, but the glaring lighting, masklike faces, and dissonant colors are Toulouse-Lautrec's.

1 ft.

19th-Century Color Theory

In the 19th century, advances in the sciences contributed to changing theories about color and how people perceive it. Many physicists and chemists immersed themselves in studying optical reception and the behavior of the human eye in response to light of differing wavelengths. They also investigated the psychological dimension of color. These new ideas about color and its perception provided a framework within which artists such as Georges Seurat worked. Although historians do not know which publications on color Seurat himself read, he no doubt relied on aspects of these evolving theories to develop pointillism (FIG. 23-15).

Discussions of color often focus on *hue* (for example, red, yellow, and blue), but it is important to consider the other facets of color—*saturation* (the hue's brightness or dullness) and *value* (the hue's lightness or darkness). Most artists during the 19th century understood the concepts of *primary colors* (red, yellow, and blue), *secondary colors* (orange, purple, and green), and *complementary colors* (red and green, yellow and purple, blue and orange; see Introduction). Chemist Michel-Eugène Chevreul (1786–1889) extended artists' understanding of color dynamics by formulating the law of *simultaneous contrasts* of colors. Chevreul asserted that juxtaposed colors affect the eye's reception of each, making the two colors as dissimilar as possible, both in hue and in value. For example, placing light green next to dark green has the effect of making the light green look even lighter and the dark green darker. Chevreul further provided an explanation of *successive contrasts*—the phenomenon of colored afterimages. When a person looks intently at a color (green, for example) and then shifts to a white area, the fatigued eye momentarily perceives the complementary color (red).

Charles Blanc (1813–1882), who coined the term *optical mixture* to describe the visual effect of juxtaposed complementary colors, asserted that the smaller the areas of adjoining complementary colors, the greater the tendency for the eye to "mix" the colors, so that the viewer perceives a grayish or neutral tint. Seurat used this principle frequently in his paintings.

Also influential for Seurat was the work of physicist Ogden Rood (1831–1902), who published his ideas in *Modern Chromatics, with Applications to Art and Industry* in 1879. Expanding on the ideas of Chevreul and Blanc, Rood constructed an accurate and understandable diagram of contrasting colors. Further (and particularly significant to Seurat), Rood explored representing color gradation. He suggested that artists could achieve gradation by placing small dots or lines of color side by side, which he observed would blend in the eye of the beholder when viewed from a distance.

The color experiments of Seurat and other late-19th-century artists were also part of a larger discourse about human vision and how people see and understand the world. The theories of physicist Ernst Mach (1838–1916) focused on the psychological experience of sensation. He believed humans perceive their environments in isolated units of sensation that the brain then recomposes into a comprehensible world. Another scientist, Charles Henry (1859–1926), also pursued research into the psychological dimension of color—how colors affect people, and under what conditions. He went even further to explore the physiological effects of perception. Seurat's work, though characterized by a systematic and scientifically minded approach, also incorporated his concerns about the emotional tone of the images.

---

the tone is new. Compare, for instance, this painting's mood with the relaxed and casual atmosphere of Renoir's *Le Moulin de la Galette* (FIG. 23-8). Toulouse-Lautrec's scene is nightlife, with its glaring artificial light, brassy music, and assortment of corrupt, cruel, and masklike faces. (He included himself in the background—the tiny man with the derby accompanying the very tall man, his cousin.) Such distortions by simplification of the figures and faces anticipated Expressionism (see Chapter 24), when artists' use of formal elements—for example, brighter colors and bolder lines than ever before—increased the impact of the images on observers.

GEORGES SEURAT The themes GEORGES SEURAT (1859–1891) addressed in his paintings were also Impressionist subjects, but he depicted them in a resolutely intellectual way. He devised a disciplined and painstaking system of painting that focused on color analysis. Seurat was less concerned with the recording of immediate color sensations than he was with their careful and systematic organization into a new kind of pictorial order. He disciplined the free and fluent play of color that characterized Impressionism into a calculated arrangement based on scientific color theory (see "19th-Century Color Theory," above). Seurat's system, known as *pointillism* or *divisionism,* involves carefully observing color and separating it into its component parts. The artist then applies these pure component colors to the canvas in tiny dots (points) or daubs. Thus, the shapes, figures, and spaces in the

image become totally comprehensible only from a distance, when the viewer's eye blends the many pigment dots.

Pointillism was on view at the eighth and last Impressionist exhibition in 1886, when Seurat showed his *A Sunday on La Grande Jatte* (FIG. 23-15). The subject of the painting is consistent with Impressionist recreational themes, and Seurat also shared the Impressionists' interest in analyzing light and color. But Seurat's rendition is strangely rigid and remote, unlike the spontaneous representations of most Impressionists. Seurat applied pointillism to produce a carefully composed and painted image. By using meticulously calculated values, the painter carved out a deep rectangular space. He played on repeated motifs both to create flat patterns and to suggest spatial depth. Reiterating the profile of the female form, the parasol, and the cylindrical forms of the figures, Seurat placed each in space to set up a rhythmic movement in depth as well as from side to side. Sunshine fills the picture, but the painter did not break the light into transient patches of color. Light, air, people, and landscape are formal elements in an abstract design in which line, color, value, and shape cohere in a precise and tightly controlled organization. Seurat's orchestration of the many forms across the monumental (almost 7-by-10-foot) canvas created a rhythmic cadence that harmonizes the entire composition.

Seurat once stated: "They see poetry in what I have done. No, I apply my method, and that is all there is to it."[8] Despite this claim,

Bio — $\frac{4.5}{7}$ You need more info about this techniques & innovations

Images $\frac{4.5}{7}$ Some good choices, but not detailed enough about techniques

Comps $\frac{4}{7}$ There too! also only 5 — missing 2

Biblio $\frac{X.5}{3.5}$ MISSING 3 (3) $\frac{13.5}{25} \frac{14}{25}$

PAGES?
PLATES?

Handout $\frac{.5}{.5}$ $\frac{14}{25}$

Leon Bakst - The Luncheon : *1924*

Both of the images have an open composition with colors that blend into one another.

5 new items, (2000 – now), **that** you believe **are influenced** by the periods listed at the beginning of the previous page.

LABEL/DATE/IDENTIFY DESIGNER-ARTIST and <u>EXPLAIN IN A FEW SENTENCES</u> HOW THESE NEW DESIGNS RELATE TO THE ORIGINAL PERIOD.

Please note: <u>DO NOT</u> SHOW ANY IMAGES THAT WERE COVERED IN CLASS LECTURES OR SEMINAR PRESENTATIONS!!!

This project is due on WEEK 7 at the beginning of class for **review and grading**. No projects will be accepted late.

THE HISTORY OF 20TH CENTURY ART

NO LECTURE WEEK 6!!!

WEEK 6 ASSIGNMENT:
Use this week to complete both the **ART NOUVEAU** and the **MACHINE AESTHETIC** timelines.

You should have two separate timelines with at least HALF of the items on each slide list in chronological order and SERVERAL items from artists discussed in <u>weekly seminar presentations</u> by your peers.
Include in this section:
*A detailed definition of the blanket movement (e.g. art nouveau, machine aesthetic)
*motifs
*names and definitions of new innovations and techniques
*detailed identifications and descriptions of the art movements and works that emerged within the blanket movement.

You should also have <u>ten</u> (10) images that will correlate with each blanket movement timeline.

5 from the period by people we covered, but things we **did not see** in class.
LABEL/DATE/IDENTIFY DESIGNER-ARTIST

And...............................*turn the page.*

1 ft.

23-15 Georges Seurat, *A Sunday on La Grande Jatte,* 1884–1886. Oil on canvas, 6′ 9″ × 10′. Art Institute of Chicago, Chicago (Helen Birch Bartlett Memorial Collection, 1926).

Seurat's color system—pointillism—involved dividing colors into their component parts and applying those colors to the canvas in tiny dots. The forms become comprehensible only from a distance.

his art is much more than a scientifically based system. *La Grande Jatte* reveals Seurat's recognition of the tenuous and shifting social and class relationships at the time. La Grande Jatte (The Big Bowl) is an island in the Seine River near Asnières, one of Paris's rapidly growing industrial suburbs. Seurat's painting captures public life on a Sunday—a congregation of people from various classes, from the sleeveless worker lounging in the left foreground to the middle-class man and woman seated next to him. Most of the people wear their Sunday best, making class distinctions less obvious.

VINCENT VAN GOGH In marked contrast to Seurat, Vincent van Gogh (1853–1890) explored the capabilities of colors and distorted forms to express his emotions as he confronted nature. The son of a Dutch Protestant pastor, van Gogh believed he had a religious calling and did missionary work in the coal-mining area of Belgium. Repeated professional and personal failures brought him close to despair. Only after he turned to painting did he find a way to communicate his experiences. When van Gogh died of a self-inflicted gunshot wound at age 37, he considered himself a failure as an artist. He felt himself an outcast not only from artistic circles but also from society at large. The hostile reception to his work, both from fellow artists and the general public, no doubt reinforced this

perception. He sold only one painting during his lifetime. Since his death, however, his reputation and the appreciation of his art have grown dramatically. Subsequent painters, especially the Fauves and German Expressionists (see Chapter 24), built on the use of color and the expressiveness of van Gogh's art. This kind of influence is an important factor in determining artistic significance, and it is no exaggeration to state that today van Gogh is one of the most revered artists in history.

NIGHT CAFÉ After relocating to Arles in southern France in 1888, van Gogh painted *Night Café* (FIG. **23-16**). Although the subject is apparently benign, van Gogh invested it with a charged energy. As he stated in a letter to his brother Theo (see "The Letters of Vincent van Gogh," page 666), he wanted the painting to convey an oppressive atmosphere—"a place where one can ruin oneself, go mad, or commit a crime."[9] The proprietor rises like a specter from the edge of the billiard table, which the painter depicted in such a steeply tilted perspective that it threatens to slide out of the painting into the viewer's space. Van Gogh communicated the "madness" of the place by selecting vivid hues whose juxtaposition augmented their intensity. His insistence on the expressive values of color led him to develop a corresponding expressiveness in his paint application. The

The Letters of Vincent van Gogh

Throughout his life, Vincent van Gogh wrote letters to his brother Theo van Gogh (1857–1891), a Parisian art dealer, on matters both mundane and philosophical. The letters are precious documents of the vicissitudes of the painter's life and reveal his emotional anguish. In many of the letters, van Gogh also forcefully stated his views about art. In one letter, he told Theo: "In both my life and in my painting, I can very well do without God but I cannot, ill as I am, do without something which is greater than I, . . . the power to create."* For van Gogh, the power to create involved the expressive use of color. "Instead of trying to reproduce exactly what I have before my eyes, I use color more arbitrarily so as to express myself forcibly."† Color in painting, he argued, is "not locally true from the point of view of the delusive realist, but color suggesting some emotion of an ardent temperament."‡

Some of van Gogh's letters contain vivid descriptions of his paintings, which are invaluable to art historians in gauging his intentions and judging his success. For example, about *Night Café* (FIG. **23-16**), he wrote:

23-16 VINCENT VAN GOGH, *Night Café*, 1888. Oil on canvas, 2′ 4$\frac{1}{2}$″ × 3′. Yale University Art Gallery, New Haven (bequest of Stephen Carlton Clark).

In *Night Café,* van Gogh explored the abilities of colors and distorted forms to express emotions. The thickness, shape, and direction of his brush strokes create a tactile counterpart to the intense colors.

I have tried to express the terrible passions of humanity by means of red and green. The room is blood red and dark yellow with a green billiard table in the middle; there are four citron-yellow lamps with a glow of orange and green. Everywhere there is a clash and contrast of the most disparate reds and greens in the figures of little sleeping hooligans, in the empty, dreary room, in violet and blue. The blood-red and the yellow-green of the billiard table, for instance, contrast with the soft, tender Louis XV green of the counter, on which there is a pink nosegay. The white coat of the landlord, awake in a corner of that furnace, turns citron-yellow, or pale luminous green.§

* Vincent van Gogh to Theo van Gogh, September 3, 1888, in W. H. Auden, ed., *Van Gogh: A Self-Portrait. Letters Revealing His Life as a Painter* (New York: Dutton, 1963), 319.
† August 11, 1888. Ibid., 313.
‡ September 8, 1888. Ibid., 321.
§ September 8, 1888. Ibid., 320.

thickness, shape, and direction of his brush strokes created a tactile counterpart to his intense color schemes. He often moved the brush vehemently back and forth or at right angles, giving a textilelike effect, even squeezing dots or streaks directly onto his canvas from his paint tube. This bold, almost slapdash attack enhanced the intensity of his colors.

STARRY NIGHT Similarly illustrative of van Gogh's "expressionist" method is *Starry Night* (FIG. **23-17**), which the artist painted in 1889, the year before his death. At this time, van Gogh was living at Saint-Paul-de-Mausole, an asylum in Saint-Rémy, near Arles, where he had committed himself. In *Starry Night,* the artist did not represent the sky's appearance. Rather, he communicated his feelings about the electrifying vastness of the universe, filled with whirling and exploding stars and galaxies of stars, the earth and humanity huddling beneath it. The church nestled in the center of the village is perhaps van Gogh's attempt to express or reconcile his conflicted views about religion. Although the style in *Starry Night* sug-

gests a very personal vision, this work does correspond in many ways to the view available to the painter from the window of his room in Saint-Paul-de-Mausole. The existence of cypress trees and the placement of the constellations have been confirmed as matching the view van Gogh would have had during his stay in the asylum. Still, the artist translated any visible objects into his unique vision. Given van Gogh's determination to "use color . . . to express [him]self forcibly," the dark, deep blue that suffuses the entire painting cannot be overlooked. Together with the turbulent brush strokes, the color suggests a quiet but pervasive depression. Van Gogh's written observation to his brother reveals his contemplative state of mind:

Perhaps death is not the hardest thing in a painter's life. . . . [L]ooking at the stars always makes me dream, as simply as I dream over the black dots representing towns and villages on a map. Why, I ask myself, shouldn't the shining dots of the sky be as accessible as the black dots on the map of France? Just as we take the train to get to Tarascon or Rouen, we take death to reach a star.[10]

23-17 Vincent van Gogh, *Starry Night*, 1889. Oil on canvas, 2′ 5″ × 3′ $\frac{1}{4}$″. Museum of Modern Art, New York (acquired through the Lillie P. Bliss Bequest).

In this late work, van Gogh painted the vast night sky filled with whirling and exploding stars, the earth huddled beneath it. The painting is an almost abstract pattern of expressive line, shape, and color.

1 ft.

PAUL GAUGUIN After painting as an amateur, Paul Gauguin (1848–1903) took lessons with Pissarro and then resigned from his prosperous brokerage business in 1883 to devote his time entirely to painting. Like van Gogh, he rejected objective representation in favor of subjective expression. He also broke with the Impressionists' studies of minutely contrasted hues because he believed that color above all must be expressive and that the artist's power to determine the colors in a painting was a central element of creativity. However, whereas van Gogh's heavy, thick brush strokes were an important component of his expressive style, Gauguin's color areas appear flatter, often visually dissolving into abstract patches or patterns.

In 1886, attracted by Brittany's unspoiled culture, its ancient Celtic folkways, and the still-medieval Catholic piety of its people, Gauguin moved to Pont-Aven. Although in the 1870s and 1880s Brittany had been transformed into a profitable market economy, Gauguin still viewed the Bretons as "natural" men and women, perfectly at ease in their unspoiled peasant environment. At Pont-Aven, he painted *Vision after the Sermon,* or *Jacob Wrestling with the Angel* (FIG. **23-18**), a work that decisively rejects both Realism and Impressionism. The painting shows Breton women, wearing their starched white Sunday caps and black dresses, visualizing the sermon they have just heard at church on Jacob's encounter with the Holy

1 ft.

23-18 Paul Gauguin, *Vision after the Sermon,* or *Jacob Wrestling with the Angel,* 1888. Oil on canvas, 2′ 4$\frac{3}{4}$″ × 3′ $\frac{1}{2}$″. National Gallery of Scotland, Edinburgh.

Gauguin admired Japanese prints, stained glass, and cloisonné enamels. Their influences are evident in this painting of Breton women, in which firm outlines enclose large areas of unmodulated color.

Post-Impressionism   **667**

Spirit (Gen. 32:24–30). The women pray devoutly before the apparition, as they would have before the roadside crucifix shrines that were familiar features of the Breton countryside. Gauguin departed from optical realism and composed the picture elements to focus the viewer's attention on the idea and intensify its message. The images are not what the Impressionist eye would have seen and replicated but what memory would have recalled and imagination would have modified. Thus the artist twisted the perspective and allotted the space to emphasize the innocent faith of the unquestioning women, and he shrank Jacob and the angel, wrestling in a ring enclosed by a Breton stone fence, to the size of fighting cocks. Wrestling matches were regular features at the entertainment held after high mass, so Gauguin's women are spectators at a contest that was, for them, a familiar part of their culture.

Gauguin did not unify the picture with a horizon perspective, light and shade, or a naturalistic use of color. Instead, he abstracted the scene into a pattern. Pure unmodulated color fills flat planes and shapes bounded by firm lines: white caps, black dresses, and the red field of combat. The shapes are angular, even harsh. The caps, the sharp fingers and profiles, and the hard contours suggest the austerity of peasant life and ritual. Gauguin admired Japanese prints, stained glass, and *cloisonné* metalwork (FIGS. 11-2 and 11-3). These art forms contributed to his own daring experiment to transform traditional painting and Impressionism into abstract, expressive patterns of line, shape, and pure color. His revolutionary method found its first authoritative expression in *Vision after the Sermon.*

WHERE DO WE COME FROM? After a brief period of association with van Gogh in Arles in 1888, Gauguin, in his restless search for provocative subjects and for an economical place to live, settled in Tahiti. The South Pacific island attracted Gauguin because it offered him a life far removed from materialistic Europe and an opportunity to reconnect with nature. Upon his arrival, he discovered that Tahiti, under French control since 1842, had been extensively colonized. Disappointed, Gauguin tried to maintain his vision of an untamed paradise by moving to the Tahitian countryside, where he expressed his fascination with primitive life and brilliant color in a series of striking decorative canvases. Gauguin often based the design, although indirectly, on native motifs, and the color owed its peculiar harmonies of lilac, pink, and lemon to the tropical flora of the island.

Despite the allure of the South Pacific, Gauguin continued to struggle with life. His health suffered, and his art had a hostile reception. In 1897, worn down by these obstacles, Gauguin decided to take his own life, but not before painting a large canvas titled *Where Do We Come From? What Are We? Where Are We Going?* (FIG. 23-19). This painting can be read as a summary of Gauguin's artistic methods and of his views on life. The scene is a tropical landscape, populated with native women and children. Despite the setting, most of the canvas surface, other than the figures, consists of broad areas of flat color, which convey a lushness and intensity.

In a letter to his friend Charles Morice, Gauguin shed light on the meaning of this painting:

> Where are we going? Near to death an old woman. . . . What are we? Day to day existence. . . . Where do we come from? Source. Child. Life begins. . . . Behind a tree two sinister figures, cloaked in garments of sombre colour, introduce, near the tree of knowledge, their note of anguish caused by that very knowledge in contrast to some simple beings in a virgin nature, which might be paradise as conceived by humanity, who give themselves up to the happiness of living.[11]

Where Do We Come From? is, therefore, a sobering, pessimistic image of the life cycle's inevitability. Gauguin's attempt to commit suicide in Tahiti was unsuccessful, but he died a few years later, in 1903, in the Marquesas Islands, his artistic genius still unrecognized.

PAUL CÉZANNE Although a lifelong admirer of Eugène Delacroix, PAUL CÉZANNE (1839–1906) allied himself early in his career with the Impressionists, especially Pissarro. He at first accepted their color theories and their faith in subjects chosen from everyday life, but his studies of the Old Masters in the Louvre persuaded him that Impressionism lacked form and structure. Cézanne declared he wanted to "make of Impressionism something solid and durable like the art of the museums."[12]

23-19 PAUL GAUGUIN, *Where Do We Come From? What Are We? Where Are We Going?* 1897. Oil on canvas, 4′ 6¾″ × 12′ 3″. Museum of Fine Arts, Boston (Tompkins Collection).

In search of a place far removed from European materialism, Gauguin moved to Tahiti, where he used native women and tropical colors to present a pessimistic view of the inevitability of the life cycle.

23-20 Paul Cézanne, *Mont Sainte-Victoire*, 1902–1904. Oil on canvas, 2′ 3½″ × 2′ 11¼″. Philadelphia Museum of Art, Philadelphia (The George W. Elkins Collection).

In his landscapes, Cézanne replaced the transitory visual effects of changing atmospheric conditions, a focus for the Impressionists, with careful analysis of the lines, planes, and colors of nature.

1 ft.

The basis of Cézanne's art was his unique way of studying nature in works such as *Mont Sainte-Victoire* (FIG. **23-20**), one of many views he painted of this mountain near his home in Aix-en-Provence. His aim was not truth in appearance, especially not photographic truth, nor was it the "truth" of Impressionism. Rather, he sought a lasting structure behind the formless and fleeting visual information the eye absorbs. Instead of employing the Impressionists' random approach when he was face-to-face with nature, Cézanne developed a more analytical style. He sought to order the lines, planes, and colors that comprised nature. He constantly and painstakingly checked his painting against the part of the real scene—he called it the "motif"—he was studying at the moment. Cézanne wrote in March 1904 that his goal was "[to do] Poussin over entirely from nature . . . in the open air, with color and light, instead of one of those works imagined in a studio, where everything has the brown coloring of feeble daylight without reflections from the sky and sun."[13] He sought to achieve Poussin's effects of distance, depth, structure, and solidity not by using traditional perspective and chiaroscuro but by recording the color patterns an optical analysis of nature provides.

With special care, Cézanne explored the properties of line, plane, and color and their interrelationships. He studied the effect of every kind of linear direction, the capacity of planes to create the sensation of depth, the intrinsic qualities of color, and the power of colors to modify the direction and depth of lines and planes. To create the illusion of three-dimensional form and space, Cézanne focused on carefully selecting colors. He understood that the visual properties—hue, saturation, and value—of different colors vary (see "19th-Century Color Theory," page 664). Cool colors tend to recede, whereas warm ones advance. By applying to the canvas small patches of juxtaposed colors, some advancing and some receding, Cézanne

created volume and depth in his works. On occasion, the artist depicted objects chiefly in one hue and achieved convincing solidity by modulating the intensity (or saturation). At other times, he juxtaposed contrasting colors—for example, green, yellow, and red—of like saturation (usually in the middle range rather than the highest intensity) to compose specific objects, such as fruit or bowls.

In *Mont Sainte-Victoire,* he replaced the transitory visual effects of changing atmospheric conditions, effects that occupied Monet, with a more concentrated, lengthier analysis of the colors in large lighted spaces. The main space stretches out behind and beyond the canvas plane and includes numerous small elements, such as roads, fields, houses, and the viaduct at the far right, each seen from a slightly different viewpoint. Above this shifting, receding perspective rises the largest mass of all, the mountain, with an effect—achieved by equally stressing background and foreground contours—of being simultaneously near and far away. This portrayal approximates the real experience a person has when viewing a landscape's forms piecemeal. The relative proportions of objects vary rather than being fixed by a strict one- or two-point perspective, such as that normally found in a photograph. Cézanne immobilized the shifting colors of Impressionism into an array of clearly defined planes that compose the objects and spaces in his scene. Describing his method in a letter to a fellow painter, he wrote:

[T]reat nature by the cylinder, the sphere, the cone, everything in proper perspective so that each side of an object or a plane is directed towards a central point. Lines parallel to the horizon give breadth . . . Lines perpendicular to this horizon give depth. But nature for us men is more depth than surface, whence the need of introducing into our light vibrations, represented by reds and yellows, a sufficient amount of blue to give the impression of air.[14]

23-21 Paul Cézanne, *Basket of Apples,* ca. 1895. Oil on canvas, $2' \frac{3}{8}'' \times 2' 7''$. Art Institute of Chicago, Chicago (Helen Birch Bartlett Memorial Collection, 1926).

Cézanne's analytical approach to painting is evident in his still lifes. He captured the solidity of bottles and fruit by juxtaposing color patches, but the resulting abstract shapes are not optically realistic.

1 ft.

BASKET OF APPLES Still life was another good vehicle for Cézanne's experiments, as he could arrange a limited number of selected objects to provide a well-ordered point of departure. So analytical was Cézanne in preparing, observing, and painting still lifes (in contrast to the Impressionist emphasis on the concept of spontaneity) that he had to abandon using real fruit and flowers because they tended to rot. In *Basket of Apples* (FIG. **23-21**), the objects have lost something of their individual character as bottles and fruit and almost become cylinders and spheres. Cézanne captured the solidity of each object by juxtaposing color patches. His interest in the study of volume and solidity is evident from the disjunctures in the painting—the table edges are discontinuous, and various objects seem to be depicted from different vantage points. In his zeal to understand three-dimensionality and to convey the placement of forms relative to the space around them, Cézanne explored his still-life arrangements from different viewpoints. This resulted in paintings that, although conceptually coherent, do not appear optically realistic. Cézanne created what might be called, paradoxically, an architecture of color.

In keeping with the modernist concern with the integrity of the painting surface, Cézanne's methods never allow the viewer to disregard the two-dimensionality of the picture plane. In this manner, Cézanne achieved a remarkable feat—presenting the viewer with two-dimensional and three-dimensional images simultaneously.

SYMBOLISM

The Impressionists and Post-Impressionists believed their emotions and sensations were important elements for interpreting nature, but the depiction of nature remained a primary focus of their efforts. By

1 ft.

23-22 Pierre Puvis de Chavannes, *Sacred Grove,* 1884. Oil on canvas, $2' 11\frac{1}{2}'' \times 6' 10''$. Art Institute of Chicago, Chicago (Potter Palmer Collection).

The Symbolists revered Puvis de Chavannes for his rejection of Realism. His statuesque figures in timeless poses inhabit a tranquil landscape, their gestures suggesting a symbolic ritual significance.

the end of the 19th century, the representation of nature became completely subjective. Artists no longer sought to imitate nature but created free interpretations of it, concerned solely with expressing their individual spirit. They rejected the optical world as observed in favor of a fantasy world, of forms they conjured in their free imagination, with or without reference to things conventionally seen. Color, line, and shape, divorced from conformity to the optical image, became symbols of personal emotions in response to the world. Deliberately choosing to stand outside of convention and tradition, artists spoke like prophets, in signs and symbols.

Many of the artists following this path adopted an approach to subject and form that associated them with a general European movement called *Symbolism*. Symbolists, whether painters or writers, disdained Realism as trivial. The task of Symbolist visual and verbal artists was not to see things but to see through them to a significance and reality far deeper than what superficial appearance gave. In this function, as the poet Arthur Rimbaud (1854–1891) insisted, artists became beings of extraordinary insight. (One group of Symbolist painters called itself the *Nabis*, the Hebrew word for "prophet.") Rimbaud, whose poems had great influence on the artistic community, went so far as to say, in his *Letter from a Seer* (1871), that to achieve the seer's insight, artists must become deranged. In effect, they must systematically unhinge and confuse the everyday faculties of sense and reason, which served only to blur artistic vision. The artists' mystical vision must convert the objects of the commonsense world into symbols of a reality beyond that world and, ultimately, a reality from within the individual. Elements of Symbolism appeared in the works of van Gogh and Gauguin, but their art differed from mainstream Symbolism in their insistence on showing unseen powers as linked to a physical reality, instead of attempting to depict an alternate, wholly interior life.

The extreme subjectivism of the Symbolists led them to cultivate all the resources of fantasy and imagination, no matter how deeply buried or obscure. Moreover, they urged artists to stand against the vulgar materialism and conventional mores of industrial and middle-class society. Above all, the Symbolists wished to purge literature and art of anything utilitarian, to cultivate an exquisite aesthetic sensitivity, and to make the slogan "art for art's sake" into a doctrine and a way of life. The subjects of the Symbolists, conditioned by this reverent attitude toward art and exaggerated aesthetic sensation, became increasingly esoteric and exotic, mysterious, visionary, dreamlike, and fantastic. Perhaps not coincidentally, contemporary with the Symbolists, Sigmund Freud (1856–1939), the founder of psychoanalysis, began the age of psychiatry with his *Interpretation of Dreams* (1900), an introduction to the concept and the world of unconscious experience.

PIERRE PUVIS DE CHAVANNES Although he never formally identified himself with the Symbolists, the French painter PIERRE PUVIS DE CHAVANNES (1824–1898) became the "prophet" of those artists. Puvis rejected Realism and Impressionism and went his own way in the 19th century, serenely unaffected by these movements. He produced an ornamental and reflective art—a dramatic rejection of Realism's noisy everyday world. In *Sacred Grove* (FIG. 23-22), which may have influenced Seurat's *Grande Jatte* (FIG. 23-15), he deployed statuesque figures in a tranquil landscape with a classical shrine. Suspended in timeless poses, the figures' contours are simple and sharp, and their modeling is as shallow as *bas-relief*. The calm and still atmosphere suggests some consecrated place, where all movements and gestures have a permanent ritual significance. The stillness and simplicity of the forms, the linear patterns their rhythmic contours create, and the suggestion of their symbolic weight constitute a type of anti-Realism. Puvis garnered support from a wide range of artists. The conservative French Academy and the government applauded his classicism. The Symbolists revered Puvis for his vindication of imagination and his independence from the capitalist world of materialism and the machine.

GUSTAVE MOREAU In keeping with Symbolist tenets, GUSTAVE MOREAU (1826–1898) gravitated toward subjects inspired by dreaming, which was as remote as possible from the everyday world. Moreau presented these subjects sumptuously, and his natural love of sensuous design led him to incorporate gorgeous color, intricate line, and richly detailed shape. *Jupiter and Semele* (FIG. 23-23) is one of the artist's rare finished works. The mortal girl Semele, one of Jupiter's loves, begged the god to appear to her in all his majesty. When he did, the sight was so powerful that she died from it.

1 ft.

23-23 GUSTAVE MOREAU, *Jupiter and Semele*, ca. 1875. Oil on canvas, 7′ × 3′ 4″. Musée Gustave Moreau, Paris.

Moreau favored subjects inspired by dreaming. In this painting, the apparition of Jupiter with his halo of thunderbolts overwhelms the mortal Semele, who dies upon seeing so powerful a sight.

Moreau presented the theme within an operalike setting, a towering opulent architecture. (Moreau loved the music of Richard Wagner [1813–1883] and, like that great composer, dreamed of a grand synthesis of the arts.) The painter depicted the royal hall of Olympus as shimmering in iridescent color, with tabernacles filled with the glowing shapes that enclose Jupiter like an encrustation of gems. In *Jupiter and Semele,* the rich color harmonizes with the exotic hues of Byzantine *mosaics,* medieval *enamels,* Indian *miniatures,* and the designs of exotic wares then influencing modern artists. The apparition of the god with his halo of thunderbolts overwhelms Semele, who sits in Jupiter's lap. Her languorous swoon and the suspended motion of all the entranced figures show the "beautiful inertia" that Moreau said he wished to render with all "necessary richness."

ODILON REDON Like Moreau, ODILON REDON (1840–1916) was a visionary. He had been aware of an intense inner world since childhood and later wrote of "imaginary things" that haunted him. Redon adapted the Impressionist palette and stippling brush stroke for a very different purpose. In *The Cyclops* (FIG. **23-24**), Redon projected a figment of the imagination as if it were visible, coloring it whimsically with a rich profusion of fresh saturated hues that harmonized with the mood he felt fitted the subject. The fetal head of the shy, simpering Polyphemus, with its single huge loving eye, rises balloonlike above the sleeping Galatea. The image born of the dreaming world and the color analyzed and disassociated from the waking world come together here at the artist's will. The contrast with Raphael's representation of the same subject (FIG. **17-10**) could hardly be more striking. As Redon himself observed: "All my originality consists . . . in making unreal creatures live humanly by putting, as much as possible, the logic of the visible at the service of the invisible."[15]

HENRI ROUSSEAU The imagination of the French artist HENRI ROUSSEAU (1844–1910) engaged a different but equally powerful world of personal fantasy. Gauguin had journeyed to the South Seas in search of primitive innocence. Rousseau was a "primitive" without leaving Paris—an untrained amateur painter. Rousseau produced an art of dream and fantasy in a style that had its own sophistication and made its own departure from the artistic currency of the time. He compensated for his apparent visual, conceptual, and technical naïveté with a natural talent for design and an imagination teeming with exotic images of mysterious tropical landscapes. In

23-24 ODILON REDON, *The Cyclops,* 1898. Oil on canvas, 2′ 1″ × 1′ 8″. Kröller-Müller Foundation, Otterlo.

In *The Cyclops,* the Symbolist painter Odilon Redon projected a figment of the imagination as if it were visible, coloring it whimsically with a rich profusion of hues adapted from the Impressionist palette.

Sleeping Gypsy (FIG. **23-25**), the recumbent figure occupies a desert world, silent and secret, and dreams beneath a pale, perfectly round moon. In the foreground, a lion that resembles a stuffed, but somehow menacing, animal doll sniffs at the gypsy. A critical encounter

23-25 HENRI ROUSSEAU, *Sleeping Gypsy,* 1897. Oil on canvas, 4′ 3″ × 6′ 7″. Museum of Modern Art, New York (gift of Mrs. Simon Guggenheim).

In *Sleeping Gypsy,* Henri Rousseau depicted a doll-like but menacing lion sniffing at a recumbent dreaming figure in a mysterious landscape. The painting conjures the vulnerable subconscious during sleep.

ness, fear, desire, despair—became the theme of most of his art. Because Munch's goal was to describe the conditions of "modern psychic life," as he put it, Realist and Impressionist techniques were inappropriate, focusing as they did on the tangible world. In the spirit of Symbolism, Munch developed a style of putting color, line, and figural distortion to expressive ends. Influenced by Gauguin, Munch produced both paintings and prints whose high emotional charge was a major source of inspiration for the German Expressionists in the early 20th century (see Chapter 24).

Munch's *The Scream* (FIG. **23-27**) exemplifies his style. The image—a man standing on a bridge or jetty in a landscape—comes from the real world, but Munch's treatment of the image departs significantly from visual reality. *The Scream* evokes a visceral, emotional response from the viewer because of the painter's dramatic presentation. The man in the foreground, simplified to almost skeletal form, emits a primal scream. The landscape's sweeping curvilinear lines reiterate the curvilinear shape of the mouth and head, almost like an echo, as the cry seems to reverberate through the setting. The fiery red and yellow stripes that give the sky an eerie glow also contribute to this work's resonance. Munch wrote a revealing epigraph to accompany the painting: "I stopped and leaned against the balustrade, almost dead with fatigue. Above the blue-black fjord hung the clouds, red as blood and tongues of fire. My friends had left me, and alone, trembling with anguish, I became aware of the vast, infinite cry of nature."[16] Appropriately, the original title of this work was *Despair*.

23-26 AUBREY BEARDSLEY, *The Peacock Skirt*, 1894. Pen-and-ink illustration for Oscar Wilde's *Salomé*, $9'' \times 6\frac{5}{8}''$. Fogg Art Museum, Harvard University, Cambridge (bequest of Grenville L. Winthrop).

Banishing the Impressionist and Post-Impressionist emphasis on color, Aubrey Beardsley, a master of calligraphic line and curvilinear shapes, confined himself to patterns of black and white without shading.

impends—an encounter of the type that recalls the uneasiness of a person's vulnerable subconscious self during sleep.

AUBREY BEARDSLEY Not all Symbolist artists were French. AUBREY BEARDSLEY (1872–1898) was one of a circle of English artists whose work was at the intersection of Symbolism and Art Nouveau (see page 846). For *Salomé*, an illustration for a book by Oscar Wilde (1854–1900), Beardsley drew *The Peacock Skirt* (FIG. **23-26**), a dazzlingly decorative composition perfectly characteristic of his style. The Japanese print influence is obvious, although Beardsley assimilated it into his unique manner. Banishing Realism as well as the Impressionists' and Post-Impressionists' emphasis on color, he confined himself to lines and to patterns of black and white, eliminating all shading. His tense, elastic line encloses sweeping curvilinear shapes that lie flat on the surface—some left almost vacant, others filled with swirling complexes of mostly organic motifs. Beardsley's unfailing sense of linear rhythms and harmonies supports his mastery of calligraphic line.

EDVARD MUNCH Also linked in spirit to the Symbolists was the Norwegian painter and graphic artist EDVARD MUNCH (1863–1944). Munch felt deeply the pain of human life. His belief that humans were powerless before the great natural forces of death and love and the emotions associated with them—jealousy, loneli-

23-27 EDVARD MUNCH, *The Scream*, 1893. Tempera and pastels on cardboard, $2' 11\frac{3}{4}'' \times 2' 5''$. National Gallery, Oslo.

Although grounded in the real world, *The Scream* departs significantly from visual reality. Munch used color, line, and figural distortion to evoke a strong emotional response from the viewer.

In this opulent Viennese fin-de-siècle painting, Gustav Klimt revealed only a small segment of each lover's body. The rest of his painting dissolves into shimmering, extravagant flat patterning.

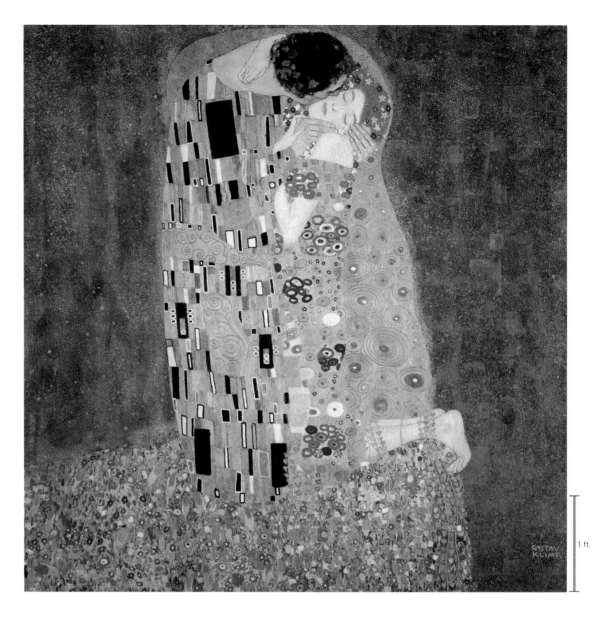

1 ft.

FIN-DE-SIÈCLE Historians have adopted the term *fin-de-siècle,* which means "end of the century," to describe the culture of the late 1800s. This designation is not merely chronological but also refers to a certain sensibility. The increasingly large and prosperous middle classes aspired to the advantages the aristocracy traditionally enjoyed. They too strove to live "the good life," which evolved into a culture of decadence and indulgence. Characteristic of the fin-de-siècle period was an intense preoccupation with sexual drives, powers, and perversions. People at the end of the century also immersed themselves in an exploration of the unconscious. This culture was unrestrained and freewheeling, but the determination to enjoy life masked an anxiety prompted by significant political upheaval and an uncertain future. The country most closely associated with fin-de-siècle culture was Austria.

GUSTAV KLIMT The Viennese artist Gustav Klimt (1863–1918) captured this period's flamboyance in his work but tempered it with unsettling undertones. In *The Kiss* (FIG. 23-28), Klimt depicted a couple locked in an embrace. All that is visible of the couple, however, is a small segment of each person's body. The rest of the painting dissolves into shimmering, extravagant flat patterning. This patterning has clear ties to Art Nouveau and to the Arts and Crafts movement (see page 678) and also evokes the conflict between two- and three-dimensionality intrinsic to the work of Degas and other modernists.

Paintings such as *The Kiss* were visual manifestations of fin-de-siècle spirit because they captured a decadence conveyed by opulent and sensuous images.

GERTRUDE KÄSEBIER Photography, which during the 19th century most people regarded as the ultimate form of Realism, could also be manipulated by artists to produce effects more akin to painting than to factual records of contemporary life. After the first great breakthroughs, which bluntly showed what was before the eye, some photographers began to pursue new ways of using the medium as a vehicle of artistic expression. One of the leading practitioners of what might be called the pictorial style in photography was the American Gertrude Käsebier (1852–1934). Käsebier took up photography in 1897 after raising a family and working as a portrait painter. She soon became famous for photographs with symbolic themes, such as *Blessed Art Thou among Women* (FIG. 23-29). The title repeats the phrase the angel Gabriel used in the New Testament to announce to the Virgin Mary that she will be the mother of Jesus. In the context of Käsebier's photography, the words suggest a parallel between the biblical "Mother of God" and the modern mother in the image, who both protects and sends forth her daughter. The white setting and the mother's pale gown shimmer in soft focus behind the serious girl, who is dressed in darker tones and captured

23-29 Gertrude Käsebier, *Blessed Art Thou among Women*, 1899. Platinum print on Japanese tissue, $9\frac{3}{8}'' \times 5\frac{1}{2}''$. Museum of Modern Art, New York (gift of Mrs. Hermine M. Turner).

Gertrude Käsebier was able to inject a sense of the spiritual and the divine into scenes from everyday life. The soft focus of this photograph invests the whole scene with an aura of otherworldly peace.

23-30 Augustus Saint-Gaudens, Adams Memorial, Rock Creek Cemetery, Washington, 1891. Bronze, 5′ 10″ high. Smithsonian American Art Museum, Washington, D.C.

For the Adams Memorial, Augustus Saint-Gaudens chose a classical mode of representation. A woman of majestic bearing sits in mourning. The gesture of her right arm derives from ancient Roman statuary.

with sharper focus. Käsebier deliberately combined an out-of-focus background with a sharp or almost-sharp foreground in order to achieve an expressive effect by blurring the entire image slightly. In *Blessed Art Thou*, the soft focus invests the whole scene with an aura of otherworldly peace. The photograph showcases Käsebier's ability to inject a sense of the spiritual and the divine into scenes from everyday life.

SCULPTURE

The three-dimensional art of sculpture was not suited to capturing the optical sensations many painters favored in the later 19th century. Its very nature—its tangibility and solidity—suggests permanence. Consequently, the sculptors of this period pursued artistic goals markedly different from those of contemporaneous painters and photographers.

AUGUSTUS SAINT-GAUDENS One artist who used sculpture to express timeless ideals rather than to depict transitory moments was the American AUGUSTUS SAINT-GAUDENS (1848–1907), who trained in France. When Saint-Gaudens received the commission to produce a memorial monument honoring Mrs. Henry Adams (FIG. 23-30), he chose a classical mode of representation, sculpting a woman of majestic bearing sitting in mourning. The voluminous garment that enfolds her body also partly shadows her classically beautiful face. The gesture of the woman's right arm, which reproduces a common motif in ancient Roman portraits of women, only slightly stirs the immobility of her form, set in an attitude of eternal vigilance.

23-31 Jean-Baptiste Carpeaux, *Ugolino and His Children,* 1865–1867. Marble, 6′ 5″ high. Metropolitan Museum of Art, New York (Josephine Bay Paul and C. Michael Paul Foundation, Inc., and the Charles Ulrich and Josephine Bay Foundation, Inc., gifts, 1967).

Based on Dante's *Inferno,* this group represents Ugolino biting his hands in despair as he and his sons await death by starvation. The twisted forms suggest the self-devouring torment of frustration.

1 ft.

JEAN-BAPTISTE CARPEAUX   In France, Jean-Baptiste Carpeaux (1827–1875) combined an interest in Realism with a love of ancient, Renaissance, and Baroque sculpture. He based his group *Ugolino and His Children* (FIG. **23-31**) on a passage in Dante's *Inferno* (33.58–75) in which Count Ugolino and his four sons starve to death while shut up in a tower. In Hell, Ugolino relates to Dante how, in a moment of extreme despair, he bit both his hands in grief. His children, thinking he did it because of his hunger, offered him their own flesh as food. In Carpeaux's statuary group, the powerful forms—twisted, intertwined, and densely concentrated—suggest the self-devouring torment of frustration and despair that wracks the unfortunate Ugolino. A careful student of Michelangelo's male figures, Carpeaux also said he had the *Laocoön* group (FIG. **5-88**) in mind. Certainly, the storm and stress of *Ugolino and His Children* recall similar characteristics of that ancient work. Regardless of these influences, the sense of vivid reality in the anatomy of Carpeaux's figures shows the artist's interest in study from life.

AUGUSTE RODIN   The leading French sculptor of the later 19th century was Auguste Rodin (1840–1917), who conceived and executed his sculptures with a Realist sensibility. Like Muybridge and Eakins (see Chapter 22), Rodin was fascinated by the human body in motion (see "Rodin on Movement in Art and Photography," page 677). He was also well aware of the innovations of the Impressionists. Although color was not a significant factor in Rodin's work, the influence of Impressionism is evident in the artist's abiding concern for the effect of light on the three-dimensional surface. When focusing on the human form, he joined his profound knowledge of anatomy and movement with special attention to the body's exterior, saying, "The sculptor must learn to reproduce the surface, which means all that vibrates on the surface, soul, love, passion, life. . . . Sculpture is thus the art of hollows and mounds, not of smoothness, or even polished planes."[17] Primarily a modeler of pliable material rather than a carver of hard wood or stone, Rodin worked his surfaces with fingers sensitive to the subtlest variations of surface, catching the fugitive play of constantly shifting light on the body. In his studio, he often would have a model move around in front of him while he modeled sketches with coils of clay.

In *Walking Man* (FIG. **23-32**), a preliminary study for the sculptor's *Saint John the Baptist Preaching,* Rodin succeeded in representing the momentary in cast bronze. He portrayed the headless and armless figure in midstride at the moment when weight is transferred across the pelvis from the back leg to the front. In addition to capturing the sense of the transitory, Rodin demonstrated his mastery of realistic detail in his meticulous rendition of muscle, bone, and tendon.

BURGHERS OF CALAIS   Rodin also made many nude and draped studies for each of the figures in one of his most ambitious works—the life-size group *Burghers of Calais* (FIG. **23-33**). This cast bronze monument commemorated a heroic episode in the Hundred Years' War. During the English siege of Calais, France, in 1347, six of the city's leading citizens agreed to offer their lives in return for the English king's promise to lift the siege and spare the rest of the populace. Each of the bedraggled-looking figures is a convincing study of despair, resignation, or quiet defiance. Rodin enhanced the psychic effects through his choreographic placement of the group members. Rather than clustering in a tightly formal composition, the *burghers* (middle-class citizens) seem to wander aimlessly. The roughly textured surfaces add to the pathos of the figures and compel the viewer's continued interest. Rodin designed the monument without the traditional high base in the hope that the citizens of Calais would be inspired by the sculptural representation of their ancestors stand-

Rodin on Movement in Art and Photography

Photography had a profound effect on 19th-century art, and many artists used photographs as an aid in capturing "reality" on canvas or in stone. Eadweard Muybridge's photographs of a galloping horse (FIG. 22-54), for example, definitively established that at certain times all four hooves of the animal are in the air. But not all artists believed that photography was "true to life." The sculptor Auguste Rodin (FIGS. 23-32 and 23-33) was one of the "doubters."

> I have always sought to give some indication of movement [in my statues]. I have very rarely represented complete repose. I have always endeavoured to express the inner feelings by the mobility of the muscles. . . . The illusion of life is obtained in our art by good modelling and by movement. . . . [M]ovement is the transition from one attitude to another. . . . Have you ever attentively examined instantaneous photographs of walking figures? . . . [Photographs] present the odd appearance of a man suddenly stricken with paralysis and petrified in his pose. . . . If, in fact, in instantaneous photographs, the figures, though taken while moving, seem suddenly fixed in mid-air, it is because, all parts of the body being reproduced exactly at the same twentieth or fortieth of a second, there is no progressive development of movement as there is in art. . . . [I]t is the artist who is truthful and it is photography which lies, for in reality time does not stop.*

* Translated by Robin Fedden, in Elizabeth Gilmore Holt, ed., *From the Classicists to the Impressionists: Art and Architecture in the 19th Century* (New Haven: Yale University Press, 1966; reprint 1986), 406–409.

1 ft.

23-32 AUGUSTE RODIN, *Walking Man*, 1905. Bronze, 6′ 11¾″ high. Musée d'Orsay, Paris.

In this study for a statue of Saint John the Baptist, Rodin depicted a headless and armless figure in mid-stride. *Walking Man* demonstrates Rodin's mastery of anatomy and his ability to capture transitory motion.

1 ft.

ing eye-level in the city center and preparing eternally to set off on their sacrificial journey. However, the city officials who commissioned the group found Rodin's Realist vision so offensive that they banished the monument to a remote site and modified the work's impact by placing it high on an isolating pedestal.

Rodin's ability to capture the quality of the transitory through his highly textured surfaces while revealing larger themes and deeper, lasting sensibilities is one of the reasons he had a strong influence on 20th-century artists. Because many of his works, such as *Walking Man*, were deliberate fragments, he was also instrumental in creating a taste for the incomplete, an aesthetic that many later sculptors embraced enthusiastically.

23-33 AUGUSTE RODIN, *Burghers of Calais*, 1884–1889. Bronze, 6′ 10½″ high, 7′ 11″ long, 6′ 6″ deep. Musée Rodin, Paris.

Rodin's bronze group commemorates an episode during the Hundred Years' War, when six Calais citizens offered their lives to save their city. Each highly textured figure is a convincing character study.

ARCHITECTURE AND DECORATIVE ARTS

The decisive effects of industrialization were impossible to ignore, and although many artists embraced this manifestation of "modern life" or at least explored its effects, other artists decried the impact of rampant industrialism. The latter response came from the Arts and Crafts movement in England. This movement, which developed during the last decades of the 19th century, was shaped by the ideas of John Ruskin, the critic who skewered Whistler's *Nocturne* (FIG. 23-13), and the artist William Morris. Both men shared a distrust of machines and industrial capitalism, which they believed alienated workers from their own nature. Accordingly, they advocated an art "made by the people for the people as a joy for the maker and the user."[18] This condemnation of capitalism and support for manual laborers were compatible with socialism, and many artists in the Arts and Crafts movement, especially in England, considered themselves socialists and participated in the labor movement.

This democratic, or at least populist, attitude carried over to the art they produced as well. Members of the Arts and Crafts movement dedicated themselves to producing functional objects with high aesthetic value for a wide public. The style they advocated was based on natural, rather than artificial, forms and often consisted of repeated designs of floral or geometric patterns. For Ruskin, Morris, and others in the Arts and Crafts movement, high-quality artisanship and honest labor were crucial.

WILLIAM MORRIS In order to promote these ideals, WILLIAM MORRIS (1834–1896) formed a decorating firm dedicated to Arts and Crafts principles: Morris, Marshall, Faulkner, and Company, Fine Arts Workmen in Painting, Carving, Furniture, and Metals. His company did a flourishing business producing wallpaper, textiles, tiles, furniture, books, rugs, stained glass, and pottery. In 1867, Morris received the commission to decorate the Green Dining Room (FIG. 23-34) at London's South Kensington Museum (now the Victoria & Albert Museum), the center of public art education and home of decorative art collections. The range of room features—windows, lights, and *wainscoting* (paneling on the lower part of interior walls)—that Morris decorated to create this unified, beautiful, and functional environment is all-encompassing. Nothing escaped his eye. Morris's design for this room also reveals the penchant of Arts and Crafts designers for intricate patterning.

CHARLES RENNIE MACKINTOSH Numerous Arts and Crafts societies in America, England, and Germany carried on this ideal of artisanship. In Scotland, CHARLES RENNIE MACKINTOSH (1868–1929) designed a number of tearooms, including the Ladies Luncheon Room (FIG. 23-35) located in the Ingram Street Tea Room in Glasgow. The room decor is consistent with Morris's vision of a functional, exquisitely designed art. The chairs, stained-glass windows, and large panels of colored gesso with twine, glass beads, thread, mother-of-pearl, and tin leaf (made by MARGARET MACDONALD MACKINTOSH [1864–1933], an artist-designer and Mackintosh's wife, who collaborated with him on many projects) are all pristinely geometric and rhythmical in design.

ART NOUVEAU An important international architectural and design movement that developed out of the ideas the Arts and Crafts movement promoted was *Art Nouveau* (New Art), which took its name from a shop in Paris called L'Art Nouveau. Known by that name in France, Belgium, Holland, England, and the United States, the style had other names elsewhere: *Jugendstil* in Austria and Germany (after the magazine *Der Jugend*, "youth"), *Modernismo* in Spain, and *Floreale* in Italy. Proponents of this movement tried to

23-34 WILLIAM MORRIS, Green Dining Room, South Kensington Museum (now Victoria & Albert Museum), London, England, 1867.

William Morris was a founder of the Arts and Crafts movement. His Green Dining Room exemplifies the group's dedication to creating intricately patterned yet unified and functional environments.

23-35 Charles Rennie Mackintosh and Margaret Macdonald Mackintosh, reconstruction (1992–1995) of Ladies Luncheon Room, Ingram Street Tea Room, Glasgow, Scotland, 1900–1912. Glasgow Art Galleries and Museum, Glasgow.

Charles Mackintosh's Ladies Luncheon Room features functional and exquisitely designed decor, including stained-glass windows and pristinely geometric furnishings by Margaret Macdonald Mackintosh.

synthesize all the arts in a determined attempt to create art based on natural forms that could be mass-produced for a large audience. The Art Nouveau style adapted the twining-plant form to the needs of architecture, painting, sculpture, and all of the decorative arts.

23-36 Victor Horta, staircase in the Van Eetvelde House, Brussels, Belgium, 1895.

The Art Nouveau movement was an attempt to create art and architecture based on natural forms. In this room, every detail conforms to the theme of the twining plant and functions as part of a living whole.

VICTOR HORTA The mature Art Nouveau style of the 1890s appears in the houses the Belgian architect Victor Horta (1861–1947) designed. The staircase (FIG. 23-36) in the Van Eetvelde House, which Horta built in Brussels in 1895, is a characteristic example. Every detail functions as part of a living whole. Furniture, drapery folds, veining in the lavish stone paneling, and the patterning of the door moldings join with real plants to provide graceful counterpoints for the twining-plant theme. Metallic tendrils curl around the railings and posts, delicate metal tracery fills the glass dome, and floral and leaf motifs spread across the fabric panels of the screen.

The Art Nouveau style reflects several influences. In addition to the rich, foliated two-dimensional ornament of Arts and Crafts design and that movement's respect for materials, the sinuous whiplash curve of Japanese print designs inspired Art Nouveau artists. Art Nouveau also borrowed from the expressively patterned styles of van Gogh (FIGS. 23-16 and 23-17), Gauguin (FIGS. 23-18 and 23-19), and their Post-Impressionist and Symbolist contemporaries.

23-37 Louis Comfort Tiffany, lotus table lamp, ca. 1905. Leaded Favrile glass, mosaic, and bronze, 2′ 10½″ high. Private collection.

Tiffany's lamps of leaded Favrile stained glass (a patented Tiffany technique), mosaic, and bronze, based on the curvilinear floral forms of the lotus, exemplify the sensuous opulence of the Art Nouveau style.

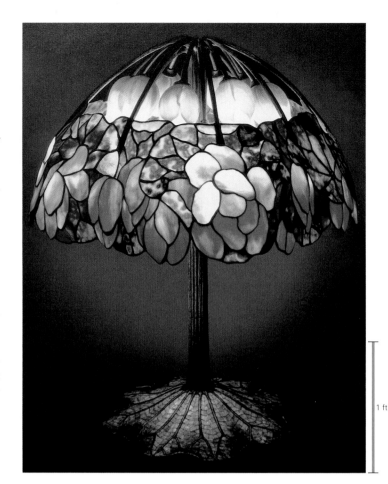

LOUIS COMFORT TIFFANY   The sensuous opulence of Art Nouveau is also on display in the stained-glass lamps of Louis Comfort Tiffany (1848–1933). His lotus table lamp (FIG. 23-37), constructed of leaded glass (often *Favrile*, a type of glass Tiffany patented), mosaic, and bronze, is based on the curvilinear floral forms of the lotus. Intended for wealthy buyers, this was the most expensive lamp Tiffany Studios produced in 1906. Because of the careful attention to detail required to produce lamps of this type, Tiffany's workshop could make only one at a time. This ensured the high-quality artisanship the Arts and Crafts movement so prized.

ANTONIO GAUDI   Art Nouveau achieved its most personal expression in the work of the Spanish architect Antonio Gaudi (1852–1926). Before becoming an architect, Gaudi had trained as an ironworker. Like many young artists of his time, he longed to create a style that was both modern and appropriate to his country. Taking inspiration from Moorish-Spanish architecture and from the simple architecture of his native Catalonia, Gaudi developed a personal aesthetic. He conceived a building as a whole and molded it almost as a sculptor might shape a figure from clay. Although work on his designs proceeded slowly under the guidance of his intuition and imagination, Gaudi was a master who invented many new structural techniques that facilitated construction of his visions. His Barcelona apartment house, Casa Milá (FIG. 23-38), is a wondrously free-form mass wrapped around a street corner. Lacy iron railings enliven the swelling curves of the cut-stone facade. Dormer windows peep from the undulating tiled roof, on which fantastically writhing chimneys poke energetically into the air above. The rough surfaces of the stone walls suggest naturally worn rock. The entrance portals look like eroded sea caves, but their design also may reflect the excitement that swept Spain following the 1879 discovery of Paleolithic cave paintings (FIG. 1-9) at Altamira. Gaudi felt that each of his buildings was symbolically a living thing. The passionate naturalism of his Casa Milá is the spiritual kin of early-20th-century Expressionist painting and sculpture (see Chapter 24).

23-38 Antonio Gaudi, Casa Milá, Barcelona, Spain, 1907.

The Spanish Art Nouveau architect Antonio Gaudi conceived this apartment house as if it were a gigantic sculpture to be molded from clay. Twisting chimneys cap the undulating roof and walls.

ALEXANDRE-GUSTAVE EIFFEL In the later 19th century, new technologies and the changing needs of urbanized, industrialized society affected architecture throughout the Western world. Since the 18th century, bridges had been built of cast iron (FIG. 21-11), which permitted engineering advancements in the construction of larger, stronger, and more fire-resistant structures. Steel, available after 1860, allowed architects to enclose ever larger spaces, such as those found in railroad stations (FIG. 23-4) and exposition halls. The Realist impulse also encouraged architectural designs that honestly expressed a building's purpose, rather than elaborately disguising its function. The elegant metal skeleton structures of the French engineer-architect ALEXANDRE-GUSTAVE EIFFEL (1832–1923) constituted responses to this idea and were an important contribution to the development of the 20th-century skyscraper. A native of Burgundy, Eiffel trained in Paris before beginning a distinguished career designing exhibition halls, bridges, and the interior armature for France's anniversary gift to the United States—Frédéric Auguste Bartholdi's *Statue of Liberty.*

Eiffel designed his best-known work, the Eiffel Tower (FIG. 23-1), for a great exhibition in Paris in 1889. Originally seen as a symbol of modern Paris and still considered a symbol of 19th-century civilization, the elegant iron tower thrusts its needle shaft 984 feet above the city, making it at the time of its construction (and for some time thereafter) the world's tallest structure. The tower rests on four giant supports connected by gracefully arching open-frame skirts that provide a pleasing mask for the heavy horizontal girders needed to strengthen the legs. Visitors can take two elevators to the top, or they can use the internal staircase. Either way, the view of Paris and the Seine from the tower is incomparable, as is the design of the tower itself. The transparency of Eiffel's structure blurs the distinction between interior and exterior to an extent never before achieved or even attempted. This interpenetration of inner and outer space became a hallmark of 20th-century art and architecture. Eiffel's tower and the earlier iron skeletal frames designed by Labrouste (FIG. 22-47) and Paxton (FIG. 22-48) jolted the architectural profession into a realization that modern materials and processes could germinate a completely new style and a radically innovative approach to architectural design.

AMERICAN SKYSCRAPERS The desire for greater speed and economy in building, as well as for a reduction in fire hazards, prompted the use of cast and wrought iron for many building programs, especially commercial ones. Designers in both England and the United States enthusiastically developed cast-iron architecture until a series of disastrous fires in the early 1870s in New York, Boston, and Chicago demonstrated that cast iron by itself was far from impervious to fire. This discovery led to encasing the metal in masonry, combining the first material's strength with the second's fire resistance.

In cities, convenience required closely grouped buildings, and increased property values forced architects literally to raise the roof. Even an attic could command high rentals if the builders installed one of the new elevators, used for the first time in the Equitable Building in New York (1868–1871). Metal, which could support these towering structures, gave birth to the American skyscraper.

HENRY HOBSON RICHARDSON One of the pioneers in designing these modern commercial structures was HENRY HOBSON RICHARDSON (1838–1886), but he also had profound respect for earlier architectural styles. Because Richardson had a special fondness for the Romanesque architecture of the Auvergne area in France, he frequently used heavy round arches and massive masonry walls. Architectural historians sometimes consider his work to constitute a

23-39 HENRY HOBSON RICHARDSON, Marshall Field wholesale store, Chicago, 1885–1887 (demolished 1930).

Richardson was a pioneer in designing commercial structures using a cast-iron skeleton encased in fire-resistant masonry. This construction technique permitted him to open up the walls with large windows.

Romanesque revival related to the Neo-Gothic style (FIG. 22-44), but this designation does not do credit to the originality and quality of most of the buildings Richardson designed during his brief 18-year practice. Trinity Church in Boston and his smaller public libraries, residences, railroad stations, and courthouses in New England and elsewhere best demonstrate his vivid imagination and the solidity (the sense of enclosure and permanence) so characteristic of his style. However, his most important and influential building was the Marshall Field wholesale store (FIG. 23-39) in Chicago, begun in 1885 and later demolished. This vast building, occupying a city block and designed for the most practical of purposes, recalled historical styles without imitating them at all. The tripartite elevation of a Renaissance palace (FIG. 16-36) or of the Roman aqueduct (FIG. 7-33) near Nîmes, France, may have been close to Richardson's mind. Yet he used no classical ornament, made much of the massive courses of masonry, and, in the strong horizontality of the windowsills and the interrupted courses that defined the levels, stressed the long sweep of the building's lines as well as its ponderous weight. Although the structural frame still lay behind and in conjunction with the masonry screen, the great glazed arcades opened up the walls of the monumental store. They pointed the way to the modern total penetration of walls and the transformation of them into mere screens or curtains that serve both to echo the underlying structural grid and to protect it from the weather.

LOUIS HENRY SULLIVAN As skyscrapers proliferated, architects refined the visual vocabulary of these buildings. LOUIS HENRY SULLIVAN (1856–1924), whom many architectural historians call the first truly modern architect, arrived at a synthesis of industrial structure and ornamentation that perfectly expressed the spirit

23-40 LOUIS HENRY SULLIVAN, Guaranty (Prudential) Building, Buffalo, New York, 1894–1896.

Louis Sullivan used the latest technologies to create this light-filled, well-ventilated Buffalo office building. He added ornate surface embellishments to impart a sense of refinement and taste.

23-41 LOUIS HENRY SULLIVAN, Carson, Pirie, Scott Building, Chicago, 1899–1904.

Sullivan's slogan was "form follows function." He tailored the design of this steel, glass, and stone Chicago department store to meet the needs of its employees and customers.

of late-19th-century commerce. To achieve this, he employed the latest technological developments to create light-filled, well-ventilated office buildings and adorned both exteriors and interiors with ornate embellishments. Such decoration served to connect commerce and culture and imbued these white-collar workspaces with a sense of refinement and taste. These characteristics are evident in the Guaranty (Prudential) Building (FIG. **23-40**) in Buffalo, New York, built between 1894 and 1896. The structure is steel, sheathed with terracotta. The imposing scale of the building and the regularity of the window placements served as an expression of the large-scale, refined, and orderly office work that took place within. Sullivan tempered the severity of the structure with lively ornamentation, both on the piers and cornice on the exterior of the building and on the stairway balustrades, elevator cages, and ceiling in the interior. The

Guaranty Building illustrates Sullivan's famous dictum that "form follows function," which became the slogan of many early-20th-century architects. Still, Sullivan did not advocate a rigid and doctrinaire correspondence between exterior and interior design. Rather, he espoused a free and flexible relationship—one his pupil Frank Lloyd Wright (see Chapter 24) later described as similar to that between the hand's bones and tissue.

Sullivan also designed the Carson, Pirie, Scott Building (FIG. **23-41**) in Chicago. Built between 1899 and 1904, this department store required broad, open, well-illuminated display spaces. Sullivan again used a minimal structural steel skeleton to achieve this goal. The architect gave over the lowest two levels of the building to an ornament in cast iron (of his invention) made of wildly fantastic motifs. He regarded the display windows as pictures and as such felt they merited elaborate frames. As in the Guaranty Building, Sullivan revealed his profound understanding of the maturing consumer economy and tailored the Chicago department store to meet the functional and symbolic needs of its users.

Thus, in architecture as well as in the pictorial arts, the late 19th century was a period during which artists challenged traditional modes of expression, often emphatically rejecting the past. Architects and painters as different as Sullivan, Monet, van Gogh, and Cézanne, each in his own way, contributed significantly to the entrenchment of modernism as the new cultural orthodoxy of the early 20th century (see Chapter 24).

EUROPE AND AMERICA, 1870 TO 1900

IMPRESSIONISM

▮ A hostile critic applied the term *Impressionism* to the paintings of Claude Monet because of their sketchy quality. The Impressionists—Monet, Pierre-Auguste Renoir, Edgar Degas, and others— strove to capture fleeting moments and transient effects of light and climate on canvas. Monet, for example, repeatedly painted Rouen Cathedral at different times of day.

▮ The Impressionists also focused on recording the contemporary urban scene in Paris. They frequently painted bars, dance halls, the ballet, wide boulevards, and railroad stations.

▮ Complementing the Impressionists' sketchy, seemingly spontaneous brush strokes are the compositions of their paintings. Reflecting the influence of Japanese prints and photography, Impressionist works often have arbitrarily cut-off figures and settings seen at sharply oblique angles.

Monet, *Rouen Cathedral*, 1894

POST-IMPRESSIONISM

▮ Post-Impressionism is not a unified style. The term refers to the group of late-19th-century artists who followed the Impressionists and took painting in new directions.

▮ Georges Seurat refined the Impressionist approach to color and light into pointillism—the disciplined application of pure color in tiny daubs that become recognizable forms only when seen from a distance. Vincent van Gogh explored the capabilities of colors and distorted forms to express emotions, as in his dramatic depiction of the sky in *Starry Night*. Paul Gauguin, another admirer of Japanese prints, moved away from Impressionism in favor of large areas of flat color bounded by firm lines. Paul Cézanne replaced the transitory visual effects of the Impressionists with a rigorous analysis of the lines, planes, and colors that make up landscapes and still lifes.

Van Gogh,
Starry Night, 1889

SYMBOLISM

▮ The Symbolists disdained Realism as trivial and sought to depict a reality beyond that of the everyday world. They rejected materialism and celebrated fantasy and imagination. Their subjects were often mysterious, exotic, and sensuous.

▮ Gustave Moreau, Odilon Redon, and Henri Rousseau were the leading French Symbolists. Rousseau's *Sleeping Gypsy,* which depicts the world of the subconscious during sleep, is a characteristic example of Symbolist painting.

Rousseau, *Sleeping Gypsy*, 1897

SCULPTURE

▮ Sculpture is not suited to capturing transitory optical effects or exploring the properties of color and line, and late-19th-century sculptors pursued goals different from those of the Impressionists and Post-Impressionists. The leading figure of the era was Auguste Rodin, who explored Realist themes and the representation of movement, as in his moving portrayal of six leading citizens of Calais who sacrificed their lives for their countrymen. He also made statues that were deliberate fragments, creating a taste for the incomplete that appealed to many later sculptors.

Rodin, *Burghers of Calais*, 1884–1889

ARCHITECTURE AND DECORATIVE ARTS

▮ Not all artists embraced the industrialization that transformed daily life during the 19th century. The Arts and Crafts movement in England and the international Art Nouveau style formed in opposition to modern mass production. Both schools advocated natural forms and high-quality craftsmanship.

▮ New technologies and the changing needs of industrialized society transformed Western architecture in the late 19th century. The exposed iron skeleton of the Eiffel Tower, which blurs the distinction between interior and exterior, jolted architects into a realization that modern materials and processes could revolutionize architectural design. In the United States, Henry Hobson Richardson and Louis Sullivan were pioneers in designing the first metal, stone, and glass skyscrapers.

Eiffel, Eiffel Tower, Paris, 1889

1 ft.

24-1 MARCEL DUCHAMP, *Nude Descending a Staircase, No. 2,* 1912. Oil on canvas, 4′ 10″ × 2′ 11″. Philadelphia Museum of Art, Philadelphia (Louise and Walter Arensberg Collection).

The Armory Show of 1913 introduced European avant-garde art to America. Duchamp's figure in motion down a staircase in a time continuum reveals the artist's indebtedness to Cubism and Futurism.

24

EUROPE
AND AMERICA,
1900 TO 1945

The first half of the 20th century was a period of significant upheaval worldwide. Between 1900 and 1945, the major industrial powers expanded their colonial empires, fought two global wars, witnessed the rise of Communism, Fascism, and Nazism, and suffered the Great Depression. These decades were also a time of radical change in the arts when painters and sculptors challenged some of the most basic assumptions about the purpose of art and what form an artwork should take.

During the 19th century, the development of modern nation-states and advanced industrial societies in Europe and America had led to frenzied imperialist expansion. By the beginning of the 20th century (MAP 24-1), Britain, France, Germany, Belgium, Italy, Spain, and Portugal all had footholds in Africa. In Asia, Britain ruled India, the Dutch controlled Indonesia's vast archipelago, the French held power in Indochina, and the Russians ruled Central Asia and Siberia. Japan began rising as a new and formidable Pacific power that would stake its claims to empire in the 1930s. This imperialism was capitalist and expansionist, establishing colonies as raw-material sources, as manufacturing markets, and as territorial acquisitions. Early-20th-century colonialism also often had the missionary dimension of bringing the "light" of Christianity and civilization to "backward peoples" and educating "inferior races."

Nationalism and rampant imperialism also led to competition. Eventually, countries negotiated alliances to protect their individual state interests. The conflicts between the two major blocs—the Triple Alliance (Germany, Austria-Hungary, and Italy) and the Triple Entente (Russia, France, and Great Britain)—led to World War I, which began in 1914. The slaughter and devastation of the Great War lasted until 1918. Not only were more than nine million soldiers killed in battle, but the introduction of poison gas in 1915 added to the horror of humankind's inhumanity to itself. Although the United States tried to remain neutral, it finally felt compelled to enter the war in 1917. In 1919, the 27 Allied nations negotiated the official end of World War I, whose legacy was widespread misery, social disruption, and economic collapse—the ultimate effects of nationalism, imperialism, and expansionist goals.

The Russian Revolution exacerbated the global chaos when it erupted in 1917. Dissatisfaction with the regime of Tsar Nicholas II (r. 1894–1917) had led workers to stage a general strike, and the monarchy's rule ended with the tsar's abdication in March. In late 1917 the Bolsheviks wrested control of the country

MAP 24-1 Colonial empires around 1900.

from the ruling provisional government. The Bolsheviks, a faction of Russian Social Democrats led by Vladimir Lenin (1870–1924), promoted violent revolution. Once in power, Lenin nationalized the land and turned it over to the local rural soviets (councils of workers and soldiers' deputies). After extensive civil war, the Communists, as they now called themselves, succeeded in retaining control of Russia and taking over an assortment of satellite countries in Eastern Europe. This new state took the official name the Union of Soviet Socialist Republics (USSR, or Soviet Union) in 1923.

Economic upheaval followed on the heels of war and revolution. The Great Depression of the 1930s dealt a serious blow to the stability of Western countries. Largely due to the international scope of banking and industrial capitalism, the economic depression deeply affected the United States and many European countries. By 1932 unemployment in the British workforce stood at 25 percent, and 40 percent of German workers were without jobs. Production in the United States plummeted by 50 percent.

This economic disaster, along with the failure of postwar treaties and the League of Nations to keep the peace, provided a fertile breeding ground for destabilizing forces to emerge once again. In the 1920s and 1930s, totalitarian regimes came to the fore in several European countries. Benito Mussolini (1883–1945) headed the nationalistic Fascist regime in Italy. Joseph Stalin (1879–1953) consolidated his control of the Soviet Union by 1929. Concurrently, in Germany Adolf Hitler (1889–1945) built the National Socialist German Workers Party (also known as the Nazi Party) into a mass political movement and eliminated all opposition.

These ruthless seizures of power led to the many conflicts that evolved into World War II. This catastrophic struggle erupted in 1939 when Germany invaded Poland, and Britain and France declared war on Germany. Eventually, the conflict earned its designation as a world war. While Germany and Italy fought most of Europe and the Soviet Union, Japan invaded China and occupied Indochina. After the Japanese bombing of Pearl Harbor in Hawaii in 1941, the United States declared war on Japan. Germany, in loose alliance with Japan, declared war on the United States, which joined the conflict in Europe on the side of Britain and France. Although most of the concerns of individual countries participating in World War II were territorial and nationalistic, other agendas surfaced as well. The Nazis, propelled by Hitler's staunch anti-Semitism, sought to build a racially exclusive Aryan state. This resolve led to the horror of the Holocaust, the killing of nearly two out of every three European Jews.

World War II drew to an end in 1945, when the Allied forces defeated Germany, and the United States dropped atomic bombs on Hiroshima and Nagasaki in Japan. The shock of the war's physical, economic, and psychological devastation immediately tempered the elation people felt at the conclusion of these global hostilities.

EUROPE, 1900 TO 1920

Like other members of society, artists deeply felt the effects of the political and economic disruptions of the early 20th century. As the old social orders collapsed and new ones, from communism to corporate capitalism, took their places, artists searched for new definitions of and uses for art in a changed world.

Already in the 19th century, each successive modernist movement—Realism, Impressionism, and Post-Impressionism—had challenged artistic conventions with ever-greater intensity. This relentless challenge gave rise to the *avant-garde* ("front guard"), a term derived from 19th-century French military usage. The avant-garde were soldiers sent ahead of the army's main body to reconnoiter and make occasional raids on the enemy. Politicians who deemed themselves visionary and forward-thinking subsequently adopted the term. It then migrated to the art world in the 1880s, where it referred to artists who were ahead of their time and who transgressed the limits of established art forms.

These artists were the vanguard, or trailblazers. The avant-garde rejected the classical, academic, and traditional, and zealously explored the premises and formal qualities of painting, sculpture, and other media. The Post-Impressionists were the first artists labeled avant-garde. Although the general public found avant-garde art incomprehensible, the principles underlying late-19th-century modernism appealed to increasing numbers of artists as the 20th century dawned. Avant-garde artists in all their diversity became a major force during the first half of the 20th century and beyond.

Avant-garde principles emerged forcefully in European art of the early 1900s in the general movement that art historians call *Expressionism,* a term used over the years in connection with a wide range of art. At its essence, Expressionism refers to art that is the result of the artist's unique inner or personal vision and that often has an emotional dimension. This contrasts strongly with most Western art produced since the Renaissance that focused on visually describing the empirical world. The term "Expressionism" first gained currency after *Der Sturm,* an avant-garde periodical initially published in Munich, popularized it.

Fauvism

One of the first movements to tap into this pervasive desire for expression was *Fauvism.* In 1905, at the third Salon d'Automne in Paris, a group of young painters exhibited canvases so simplified in design and so shockingly bright in color that a startled critic, Louis Vauxcelles (1870–1943), described the artists as *fauves* (wild beasts). The Fauves were totally independent of the French Academy and the "official" Salon (see "Academic Salons and Independent Art Exhibitions," Chapter 23, page 655). Driving the Fauve movement was a desire to develop an art having the directness of Impressionism but also embracing intense color juxtapositions and their emotional capabilities.

Building on the legacy of artists such as van Gogh and Gauguin (see Chapter 23), Fauve artists went even further in liberating color from its descriptive function and using it for both expressive and structural ends. They produced portraits, landscapes, still lifes, and nudes of spontaneity and verve, with rich surface textures, lively linear patterns, and, above all, bold colors. The Fauves employed startling contrasts of vermilion and emerald green and of cerulean blue and vivid orange held together by sweeping brush strokes and bold patterns. Thus, these artists explored both facets of Expressionism. They combined outward expression, in the form of a bold release of internal feelings through wild color and powerful, even brutal, brushwork, and inward expression, awakening the viewer's emotions by these very devices.

The Fauve painters never officially organized, and the looseness of both personal connections and stylistic affinities caused the Fauve movement to begin to disintegrate almost as soon as it emerged. Within five years, most of the artists had departed from a strict adherence to Fauve principles and developed their own, more personal styles. During the brief existence of the movement, however, the Fauve artists made a remarkable contribution to the direction of painting by demonstrating color's structural, expressive, and aesthetic capabilities.

HENRI MATISSE The dominant figure of the Fauve group was Henri Matisse (1869–1954), who believed that color could play a primary role in conveying meaning and focused his efforts on developing this premise. In an early painting, *Woman with the Hat* (FIG. 24-2), Matisse depicted his wife Amélie in a rather conventional manner compositionally, but the seemingly arbitrary colors immediately startle the viewer, as does the sketchiness of the forms. The entire image—the woman's face, clothes, hat, and background—consists of patches and splotches of color juxtaposed in ways that sometimes produce jarring contrasts. Matisse explained his approach: "What characterized fauvism was that we rejected imitative colors, and that with pure colors we obtained stronger reactions."[1] For Matisse and the Fauves, therefore, color became the formal element most responsible for pictorial coherence and the primary conveyor of meaning (see "Matisse on Color," page 688).

24-2 Henri Matisse, *Woman with the Hat,* 1905. Oil on canvas, 2′ 7¾″ × 1′ 11½″. San Francisco Museum of Modern Art, San Francisco (bequest of Elise S. Haas).

Matisse portrayed his wife Amélie using patches and splotches of seemingly arbitrary colors. He and the other Fauve painters used color not to imitate nature but to produce a reaction in the viewer.

Matisse on Color

In an essay entitled "Notes of a Painter," published in the Parisian journal *La Grande Revue* on Christmas Day, 1908, Henri Matisse responded to his critics and set forth his principles and goals as a painter. The excerpts that follow help explain what Matisse was trying to achieve in paintings such as *Harmony in Red* (FIG. 24-3).

What I am after, above all, is expression.... Expression, for me, does not reside in passions glowing in a human face or manifested by violent movement. The entire arrangement of my picture is expressive: the place occupied by the figures, the empty spaces around them, the proportions, everything has its share. Composition is the art of arranging in a decorative manner the diverse elements at the painter's command to express his feelings....

Both harmonies and dissonances of colour can produce agreeable effects.... Suppose I have to paint an interior: I have before me a cupboard; it gives me a sensation of vivid red, and I put down a red which satisfies me. A relation is established between this red and the white of the canvas. Let me put a green near the red, and make the floor yellow; and again there will be relationships between the green or yellow and the white of the canvas which will satisfy me.... A new combination of colours will succeed the first and render the totality of my representation. I am forced to transpose until finally my picture may seem completely changed when, after successive modifications, the red has succeeded the green as the dominant colour. I cannot copy nature in a servile way; I am forced to interpret nature and submit it to the spirit of the picture. From the relationship I have found in all the tones there must result a living harmony of colours, a harmony analogous to that of a musical composition....

The chief function of colour should be to serve expression as well as possible.... My choice of colours does not rest on any scientific theory; it is based on observation, on sensitivity, on felt experiences. ... I simply try to put down colours which render my sensation. There is an impelling proportion of tones that may lead me to change the shape of a figure or to transform my composition. Until I have achieved this proportion in all parts of the composition I strive towards it and keep on working. Then a moment comes when all the parts have found their definite relationships, and from then on it would be impossible for me to add a stroke to my picture without having to repaint it entirely.*

* Translated by Jack D. Flam, *Matisse on Art* (London: Phaidon, 1973), 32–40.

1 ft.

24-3 HENRI MATISSE, *Red Room* (*Harmony in Red*), 1908–1909. Oil on canvas, 5′ 11″ × 8′ 1″. State Hermitage Museum, Saint Petersburg.

Matisse believed painters should choose compositions and colors that express their feelings. Here, the table and wall seem to merge because they are the same color and have identical patterning.

24-4 André Derain, *The Dance*, 1906. Oil on canvas, $6' \frac{7}{8}'' \times 6' 10\frac{1}{4}''$. Fridart Foundation, London.

Derain worked closely with Matisse, but the tropical setting and the bold colors of *The Dance* also reflect Derain's study of Gauguin's paintings (FIGS. 23-18 and 23-19), as does the flattened perspective.

1 ft.

HARMONY IN RED The maturation of Matisse's color discoveries coalesced in his *Red Room* (*Harmony in Red;* FIG. 24-3). The subject is the interior of a comfortable, prosperous household with a maid placing fruit and wine on the table, but Matisse's canvas is radically different from traditional paintings of domestic interiors (FIG. 20-19). The Fauve painter depicted objects in simplified and schematized fashion and flattened out the forms. For example, Matisse eliminated the front edge of the table, making the table, with its identical patterning, as flat as the wall behind it. The window at the upper left could also be a painting on the wall, further flattening the space. Everywhere, the colors contrast richly and intensely. Matisse's process of overpainting reveals the importance of color for striking the right chord in the viewer. Initially, this work was predominantly green, and then he repainted it blue. Neither seemed appropriate to Matisse, and not until he repainted this work in red did he feel he had found the right color for the "harmony" he wished to compose.

ANDRÉ DERAIN Another Fauve painter was ANDRÉ DERAIN (1880–1954), who worked closely with Matisse. Like Matisse, Derain worked to use color to its fullest potential—to produce aesthetic and compositional coherence, to increase luminosity, and to elicit emotional responses from the viewer. *The Dance* (FIG. 24-4), in which several figures, some nude, others clothed, frolic in a lush landscape, is typical of Derain's art. The tropical setting and the bold colors reflect in part Derain's study of Paul Gauguin's paintings (FIGS. 23-18 and 23-19), as does the flattened perspective. Color delineates space, and Derain indicated light and shadow not by differences in value but by contrasts of hue. For the Fauves, as for Gauguin and van Gogh, color does not describe the local tones of objects but expresses the picture's content.

German Expressionism

The immediacy and boldness of the Fauve images appealed to many artists, including the German Expressionists. However, although color plays a prominent role in contemporaneous German painting, the expressiveness of the German images is due as much to wrenching distortions of form, ragged outline, and agitated brush strokes. This approach resulted in savagely powerful, emotional canvases in the years leading to World War I.

ERNST LUDWIG KIRCHNER The first group of German artists to explore Expressionist ideas gathered in Dresden in 1905 under the leadership of ERNST LUDWIG KIRCHNER (1880–1938). The group members thought of themselves as paving the way for a more perfect age by bridging the old age and the new. They derived their name, *Die Brücke* (The Bridge), from this concept. Kirchner's early studies in architecture, painting, and the graphic arts had instilled in him a deep admiration for German medieval art. Like the British artists associated with the Arts and Crafts movement, such as William Morris (FIG. 23-34), members of Die Brücke modeled themselves on their ideas of medieval craft guilds by living together and practicing all the arts equally. Kirchner described their lofty goals in a ringing statement published in the form of a woodcut in 1913 and titled *Chronik der Brücke:*

> With faith in progress and in a new generation of creators and spectators we call together all youth. As youth, we carry the future and want to create for ourselves freedom of life and of movement against the long-established older forces. Everyone who reproduces that which drives him to creation with directness and authenticity belongs to us.[2]

These artists protested the hypocrisy and materialistic decadence of those in power. Kirchner, in particular, focused much of his attention on the detrimental effects of industrialization, such as the alienation of individuals in cities, which he felt fostered a mechanized and impersonal society. The tensions leading to World War I further exacerbated the discomfort and anxiety evidenced in the works of Die Brücke artists.

24-5 ERNST LUDWIG KIRCHNER, *Street, Dresden,* 1908 (dated 1907). Oil on canvas, 4' 11¼" × 6' 6⅞". Museum of Modern Art, New York.

Kirchner's perspectival distortions, disquieting figures, and color choices reflect the influence of the Fauves and of Edvard Munch (FIG. 23-27), who made similar expressive use of formal elements.

Kirchner's *Street, Dresden* (FIG. 24-5) provides a glimpse into the frenzied urban activity of a bustling German city before World War I. Rather than offering the distant, panoramic urban view of the Impressionists (FIG. 23-5), Kirchner's street scene is jarring and dissonant in both composition and color. The women in the foreground loom large, approaching somewhat menacingly. The steep perspective of the street, which threatens to push the women directly into the viewer's space, increases their confrontational nature. Harshly rendered, the women's features make them appear ghoulish, and the garish, clashing colors—juxtapositions of bright orange, emerald green, chartreuse, and pink—add to the expressive impact of the image. Kirchner's perspectival distortions, disquieting figures, and color choices reflect the influence of the work of Edvard Munch, who made similar expressive use of formal elements in *The Scream* (FIG. 23-27).

EMIL NOLDE Much older than most Die Brücke artists was EMIL NOLDE (1867–1956), but because he pursued similar ideas in his work, the younger artists invited him to join their group in 1906. (Die Brücke dissolved by 1913, and each member continued to work independently.) The content of Nolde's work centered, for the most part, on religious imagery. In contrast to the quiet spirituality and restraint of traditional religious images, however, Nolde's paintings, for example, *Saint Mary of Egypt among Sinners* (FIG. 24-6), are visceral and forceful. Mary, before her conversion, entertains lechers whose lust magnifies their brutal ugliness. The distortions of form and color (especially the jolting juxtaposition of blue and orange) and the rawness of the brush strokes amplify the harshness of the leering faces.

Borrowing ideas from van Gogh, Munch, the Fauves, and African and Oceanic art (see "Primitivism and Colonialism," page 696), Nolde and the other Die Brücke artists created images that derive much of their power from a dissonance and seeming lack of finesse. The harsh colors, aggressively brushed paint, and distorted forms expressed the artists' feelings about the injustices of society and their belief in a healthful union of human beings and nature. Their use of these diverse sources reflects the expanding scope of global contact brought about by colonialism and international capitalism.

24-6 EMIL NOLDE, *Saint Mary of Egypt among Sinners,* 1912. Left panel of a triptych, oil on canvas, 2' 10" × 3' 3". Hamburger Kunsthalle, Hamburg.

In contrast to the quiet spirituality of traditional religious images, Nolde's paintings produce visceral emotions and feature distortions of form, jarring juxtapositions of color, and raw brush strokes.

Science and Art in the Early 20th Century

In the early 20th century, societies worldwide contended with discoveries and new ways of thinking in a wide variety of fields, including science. These new ideas forced people to revise radically how they understood their world. In particular, the values and ideals that were the legacy of the Enlightenment (see Chapter 21) began to yield to innovative views. Thus, intellectuals countered 18th- and 19th-century assumptions about progress and reason with ideas challenging traditional notions about the physical universe, the structure of society, and human nature. Artists participated in this reassessment. Modernist artists, in particular, often acknowledged these new discoveries and shifting theoretical bases in their work. Accordingly, much of the history of early-20th-century Western art is a history of the rejection of traditional limitations and definitions both of art and of the universe.

One of the fundamental Enlightenment beliefs was faith in science. Because of its basis in empirical, or observable, fact, science provided a

24-7 VASSILY KANDINSKY, *Improvisation 28* (second version), 1912. Oil on canvas, 3′ 7⅞″ × 5′ 3⅞″. Solomon R. Guggenheim Museum, New York (gift of Solomon R. Guggenheim, 1937).

The scientific theories of Einstein and Rutherford convinced Kandinsky that material objects had no real substance. He was one of the first painters to explore complete abstraction in his canvases.

mechanistic conception of the universe, which reassured a populace that was finding traditional religions less certain. As promoted in the classic physics of Isaac Newton (1642–1727), the universe was a huge machine consisting of time, space, and matter. The early 20th century witnessed an astounding burst of scientific activity challenging this model of the universe. It amounted to what has been called "the second scientific and technological revolution." Particularly noteworthy was the work of various physicists: Max Planck (1858–1947), Albert Einstein (1879–1955), Ernest Rutherford (1871–1937), and Niels Bohr (1885–1962). With their discoveries, each of these scientists shattered the existing faith in the objective reality of matter and, in so doing, paved the way for a new model of the universe. Planck's quantum theory (1900) raised questions about the emission of atomic energy. In his 1905 paper, "The Electrodynamics of Moving Bodies," Einstein carried

Planck's work further by introducing his theory of relativity. He argued that space and time are not absolute, as postulated in Newtonian physics. Rather, Einstein explained, time and space are relative to the observer and linked in what he called a four-dimensional space-time continuum. He also concluded that matter, rather than a solid, tangible reality, was actually another form of energy. Einstein's famous equation $E = mc^2$, where E stands for energy, m for mass, and c for the speed of light, provided a formula for understanding atomic energy. Rutherford's and Bohr's exploration of atomic structure between 1906 and 1913 contributed to this new perception of matter and energy. Together, all these scientific discoveries constituted a changed view of physical nature and contributed to the growing interest in abstraction, as opposed to the mimetic representation of the world, among early-20th-century artists like Vassily Kandinsky (FIG. 24-7).

VASSILY KANDINSKY A second major German Expressionist group, *Der Blaue Reiter* (The Blue Rider), formed in Munich in 1911. The two founding members, Vassily Kandinsky and Franz Marc, whimsically selected this name because of their mutual interest in the color blue and horses. Like Die Brücke, this group produced paintings that captured their feelings in visual form while also eliciting intense visceral responses from viewers.

Born in Russia, VASSILY KANDINSKY (1866–1944) moved to Munich in 1896 and soon developed a spontaneous and aggressively avant-garde expressive style. Indeed, Kandinsky was one of the first artists to explore complete abstraction, as in *Improvisation 28* (FIG. 24-7), painted in 1912. Kandinsky fueled his elimination of repre-

sentational elements with his interest in theosophy (a religious and philosophical belief system incorporating a wide range of tenets from, among other sources, Buddhism and mysticism) and the occult, as well as with advances in the sciences. A true intellectual, widely read in philosophy, religion, history, and the other arts, especially music, Kandinsky was also one of the few early modernists to read with some comprehension the new scientific theories of the era (see "Science and Art in the Early 20th Century," above). Scientists' exploration of atomic structure, for example, convinced Kandinsky that material objects had no real substance, thereby shattering his faith in a world of tangible things. The painter articulated his ideas in an influential treatise, *Concerning the Spiritual in Art*, published in

24-8 Franz Marc, *Fate of the Animals,* 1913. Oil on canvas, 6′ 4¾″ × 8′ 9½″. Kunstmuseum, Basel.

Marc developed a system of correspondences between specific colors and feelings or ideas. In this apocalyptic scene of animals trapped in a forest, the colors of severity and brutality dominate.

1 ft.

1912. Artists, Kandinsky believed, must express the spirit and their innermost feelings by orchestrating color, form, line, and space. He produced numerous works like *Improvisation 28,* conveying feelings with color juxtapositions, intersecting linear elements, and implied spatial relationships. Ultimately, Kandinsky saw these abstractions as evolving blueprints for a more enlightened and liberated society emphasizing spirituality.

FRANZ MARC Like many of the other German Expressionists, Franz Marc (1880–1916), the cofounder of Der Blaue Reiter, grew increasingly pessimistic about the state of humanity, especially as World War I loomed on the horizon. His perception of human beings as deeply flawed led him to turn to the animal world for his subjects. Animals, he believed, were more pure than humanity and thus more appropriate as a vehicle to express an inner truth. In his quest to imbue his paintings with greater emotional intensity, Marc focused on color and developed a system of correspondences between specific colors and feelings or ideas. In a letter to a fellow Blaue Reiter, Marc explained: "Blue is the *male* principle, severe and spiritual. Yellow is the *female* principle, gentle, happy and sensual. Red is *matter,* brutal and heavy."[3] Marc's attempts to create, in a sense, an iconography (or representational system) of color linked him to other avant-garde artists struggling to redefine the practice of art.

Fate of the Animals (FIG. **24-8**) represents the culmination of Marc's color explorations. Painted in 1913, when the tension of impending cataclysm had pervaded society, the animals appear trapped in a forest amid falling trees, some apocalyptic event destroying both the forest and the animals inhabiting it. The painter distorted the entire scene and shattered it into fragments. Significantly, the lighter and brighter colors—the passive, gentle, and cheerful ones—are absent, and the colors of severity and brutality dominate the work. On the back of the canvas Marc wrote "All being is flaming suffering." The artist discovered just how well his painting portended war's anguish and tragedy when he ended up at the front the following year.

His experiences in battle prompted him to write to his wife that *Fate of the Animals* "is like a premonition of this war—horrible and shattering. I can hardly conceive that I painted it."[4] His contempt for people's inhumanity and his attempt to express that through his art ended, with tragic irony, in his death in action in 1916.

KÄTHE KOLLWITZ The emotional range of German Expressionism extends from passionate protest and satirical bitterness to the poignantly expressed pity for the poor in the prints of Käthe Kollwitz (1867–1945), who had no formal association with any Expressionist group. The graphic art of Gauguin and Munch stimulated a revival of the print medium in Germany, especially the woodcut, and these proved inspiring models. Kollwitz worked in a variety of printmaking techniques, including woodcut, lithography, and etching, and explored a range of issues from the overtly political to the deeply personal. One image she explored in depth, producing a number of print variations, was that of a mother with her dead child. Although she initially derived the theme from the Christian *Pietà,* she transformed it into a universal statement of maternal loss and grief. In *Woman with Dead Child* (FIG. **24-9**), an etching and lithograph, she disavowed the reverence and grace that pervaded most Christian depictions of Mary holding the dead Christ (FIG. **17-12**) and replaced those attributes with an animalistic passion, shown in the way the mother ferociously grips the body of her dead child. The primal nature of the image is in keeping with the aims of the Expressionists, and the scratchy lines the etching needle produced serve as evidence of Kollwitz's very personal touch. The impact of this image is undeniably powerful. Not since the Gothic age in Germany (FIG. **13-51**) had any artist produced a mother-and-son group of comparable emotional power. That Kollwitz used her son Peter as the model for the dead child no doubt made the image all the more personal to her. The image stands as a poignant premonition. Peter died fighting in World War I at age 21.

WILHELM LEHMBRUCK The Great War also deeply affected Wilhelm Lehmbruck (1881–1919). His figurative sculptures exude

24-9 KÄTHE KOLLWITZ, *Woman with Dead Child*, 1903. Etching and soft-ground etching, overprinted lithographically with a gold tone plate, 1′ 4⅝″ × 1′ 7⅛″. British Museum, London.

The theme of the mother mourning over her dead child comes from images of the *Pietà* in Christian art, but Kollwitz transformed it into a powerful universal statement of maternal loss and grief.

a quiet mood but still possess a compelling emotional sensibility. Lehmbruck studied sculpture, painting, and the graphic arts in Düsseldorf before moving to Paris in 1910, where he developed the style of his *Seated Youth* (FIG. **24-10**). His sculpture combines the expressive qualities he much admired in the work of fellow sculptors, especially the psychological energies of Rodin (FIGS. **23-32** and **23-33**). In *Seated Youth*, the poignant elongation of human proportions, the slumped shoulders, and the hands that hang uselessly all impart an undertone of anguish to the rather classical figure. Lehmbruck's figure communicates by pose and gesture alone. Although its extreme proportions may recall Mannerist attenuation (FIG. **17-43**), its distortions announce a new freedom in interpreting the human figure. For Lehmbruck, as for Rodin, the human figure could express every human condition and emotion. The quiet, contemplative nature of this sculpture serves both as a personal expression of Lehmbruck's increasing depression and as a powerful characterization of the general sensibility in the wake of World War I. Appropriately, the original title of *Seated Youth* was *The Friend*, in reference to the artist's many friends who lost their lives in the war. After Lehmbruck's tragic suicide in 1919, officials placed this sculpture as a memorial in the soldiers' cemetery in Lehmbruck's native city of Duisburg.

24-10 WILHELM LEHMBRUCK, *Seated Youth*, 1917. Composite tinted plaster, 3′ 4⅝″ × 2′ 6″ × 3′ 9″. National Gallery of Art, Washington, D.C. (Andrew W. Mellon Fund).

The poignant elongation of human proportions, the slumped shoulders, and the hands that hang uselessly all impart an undertone of anguish to Lehmbruck's rather classical figure.

Gertrude and Leo Stein and the Avant-Garde

One of the many unexpected developments in the history of art is that two Americans—Gertrude (1874–1946) and Leo (1872–1947) Stein—played pivotal roles in the history of the European avant-garde because they provided a hospitable environment in their Paris home. Artists, writers, musicians, collectors, and critics interested in progressive art and ideas could meet there to talk and socialize. Born in Pennsylvania, the Stein siblings moved to 27 rue de Fleurus in Paris in 1903. Gertrude's experimental writing stimulated her interest in the latest developments in the arts. Conversely, the avant-garde ideas discussed at the Steins' house influenced her unique poetry, plays, and other works. She is perhaps best known for *The Autobiography of Alice B. Toklas* (1933), a unique memoir written in the persona of her longtime lesbian companion.

The Steins' interest in the exciting, invigorating debates taking place in avant-garde circles led them to welcome visitors to their Saturday salons, which included lectures, thoughtful discussions, and spirited arguments. Often, these gatherings lasted until dawn and included not only their French friends but also visiting Americans, Britons, Swedes, Germans, Hungarians, Spaniards, Poles, and Russians. Among the hundreds who welcomed the opportunity to visit the Steins were artists Henri Matisse, Pablo Picasso, Georges Braque, Mary Cassatt, Marcel Duchamp, Alfred Stieglitz, and Arthur B. Davis; writers Ernest Hemingway, F. Scott Fitzgerald, John dos Passos, Jean Cocteau, and Guillaume Apollinaire; art dealers Daniel Kahnweiler and Ambroise Vollard; critics Roger Fry and Clive Bell; and collectors Sergei Shchukin and Ivan Morosov.

The Steins were avid art collectors, and the works decorating their walls attracted many visitors. One of the first paintings Leo purchased was Matisse's notorious *Woman with the Hat* (FIG. 24-2), and he subsequently bought numerous important paintings by Matisse and Picasso, along with works by Gauguin, Cézanne, Renoir, and Braque. Picasso, who developed a close friendship with Gertrude, painted her portrait (FIG. 24-11) in 1907. Gertrude loved the painting so much that she kept it by her all her life and donated it to the Metropolitan Museum of Art only upon her death in 1946.

24-11 PABLO PICASSO, *Gertrude Stein,* 1906–1907. Oil on canvas, $3' 3\frac{3}{8}'' \times 2' 8''$. Metropolitan Museum of Art, New York (bequest of Gertrude Stein, 1947).

Picasso had left this portrait of his friend and patron unfinished until he decided to incorporate the planar simplicity of ancient Iberian stone sculptures into his depiction of her face.

Primitivism and Cubism

The Expressionist departure from any strict adherence to illusionism in art was a path that other artists followed. Among those who most radically challenged prevailing artistic conventions and moved most aggressively into the realm of abstraction was Pablo Picasso.

PABLO PICASSO Born in Spain four years after Gustave Courbet's death, PABLO PICASSO (1881–1973) mastered all aspects of late-19th-century Realist technique by the time he entered the Barcelona Academy of Fine Art in the late 1890s. His prodigious talent led him to experiment with a wide range of visual expression, first in Spain and then in Paris, where he settled in 1904. An artist whose importance to the history of art is uncontested, Picasso made staggering contributions to new ways of representing the surrounding world. Perhaps the most prolific artist in history, he explored virtually every artistic medium during his lengthy career, but remained a traditional artist in making careful preparatory studies for each major work. Picasso epitomized modernism, however, in his enduring quest for innovation, which resulted in sudden shifts from one style to another. By the time he settled permanently in Paris, Picasso's work had evolved from Spanish painting's sober Realism through an Impressionistic phase to the so-called Blue Period (1901–1904), when, in a melancholy state of mind, he used primarily blue colors to depict worn, pathetic, and alienated figures.

GERTRUDE STEIN By 1906, Picasso was searching restlessly for new ways to depict form. He found clues in the ancient Iberian sculpture of his homeland and other "primitive" cultures. Inspired by these sources, Picasso returned to a portrait of *Gertrude Stein* (FIG. 24-11), his friend and patron (see "Gertrude and Leo Stein and the Avant-Garde," above). Picasso had begun the painting earlier that year but left it unfinished after more than 80 sittings. When he resumed work on the portrait, Picasso painted Stein's head as a simplified planar form, incorporating aspects derived from Iberian stone heads. Although the disparity between the style of the face and the rest of Stein's image is striking, together they provide an insightful portrait of a forceful, vivacious woman. More important, Picasso had discovered a new approach to the representation of the human form.

24-12 Pablo Picasso, *Les Demoiselles d'Avignon*, 1907. Oil on canvas, 8′ × 7′ 8″. Museum of Modern Art, New York (acquired through the Lillie P. Bliss Bequest).

African and ancient Iberian sculpture and the late paintings of Cézanne influenced this pivotal work, with which Picasso opened the door to a radically new method of representing forms in space.

DEMOISELLES D'AVIGNON The influence of "primitive" art also surfaces in *Les Demoiselles d'Avignon* (*The Young Ladies of Avignon;* FIG. 24-12), which opened the door to a radically new method of representing form in space. Picasso began the work as a symbolic picture to be titled *Philosophical Bordello,* portraying two male clients (who, based on surviving drawings, had features resembling Picasso's) intermingling with women in the reception room of a brothel on Avignon Street in Barcelona. One was a sailor. The other carried a skull, an obvious reference to death. By the time the artist finished, he had eliminated the male figures and simplified the room's details to a suggestion of drapery and a schematic foreground still life. Picasso had become wholly absorbed in the problem of finding a new way to represent the five female figures in their interior space. Instead of depicting the figures as continuous volumes, he fractured their shapes and interwove them with the equally jagged planes that represent drapery and empty

space. Indeed, the space, so entwined with the bodies, is virtually illegible. Here Picasso pushed Cézanne's treatment of form and space (FIGS. 23-20 and 23-21) to a new level. The tension between Picasso's representation of three-dimensional space and his conviction that a painting is a two-dimensional design lying flat on the surface of a stretched canvas is a tension between representation and abstraction.

The artist extended the radical nature of *Les Demoiselles d'Avignon* even further by depicting the figures inconsistently. Ancient Iberian sculptures inspired the calm, ideal features of the three young women at the left, as they had the head of Gertrude Stein (FIG. 24-11). The energetic, violently striated features of the two heads to the right emerged late in Picasso's production of the work and grew directly from his increasing fascination with the power of African sculpture (see "Primitivism and Colonialism," page 696), which the artist studied in Paris's Trocadéro ethnography museum as well as collected and kept in his

Primitivism and Colonialism

Many scholars have noted that one major source for much of early-20th-century art is non-Western culture. Many modernist artists incorporated stylistic elements from the artifacts of Africa, Oceania, and the native peoples of the Americas—a phenomenon art historians call *primitivism*. Some of them, for example, Henri Matisse and Pablo Picasso (FIG. 24-13), were enthusiastic collectors of "primitive art," but all of them could view the numerous non-Western objects displayed in European and American collections and museums. During the second half of the 19th century, anthropological and ethnographic museums began to proliferate. In 1882, the Musée d'Ethnographie du Trocadéro (now the Musée du quai Branly) in Paris opened its doors to the public. The Musée Permanent des Colonies (now the Musée National des Arts d'Afrique et d'Océanie) in Paris also provided the public with a wide array of objects—weapons, tools, basketwork, headdresses—from colonial territories, as did the Musée Africain in Marseilles. In Berlin, the Museum für Völkerkunde housed close to 10,000 African objects by 1886, when it opened for public viewing. The Expositions Universelles, regularly scheduled exhibitions in France designed to celebrate industrial progress, included products from Oceania and Africa after 1851, familiarizing the public with these cultures. By the beginning of the 20th century, significant non-Western collections were on view in museums in Liverpool, Glasgow, Edinburgh, London, Hamburg, Stuttgart, Vienna, Berlin, Munich, Leiden, Copenhagen, and Chicago.

The formation of these collections was a by-product of the rampant colonialism central to the geopolitical dynamics of the 19th century and much of the 20th century. Most of the Western powers maintained colonies (MAP 24-1). For example, the United States, Holland, and France all kept a colonial presence in the Pacific. Britain, France, Germany, Belgium, Holland, Spain, and Portugal divided up the African continent. People often perceived these colonial cultures as "primitive" and referred to many of the non-Western artifacts displayed in museums as "artificial curiosities" or "fetish objects." Indeed, the exhibition of these objects collected during expeditions to the colonies served to reinforce the perceived "need" for a colonial presence in these countries. These objects, which often seemed to depict strange gods or creatures, bolstered the view that these peoples were "barbarians" who needed to be "civilized" or "saved," and this perception thereby justified colonialism—including its missionary dimension—worldwide.

Whether avant-garde artists were aware of the imperialistic implications of their appropriation of non-Western culture is unclear. Certainly, however, many artists reveled in the energy and freshness of non-Western images and forms. These different cultural products provided Western artists with new ways of looking at their own art. Matisse always maintained he saw African sculptures as simply "good sculptures . . . like any other."* Picasso, in contrast, believed "the masks weren't just like any other pieces of sculpture. Not at all.

24-13 FRANK GELETT BURGESS, Pablo Picasso in his studio, Paris, France, 1908. Collection of the Musée Picasso, Paris.

Picasso was familiar with ancient Iberian art from his homeland and studied African and other "primitive" art in Paris's Trocadéro museum. He kept his own collection of primitive art in his studio.

They were magic things. . . . mediators" between humans and the forces of evil, and he sought to capture their power as well as their forms in his paintings. "[In the Trocadéro] I understood why I was a painter. . . . All alone in that awful museum, with masks, dolls . . . *Les Demoiselles d'Avignon* [FIG. 24-12)] must have come to me that day."† Further, "primitive" art seemed to embody a directness, closeness to nature, and honesty that appealed to modernist artists determined to reject conventional models. Non-Western art served as an important revitalizing and energizing force in Western art.

* Jean-Louis Paudrat, "From Africa," in William Rubin, ed., *"Primitivism" in 20th Century Art: Affinity of the Tribal and the Modern* (New York: Museum of Modern Art, 1984), 1:141.
† Ibid.

Paris studio (FIG. 24-13). Perhaps responding to the energy of these two new heads, Picasso also revised their bodies. He broke them into more ambiguous planes suggesting a combination of views, as if the observer sees the figures from more than one place in space at once. The woman seated at the lower right shows these multiple angles most clearly, seeming to present the viewer simultaneously with a three-quarter back view from the left, another from the right, and a front view of the head that suggests seeing the figure frontally as well. Gone is the traditional concept of an orderly, constructed, and unified pictorial space that mirrors the world. In its place are the rudimentary beginnings of a new representation of the world as a dynamic interplay of time and space. Clearly, *Les Demoiselles d'Avignon* represents a dramatic departure from the careful presentation of a visual reality. Explained Picasso: "I paint forms as I think them, not as I see them."[5]

GEORGES BRAQUE AND CUBISM For many years, Picasso showed *Les Demoiselles* only to other painters. One of the first to see it was GEORGES BRAQUE (1882–1963), a Fauve painter who found it so challenging that he began to rethink his own painting style. Using the painting's revolutionary ideas as a point of departure, together Braque and Picasso formulated *Cubism* around 1908. Cubism represented a radical turning point in the history of art, nothing less than a dismissal of the pictorial illusionism that had dominated Western art since the Renaissance. The Cubists rejected naturalistic depictions, preferring compositions of shapes and forms abstracted from the conventionally perceived world. These artists pursued the analysis of form central to Cézanne's artistic explorations, and they dissected life's continuous optical spread into its many constituent features, which they then recomposed, by a new logic of design, into a coherent aesthetic object. For the Cubists, the art of painting had to move far beyond the description of visual reality. This rejection of accepted artistic practice illustrates both the period's aggressive avantgarde critique of pictorial convention and the public's dwindling faith in a safe, concrete Newtonian world in the face of the physics of Einstein and others (see "Science and Art," page 691).

The new style received its name after Matisse described some of Braque's work to the critic Louis Vauxcelles as having been painted "with little cubes." In his review, Vauxcelles described the new paintings as "cubic oddities."[6] The French writer and theorist Guillaume Apollinaire (1880–1918) summarized well the central concepts of Cubism in 1913:

> Authentic cubism [is] the art of depicting new wholes with formal elements borrowed not from the reality of vision, but from that of conception. This tendency leads to a poetic kind of painting which stands outside the world of observation; for, even in a simple cubism, the geometrical surfaces of an object must be opened out in order to give a complete representation of it. . . . Everyone must agree that a chair, from whichever side it is viewed, never ceases to have four legs, a seat and a back, and that, if it is robbed of one of these elements, it is robbed of an important part.[7]

Art historians refer to the first phase of Cubism, developed jointly by Picasso and Braque, as *Analytic Cubism*. Because Cubists could not achieve Apollinaire's total view through the traditional method of drawing or painting models from one position, these artists began to dissect the forms of their subjects. They presented that dissection for the viewer to inspect across the canvas surface. In simplistic terms, Analytic Cubism involves analyzing the structure of forms.

THE PORTUGUESE Georges Braque's painting *The Portuguese* (FIG. **24-14**) exemplifies Analytic Cubism. The artist derived the subject from his memories of a Portuguese musician seen years earlier in a bar in Marseilles. Braque concentrated his attention on dissecting the form and placing it in dynamic interaction with the space around it. Unlike the Fauves and German Expressionists, who used vibrant colors, the Cubists chose subdued hues—here solely brown tones—in order to focus the viewer's attention on form. In *The Portuguese*, the artist carried his analysis so far that the viewer must work diligently to discover clues to the subject. The construction of large intersecting planes suggests the forms of a man and a guitar. Smaller shapes interpenetrate and hover in the large planes. The way Braque treated light and shadow reveals his departure from conventional artistic practice. Light and dark passages suggest both chiaroscuro modeling and transparent planes that allow the viewer to see through one level to another. As the observer looks, solid forms emerge only to be canceled almost immediately by a different reading of the subject.

24-14 GEORGES BRAQUE, *The Portuguese*, 1911. Oil on canvas, 3′ 10$\frac{1}{8}$″ × 2′ 8″. Kunstmuseum, Basel (gift of Raoul La Roche, 1952).

The Cubists rejected the pictorial illusionism that had dominated Western art for centuries. In this painting, Braque concentrated on dissecting form and placing it in dynamic interaction with space.

The stenciled letters and numbers add to the painting's complexity. Letters and numbers are flat shapes, but as elements of a Cubist painting such as *The Portuguese*, they allow the artist to play with the viewer's perception of two- and three-dimensional space. The letters and numbers lie flat on the painted canvas surface, yet the image's shading and shapes seem to flow behind and underneath them, pushing the letters and numbers forward into the viewing space. Occasionally, they seem attached to the surface of some object within the painting. Ultimately, the constantly shifting imagery makes it impossible to arrive at any definitive or final reading of the image. Examining this kind of painting is a disconcerting excursion into ambiguity and doubt, especially since the letters and numbers seem to anchor the painting in the world of representation, thereby exacerbating the tension between representation and abstraction. Analytical Cubist paintings radically disrupt expectations about the representation of space and time.

ROBERT DELAUNAY Artists and art historians generally have regarded the suppression of color as crucial to Cubism's success, but ROBERT DELAUNAY (1885–1941), a contemporary of Picasso and Braque, worked toward a kind of color Cubism. Apollinaire called this art style *Orphism*, after Orpheus, the Greek god with magical powers of music-making. Apollinaire believed art, like music, was

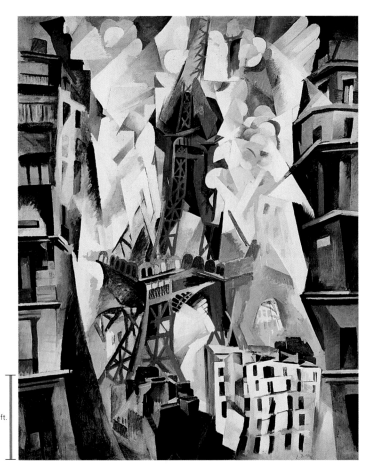

24-15 ROBERT DELAUNAY, *Champs de Mars,* or *The Red Tower,* 1911. Oil on canvas, 5′ 3″ × 4′ 3″. Art Institute of Chicago, Chicago.

Orphism is a kind of color Cubism. Delaunay broke the Eiffel Tower into a kaleidoscopic array of colored pieces. Some scholars have interpreted the painting as a commentary on the collapse of society.

distinct from the representation of the visible world. Delaunay developed his ideas about color use in dialogue with his Russian-born wife, Sonia (1885–1974), also an artist. She created paintings, quilts, other textile arts, and book covers that exploited the expressive capabilities of color. As a result of their artistic explorations, both Delaunays became convinced that the rhythms of modern life could best be expressed through color harmonies and dissonances. *Champs de Mars,* or *The Red Tower* (FIG. **24-15**), is one of many paintings Delaunay produced between 1909 and 1912 depicting the Eiffel Tower (FIG. **23-1**). The title *Champs de Mars* refers to the Parisian field on which the Eiffel Tower stands, named after the Campus Martius (Field of Mars) located outside the walls of Republican Rome.

The artist broke Eiffel's tower into a kaleidoscopic array of colored pieces, which variously leap forward or pull back according to the relative hues and values of the broken shapes. The structure ambiguously rises and collapses. Delaunay's experiments with color dynamics strongly influenced the Futurists (discussed later) and the German Expressionists (he exhibited with Der Blaue Reiter as well as with Cubists). These artists found in his art a means for intensifying expression by suggesting violent motion through shape and color.

Some scholars have interpreted Delaunay's fragmentation of the Eiffel Tower in *Champs de Mars* in political terms as a commentary on societal collapse in the years leading to World War I. Delaunay himself described the collapsing-tower imagery as "the synthesis of a period of destruction; likewise a prophetic vision with social repercussions: war, and the base crumbles."[8] This statement encapsulates well the social and artistic climate during these years—the destruction of old world

24-16 PABLO PICASSO, *Still Life with Chair-Caning,* 1912. Oil and oilcloth on canvas, $10\frac{5}{8}″ \times 1′ 1\frac{3}{4}″$. Musée Picasso, Paris.

This painting includes a piece of oilcloth imprinted with the photolithographed pattern of a cane chair seat. Framed with a piece of rope, the still life challenges the viewer's understanding of reality.

orders and of artistic practices deemed obsolete, as well as the avant-garde's prophetic nature and its determination to subvert tradition.

SYNTHETIC CUBISM In 1912, Cubism entered a new phase called *Synthetic Cubism,* in which artists constructed paintings and drawings from objects and shapes cut from paper or other materials to represent parts of a subject. The work marking the point of departure for this new style was Picasso's *Still Life with Chair-Caning* (FIG. **24-16**), a painting in which the artist imprinted a photolithographed pattern of a cane chair seat on the canvas and then pasted a piece of oilcloth on it. Framed with a piece of rope, this work challenges the viewer's understanding of reality. The photographically replicated chair-caning seems so "real" that one expects the holes to break any brush strokes laid upon it. But the chair-caning, although optically suggestive of the real, is only an illusion or representation of an object. In contrast, the painted abstract areas do not refer to tangible objects in the real world. Yet the fact they do not imitate anything makes them more "real" than the chair-caning. No pretense exists. Picasso extended the visual play by making the letter *U* escape from the space of the accompanying *J* and *O* and partially covering it with a cylindrical shape that pushes across its left side. The letters *JOU* appear in many Cubist paintings. These letters formed part of the masthead of the daily French newspapers (*journaux*) often found among the objects represented. Picasso and Braque especially delighted in the punning references to *jouer* and *jouir*—the French verbs meaning "to play" and "to enjoy."

COLLAGE After *Still Life with Chair-Caning,* both Picasso and Braque continued to explore the medium of *collage* introduced into the realm of high art in that work. From the French word "coller" ("to stick"), a collage is a composition of bits of objects, such as newspaper or cloth, glued to a surface. Its possibilities can be seen in Braque's *Bottle, Newspaper, Pipe, and Glass* (FIG. **24-17**), done in a variant of collage called *papier collé* ("stuck paper")—gluing assorted paper shapes to a drawing or painting. Here, charcoal lines and shadows provide clues to the Cubist multiple views of various surfaces and objects. Roughly rectangular strips of variously printed and colored paper dominate the composition. The paper imprinted with wood grain and

1 in.

24-17 GEORGES BRAQUE, *Bottle, Newspaper, Pipe, and Glass,* 1913. Charcoal and various papers pasted on paper, 1′ 6$\frac{7}{8}$″ × 2′ 1$\frac{1}{4}$″. Private collection, New York.

This Cubist collage of glued paper is a visual game to be deciphered. The pipe in the foreground, for example, seems to lie on the newspaper, but it is actually cut through the printed paper.

ety. Many artists and writers of the period allied themselves with various anarchist groups whose social critiques and utopian visions appealed to progressive thinkers. It was, therefore, not a far leap to see radical art, like Cubism, as having political ramifications. Indeed, many critics in the French press consistently equated Cubism with anarchism, revolution, and disdain for tradition. Picasso himself, however, never viewed Cubism as a protest movement or even different in kind from traditional painting (see "Picasso on Cubism," page 700).

moldings provides an illusion whose concreteness contrasts with the lightly rendered objects on the right. Five pieces of paper overlap each other in the center of the composition to create a layering of flat planes that both echo the space the lines suggest and establish the flatness of the work's surface. All shapes in the image seem to oscillate, pushing forward and dropping back in space. Shading carves space into flat planes in some places and turns planes into transparent surfaces in others. The pipe in the foreground illustrates this complex visual interplay especially well. Although it appears to lie on the newspaper, it is in fact a form cut through the printed paper to reveal the canvas surface, which Braque lightly modeled with charcoal. The artist thus kept his audience aware that *Bottle, Newspaper, Pipe, and Glass* is an artwork, a visual game to be deciphered, and not an attempt to reproduce nature. Picasso explained the goals of Cubist collage:

> Not only did we try to displace reality; reality was no longer in the object.... [In] the *papier collé* ... [w]e didn't any longer want to fool the eye; we wanted to fool the mind.... If a piece of newspaper can be a bottle, that gives us something to think about in connection with both newspapers and bottles, too.[9]

Like all collage, the papier collé technique was modern in its medium—mass-produced materials never before found in "high" art—and modern in the way the artist embedded the art's "message" in the imagery and in the nature of these everyday materials.

Although most discussions of Cubism and collage focus on the formal innovations they represented, it is important to note that the public also viewed the revolutionary and subversive nature of Cubism in sociopolitical terms. The public saw Cubism's challenge to artistic convention and tradition as an attack on 20th-century soci-

PICASSO, *GUITAR* Cubism did not just open new avenues for representing form on two-dimensional surfaces. It also inspired new approaches to sculpture. Picasso explored Cubism's possibilities in sculpture throughout the years he and Braque developed the style. Picasso created *Guitar* (FIG. **24-18**) in 1912. As in his Cubist paintings, this sculpture operates at the intersection of two- and three-dimensionality. Picasso took the form of a guitar (an image that

1 in.

24-18 PABLO PICASSO, maquette for *Guitar,* 1912. Cardboard, string, and wire (restored), 2′ 1$\frac{1}{4}$″ × 1′ 1″ × 7$\frac{1}{2}$″. Museum of Modern Art, New York.

In this model for a sculpture of sheet metal, Picasso presented what is essentially a cutaway view of a guitar, allowing the viewer to examine both surface and interior space, both mass and void.

Picasso on Cubism

In 1923, Picasso granted an interview to the Mexican-born painter and critic Marius de Zayas (1880–1961), who had settled in New York City in 1907 and in 1911 had been instrumental in putting together the first exhibition in the United States of Picasso's paintings. In their conversation, the approved English translation of which appeared in the journal *The Arts* under the title "Picasso Speaks," the artist set forth his views about Cubism and the nature of art in general.

> We all know that Art is not truth. Art is a lie that makes us realize truth, at least the truth that is given us to understand. The artist must know the manner whereby to convince others of the truthfulness of his lies. . . . They speak of naturalism in opposition to modern painting. I would like to know if anyone has ever seen a natural work of art. Nature and art, being two different things, cannot be the same thing. Through art we express our conception of what nature is not. . . .
>
> Cubism is no different from any other school of painting. The same principles and the same elements are common to all. . . . Many think that Cubism is an art of transition, an experiment which is to bring

ulterior results. Those who think that way have not understood it. Cubism is not either a seed or a foetus, but an art dealing primarily with forms, and when a form is realized it is there to live its own life. . . . Mathematics, trigonometry, chemistry, psychoanalysis, music, and whatnot, have been related to Cubism to give it an easier interpretation. All this has been pure literature, not to say nonsense, . . . Cubism has kept itself within the limits and limitations of painting, never pretending to go beyond it. Drawing, design, and color are understood and practiced in Cubism in the spirit and manner that they are understood and practiced in all other schools. Our subjects might be different, as we have introduced into painting objects and forms that were formerly ignored. . . . [I]n our subjects, we keep the joy of discovery, the pleasure of the unexpected; our subject itself must be a source of interest.*

* Marius de Zayas, "Picasso Speaks," *The Arts* (May 1923), 315–326. Reprinted in Herschel B. Chipp, *Theories of Modern Art: A Source Book by Artists and Critics* (Berkeley and Los Angeles: University of California Press, 1968), 263–266.

---

surfaces in many of his paintings as well) and explored its volume via flat planar cardboard surfaces. (FIG. 24-18 reproduces the maquette, or model. The finished sculpture was to be made of sheet metal.) By presenting what is essentially a cutaway view of a guitar, Picasso allowed the viewer to examine both surface and interior space, both mass and void. This approach, of course, was completely in keeping with the Cubist program. Some scholars have suggested that Picasso derived the cylindrical form that serves as the sound hole on the guitar from the eyes on masks from the Ivory Coast of Africa. African masks were a continuing and persistent source of inspiration for the artist (see "Primitivism," page 696). Here, however, Picasso seems to have transformed the anatomical features of African masks into a part of a musical instrument—dramatic evidence of his unique, innovative artistic vision. Ironically—and intentionally—the sound hole, the central void in a real guitar, is, in Picasso's guitar, the only solid form.

JACQUES LIPCHITZ One of the most successful sculptors to adapt into three dimensions the planar, fragmented dissolution of form central to Analytic Cubist painting was JACQUES LIPCHITZ (1891–1973). Born in Lithuania, Lipchitz resided for many years in France and the United States. He worked out his ideas for many of his sculptures in clay before creating them in bronze or in stone. *Bather* (FIG. 24-19) is typical of his Cubist style. Lipchitz broke the continuous form of the human body into cubic volumes and planes. The interlocking and gracefully intersecting irregular facets and curves recall the paintings of Picasso and Braque and represent a parallel analysis of dynamic form in space. Lipchitz later produced less volumetric sculptures that included empty spaces outlined by metal shapes. In these sculptures, Lipchitz pursued even further the Cubist notion of spatial ambiguity and the relationship between solid forms and space.

ALEKSANDR ARCHIPENKO The Russian sculptor ALEKSANDR ARCHIPENKO (1887–1964) explored similar ideas, as seen in *Woman Combing Her Hair* (FIG. 24-20). In this statuette Archipenko introduced, in place of the head, a void with a shape of its

24-19 JACQUES LIPCHITZ, *Bather*, 1917. Bronze, $2' 10\frac{3}{4}'' \times 1' 1\frac{1}{4}'' \times 1' 1''$. Nelson-Atkins Museum of Art, Kansas City (gift of the Friends of Art).

The interlocking and gracefully intersecting irregular facets and curves of Lipchitz's *Bather* recall the Cubist paintings of Picasso and Braque and represent a parallel analysis of dynamic form in space.

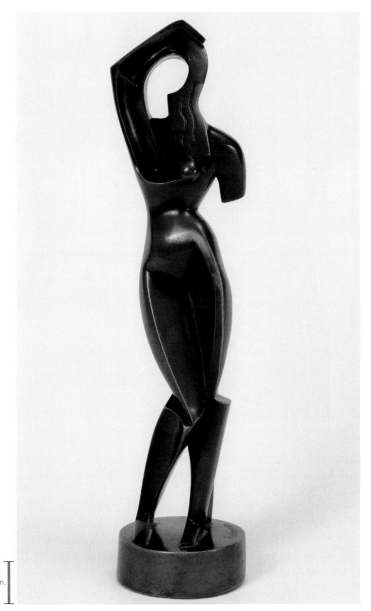

24-20 ALEKSANDR ARCHIPENKO, *Woman Combing Her Hair*, 1915. Bronze, 1′ 1¾″ × 3¼″ × 3⅛″. Museum of Modern Art, New York (acquired through the Lillie P. Bliss Bequest).

In this statuette Archipenko introduced, in place of the head, a void with a shape of its own that figures importantly in the whole design. The void is not simply the negative counterpart of the volume.

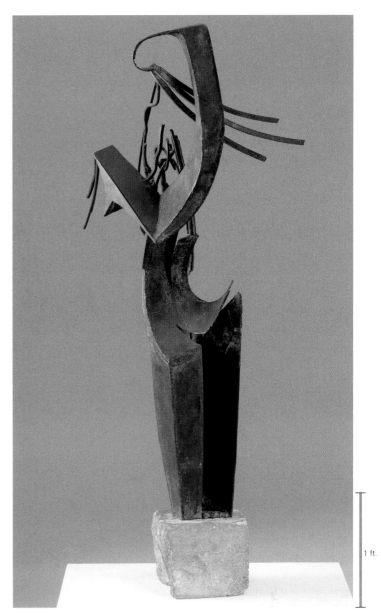

1 ft.

24-21 JULIO GONZÁLEZ, *Woman Combing Her Hair*, 1936. Iron, 4′ 4″ × 1′ 11½″ × 2′ ⅝″. Museum of Modern Art, New York (Mrs. Simon Guggenheim Fund).

Using prefabricated metal pieces, González reduced his figure to an interplay of curves, lines, and planes—virtually a complete abstraction without any vestiges of traditional representational art.

own that figures importantly in the whole design. Enclosed spaces have always existed in figurative sculpture—for example, the space between the arm and the body when the hand rests on the hip (FIG. **16-13**). But here the space penetrates the figure's continuous mass and is a defined form equal in importance to the mass of the bronze. It is not simply the negative counterpart to the volume. Archipenko's figure shows the same fluid intersecting planes seen in Cubist painting, and the relation of the planes to each other is similarly complex. Thus, in both painting and sculpture, the Cubists broke through traditional limits and transformed the medium.

JULIO GONZÁLEZ   A friend of Picasso, JULIO GONZÁLEZ (1876–1942) shared his interest in the artistic possibilities of new materials and new methods borrowed from both industrial technology and traditional metalworking. Born into a family of metalworkers in Barcelona, González helped Picasso construct a number of welded sculptures. This contact with Picasso in turn allowed González

to refine his own sculptural vocabulary. Using prefabricated bars, sheets, or rods of welded or wrought iron and bronze, González created dynamic sculptures with both linear elements and volumetric forms. A comparison between his *Woman Combing Her Hair* (FIG. **24-21**) and Archipenko's version of the same subject (FIG. **24-20**) is instructive. Archipenko's figure still incorporates the basic shapes of a woman's body. González reduced his figure to an interplay of curves, lines, and planes—virtually a complete abstraction without any vestiges of traditional representational art. Although González's sculpture received limited exposure during his lifetime, his work had a great impact on later abstract artists working in welded metal.

FERNAND LÉGER AND PURISM   Le Corbusier is today best known as one of the most important modernist architects (FIG. **24-75**), but he was also a painter. In 1918 he founded a movement called *Purism,* which opposed Synthetic Cubism on the grounds that it was becoming merely an esoteric, decorative art out of touch with

24-22 FERNAND LÉGER, *The City*, 1919. Oil on canvas, 7' 7" × 9' 9½". Philadelphia Museum of Art, Philadelphia (A. E. Gallatin Collection).

Léger was a champion of the "machine aesthetic." In *The City*, he depicted the mechanical commotion of urban life, incorporating the effects of billboard advertisements, flashing lights, and noisy traffic.

1 ft.

the machine age. Purists maintained that machinery's clean functional lines and the pure forms of its parts should direct the artist's experiments in design, whether in painting, architecture, or industrially produced objects. This "machine aesthetic" inspired FERNAND LÉGER (1881–1955), a French painter who early on had painted with the Cubists. He devised an effective compromise of tastes, bringing together meticulous Cubist analysis of form with Purism's broad simplification and machinelike finish of the design components. He retained from his Cubist practice a preference for cylindrical and tube-shaped motifs, suggestive of machined parts such as pistons and cylinders.

Léger's works have the sharp precision of the machine, whose beauty and quality he was one of the first artists to discover. For example, in his film *Ballet Mécanique* (1924), Léger contrasted inanimate objects such as functioning machines with humans in dancelike variations. Preeminently the painter of modern urban life, Léger incorporated into his work the massive effects of modern posters and billboard advertisements, the harsh flashing of electric lights, the noise of traffic, and the robotic movements of mechanized people. These effects appear in *The City* (FIG. **24-22**), an early work that incorporates the aesthetic of Synthetic Cubism. Its monumental scale suggests that Léger, had he been given the opportunity, would have been one of the great mural painters of his age. In a definitive way, he depicted the mechanical commotion of urban life.

Futurism

Artists associated with another major early-20th-century movement, *Futurism*, pursued many of the ideas the Cubists explored. Equally important to the Futurists, however, was their well-defined sociopolitical agenda. Inaugurated and given its name by the charismatic Italian poet and playwright Filippo Tommaso Marinetti (1876–1944) in 1909, Futurism began as a literary movement but soon encompassed the visual arts, cinema, theater, music, and architecture. Indignant over the political and cultural decline of Italy, the Futurists published numerous

manifestos in which they aggressively advocated revolution, both in society and in art. Like Die Brücke and other avant-garde artists, the Futurists aimed at ushering in a new, more enlightened era.

In their quest to launch Italian society toward a glorious future, the Futurists championed war as a means of washing away the stagnant past. Indeed, they saw war as a cleansing agent. Marinetti declared: "We will glorify war—the only true hygiene of the world."[10] The Futurists agitated for the destruction of museums, libraries, and

1 ft.

24-23 GIACOMO BALLA, *Dynamism of a Dog on a Leash*, 1912. Oil on canvas, 2' 11⅜" × 3' 7¼". Albright-Knox Art Gallery, Buffalo (bequest of A. Conger Goodyear, gift of George F. Goodyear, 1964).

The Futurists' interest in motion and in the Cubist dissection of form is evident in Balla's painting of a passing dog and its owner. Simultaneity of views was central to the Futurist program.

Futurist Manifestos

On April 11, 1910, a group of young Italian artists published *Futurist Painting: Technical Manifesto* in Milan in an attempt to apply the writer Filippo Tommaso Marinetti's views on literature to the visual arts. Signed jointly by Umberto Boccioni (FIG. 24-24), Carlo Carrà, Luigi Russolo, Giacomo Balla (FIG. 24-23), and Gino Severini, the manifesto also appeared in an English translation supervised by Marinetti himself. It states in part:

> On account of the persistency of an image on the retina, moving objects constantly multiply themselves [and] their form changes.... Thus a running horse has not four legs, but twenty....

> What was true for the painters of yesterday is but a falsehood today.... To paint a human figure you must not paint it; you must render the whole of its surrounding atmosphere.... [T]he vivifying current of science [must] soon deliver painting from academic tradition.... The shadows which we shall paint shall be more luminous than the highlights of our predecessors, and our pictures, next to those of the museums, will shine like blinding daylight compared with deepest night....

> We declare ... that all forms of imitation must be despised, all forms of originality glorified ... that all subjects previously used must be swept aside in order to express our whirling life of steel, of pride, of fever and of speed ... that movement and light destroy the materiality of bodies.*

Two years later, Boccioni published a *Technical Manifesto of Futurist Sculpture*, in which he argued that traditional sculpture was "a monstrous anachronism" and that modern sculpture should be

> a translation, in plaster, bronze, glass, wood or any other material, of those atmospheric planes which bind and intersect things.... Let's ... proclaim the absolute and complete abolition of finite lines and the contained statue. Let's split open our figures and place the environment inside them. We declare that the environment must form part of the plastic whole.†

Boccioni's own work (FIG. 24-24) is the perfect expression of these principles and goals.

1 ft.

24-24 UMBERTO BOCCIONI, *Unique Forms of Continuity in Space,* 1913 (cast 1931). Bronze, 3' 7$\frac{7}{8}$" × 2' 10$\frac{7}{8}$" × 1' 3$\frac{3}{4}$". Museum of Modern Art, New York (acquired through the Lillie P. Bliss Bequest).

Boccioni's Futurist manifesto for sculpture advocated abolishing the enclosed statue. This running figure is so expanded and interrupted that it almost disappears behind the blur of its movement.

* *Futurist Painting: Technical Manifesto* (*Poesia*, April 11, 1910). Translated by Filippo Tommaso Marinetti, in Umbro Apollonio, ed., *Futurist Manifestos* (Boston: Museum of Fine Arts, 1970), 27–31.

† Translated by Robert Brain, in ibid., 51–65.

---

similar repositories of accumulated culture, which they described as mausoleums. They also called for radical innovation in the arts. Of particular interest to the Futurists were the speed and dynamism of modern technology. Marinetti insisted that a racing "automobile adorned with great pipes like serpents with explosive breath . . . is more beautiful than the *Victory of Samothrace*" (FIG. 5-82, by then representative of classicism and the glories of past civilizations).[11] Appropriately, Futurist art often focuses on motion in time and space, incorporating the Cubist discoveries derived from the analysis of form.

GIACOMO BALLA The Futurists' interest in motion and in the Cubist dissection of form is evident in *Dynamism of a Dog on a Leash* (FIG. 24-23) by GIACOMO BALLA (1871–1958). Here, observers focus their gaze on a passing dog and its owner, whose skirts the artist placed just within visual range. Balla achieved the effect of motion by repeating shapes, as in the dog's legs and tail and in the swinging line of the leash. Simultaneity of views, as demonstrated here, was central to the Futurist program (see "Futurist Manifestos," above).

UMBERTO BOCCIONI One of the artists who cosigned the Futurist manifesto was UMBERTO BOCCIONI (1882–1916), who produced what is perhaps the definitive work of Futurist sculpture, *Unique Forms of Continuity in Space* (FIG. 24-24). This piece highlights the formal and spatial effects of motion rather than their source, the striding human figure. The figure is so expanded, interrupted, and broken in plane and contour that it almost disappears behind the blur of its movement. Boccioni's search for sculptural means for expressing dynamic action reached majestic expression here. In its power and sense of vital activity, this sculpture surpasses similar efforts in Futurist painting to create images symbolic of the dynamic quality of modern life. To be convinced by it, people need only reflect on how details of an adjacent landscape appear in their peripheral vision when they are traveling at great speed on a highway or in a low-flying airplane. Although Boccioni's figure bears a curious resemblance to the ancient *Nike of Samothrace* (FIG. 5-82), even a cursory comparison reveals how far the modern work departs from the ancient one.

24-25 GINO SEVERINI, *Armored Train*, 1915. Oil on canvas, 3′ 10″ × 2′ 10⅛″. Collection of Richard S. Zeisler, New York.

Severini's glistening armored train with protruding cannon reflects the Futurist faith in the cleansing action of war. The painting captures the dynamism and motion central to the Futurist manifesto.

This Futurist representation of motion in sculpture has its limitations. The eventual development of the motion picture, based on the rapid sequential projection of fixed images, produced more convincing illusions of movement. And several decades later in sculpture, Alexander Calder (FIG. **24-61**) pioneered the development of kinetic sculpture—with parts that really move. However, in the early 20th century, Boccioni's sculpture was notable for its ability to capture the sensation of motion.

GINO SEVERINI The painting *Armored Train* (FIG. **24-25**) by GINO SEVERINI (1883–1966) nicely encapsulates the Futurist program, both artistically and politically. The artist depicted a high-tech armored train with its rivets glistening and a huge booming cannon protruding from the top. Submerged in the bowels of the train, a row of soldiers train guns at an unseen target. Severini's painting reflects the Futurist faith in the cleansing action of war. Not only are the colors predominantly light and bright, but the artist also omitted death and destruction—the tragic consequences of war—from the image. This sanitized depiction of war contrasts sharply with Francisco Goya's *Third of May, 1808* (FIG. **22-13**), which also depicts a uniform row of anonymous soldiers in the act of shooting. Goya, however, graphically presented the dead and those about to be shot, and the dark tones of the work cast a dramatic and sobering pall. *Armored Train* captures the dynamism and motion central to Futurism.

In Cubist fashion, Severini depicted all of the objects, from the soldiers to the smoke emanating from the cannon, broken into facets and planes, suggesting action and movement. Once World War I broke out, the Futurist group began to disintegrate, largely because so many of them felt compelled (given the Futurist support for the war) to join the Italian army. Some of them, including Umberto Boccioni, died in the war. The ideas the Futurists promoted became integral to the Fascism that emerged in Italy shortly thereafter.

Dada

Although the Futurists celebrated World War I and the changes they hoped it would effect, the mass destruction and chaos that conflict unleashed horrified other artists. Humanity had never before witnessed such wholesale slaughter on so grand a scale over such an extended period. Millions died or sustained grievous wounds in great battles. For example, in 1916, the battle of Verdun (lasting five months) left 500,000 casualties. On another day in 1916, the British lost 60,000 men in the opening battle of the Somme. The new technology of armaments, bred of the age of steel, made it a "war of the guns" (as in Severini's *Armored Train*; FIG. **24-25**). In the face of massed artillery hurling millions of tons of high explosives and gas shells and in the sheets of fire from thousands of machine guns, attack was suicidal, and battle movement congealed into the stalemate of trench warfare, stretching from the English Channel almost to Switzerland. The mud, filth, and blood of the trenches, the pounding and shattering of incessant shell fire, and the terrible deaths and mutilations were a devastating psychological, as well as physical, experience for a generation brought up with the doctrine of progress and a belief in the fundamental values of civilization.

With the war as a backdrop, many artists contributed to an artistic and literary movement that became known as *Dada*. This movement emerged, in large part, in reaction to what many of these artists saw as nothing more than an insane spectacle of collective homicide. Although Dada began independently in New York and Zurich, it also emerged in Paris, Berlin, and Cologne, among other cities. Dada was more a mind-set or attitude than a single identifiable style. As André Breton (1896–1966), founder of the slightly later Surrealist movement, explained: "Cubism was a school of painting, futurism a political movement: DADA is a state of mind."[12] The Dadaists believed reason and logic had been responsible for the unmitigated disaster of global warfare, and they concluded that the only route to salvation was through political anarchy, the irrational, and the intuitive. Thus, an element of absurdity is a cornerstone of Dada, even reflected in the movement's name. There are many explanations for the choice of "Dada," but according to an often repeated anecdote, the Dadaists chose the word at random from a French-German dictionary. Dada is French for a child's hobbyhorse. The word satisfied the Dadaists' desire for something irrational and nonsensical.

The Dadaists' pessimism and disgust surfaced in their disdain for convention and tradition. These artists made a concerted and sustained attempt to undermine cherished notions and assumptions about art. Because of this destructive dimension, art historians often describe Dada as a nihilistic enterprise. Dada's nihilism and its derisive iconoclasm can be read at random from the Dadaists' numerous manifestos and declarations of intent:

> Dada knows everything. Dada spits on everything. Dada says
> "knowthing," Dada has no fixed ideas. Dada does not catch flies.
> Dada is bitterness laughing at everything that has been accomplished,
> sanctified.... Dada is never right.... No more painters, no more
> writers, no more religions, no more royalists, no more anarchists,
> no more socialists, no more police, no more airplanes, no more uri-
> nary passages.... Like everything in life, Dada is useless, everything

happens in a completely idiotic way. . . . We are incapable of treating seriously any subject whatsoever, let alone this subject: ourselves.[13]

Although cynicism and pessimism inspired the Dadaists, the movement they developed was phenomenally influential and powerful. By attacking convention and logic, the Dada artists unlocked new avenues for creative invention, thereby fostering a more serious examination of the basic premises of art than had prior movements. But the Dadaists could also be lighthearted in their subversiveness. Although horror and disgust about the war initially prompted Dada, an undercurrent of humor and whimsy—sometimes sardonic or irreverent—runs through much of the art. For example, Marcel Duchamp (see page 706) painted a mustache and goatee on a reproduction of Leonardo da Vinci's *Mona Lisa*. The French painter Francis Picabia (1879–1953), Duchamp's collaborator in setting up Dada in New York, nailed a toy monkey to a board and labeled it *Portrait of Cézanne*.

In its emphasis on the spontaneous and intuitive, Dada paralleled the views of Sigmund Freud (1856–1939) and Carl Jung (1875–1961). Freud was a Viennese doctor who developed the fundamental principles for what became known as psychoanalysis. In his book *The Interpretation of Dreams* (1900), Freud argued that the unconscious and inner drives (of which people are largely unaware) control human behavior. Jung, a Swiss psychiatrist who developed Freud's theories further, believed that the unconscious is composed of two facets, a personal unconscious and a collective unconscious. The collective unconscious comprises memories and associations all humans share, such as archetypes and mental constructions. According to Jung, the collective unconscious accounts for the development of myths, religions, and philosophies.

Particularly interested in the exploration of the unconscious as Freud advocated, the Dada artists believed that art was a powerfully practical means of self-revelation and catharsis, and that the images arising out of the subconscious mind had a truth of their own, independent of conventional vision. A Dada filmmaker, Hans Richter (1888–1976), summarized the attitude of the Dadaists:

> Possessed, as we were, of the ability to entrust ourselves to "chance," to our conscious as well as our unconscious minds, we became a sort of public secret society. . . . We laughed at everything. . . . But laughter was only the expression of our new discoveries, not their essence and not their purpose. Pandemonium, destruction, anarchy, anti-everything of the World War? How could Dada have been anything but destructive, aggressive, insolent, on principle and with gusto?[14]

JEAN ARP A Dada artist whose works illustrate Richter's element of chance was Zurich-based JEAN (HANS) ARP (1887–1966). Arp pioneered the use of chance in composing his images. Tiring of the look of some Cubist-related collages he was making, he took some sheets of paper, tore them into roughly shaped squares, haphazardly dropped them onto a sheet of paper on the floor, and glued them into the resulting arrangement. The rectilinearity of the shapes guaranteed a somewhat regular design (which Arp no doubt enhanced by adjusting the random arrangement into a quasi-grid), but chance had introduced an imbalance that seemed to Arp to restore to his work a special mysterious vitality he wanted to preserve. *Collage Arranged According to the Laws of Chance* (FIG. **24-26**) is a work he created by this method. The operations of chance were for Dadaists a crucial part of this kind of improvisation. As Richter stated: "For us chance was the 'unconscious mind' that Freud had discovered in 1900. . . . Adoption of chance had another purpose, a secret one. This was to restore to the work of art its primeval magic power and to find a way back to the immediacy it had lost through contact with . . . classicism."[15] Arp's renunciation of artis-

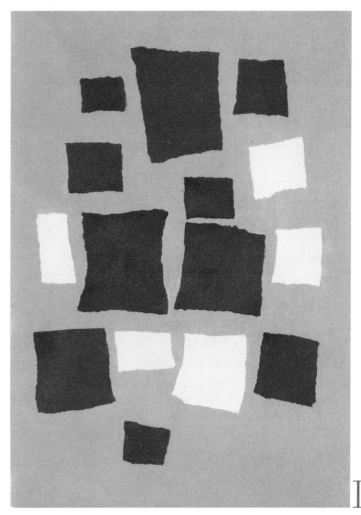

24-26 JEAN (HANS) ARP, *Collage Arranged According to the Laws of Chance,* 1916–1917. Torn and pasted paper, $1' 7\frac{1}{8}'' \times 1' 1\frac{5}{8}''$. Museum of Modern Art, New York.

In this collage, Arp dropped torn paper squares onto a sheet of paper and then glued them into the resulting arrangement. His reliance on chance in composing images reinforced the anarchy inherent in Dada.

tic control and reliance on chance when creating his compositions reinforced the anarchy and subversiveness inherent in Dada.

CABARET VOLTAIRE Among the manifestations of Dada that matured in 1916 in Zurich were the performances presented at the Cabaret Voltaire, founded by Dadaist Hugo Ball (1886–1927), a poet, musician, and theatrical producer. The first Dada performances were fairly tame, consisting of musical presentations and poetry readings. In keeping with Dada thought, however, they quickly became more aggressive, anarchic, and illogical. Tristan Tzara (1896–1963) described one of these performances in characteristically absurd Dadaist language:

> Boxing resumed: Cubist dance, costumes by Janco, each man his own big drum on his head, noise, Negro music/trabatgea bonooooooo oo ooooo/5 literary experiments; Tzara in tails stands before the curtain, stone sober for the animals, and explains the new aesthetic: gymnastic poem, concert of vowels, bruitist poem, static poem chemical arrangement of ideas, 'Biriboom biriboom' saust der Ochs im Kreis herum (the ox dashes round in a ring) (Huelsenbeck), vowel poem a a ò, i e o, a i ï, new interpretation of subjective folly of the arteries the dance of the heart on burning buildings and acrobatics in the audience.[16]

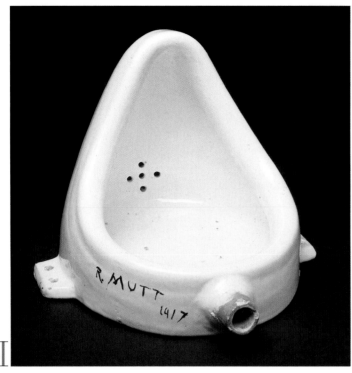

1 in.

24-27 MARCEL DUCHAMP, *Fountain* (second version), 1950 (original version produced 1917). Readymade glazed sanitary china with black paint, 1′ high. Philadelphia Museum of Art, Philadelphia.

Duchamp's "readymade" sculptures were mass-produced objects that the Dada artist modified. In *Fountain*, he conferred the status of art on a urinal and forced people to see the object in a new light.

MARCEL DUCHAMP Perhaps the most influential Dadaist was MARCEL DUCHAMP (1887–1968), a Frenchman who became the central artist of New York Dada but was also active in Paris. In 1913 he exhibited his first "readymade" sculptures, which were mass-produced common objects—"found objects" the artist selected and sometimes "rectified" by modifying their substance or combining them with another object. The creation of readymades, he insisted, was free from any consideration of either good or bad taste, qualities shaped by a society he and other Dada artists found aesthetically bankrupt. Perhaps his most outrageous readymade was *Fountain* (FIG. **24-27**), a porcelain urinal presented on its back, signed "R. Mutt," and dated. The "artist's signature" was, in fact, a witty pseudonym derived from the Mott plumbing company's name and that of the short half of the then-popular Mutt and Jeff comic-strip team. As with Duchamp's other readymades, he did not select this object for exhibition because of its aesthetic qualities. The "art" of this "artwork" lies in the artist's choice of object, which has the effect of conferring the status of art on it and forces the viewer to see the object in a new light. As he wrote in a "defense" published in 1917, after an exhibition committee rejected *Fountain* for display: "Whether Mr. Mutt with his own hands made the fountain or not has no importance. He CHOSE it. He took an ordinary article of life, placed it so that its useful significance disappeared under the new title and point of view—created a new thought for that object."[17] It is hard to imagine a more aggressively avant-garde approach to art. Dada persistently presented staggering challenges to artistic conventions.

THE LARGE GLASS Among the most visually and conceptually challenging of Duchamp's works is *The Bride Stripped Bare by Her Bachelors, Even* (FIG. **24-28**), often referred to as *The Large Glass*. Begun in 1915 and abandoned by Duchamp as unfinished in 1923,

1 ft.

24-28 MARCEL DUCHAMP, *The Bride Stripped Bare by Her Bachelors, Even* (*The Large Glass*), 1915–1923. Oil, lead, wire, foil, dust, and varnish on glass, 9′ 1½″ × 5′ 9⅛″. Philadelphia Museum of Art, Philadelphia (Katherine S. Dreier Bequest).

The Large Glass is a simultaneously playful and serious examination of humans as machines. The bride is a motor fueled by "love gasoline," and the male figures in the lower half also move mechanically.

The Large Glass is a simultaneously playful and serious examination of humans as machines. Consisting of oil paint, wire, and lead foil sandwiched in between two large glass panels, the artwork presents the viewer with an array of images, some apparently mechanical, others diagrammatic, and yet others seemingly abstract in nature. Duchamp provided some clues to the intriguing imagery in a series of notes that accompanied the work. The top half of the work represents "the bride," whom Duchamp has depicted as "basically a motor" fueled by "love gasoline." In contrast, the bachelors appear as uniformed male figures in the lower half of the work. They too move mechanically. The chocolate grinder in the center of the lower glass pane represents masturbation ("the bachelor grinds his own chocolate"). In *The Large Glass*, Duchamp provided his own whimsical but insightful ruminations into the ever-confounding realm of desire and sexuality. In true Dadaist fashion, chance completed the work. During the transportation of *The Large Glass* from an exhibition in 1927, the glass panes shattered. Rather than replace the broken glass, Duchamp painstakingly pieced together the glass fragments. After encasing the recon-

1 ft.

sity a technique that had been used in private and popular arts long before the 20th century to create a composition by pasting together pieces of paper. A few years earlier, the Cubists had named the process "collage." The Berliners christened their version of the technique *photomontage.* Unlike Cubist collage (FIGS. 24-16 and 24-17), the parts of a Dada collage consisted almost entirely of "found" details, such as pieces of magazine photographs, usually combined into deliberately antilogical compositions. Collage lent itself well to the Dada desire to use chance when creating art and antiart, but not all Dada collage was as savagely aggressive as that of the Berlin photomontagists.

structed work, broken panes and all, between two heavier panes of glass, Duchamp declared the work completed "by chance."

Duchamp (and the generations of later artists who were profoundly influenced by his art and especially his attitude) considered life and art matters of chance and choice freed from the conventions of society and tradition. Within his approach to art and life, each act was individual and unique. Every person's choice of found objects would be different, for example, and each person's throw of the dice would be at a different instant and probably would yield a different number. This philosophy of utter freedom for artists was fundamental to the history of art in the 20th century. Duchamp spent much of World War I in New York, inspiring a group of American artists and collectors with his radical rethinking of the role of artists and of the nature of art.

HANNAH HÖCH Dada spread throughout much of western Europe, arriving as early as 1917 in Berlin, where it soon took on an activist political edge, partially in response to the economic, social, and political chaos in that city in the years at the end of and immediately after World War I. The Berlin Dadaists developed to a new inten-

One of the Berlin Dadaists who perfected the photomontage technique was HANNAH HÖCH (1889–1978). Höch's photomontages advanced the absurd illogic of Dada by presenting the viewer with chaotic, contradictory, and satiric compositions. They also provided insightful and scathing commentary on two of the most dramatic developments during the Weimar Republic (1918–1933) in Germany—the redefinition of women's social roles and the explosive growth of mass print media. She revealed these combined themes in *Cut with the Kitchen Knife Dada through the Last Weimar Beer Belly Cultural Epoch of Germany* (FIG. 24-29). In this work Höch arranged an eclectic mixture of cutout photos in seemingly haphazard fashion. On closer inspection, however, the viewer can see that the artist carefully placed photographs of some of her fellow Dadaists among images of Marx, Lenin, and other revolutionary figures in the lower right section, aligning this movement with other revolutionary forces. She promoted Dada in prominently placed cutout lettering—"Die grosse Welt dada" (the great Dada world). Certainly, juxtaposing the heads of German military leaders with exotic dancers' bodies provided the wickedly humorous critique central to much of Dada. Höch also positioned herself in this topsy-turvy world she created.

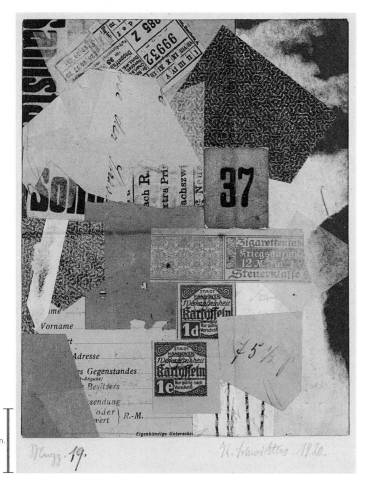

1 in.

24-30 KURT SCHWITTERS, *Merz 19*, 1920. Paper collage, $7\frac{1}{4}'' \times 5\frac{7}{8}''$. Yale University Art Gallery, New Haven (gift of Collection Société Anonyme).

Inspired by Cubist collage but working nonobjectively, Schwitters found visual poetry in the cast-off junk of modern society, which he pasted and nailed together into striking Dada compositions.

A photograph of her head appears in the lower right corner, juxtaposed with a map of Europe showing the progress of women's enfranchisement. Aware of the power both women and Dada had to destabilize society, Höch made forceful visual manifestations of that belief.

KURT SCHWITTERS The Hanover Dada artist KURT SCHWITTERS (1887–1948) followed a gentler muse. Inspired by Cubist collage but working nonobjectively, Schwitters found visual poetry in the cast-off junk of modern society and scavenged in trash bins for materials, which he pasted and nailed together into designs such as *Merz 19* (FIG. **24-30**). The term "Merz," which Schwitters used as a generic title for a whole series of collages, derived nonsensically from the German word Kommerzbank (commerce bank) and appeared as a word fragment in one of his compositions. Although nonobjective, his collages still resonate with the meaning of the fragmented found objects they contain. The recycled elements of Schwitters's collages, like Duchamp's readymades, acquire new meanings through their new uses and locations. Elevating objects that are essentially trash to the status of high art certainly fits within the parameters of the Dada program and parallels the absurd dimension of much of Dada art. Contradiction, paradox, irony, and even blasphemy are Dada's bequest. They are, in the view of Dada and its successors, the free and defiant artist's weapons in what has been called the hundred years' war with the public.

AMERICA, 1900 TO 1930

Avant-garde experiments in the arts were not limited to Europe. A wide range of artists engaged in a lively exchange of artistic ideas and significant transatlantic travel. In the latter part of the 19th century, American artists such as John Singer Sargent (see Chapter 22), James Abbott McNeil Whistler, and Mary Cassatt (see Chapter 23) spent much of their productive careers in Europe, whereas many European artists ended their careers in America, especially in anticipation of and, later, in the wake of World War I. Visionary patrons sup-

24-31 JOHN SLOAN, *Sixth Avenue and Thirtieth Street, New York City,* 1907. Oil on canvas, $2' \frac{1}{4}'' \times 2' 8''$. Philadelphia Museum of Art, Philadelphia (gift of Meyer P. Potamkin and Vivian O. Potamkin, 2000).

A prominent member of the American Realist group called The Eight, Sloan captured in his paintings the bleak and seedy aspects of the rapidly changing urban landscape of New York City.

1 in.

Art "Matronage" in America

Until the 20th century, the dearth of women artists was often due to professional institutions that restricted women's access to artistic training. For example, the proscription against women participating in life-drawing classes, a staple of academic artistic training, in effect denied women the opportunity to become professional artists. Further, the absence of women from the art historical canon is also partly because art historians have not considered as "high art" many of the art objects women have traditionally produced (for example, quilts or basketry).

By the early 20th century, many of the impediments to women becoming recognized artists had been removed. Today, women are a major presence in the art world. One development in the early 20th century that laid the groundwork for this change was the prominent role women played as art patrons. These "art matrons" provided financial, moral, and political support to cultivate the advancement of the arts in America. Among these women were Gertrude Vanderbilt Whitney, Lillie P. Bliss, Mary Quinn Sullivan, Abby Aldrich Rockefeller, Isabella Stewart Gardner, Peggy Guggenheim, and Jane Stanford.*

Gertrude Vanderbilt Whitney (1875–1942) was a practicing sculptor and enthusiastic collector. To assist young American artists such as Robert Henri and John Sloan (FIG. 24-31) to exhibit their work, she opened the Whitney Studio in 1914. By 1929, dissatisfied with the recognition accorded young, progressive American artists, she offered her entire collection of 500 works to the Metropolitan Museum of Art. Her offer rejected, she founded her own museum, the Whitney Museum of American Art in New York City. She chose as the first director a visionary and energetic woman, Juliana Force (1876–1948), who inaugurated a pioneering series of monographs on living American artists and organized lecture series by influential art historians and critics. Through the efforts of these two women, the Whitney Museum became a major force in American art.

A trip to Paris in 1920 whetted the interest of Peggy Guggenheim (1898–1979) in avant-garde art. Like Whitney, she collected art and eventually opened a gallery in England to exhibit the work of in-novative artists. She continued her support for avant-garde art after her return to the United States. Guggenheim's New York gallery, called Art of This Century, was instrumental in advancing the careers of many artists, including her husband, Max Ernst (FIG. 24-47). She eventually moved her art collection to a lavish Venetian palace, where the public can still view these important artworks.

Other women contributed significantly to the arts, including Lillie P. Bliss (1864–1931), Mary Quinn Sullivan (1877–1939), and Abby Aldrich Rockefeller (1874–1948). Philanthropists, art collectors, and educators, these visionary and influential women saw the need for a museum to collect and exhibit modernist art. Together they established the Museum of Modern Art in New York City in 1929, which became (and continues to be) the most influential museum of modern art in the world (see "The Museum of Modern Art," page 730).

Isabella Stewart Gardner (1840–1924) and Jane Stanford (1828–1905) also undertook the ambitious project of founding museums. The Isabella Stewart Gardner Museum in Boston, established in 1903, contains an impressive collection of art that is comprehensive in scope. The Stanford Museum, the first American museum west of the Mississippi, got its start in 1905 on the grounds of Stanford University, which Leland Stanford Sr. and Jane Stanford founded after the tragic death of their son. The Stanford Museum houses a wide range of objects, including archaeological and ethnographic artifacts. These two driven women committed much of their time, energy, and financial resources to ensure the success of these museums. Both were intimately involved in the day-to-day operations of their institutions.

The museums these women established flourish today, attesting to the extraordinary vision of these "art matrons" and the remarkable contributions they made to the advancement of art in the United States.

* Art historian Wanda Corn coined the term "art matronage" in the catalog *Cultural Leadership in America: Art Matronage and Patronage* (Boston: Isabella Stewart Gardner Museum, 1997).

ported the efforts of American artists to pursue modernist ideas (see "Art 'Matronage' in America," above).

Painting and Sculpture

The art scene in America before the establishment of a significant and consistent dialogue with European modernists was, of course, quite varied. However, many American artists active in the early 20th century were committed to presenting what they considered to be a realistic, unvarnished look at life. In this regard, their work parallels that of the French Realists in the mid-19th century (see Chapter 22).

JOHN SLOAN AND THE EIGHT One group of American Realist artists, The Eight, consisted of eight painters who gravitated into the circle of the influential and evangelical artist and teacher Robert Henri (1865–1929). Henri urged his followers to make "pictures from life,"[18] and accordingly, these artists pursued with zeal the production of images depicting the rapidly changing urban landscape of New York City. Because these vignettes often captured the bleak and seedy aspects of city life, The Eight eventually became known as the Ash Can School. Some critics referred to them as "the apostles of ugliness."

A prominent member of The Eight was JOHN SLOAN (1871–1951). A self-described "incorrigible window watcher,"[19] Sloan constantly wandered the streets of New York, observing human drama. He focused much of his attention on the working class, which he perceived as embodying the realities of life. So sympathetic was Sloan to the working class that he joined the Socialist Party in 1909 and eventually ran for public office on the Socialist ticket. In paintings such as *Sixth Avenue and Thirtieth Street* (FIG. 24-31), Sloan revealed his ability to capture both the visual and social realities of American urban life shortly after the turn of the century. When he painted this image in 1907, Sloan was living on West 23rd Street, on the outskirts

The Armory Show

From February 17 to March 15, 1913, the American public flocked in large numbers to view the International Exhibition of Modern Art (FIG. 24-32) at the 69th Regiment Armory in New York City. The "Armory Show," as it came universally to be called, was an ambitious endeavor organized primarily by two artists, Walt Kuhn (1877–1949) and Arthur B. Davies (1862–1928). The show contained more than 1,600 artworks by American and European artists. Among the European artists represented were Matisse, Derain, Picasso, Braque, Duchamp, Kandinsky, Kirchner, Lehmbruck, and Brancusi. In addition to exposing American artists and the public to the latest in European artistic developments, this show also provided American artists with a prime showcase for their work. The foreword to the exhibition catalogue spelled out the goals of the organizers:

> The American artists exhibiting here consider the exhibition of equal importance for themselves as for the public. The less they find their work showing signs of the developments indicated in the Europeans, the more reason they will have to consider whether or not painters or sculptors here have fallen behind . . . the forces that have manifested themselves on the other side of the Atlantic.*

24-32 Installation photo of the Armory Show, New York National Guard's 69th Regiment, New York, 1913. Museum of Modern Art, New York.

The groundbreaking Armory Show introduced European modernism to the American public. Works like Duchamp's *Nude Descending a Staircase* (FIG. 24-1) received a hostile reception in the press.

On its opening, this provocative exhibition served as a lightning rod for commentary, immediately attracting heated controversy. The *New York Times* described the show as "pathological" and called the modernist artists "cousins to the anarchists," while the magazine *Art and Progress* compared them to "bomb throwers, lunatics, depravers."[†] Other critics demanded the exhibition be closed as a menace to public morality. The *New York Herald,* for example, asserted: "The United States is invaded by aliens, thousands of whom constitute so many perils to the health of the body politic. Modernism is of precisely the same heterogeneous alien origin and is imperiling the republic of art in the same way."[‡]

Nonetheless, the exhibition was an important milestone in the history of art in the United States. The Armory Show traveled to Chicago and Boston after it closed in New York and was a significant catalyst for the reevaluation of the nature and purpose of American art.

---

* Quoted in Herschel B. Chipp, *Theories of Modern Art: A Source Book by Artists and Critics* (Berkeley and Los Angeles: University of California Press, 1968), 503.
[†] Quoted in Sam Hunter, John Jacobus, and Daniel Wheeler, *Modern Art,* rev. 3d ed. (Upper Saddle Hill, N.J.: Prentice Hall, 2005), 250.
[‡] Quoted in Francis K. Pohl, *Framing America: A Social History of American Art* (New York: Thames & Hudson, 2002), 321.

---

of the Tenderloin District, an area cluttered with brothels, dance halls, saloons, gambling dens, and cheap hotels. *Sixth Avenue* depicts a bustling intersection. Bracketing the throngs of people filling the intersection are elevated train tracks on the left and a row of storefronts and apartment buildings on the right side of the painting. These two defining elements of city life converge in the far center background. Sloan's paintings also capture a slice of American urban life in the cross-section of people depicted. In the foreground of *Sixth Avenue,* Sloan prominently placed three women. One, in a shabby white dress, is a drunkard, stumbling along with her pail of beer. Two streetwalkers stare at her. In turn, two well-dressed men gaze at the prostitutes. Sloan's depiction of the women allied him with reformers of the time, who saw streetwalkers not as immoral but as victims of an unfair social and economic system. At a time

when traditional art centered on genteel and proper society, Sloan's forthright depiction of prostitutes was categorically "Realist."

ARMORY SHOW One of the major vehicles for disseminating information about European artistic developments in the United States was the Armory Show (FIG. 24-32), held in early 1913 (see "The Armory Show," above). The exhibition received a hostile response from the press. The work the journalists and critics most maligned was Marcel Duchamp's *Nude Descending a Staircase, No. 2* (FIG. 24-1). The painting, a single figure in motion down a staircase in a time continuum, suggests the effect of a sequence of overlaid film stills. Unlike Duchamp's contributions to the Dada movement (FIGS. 24-27 and 24-28), *Nude Descending a Staircase* has much in common with the work of the Cubists and the Futurists.

The monochromatic palette is reminiscent of Analytic Cubism, as is Duchamp's faceted presentation of the human form. The artist's interest in depicting the figure in motion reveals an affinity for the Futurists' ideas. One critic described this work as "an explosion in a shingle factory,"[20] and newspaper cartoonists had a field day lampooning the painting.

MAN RAY One American artist to incorporate the latest European trends in his work was Emmanuel Radnitzky, known as MAN RAY (1890–1976), who was a close associate of Duchamp in the 1920s. Man Ray produced art with a decidedly Dada spirit, often incorporating found objects in his paintings, sculptures, movies, and photographs. Trained as an architectural draftsman and engineer, Man Ray earned his living as a graphic designer and portrait photographer. He brought to his personal work an interest in mass-produced objects and technology, as well as a dedication to exploring the psychological realm of human perception of the exterior world. Like Schwitters, Man Ray used chance and the dislocation of ordinary things from their everyday settings to surprise his viewers into new awareness. His displacement of found objects was particularly effective in works such as *Cadeau* (*Gift*; FIG. **24-33**). For this sculpture, Man Ray—with characteristic Dada humor—equipped a laundry iron with a row of wicked-looking spikes, subverting its proper function of smoothing and pressing.

MARSDEN HARTLEY Other American artists developed personal styles that intersected with movements such as Cubism. MARSDEN HARTLEY (1877–1943) traveled to Europe in 1912, visiting Paris, where he became acquainted with the work of the Cubists, and Munich, where he gravitated to the Blaue Reiter circle. Kandinsky's work particularly impressed Hartley, and he developed a style he called "Cosmic Cubism." He took these influences with him when he landed in Berlin in 1913. With the heightened militarism in Germany and the eventual outbreak of World War I, Hartley immersed himself in military imagery. Among his most famous paintings of this period is *Portrait of a German Officer* (FIG. **24-34**). It depicts an array of military-related images: German imperial flags, regimental insignia, badges, and emblems such as the Iron Cross. Although this image resonates in the general context of wartime militarism, elements in the painting did have personal significance for Hartley. In particular, the painting includes references to his lover, Lieutenant Karl von Freyberg, who lost his life in battle a few months before Hartley painted this work. Von Freyberg's initials appear in the lower

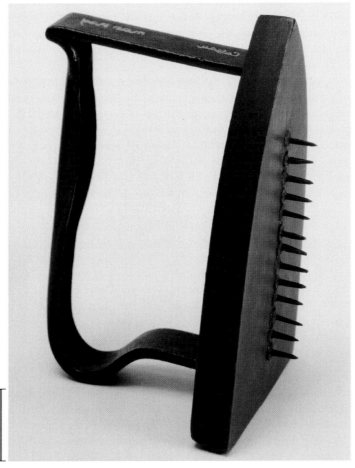

1 in.

24-33 MAN RAY, *Cadeau* (*Gift*), ca. 1958 (replica of 1921 original). **Painted flatiron with row of 13 tacks with heads glued to the bottom, $6\frac{1}{8}'' \times 3\frac{5}{8}'' \times 4\frac{1}{2}''$. Museum of Modern Art, New York (James Thrall Soby Fund).**

With characteristic Dada humor, the American artist Man Ray equipped a laundry iron with a row of wicked-looking spikes, subverting its proper function of smoothing and pressing.

1 ft.

24-34 MARSDEN HARTLEY, *Portrait of a German Officer*, 1914. Oil on canvas, $5'\,8\frac{1}{4}'' \times 3'\,5\frac{3}{8}''$. Metropolitan Museum of Art, New York (Alfred Stieglitz Collection).

In this elegy to a lover killed in battle, Hartley arranged military-related images against a somber black background. The flattened, planar presentation reveals the influence of Synthetic Cubism.

left corner. His age when he died (24) appears in the lower right corner, and his regiment number (4) appears in the center of the painting. Also incorporated is the letter *E* for von Freyberg's regiment, the Bavarian Eisenbahn. The influence of Synthetic Cubism is evident in the flattened, planar presentation of the elements, which almost appear as abstract patterns. The somber black background against which the artist placed the colorful stripes, patches, and shapes casts an elegiac pall over the painting.

STUART DAVIS Philadelphia-born STUART DAVIS (1894–1964) created what he believed was a modern American art style by combining the flat shapes of Synthetic Cubism with his sense of jazz tempos and his perception of the energy of fast-paced American culture.

1 in.

24-35 STUART DAVIS, *Lucky Strike,* 1921. Oil on canvas, 2′ 9$\frac{1}{4}$″ × 1′ 6″. Museum of Modern Art, New York (gift of the American Tobacco Company, Inc.). Art © Estate of Stuart Davis/Licensed by VAGA, New York.

Tobacco products fascinated Davis, a heavy smoker. In *Lucky Strike,* he depicted a cigarette package in fragmented form, reminiscent of Cubism, and imbued his painting with an American jazz rhythm.

Lucky Strike (FIG. **24-35**) is one of several tobacco still lifes Davis began in 1921. Davis was a heavy smoker, and tobacco products and their packaging fascinated him. He insisted that the late-19th-century introduction of packaging was evidence of high civilization and therefore, he concluded, of the progressiveness of American culture. Davis depicted the Lucky Strike package in fragmented form, reminiscent of Synthetic Cubist collages. However, although the work does incorporate flat printed elements, these are illusionistically painted rather than glued onto the canvas surface. The discontinuities and the interlocking planes imbue *Lucky Strike* with a dynamism and rhythm not unlike American jazz or the pace of life in a lively American metropolis. This work is both resolutely American and modern.

AARON DOUGLAS Also deriving his personal style from Synthetic Cubism was African American artist AARON DOUGLAS (1898–1979), who used the style to represent symbolically the historical and cultural memories of African Americans. Born in Kansas, Douglas studied in Nebraska and Paris before settling in New York City, where he became part of the flowering of art and literature in the 1920s known as the Harlem Renaissance. Spearheaded by writers and editors Alain Locke and Charles Johnson, the Harlem Renaissance was a manifestation of the desire of African Americans to promote their cultural accomplishments. They also aimed to cultivate pride among fellow African Americans and to foster racial tolerance across the United States. Expansive and diverse, the fruits of the Harlem Renaissance included the writings of authors such as Langston Hughes, Countee Cullen, and Zora Neale Hurston; the jazz and blues of Duke Ellington, Bessie Smith, Eubie Blake, Fats Waller, and Louis Armstrong; the photographs of James Van Der Zee and Prentice H. Polk; and the paintings and sculptures of Meta Warrick Fuller and Augusta Savage.

Aaron Douglas arrived in New York City in 1924 and became one of the most sought-after graphic artists in the African American community. Encouraged to create art that would express the cultural history of his race, Douglas incorporated motifs from African sculpture into compositions painted in a version of Synthetic Cubism that stressed transparent angular planes. *Noah's Ark* (FIG. **24-36**) was one of seven paintings based on a book of poems by James Weldon Johnson (1871–1938) called *God's Trombones: Seven Negro Sermons in Verse.* Douglas used flat planes to evoke a sense of mystical space and miraculous happenings. In *Noah's Ark,* lightning strikes and rays of light crisscross the pairs of animals entering the ark, while men load supplies in preparation for departure. The artist suggested deep space by differentiating the size of the large human head and shoulders of the worker at the bottom and the small person at work on the far deck of the ship. Yet the composition's unmodulated color shapes create a pattern on the Masonite surface that cancels any illusion of three-dimensional depth. Here, Douglas used Cubism's formal language to express a powerful religious vision.

PRECISIONISM It is obvious from viewing American art in the period immediately after the Armory Show that the latest European avant-garde art, from Cubism to Dada, intrigued American artists. However, the Americans did not just passively absorb the ideas transported across the Atlantic. The challenge was to understand the ideas modernist European art presented and then filter them through an American sensibility. Ultimately, many American artists, including a group that became known as Precisionists, set as their goal the development of a uniquely American art.

Precisionism was not an organized movement, but the Precisionists did share certain thematic and stylistic traits in their art, which developed in the 1920s out of a fascination with the machine's precision and importance in modern life. Although many European

24-36 AARON DOUGLAS, *Noah's Ark,* ca. 1927. Oil on Masonite, 4′ × 3′. Fisk University Galleries, University of Tennessee, Nashville.

In *Noah's Ark* and other paintings of the cultural history of African Americans, Douglas incorporated motifs from African sculpture and the transparent angular planes characteristic of Synthetic Cubism.

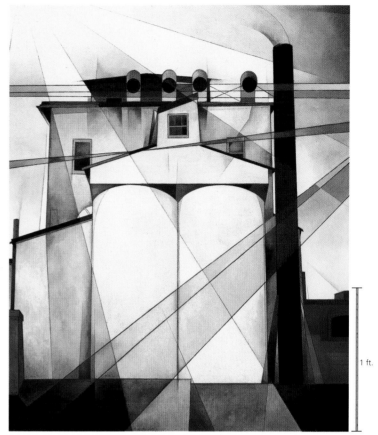

24-37 CHARLES DEMUTH, *My Egypt,* 1927. Oil on composition board, 2′ 11¾″ × 2′ 6″. Collection of Whitney Museum of American Art, New York (purchased with funds from Gertrude Vanderbilt Whitney).

Demuth was one of the leading Precisionists—American artists who extolled the machine age. This painting depicts grain elevators reduced to geometric forms amid Cubist transparent diagonal planes.

artists, especially the Futurists, had demonstrated interest in burgeoning technology, Americans generally seemed more enamored by the prospects of a mechanized society than did Europeans. Even the Frenchman Francis Picabia, Duchamp's collaborator, noted: "Since machinery is the soul of the modern world, and since the genius of machinery attains its highest expression in America, why is it not reasonable to believe that in America the art of the future will flower most brilliantly?"[21] Precisionism, however, expanded beyond the exploration of machine imagery. Many artists associated with this group gravitated toward Synthetic Cubism's flat, sharply delineated planes as an appropriate visual idiom for their imagery, adding to the clarity and precision of their work. Eventually, Precisionism came to be characterized by a merging of a familiar native style in American architecture and artifacts with a modernist vocabulary derived largely from Synthetic Cubism.

CHARLES DEMUTH One of the leading Precisionists was CHARLES DEMUTH (1883–1935), who spent the years 1912–1914 in Paris and thus had firsthand exposure to Cubism and other avant-garde directions in art. He incorporated the spatial discontinuities characteristic of Cubism into his work, focusing much of it on industrial sites near his native Lancaster, Pennsylvania. *My Egypt* (FIG. 24-37) is a prime example of Precisionist painting. Demuth depicted the John W. Eshelman and Sons grain elevators, which he

reduced to simple geometric forms. The grain elevators remain insistently recognizable and solid. However, the "beams" of transparent planes and the diagonal force lines threaten to destabilize the image and correspond to Cubist fragmentation of space. The degree to which Demuth intended to extol the American industrial scene is unclear. The title, *My Egypt,* is sufficiently ambiguous in tone to accommodate differing readings. On the one hand, Demuth could have been suggesting a favorable comparison between the Egyptian pyramids and American grain elevators as cultural icons. On the other hand, the title could be read cynically, as a negative comment on the limitations of American culture.

GEORGIA O'KEEFFE The work of Wisconsin-born GEORGIA O'KEEFFE (1887–1986), like that of many artists, changed stylistically throughout her career. During the 1920s, O'Keeffe was a Precisionist. She had moved from the tiny town of Canyon to New York City in 1918, and although she had visited the city before, what she found there excited her. "You have to live in today," she told a friend. "Today the city is something bigger, more complex than ever before in history. And nothing can be gained from running away. I couldn't even if I could."[22] While in New York, O'Keeffe met Alfred Stieglitz (FIG. 24-39), who played a major role in promoting the avant-garde in the United States. Stieglitz had established an art gallery at 291 Fifth Avenue in New York. In "291," as the gallery came to be called, he exhibited the latest in both European and American art. Thus, 291, like the Armory Show, played an important role in the history of early-20th-century art in America. Stieglitz had seen and exhibited some of O'Keeffe's earlier

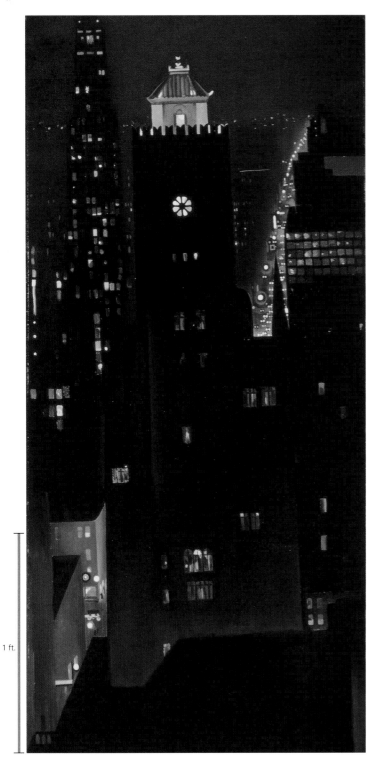

1 ft.

24-38 GEORGIA O'KEEFFE, *New York, Night*, 1929. Oil on canvas, 3′ 4⅛″ × 1′ 7⅛″. Sheldon Memorial Art Gallery, Lincoln (Nebraska Art Association, Thomas C. Woods Memorial Collection).

O'Keeffe's Precisionist representation of New York's soaring skyscrapers reduces the buildings to large, simple, dark planes punctuated by small windows that add rhythm and energy to the image.

work and drew her into his circle of avant-garde painters and photographers. Stieglitz became one of O'Keeffe's staunchest supporters and, eventually, her husband. The interest of Stieglitz and his circle in capturing the sensibility of the machine age intersected with O'Keeffe's fascination with the fast pace of city life, and she produced paintings during this period, such as *New York, Night* (FIG. 24-38), that depict the soaring skyscrapers dominating the city. Like other Precisionists,

O'Keeffe reduced her images to simple planes, here punctuated by small rectangular windows that add rhythm and energy to the image, countering the monolithic darkness of the looming buildings.

Despite O'Keeffe's affiliation with the Precisionist movement and New York, she is probably best known for her paintings of cow skulls and of flowers, for example, *Jack in the Pulpit No. 4* (FIG. I-4), which reveals her interest in stripping subjects to their purest forms and colors to heighten their expressive power. In this work, O'Keeffe reduced the incredible details of a flower to a symphony of basic colors, shapes, textures, and vital rhythms. Exhibiting the natural flow of curved planes and contour, O'Keeffe simplified the form almost to the point of complete abstraction. The fluid planes unfold like undulant petals from a subtly placed axis—the white jetlike streak—in a vision of the slow, controlled motion of growing life. O'Keeffe's painting, in its graceful, quiet poetry, reveals the organic reality of the object by strengthening its characteristic features.

Photography

ALFRED STIEGLITZ As an artist, ALFRED STIEGLITZ (1864–1946) is best known for his photographs. Taking his camera everywhere he went, he photographed whatever he saw around him, from the bustling streets of New York City to cloudscapes in upstate New York and the faces of friends and relatives. He believed in making only "straight, unmanipulated" photographs. Thus, he exposed and printed them using basic photographic processes, without resorting to techniques such as double-exposure or double-printing that would add information not present in the subject when he released the shutter. Stieglitz said he wanted the photographs he made with this direct technique "to hold a moment, to record something so completely that those who see it would relive an equivalent of what has been expressed."[23]

Stieglitz began a lifelong campaign to win a place for photography among the fine arts while he was a student of photochemistry in Germany. Returning to New York, he founded the Photo-Secession group, which mounted traveling exhibitions in the United States and sent loan collections abroad, and he also published an influential journal titled *Camera Work*. In his own works, Stieglitz specialized in photographs of his environment and saw these subjects in terms of arrangements of forms and of the "colors" of his black-and-white materials. His aesthetic approach crystallized during the making of *The Steerage* (FIG. 24-39), taken during a voyage to Europe with his first wife and daughter in 1907. Traveling first class, Stieglitz rapidly grew bored with the company of the prosperous passengers in that section of the ship. He walked as far forward on the first-class level as he could, when the rail around the opening onto the lower deck brought him up short. This level was for the steerage passengers the government sent back to Europe after refusing them entrance into the United States. Later, Stieglitz described what happened next:

The scene fascinated me: A round hat; the funnel leaning left, the stairway leaning right; the white drawbridge, its railing made of chain; white suspenders crossed on the back of a man below; circular iron machinery; a mast that cut into the sky, completing a triangle. I stood spellbound. I saw shapes related to one another—a picture of shapes, and underlying it, a new vision that held me: simple people; the feeling of ship, ocean, sky; a sense of release that I was away from the mob called rich. Rembrandt came into my mind and I wondered would he have felt as I did. . . . I had only one plate holder with one unexposed plate. Could I catch what I saw and felt? I released the shutter. If I had captured what I wanted, the photograph would go far beyond any of my previous prints. It would be a picture based on related shapes and deepest human feeling—a step in my own evolution, a spontaneous discovery.[24]

1 in.

24-39 Alfred Stieglitz, *The Steerage*, 1907 (print 1915). Photogravure (on tissue), $1' \frac{3}{8}'' \times 10\frac{1}{8}''$. Amon Carter Museum, Fort Worth.

Stieglitz waged a lifelong campaign to win a place for photography among the fine arts. This 1907 image is a haunting mixture of found patterns of forms and human activity. It stirs deep emotions.

This description reveals Stieglitz's abiding interest in the formal elements of the photograph—an insistently modernist focus. The finished print fulfilled Stieglitz's vision so well that it shaped his future photographic work, and its haunting mixture of found patterns and human activity has continued to stir viewers' emotions to this day.

EDWARD WESTON Stieglitz's concern for positioning photography as an art form with the same fine-art status as painting and sculpture was also the aim of EDWARD WESTON (1886–1958). In addition to making "straight" photographs, like those of Stieglitz, Weston experimented with photographs that moved toward greater abstraction, paralleling developments in other media. *Nude* (FIG. 24-40) is an example of the latter photographic style. The image's simplicity and the selection of a small segment of the human body as the subject result in a lyrical photograph of dark and light areas that at first glance suggests a landscape. Further inspection reveals the fluid curves and underlying skeletal armature of the human form. This photograph, in its reductiveness, formally expresses a study of the body that verges on the abstract.

1 in.

24-40 Edward Weston, *Nude*, 1925. Platinum print, $7\frac{1}{2}'' \times 9\frac{1}{2}''$. Center for Creative Photography, University of Arizona, Tucson.

Weston experimented with photographs that moved toward abstraction. By selecting only a segment of a nude body as his subject, the artist converted the human form to a landscape.

EUROPE, 1920 TO 1945

Because World War I was fought entirely on European soil, European artists experienced its devastating effects to a much greater degree than did their American counterparts. The war had a profound impact on Europe's geopolitical terrain, on individual and national psyches, and on the art of the 1920s and 1930s.

Picasso in the 1930s

The previous discussion of Pablo Picasso focused on his immersion in aesthetic issues, but he was acutely aware of politics throughout his life. As Picasso watched his homeland descend into civil war in the late 1930s, his involvement in political issues grew even stronger. He declared: "[P]ainting is not made to decorate apartments. It is an instrument for offensive and defensive war against the enemy."[25]

GUERNICA In January 1937, the Spanish Republican government-in-exile in Paris asked Picasso to produce a major work for the Spanish Pavilion at the Paris International Exposition that summer. Picasso was well aware of the immense visibility and large international audience this opportunity afforded him, but he did not formally accept this invitation until he received word that Guernica, capital of the Basque region (an area in southern France and northern Spain populated by Basque speakers), had been almost totally destroyed in an air raid on April 26 by Nazi bombers acting on behalf of the rebel general Francisco Franco (1892–1975). Not only did the Germans attack the city itself, but because they dropped their bombs at the busiest hour of a market day, they also killed or wounded many of Guernica's 7,000 citizens. The event jolted Picasso into action. By the end of June, he had completed *Guernica* (FIG. 24-41), a mural-sized canvas of immense power.

Despite the painting's title, Picasso made no specific reference to the event in *Guernica*—no bombs, no German planes. Rather, the collected images in *Guernica* combine to create a visceral outcry of human grief. In the center, along the lower edge of the painting, lies a slain warrior clutching a broken and useless sword. A gored horse tramples him and rears back in fright as it dies. On the left, a shrieking, anguished woman cradles her dead child. On the far right, a woman on fire runs screaming from a burning building, while another woman flees mindlessly. In the upper right corner, a woman, represented by only a head, emerges from the burning building, thrusting forth a light to illuminate the horror. Overlooking the destruction is a bull, which, according to the artist, represents "brutality and darkness."[26]

Picasso used aspects of his Cubist discoveries to expressive effect in *Guernica*, particularly the fragmentation of objects and the dislocation of anatomical features. This Cubist fragmentation gave visual form to the horror. What happened to these figures in the artist's act of painting—the dissections and contortions of the human form—paralleled what happened to them in real life. To emphasize the scene's severity and starkness, Picasso reduced his palette to black, white, and shades of gray.

Revealing his political commitment and his awareness of the power of art, Picasso refused to allow exhibition of *Guernica* in Spain while Generalissimo Franco was in power. At the artist's request, *Guernica* hung in the Museum of Modern Art in New York City after the 1937 World's Fair concluded. Not until after Franco's death in 1975 did Picasso allow the mural to be exhibited in his homeland. It hangs today in the Centro de Arte Reina Sofia in Madrid as a testament to a tragic chapter in Spanish history.

Neue Sachlichkeit

In Germany, World War I gave rise to an artistic movement called *Neue Sachlichkeit* (New Objectivity). The artists associated with Neue Sachlichkeit served, at some point, in the German army, and their military experiences deeply influenced their worldviews and informed their art. "New Objectivity" captures the group's aim—to present a clear-eyed, direct, and honest image of the war and its effects.

GEORGE GROSZ   One of the Neue Sachlichkeit artists was GEORGE GROSZ (1893–1958), who was, for a time, associated with the Dada group in Berlin. Grosz observed the onset of World War I with horrified fascination, but that feeling soon turned to anger and frustration. He reported:

1 ft.

24-41 PABLO PICASSO, *Guernica*, 1937. Oil on canvas, 11′ 5$\frac{1}{2}$″ × 25′ 5$\frac{3}{4}$″. Museo Nacional Centro de Arte Reina Sofia, Madrid.

Picasso used Cubist techniques, especially the fragmentation of objects and dislocation of anatomical features, to expressive effect in this condemnation of the Nazi bombing of the Basque capital.

24-42 GEORGE GROSZ, *Fit for Active Service,* 1916–1917. Pen and brush and ink on paper, 1′ 8″ × 1′ 2⅜″. Museum of Modern Art, New York (gift of the American Tobacco Company, Inc.). Art © Estate of George Grosz/Licensed by VAGA, New York.

In a drawing that is an indictment of the German army and based on Grosz's personal experience, a doctor proclaims the skeleton before him "fit for service," and no one disputes his evaluation.

Of course, there was a kind of mass enthusiasm at the start. But this intoxication soon evaporated, leaving a huge vacuum. . . . And then after a few years when everything bogged down, when we were defeated, when everything went to pieces, all that remained, at least for me and most of my friends, were disgust and horror.[27]

Grosz produced numerous paintings and drawings, such as *Fit for Active Service* (FIG. **24-42**), that were caustic indictments of the military. In these works, he often depicted army officers as heartless or incompetent. This particular drawing may relate to Grosz's personal experience. On the verge of a nervous breakdown in 1917, he was sent to a sanatorium where doctors examined him and, much to his horror, declared him "fit for service." In this biting and sarcastic drawing, an army doctor proclaims the skeleton before him "fit for service." The other officers or doctors attending do not dispute this evaluation. The spectacles perched on the skeleton's face, very similar to the gold-rimmed glasses Grosz wore, further suggest he based this scene on his experiences. Grosz's searing wit is all the more evident upon comparing *Fit for Active Service* with Marsden Hartley's *Portrait of a German Officer* (FIG. **24-34**). Although Hartley's painting deals with the death of his lover in battle, the incorporation of colorful German military insignia and emblems imbues the painting with a more heroic, celebratory tone. In contrast, the simplicity of Grosz's line drawing contributes to the directness and immediacy of the work, which scathingly portrays the German army.

MAX BECKMANN Like Grosz, MAX BECKMANN (1884–1950) enlisted in the German army and initially rationalized the war. He believed the chaos would lead to a better society, but over time the massive death and destruction increasingly disillusioned him. Soon his work began to emphasize the horrors of war and of a society he saw descending into madness. His disturbing view of society is evident in *Night* (FIG. **24-43**), which depicts a cramped room three intruders have forcibly invaded. A bound woman, apparently raped, is splayed across the foreground of the painting. Her husband appears on the left. One of the intruders hangs him, while another one twists his left arm out of its socket. An unidentified woman cowers in the background. On the far right, the third intruder prepares to flee with the child.

Although this image does not depict a war scene, the violence and wrenching brutality pervading the home are a searing and horrifying comment on society's condition. Beckmann also injected a personal

24-43 MAX BECKMANN, *Night,* 1918–1919. Oil on canvas, 4′ 4⅜″ × 5′ 1¼″. Kunstsammlung Nordrhein-Westfalen, Düsseldorf.

Beckmann's treatment of forms and space in *Night* matched his view of the brutality of early-20th-century society. Objects seem dislocated and contorted, and the space appears buckled and illogical.

1 ft.

24-44 OTTO DIX, *Der Krieg* (*The War*), 1929–1932. Oil and tempera on wood, 6′ 8⅓″ × 13′ 4¾″. Staatliche Kunstsammlungen, Gemäldegalerie Neue Meister, Dresden.

In this triptych recalling earlier altarpieces, Dix captured the panoramic devastation that war inflicts on the terrain and on humans. He depicted himself as a soldier dragging a comrade to safety.

reference by using himself, his wife, and his son as the models for the three family members. The stilted angularity of the figures and the roughness of the paint surface contribute to the image's savageness. In addition, the artist's treatment of forms and space reflects the world's violence. Objects seem dislocated and contorted, and the space appears buckled and illogical. For example, the woman's hands are bound to the window that opens from the room's back wall, but her body appears to hang vertically, rather than lying across the plane of the intervening table.

OTTO DIX The third artist most closely associated with Neue Sachlichkeit was OTTO DIX (1891–1959). Having served as both a machine gunner and an aerial observer, Dix was well acquainted with war's effects. Like Grosz, he initially tried to find redeeming value in the apocalyptic event: "The war was a horrible thing, but there was something tremendous about it, too. . . . You have to have seen human beings in this unleashed state to know what human nature is. . . . I need to experience all the depths of life for myself, that's why I go out, and that's why I volunteered."[28] This idea of experiencing the "depths of life" stemmed from Dix's interest in the philosophy of Friedrich Nietzsche (1844–1900). In particular, Dix avidly read Nietzsche's *The Joyous Science,* deriving from it a belief in life's cyclical nature—procreation and death, building up and tearing down, and growth and decay.

As the war progressed, however, Dix's faith in the potential improvement of society dissipated, and he began to produce unflinch-

ingly direct and provocative artworks. His *Der Krieg* (*The War;* FIG. **24-44**) vividly captures the panoramic devastation that war inflicts, both on the terrain and on humans. In the left panel, armed and uniformed soldiers march off into the distance. Dix graphically displayed the horrific results in the center and right panels, where mangled bodies, many riddled with bullet holes, are scattered throughout the eerily lit apocalyptic landscape. As if to emphasize the intensely personal nature of this scene, the artist painted himself into the right panel as the ghostly but determined soldier who drags a comrade to safety. In the bottom panel, in a coffinlike bunker, lie soldiers asleep—or perhaps dead. Dix significantly chose to present this sequence of images in a triptych format, and the work recalls triptychs such as Matthias Grünewald's *Isenheim Altarpiece* (FIG. **18-2**). However, Dix's work presents a bleaker outlook than that piece: The hope of salvation extended to viewers of the *Isenheim Altarpiece* through Christ's eventual Resurrection is absent from *Der Krieg.* Like his fellow Neue Sachlichkeit artists, Dix felt compelled to lay bare the realities of his time, which the war's violence dominated. Even years later, Dix still maintained:

You have to see things the way they are. You have to be able to say yes to the human manifestations that exist and will always exist. That doesn't mean saying yes to war, but to a fate that approaches you under certain conditions and in which you have to prove yourself. Abnormal situations bring out all the depravity, the bestiality of human beings. . . . I portrayed states, states that the war brought about, and the results of war, as states.[29]

ERNST BARLACH A work more spiritual in its expression is the *War Monument* (FIG. 24-45), which the German sculptor ERNST BARLACH (1870–1938) created for the cathedral in his hometown of Güstrow in 1927. Working often in wood, Barlach sculpted single figures usually dressed in flowing robes and portrayed in strong, simple poses that embody deep human emotions and experiences such as grief, vigilance, or self-comfort. Barlach's works combine sharp, smoothly planed forms with intense expression. The cast-bronze hovering figure of his *War Monument* is one of the most poignant memorials of World War I. Unlike traditional war memorials depicting heroic military figures, often engaged in battle, the hauntingly symbolic figure that Barlach created speaks to the experience of all caught in the conflict of war. The floating human form, suspended above a tomb inscribed with the dates 1914–1918 (and later also 1939–1945), suggests a dying soul at the moment when it is about to awaken to everlasting life—the theme of death and transfiguration. The rigid economy of surfaces concentrates attention on the simple but expressive head. So powerful was this sculpture that the Nazis had it removed from the cathedral in 1937 and melted down for ammunition. Luckily, a friend hid another version Barlach made. A Protestant parish in Cologne purchased this surviving cast, from which bronzeworkers made a new cast for the Güstrow cathedral.

24-45 ERNST BARLACH, *War Monument,* Cathedral, Güstrow, Germany, 1927. Bronze.

In this World War I memorial, a human form floating above a tomb suggests a dying soul at the moment when it is about to awaken to everlasting life. The Nazis melted down the piece for ammunition.

Surrealism

The exuberantly aggressive momentum of the Dada movement that emerged during World War I was of short duration. By 1924, with the publication in France of the *First Surrealist Manifesto,* most of the artists associated with Dada joined the *Surrealism* movement and its determined exploration of ways to express in art the world of dreams and the unconscious. Not surprisingly, the Surrealists incorporated many of the Dadaists' improvisational techniques. They believed these methods important for engaging the elements of fantasy and activating the unconscious forces that lie deep within every human being. The Surrealists sought to explore the inner world of the psyche, the realm of fantasy and the unconscious. Inspired in part by the ideas of the psychoanalysts Sigmund Freud and Carl Jung, the Surrealists had a special interest in the nature of dreams. They viewed dreams as occurring at the level connecting all human consciousness and as constituting the arena in which people could move beyond their environment's constricting forces to reengage with the deeper selves society had long suppressed. In the words of André Breton, one of the leading Surrealist thinkers:

> Surrealism is based on the belief in the superior reality of certain forms of association heretofore neglected, in the omnipotence of dreams, in the undirected play of thought. . . . I believe in the future resolution of the states of dream and reality, in appearance so contradictory, in a sort of absolute reality, or surreality.[30]

Thus, the Surrealists' dominant motivation was to bring the aspects of outer and inner "reality" together into a single position, in much the same way life's seemingly unrelated fragments combine in the vivid world of dreams. The projection in visible form of this new conception required new techniques of pictorial construction. The Surrealists adapted some Dada devices and invented new methods such as automatic writing (spontaneous writing using free association), not so much to reveal a world without meaning as to provoke reactions closely related to subconscious experience.

Surrealism developed along two lines. In *Naturalistic Surrealism,* artists present recognizable scenes that seem to have metamorphosed into a dream or nightmare image. The artists Salvador Dalí (FIG. 24-49) and René Magritte (FIG. 24-50) were the most famous practitioners of this variant of Surrealism. In contrast, some artists gravitated toward an interest in *Biomorphic Surrealism.* In Biomorphic (life forms) Surrealism, *automatism*—the creation of art without conscious control—predominated. Biomorphic Surrealists such as Joan Miró (FIG. 24-52) produced largely abstract compositions, although the imagery sometimes suggests organisms or natural forms.

GIORGIO DE CHIRICO The Italian painter GIORGIO DE CHIRICO (1888–1978) produced emphatically ambiguous works that position him as a precursor of Surrealism. De Chirico's paintings of cityscapes and shop windows were part of a movement called *Pittura Metafisica,* or Metaphysical Painting. Returning to Italy after study in Munich, de Chirico found hidden reality revealed through strange juxtapositions, such as those seen on late autumn afternoons in the city of Turin, when the long shadows of the setting sun transformed vast open squares and silent public monuments into what the painter called "metaphysical towns." De Chirico translated this vision into paint in works such as *Melancholy and Mystery of a Street* (FIG. 24-46), where the spaces and buildings evoke a disquieting sense of foreboding. The choice of the term "metaphysical" to describe de Chirico's paintings suggests that these images transcend their physical appearances. *Melancholy and Mystery of a Street,* for all of its clarity and simplicity, takes on a rather sinister air. Only a few inexplicable and incongruous elements punctuate the scene's solitude—a small

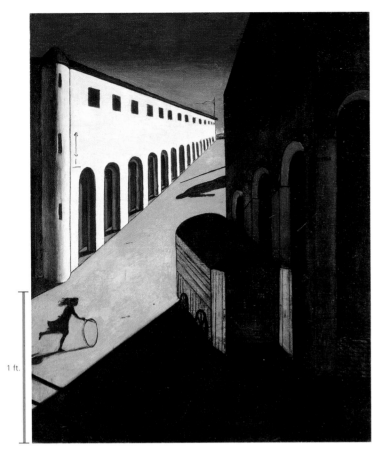

1 ft.

24-46 Giorgio de Chirico, *Melancholy and Mystery of a Street*, 1914. Oil on canvas, 2′ 10¼″ × 2′ 4½″. Private collection.

De Chirico's Metaphysical Painting movement was a precursor of Surrealism. In this street scene, filled with mysterious forms and shadows, the painter evoked a disquieting sense of foreboding.

1 ft.

24-47 Max Ernst, *Two Children Are Threatened by a Nightingale*, 1924. Oil on wood with wood construction, 2′ 3½″ × 1′ 10½″ × 4½″. Museum of Modern Art, New York.

In this early Surrealist painting with an intentionally ambiguous title, Ernst used traditional perspective to represent the setting, but the three sketchily rendered figures belong to a dream world.

girl with her hoop in the foreground, the empty van, and the ominous shadow of a man emerging from behind the building. The sense of strangeness de Chirico could conjure with familiar objects and scenes recalls Nietzsche's "foreboding that underneath this reality in which we live and have our being, another and altogether different reality lies concealed."[31]

De Chirico's paintings were reproduced in periodicals almost as soon as he completed them, and his works quickly influenced artists outside Italy, including both the Dadaists and, later, the Surrealists. The incongruities in his work intrigued the Dadaists, whereas the eerie mood and visionary quality of paintings such as *Melancholy and Mystery of a Street* excited and inspired Surrealist artists who sought to portray the world of dreams.

MAX ERNST Originally a Dada activist in Germany, Max Ernst (1891–1976) became one of the early adherents of the Surrealist circle that André Breton anchored. As a child living in a small community near Cologne, Ernst had found his existence fantastic and filled with marvels. In autobiographical notes, written mostly in the third person, he said of his birth: "Max Ernst had his first contact with the world of sense on the 2nd April 1891 at 9:45 A.M., when he emerged from the egg which his mother had laid in an eagle's nest and which the bird had incubated for seven years."[32] Ernst's service in the German army during World War I swept away his early success as an Expressionist. In his own words:

> Max Ernst died on 1st August 1914. He returned to life on 11th November 1918, a young man who wanted to become a magician and

find the central myth of his age. From time to time he consulted the eagle which had guarded the egg of his prenatal existence. The bird's advice can be detected in his work.[33]

Before joining the Surrealists, Ernst explored every means to achieve the sense of the psychic in his art. Like other Dadaists, he set out to incorporate found objects and chance into his works. Using a process called *frottage,* he created some works by combining the patterns achieved by rubbing a crayon or another medium across a sheet of paper placed over a surface having a strong, evocative textural pattern. In other works, Ernst joined fragments of images he had cut from old books, magazines, and prints to form one hallucinatory collage.

Ernst soon began making paintings that shared the mysterious dreamlike effect of his collages. In 1920 his works brought him into contact with Breton, who instantly recognized Ernst's affinity with the Surrealist group. In 1922, Ernst moved to Paris. His *Two Children Are Threatened by a Nightingale* (FIG. **24-47**) manifests many of the creative bases of Surrealism. Here, Ernst displayed a private dream that challenged the post-Renaissance idea that a painting should resemble a window looking into a "real" scene rendered illusionistically three-dimensional through mathematical perspective. In *Two Children,* the artist painted the landscape, the distant city, and the tiny flying bird in conventional fashion, following all the established rules of linear and atmospheric perspective. The three sketchily rendered figures, however, clearly belong to a dream world, and the literally three-dimensional miniature gate, the odd button knob, and the strange

Degenerate Art

Although avant-garde artists often had to endure public ridicule both in Europe and America (see "The Armory Show," page 710), they suffered outright political persecution in Germany in the 1930s and 1940s. The most dramatic example of this abuse was the infamous *Entartete Kunst* (Degenerate Art) exhibition that Adolf Hitler (1889–1945) and the Nazis mounted in 1937.

Hitler aspired to become an artist himself and produced numerous drawings and paintings. These works reflected his firm belief that 19th-century realistic genre painting represented the zenith of Aryan art development. Accordingly, he denigrated anything that did not conform to that standard—in particular, avant-garde art. Turning his criticism into action, Hitler ordered the confiscation of more than 16,000 artworks he considered "degenerate." To publicize his condemnation of this art, he directed his minister for public enlightenment and propaganda, Joseph Goebbels (1897–1945), to organize a massive exhibition of this "degenerate art." Hitler defined it as works that "insult German feeling, or destroy or confuse natural form, or simply reveal an absence of adequate manual and artistic skill."* The term "degenerate" also had other specific connotations at the time. The Nazis used it to designate supposedly inferior racial, sexual, and moral types. Hitler's order to Goebbels to target 20th-century avant-garde art for inclusion in this exhibition aimed to impress on viewers the general inferiority of the artists producing this work. To make this point even more dramatically, Hitler mandated the organization of another exhibition, the *Grosse Deutsche Kunstausstellung* (Great German Art Exhibition), which ran concurrently and presented an extensive array of Nazi-approved conservative art.

Entartete Kunst opened in Munich on July 19, 1937, and included more than 650 paintings, sculptures, prints, and books. The exhibition was immensely popular. Roughly 20,000 viewers visited the show daily. By the end of its four-month run, it had attracted more than two million viewers, and nearly a million more viewed it as it traveled through Germany and Austria. Among the 112 artists whose works the Nazis presented for ridicule were Ernst Barlach, Max Beckmann, Otto Dix, Max Ernst, George Grosz, Vassily Kandinsky, Ernst Kirchner, Paul Klee, Wilhelm Lehmbruck, Franz Marc, Emil Nolde, and Kurt Schwitters. A memorable photograph (FIG. 24-48) recorded Hitler visiting the exhibition, pausing in front of the Dada wall where the organizers initially deliberately hung askew works by Schwitters, Klee, and Kandinsky. No avant-garde or even modernist artist was safe from Hitler's attack. (Only six of the artists in the exhibition were Jewish.) Indeed, despite his status as a charter member of the Nazi Party, Emil Nolde received particularly harsh treatment. The Nazis confiscated more than 1,000 of Nolde's works from German

24-48 Adolf Hitler, accompanied by Nazi commission members, including photographer Heinrich Hoffmann, Wolfgang Willrich, Walter Hansen, and painter Adolf Ziegler, viewing the *Entartete Kunst* show on July 16, 1937.

For Hitler's visit, the curators deliberately hung askew the works of Kandinsky, Klee, and Schwitters (although they subsequently straightened them for the duration of the exhibition).

museums and included 27 of them in the exhibition, more than for almost any other artist.

Clearly, artists needed considerable courage to defy tradition and produce avant-garde art. Especially in Germany in the 1930s and 1940s, in the face of Nazi persecution, commitment to the avant-garde demanded a resoluteness that extended beyond issues of aesthetics and beyond the confines of the art world. This persecution exacted an immense toll on these artists. Kirchner, for example, responded to the stress of Nazi pressure by destroying all his woodblocks and burning many of his works. A year later, in 1938, he committed suicide. Beckmann and his wife fled to Amsterdam on the exhibit's opening day, never to return to their homeland. Although *Entartete Kunst* was just a fragment of the tremendous destruction of life and spirit Hitler and the Nazis wrought, Hitler's insistence on suppressing and discrediting this art dramatically demonstrates art's power to affect viewers.

* Stephanie Barron, *"Degenerate Art": The Fate of the Avant-Garde in Nazi Germany* (Los Angeles: Los Angeles County Museum of Art, 1991), 19.

closed building "violate" the bulky frame's space. Additional dislocation occurs in the traditional museum identification label, which Ernst displaced into a cutaway part of the frame. Handwritten, it announces the work's title (taken from a poem Ernst wrote before he painted this), adding another note of irrational mystery.

As is true of many Surrealist works, the title, *Two Children Are Threatened by a Nightingale,* is ambiguous and relates uneasily to what the spectator sees. The viewer must struggle to decipher connections between the image and words. When Surrealists (and

Dadaists and Metaphysical artists before them) used such titles, they intended the seeming contradiction between title and picture to throw the spectator off balance with all expectations challenged. Much of the impact of Surrealist works begins with the viewer's sudden awareness of the incongruity and absurdity of what the artist pictured. These were precisely the qualities that subjected the Dadaists and Surrealists to public condemnation and, in Germany under Adolf Hitler (FIG. 24-48), to governmental persecution (see "Degenerate Art," above).

24-49 SALVADOR DALÍ, *The Persistence of Memory,* 1931. Oil on canvas, $9\frac{1}{2}''$ × 1' 1". Museum of Modern Art, New York.

Dalí aimed to paint "images of concrete irrationality." In this realistically rendered landscape featuring three "decaying" watches, he created a haunting allegory of empty space where time has ended.

SALVADOR DALÍ The Surrealists' exploration of the human psyche and dreams reached new heights in the works of Spain's SALVADOR DALÍ (1904–1989). In his paintings, sculptures, jewelry, and designs for furniture and movies, Dalí probed a deeply erotic dimension, studying the writings of Richard von Krafft-Ebing (1840–1902) and Sigmund Freud and inventing what he called the "paranoiac-critical method" to assist his creative process. As he described it, in his painting he aimed "to materialize the images of concrete irrationality with the most imperialistic fury of precision . . . in order that the world of imagination and of concrete irrationality may be as objectively evident . . . as that of the exterior world of phenomenal reality."[34]

All these aspects of Dalí's style appear in *The Persistence of Memory* (FIG. **24-49**), a haunting allegory of empty space where time has ended. In the painting, an eerie, never-setting sun illuminates the barren landscape. An amorphous creature draped with a limp pocket watch sleeps in the foreground. Another watch hangs from the branch of a dead tree that springs unexpectedly from a blocky architectural form. A third watch hangs half over the edge of the rectangular form, beside a small timepiece resting face down on the block's surface. Ants swarm mysteriously over the small watch, while a fly walks along the face of its large neighbor, almost as if this assembly of watches were decaying organic life—soft and sticky. Dalí rendered every detail of this dreamscape with precise control, striving to make the world of his paintings as convincingly real as the most meticulously rendered landscape based on a real scene from nature.

RENÉ MAGRITTE The Belgian painter RENÉ MAGRITTE (1898–1967) also expressed in exemplary fashion the Surrealist idea and method—the dreamlike dissociation of image and meaning. His works administer disruptive shocks because they subvert the viewer's expectations based on logic and common sense. The danger of relying on rationality when viewing a Surrealist work is glaringly apparent in Magritte's *The Treachery (or Perfidy) of Images* (FIG. **24-50**). Magritte presented a meticulously rendered *trompe l'oeil* depiction of a briar pipe. The caption beneath the image, however, contradicts what seems obvious: "Ceci n'est pas une pipe" ("This is not a pipe"). The discrepancy between image and caption clearly challenges the assumptions underlying the reading of visual art. Like the other Surrealists' work, this painting wreaks havoc on the viewer's reliance on the conscious and the rational.

MERET OPPENHEIM Sculpture especially appealed to the Surrealists because its concrete tangibility made their art all the more disquieting. *Object* (FIG. **24-51**), also called *Le Déjeuner en fourrure* (*Luncheon in Fur*), by Swiss artist MERET OPPENHEIM (1913–1985) captures the incongruity, humor, visual appeal, and, often, eroticism characterizing Surrealism. The artist presented a fur-lined teacup inspired by a conversation she had with Picasso. After admiring a bracelet Oppenheim had made from a piece of brass covered with fur, Picasso noted that anything might be covered with fur. When her tea grew cold, Oppenheim responded to Picasso's com-

24-50 RENÉ MAGRITTE, *The Treachery (or Perfidy) of Images,* 1928–1929. Oil on canvas, 1' $11\frac{5}{8}''$ × 3' 1". Los Angeles County Museum of Art, Los Angeles (purchased with funds provided by the Mr. and Mrs. William Preston Harrison Collection).

The discrepancy between Magritte's meticulously painted briar pipe and his caption, "This is not a pipe," challenges the viewer's reliance on the conscious and the rational in the reading of visual art.

24-51 MERET OPPENHEIM, *Object (Le Déjeuner en fourrure)*, 1936. Fur-covered cup, 4⅜″ diameter; saucer, 9⅜″ diameter; spoon, 8″ long. Museum of Modern Art, New York.

The Surrealists loved the concrete tangibility of sculpture, which made their art even more disquieting. Oppenheim's functional fur-covered object captures the Surrealist flair for magical transformation.

porates a sensuality and eroticism (seen here in the seductively soft, tactile fur lining the concave form) that are also components of much of Surrealist art.

JOAN MIRÓ Like the Dadaists, the Surrealists used many methods to free the creative process from reliance on the kind of conscious control they believed society had shaped too much. Dalí used his paranoiac-critical approach to encourage the free play of association as he worked. Other Surrealists used automatism and various types of planned "accidents" to provoke reactions closely related to subconscious experience. The Spanish artist JOAN MIRÓ (1893–1983) was a master of this approach. Although Miró resisted formal association with any movement or group, including the Surrealists, André Breton identified him as "the most Surrealist of us all."[35] From the beginning, Miró's work contained an element of fantasy and hallucination. After Surrealist poets in Paris introduced him to the use of chance to create art, the young Spaniard devised a new painting method that allowed him to create works such as *Painting* (FIG. **24-52**). Miró began this painting by making a scattered collage composition with assembled fragments cut from a catalogue for machinery. The shapes in the collage became motifs the artist freely reshaped to create black silhouettes—solid or in outline, with dramatic accents of white and vermilion. They suggest, in the painting, a host of amoebic organisms or constellations in outer space floating in an immaterial background space filled with soft reds, blues, and greens.

ment by ordering "un peu plus de fourrure" (a little more fur), and the sculpture had its genesis. *Object* takes on an anthropomorphic quality, animated by the quirky combination of the fur with a functional object. Further, the sculpture captures the Surrealist flair for alchemical, seemingly magical or mystical, transformation. It incor-

Miró described his creative process as a back-and-forth switch between unconscious and conscious image-making: "Rather than setting out to paint something, I begin painting and as I paint the picture begins to assert itself, or suggest itself under my brush. The form becomes a sign for a woman or a bird as I work.... The first stage is free, unconscious.... The second stage is carefully calculated."[36] Even the artist could not always explain the meanings of pictures such as *Painting*. They are, in the truest sense, spontaneous and intuitive expressions of the little-understood, submerged unconscious part of life.

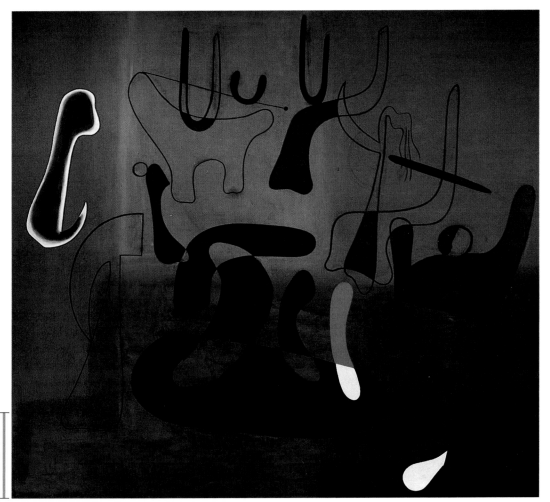

24-52 JOAN MIRÓ, *Painting*, 1933. Oil on canvas, 5′ 8″ × 6′ 5″. Museum of Modern Art, New York (Loula D. Lasker Bequest by exchange).

Miró promoted automatism, the creation of art without conscious control. He began this painting with a scattered collage and then added forms suggesting floating amoebic organisms.

1 in.

24-53 PAUL KLEE, *Twittering Machine,* 1922. Watercolor and pen and ink, on oil transfer drawing on paper, mounted on cardboard, 2′ 1″ × 1′ 7″. Museum of Modern Art, New York.

Although based on forms in the tangible world easily read as birds, Klee's *Twittering Machine* is a fanciful vision of a mysterious world presented in a simplified, almost childlike manner.

PAUL KLEE Perhaps the most inventive artist using fantasy images to represent the nonvisible world was the Swiss-German painter PAUL KLEE (1879–1940). Like Miró, he shunned formal association with groups such as the Dadaists and Surrealists but pursued their interest in the subconscious. Klee sought clues to humanity's deeper nature in primitive shapes and symbols. Like Jung, Klee seems to have accepted the existence of a collective unconscious that reveals itself in archaic signs and patterns and that is everywhere evident in the art of "primitive" cultures (see "Primitivism," page 696). The son of a professional musician and himself an accomplished violinist, Klee thought of painting as similar to music in its ability to express emotions through color, form, and line. In 1920, Klee set down his *Creative Credo,* which reads in part:

> Art does not reproduce the visible; rather it makes visible. . . . The formal elements of graphic art are dot, line, plane, and space— the last three charged with energy of various kinds. . . . Formerly we used to represent things visible on earth, things we either liked to look at or would have liked to see. Today we reveal the reality that is behind visible things.[37]

To penetrate the reality behind visible things, Klee studied nature avidly, taking special interest in analyzing processes of growth and change. He coded these studies in diagrammatic form in notebooks. The root of his work was thus nature, but nature filtered

through his mind. Upon starting an image, he would allow the pencil or brush to lead him until an image emerged, to which he would then respond to complete the idea.

Twittering Machine (FIG. **24-53**) reveals Klee's fanciful vision. The painting, although based on forms in the tangible world easily read as birds, is far from illusionistic. Klee presented the scene in a simplified, almost childlike manner, imbuing the work with a poetic lyricism. The small size of Klee's works enhanced their impact. A viewer must draw near to decipher the delicately rendered forms and enter this mysterious dream world. The inclusion of a crank-driven mechanism adds a touch of whimsy. Perhaps no other artist of the 20th century matched Klee's subtlety as he deftly created a world of ambiguity and understatement that draws each viewer into finding a unique interpretation of the work.

Suprematism, Constructivism, and De Stijl

The pessimism and cynicism of movements such as Dada reflect the historical circumstances of the early 20th century. However, not all artists reacted to the profound turmoil of the times by retreating from society. Some avant-garde artists promoted utopian ideals, believing staunchly in art's ability to contribute to improving society and all humankind. These efforts often surfaced in the face of significant political upheaval, illustrating the link established early on between revolution in politics and revolution in art. Among the art movements espousing utopian notions were Suprematism and Constructivism in Russia and De Stijl in Holland.

KAZIMIR MALEVICH Despite Russia's distance from Paris, the center of the international art world in the early 20th century, Russians had a long history of cultural contact and interaction with western Europe. Wealthy Russians, such as Ivan Morozov (1871–1921) and Sergei Shchukin (1854–1936), amassed extensive collections of Impressionist, Post-Impressionist, and avant-garde paintings. Shchukin became particularly enamored with the work of both Picasso and Matisse. By the mid-1910s, he had acquired 37 paintings by Matisse and 51 by Picasso. Because of their access to collections such as these, Russian artists were familiar with early-20th-century artistic developments, especially Fauvism, Cubism, and Futurism.

Among the Russian artists who pursued the avant-garde direction Cubism introduced was KAZIMIR MALEVICH (1878–1935). Malevich developed an abstract style to convey his belief that the supreme reality in the world is pure feeling, which attaches to no object. Thus, this belief called for new, nonobjective forms in art—shapes not related to objects in the visible world. Malevich had studied painting, sculpture, and architecture and had worked his way through most of the avant-garde styles of his youth before deciding none could express the subject he found most important—"pure feeling." He christened his new artistic approach *Suprematism,* explaining: "Under Suprematism I understand the supremacy of pure feeling in creative art. To the Suprematist, the visual phenomena of the objective world are, in themselves, meaningless; the significant thing is feeling, as such, quite apart from the environment in which it is called forth."[38]

The basic form of Malevich's new Suprematist nonobjective art was the square. Combined with its relatives, the straight line and the rectangle, the square soon filled his paintings, such as *Suprematist Composition: Airplane Flying* (FIG. **24-54**). In this work, the brightly colored shapes float against and within a white space, and the artist placed them in dynamic relationship to one another. Malevich believed all people would easily understand his new art because of the universality of its symbols. It used the pure language of shape and color, to which everyone could respond intuitively.

24-54 KAZIMIR MALEVICH, *Suprematist Composition: Airplane Flying*, 1915 (dated 1914). Oil on canvas, $1' 10\frac{7}{8}'' \times 1' 7''$. Museum of Modern Art, New York.

Malevich developed an abstract style he called Suprematism to convey that the supreme reality in the world is pure feeling. In this work, the brightly colored rectilinear shapes float against white space.

Having formulated his artistic approach, Malevich welcomed the Russian Revolution, which broke out in 1917, as a political act that would wipe out past traditions and begin a new culture. He believed his art could play a major role because of its universal accessibility. In actuality, after a short period when the new regime heralded avant-garde art, the political leaders of the postrevolution Soviet Union decided the new society needed a more "practical" art. Soviet authorities promoted a "realistic," illusionistic art that they believed a wide public could understand and that they hoped would teach citizens about their new government. This horrified Malevich. To him, true art could never have a practical connection with life. As he explained, "Every social idea, however great and important it may be, stems from the sensation of hunger; every art work, regardless of how small and insignificant it may seem, originates in pictorial or plastic feeling. It is high time for us to realize that the problems of art lie far apart from those of the stomach or the intellect."[39] Disappointed and unappreciated in his own country, Malevich eventually gravitated toward other disciplines, such as mathematical theory and geometry, logical fields given his interest in pure abstraction.

NAUM GABO Like Malevich, the Russian-born sculptor NAUM GABO (1890–1977) wanted to create an innovative art to express a new reality, and, also like Malevich, Gabo believed art should spring from sources separate from the everyday world. For Gabo, the new reality was the space-time world described by early-20th-century scientists (see "Science and Art," page 691). As he wrote in *The Realistic Manifesto*, published with his brother Anton Pevsner (1886–1962) in 1920:

24-55 NAUM GABO, *Column*, ca. 1923 (reconstructed 1937). Perspex, wood, metal, glass, $3' 5'' \times 2' 5'' \times 2' 5''$. Solomon R. Guggenheim Museum, New York.

Gabo's Constructivist sculptures rely on the relationship of mass and space to suggest the nature of space-time. Space seems to flow through as well as around the transparent materials he used.

Space and time are the only forms on which life is built and hence art must be constructed. . . . The realization of our perceptions of the world in the forms of space and time is the only aim of our pictorial and plastic art. . . . We renounce the thousand-year-old delusion in art that held the static rhythms as the only elements of the plastic and pictorial arts. We affirm in these arts a new element, the kinetic rhythms, as the basic forms of our perception of real time.[40]

Gabo was one of the Russian sculptors known as Constructivists. The name *Constructivism* may have come originally from the title *Construction,* which the Russian artist Vladimir Tatlin (FIG. **24-70**) used for some relief sculptures he made in 1913 and 1914. Gabo explained that he called himself a Constructivist partly because he built up his sculptures piece by piece in space, instead of carving or modeling them in the traditional way. Although Gabo experimented briefly with real motion in his work, most of his sculptures relied on the relationship of mass and space to suggest the nature of space-time. To indicate the volumes of mass and space more clearly in his sculpture, Gabo used some of the new synthetic plastic materials, including celluloid, nylon, and Lucite, to create constructions whose space seems to flow through as well as around the transparent materials. In works such as *Column* (FIG. **24-55**), the sculptor opened up the column's circular mass so that the viewer can experience the volume of space it occupies. Two transparent planes extend through its diameter, crossing at right angles at the center of the implied cylindrical column shape. The opaque colored planes at the base and the inclined open ring set up counter-rhythms to the crossed upright planes. They establish the sense of dynamic kinetic movement that Gabo always sought to express as an essential part of reality.

DE STIJL The utopian spirit and ideals of the Suprematists and Constructivists extended beyond Russia. In Holland, a group of young artists formed a new movement in 1917 and began publishing a magazine, calling both movement and magazine *De Stijl* (The Style). The group's cofounders were the painters Piet Mondrian (1872–1944) and Theo van Doesburg (1883–1931). In addition to promoting utopian ideals, De Stijl artists believed in the birth of a new age in the wake of World War I. They felt it was a time of balance between individual and universal values, when the machine would assure ease of living. In their first manifesto of De Stijl, the artists declared: "There is an old and a new consciousness of time. The old is connected with the individual. The new is connected with the universal."[41] The goal, according to van Doesburg and architect Cor van Eesteren (1897–1988), was a total integration of art and life:

> We must realize that life and art are no longer separate domains. That is why the "idea" of "art" as an illusion separate from real life must disappear. The word "Art" no longer means anything to us. In its place we demand the construction of our environment in accordance with creative laws based upon a fixed principle. These laws, following those of economics, mathematics, technique, sanitation, etc., are leading to a new, plastic unity.[42]

PIET MONDRIAN Toward this goal of integration, Mondrian created a new style based on a single ideal principle. The choice of the term "De Stijl" reflected Mondrian's confidence that this style—*the* style—revealed the underlying eternal structure of existence. Accordingly, De Stijl artists reduced their artistic vocabulary to simple geometric elements. Time spent in Paris, just before World War I, introduced Mondrian to modes of abstraction such as Cubism. However, as his attraction to contemporary theological writings grew, Mondrian sought to purge his art of every overt reference to individual objects in the external world. He initially favored the teachings of theosophy, a tradition basing knowledge of nature and the human condition on knowledge of the divine nature or spiritual powers. (His fellow theosophist, Vassily Kandinsky [FIG. 24-7], pursued a similar path.) Mondrian, however, quickly abandoned the strictures of theosophy and turned toward a conception of nonobjective design—"pure plastic art"—that he believed expressed universal reality. He articulated his credo with great eloquence in 1914:

> What first captivated us does not captivate us afterward (like toys). If one has loved the surface of things for a long time, later on one will look for something more. . . . The interior of things shows through the surface; thus as we look at the surface the inner image is formed in our soul. It is this inner image that should be represented. For the natural surface of things is beautiful, but the imitation of it is without life. . . . Art is higher than reality and has no direct relation to reality. . . . To approach the spiritual in art, one will make as little use as possible of reality, because reality is opposed to the spiritual. . . . [W]e find ourselves in the presence of an abstract art. Art should be above reality, otherwise it would have no value for man.[43]

Mondrian soon moved beyond Cubism because he felt "Cubism did not accept the logical consequences of its own discoveries; it was not developing towards its own goal, the expression of pure plastics."[44] Caught by the outbreak of hostilities while on a visit to

24-56 Piet Mondrian, *Composition with Red, Blue and Yellow*, 1930. Oil on canvas, $1' 6\frac{1}{8}'' \times 1' 6\frac{1}{8}''$. Kunsthaus, Zürich. © 2008 Mondrian/Holtzman Trust c/o HCR International, VA, USA.

Mondrian created numerous "pure plastic" paintings in which he locked primary colors into a grid of intersecting vertical and horizontal lines. By altering the grid patterns, he created a dynamic tension.

Holland, Mondrian remained there during World War I, developing his theories for what he called *Neoplasticism*—the new "pure plastic art." He believed all great art had polar but coexistent goals, the attempt to create "universal beauty" and the desire for "aesthetic expression of oneself."[45] The first goal is objective in nature, whereas the second is subjective, existing within the individual's mind and heart. To create such a universal expression, an artist must communicate "a real equation of the universal and the individual."[46]

To express this vision, Mondrian eventually limited his formal vocabulary to the three primary colors (red, yellow, and blue), the three primary values (black, white, and gray), and the two primary directions (horizontal and vertical). Basing his ideas on a combination of teachings, he concluded that primary colors and values are the purest colors and therefore are the perfect tools to help an artist construct a harmonious composition. Using this system, he created numerous paintings locking color planes into a grid of intersecting vertical and horizontal lines, as in *Composition with Red, Blue, and Yellow* (FIG. 24-56). In each of these paintings, Mondrian altered the grid patterns and the size and placement of the color planes to create an internal cohesion and harmony. This did not mean inertia. Rather, Mondrian worked to maintain a dynamic tension in his paintings from the size and position of lines, shapes, and colors.

Sculpture

It was impossible for early-20th-century artists to ignore the increasingly intrusive expansion of mechanization and growth of technology. However, not all artists embraced these developments, as had the Futurists. In contrast, many artists attempted to overcome the

Brancusi, Hepworth, and Moore
on Abstract Sculpture

Many early-20th-century sculptors rejected the notion that reproducing the physical world of nature was the purpose of sculpture. Instead, they championed abstraction as the sculptor's proper goal. Among those who not only produced enduring masterpieces of abstract sculpture but also wrote eloquently about the theoretical basis of their work were Constantin Brancusi (FIG. 24-57), Barbara Hepworth (FIG. 24-58), and Henry Moore (FIG. 24-59). Some excerpts from their writings on sculpture illustrate their commitment to abstraction as their guiding principle.

▌ *Constantin Brancusi* Simplicity is not an objective in art, but one achieves simplicity despite oneself by entering into the real sense of things.* What is real is not the external form but the essence of things. Starting from this truth it is impossible for anyone to express anything essentially real by imitating its exterior surface.[†]

▌ *Barbara Hepworth* The forms which have had special meaning for me since childhood have been the standing form (which is the translation of my feeling towards the human being standing in landscape); the two forms (which is the tender relationship of one living thing beside another); and the closed form, such as the oval, spherical, or pierced form (sometimes incorporating colour) which translates for me the association and meaning of gesture in the landscape. . . . In all these shapes the translation of what one feels about man and nature must be conveyed by the sculptor in terms of mass, inner tension, and rhythm, scale in relation to our human size, and the quality of surface which speaks through our hands and eyes.[‡]

▌ *Henry Moore* Since the Gothic, European sculpture had become overgrown with moss, weeds—all sorts of surface excrescences which completely concealed shape. It has been Brancusi's special mission to get rid of this overgrowth, and to make us once more shape-conscious. To do this he has had to concentrate on very simple direct shapes. . . . Abstract qualities of design are essential to the value of a work. . . . Because a work does not aim at reproducing natural appearances, it is not, therefore, an escape from life—but may be a penetration into reality. . . . My sculpture is becoming less representational, less an outward visual copy . . . but only because I believe that in this way I can present the human psychological content of my work with greatest directness and intensity.[§]

* Quoted in Herschel B. Chipp, *Theories of Modern Art: A Source Book by Artists and Critics* (Berkeley and Los Angeles: University of California Press, 1968), 364–365.
[†] Quoted in George Heard Hamilton, *Painting and Sculpture in Europe, 1880–1940,* 6th ed. (New Haven: Yale University Press, 1993), 426.
[‡] Barbara Hepworth, *A Pictorial Autobiography* (London: Tate Gallery, 1978), 9, 53.
[§] Quoted in Robert L. Herbert, *Modern Artists on Art,* 2d ed. (Mineola, N.Y.: Dover, 2000), 173–179.

24-57 CONSTANTIN BRANCUSI, *Bird in Space,* 1924. Bronze, 4′ 2$\frac{5}{16}$″ high. Philadelphia Museum of Art, Philadelphia (Louise and Walter Arensberg Collection, 1950).

Although not a literal depiction of a bird, Brancusi's softly curving, light-reflecting abstract sculpture in polished bronze suggests a bird about to soar in free flight through the heavens.

1 ft.

predominance of mechanization in society by immersing themselves in a search for the organic and natural.

CONSTANTIN BRANCUSI Romanian artist CONSTANTIN BRANCUSI (1876–1957) was one of many sculptors eager to produce works emphasizing the natural or organic. Often composed of softly curving surfaces and ovoid forms, his sculptures refer, directly or indirectly, to the cycle of life. Brancusi sought to move beyond surface appearances to capture the essence or spirit of the object depicted (see "Brancusi, Hepworth, and Moore on Abstract Sculpture," above). Brancusi's ability to design rhythmic, elegant sculptures conveying the essence of his subjects is evident in *Bird in Space* (FIG. 24-57). Clearly not a literal depiction of a bird, the work is the final result of a long process. Brancusi started with the image of a bird at rest with its wings folded at its sides and ended with an abstract columnar form sharply tapered at each end. Despite the abstraction, the sculpture retains the suggestion of a bird about to soar in free flight through the heavens. The highly reflective surface of the polished bronze does not allow the eye to linger on the sculpture itself (as do, for example, Rodin's agitated and textured surfaces; FIGS. 23-32 and 23-33). Instead, the viewer's eye follows the gleaming reflection along the delicate curves to glide right off the tip of the work, thereby inducing a feeling of flight. Brancusi stated, "All my life I have sought the essence of flight. Don't look for mysteries. I give you pure joy. Look at the sculptures until you see them. Those nearest to God have seen them."[47]

BARBARA HEPWORTH British artist BARBARA HEPWORTH (1903–1975) developed her own kind of essential sculptural form, combining pristine shape with a sense of organic vitality. She sought a sculptural idiom that would express her sense both of nature and the landscape and of the person who is in and observes nature (see "Brancusi, Hepworth, and Moore," above). By 1929, Hepworth arrived at a breakthrough that evolved into an enduring and commanding

24-58 Barbara Hepworth, *Oval Sculpture (No. 2),* 1943. Plaster cast, 11¼″ × 1′ 4¼″ × 10″. Tate Gallery, London.

Hepworth's major contribution to the history of sculpture was the introduction of the hole, or negative space, as an abstract element that is as integral and important to the sculpture as its mass.

element in her work from that point forward, and that represents her major contribution to the history of sculpture: the use of the hole, or void. Particularly noteworthy is that Hepworth introduced the hole, or negative space, in her sculpture as an abstract element—it does not represent anything specific—and one that is as integral and important to the sculpture as its mass. *Oval Sculpture (No. 2)* is a plaster cast (FIG. 24-58) of an earlier wooden sculpture Hepworth carved in 1943. Pierced in four places, *Oval Sculpture* is as much defined by the smooth, curving holes as by the volume of white plaster. Like the forms in all of Hepworth's mature works, those in *Oval Sculpture* are basic and universal, expressing a sense of eternity's timelessness.

HENRY MOORE British sculptor HENRY MOORE (1898–1986) shared Hepworth's interest in the hole, or void, and Brancusi's profound love of nature and knowledge of organic forms and materials. Moore maintained that every "material has its own individual qualities" and that these qualities could play a role in the creative process: "It is only when the sculptor works direct, when there is an active relationship with his material, that the material can take its part in the shaping of an idea."[48] Accordingly, the forms and lines of Moore's lead and stone sculptures tend to emphasize the material's hardness and solidity, whereas his fluid wood sculptures draw attention to the flow of the wood grain. One major recurring theme in Moore's work is the reclining female figure with simplified and massive forms. A tiny photograph of a Chacmool from ancient Mexico originally inspired this motif.

Although viewers can recognize a human figure in most of Moore's works, the artist simplified and abstracted the figure, attempting to express a universal truth beyond the physical world (see "Brancusi, Hepworth, and Moore," page 727). *Reclining Figure* (FIG. 24-59) reveals Moore's expressive handling of the human form and his responsiveness to his chosen material—here, elm wood. The contours of the sculpture follow the grain of the wood. The figure's massive shapes suggest Surrealist biomorphic forms (FIG. 24-52), but Moore's recumbent woman is also a powerful earth mother whose undulant forms and hollows suggest nurturing human energy. Similarly, they evoke the contours of the Yorkshire hills of Moore's childhood and the wind-polished surfaces of weathered wood and stone. The sculptor heightened the allusions to landscape and to Surrealist organic forms in his work by interplaying mass and void, based on the intriguing qualities of cavities in nature. As he explained, "The hole connects one side to the other, making it immediately more three-dimensional. . . . The mystery of the hole—the mysterious fascination of caves in hillsides and cliffs."[49] The concern with the void—the holes—recalls the sculpture of artists such as Barbara Hepworth (FIG. 24-58), whose work influenced him, and Aleksandr Archipenko (FIG. 24-20). Above all, *Reclining Figure* combines the organic vocabulary central to Moore's philosophy—bone shapes, eroded rocks, and geologic formations—to communicate the human form's fluidity, dynamism, and evocative nature.

24-59 Henry Moore, *Reclining Figure,* 1939. Elm wood, 3′ 1″ × 6′ 7″ × 2′ 6″. Detroit Institute of Arts, Detroit (Founders Society purchase with funds from the Dexter M. Ferry Jr. Trustee Corporation).

The reclining female figure was a major theme in Moore's sculptures. He simplified and abstracted the massive form in a way that recalls Biomorphic Surrealism. The contours follow the grain of the wood.

10 ft.

24-60 Vera Mukhina, *The Worker and the Collective Farm Worker,* Soviet Pavilion, Paris Exposition, 1937. Stainless steel, 78′ high. Art © Estate of Vera Mukhina/RAO, Moscow/VAGA, New York.

In contrast to contemporaneous abstract sculpture, Mukhina's realistic representation of a male factory worker and a female farm worker glorifies the communal labor of the Soviet people.

VERA MUKHINA Not all sculptors of this period pursued abstraction, however. *The Worker and the Collective Farm Worker* (FIG. **24-60**) by Russian artist Vera Mukhina (1889–1963) presents a vivid contrast to the work of Brancusi, Hepworth, and Moore. Produced in 1937 for the International Exposition in Paris— the same venue in which Picasso displayed *Guernica* (FIG. **24-41**)— Mukhina's monumental stainless-steel sculpture glorifies the communal labor of the Soviet people. Whereas Picasso employed Cubist abstraction to convey the horror of wartime bombing, Mukhina relied on realism to represent exemplars of the Soviet citizenry. Her sculpture, which stood atop the Soviet Pavilion at the exposition, depicts a male factory worker holding aloft the tool of his trade, the hammer. Alongside him is a female farm worker raising her sickle to the sky. The juxtaposed hammer and sickle, appearing as they do at the apex of the sculpture, replicate their appearance on the Soviet flag, thereby celebrating the Soviet system. The artist augmented the heroic tenor of this sculpture by emphasizing the solidity of the figures, who stride forward with their clothes billowing dramatically behind them. Mukhina had studied in Paris and was familiar with abstraction, especially Cubism, but felt that a commitment to real-

ism produced the most powerful sculpture. The Soviet government officially approved this realist style, and Mukhina earned high praise for her sculpture. Indeed, Russian citizens celebrated the work as a national symbol for decades.

AMERICA, 1930 TO 1945

The Armory Show of 1913 (see "The Armory Show," page 710) was an important vehicle for exposing American artists to modernist European art. Equally significant was the emigration of European artists across the Atlantic Ocean. The havoc Hitler and the National Socialists wreaked in the early 1930s (see "Degenerate Art," page 721) forced artists to flee. The United States, among other countries, offered both survival and a more hospitable environment for producing their art. Léger, Lipchitz, Beckmann, Grosz, Ernst, and Dalí, among many others, all made their way to American cities.

Museums in the United States, wanting to demonstrate their familiarity and connection with the most progressive European art, mounted exhibitions centered on the latest European artistic developments. In 1938, for example, the City Art Museum of Saint Louis presented an exhibition of Beckmann's work, and the Art Institute of Chicago organized *George Grosz: A Survey of His Art from 1918–1938.* This interest in exhibiting the work of persecuted artists driven from their homelands also had political overtones. In the highly charged atmosphere of the late 1930s leading to the onset of World War II, people often perceived support for these artists and their work as support for freedom and democracy. In 1942, Alfred H. Barr Jr. (1902–1981), director of the Museum of Modern Art, stated:

> Among the freedoms which the Nazis have destroyed, none has been more cynically perverted, more brutally stamped upon, than the Freedom of Art. For not only must the artist of Nazi Germany bow to political tyranny, he must also conform to the personal taste of that great art connoisseur, Adolf Hitler. . . . But German artists of spirit and integrity have refused to conform. They have gone into exile or slipped into anxious obscurity. . . . Their paintings and sculptures, too, have been hidden or exiled. . . . But in free countries they can still be seen, can still bear witness to the survival of a free German culture.[50]

Despite this moral support for exiled artists, once the United States formally entered the war, Germany officially became the enemy. Then it was much more difficult for the American art world to promote German artists, however persecuted. Many émigré artists, including Léger, Grosz, Ernst, and Dalí, returned to Europe after the war ended. Their collective presence in the United States until then, however, was critical for the development of American art and contributed to the burgeoning interest in the avant-garde among American artists.

Sculpture and Photography

ALEXANDER CALDER One American artist who rose to international prominence at this time was Alexander Calder (1898–1976). Both the artist's father and grandfather were sculptors, but Calder initially studied mechanical engineering. Fascinated all his life by motion, he explored that phenomenon and its relationship to three-dimensional form in much of his sculpture. As a young artist in Paris in the late 1920s, Calder invented a circus filled with wire-based miniature performers that he activated into realistic analogues of their real-life counterparts' motion. After a visit to Mondrian's studio in the early 1930s, Calder set out to put the Dutch painter's brightly colored rectangular shapes (FIG. **24-56**) into motion. (Marcel Duchamp, intrigued by Calder's early motorized and hand-cranked examples of moving abstract pieces, named them *mobiles.*) Calder's

The Museum of Modern Art
and the Avant-Garde

Established in 1929, the Museum of Modern Art (often called MoMA) in New York City owes its existence to a trio of women—Lillie P. Bliss, Mary Quinn Sullivan, and Abby Aldrich Rockefeller (see "Art 'Matronage' in America," page 709). These women saw the need for a museum to collect and exhibit modernist art. Together they founded what quickly became the most influential museum of modern art in the world. Their success was extraordinary considering the skepticism and hostility greeting much of modernist art at the time of the museum's inception. Indeed, at that time, few American museums exhibited late-19th- and 20th-century art at all.

In its quest to expose the public to the energy and challenge of modernist, particularly avant-garde, art, MoMA developed unique and progressive exhibitions. Among those the museum mounted during the early years of its existence were *Cubism and Abstract Art* and *Fantastic Art, Dada, Surrealism* (1936). Two other noteworthy shows were *American Sources of Modern Art (Aztec, Maya, Inca)* in 1933 and *African Negro Art* in 1935, among the first exhibitions to deal with "primitive" artifacts in artistic rather than anthropological terms (see "Primitivism," page 696).

The organization of MoMA's administrative structure and the scope of the museum's early activities were also remarkable. MoMA's first director, Alfred H. Barr Jr., insisted on establishing departments not only for painting and sculpture but also for photography, prints and drawing, architecture, and the decorative arts. He developed a library of books on modern art and a film library, both of which have become world-class collections, as well as an extensive publishing program.

It is the museum's art collection, however, that has drawn the most attention. By cultivating an influential group of patrons, MoMA has developed an extensive and enviable collection of late-19th- and

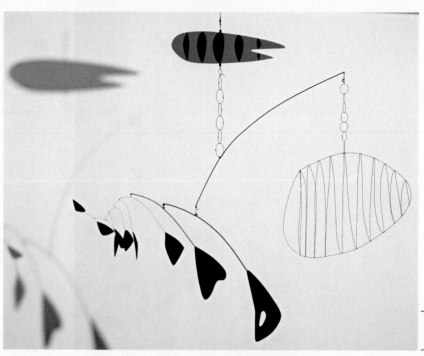

24-61 Alexander Calder, *Lobster Trap and Fish Tail*, 1939. Painted sheet aluminum and steel wire, 8′ 6″ × 9′ 6″. Museum of Modern Art, New York.

Using his thorough knowledge of engineering to combine nonobjective organic forms and motion, Calder created a new kind of sculpture—the mobile—that expressed reality's innate dynamism.

20th-century art. Its collection includes such important works as van Gogh's *Starry Night* (FIG. 23-17), Picasso's *Les Demoiselles d'Avignon* (FIG. 24-12), and Dali's *The Persistence of Memory* (FIG. 24-49), as well as many others illustrated in this book, including 19 in this chapter alone. MoMA has also served as an art patron itself, commissioning works like Calder's *Lobster Trap and Fish Tail* (FIG. 24-61) in 1939, just a decade after the institution's founding.

engineering skills soon helped him to fashion a series of balanced structures hanging from rods, wires, and colored, organically shaped plates. This new kind of sculpture, which combined nonobjective organic forms and motion, succeeded in expressing the innate dynamism of the natural world.

An early Calder mobile is *Lobster Trap and Fish Tail* (FIG. **24-61**), which the artist created in 1939 under a commission from the Museum of Modern Art in New York City for the stairwell of the museum's new building on 53rd Street (see "The Museum of Modern Art and the Avant-Garde," above). Calder carefully planned each nonmechanized mobile so that any air current would set the parts moving to create a constantly shifting dance in space. Mondrian's work may have provided the initial inspiration for the mobiles, but their organic

shapes resemble those in Joan Miró's Surrealist paintings (FIG. 24-52). Indeed, a viewer can read Calder's forms as either geometric or organic. Geometrically, the lines suggest circuitry and rigging, and the shapes derive from circles and ovoid forms. Organically, the lines suggest nerve axons, and the shapes resemble cells, leaves, fins, wings, and other bioforms.

GREAT DEPRESSION In the 1930s much of the Western world plunged into the Great Depression, which had particularly acute ramifications in the United States. The decade following the catastrophic stock market crash of October 1929 dramatically changed the nation, and artists were among the many economic victims. The limited art market virtually disappeared, and museums curtailed both their purchases and exhibition schedules. Many artists sought financial support from the federal government, which established numerous programs to provide relief, assist recovery, and promote reform. Among the programs supporting artists were the Treasury Relief Art Project, founded in 1934 to commission art for federal buildings, and the Works Progress Administration (WPA), founded in 1935 to relieve widespread unemployment. Under the WPA, varied activities of the Federal Art Project paid artists, writers, and theater people a regular wage in exchange for work in their professions. Another important program was the Resettlement Administration (RA), better known by its later name, the Farm Security Administration. The RA oversaw emergency aid programs for farm families caught in the Depression.

DOROTHEA LANGE The RA hired American photographer Dorothea Lange (1895–1965) in 1936 and dispatched her to photograph the rural poor attempting to survive the desperate conditions wrought by the Great Depression. At the end of an assignment to document the lives of migratory pea pickers in California, Lange stopped at a camp in Nipomo and found the migrant workers there starving because the crops had frozen in the fields. Among the pictures Lange made on this occasion was *Migrant Mother, Nipomo Valley* (FIG. 24-62), in which she captured the mixture of strength and worry in the raised hand and careworn face of a young mother, who holds a baby on her lap. Two older children cling to their

mother trustingly while shunning the camera. Lange described how she got the picture:

> [I] saw and approached the hungry and desperate mother, as if drawn by a magnet. I do not remember how I explained my presence or my camera to her, but I remember she asked me no questions. I made five exposures, working closer and closer from the same direction. . . . There she sat in that lean-to tent with her children huddled around her, and she seemed to know that my pictures might help her, and so she helped me.[51]

Within days after Lange's photograph appeared in a San Francisco newspaper, people rushed food to Nipomo to feed the hungry workers.

Painting

The political, social, and economic developments of the 1930s and 1940s also had a profound effect on American painters.

BEN SHAHN Born in Lithuania, Ben Shahn (1898–1969) came to the United States in 1906 and trained as a lithographer before broadening the media in which he worked to include easel painting, photography, and murals. He focused on the lives of ordinary people and the injustices often done to them by the structure of an impersonal, bureaucratic society. In the early 1930s, he completed a cycle of 23 paintings and prints inspired by the trial and execution of the two Italian anarchists Nicola Sacco and Bartolomeo Vanzetti. Accused of killing two men in a holdup in 1920 in South Braintree, Massachusetts, the Italians were convicted in a trial that many people thought resulted in a grave miscarriage of justice. Shahn felt he had found in this story a subject the equal of any in Western art history: "Suddenly I realized . . . I was living through another crucifixion."[52] Basing many of the works in this cycle on newspaper photographs of the events, Shahn devised a style that adapted his knowledge of Synthetic Cubism and his training in commercial art to an emotionally expressive use of flat, intense color in figural compositions filled with sharp, dry, angular forms. He called the major work in the series *The Passion of Sacco and Vanzetti* (FIG. I-5), drawing a parallel to Christ's Passion. This tall, narrow painting condenses the narrative in terms of both time and space. The two executed men lie in coffins at the bottom of the composition. Presiding over them are the three members of the commission chaired by Harvard University president A. Laurence Lowell, who declared the original trial fair and cleared the way for the executions to take place. A framed portrait of Judge Webster Thayer, who handed down the initial sentence, hangs on the wall of a simplified government building. The gray pallor of the dead men, the stylized mask-faces of the mock-pious mourning commissioners, and the sanctimonious, distant judge all contribute to the mood of anguished commentary that makes this image one of Shahn's most powerful works.

EDWARD HOPPER Trained as a commercial artist, Edward Hopper (1882–1967) studied painting and printmaking in New York and then in Paris. When he returned to the United States, he concentrated on scenes of contemporary American city and country life. His paintings depict buildings, streets, and landscapes that are curiously muted, still, and filled with empty spaces, evoking the national mind-set during the Depression era. Hopper did not paint historically specific scenes. He took as his subject the more generalized theme of the overwhelming loneliness and echoing isolation of modern life in the United States. In his paintings, motion is stopped

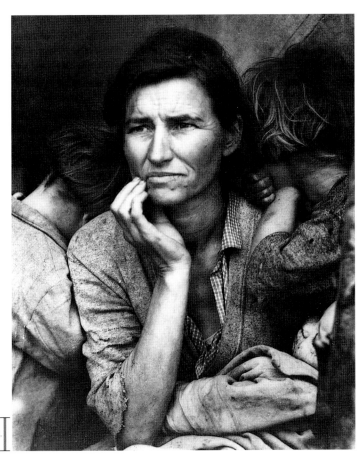

1 in.

24-62 Dorothea Lange, *Migrant Mother, Nipomo Valley,* 1935. Gelatin silver print, 1′ 1″ × 9″. Oakland Museum of California, Oakland (gift of Paul S. Taylor).

While documenting the lives of migratory farm workers during the Depression, Lange made this unforgettable photograph of a mother in which she captured the woman's strength and worry.

24-63 EDWARD HOPPER, *Nighthawks*, 1942. Oil on canvas, 2′ 6″ × 4′ 8 11/16″. Art Institute of Chicago, Chicago (Friends of American Art Collection).

The seeming indifference of Hopper's characters to one another, and the echoing spaces that surround them, evoke the overwhelming loneliness and isolation of Depression-era life in the United States.

and time suspended, as if the artist recorded the major details of a poignant personal memory. From the darkened streets outside a restaurant in *Nighthawks* (FIG. **24-63**), the viewer glimpses the lighted interior through huge plate-glass windows, which lend the inner space the paradoxical sense of being both a safe refuge and a vulnerable place for the three customers and the counterman. The seeming indifference of Hopper's characters to one another and the echoing spaces that surround them suggest the pervasive loneliness of modern humans. In *Nighthawks* and other works, Hopper created a Realist vision recalling that of 19th-century artists such as Thomas Eakins (FIG. 22-38) and Henry Ossawa Tanner (FIG. 22-40), but, consistent with more recent trends in painting, he simplified the shapes in a move toward abstraction.

JACOB LAWRENCE African American artist JACOB LAWRENCE (1917–2000) found his subjects in modern history, concentrating on the culture and history of his own people. Lawrence moved to Harlem, New York, in 1927 at about age 10. There, he came under the spell of the African art and the African American history he found in lectures and exhibitions and in the special programs sponsored by the 135th Street New York Public Library, which had outstanding collections of African American art and archival data. Inspired by the politically oriented art of Goya (FIG. 22-13), Daumier (FIG. 22-30), and Orozco (FIG. 24-67), and influenced by the many artists and writers of the Harlem Renaissance whom he met, including Aaron Douglas (FIG. 24-36), Lawrence found his subjects in the everyday life of Harlem and in African American history.

In 1941, Lawrence began a 60-painting series titled *The Migration of the Negro,* in which he defined his own vision of the continuing African American struggle against discrimination. Unlike his earlier historical paintings depicting important figures in American history,

such as the abolitionists Frederick Douglass and Harriet Tubman, this series called attention to a contemporaneous event—the ongoing exodus of black labor from the southern United States. Disillusioned with their lives in the South, hundreds of thousands of African Americans migrated north in the years following World War I, seeking improved economic opportunities and more hospitable political and social conditions. This subject had personal relevance to Lawrence:

> I was part of the migration, as was my family, my mother, my sister, and my brother. . . . I grew up hearing tales about people "coming up," another family arriving. . . . I didn't realize what was happening until about the middle of the 1930s, and that's when the *Migration* series began to take form in my mind.[53]

The "documentation" of the period, such as the RA program, ignored African Americans, and thus this major demographic shift remained largely invisible to most Americans. Of course, the conditions African Americans encountered both during their migration and in the North were often as difficult and discriminatory as those they had left behind in the South.

Lawrence's series provides numerous vignettes capturing the experiences of these migrating people. Often, a sense of bleakness and of the degradation of African American life dominates the images. *No. 49* (FIG. **24-64**) of this series bears the caption "They also found discrimination in the North although it was much different from that which they had known in the South." The artist depicted a blatantly segregated dining room with a barrier running down the room's center separating the whites on the left from the African Americans on the right. To ensure a continuity and visual integrity among all 60 paintings, Lawrence interpreted his themes systematically in rhythmic arrangements of bold, flat, and strongly colored shapes. His style drew equally from his interest in the push-pull

1 in.

24-64 JACOB LAWRENCE, *No. 49* from *The Migration of the Negro*, 1940–1941. Tempera on Masonite, 1′ 6″ × 1′. Phillips Collection, Washington, D.C.

The 49th in a series of 60 paintings documenting African American life in the North, Lawrence's depiction of a segregated dining room underscored that the migrants had not left discrimination behind.

1 ft.

24-65 GRANT WOOD, *American Gothic*, 1930. Oil on beaverboard, 2′ 5$\frac{7}{8}$″ × 2′ 7$\frac{7}{8}$″. Art Institute of Chicago, Chicago (Friends of American Art Collection). Art © Estate of Grant Wood/Licensed by VAGA, New York.

In reaction to modernist abstract painting, the Midwestern Regionalism movement focused on American subjects. Wood's painting of an Iowa farmer and his daughter is an American icon.

effects of Cubist space and his memories of the patterns made by the colored scatter rugs brightening the floors of his childhood homes. He unified the narrative with a consistent palette of bluish green, orange, yellow, and grayish brown throughout the entire series.

GRANT WOOD Although many American artists, such as the Precisionists (FIGS. 24-37 and 24-38), preferred to depict the city or rapidly developing technological advances, others avoided subjects tied to modern life. At a 1931 arts conference, GRANT WOOD (1891–1942) announced a new movement developing in the Midwest, known as *Regionalism,* which he described as focused on American subjects and as standing in reaction to the modernist abstraction of Europe and New York. Four years later, Wood published an essay "Revolt against the City" that underscored this new focus. Wood and the Regionalists, sometimes referred to as the American Scene Painters, turned their attention instead to rural life as America's cultural backbone. Wood's paintings, for example, focus on rural Iowa, where he was born and raised.

The work that catapulted Wood to national prominence was *American Gothic* (FIG. 24-65), which became an American icon. The artist depicted a farmer and his spinster daughter standing in front of a neat house with a small *lancet* window, typically found on Gothic cathedrals. The man and woman wear traditional attire. He appears in worn overalls, and she in an apron trimmed with rickrack. The dour expression on both faces gives the painting a severe quality, which Wood enhanced with his meticulous brushwork. The public and professional critics agreed that *American Gothic* was "quaint, humorous, and AMERICAN" and embodied "strength, dignity, fortitude, resoluteness, integrity," qualities that represented the true spirit of America.[54]

Wood's Regionalist vision involved more than his subjects. It extended to a rejection of avant-garde styles in favor of a clearly readable, Realist style. Surely this approach appealed to many people alienated by the increasing presence of abstraction in art. Interestingly enough, despite the accolades this painting received, it also attracted criticism. Not everyone saw the painting as a sympathetic portrayal of Midwestern life. Indeed, some in Iowa considered the depiction insulting. In addition, despite the seemingly reportorial nature of *American Gothic,* some viewed it as a political statement—one of staunch nationalism. In light of the problematic nationalism in Germany at the time, many observers found Wood's nationalistic attitude disturbing. Nonetheless, during the Great Depression, Regionalist paintings had a popular appeal because they often projected a reassuring image of America's heartland. The public saw Regionalism as a means of coping with the national crisis through a search for cultural roots. Thus, people deemed acceptable any nostalgia implicit in Regionalist paintings or mythologies these works perpetuated because they served a larger purpose.

24-66 Thomas Hart Benton, *Pioneer Days and Early Settlers*, State Capitol, Jefferson City, Missouri, 1936. Mural. Art © T. H. Benton and R. P. Benton Testamentary Trusts/UMB Bank Trustee/Licensed by VAGA, New York.

Benton's mural for Missouri's State Capitol is one of the major Regionalist artworks. Part documentary and part invention, the images include both positive and negative aspects of state history.

THOMAS HART BENTON Another major Regionalist artist was THOMAS HART BENTON (1889–1975). Whereas Wood focused his attention on Iowa, Benton turned to scenes from his native Missouri. He produced one of his major works, a series of murals titled *A Social History of the State of Missouri*, in 1936 for the Missouri State Capitol. The murals depict a collection of images from the state's true and legendary history, such as primitive agriculture, horse trading, a vigilante lynching, and an old-fashioned political meeting. Other scenes portray the mining industry, grain elevators, Native Americans, and family life. One segment, *Pioneer Days and Early Settlers* (FIG. **24-66**), shows a white man using whiskey as a bartering tool with a Native American (at left), along with scenes documenting the building of Missouri. Part documentary and part invention, Benton's images include both positive and negative aspects of Missouri's history, as these examples illustrate. Although the public perceived the Regionalists as dedicated to glorifying Midwest-

ern life, that belief distorted their aims. Indeed, Grant Wood observed, "your true regionalist is not a mere eulogist; he may even be a severe critic."[55] Benton, like Wood, championed a visually accessible style, but he developed a highly personal aesthetic that included complex compositions, a fluidity of imagery, and simplified figures depicted with a rubbery distortion.

JOSÉ CLEMENTE OROZCO During the period between the two world wars, three Mexican painters achieved international renown for their work both in Mexico and in the United States. The eldest of the three was JOSÉ CLEMENTE OROZCO (1883–1949), one of a group of Mexican artists determined to base their art on the indigenous history and culture existing in Mexico before Europeans arrived. The movement these artists formed was part of the idealistic rethinking of society that occurred in conjunction with the Mexican Revolution (1910–1920) and the lingering political turmoil of the 1920s.

24-67 José Clemente Orozco, *Epic of American Civilization: Hispano-America* (panel 16), Baker Memorial Library, Dartmouth College, Hanover, New Hampshire, ca. 1932–1934. Fresco. Copyright © Orozco Valladares Family/SOMAAP, Mexico/Licensed by VAGA, New York.

One of 24 panels depicting the history of Mexico from ancient times, this scene focuses on a heroic peasant soldier of the Mexican Revolution surrounded by symbolic figures of his oppressors.

Rivera on Art for the People

Diego Rivera was an avid proponent of a social and political role for art in the lives of common people and wrote passionately about the proper goals for an artist—goals he fully met in his murals depicting Mexican history (FIG. 24-68). Rivera's views stand in sharp contrast to the growing interest in abstraction on the part of many early-20th-century painters and sculptors.

Art has always been employed by the different social classes who hold the balance of power as one instrument of domination—hence, as a political instrument. One can analyze epoch after epoch—from the stone age to our own day—and see that there is no form of art which does not also play an essential political role.... What is it then that we really need? ... An art with revolution as its subject: because the principal interest in the worker's life has to be touched first. It is necessary that he find aesthetic satisfaction and the highest pleasure appareled in the essential interest of his life.... The subject is to the painter what the rails are to a locomotive. He cannot do without it. In fact, when he refuses to seek or accept a subject, his own plastic methods and his own aesthetic theories become his subject instead.... [H]e himself becomes the subject of his work. He be-

comes nothing but an illustrator of his own state of mind ... That is the deception practiced under the name of "Pure Art."*

* Quoted in Robert Goldwater and Marco Treves, eds., *Artists on Art from the XIV to the XX Century* (New York: Pantheon, 1945), 475–477.

24-68 DIEGO RIVERA, *Ancient Mexico,* from the *History of Mexico,* Palacio Nacional, Mexico City, 1929–1935. Fresco.

A staunch Marxist, Rivera painted vast mural cycles in public buildings to dramatize the history of his native land. This fresco depicts the conflicts between indigenous Mexicans and the Spanish colonizers.

Among the projects these politically motivated artists undertook were vast mural cycles placed in public buildings to dramatize and validate the history of Mexico's native peoples. Orozco worked on one of the first major cycles, painted in 1922 on the walls of the National Training School in Mexico City. He carried the ideas of this mural revolution to the United States, completing many commissions for wall paintings between 1927 and 1934. From 1932 to 1934, he worked on one of his finest mural cycles in Baker Library at Dartmouth College in New Hampshire, partly in honor of its superb collection of books in Spanish. The college let him choose the subject. Orozco depicted, in 14 large panels and 10 smaller ones, a panoramic and symbolic history of ancient and modern Mexico, from the early mythic days of the feathered-serpent god Quetzalcoatl to a contemporary and bitterly satiric vision of modern education.

The imagery in panel 16, *Epic of American Civilization: Hispano-America* (FIG. 24-67), revolves around the monumental figure of a heroic Mexican peasant armed to participate in the Mexican Revolution. Looming on either side of him are mounds crammed with symbolic figures of his oppressors—bankers, government soldiers, officials, gangsters, and the rich. Money-grubbers pour hoards of gold at the incorruptible peon's feet, cannons threaten him, and a bemedaled general raises a dagger to stab him in the back. Orozco's

training as an architect gave him a sense of the framed wall surface, which he easily commanded, projecting his clearly defined figures onto the solid mural plane in monumental scale. In addition, Orozco's early training as a maker of political prints and as a newspaper artist had taught him the rhetorical strength of graphic brevity, which he used here to assure that his allegory could be read easily. His special merging of the graphic and mural media effects gives his work an originality and force rarely seen in mural painting after the Renaissance and Baroque periods.

DIEGO RIVERA Like his countryman, DIEGO RIVERA (1886–1957) received great acclaim for his murals, both in Mexico and in the United States. A staunch Marxist, Rivera strove to develop an art that served his people's needs (see "Rivera on Art for the People," above). Toward that end, he sought to create a national Mexican style focusing on Mexico's history and incorporating a popular, generally accessible aesthetic in keeping with the socialist spirit of the Mexican Revolution. Rivera produced numerous large murals in public buildings, among them a series lining the staircase of the National Palace in Mexico City. In these images, painted between 1929 and 1935, he depicted scenes from Mexico's history, of which *Ancient Mexico* (FIG. 24-68) is one. This section of the mural represents the

24-69 Frida Kahlo, *The Two Fridas*, 1939. Oil on canvas, 5′ 7″ × 5′ 7″. Museo de Arte Moderno, Mexico City.

Kahlo's deeply personal paintings touch sensual and psychological memories in her audience. Here, twin self-portraits linked by clasped hands and a common artery suggest different sides of her personality.

1 ft.

conflicts between the indigenous people and the Spanish colonizers. Rivera included portraits of important figures in Mexican history and, in particular, in the struggle for Mexican independence. Although complex, the decorative, animated murals retain the legibility of folklore, and the figures consist of simple monumental shapes and areas of bold color.

FRIDA KAHLO Born to a Mexican mother and German father, the painter FRIDA KAHLO (1907–1954), who married Diego Rivera, used the details of her life as powerful symbols for the psychological pain of human existence. Art historians often consider Kahlo a Surrealist due to the psychic and autobiographical issues she dealt with in her art. Indeed, André Breton deemed her a Natural Surrealist, although Kahlo herself rejected any association with Surrealism. Kahlo began painting seriously as a young student, during convalescence from an accident that tragically left her in constant pain. Her life became a heroic and tumultuous battle for survival against illness and stormy personal relationships.

Typical of her long series of unflinching self-portraits is *The Two Fridas* (FIG. **24-69**), one of the few large-scale canvases Kahlo ever produced. The twin figures sit side by side on a low bench in a barren landscape under a stormy sky. The figures suggest different sides of the artist's personality, inextricably linked by the clasped hands and by the thin artery that stretches between them, joining their exposed hearts. The artery ends on one side in surgical forceps and on the other in a miniature portrait of her husband as a child. Her deeply personal paintings touch sensual and psychological memories in her audience.

However, to read Kahlo's paintings solely as autobiographical overlooks the powerful political dimension of her art. Kahlo was deeply nationalistic and committed to her Mexican heritage. Politically active, she joined the Communist Party in 1920 and participated in public political protests. *The Two Fridas* incorporates Kahlo's commentary on the struggle facing Mexicans in the early 20th century in defining their national cultural identity. The Frida on the right (representing indigenous culture) appears in a Tehuana dress, the traditional costume of Zapotec women from the Isthmus of Tehuantepec, whereas the Frida on the left (representing imperialist forces) wears a European-style white lace dress. The heart, depicted here in such dramatic fashion, was an important symbol in the art of the Aztecs, whom Mexican nationalists idealized as the last independent rulers of an indigenous political unit. Thus, *The Two Fridas* represents both Kahlo's personal struggles and the struggles of her homeland.

ARCHITECTURE

The first half of the 20th century was a time of great innovation in architecture too. As in painting, sculpture, and photography, new ideas came from both sides of the Atlantic.

Europe

In the years immediately following the Russian Revolution, a new art movement called *Productivism* emerged in the Soviet Union as an offshoot of the Constructivist movement. The Productivists devoted their talents to designing a better environment for human beings.

VLADIMIR TATLIN One of the most gifted leaders of the Productivism movement was VLADIMIR TATLIN (1885–1953). The revolution was the signal to Tatlin and other avant-garde artists in Russia that the hated old order was about to end. In utopian fashion, these artists aspired to play a significant role in creating a new world, one that would fully use the power of industrialization to benefit all the people. Initially, like Malevich (FIG. **24-54**) and Gabo (FIG. **24-55**), Tatlin believed that nonobjective art was ideal for the new society, free as such art was from any past symbolism. But after the 1917 revolution, Tatlin enthusiastically abandoned abstract art for "functional art" by designing products such as an efficient stove and a set of worker's clothing.

Tatlin's most famous work is his design for *Monument to the Third International* (FIG. **24-70**), commissioned by the Department of Artistic Work of the People's Commissariat for Enlightenment early in 1919 to honor the Russian Revolution. He envisioned a huge glass-and-iron building that—at 1,300 feet—would have been one-third taller than the Eiffel Tower (FIG. **23-1**). Widely influential, "Tatlin's Tower," as it became known, served as a model for those seeking to encourage socially committed and functional art. On its

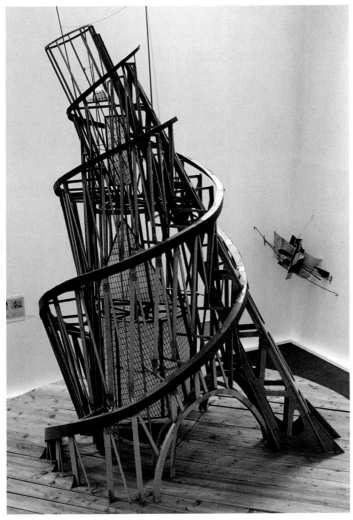

24-70 VLADIMIR TATLIN, *Monument to the Third International*, 1919–1920. Reconstruction of the lost model, 1992–1993. Kunsthalle, Düsseldorf.

"Tatlin's Tower" was an ambitious avant-garde design for a Soviet governmental building with three geometrically shaped chambers rotating at different speeds within a dynamically tilted spiral cage.

proposed site in the center of Moscow, it would have functioned as a propaganda and news center for the Soviet people. Within a dynamically tilted spiral cage, three geometrically shaped chambers were to rotate around a central axis, each chamber housing facilities for a different type of governmental activity and rotating at a different speed. The one at the bottom, a huge cylindrical glass structure for lectures and meetings, was to revolve once a year. Higher up was a cone-shaped chamber intended for administrative functions and monthly rotations. At the top, a cubic information center would have revolved daily, issuing news bulletins and proclamations via the most modern means of communication. These included an open-air news screen (illuminated at night) and a special instrument designed to project words on the clouds on any overcast day. The decreasing size of the chambers as visitors ascended the monument paralleled the decision-making hierarchy in the political system, with the most authoritative, smallest groups near the building's apex. The design thus served as a visual reinforcement of a social and political reality.

Tatlin envisioned the whole complex as a dynamic communications center perfectly suited to the exhilarating pace of the new age. In addition, the design's reductive geometry demonstrates the architect's connection to the artistic programs of the Suprematists and the Con-

structivists. Due to Russia's desperate economic situation during these years, however, Tatlin's ambitious design never materialized as a building. It existed only in metal and wood models exhibited on various official occasions before disappearing. The only records of the models are a few drawings, photographs, and recent reconstructions (FIG. 24-70).

GERRIT RIETVELD Some European architects explored the ideas Mondrian and De Stijl artists advanced. One of the masterpieces of De Stijl architecture is the Schröder House (FIG. **24-71**) in Utrecht, built in 1924 by GERRIT THOMAS RIETVELD (1888–1964). Rietveld came to the group as a cabinetmaker and made De Stijl furnishings throughout his career. His architecture carries the same spirit into a larger integrated whole and perfectly expresses Theo van Doesburg's definition of De Stijl architecture:

> The new architecture is anti-cubic, i.e., it does not strive to contain the different functional space cells in a single closed cube, but it throws the functional space (as well as canopy planes, balcony volumes, etc.) out from the centre of the cube, so that height, width, and depth plus time become a completely new plastic expression in open spaces. . . . The plastic architect . . . has to construct in the new field, time-space.[56]

The main living rooms of the Schröder House are on the second floor, with more private rooms on the ground floor. However, Rietveld's house has an open plan and a relationship to nature more like the houses of his contemporary, the American architect Frank Lloyd Wright (FIGS. 24-77 and FIG. 24-79). Rietveld designed the entire second floor with sliding partitions that can be closed to define separate rooms or pushed back to create one open space broken into units only by the furniture arrangement. This shifting quality appears also on the outside, where railings, free-floating walls, and long rectangular windows give the effect of cubic units breaking up before the viewer's eyes. Rietveld's design clearly links all the arts. Rectangular planes seem to slide across each other on the Schröder House facade like movable panels, making this structure a kind of three-dimensional projection of the rigid but carefully proportioned flat color rectangles in Mondrian's paintings (FIG. 24-56).

24-71 GERRIT THOMAS RIETVELD, Schröder House, Utrecht, the Netherlands, 1924.

The De Stijl Schröder House has an open plan and an exterior that is a kind of three-dimensional projection of the carefully proportioned flat color rectangles in Mondrian's paintings (FIG. 24-56).

WALTER GROPIUS De Stijl architects not only developed an appealing simplified geometric style but also promoted the notion that art should be thoroughly incorporated into living environments. As Mondrian had insisted, "[A]rt and life are *one;* art and life are both expressions of truth."[57] In Germany, WALTER GROPIUS (1883–1969) developed a particular vision of "total architecture." He made this concept the foundation of not only his own work but also the work of generations of pupils under his influence at a school called the *Bauhaus*. In 1919, Gropius became the director of the Weimar School of Arts and Crafts in Germany, founded in 1906. Under Gropius, the school assumed a new name—Das Staatliche Bauhaus (roughly translated as "State School of Building"). Gropius's goal was to train artists, architects, and designers to accept and anticipate 20th-century needs. He developed an extensive curriculum based on certain principles. First, Gropius staunchly advocated the importance of strong basic design (including principles of composition, two- and three-dimensionality, and color theory) and craftsmanship as fundamental to good art and architecture. He declared: "Architects, sculptors, painters, we must all go back to the crafts. . . . There is no essential difference between the artist and the craftsman."[58] To achieve this integration of art and craft, both a technical instructor and a "teacher of form"—an artist—taught in each department. Among the teachers Gropius hired were Vassily Kandinsky (FIG. 24-7) and Paul Klee (FIG. 24-53).

Second, Gropius promoted the unity of art, architecture, and design. "Architects, painters, and sculptors," he insisted, "must recognize anew the composite character of a building as an entity."[59] To encourage the elimination of boundaries that traditionally separated art from architecture and art from craft, the Bauhaus offered courses in a wide range of artistic disciplines. These included weaving, pottery, bookbinding, carpentry, metalwork, stained glass, mural painting, stage design, and advertising and typography, in addition to painting, sculpture, and architecture.

Third, because Gropius wanted the Bauhaus to produce graduates who could design progressive environments that satisfied 20th-century needs, he emphasized thorough knowledge of machine-age technologies and materials. He felt that to produce truly successful designs, the artist-architect-craftsperson had to understand industry and mass production. Ultimately, Gropius hoped for a marriage between art and industry—a synthesis of design and production.

Like the De Stijl movement, the Bauhaus philosophy had its roots in utopian principles. Gropius's declaration reveals the idealism of the entire Bauhaus enterprise: "Together let us conceive and create the new building of the future, which will embrace architecture and sculpture and painting in one unity and which will rise one day toward heaven from the hands of a million workers like a crystal symbol of a new faith."[60] In its reference to a unity of workers, this statement also reveals the undercurrent of socialism present in Germany at the time.

BAUHAUS IN DESSAU After encountering increasing hostility from a new government elected in 1924, the Bauhaus moved north to Dessau in early 1925. By this time, the Bauhaus program had matured. In a statement, Walter Gropius listed the school's goals more clearly:

▌ A decidedly positive attitude to the living environment of vehicles and machines.

▌ The organic shaping of things in accordance with their own current laws, avoiding all romantic embellishment and whimsy.

▌ Restriction of basic forms and colors to what is typical and universally intelligible.

▌ Simplicity in complexity, economy in the use of space, materials, time, and money.[61]

The building Gropius designed for the Bauhaus at Dessau visibly expressed these goals. It is, in fact, the Bauhaus's architectural manifesto. The Dessau Bauhaus consisted of workshop and class areas, a dining room, a theater, a gymnasium, a wing with studio apartments, and an enclosed two-story bridge housing administrative offices. Of the major wings, the most dramatic was the Shop Block (FIG. 24-72). Three stories tall, the Shop Block housed a printing shop and dye works facility, in addition to other work areas. The builders constructed the skeleton of reinforced concrete but set these supports well back, sheathing the entire structure in glass to create a streamlined and light effect. This design's simplicity followed Gropius's dictum that architecture should avoid "all romantic embellishment and whimsy." Further, he realized his principle of "economy in the use of space" in his interior layout of the Shop Block, which consisted of large areas of free-flowing undivided space. Gropius believed this kind of spatial organization encouraged interaction and the sharing of ideas.

MARCEL BREUER The interior decor of this Dessau building also reveals the comprehensiveness of the Bauhaus program. Because carpentry, furniture design, and weaving were all part of the Bauhaus curriculum, Gropius gave students and teachers the task of designing furniture and light fixtures for the building. One of the memorable furniture designs that emerged from the Bauhaus was the tubular steel "Wassily chair" (FIG. 24-73) crafted by Hungarian MARCEL BREUER (1902–1981) and named in honor of Bauhaus instructor Vassily

24-72 WALTER GROPIUS, Shop Block, the Bauhaus, Dessau, Germany, 1925–1926.

Gropius constructed this Bauhaus building by sheathing a reinforced concrete skeleton in glass. The design followed his dictum that architecture should avoid "all romantic embellishment and whimsy."

1 ft.

24-73 Marcel Breuer, Wassily chair, 1925. Chrome-plated tubular steel and canvas, $2' 4\frac{1}{4}'' \times 2' 6\frac{3}{4}'' \times 2' 4''$. Museum of Modern Art, New York (gift of Herbert Bayer).

The Bauhaus advocated a comprehensive approach to architecture, which included furniture design. Breuer's chair has a simple geometric look in keeping with Bauhaus aesthetics.

(sometimes spelled Wassily) Kandinsky. Breuer supposedly got the inspiration to use tubular steel while riding his bicycle and admiring the handlebars. In keeping with Bauhaus aesthetics, his chairs have a simplified, geometric look, and the leather or cloth supports add to the furniture's comfort and functionality. These chairs could also easily be mass produced and thus epitomize the goals of the Bauhaus.

LUDWIG MIES VAN DER ROHE In 1928, Gropius left the Bauhaus, and Ludwig Mies van der Rohe (1886–1969) eventually took over the directorship, moving the school to Berlin. Taking as his motto "less is more" and calling his architecture "skin and bones," the new Bauhaus director had already fully formed his aesthetic when he conceived the model (FIG. **24-74**) for a glass skyscraper building in 1921. In the glass model, which was on display at the first Bauhaus exhibition in 1923, three irregularly shaped towers flow outward from a central court designed to hold a lobby, a porter's room, and a community center. Two cylindrical entrance shafts rise at the ends of the court, each containing elevators, stairways, and toilets. Wholly transparent, the perimeter walls reveal the regular horizontal patterning of the cantilevered floor planes and their thin vertical supporting elements. The bold use of glass sheathing and inset supports was, at the time, technically and aesthetically adventurous. The weblike delicacy of the lines of the model, as well as the illusion of movement created by reflection and by light changes seen through the glass, appealed to many other architects. A few years later, Gropius pursued these principles in his design for the Bauhaus building (FIG. **24-72**) in Dessau. The glass-and-steel skyscrapers found in major cities throughout the world today are the enduring legacy of Mies van der Rohe's design.

END OF THE BAUHAUS One of Hitler's first acts after coming to power was to close the Bauhaus in 1933. During its 14-year existence, the beleaguered school graduated fewer than 500 students, yet it achieved legendary status. Its phenomenal impact extended beyond painting, sculpture, and architecture to interior design, graphic design, and advertising. Moreover, art schools everywhere began to structure their curricula in line with the program the

24-74 Ludwig Mies van der Rohe, model for a glass skyscraper, Berlin, Germany, 1922 (no longer extant).

In this technically and aesthetically adventurous design, the architect whose motto was "less is more" proposed a transparent building that revealed its cantilevered floor planes and thin supports.

Bauhaus pioneered. The numerous Bauhaus instructors who fled Nazi Germany disseminated the school's philosophy and aesthetic. Many Bauhaus members came to the United States. Gropius and Breuer ended up at Harvard University. Mies van der Rohe moved to Chicago and taught there.

LE CORBUSIER The simple geometric aesthetic that Gropius and Mies van der Rohe developed became known as the *International Style* because of its widespread popularity. The first and purest adherent of this style was the Swiss architect Charles-Edouard Jeanneret, who adopted his maternal grandfather's name—Le Corbusier (1887–1965). Trained in Paris and Berlin, he was also a painter, but Le Corbusier wielded greater influence as an architect and theorist on modern architecture. As such, he applied himself to designing a functional living space, which he described as a "machine for living."[62]

Le Corbusier maintained that the basic physical and psychological needs of every human being were sun, space, and vegetation combined with controlled temperature, good ventilation, and insulation

24-75 Le Corbusier, Villa Savoye, Poissy-sur-Seine, France, 1929.

Steel and ferroconcrete made it possible for Le Corbusier to invert the traditional practice of placing light architectural elements above heavy ones and to eliminate weight-bearing walls on the ground story.

against harmful and undesirable noise. He also advocated basing dwelling designs on human scale, because the house is humankind's assertion within nature. All these qualities characterize Le Corbusier's Villa Savoye (FIG. **24-75**), located at Poissy-sur-Seine near Paris. This country house sits conspicuously within its site, tending to dominate it, and has a broad view of the landscape. Several colors appear on the exterior—originally, a dark-green base, cream walls, and a rose-and-blue windscreen on top. They were a deliberate analogy for the colors in the contemporary machine-inspired Purist style of painting (FIG. 24-22) Le Corbusier practiced.

A cube of lightly enclosed and deeply penetrated space, the Villa Savoye has an only partially confined ground floor (containing a three-car garage, bedrooms, a bathroom, and utility rooms). Much of the house's interior is open space, with the thin columns supporting the main living floor and the roof garden area. The major living rooms in the Villa Savoye are on the second floor, wrapping around an open central court. Strip windows that run along the membranelike exterior walls provide illumination to the rooms. From the second-floor court, a ramp leads up to a flat roof-terrace and garden protected by a curving windbreak along one side. The Villa Savoye has no traditional facade. The ostensible approach to the house does not define an entrance. People must walk around and through the house to comprehend its layout. Spaces and masses interpenetrate so fluidly that inside and outside space intermingle. The machine-planed smoothness of the unadorned surfaces, the slender ribbons of continuous windows, and the buoyant lightness of the whole fabric—all combine to reverse the effect of traditional country houses (FIG. 17-29). By placing heavy elements above and light ones below, and by refusing to enclose the ground story of the Villa Savoye with masonry walls, Le Corbusier inverted traditional design practice. This openness, made possible by the use of steel and ferroconcrete as construction materials, makes the Villa Savoye's heavy upper stories appear to hover lightly on the slender column supports.

The Villa Savoye was a marvelous house for a single family, but like De Stijl architects, Le Corbusier dreamed of extending his ideas of the house as a "machine for living" to designs for efficient and humane cities. He saw great cities as spiritual workshops, and he proposed to correct the deficiencies in existing cities caused by poor traffic circulation, inadequate living units, and the lack of space for recreation and exercise. Le Corbusier suggested replacing traditional cities with three types of new communities. Vertical cities would house workers and the business and service industries. Linear-industrial cities would run as belts along the routes between the vertical cities and would serve as centers for the people and processes involved in manufacturing. Finally, separate centers would be constructed for people involved in intensive agricultural activity. Le Corbusier's cities would provide for human cultural needs in addition to serving every person's physical, mental, and emotional comfort needs.

Later in his career, Le Corbusier designed a few vertical cities, most notably the Unité d'Habitation in Marseilles (1945–1952). He also created the master plan for the entire city of Chandigarh, the capital city of Punjab, India (1950–1957). He ended his career with a personal expressive style in his design of the Chapel of Notre Dame du Haut (FIGS. **25-56** and **25-57**) at Ronchamp.

America

America also embraced the new European architecture, particularly the Bauhaus style, which rejected ornament of any kind. But other styles also won wide followings, some of which were reactions against the severity of Bauhaus design.

ART DECO According to Bauhaus principles, pure form emerged from functional structure and required no decoration. Yet popular taste still favored ornamentation, especially in public architecture. A movement in the 1920s and 1930s sought to upgrade industrial design as a "fine art." Proponents wanted to work new materials into decorative patterns that could be either machined or handcrafted and that could, to a degree, reflect the simplifying trend in architecture. A remote descendant of Art Nouveau, this movement became known as *Art Deco*, which acquired its name at the Exposition des Arts Décoratifs et Industriels Modernes (Exposition of Modern Decorative and Industrial Arts), held in Paris in 1925. Art Deco had universal application—to buildings, interiors, furniture, utensils, jewelry, fashions, illustration, and commercial products of every sort. Art Deco products have a "streamlined," elongated symmetrical aspect. Simple flat shapes alternate with shallow volumes in hard patterns. The concept of streamlining predominated in industrial-design circles in the 1930s and involved the use of organic, tapered shapes and forms. Derived from nature, these simple forms are inherently aerodynamic, making them technologically efficient (because of their reduced resistance as they move through air or water) as well as aesthetically pleasing. Designers adopted streamlined shapes for trains and cars, and the popular appeal of these designs led to their use in an array of objects, from machines to consumer products.

Art Deco's exemplary masterpiece is the stainless-steel spire of the Chrysler Building (FIG. **24-76**) in New York City, designed by WILLIAM VAN ALEN (1882–1954). The building and spire are monuments to the fabulous 1920s, when American millionaires and corporations competed with one another to raise the tallest skyscrapers in the biggest cities. Built up of diminishing fan shapes, the spire glitters triumphantly in the sky, a resplendent crown honoring the business achievements of the great auto manufacturer. As a temple of commerce, the Chrysler Building celebrated the principles and success of American business before the onset of the Great Depression.

FRANK LLOYD WRIGHT

One of the most striking personalities in the development of early-20th-century architecture was FRANK LLOYD WRIGHT (1867–1959). Born in Wisconsin, Wright moved to Chicago, where he eventually joined the firm headed by Louis Sullivan (FIGS. 23-40 and 23-41). Wright set out to create an "architecture of democracy."[63] Always a believer in architecture as "natural" and "organic," Wright saw it as serving free individuals who have the right to move within a "free" space, envisioned as a nonsymmetrical design interacting spatially with its natural surroundings. He sought to develop an organic unity of planning, structure, materials, and site. Wright identified the principle of continuity as fundamental to understanding his view of organic unity:

> Classic architecture was all fixation.... Now why not let walls, ceilings, floors become seen as component parts of each other? ... You may see the appearance in the surface of your hand contrasted with the articulation of the bony structure itself. This ideal, profound in its architectural implications ... I called ... continuity.[64]

Wright manifested his vigorous originality early, and by 1900 he had arrived at a style entirely his own. In his work during the first decade of the 20th century, his cross-axial plan and his fabric of continuous roof planes and screens defined a new domestic architecture.

ROBIE HOUSE Wright fully expressed these elements and concepts in the Robie House (FIG. 24-77), built between 1907 and 1909. Like other buildings in the Chicago area he designed at about the same time, he called this home a "prairie house." Wright conceived the long, sweeping, ground-hugging lines, unconfined by abrupt wall limits, as reaching out toward and capturing the expansiveness of the Midwest's great flatlands. Abandoning all symmetry, the architect eliminated a facade, extended the roofs far beyond the walls, and all but concealed the entrance. Wright filled the house's "wandering" plan (FIG. 24-78) with intricately joined spaces (some large and open, others closed), grouped freely around a great central

24-76 WILLIAM VAN ALEN, Chrysler Building, New York, New York, 1928–1930.

The Chrysler Building's stainless steel spire epitomizes Art Deco architecture. The skyscraper's glittering crown of diminishing fan shapes has a streamlined form that was popular during the 1920s.

24-77 FRANK LLOYD WRIGHT, Robie House, Chicago, Illinois, 1907–1909.

The Robie House is an example of Wright's "architecture of democracy," in which free individuals move within a "free" space—a nonsymmetrical design interacting spatially with its natural surroundings.

24-78 FRANK LLOYD WRIGHT, plan of the second (main) level of the Robie House, Chicago, Illinois, 1907–1909.

Typical of Wright's "prairie houses," the Robie House has a bold "wandering" asymmetrical plan with intricately joined open and closed spaces grouped freely around a great central fireplace.

Architecture **741**

24-79 Frank Lloyd Wright, Kaufmann House (Fallingwater), Bear Run, Pennsylvania, 1936–1939.

Perched on a rocky hillside over a waterfall, Wright's Fallingwater has long sweeping lines, unconfined by abrupt wall limits, reaching out and capturing the expansiveness of the natural environment.

fireplace. (He believed strongly in the hearth's age-old domestic significance.) Wright designed enclosed patios, overhanging roofs, and strip windows to provide unexpected light sources and glimpses of the outdoors as the inhabitants moved through the interior space. These elements, together with the open ground plan, created a sense of space in motion, inside and out. Wright matched his new and fundamental interior spatial arrangement in his exterior treatment. The flow of interior space determined the sharp angular placement of exterior walls.

FALLINGWATER The Robie House is an example of Wright's "naturalism"—his adjustment of a building to its site. In this particular case, however, the confines of the city lot constrained the building-to-site relationship more than did the sites of some of Wright's more expansive suburban and country homes. The Kaufmann House, nicknamed "Fallingwater" (FIG. **24-79**) and designed as a weekend retreat at Bear Run, Pennsylvania, for Pittsburgh department store magnate Edgar Kaufmann Sr., is a prime example of the latter. Perched on a rocky hillside over a small waterfall, this structure, which has become an icon of modernist architectural design, extends the Robie House's blocky masses in all four directions. Ever since the completion of this residence, architects and the public alike have marveled at the fluid interplay between interior and exterior. In designing Fallingwater, Wright, in keeping with his commitment to an "architecture of democracy," sought to incorporate the structure more fully into the site, thereby ensuring a fluid, dynamic exchange between the interior of the house and the natural environment outside. Rather than build the house overlooking or next to the waterfall, Wright decided to build it over the waterfall, because he believed the inhabitants would become desensitized to the waterfall's presence and power if they merely overlooked it. To take advantage of the location, Wright designed a series of terraces that extend on three levels from a central core structure. The contrast in textures between concrete, painted metal, and natural stones in the house's terraces and walls enlivens its shapes, as does Wright's use of full-length strip windows to create a stunning interweaving of interior and exterior space.

The implied message of Wright's new architecture was space, not mass—a space designed to fit the patron's life and enclosed and divided as required. Wright took special pains to meet his clients' requirements, often designing all the accessories of a house (including, in at least one case, gowns for his client's wife). In the late 1930s, he acted on a cherished dream to provide good architectural design for less prosperous people by adapting the ideas of his prairie house to plans for smaller, less-expensive dwellings. These residences, known as Usonian houses, became templates for suburban housing developments in the post–World War II housing boom.

The publication of Wright's plans brought him a measure of fame in Europe, especially in Holland and Germany. The issuance in Berlin in 1910 of a portfolio of his work and an exhibition of his designs the following year stimulated younger architects to adopt some of his ideas about open plans that afforded clients freedom. Some 40 years before his career ended, his work was already of revolutionary significance. Mies van der Rohe wrote in 1940 that the "dynamic impulse from [Wright's] work invigorated a whole generation. His influence was strongly felt even when it was not actually visible."[65]

Frank Lloyd Wright's influence in Europe was exceptional, however, for any American artist before World War II. But in the decades following that global conflict, American painters, sculptors, and architects often took the lead in establishing new styles that artists elsewhere quickly emulated. This new preeminence of America in the arts is the subject of Chapter 25.

EUROPE AND AMERICA, 1900 TO 1945

EUROPE, 1900 to 1920

▮ During the early 20th century, avant-garde artists searched for new definitions of art in a changed world. Matisse and the Fauves used bold colors as the primary means of conveying feeling. German Expressionist paintings feature clashing colors, disquieting figures, and perspectival distortions.
▮ Pablo Picasso and Georges Braque radically challenged prevailing artistic conventions with Cubism, in which artists dissect forms and place them in interaction with the space around them.
▮ The Futurists focused on motion in time and space in their effort to create paintings and sculptures that captured the dynamic quality of modern life. The Dadaists celebrated the spontaneous and intuitive, often incorporating found objects in their artworks.

Picasso, *Les Demoiselles d'Avignon*, 1907

AMERICA, 1900 to 1930

▮ The Armory Show of 1913 introduced avant-garde European art to American artists. Man Ray, for example, embraced Dada's fondness for chance and the displacement of ordinary items, and Stuart Davis adopted the Cubist interest in fragmented form.
▮ The Harlem Renaissance brought African American artists to the forefront, including Aaron Douglas, whose paintings drew on Cubist principles. Charles Demuth, Georgia O'Keeffe, and the Precisionists used European modernist techniques to celebrate contemporary American subjects.
▮ Photography emerged as an important American art form in the work of Alfred Stieglitz, who emphasized the careful arrangement of forms and patterns of light and dark. Edward Weston experimented with photographs of segments of the human body that verge on abstraction.

Weston, *Nude*, 1925

EUROPE, 1920 to 1945

▮ World War I gave rise to the Neue Sachlichkeit movement in Germany. "New Objectivity" artists depicted the horrors of war and explored the themes of death and transfiguration.
▮ The Surrealists investigated ways to express in art the world of dreams and the unconscious. Natural Surrealists aimed for "concrete irrationality" in their naturalistic paintings of dreamlike scenes. Biomorphic Surrealists experimented with automatism and employed abstract imagery.
▮ Many European modernists pursued utopian ideals. The Suprematists developed an abstract style to express pure feeling. The Constructivists used nonobjective forms to suggest the nature of space-time. De Stijl artists employed simple geometric forms in their search for "pure plastic art."
▮ Sculptors, including Hepworth and Moore, also increasingly turned to abstraction and emphasized voids as well as masses in their work. Brancusi captured the essence of flight in *Bird in Space,* a glistening abstract sculpture that does not mimic the form of a bird.

Brancusi, *Bird in Space*, 1924

AMERICA, 1930 to 1945

▮ Although Calder created abstract works between the wars, other American artists favored figural art. Lange and Shahn chronicled social injustice. Hopper explored the loneliness of the Depression era. Lawrence recorded the struggle of African Americans. Wood depicted life in rural Iowa.
▮ Mexican artists Orozco and Rivera painted epic mural cycles of the history of Mexico. Kahlo's powerful and frequently autobiographical paintings explored the human psyche.

Kahlo, *The Two Fridas*, 1939

ARCHITECTURE

▮ Under Walter Gropius, the Bauhaus in Germany promoted the vision of "total architecture," which called for the integration of all the arts in constructing modern living environments. Bauhaus buildings were simple glass and steel designs devoid of "romantic embellishment and whimsy."
▮ In France, Le Corbusier used modern construction materials in his "machines for living"—simple houses with open plans and unadorned surfaces.
▮ The leading American architect of the first half of the 20th century was Frank Lloyd Wright, who promoted the "architecture of democracy," in which free individuals move in a "free" space. Fallingwater is a bold asymmetrical design integrating the building with the natural environment.

Wright, Fallingwater, 1936–1939

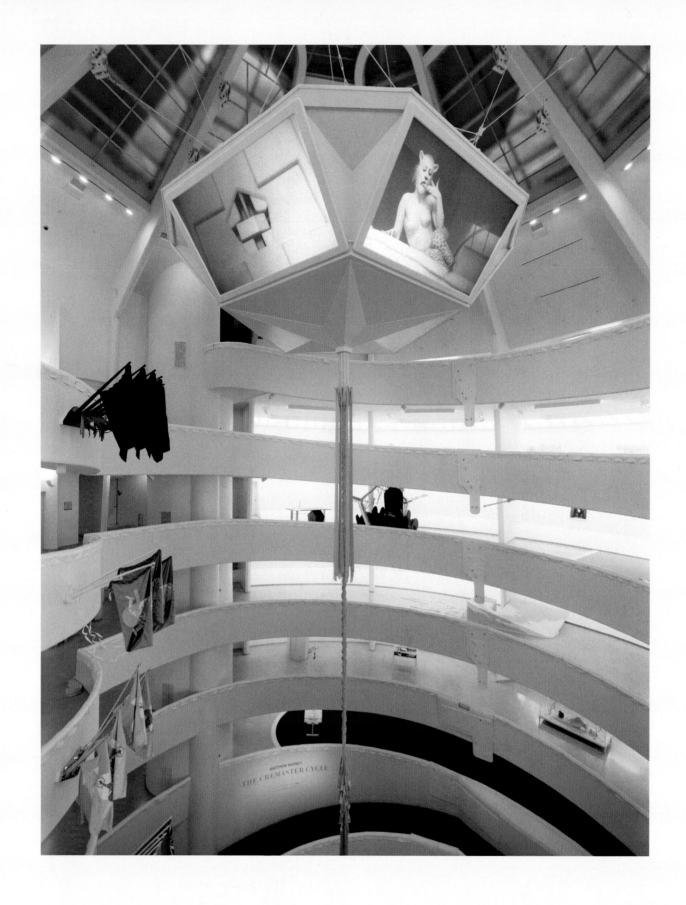

25-1 MATTHEW BARNEY, *Cremaster* cycle, installation at the Solomon R. Guggenheim Museum, New York, 2003.

Barney's vast multimedia installations of drawings, photographs, sculptures, and videos typify the relaxation at the opening of the 21st century of the traditional boundaries among artistic media.

25

EUROPE AND AMERICA AFTER 1945

World War II, with the global devastation it unleashed on all dimensions of life—psychological, political, physical, and economic—set the stage for the second half of the 20th century. The dropping of atomic bombs by the United States on the Japanese cities of Hiroshima and Nagasaki in 1945 signaled a turning point not only in the war but in the geopolitical balance and the nature of international conflict as well. For the rest of the century, nuclear war became a very real threat. Indeed, the two nuclear superpowers, the United States and the Soviet Union, divided the post–World War II world into spheres of influence, and each regularly intervened politically, economically, and militarily wherever and whenever it considered its interests to be at stake.

Persistent conflict throughout the world in the later 20th century resulted in widespread disruption and dislocation. In 1947 the British left India, dividing the subcontinent into the new, still hostile nations of India and Pakistan. After a catastrophic war, Communists came to power in China in 1949. North Korea invaded South Korea in 1950 and fought a grim war with the United States and its allies that ended in 1953. The Soviet Union brutally suppressed uprisings in its subject nations—East Germany, Poland, Hungary, and Czechoslovakia. The United States intervened in disputes in Central and South America. Almost as soon as many previously colonized nations of Africa—Kenya, Uganda, Nigeria, Angola, Mozambique, the Sudan, Rwanda, and the Congo—won their independence, civil wars devastated them. In Indonesia civil conflict left more than 100,000 dead. Algeria expelled France in 1962 after the French waged a prolonged, vicious war with Algeria's Muslim natives. After 15 years of bitter war in Southeast Asia, the United States suffered defeat in Vietnam. From 1979 to 1989 the Soviets unsuccessfully tried to occupy Afghanistan. Arab nations fought wars with Israel in 1967, 1973, and the early 1980s. The Palestinian conflict remains the subject of almost daily newspaper headlines. A revitalized Islam, which inspired a fundamentalist religious revolution in Iran, has encouraged "holy war" with the West, using a new weapon, international terrorism—most dramatically in the attacks on New York City and Washington, D.C., on September 11, 2001. In response, the United States and allied Western nations launched invasions of Afghanistan and Iraq. Conflict and unrest continue to plague large areas of the globe today.

Upheaval has also characterized the cultural sphere in the decades since the end of World War II. In the United States, for example, various groups forcefully questioned the status quo. During the 1960s and 1970s, the struggle for civil rights for African Americans, for free speech on university campuses, and for disengagement from the Vietnam War led to a rebellion of the young, who took to the streets in often raucous demonstrations, with violent repercussions. The prolonged ferment produced a new system of values, a "youth culture," expressed in the radical rejection not only of national policies but often also of the society generating them. Young Americans derided their elders' lifestyles and adopted unconventional dress, manners, habits, and morals deliberately subversive of mainstream social standards. The youth era witnessed the sexual revolution, the widespread use and abuse of drugs, and the development of rock music, then an exclusively youthful art form. Young people "dropped out" of regulated society, embraced alternative belief systems, and rejected Western university curricula as irrelevant.

This counterculture had considerable societal impact and widespread influence beyond its political phase. The civil rights movement of the 1960s and later the women's liberation movement of the 1970s reflected the spirit of rebellion, coupled with the rejection of racism and sexism. In keeping with the growing resistance to established authority, women systematically began to challenge the male-dominated culture, which they perceived as having limited their political power and economic opportunities for centuries. Feminists charged that the institutions of Western society, particularly the nuclear family headed by the patriarch, perpetuated male power and subordination of women. They further contended that monuments of Western culture—its arts and sciences as well as its political, social, and economic institutions—masked the realities of male power.

The central issue that fueled these rebellions and changes—from international political conflicts to the rise of feminism—was power. Increasingly, individuals and groups sought not just to uncover the dynamics of power, but to combat actively the inappropriate exercise of power or change the balance of power. For example, following patterns developed first in the civil rights movement and later in feminism, various ethnic groups and gays and lesbians all mounted challenges to discriminatory policies and attitudes. These groups fought for recognition, respect, and legal protection and battled discrimination with political action. In addition, the growing scrutiny in numerous academic fields—cultural studies, literary theory, and colonial and postcolonial studies—of the dynamics and exercise of power also contributed to the dialogue on these issues. As a result of this concern for the dynamics of power, identity (both individual and group) has emerged as a potent arena for discussion and action. Explorations into the politics of identity now aim to increase personal and public understanding of how self-identifications, along with imposed or inherited identities, affect lives.

As has been true since human beings first began to make sculptures and paintings and erect buildings, European and American art and architecture since 1945 have reflected the changing cultural world in which artists and architects live and work.

PAINTING AND SCULPTURE, 1945 TO 1970

The end of World War II in 1945 left devastated cities, ruptured economies, and governments in chaos throughout Europe. These factors, coupled with the massive loss of life and the indelible horror of the Holocaust and of Hiroshima and Nagasaki, resulted in a pervasive sense of despair, disillusionment, and skepticism. Although many groups (for example, the Futurists in Italy; see Chapter 24) had tried to find redemptive value in World War I, it was virtually impossible to do the same with World War II, coming as it did so soon after the war that was supposed to "end all wars." Additionally, World War I was largely a European conflict that left roughly 10 million people dead, whereas World War II was a truly global catastrophe that claimed 35 million lives.

Postwar Expressionism in Europe

The cynicism that emerged across Europe in the 1940s found voice in existentialism, a philosophy asserting the absurdity of human existence and the impossibility of achieving certitude. As existentialism gained widespread popularity, many adherents also promoted atheism and questioned the possibility of situating God within a systematic philosophy. Most scholars trace the roots of existentialism to the Danish theologian Søren Kierkegaard (1813–1855), but in the postwar period, the writings of French author Jean-Paul Sartre (1905–1980) most clearly captured the existentialist spirit. According to Sartre, if God does not exist, then individuals must constantly struggle in isolation with the anguish of making decisions in a world without absolutes or traditional values. This spirit of pessimism and despair emerged frequently in European art of the immediate postwar period.

1 ft.

25-2 ALBERTO GIACOMETTI, *Man Pointing* (no. 5 of 6), 1947. Bronze, 5′ 10″ × 3′ 1″ × 1′ 5⅝″. Des Moines Art Center, Des Moines (Nathan Emory Coffin Collection).

The writer Jean-Paul Sartre considered Giacometti's thin and virtually featureless sculpted figures as the epitome of existentialist humanity—alienated, solitary, and lost in the world's immensity.

A brutality or roughness appropriately expressing both the artist's state of mind and the larger cultural sensibility characterized the work of many European sculptors and painters.

ALBERTO GIACOMETTI The sculpture of Swiss artist ALBERTO GIACOMETTI (1901–1966) perhaps best expresses the spirit of existentialism. Although Giacometti never claimed he pursued existentialist ideas in his art, his works capture the essence of that philosophy. Indeed, Sartre, Giacometti's friend, saw the artist's figural sculptures as the epitome of existentialist humanity—alienated, solitary, and lost in the world's immensity. Giacometti's sculptures of the 1940s, such as *Man Pointing* (FIG. 25-2), are thin, virtually featureless figures with rough, agitated surfaces. Rather than conveying the solidity and mass of conventional bronze sculpture, these severely attenuated figures seem swallowed up by the space surrounding them, imparting a sense of isolation and fragility. Giacometti's sculptures are evocative and moving, speaking to the pervasive despair in the aftermath of world war.

FRANCIS BACON Created in the year after World War II ended, *Painting* (FIG. 25-3) by British artist FRANCIS BACON (1910–1992) is an indictment of humanity and a reflection of war's butchery. The painting is a compelling and revolting image of a powerful, stocky man with a gaping mouth and a vivid red stain on his upper lip, as if he were a carnivore devouring the raw meat sitting on the railing surrounding him. Bacon may have based his depiction of this central figure on news photos of similarly dressed European and American officials. The umbrella in particular recalls images of Neville Chamberlain (1869–1940), the wartime British prime minister who frequently appeared in photographs with an umbrella. Bacon added to the visceral impact of the painting by depicting the flayed carcass hanging behind the central figure as if it were a crucified human form. Although the specific sources for the imagery in *Painting* may not be entirely clear, the work is unmistakably "an attempt to remake the violence of reality itself," as Bacon often described his art, based on what he referred to as "the brutality of fact."[1]

25-3 FRANCIS BACON, *Painting,* 1946. Oil and pastel on linen, $6' 5\frac{7}{8}'' \times 4' 4''$. Museum of Modern Art, New York.

Painted in the aftermath of World War II, this intentionally revolting image of a powerful figure presiding over a slaughter is Bacon's indictment of humanity and a reflection of war's butchery.

JEAN DUBUFFET Although less specific, the works of French artist JEAN DUBUFFET (1901–1985) also express a tortured vision of the world through manipulated materials. In works such as *Vie Inquiète* (*Uneasy Life;* FIG. 25-4), Dubuffet presented a scene incised into thickly encrusted, parched-looking surfaces. He first built up an *impasto* (a layer of thickly applied pigment) of plaster, glue, sand, asphalt, and other common materials. Over that he painted or incised crude images of the type produced by children, the insane, and graffiti scrawlers. Scribblings interspersed with the images heighten the impression of smeared and gashed surfaces of crumbling walls and worn pavements marked by random individuals.

25-4 JEAN DUBUFFET, *Vie Inquiète* (*Uneasy Life*), 1953. Oil on canvas, $4' 3'' \times 6' 4''$. Tate Gallery, London.

Dubuffet expressed a tortured vision of the world through thickly encrusted painted surfaces and crude images of the kind children and the insane produce. He called it "art brut"—untaught and coarse art.

Dubuffet believed the art of children, the mentally unbalanced, prisoners, and outcasts was more direct and genuine because those who created it did so unrestrained by conventional standards of art. He promoted "art brut"—untaught and coarse art.

Abstract Expressionism

In the 1940s, the center of the Western art world shifted from Paris to New York because of the devastation World War II had inflicted across Europe and the resulting influx of émigré artists escaping to the United States. American artists picked up the European avant-garde's energy, which movements such as Cubism and Dada had fostered, but in the postwar years, modernism increasingly became synonymous with a strict *formalism*—an emphasis on an artwork's visual elements rather than its subject. The most important champion of New York formalist painting was the American art critic Clement Greenberg (1909–1994), who wielded considerable influence from the 1940s through the 1970s. Greenberg helped redefine the parameters of modernism by advocating the rejection of illusionism and the exploration of the properties of each artistic medium. So dominant was Greenberg that scholars often refer to the general modernist tenets during this period as Greenbergian formalism.

Although Greenberg modified his complex ideas about art over the years, he consistently expounded certain basic concepts. In particular, he promoted the idea of purity in art. "Purity in art consists in the acceptance, willing acceptance, of the limitations of the medium of the specific art."[2] In other words, Greenberg believed artists should strive for a more explicit focus on the properties exclusive to each medium—for example, two-dimensionality or flatness in painting, and three-dimensionality in sculpture.

It follows that a modernist work of art must try, in principle, to avoid communication with any order of experience not inherent in the most literally and essentially construed nature of its medium. Among other things, this means renouncing illusion and explicit subject matter. The arts are to achieve concreteness, "purity," by dealing solely with their respective selves—that is, by becoming "abstract" or nonfigurative.[3]

Abstract Expressionism, the first major American avant-garde movement, emerged in New York in the 1940s. As the name suggests, the artists associated with the New York School of Abstract Expressionism produced paintings that are, for the most part, abstract but express the artist's state of mind with the goal also of striking emotional chords in the viewer. The Abstract Expressionists turned inward to create, and the resulting works convey a rough spontaneity and palpable energy. The New York School painters wanted the viewer to grasp the content of their art intuitively, in a state free from structured thinking. The artist Mark Rothko (FIG. 25-9) eloquently wrote:

We assert man's absolute emotions. We don't need props or legends. We create images whose realities are self evident. Free ourselves from memory, association, nostalgia, legend, myth. Instead of making cathedrals out of Christ, man or life, we make it out of ourselves, out of our own feelings. The image we produce is understood by anyone who looks at it without nostalgic glasses of history.[4]

1 ft.

25-5 JACKSON POLLOCK, *Number 1, 1950* (*Lavender Mist*), 1950. Oil, enamel, and aluminum paint on canvas, 7′ 3″ × 9′ 10″. National Gallery of Art, Washington, D.C. (Ailsa Mellon Bruce Fund).

Pollock's paintings emphasize the creative process. His mural-size canvases consist of rhythmic drips, splatters, and dribbles of paint that envelop viewers, drawing them into a lacy spider web.

Jackson Pollock on Easel and Mural Painting

In two statements made in 1947, one as part of his application for a Guggenheim Fellowship and one in a published essay, Jackson Pollock explained the motivations for his new kind of "action painting" and described the manner in which he applied pigment to canvas (FIG. 25-6).

> I intend to paint large movable pictures which will function between the easel and mural. . . . I believe the easel picture to be a dying form, and the tendency of modern feeling is towards the wall picture or mural.*

My painting does not come from the easel. I hardly ever stretch my canvas before painting. I prefer to tack the unstretched canvas to the hard wall or the floor. I need the resistance of a hard surface. On the floor I am more at ease. I feel nearer, more a part of the painting, since this way I can walk around it, work from the four sides and literally be *in* the painting. This is akin to the method of the Indian sand painters of the West. I continue to get further away from the usual painter's tools such as easel, palette, brushes, etc. I prefer sticks, trowels, knives and dripping fluid paint or a heavy impasto with sand, broken glass and other foreign matter added. When I am *in* my painting, I'm not aware of what I'm doing. . . . [T]he painting has a life of its own. I try to let it come through. . . . The source of my painting is the unconscious.†

* Quoted in Francis V. O'Connor, *Jackson Pollock* (New York: Museum of Modern Art, 1967), 39.
† Ibid., 39–40.

25-6 HANS NAMUTH, Jackson Pollock painting in his studio in Springs, Long Island, New York, 1950. Center for Creative Photography, University of Arizona, Tucson.

"Gestural abstraction" nicely describes Pollock's working technique. Using sticks or brushes, he flung, poured, and dripped paint onto a section of canvas he simply unrolled across his studio floor.

The Abstract Expressionist movement developed along two lines—*gestural abstraction* and *chromatic abstraction*. The gestural abstractionists relied on the expressiveness of energetically applied pigment. In contrast, the chromatic abstractionists focused on color's emotional resonance.

JACKSON POLLOCK The artist whose work best exemplifies gestural abstraction is JACKSON POLLOCK (1912–1956), who developed his signature style in the mid-1940s. By 1950, Pollock had refined his technique and was producing large-scale abstract paintings such as *Number 1, 1950* (*Lavender Mist;* FIG. 25-5). These works consist of rhythmic drips, splatters, and dribbles of paint. The mural-sized fields of energetic skeins of pigment envelop viewers, drawing them into a lacy spider web. Using sticks or brushes, Pollock flung, poured, and dripped paint (not only traditional oil paints but aluminum paints and household enamels as well) onto a section of canvas he simply unrolled across his studio floor (FIG. 25-6). This working method earned Pollock the derisive nickname "Jack the Dripper."

Responding to the image as it developed, he created art that was both spontaneous and choreographed. Pollock's painting technique highlights a particularly avant-garde aspect of gestural abstraction—its emphasis on the creative process. Indeed, Pollock literally immersed himself in the painting during its creation.

Art historians have linked Pollock's ideas about improvisation in the creative process to his interest in what psychiatrist Carl Jung called the collective unconscious. The improvisational nature of Pollock's work and his reliance on the subconscious also have parallels in the "psychic automatism" of Surrealism and the work of Vassily Kandinsky (FIG. 24-7), whom critics described as an "abstract expressionist" as early as 1919. In addition to Pollock's unique working methods and the expansive scale of his canvases, the lack of a well-defined compositional focus in his paintings significantly departed from conventional easel painting (see "Jackson Pollock on Easel and Mural Painting," above). A towering figure in 20th-century art, Pollock tragically died in a car accident at age 44, cutting short the development of his innovative artistic vision.

25-7 Willem de Kooning, *Woman I*, 1950–1952. Oil on canvas, 6′ 3⅞″ × 4′ 10″. Museum of Modern Art, New York.

Although rooted in figuration, including pictures of female models on advertising billboards, de Kooning's *Woman I* displays the energetic application of pigment typical of gestural abstraction.

WILLEM DE KOONING Despite the public's skepticism about Pollock's art, other artists enthusiastically pursued similar avenues of expression. Dutch-born WILLEM DE KOONING (1904–1997) also developed a gestural abstractionist style. Even images such as *Woman I* (FIG. 25-7), although rooted in figuration, display the sweeping gestural brush strokes and energetic application of pigment typical of gestural abstraction. Out of the jumbled array of slashing lines and agitated patches of color appears a ferocious-looking woman with staring eyes and ponderous breasts. Her toothy smile, modeled on an ad for Camel cigarettes, becomes a grimace. Female models on advertising billboards partly inspired *Woman I*, one of a series of female images, but de Kooning's female forms also suggest fertility figures and a satiric inversion of the traditional image of Venus, goddess of love.

Process was important to de Kooning, as it was to Pollock. Continually working on *Woman I* for almost two years, de Kooning painted an image and then scraped it away the next day and began anew. His wife Elaine, also a painter, estimated that he painted approximately 200 scraped-away images of women on this canvas before settling on the final one.

In addition to this *Woman* series, de Kooning created nonrepresentational works dominated by huge swaths and splashes of pigment. His images suggest rawness and intensity. His dealer, Sidney Janis (1896–1989), confirmed this impression, recalling that de Kooning occasionally brought him paintings with ragged holes in them, the result of overly vigorous painting. Like Pollock, de Kooning was very much "in" his paintings. That kind of physical interaction between the painter and the canvas led the critic Harold Rosenberg (1906–1978) to describe the work of the New York School as *action painting*. In his influential 1952 article "The American Action Painters," Rosenberg described the attempts of Pollock, de Kooning, and others to get "inside the canvas."

At a certain moment the canvas began to appear to one American painter after another as an arena in which to act—rather than as a space in which to reproduce, re-design, analyze or "express" an

25-8 Barnett Newman, *Vir Heroicus Sublimis*, 1950–1951. Oil on canvas, 7′ 11⅜″ × 17′ 9¼″. Museum of Modern Art, New York (gift of Mr. and Mrs. Ben Heller).

Newman's canvases consist of a single slightly modulated color field split by "zips" (narrow bands) running from one edge of the painting to the other, energizing the color field and giving it scale.

25-9 Mark Rothko, *No. 14*, 1960. Oil on canvas, 9′ 6″ × 8′ 9″. San Francisco Museum of Modern Art, San Francisco (Helen Crocker Russell Fund Purchase).

Rothko's chromatic abstractionist paintings—consisting of hazy rectangles of pure color hovering in front of a colored background—are compositionally simple but compelling visual experiences.

1 ft.

his family to the United States when he was 10. His early paintings were figural in orientation, but he soon arrived at the belief that references to anything specific in the physical world conflicted with the sublime idea of the universal, supernatural "spirit of myth," which he saw as the core of meaning in art. In a statement cowritten with Newman and artist Adolph Gottlieb (1903–1974), Rothko expressed his beliefs about art:

> We favor the simple expression of the complex thought. We are for the large shape because it has the impact of the unequivocal. . . . We assert that . . . only that subject matter is valid which is tragic and timeless. That is why we profess spiritual kinship with primitive and archaic art.[8]

Rothko's paintings became compositionally simple, and he increasingly focused on color as the primary conveyor of meaning. In works such as *No. 14* (FIG. 25-9), Rothko created compelling visual experiences consisting of two or three large rectangles of pure color with hazy, brushy edges that seem to float on the canvas surface, hovering in front of a colored background. These paintings appear as shimmering veils of intensely luminous colors suspended in front of the canvases. Although the color juxtapositions are visually captivating, Rothko intended them as more than decorative. He saw color as a doorway to another reality, and insisted that color could express "basic human emotions—tragedy, ecstasy, doom. . . . The people who weep before my pictures are having the same religious experience I had when I painted them. And if you, as you say, are moved only by their color relationships, then you miss the point."[9] Like the other Abstract Expressionists, Rothko produced highly evocative, moving paintings that relied on formal elements rather than specific representational content to elicit emotional responses in the viewer.

Post-Painterly Abstraction

Post-Painterly Abstraction, another American art movement, developed out of Abstract Expressionism. Indeed, many of the artists associated with Post-Painterly Abstraction produced Abstract Expressionist work early in their careers. Yet Post-Painterly Abstraction, a term Clement Greenberg coined, manifests a radically different sensibility from Abstract Expressionism. Whereas Abstract Expressionism conveys a feeling of passion and visceral intensity, a cool, detached rationality emphasizing tighter pictorial control characterizes Post-Painterly Abstraction. Greenberg saw this art as contrasting with "painterly" art, characterized by loose, visible pigment application. Evidence of the artist's hand, so prominent in gestural abstraction, is conspicuously absent in Post-Painterly Abstraction. Greenberg championed this art form because it seemed to embody his idea of purity in art.

object, actual or imagined. What was to go on the canvas was not a picture but an event. The painter no longer approached his easel with an image in his mind; he went up to it with material in his hand to do something to that other piece of material in front of him. The image would be the result of this encounter.[5]

BARNETT NEWMAN In contrast to the aggressively energetic images of the gestural abstractionists, the work of the chromatic abstractionists exudes a quieter aesthetic, exemplified by the work of Barnett Newman and Mark Rothko. The emotional resonance of their works derives from their eloquent use of color. In his early paintings, BARNETT NEWMAN (1905–1970) presented organic abstractions inspired by his study of biology and his fascination with Native American art. He soon simplified his compositions so that each canvas, such as *Vir Heroicus Sublimis* (FIG. 25-8)—Latin, "sublime heroic man"— consists of a single slightly modulated color field split by narrow bands the artist called "zips," which run from one edge of the painting to the other. As Newman explained it, "The streak was always going through an atmosphere; I kept trying to create a world around it."[6] He did not intend the viewer to perceive the zips as specific entities, separate from the ground, but as accents energizing the field and giving it scale. By simplifying his compositions, Newman increased color's capacity to communicate and to express his feelings about the tragic condition of modern life and the human struggle to survive. He claimed that "the artist's problem . . . [is] the idea-complex that makes contact with mystery—of life, of men, of nature, of the hard black chaos that is death, or the grayer, softer chaos that is tragedy."[7] Confronted by one of Newman's monumental colored canvases, viewers truly feel as if they are in the presence of the epic.

MARK ROTHKO The work of MARK ROTHKO (1903–1970) also deals with universal themes. Born in Russia, Rothko moved with

25-10 ELLSWORTH KELLY, *Red Blue Green,* 1963. Oil on canvas, 6′ 11$\frac{5}{8}$″ × 11′ 3$\frac{7}{8}$″. Museum of Contemporary Art, San Diego (gift of Dr. and Mrs. Jack M. Farris).

Hard-edge painting is one variant of Post-Painterly Abstraction. Kelly used razor-sharp edges and clearly delineated areas of color to distill painting to its essential two-dimensional elements.

ELLSWORTH KELLY Attempting to arrive at pure painting, the Post-Painterly Abstractionists distilled painting down to its essential elements, producing spare, elemental images. An example of one variant of Post-Painterly Abstraction, *hard-edge painting,* is *Red Blue Green* (FIG. **25-10**) by ELLSWORTH KELLY (b. 1923). With its razor-sharp edges and clearly delineated shapes, this work is completely abstract and extremely simple compositionally. Further, the painting contains no suggestion of the illusion of depth—the color shapes appear resolutely two-dimensional.

FRANK STELLA Another artist associated with the hard-edge painters of the 1960s is FRANK STELLA (b. 1936). In works such as *Mas o Menos* (*More or Less*; FIG. **25-11**), Stella eliminated many of

the variables associated with painting. His simplified images of thin, evenly spaced pinstripes on colored grounds have no central focus, no painterly or expressive elements, only limited surface modulation, and no tactile quality. Stella's systematic painting illustrates Greenberg's insistence on purity in art. The artist's famous comment on his work, "What you see is what you see," reinforces the notions that painters interested in producing advanced art must reduce their work to its essential elements and that the viewer must acknowledge that a painting is simply pigment on a flat surface.

HELEN FRANKENTHALER *Color-field painting,* another variant of Post-Painterly Abstraction, also emphasized painting's basic properties. However, rather than produce sharp, unmodulated

25-11 FRANK STELLA, *Mas o Menos* (*More or Less*), 1964. Metallic powder in acrylic emulsion on canvas, 9′ 10″ × 13′ 8$\frac{1}{2}$″. Musée National d'Art Moderne, Centre Georges Pompidou, Paris (purchase 1983 with participation of Scaler Foundation).

Stella tried to achieve purity in painting using evenly spaced pinstripes on colored grounds. His canvases have no central focus, no painterly or expressive elements, and no tactile quality.

Helen Frankenthaler
on Color-Field Painting

In 1965 the art critic Henry Geldzahler interviewed Helen Frankenthaler about her work as an abstract painter. In the following excerpt, Frankenthaler describes her approach to placing color on canvas (FIG. 25-12) and compares her method with the way earlier modernist artists used color in their paintings.

I will sometimes start a picture feeling "What will happen if I work with three blues and another color, and maybe more or less of the other color than the combined blues?" And very often midway through the picture I have to change the basis of the experience. . . .

When you first saw a Cubist or Impressionist picture there was a whole way of instructing the eye or the subconscious. Dabs of color had to stand for real things; it was an abstraction of a guitar or a hillside. The opposite is going on now. If you have bands of blue, green, and pink, the mind doesn't think sky, grass and flesh. These are colors and the question is what are they doing with themselves and with each other. Sentiment and nuance are being squeezed out.*

* Henry Geldzahler, "Interview with Helen Frankenthaler," *Artforum* 4, no. 2 (October 1965), 37–38.

25-12 HELEN FRANKENTHALER, *The Bay,* 1963. Acrylic on canvas, 6′ 8$\frac{7}{8}$″ × 6′ 9$\frac{7}{8}$″. Detroit Institute of Arts, Detroit.

Color-field painters like Frankenthaler poured paint onto unprimed canvas, allowing the pigments to soak into the fabric. Her works underscore that a painting is simply pigment on a flat surface.

1 ft.

shapes as the hard-edge artists had done, the color-field painters poured diluted paint onto unprimed canvas, allowing the pigments to soak in. It is hard to conceive of another painting method that results in such literal flatness. The images created, such as *The Bay* (FIG. 25-12) by HELEN FRANKENTHALER (b. 1928), appear spontaneous and almost accidental (see "Helen Frankenthaler on Color-Field Painting," above). These works differ from those of Rothko and Newman in that Frankenthaler subordinated the emotional component, so integral to Abstract Expressionism, to resolving formal problems.

MORRIS LOUIS Another artist who pursued color-field painting was MORRIS LOUIS (1912–1962). Clement Greenberg, an admirer of Frankenthaler's paintings, took Louis to her studio, and there she introduced him to the possibilities presented by the staining technique. Louis used this method of pouring diluted paint onto the surface of unprimed canvas in several series of paintings. *Saraband* (FIG. 25-13) is one of the works in Louis's *Veils* series. By holding up the canvas edges and pouring on diluted acrylic resin, Louis created billowy, fluid, transparent shapes that run down the length of the canvas. Like Frankenthaler, Louis reduced painting to the concrete fact of the paint-impregnated material.

1 ft.

25-13 MORRIS LOUIS, *Saraband,* 1959. Acrylic resin on canvas, 8′ 5$\frac{1}{8}$″ × 12′ 5″. Solomon R. Guggenheim Museum, New York.

Louis created his color-field paintings by holding up the canvas edges and pouring diluted acrylic resin to produce billowy, fluid, transparent shapes that run down the length of the fabric.

Painting and Sculpture, 1945 to 1970   **753**

David Smith on Outdoor Sculpture

From ancient times, sculptors have frequently created statues for display in the open air, whether a portrait of a Roman emperor on horseback in a forum (FIG. 7-43, no. 6) or Michelangelo's *David* (FIG. 17-13) in Florence's Piazza della Signoria. But rarely have sculptors taken into consideration the effects of sunlight in the conception of their works. David Smith (FIG. 25-14) was an exception.

> I like outdoor sculpture and the most practical thing for outdoor sculpture is stainless steel, and I make them and I polish them in such a way that on a dull day, they take on the dull blue, or the color of the sky in the late afternoon sun, the glow, golden like the rays, the colors of nature. And in a particular sense, I have used atmosphere in a reflective way on the surfaces. They are colored by the sky and the surroundings, the green or blue of water. Some are down by the water and some are by the mountains. They reflect the colors. They are designed for the outdoors.*

* Quoted in Cleve Gray, ed., *David Smith by David Smith* (New York: Holt, Rinehart, and Winston, 1968), 133.

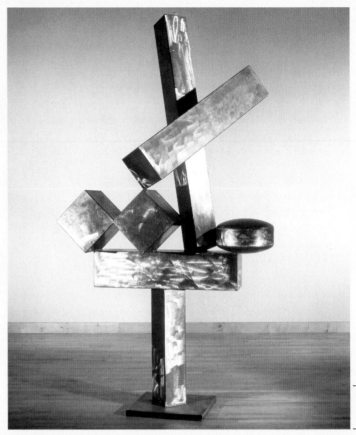

25-14 DAVID SMITH, *Cubi XIX*, 1964. Stainless steel, 9′ 4$\frac{3}{4}$″ × 4′ 10$\frac{1}{4}$″ × 3′ 4″. Tate Gallery, London. Art © Estate of David Smith/Licensed by VAGA, New York.

David Smith designed his abstract metal sculptures of simple geometric forms to reflect the natural light and color of their outdoor settings, not the sterile illumination of a museum gallery.

1 ft.

CLYFFORD STILL Another American painter whose work art historians usually classify as Post-Painterly Abstraction was CLYFFORD STILL (1904–1980), a pioneering abstract painter who produced a large series of canvases titled simply with their dates, underscoring his rejection of the very notion that the purpose of art is to represent places, people, or objects. Nonetheless, Still's paintings remind many viewers of vast landscapes seen from the air. But the artist's canvases make no reference to any forms in nature. His paintings, for example, *1948-C* (FIG. I-1), are pure exercises in the expressive use of color, shape, and texture.

Sculpture

Painters were not the only artists interested in Greenberg's formalist ideas. American sculptors also aimed for purity in their medium. While painters worked to emphasize flatness, sculptors, understandably, chose to focus on three-dimensionality as the unique characteristic and inherent limitation of the sculptural idiom.

DAVID SMITH American sculptor DAVID SMITH (1906–1965) produced metal sculptures that have affinities with the Abstract Expressionist movement in painting. Smith learned to weld in an automobile plant in 1925 and later applied to his art the technical expertise in handling metals he gained from that experience. In addition, working in large scale at the factories helped him visualize the possibilities for monumental metal sculpture. After experimenting with a variety of sculptural styles and materials, Smith created his *Cubi* series in the early 1960s. These works, for example *Cubi XIX* (FIG. 25-14), consist

of simple geometric forms—cubes, cylinders, and rectangular bars. Made of stainless steel sections piled atop one another and then welded together, these large-scale sculptures make a striking visual statement. Smith added gestural elements reminiscent of Abstract

25-15 TONY SMITH, *Die*, 1962. Steel, 6′ × 6′ × 6′. Museum of Modern Art, New York (gift of Jane Smith in honor of Agnes Gund).

By rejecting illusionism and symbolism and reducing sculpture to basic geometric forms, Minimalist sculptors like Tony Smith emphasized their art's "objecthood" and concrete tangibility.

1 ft.

Donald Judd on Sculpture
and Industrial Materials

In a 1965 essay entitled "Specific Objects," the Minimalist sculptor Donald Judd described the advantages of sculpture over painting and the attractions of using industrial materials for his works (FIG. 25-16).

> Three dimensions are real space. That gets rid of the problem of illusionism . . . one of the salient and most objectionable relics of European art. The several limits of painting are no longer present. A work can be as powerful as it can be thought to be. Actual space is intrinsically more powerful and specific than paint on a flat surface. . . . The use of three dimensions makes it possible to see all sorts of materials and colors. Most of [my] work involves new materials, either recent inventions or things not used before in art. Little was done until lately with the wide range of industrial products. . . . Materials vary greatly and are simply materials—formica, aluminum, cold-rolled steel, plexiglas, red and common brass, and so forth. They are specific. If they are used directly, they are more specific. Also, they are usually aggressive. There is an objectivity to the obdurate identity of a material. . . . The form of a work of art and its materials are closely related. In earlier work the structure and the imagery were executed in some neutral and homogeneous material.*

* Donald Judd, *Complete Writings 1959–1975* (New York: New York University Press, 1975), 181–189.

25-16 Donald Judd, *Untitled,* 1969. Brass and colored fluorescent Plexiglas on steel brackets, 10 units, $6\frac{1}{8}'' \times 2' \times 2'\ 3''$ each, with 6″ intervals. Hirshhorn Museum and Sculpture Garden, Smithsonian Institution, Washington, D.C. (gift of Joseph H. Hirshhorn, 1972). Art © Judd Foundation/Licensed by VAGA, New York.

Judd's Minimalist sculpture incorporates boxes fashioned from undisguised industrial materials. The artist used Plexiglas because its translucency gives the viewer access to the work's interior.

1 ft.

Expressionism by burnishing the metal with steel wool, producing swirling random-looking patterns that draw attention to the two-dimensionality of the sculptural surface. This treatment, which captures the light hitting the sculpture, activates the surface and imparts a texture to his pieces. Meant to be seen outdoors (see "David Smith on Outdoor Sculpture," page 754), Smith's sculptures unfortunately lose much of their character in the sterile lighting of a museum.

TONY SMITH A predominantly sculptural movement that emerged in the 1960s among artists seeking Greenbergian purity of form was *Minimalism.* One leading Minimalist was TONY SMITH (1912–1980), who created simple volumetric sculptures such as *Die* (FIG. 25-15). Difficult to describe other than as three-dimensional objects, Minimalist artworks often lack identifiable subjects, colors, surface textures, and narrative elements. By rejecting illusionism and reducing sculpture to basic geometric forms, Minimalists emphatically stress their art's "objecthood" and concrete tangibility. In so doing, they reduce experience to its most fundamental level, preventing viewers from drawing on assumptions or preconceptions when dealing with the art before them.

DONALD JUDD Another Minimalist sculptor, DONALD JUDD (1928–1994), embraced a spare, universal aesthetic corresponding to

the core tenets of the movement. Judd's determination to arrive at a visual vocabulary that avoided deception or ambiguity propelled him away from representation and toward precise and simple sculpture. For Judd, a work's power derived from its character as a whole and from the specificity of its materials (see "Donald Judd on Sculpture and Industrial Materials," above). *Untitled* (FIG. 25-16) presents basic geometric boxes constructed of brass and red Plexiglas, undisguised by paint or other materials. The artist did not intend the work to be metaphorical or symbolic but a straightforward declaration of sculpture's objecthood. Judd used Plexiglas because its translucency permits the viewer to access the interior, thereby rendering the sculpture both open and enclosed. This aspect of the design reflects Judd's desire to banish ambiguity or falseness from his works.

Interestingly, despite the ostensible connections between Minimalism and Greenbergian formalism, Greenberg did not embrace this direction in art. In his view,

> Minimal Art remains too much a feat of ideation [the mental formation of ideas], and not enough anything else. Its idea remains an idea, something deduced instead of felt and discovered. The geometrical and modular simplicity may announce and signify the artistically furthest-out, but the fact that the signals are understood for

25-17 Louise Nevelson, *Tropical Garden II*, 1957–1959. Wood painted black, 5′ 11½″ × 10′ 11¾″ × 1′. Musée National d'Art Moderne, Centre Georges Pompidou, Paris.

1 ft.

25-17 Louise Nevelson, *Tropical Garden II*, 1957–1959. Wood painted black, 5′ 11½″ × 10′ 11¾″ × 1′. Musée National d'Art Moderne, Centre Georges Pompidou, Paris.

The monochromatic color scheme unifies the diverse sculpted forms and found objects in Nevelson's "walls" and creates a mysterious field of shapes and shadows that suggest magical environments.

what they want to mean betrays them artistically. There is hardly any aesthetic surprise in Minimal Art. . . . Aesthetic surprise hangs on forever—it is there in Raphael as it is in Pollock—and ideas alone cannot achieve it.[10]

LOUISE NEVELSON Although Minimalism was a dominant sculptural trend in the 1960s, many sculptors pursued other styles. Russian-born Louise Nevelson (1899–1988) created sculpture that combines a sense of the architectural fragment with the power of Dada and Surrealist found objects to express her personal sense of life's underlying significance. Multiplicity of meaning was important to Nevelson. She sought "the in-between place. . . . The dawns and the dusks"[11]—the transitional realm between one state of being and another. Beginning in the late 1950s, she assembled sculptures of found wooden objects and forms, enclosing small sculptural compositions in boxes of varied sizes, and joined the boxes to one another to form "walls," which she then painted in a single hue—usually black, white, or gold. This monochromatic color scheme unifies the diverse parts of pieces such as *Tropical Garden II* (FIG. **25-17**) and creates a mysterious field of shapes and shadows. The structures suggest magical environments resembling the treasured secret hideaways dimly remembered from childhood. Yet the boxy frames and the precision of the manufactured found objects create a rough geometric structure

that the eye roams over freely, lingering on some details. The parts of a Nevelson sculpture and their interrelation recall the *Merz* constructions of Kurt Schwitters (FIG. **24-30**). The effect is also rather like viewing the side of an apartment building from a moving elevated train or like looking down on a city from the air.

LOUISE BOURGEOIS In contrast to the architectural nature of Nevelson's work, a sensuous organic quality recalling the evocative Biomorphic Surrealist forms of Joan Miró (FIG. **24-52**) pervades the work of French-American artist Louise Bourgeois (b. 1911). *Cumul I* (FIG. **25-18**) is a collection of round-headed units huddled, with their heads protruding, within a collective cloak dotted with holes. The units differ in size, and their position within the group lends a distinctive personality to each. Although the shapes remain abstract, they refer strongly to human bodies. Bourgeois uses a wide variety of materials in her works, including wood, plaster, latex, and plastics, in addition to alabaster, marble, and bronze. She exploits each material's qualities to suit the expressiveness of the piece.

In *Cumul I*, the alternating high gloss and matte finish of the marble increases the sensuous distinction between the group of swelling forms and the soft folds swaddling them. Like Barbara Hepworth (FIG. **24-58**), Bourgeois connects her sculpture with the body's multiple relationships to landscape: "[My pieces] are anthropomorphic and they are landscape also, since our body could be considered from a topographical point of view, as a land with mounds and valleys and caves and holes."[12] However, Bourgeois's sculptures are more personal and more openly sexual than those of Hepworth. *Cumul I* represents perfectly the allusions Bourgeois seeks: "There has always been sexual suggestiveness in my work. Sometimes I am totally concerned with female shapes—characters of breasts like clouds—but often I merge the activity—phallic breasts, male and female, active and passive."[13]

1 ft.

25-18 Louise Bourgeois, *Cumul I*, 1969. Marble, 1′ 10⅜″ × 4′ 2″ × 4′. Musée National d'Art Moderne, Centre Georges Pompidou, Paris. Art © Louise Bourgeois/Licensed by VAGA, New York.

Bourgeois's sculptures consist of sensuous organic forms that recall the Biomorphic Surrealist forms of Miró (FIG. **24-52**). Although the shapes remain abstract, they refer strongly to human figures.

EVA HESSE A Minimalist in the early part of her career, Eva Hesse (1936–1970) later moved away from the severity characterizing much of Minimalist art. She created sculptures that, although spare and simple, have a compelling presence. Using nontraditional sculptural materials such as fiberglass, cord, and latex, Hesse produced sculptures whose pure Minimalist forms appear to crumble,

25-19 EVA HESSE, *Hang-Up,* 1965–1966. Acrylic on cloth over wood and steel, 6′ × 7′ × 6′ 6″. Art Institute of Chicago, Chicago (gift of Arthur Keating and Mr. and Mrs. Edward Morris by exchange).

Hesse created spare and simple sculptures with parts that extend into the room. She wanted her works to express the strangeness and absurdity that she considered the central conditions of modern life.

public, sought to harness the communicative power of art to reach a wide audience. However, they did not create reactionary or academic work. Their art still incorporated avant-garde elements, but their focus was not on the formalist issues characteristic of the modernist mindset.

The artists of the *Pop Art* movement reintroduced all of the devices the postwar avant-garde artists, in search of purity, had purged from their abstract and often reductive works. Thus, Pop artists revived the tools traditionally used to convey meaning in art, such as signs, symbols, metaphors, allusions, illusions, and figural imagery. They not only embraced representation but also produced an art firmly grounded in consumer culture and the mass media, thereby making it much more accessible and understandable to the average person. Indeed, the name "Pop Art" (credited to the British art critic Lawrence Alloway) is short for "popular art" and referred to the popular mass culture and familiar imagery of the contemporary urban environment. This was an art form rooted in the sensibilities and visual language of a late-20th-century mass audience.

RICHARD HAMILTON Art historians trace the roots of Pop Art to a group of young British artists, architects, and writers who formed the Independent Group at the Institute of Contemporary Art in London in the early 1950s. They sought to initiate fresh thinking in art, in part by sharing their fascination with the aesthetics and content of such facets of popular culture as advertising, comic books, and movies. In 1956 an Independent Group member, RICHARD HAMILTON (b. 1922), made a small collage, *Just What Is It That Makes Today's Homes So Different, So Appealing?* (FIG. **25-20**), which exemplifies many of the attitudes of British Pop Art. Trained as an engineering draftsman, exhibition designer, and painter, Hamilton studied the way advertising shapes public attitudes. Long intrigued by

sag, and warp under the pressures of atmospheric force and gravity. Born Jewish in Hitler's Germany, the young Hesse hid with a Christian family when her parents and elder sister had to flee the Nazis. She did not reunite with them until the early 1940s, just before her parents divorced. Those extraordinary circumstances helped give her a lasting sense that the central conditions of modern life are strangeness and absurdity. Struggling to express these qualities in her art, she created informal sculptural arrangements with units often hung from the ceiling, propped against the walls, or spilled out along the floor. She said she wanted her pieces to be "non art, non connotative, non anthropomorphic, non geometric, non nothing, everything, but of another kind, vision, sort."[14]

Hang-Up (FIG. **25-19**) fulfills these requirements. The piece looks like a carefully made empty frame sprouting a strange feeler that extends into the room and doubles back to the frame. Hesse wrote that in this work, for the first time, her "idea of absurdity or extreme feeling came through. . . . [*Hang-Up*] has a kind of depth I don't always achieve and that is the kind of depth or soul or absurdity of life or meaning or feeling or intellect that I want to get."[15] The sculpture possesses a disquieting and touching presence, suggesting the fragility and grandeur of life amid the pressures of the modern age. Hesse was herself a touching and fragile presence in the art world. She died of a brain tumor at age 34.

Pop Art

Despite their differences, the Abstract Expressionists, Post-Painterly Abstractionists, and Minimalists all adopted an artistic vocabulary of resolute abstraction. Other artists, however, observing that the insular and introspective attitude of the avant-garde had alienated the

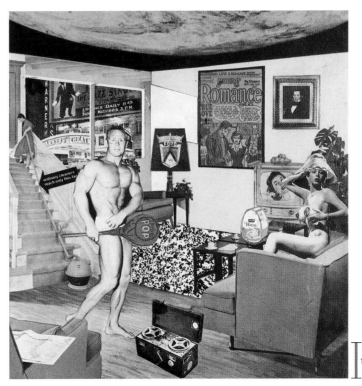

25-20 RICHARD HAMILTON, *Just What Is It That Makes Today's Homes So Different, So Appealing?* 1956. Collage, $10\frac{1}{4}″ × 9\frac{3}{4}″$. Kunsthalle Tübingen, Tübingen.

The fantasy interior in Hamilton's collage reflects the values of modern consumer culture through figures and objects cut from glossy magazines. Toying with mass-media imagery typifies British Pop Art.

25-21 JASPER JOHNS, *Flag*, 1954–1955, dated on reverse 1954. Encaustic, oil, and collage on fabric mounted on plywood, 3′ 6$\frac{1}{4}$″ × 5′ $\frac{5}{8}$″. Museum of Modern Art, New York (gift of Philip Johnson in honor of Alfred H. Barr Jr.). Art © Jasper Johns/Licensed by VAGA, New York.

American Pop artist Jasper Johns wanted to draw attention to common objects that people view frequently but rarely scrutinize. He made several series of paintings of targets, flags, numbers, and alphabets.

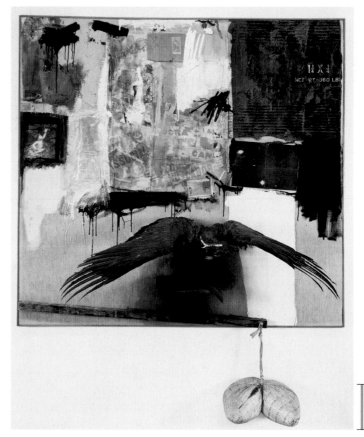

25-22 ROBERT RAUSCHENBERG, *Canyon*, 1959. Oil, pencil, paper, fabric, metal, cardboard box, printed paper, printed reproductions, photograph, wood, paint tube, and mirror on canvas, with oil on bald eagle, string, and pillow, 6′ 9$\frac{3}{4}$″ × 5′ 10″ × 2′. Sonnabend Collection. Art © Robert Rauschenberg/Licensed by VAGA, New York.

Rauschenberg's "combines" intersperse painted passages with sculptural elements. *Canyon* incorporates pigment on canvas with pieces of printed paper, photographs, a pillow, and a stuffed eagle.

Duchamp's ideas, Hamilton consistently combined elements of popular art and fine art, seeing both as belonging to the whole world of visual communication. He created *Just What Is It?* for the poster and catalogue of one section of an exhibition titled *This Is Tomorrow,* which included images from Hollywood cinema, science fiction, the mass media, and one reproduction of a van Gogh painting (to represent popular fine artworks).

The fantasy interior in Hamilton's collage reflects the values of modern consumer culture through figures and objects cut from glossy magazines. *Just What Is It?* includes references to mass media (the television, the theater marquee outside the window, the newspaper), advertising (Hoover vacuums, Ford cars, Armour hams, Tootsie Pops), and popular culture (the girlie magazine, bodybuilder Charles Atlas, romance comic books). Scholars have written much about the possible deep message of this piece, and few would deny the work's sardonic effect, whether or not the artist intended to make a pointed comment. Artworks of this sort stimulated the viewer's wide-ranging speculation about society's values, and this kind of intellectual toying with mass-media meaning and imagery typified Pop Art in England and Europe.

JASPER JOHNS Although Pop Art originated in England, the movement found its greatest articulation and success in the United States, in large part because the more fully matured American consumer culture provided a fertile environment in which the movement flourished through the 1960s. Indeed, Independent Group members claimed their inspiration came from Hollywood, Detroit, and New York's Madison Avenue, paying homage to America's predominance in the realms of mass media, mass production, and advertising. One of the artists pivotal to the early development of American Pop was JASPER JOHNS (b. 1930), who sought to draw attention to common objects in the world—what he called things "seen but not looked at."[16] To this end, he created several series of paintings of targets, flags, numbers, and alphabets. For example, *Flag* (FIG. **25-21**) depicts an object people view frequently but rarely scrutinize. The highly textured surface of the work is the result of Johns's use of *encaustic,* an ancient method of painting with liquid

wax and dissolved pigment (see "Encaustic Painting," Chapter 7, page 195). First, the artist embedded a collage of newspaper scraps or photographs in wax. He then painted over them with the encaustic. Because the wax hardened quickly, Johns could work rapidly, and the translucency of the wax allows the viewer to see the layered painting process.

ROBERT RAUSCHENBERG Johns's friend ROBERT RAUSCHENBERG (1925–2008) began using mass-media images in his work in the 1950s. Rauschenberg set out to create works that would be open and indeterminate, and he began by making *combines,* which intersperse painted passages with sculptural elements. Combines are, in a sense, Rauschenberg's personal variation on *assemblages,* artworks constructed from already existing objects. At times, these combines seem to be sculptures with painting incorporated into certain sections. Others seem to be paintings with three-dimensional objects attached to the surface. In the 1950s, assemblages usually contained an array of art reproductions, magazine and newspaper clippings, and passages painted in an Abstract Expressionist style. In the early 1960s, Rauschenberg adopted the commercial medium of *silk-screen printing,* first in black and white and then in color, and began filling entire canvases with appropriated news images and anonymous photographs of city scenes.

Canyon (FIG. **25-22**) is typical of Rauschenberg's combines. Pieces of printed paper and photographs cover parts of the canvas.

Roy Lichtenstein on Pop Art

In 1963, Roy Lichtenstein was one of eight painters interviewed for a profile on Pop Art in *Art News*. G. R. Swenson posed the questions. Part of Lichtenstein's response follows.

[Pop Art is] the use of commercial art as a subject matter in painting.... [Pop artists portray] what I think to be the most brazen and threatening characteristics of our culture, things we hate, but which are also so powerful in their impingement on us.... I paint directly... [without] perspective or shading. It doesn't look like a painting *of* something, it looks like the thing itself. Instead of looking like a painting *of* a billboard... Pop Art seems to be the actual thing. It is an intensification, a stylistic intensification of the excitement which the subject matter has for me; but the style is... cool. One of the things a cartoon does is to express violent emotion and passion in a completely mechanized and removed style. To express this thing in a painterly style would dilute it.... Everybody has called Pop Art "American" painting, but it's actually industrial painting. America was hit by industrialism and capitalism harder and sooner... I think the meaning of my work is that it's industrial, it's what all the world will soon become. Europe will be the same way, soon, so it won't be American; it will be universal.*

* Roy Lichtenstein quoted in G. R. Swenson, "What Is Pop Art? Interviews with Eight Painters," *Art News* 62, no. 7 (November 1963), 25, 64.

25-23 Roy Lichtenstein, *Hopeless*, 1963. Oil on canvas, 3′ 8″ × 3′ 8″. Kunstmuseum, Basel. © Estate of Roy Lichtenstein.

Comic books appealed to Lichtenstein because they were a mainstay of American popular culture, meant to be read and discarded. The Pop artist immortalized their images on large canvases.

Much of the unevenly painted surface consists of pigment roughly applied in a manner reminiscent of de Kooning's work (FIG. 25-7). A stuffed bald eagle attached to the lower part of the combine spreads its wings as if lifting off in flight toward the viewer. Completing the combine, a pillow dangles from a string attached to a wood stick below the eagle. The artist presented the work's components in a jumbled fashion. He tilted or turned some of the images sideways, and each overlays part of another image. The compositional confusion may resemble that of a Dada collage, but the parts of Rauschenberg's combines maintain their individuality more than those in, for example, a Schwitters piece (FIG. 24-30). The eye scans a Rauschenberg canvas much as it might survey the environment on a walk through a city. The various recognizable images and objects seem unrelated and defy a consistent reading, although Rauschenberg chose all the elements of his combines with specific meanings in mind. For example, Rauschenberg based *Canyon* on a Rembrandt painting of Jupiter in the form of an eagle carrying the boy Ganymede heavenward. The photo in the combine is a reference to the Greek boy, and the hanging pillow is a visual pun on his buttocks.

ROY LICHTENSTEIN As the Pop movement matured, the images became more concrete and tightly controlled. American artist ROY LICHTENSTEIN (1923–1997) turned his attention to commercial art and especially to the comic book as a mainstay of popular culture (see "Roy Lichtenstein on Pop Art," above). In paintings such as *Hopeless* (FIG. 25-23), Lichtenstein excerpted an image from a comic book, a form of entertainment meant to be read and discarded, and immortalized the image on a large canvas. Aside from that modification, Lichtenstein remained remarkably faithful to the original comic strip image. His subject was one of the melodramatic scenes common to popular romance comic books of the time. Lichtenstein also used the visual vocabulary of the comic strip, with its dark black outlines and unmodulated color areas, and retained the familiar square dimensions. Moreover, his printing technique, *benday dots,* called attention to the mass-produced derivation of the image. Named after its inventor, the newspaper printer Benjamin Day (1810–1889), the benday dot system involves the modulation of colors through the placement and size of colored dots. Lichtenstein thus transferred the visual shorthand language of the comic book to the realm of monumental painting.

25-24 ANDY WARHOL, *Green Coca-Cola Bottles,* 1962. Oil on canvas, 6' 10½" × 4' 9". Whitney Museum of American Art, New York.

Warhol was the quintessential American Pop artist. Here, he selected an icon of mass-produced consumer culture and then multiplied it, reflecting Coke's omnipresence in American society.

ANDY WARHOL The quintessential American Pop artist was ANDY WARHOL (1928–1987). An early successful career as a commercial artist and illustrator grounded Warhol in the sensibility and visual rhetoric of advertising and the mass media, knowledge that proved useful for his Pop artworks. In paintings such as *Green Coca-Cola Bottles* (FIG. 25-24), Warhol selected an icon of mass-produced, consumer culture of the time. The reassuringly familiar curved Coke bottle especially appealed to Warhol:

> What's great about this country is that America started the tradition where the richest consumers buy essentially the same things as the poorest. You can be watching TV and see Coca-Cola, and you can know that the President drinks Coke, Liz Taylor drinks Coke, and just think, you can drink Coke, too. A Coke is a Coke and no amount of money can get you a better Coke.[17]

As did other Pop artists, Warhol used a visual vocabulary and a printing technique that reinforced the image's connections to consumer culture. The repetition and redundancy of the Coke bottle reflect the omnipresence and dominance of this product in American society. The silk-screen technique allowed Warhol to print the image endlessly (although he varied each bottle slightly). So immersed was Warhol in a culture of mass production that he not only produced numerous canvases of the same image but also named his studio "the Factory."

Warhol often produced images of Hollywood celebrities, such as Marilyn Monroe. Like his other paintings, these works emphasize the commodity status of the subjects depicted. Warhol created *Marilyn Diptych* (FIG. 25-25) in the weeks following the movie star's suicide in August 1962, capitalizing on the media frenzy her death prompted. Warhol selected a Hollywood publicity photo, one that provides no insight into the real Norma Jean Baker (the actress's name before she assumed the persona of Marilyn Monroe). Rather, the viewer sees only a mask—the image the Hollywood myth machine generated. The garish colors and the flat application of paint contribute to that image's masklike quality. The repetition of Monroe's face reinforces her status as a consumer product on a par with Coke bottles, her glamorous, haunting visage seemingly confronting the viewer endlessly, as it did the American public in the aftermath of her death. The right half of this work, with its poor registration of pigment, suggests a sequence of film stills, a reference to the realm from which Monroe derived her fame.

Warhol's ascendance to the rank of celebrity artist underscored his remarkable and astute understanding of the dynamics and visual language of mass culture. He predicted

25-25 ANDY WARHOL, *Marilyn Diptych,* 1962. Oil, acrylic, and silkscreen enamel on canvas, each panel 6' 8" × 4' 9". Tate Gallery, London.

Warhol's repetition of Monroe's face reinforced her status as a consumer product, her glamorous visage confronting the viewer endlessly, as it did the American public in the aftermath of her death.

25-26 Claes Oldenburg, various works exhibited at the Green Gallery, New York, 1962.

Oldenburg's painted plaster and stuffed vinyl sculptures magnify familiar items of American consumer culture. The title of one of his shows, *The Store,* was a comment on art itself as a commodity.

that the age of mass media would enable everyone to become famous for 15 minutes. His own fame has lasted much longer.

CLAES OLDENBURG The Swedish-born Pop artist Claes Oldenburg (b. 1929) has produced sculptures that incisively comment on American consumer culture. His early works consisted of reliefs of food and clothing items. Oldenburg constructed these sculptures of plaster layered on chicken wire and muslin, painting them with cheap commercial house enamel. In later works, focused on the same subjects, he shifted to large-scale stuffed sculptures of sewn vinyl or canvas. Examples of both types of sculptures appear in the photograph (FIG. **25-26**) of his one-person show at the Green Gallery in New York in 1962. Oldenburg had included many of the works in this exhibition in an earlier show he mounted titled *The Store*—an appropriate comment on the function of art as a commodity in a consumer society. Over the years, Oldenburg's sculpture has become increasingly monumental. In recent decades, he and his wife and collaborator, Dutch American Coosje van Bruggen (b. 1942), have become particularly well known for their mammoth outdoor sculptures of familiar, commonplace objects, such as cue balls, shuttlecocks, clothespins, and torn notebooks.

Superrealism

Like the Pop artists, the artists associated with *Superrealism* sought a form of artistic communication that was more accessible to the public than the remote, unfamiliar visual language of the Abstract Expressionists, Post-Painterly Abstractionists, and Minimalists. The Superrealists expanded Pop's iconography in both painting and sculpture by making images in the late 1960s and 1970s involving scrupulous fidelity to optical fact. Because many Superrealists used photographs as sources for their imagery, art historians also refer to this postwar art movement as *Photorealism.*

AUDREY FLACK American artist Audrey Flack (b. 1931) was one of Superrealism's pioneers. Her paintings, such as *Marilyn* (FIG. **25-27**), were not simply technical exercises in recording objects in

minute detail but were also conceptual inquiries into the nature of photography and the extent to which photography constructs an understanding of reality. Flack observed that "[photography is] my whole life, I studied art history, it was always photographs, I never saw the paintings, they were in Europe. . . . Look at TV and at magazines

25-27 Audrey Flack, *Marilyn,* 1977. Oil over acrylic on canvas, 8′ × 8′. University of Arizona Museum, Tucson (museum purchase with funds provided by the Edward J. Gallagher Jr. Memorial Fund).

Flack's pioneering Photorealist still lifes record objects with great optical fidelity. *Marilyn* alludes to Dutch vanitas paintings (FIG. **20-21**) and incorporates multiple references to the transience of life.

Chuck Close on Portrait Painting and Photography

In a 1970 interview, the art critic Cindy Nemser asked Chuck Close about the scale of his huge portraits (FIG. 25-28) and the relationship of his paintings to the photographs that lie behind them. He answered in part:

The large scale allows me to deal with information that is overlooked in an eight-by-ten inch photograph ... My large scale forces the viewer to focus on one area at a time. In that way he is made aware of the blurred areas that are seen with peripheral vision. Normally we never take those peripheral areas into account. When we focus on an area it is sharp. As we turn our attention to adjacent areas they sharpen up too. In my work, the blurred areas don't come into focus, but they are too large to be ignored. ... In order to ... make [my painted] information stack up with photographic information, I tried to purge my work of as much of the baggage of traditional portrait painting as I could. To avoid a painterly brush stroke and surface, I use some pretty devious means, such as razor blades, electric drills and airbrushes. I also work as thinly as possible and I don't use white paint as it tends to build up and become chalky and opaque. In fact, in a nine-by-seven foot picture, I only use a couple of tablespoons of black paint to cover the entire canvas.*

* Cindy Nemser, "Chuck Close: Interview with Cindy Nemser," *Artforum* 8, no. 5 (January 1970), 51–55.

25-28 CHUCK CLOSE, *Big Self-Portrait*, 1967–1968. Acrylic on canvas, 8′ 11″ × 6′ 11″. Walker Art Center, Minneapolis (Art Center Acquisition Fund, 1969).

Close's goal was to translate photographic information into painted information. In his portraits, he deliberately avoided creative compositions, flattering lighting effects, and revealing facial expressions.

1 ft.

and reproductions, they're all influenced by photo-vision."[18] The photograph's formal qualities also intrigued her, and she used photographic techniques by first projecting an image in slide form onto the canvas. By next using an *airbrush* (a device that uses compressed air to spray paint, originally designed as a photo-retouching tool), Flack could duplicate the smooth gradations of tone and color found in photographs. Most of her paintings are still lifes that present the viewer with a collection of familiar objects painted with great optical fidelity. *Marilyn* is a still life that incorporates photographs of the actress's face. Flack's commentary on Monroe's tragic death differs from that in Warhol's *Marilyn Diptych* (FIG. 25-25). Flack alludes to Dutch vanitas paintings (FIG. 20-21), and her still life includes multiple references to death. In addition to the black-and-white photographs of a youthful, smiling Monroe, fresh fruit, an hourglass, a burning candle, a watch, and a calendar all refer to the passage of time and the transience of life on earth.

CHUCK CLOSE Also usually considered a Superrealist is American artist CHUCK CLOSE (b. 1940), best known for his large-scale portraits, such as *Big Self-Portrait* (FIG. 25-28). However, Close felt his connection to the Photorealists was tenuous, because for him realism, rather than an end in itself, was the result of an intellectually rigorous, systematic approach to painting. He based his paintings of

the late 1960s and early 1970s on photographs, and his main goal was to translate photographic information into painted information. Because he aimed simply to record visual information about his subject's appearance, Close deliberately avoided creative compositions, flattering lighting effects, and revealing facial expressions. Not interested in providing great insight into the personalities of those portrayed, Close painted anonymous and generic people, mostly friends. By reducing the variables in his paintings (even their canvas size is a constant 9 by 7 feet), he could focus on employing his methodical presentations of faces, thereby encouraging the viewer to deal with the formal aspects of his works. Indeed, because of the large scale of Close paintings, careful scrutiny causes the images to dissolve into abstract patterns (see "Chuck Close on Portrait Painting and Photography," above).

DUANE HANSON Not surprisingly, many sculptors also were Superrealists, including DUANE HANSON (1925–1996), who perfected a casting technique that allowed him to create life-size figural sculptures that many viewers initially mistake for real people. Hanson first made plaster molds from live models and filled the molds with polyester resin. After the resin hardened, the artist removed the outer molds and cleaned, painted with an airbrush, and decorated the sculptures with wigs, clothes, and other accessories. These works,

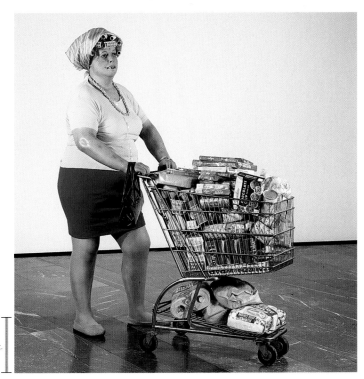

1 ft.

25-29 DUANE HANSON, *Supermarket Shopper,* 1970. Polyester resin and fiberglass polychromed in oil, with clothing, steel cart, and groceries, life-size. Nachfolgeinstitut, Neue Galerie, Sammlung Ludwig, Aachen. Art © Estate of Duane Hanson/Licensed by VAGA, New York.

Hanson used molds from live models to create his Superrealistic life-size painted plaster sculptures. His aim was to capture the emptiness and loneliness of average Americans in familiar settings.

such as *Supermarket Shopper* (FIG. 25-29), depict stereotypical average Americans, striking chords with the public precisely because of their familiarity. Hanson explained his choice of imagery: "The subject matter that I like best deals with the familiar lower and middle-class American types of today. To me, the resignation, emptiness and loneliness of their existence captures the true reality of life for these people. . . . I want to achieve a certain tough realism which speaks of the fascinating idiosyncrasies of our time."[19]

PAINTING AND SCULPTURE SINCE 1970

The Pop artists and Superrealists were not the only artists to challenge modernist formalist doctrine. By the 1970s, the range of art produced in both traditional and new media in reaction to Abstract Expressionism, Minimalism, and other formalist movements had become so diverse that only a broad general term can describe the phenomenon: *postmodernism.* There is no agreement about the definition of postmodern art. Some scholars, such as Fredric Jameson, assert that a major characteristic of postmodernism is the erosion of the boundaries between high culture and popular culture—a separation Clement Greenberg and the modernists had staunchly defended. With the appearance of Pop Art, that separation became more difficult to maintain. For Jameson, the intersection of high and mass culture is, in fact, a defining feature of the new postmodernism. He attributed the emergence of postmodernism to "a new type of social life and a new economic order—what is often euphemistically called modernization, postindustrial or consumer society, the society of the media or the spectacle, or multinational capitalism."[20]

For many recent artists, postmodernism involves examining the process by which meaning is generated and the negotiation or dialogue that transpires between viewers and artworks. This kind of examination of the nature of art parallels the literary field of study known as critical theory. Critical theorists view art and architecture, as well as literature and the other humanities, as a culture's intellectual products, or "constructs." These constructs unconsciously suppress or conceal the true premises that inform the culture, primarily the values of those politically in control. Thus, cultural products function in an ideological capacity, obscuring, for example, racist or sexist attitudes. When revealed by analysis, the facts behind these constructs, according to critical theorists, contribute to a more substantial understanding of artworks, buildings, books, and the overall culture.

Many critical theorists use an analytical strategy called *deconstruction,* after a method developed in the 1960s and 1970s by French intellectuals, notably Michel Foucault (1926–1984) and Jacques Derrida (1930–2004). For those employing deconstruction, all cultural constructs are "texts." Acknowledging the lack of fixed or uniform meanings in these texts, critical theorists accept a variety of interpretations as valid. Further, as cultural products, how texts signify and what they signify are entirely conventional. They can refer to nothing outside of themselves, only to other texts. Thus, no extratextual reality exists that people can reference. The enterprise of deconstruction is to reveal the contradictions and instabilities of these texts, or cultural language (written or visual).

With primarily political and social aims, deconstructive analysis has the ultimate goal of effecting political and social change. Accordingly, critical theorists who employ this approach seek to uncover—to deconstruct—the facts of power, privilege, and prejudice underlying the practices and institutions of any given culture. In the process, deconstruction reveals the precariousness of structures and systems, such as language and cultural practices, along with the assumptions underlying them. Yet because of the lack of fixed meaning in texts, many politically committed thinkers assert that deconstruction does not provide a sufficiently stable basis for dissent.

Critical theorists do not agree upon any philosophy or analytical method, because in principle they oppose firm definitions. They do share a healthy suspicion of all traditional truth claims and value standards, all hierarchical authority and institutions. For them, deconstruction means destabilizing established meanings, definitions, and interpretations while encouraging subjectivity and individual differences.

Certainly, one thing all postmodern artists have in common is a self-consciousness about their place in the historical continuum of art. Consequently, many of them resurrect artistic traditions to comment on and reinterpret those styles or idioms. However defined, postmodern art comprises a dizzying array of artworks in different media. Only a representative sample can be presented here.

Neo-Expressionism

One of the first coherent movements to emerge during the postmodern era was *Neo-Expressionism.* This movement's name reflects postmodern artists' interest in reexamining earlier art production and connects this art to the powerful, intense works of the German Expressionists (see Chapter 24) and the Abstract Expressionists, among other artists.

SUSAN ROTHENBERG In the 1970s, SUSAN ROTHENBERG (b. 1945) produced a major series of large paintings with the horse as the central image. The horse theme resonates with history and metaphor—from the Parthenon frieze and Roman and Renaissance equestrian portraits to the paintings of German Expressionist Franz

25-30 Susan Rothenberg, *Tattoo,* 1979. Acrylic paint on canvas, 5′ 7″ × 8′ 7″. Walker Art Center, Minneapolis (purchased with the aid of funds from Mr. and Mrs. Edmond R. Ruben, Mr. and Mrs. Julius E. Davis, the Art Center Acquisition Fund, and the National Endowment for the Arts, 1979).

Rothenberg's Neo-Expressionist paintings feature loose brush-work, agitated surfaces, and hazy, semiabstract forms. This work's title refers to the horse's head drawn within the outline of its leg.

1 ft.

Marc (FIG. 24-8). Like Marc, Rothenberg saw horses as metaphors for humanity: "The horse was a way of not doing people, yet it was a symbol of people, a self-portrait, really."[21] Rothenberg, however, distilled the image to a ghostly outline or hazy depiction that is more poetic than descriptive. As such, her works fall in the nebulous area between representation and abstraction. In paintings such as *Tattoo* (FIG. 25-30), the loose brushwork and agitated surface contribute to the expressiveness of the image and account for Rothenberg's cat-

egorization as a Neo-Expressionist. The title, *Tattoo,* refers to the horse's head drawn within the outline of its leg—"a tattoo or memory image," according to the artist.[22]

JULIAN SCHNABEL The work of another American artist, Julian Schnabel (b. 1951), forcefully restates the premises of Abstract Expressionism. When executing his artworks in the 1980s, however, Schnabel experimented widely with materials and sup-

25-31 Julian Schnabel, *The Walk Home,* 1984–1985. Oil, plates, copper, bronze, fiberglass, and Bondo on wood, 9′ 3″ × 19′ 4″. Broad Art Foundation and the Pace Gallery, New York.

Schnabel's paintings recall the work of the gestural abstractionists, but he employs an amalgamation of media, bringing together painting, mosaic, and low-relief sculpture.

1 ft.

1 ft.

25-32 ANSELM KIEFER, *Nigredo*, 1984. Oil paint on photosensitized fabric, acrylic emulsion, straw, shellac, relief paint on paper pulled from painted wood, 11′ × 18′. Philadelphia Museum of Art, Philadelphia (gift of Friends of the Philadelphia Museum of Art).

Kiefer's paintings have thickly encrusted surfaces incorporating materials such as straw. Here, the German artist used perspective to pull the viewer into an incinerated landscape alluding to the Holocaust.

ports—from fragmented china plates bonded to wood, to paint on velvet and tarpaulin. He had a special interest in the physicality of the objects, and by attaching broken crockery, as in *The Walk Home* (FIG. 25-31), he found an extension of what paint could do. Superficially, the painting recalls the work of the gestural abstractionists—the spontaneous drips of Pollock (FIG. 25-5) and the energetic brush strokes of de Kooning (FIG. 25-7). The thick, mosaic-like texture, an amalgamation of media, brings together painting, mosaic, and low-relief sculpture. In effect, Schnabel reclaimed older media for his expressionistic method, which considerably amplifies his bold, distinctive statement.

ANSELM KIEFER Neo-Expressionism was by no means a solely American movement. German artist ANSELM KIEFER (b. 1945) has produced some of the most lyrical and engaging works of the contemporary period. Like Schnabel's, Kiefer's paintings, such as *Nigredo* (FIG. 25-32), are monumental in scale, recall Abstract Expressionist canvases, and draw the viewer to their textured surfaces, made more complex by the addition of materials such as straw and lead. It is not merely the impressive physicality of Kiefer's paintings that accounts for the impact of his work, however. His images function on a mythological or metaphorical level as well as on a historically specific one. Kiefer's works of the 1970s and 1980s often involve a reexamination of German history, particularly the painful Nazi era of 1933–1945, and evoke the feeling of despair. Kiefer believes that Germany's participation in World War II and the Holocaust left permanent scars on the souls of the German people and on the souls of all humanity.

Nigredo ("blackening") pulls the viewer into an expansive landscape depicted using Renaissance perspectival principles. This landscape, however, is far from pastoral or carefully cultivated. Rather, it is bleak and charred. Although it makes no specific reference to the Holocaust, this incinerated landscape indirectly alludes to the horrors of that event. More generally, the blackness of the landscape may refer to the notion of alchemical change or transformation, a concept of great interest to Kiefer. Black is one of the four symbolic colors of the alchemist—a color that refers both to death and to the

molten, chaotic state of substances broken down by fire. The alchemist, however, focuses on the transformation of substances, and thus the emphasis on blackness is not absolute but can also be perceived as part of a process of renewal and redemption. Kiefer thus imbued his work with a deep symbolic meaning that, when combined with the intriguing visual quality of his parched, congealed surfaces, results in paintings of enduring power.

Feminist Art

With the renewed interest in representation that the Pop artists and Superrealists introduced in the 1960s and 1970s, painters and sculptors once again began to embrace the persuasive powers of art to communicate with a wide audience. In recent decades, artists have investigated more insistently the dynamics of power and privilege, especially in relation to issues of gender, race, ethnicity, class, and sexual orientation.

In the 1970s, the feminist movement focused public attention on the history of women and their place in society. In art, two women—Judy Chicago and Miriam Schapiro—largely spearheaded the American feminist art movement. Chicago and a group of students at California State University, Fresno, founded the Feminist Art Program, and Chicago and Schapiro coordinated it at the California Institute of the Arts in Valencia. In 1972, as part of this program, teachers and students joined to create projects such as Womanhouse, an abandoned house in Los Angeles they completely converted into a suite of "environments," each based on a different aspect of women's lives and fantasies.

JUDY CHICAGO In her own work in the 1970s, JUDY CHICAGO (Judy Cohen, b. 1939) wanted to educate viewers about women's role in history and the fine arts. She aimed to establish a respect for women and their art, to forge a new kind of art expressing women's experiences, and to find a way to make that art accessible to a large audience. Inspired early in her career by the work of Barbara Hepworth (FIG. 24-58), Georgia O'Keeffe (FIGS. I-4 and 24-38), and Louise Nevelson (FIG. 25-17), Chicago developed a personal painting style that consciously included abstract organic vaginal images. In the early 1970s, Chicago began planning an ambitious piece, *The*

Judy Chicago on *The Dinner Party*

One of the acknowledged masterpieces of feminist art is Judy Chicago's *The Dinner Party* (FIG. 25-33), which required a team of nearly 400 to create and assemble. In 1979, Chicago published a book explaining the genesis and symbolism of the work.

[By 1974] I had discarded [my original] idea of painting a hundred abstract portraits on plates, each paying tribute to a different historic female figure.... In my research I realized over and over again that women's achievements had been left out of history.... My new idea was to try to symbolize this.... [I thought] about putting the plates on a table with silver, glasses, napkins, and tablecloths, and over the next year and a half the concept of *The Dinner Party* slowly evolved. I began to think about the piece as a reinterpretation of the Last Supper from the point of view of women, who, throughout history, had prepared the meals and set the table. In my "Last Supper," however, the women would be the honored guests. Their representation in the form of plates set on the table would express the way women had been confined, and the piece would thus reflect both women's achievements and their oppression.... My goal with *The Dinner Party* was ... to forge a new kind of art expressing women's experience.... [It] seemed appropriate to relate our history through

10 ft.

25-33 JUDY CHICAGO, *The Dinner Party,* 1979. Multimedia, including ceramics and stitchery, 48′ long on each side. Brooklyn Museum, Brooklyn.

Chicago's *Dinner Party* honors 39 women from antiquity to 20th-century America. The triangular form and the materials—painted china and fabric—are traditionally associated with women.

art, particularly through techniques traditionally associated with women—china-painting and needlework.*

* Judy Chicago, *The Dinner Party: A Symbol of Our Heritage* (Garden City, N.Y.: Anchor Press, 1979) 11–12.

Dinner Party (FIG. 25-33), using craft techniques (such as china painting and needlework) traditionally practiced by women, to celebrate the achievements and contributions women made throughout history (see "Judy Chicago on *The Dinner Party,*" above). She originally conceived the work as a feminist Last Supper for 13 "honored guests," as in the New Testament, but all women. There also are 13 women in a witches' coven, and Chicago's *Dinner Party* refers to witchcraft and the worship of the Mother Goddess. But because Chicago had uncovered so many worthy women in the course of her research, she expanded the number of guests threefold to 39 and placed them around a triangular table 48 feet long on each side. The triangular form refers to the ancient symbol for both woman and the Goddess. The notion of a dinner party also alludes to women's traditional role as homemakers.

The Dinner Party rests on a white tile floor inscribed with the names of 999 additional women of achievement to signify that the accomplishments of the 39 honored guests rest on a foundation other women laid. Among those with place settings at the table are O'Keeffe, the Egyptian pharaoh Hatshepsut (see "Hatshepsut," Chapter 3, page 54), the British writer Virginia Woolf, the Native American guide

Sacagawea, and the American suffragist Susan B. Anthony. Each woman's place has identical eating utensils and a goblet but a unique oversized porcelain plate and a long place mat or table runner covered with imagery that reflects significant facts about that woman's life and culture. The plates range from simple concave shapes with china-painted imagery to dishes whose sculptured three-dimensional designs almost seem to struggle to free themselves. The designs on each plate incorporate both butterfly and vulval motifs—the butterfly as the ancient symbol of liberation and the vulva as the symbol of female sexuality. Each table runner combines traditional needlework techniques, including needlepoint, embroidery, crochet, beading, patchwork, and appliqué. *The Dinner Party* is, however, more than the sum of its parts. It provides viewers with a powerful launching point for considering broad feminist concerns.

MIRIAM SCHAPIRO After enjoying a thriving career as a hard-edge painter in California in the late 1960s, MIRIAM SCHAPIRO (b. 1923) became fascinated with the hidden metaphors for womanhood she then saw in her abstract paintings. Intrigued by the materials

25-34 MIRIAM SCHAPIRO, *Anatomy of a Kimono* (section), 1976. Fabric and acrylic on canvas, 6′ 8″ high. Collection of Bruno Bishofberger, Zurich.

Schapiro calls her huge sewn collages *femmages* to make the point that women had been doing collages of fabric long before Picasso (FIG. 24-16). This femmage incorporates patterns from Japanese kimonos.

she had used to create a doll's house for her part in Womanhouse, in the 1970s Schapiro began to make huge sewn collages, assembled from fabrics, quilts, buttons, sequins, lace, and rickrack collected at antique shows. She called these works *femmages* to make the point that women had been doing collages using these materials long before Pablo Picasso (FIG. 24-16) introduced them to the art world. *Anatomy of a Kimono* (FIG. 25-34) is one of a series of monumental femmages based on the patterns of Japanese kimonos, fans, and robes. This vast composition repeats the kimono shape in a sumptuous array of fabric fragments.

CINDY SHERMAN Early attempts at dealing with feminist issues in art tended toward essentialism, emphasizing universal differences—either biological or experiential—between women and men. More recent discussions have gravitated toward the notion of gender as a socially constructed concept, and an extremely unstable one at that. Identity is multifaceted and changeable, making the discussion of feminist issues more challenging. Consideration of the many variables, however, results in a more complex understanding of gender roles.

American artist CINDY SHERMAN (b. 1954) addresses in her work the way much of Western art presents female beauty for the enjoyment of the "male gaze," a primary focus of contemporary feminist theory. Since 1977, Sherman has produced a series of more than 80 black-and-white photographs titled *Untitled Film Stills*. She got the idea for the series after examining soft-core pornography magazines and noting the stereotypical ways they depicted women. She decided to produce her own series of photographs, designing, acting in, directing, and photographing the works. In so doing, she took control of her own image and constructed her own identity, a primary feminist concern. In works from the series, such as *Untitled Film Still #35* (FIG. 25-35), Sherman appears, often in costume and wig, in a photograph that seems to be a film still. Most of the images in this series recall popular film genres but are sufficiently generic that the viewer cannot relate them to specific movies. Sherman often reveals the constructed nature of these images with the shutter release cable she holds in her hand to take the pictures. (The cord runs across the floor in *#35*.) Although the artist is still the object of the viewer's gaze in these images, the identity is one she alone chose to assume.

25-35 CINDY SHERMAN, *Untitled Film Still #35*, 1979. Gelatin silverprint, 10″ × 8″. Private collection.

Sherman here assumed a role for one of a series of 80 photographs resembling film stills in which she addressed the way women have been presented in Western art for the enjoyment of the "male gaze."

1 ft.

25-36 Barbara Kruger, *Untitled* (*Your Gaze Hits the Side of My Face*), 1981. Photograph, red painted frame, 4′ 7″ × 3′ 5″. Courtesy Mary Boone Gallery, New York.

Kruger, like Sherman, has explored the male gaze in her art. Using the layout techniques of mass media, she constructed this word-and-photograph collage to challenge culturally constructed notions of gender.

BARBARA KRUGER Another artist who has examined the male gaze and the culturally constructed notion of gender in her art is Barbara Kruger (b. 1945). Kruger's work explores the strategies and techniques of contemporary mass media and draws on her early training as a graphic designer who contributed to *Mademoiselle* magazine. *Untitled* (*Your Gaze Hits the Side of My Face;* FIG. **25-36**) incorporates layout techniques the mass media use to sell consumer goods. Although Kruger favored the reassuringly familiar format and look of advertising, her goal was to subvert the typical use of such imagery. Rather, she aimed to expose the deceptiveness of the media messages the viewer complacently absorbs. Kruger wanted to undermine the myths—particularly those about women—the media constantly reinforce. Her huge (often 4 by 6 feet) word-and-photograph collages challenge the cultural attitudes embedded in commercial advertising.

In *Your Gaze,* Kruger overlaid a photograph of a classically beautiful sculpted head of a woman with a vertical row of text composed of eight words. The words cannot be taken in with a single glance, and reading them is a staccato exercise, with an overlaid cumulative quality that delays understanding and intensifies the meaning (rather like reading a series of roadside billboards from a speeding car). Kruger's use of text in her work is significant. Many cultural theorists have asserted that language is one of the most powerful vehicles for internalizing stereotypes and conditioned roles.

25-37 Ana Mendieta, *Flowers on Body,* 1973. Color photograph of earth/body work with flowers, executed at El Yagul, Mexico. Courtesy of the Estate of Ana Mendieta and Galerie Lelong, New York.

In this earth/body sculpture, Mendieta appears covered with flowers in a womblike cavity to address issues of birth and death as well as the human connection to the earth.

ANA MENDIETA Cuban-born artist Ana Mendieta (1948–1985), like Sherman, used her body as a component in her artworks. Although gender issues concerned her, Mendieta's art also dealt with issues of spirituality and cultural heritage. The artist's best-known series, *Silueta* (*Silhouettes*), consists of approximately 200 earth/body works completed between 1973 and 1980. These works represented Mendieta's attempt to carry on, as she described, "a dialogue between the landscape and the female body (based on my own silhouette)."[23]

Flowers on Body (FIG. **25-37**) is a documentary photograph of the first of the earth/body sculptures in the *Silueta* series. In this work, Mendieta appears covered with flowers in an earthen, womblike cavity. Executed at El Yagul, a Mexican archaeological site, the work speaks to the issues of birth and death, the female experience of childbirth, and the human connection to the earth. Objects and locations from nature play an important role in Mendieta's art. She explained the centrality of this connection to nature:

> I believe this has been a direct result of my having been torn from
> my homeland during my adolescence. I am overwhelmed by the

1 ft.

25-38 HANNAH WILKE, S.O.S.—*Starification Object Series*, 1974. Ten black-and-white photographs with 15 chewing-gum sculptures in Plexiglas cases mounted on ragboard, from a series originally made for *S.O.S. Mastication Box* and used in an exhibition-performance at the Clocktower, January 1, 1975, 3′ 5″ × 5′ 8″. Courtesy Ronald Feldman Fine Arts, New York. Art © Marsie, Emanuelle, Damon and Andrew Scharlatt/Licensed by VAGA, New York.

In this photographic series, Wilke posed topless decorated with chewing-gum sculptures of vulvas that allude to female pleasure but also to pain, because they resemble scars.

feeling of having been cast from the womb (nature). My art is the way I re-establish the bonds that unite me to the universe. It is a return to the maternal source. Through my earth/body sculptures I become one with the earth.[24]

Beyond their sensual, moving presence, Mendieta's works also generate a palpable spiritual force. In longing for her homeland, she sought the cultural understanding and acceptance of the spiritual powers inherent in nature that modern Western societies often seem to reject in favor of scientific and technological developments. Mendieta's art is lyrical and passionate and operates at the intersection of cultural, spiritual, physical, and feminist concerns.

HANNAH WILKE Like Mendieta, HANNAH WILKE (1940–1993) used her own nude body as her artistic material. In her 1974–1982 series *S.O.S.—Starification Object Series* (FIG. 25-38), Wilke's images of herself trigger readings that are simultaneously metaphorical and real, stereotypical and unique, erotic and disconcerting, and that deal with both pleasure and pain. In these 10 black-and-white photographs documenting a performance, Wilke appears topless in a variety of poses, some seductive and others more confrontational. In each, pieces of chewed gum shaped into small vulvas decorate her body. While these tiny vaginal sculptures allude to female pleasure, they also appear as scars, suggesting pain. Ultimately, Wilke hoped that women would "take control of and have pride in the sensuality of their own bodies and create a sexuality in their own terms, without deferring to concepts degenerated by culture."[25]

GUERRILLA GIRLS Some feminist artists have taken the world of the woman artist as their subject, rather than women in society at large. The New York–based GUERRILLA GIRLS, formed in 1984, bill themselves as the "conscience of the art world." This group sees its duty as calling attention to injustice in the art world, especially what it perceives as the sexist and racist orientation of the major art institutions. The women who are members of the Guerrilla Girls have chosen to remain anonymous. To protect their identities, they wear gorilla masks in public. The Guerrilla Girls employ guerrilla tactics by demonstrating in public, putting on performances, and placing posters and flyers in public locations. This distribution network expands the impact of their messages. One poster that reflects the Guerrilla Girls' agenda facetiously lists "the advantages of being a woman artist" (FIG. 25-39). In fact, the list itemizes the numerous obstacles women artists face in the contemporary art world. The Guerrilla Girls hope their publicizing of these obstacles will inspire improvements in the situation for women artists.

THE ADVANTAGES OF BEING A WOMAN ARTIST:

Working without the pressure of success
Not having to be in shows with men
Having an escape from the art world in your 4 free-lance jobs
Knowing your career might pick up after you're eighty
Being reassured that whatever kind of art you make it will be labeled feminine
Not being stuck in a tenured teaching position
Seeing your ideas live on in the work of others
Having the opportunity to choose between career and motherhood
Not having to choke on those big cigars or paint in Italian suits
Having more time to work when your mate dumps you for someone younger
Being included in revised versions of art history
Not having to undergo the embarrassment of being called a genius
Getting your picture in the art magazines wearing a gorilla suit

A PUBLIC SERVICE MESSAGE FROM **GUERRILLA GIRLS** CONSCIENCE OF THE ART WORLD

1 in.

25-39 GUERRILLA GIRLS, *The Advantages of Being a Woman Artist*, 1988. Offset print, 1′ 5″ × 1′ 10″. Collection of the artists.

The anonymous Guerrilla Girls wear gorilla masks in public performances and produce posters in which they call attention to injustice in the art world, especially what they perceive as sexist or racist treatment.

Other Social and Political Art

Feminist issues are by no means the only social and political concerns that contemporary artists have addressed in their work. Race, ethnicity, and sexual orientation are among the other pressing issues that have given rise to important artworks during the past few decades.

KIKI SMITH American sculptor KIKI SMITH (b. 1954) has explored the question of who controls the human body, an interest that grew out of her training as an emergency medical service technician in New York City. Smith, however, also wants to reveal the socially constructed nature of the body, and she encourages the viewer to consider how external forces shape people's perceptions of their bodies. In works such as *Untitled* (FIG. 25-40), the artist dramatically departed from conventional representations of the body, both in art and in the media. She suspended two life-size wax figures, one male and one female, both nude, from metal stands. Smith marked each of the sculptures with long white drips—body

fluids running from the woman's breasts and down the man's leg. She commented:

> Most of the functions of the body are hidden ... from society.... [W]e separate our bodies from our lives. But, when people are dying, they are losing control of their bodies. That loss of function can seem humiliating and frightening. But, on the other hand, you can look at it as a kind of liberation of the body. It seems like a nice metaphor—a way to think about the social—that people lose control despite the many agendas of different ideologies in society, which are trying to control the body(ies) ... medicine, religion, law, etc. Just thinking about control—who has control of the body? ... Does the mind have control of the body? Does the social?[26]

FAITH RINGGOLD Other artists, reflecting their own identities and backgrounds, have used their art to address issues associated with African American women. Inspired by the civil rights movement, FAITH RINGGOLD (b. 1930) produced numerous works in the 1960s that provided incisive commentary on the realities of racial prejudice. She increasingly incorporated references to gender as well and, in the 1970s, turned to fabric as the predominant material in her art. Using fabric enabled her to make more pointed reference to the domestic sphere, traditionally associated with women, and to collaborate with her mother, Willi Posey, a fashion designer. After her mother's death in 1981, Ringgold created *Who's Afraid of Aunt Jemima?* (FIG. 25-41), a quilt composed of dyed, painted, and pieced fabric. A moving tribute to her mother, this work combines the personal and the political. The quilt includes a narrative—the witty story of the family of Aunt Jemima, most familiar as the stereotypical black "mammy" but here a successful African American businesswoman. Ringgold conveyed this

25-40 KIKI SMITH, *Untitled,* 1990. Beeswax and microcrystalline wax figures on metal stands, female figure installed height 6′ 1½″; male figure 6′ 4 15/16″. Whitney Museum of American Art, New York (purchased with funds from the Painting and Sculpture Committee).

Asking "who controls the body?" Kiki Smith sculpted two life-size wax figures of a nude man and woman with body fluids running from the woman's breasts and down the man's leg.

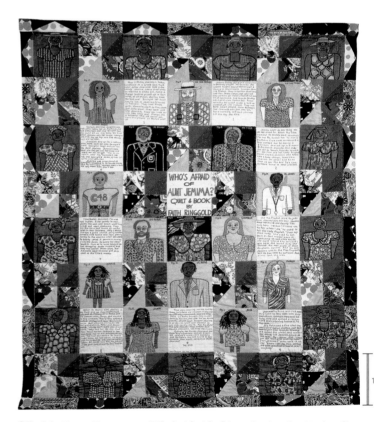

25-41 FAITH RINGGOLD, *Who's Afraid of Aunt Jemima?* 1983. Acrylic on canvas with fabric borders, quilted, 7′ 6″ × 6′ 8″. Private collection.

In this quilt, a medium associated with women, Ringgold presented a tribute to her mother that also addresses African American culture and the struggles of women to overcome oppression.

Daring Sensible Severe Long & Silly Boyish Ageless Silly Magnetic Country Fresh Sweet

1 ft.

25-42 LORNA SIMPSON, *Stereo Styles*, 1988. 10 black-and-white Polaroid prints and 10 engraved plastic plaques, 5′ 4″ × 9′ 8″ overall. Private collection.

In *Stereo Styles,* Simpson presents photographs of African American hairstyles as racial symbols associated with personality traits. She also comments on those coiffures as fashion commodities.

narrative using both text (written in black dialect) and embroidered portraits interspersed with traditional patterned squares. This work, while resonating with autobiographical references, also speaks to the larger issues of the history of African American culture and the struggles of women to overcome oppression.

LORNA SIMPSON The issues of racism and sexism are also central to the work of LORNA SIMPSON (b. 1960). Simpson has spent much of her career producing photographs that explore feminist and African American strategies to reveal and subvert conventional representations of gender and race. Like Sherman (FIG. **25-35**), she deals with the issue of "the gaze," trying to counteract the process of objectification to which both women and African Americans are subject. In *Stereo Styles* (FIG. **25-42**), a series of Polaroid photographs and engravings, Simpson focuses on African American hairstyles, often used to symbolize the entire race. Hair is a physical code tied to issues of social status and position. Kobena Mercer, who has studied the cultural importance of hair, observed that "Hair is never a straightforward biological 'fact' because it is almost always groomed, . . . cut, . . . and generally 'worked upon' by human hands. Such practices socialize hair, making it the medium of significant 'statements' about self and society."[27] On the issue of race, Mercer argued, "where race structures social relations of power, hair—as visible as skin color, but also the most tangible sign of racial difference—takes on another forcefully symbolic dimension."[28] In *Stereo Styles,* Simpson also commented on the appropriation of African-derived hairstyles as a fashion commodity, and the personality traits listed correlate with specific hairstyles.

MELVIN EDWARDS American MELVIN EDWARDS (b. 1937) also has sought to reveal a history of collective oppression through his art. One of Edwards's major sculptural series focused on the metaphor of lynching to provoke thought about the legacy of racism. This *Lynch Fragment* series encompassed more than 150 welded-steel sculptures produced in the years after 1963. Lynching

as an artistic theme prompts an immediate and visceral response, conjuring chilling and gruesome images from the past. Edwards sought to extend this emotional resonance further in his art. He constructed the series' relatively small welded sculptures, such as *Tambo* (FIG. **25-43**), from found metal objects—for example, chains, hooks, hammers, spikes, knife blades, and handcuffs. Although Edwards often intertwined or welded together the individual metal

25-43 MELVIN EDWARDS, *Tambo,* 1993. Welded steel, 2′ 4$\frac{1}{8}$″ × 2′ 1$\frac{1}{4}$″. Smithsonian American Art Museum, Washington, D.C.

Edwards's welded sculptures of chains, spikes, knife blades, and other found objects allude to the lynching of African Americans and the continuing struggle for civil rights and an end to racism.

1 ft.

Public Funding of Controversial Art

Although art can be beautiful and uplifting, throughout history art has also challenged and offended. Since the early 1980s, a number of heated controversies about art have surfaced in the United States. There have been many calls to remove the "offensive" works from public view (see "Richard Serra's *Tilted Arc*," page 792) and, in reaction, accusations of censorship. The central questions in all cases have been whether there are limits to what art can appropriately be exhibited, and whether governmental authorities have the right to monitor and pass judgment on creative endeavors. A related question is whether the acceptability of a work should be a criterion in determining the public funding of art.

Two exhibits in 1989 placed the National Endowment for the Arts (NEA), a government agency charged with distributing federal funds to support the arts, squarely in the middle of this debate. One of the exhibitions, devoted to recipients of the Awards for the Visual Arts (AVA), took place at the Southeastern Center for Contemporary Art in North Carolina. Among the award winners was Andres Serrano, whose *Piss Christ*, a photograph of a crucifix submerged in urine, sparked an uproar. Responding to this artwork, Reverend Donald Wildmon, an evangelical minister from Mississippi and head of the American Family Association, expressed outrage that such work was in an exhibition funded by the NEA and the Equitable Life Assurance Society (a sponsor of the AVA). He demanded that the work be removed and launched a letter-writing campaign that led Equitable Life to cancel its sponsorship of the awards. To Wildmon and other staunch conservatives, this exhibition, along with the *Robert Mapplethorpe: The Perfect Moment* show, served as evidence of cultural depravity and immorality, which they insisted should not be funded by government agencies such as the NEA. Mapplethorpe was a photographer well known for his elegant, spare photographs of flowers and vegetables as well as his erotic, homosexually oriented images. As a result of media furor over *The Perfect Moment*, the director of the Corcoran Museum of Art canceled the scheduled exhibition of this traveling show. But the director of the Contemporary Arts Center in Cincinnati decided to mount the show. The government indicted him on charges of obscenity, but a jury acquitted him six months later.

These controversies intensified public criticism of the NEA and its funding practices. The next year, the head of the NEA, John Frohnmayer, vetoed grants for four lesbian, gay, or feminist performance artists—Karen Finley, John Fleck, Holly Hughes, and Tim Miller—who became known as the "NEA Four." Infuriated by what they perceived as overt censorship, the artists filed suit, eventually settling the case and winning reinstatement of their grants. Congress responded by dramatically reducing the NEA's budget, and the agency no longer awards grants or fellowships to individual artists.

Controversies have also erupted on the municipal level. In 1999, Rudolph Giuliani, then mayor of New York, joined a number of individuals and groups protesting the inclusion of several artworks in the exhibition *Sensation: Young British Artists from the Saatchi Collec-*

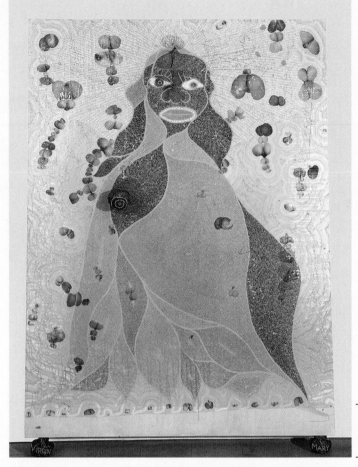

25-44 CHRIS OFILI, *The Holy Virgin Mary*, 1996. Paper collage, oil paint, glitter, polyester resin, map pins, elephant dung on linen, 7′ 11″ × 5′ 11$\frac{5}{16}$″. Saatchi Collection, London.

Ofili, a British-born Catholic of Nigerian descent, represented the Virgin Mary with African elephant dung on one breast and surrounded by genitalia and buttocks. The painting produced a public outcry.

tion at the Brooklyn Museum. Chris Ofili's *The Holy Virgin Mary* (FIG. **25-44**), a collage of Mary incorporating cutouts from pornographic magazines and shellacked clumps of elephant dung, became the flashpoint for public furor. Denouncing the show as "sick stuff," the mayor threatened to cut off all city subsidies to the museum.

Art that seeks to unsettle and challenge is critical to the cultural, political, and psychological life of a society. The regularity with which such art raises controversy suggests that it operates at the intersection of two competing principles: free speech and artistic expression on the one hand and a reluctance to impose images upon an audience that finds them repugnant or offensive on the other. What these controversies do demonstrate, beyond doubt, is the enduring power of art.

---

components so as to diminish immediate identifiability, the sculptures still retain a haunting connection to the overall theme. These works refer to a historical act that evokes a collective memory of oppression, but they also speak to the continuing struggle for civil rights and an end to racism. While growing up in Los Angeles,

Edwards experienced racial conflict firsthand. Among the metal objects incorporated into his *Lynch Fragments* sculptures are items he found in the streets in the aftermath of the Watts riots in 1965. The inclusion of these found objects imbued his disquieting, haunting works with an even greater intensity.

25-45 David Hammons, *Public Enemy,* installation at Museum of Modern Art, New York, 1991. Photographs, balloons, sandbags, guns, and other mixed media.

Hammons intended this multimedia installation, with Theodore Roosevelt flanked by an African American and a Native American as servants, to reveal the racism embedded in America's cultural heritage.

CHRIS OFILI Another contemporary artist who has explored his ethnic and racial heritage in his art is CHRIS OFILI (b. 1968). One theme Ofili has treated is religion, interpreted through the eyes of a British-born Catholic of Nigerian descent. Ofili's *The Holy Virgin Mary* (FIG. 25-44) depicts Mary in a manner that departs radically from conventional Renaissance representations. Ofili's work presents the Virgin in simplified form, and she appears to float in an indeterminate space. The artist employed brightly colored pigments, applied to the canvas in multiple layers of beadlike dots (inspired by images from ancient caves in Zimbabwe). Surrounding the Virgin are tiny images of genitalia and buttocks cut from pornographic magazines, which, to the artist, parallel the putti that often surround Mary in Renaissance paintings. Another reference to Ofili's African heritage surfaces in the clumps of elephant dung—one attached to the Virgin's breast, and two more on which the canvas rests, serving as supports. The dung allowed Ofili to incorporate Africa into his work in a literal way. Still, he wants the viewer to move beyond the cultural associations of the materials and see those materials in new ways.

Not surprisingly, *The Holy Virgin Mary* has elicited strong reactions. Its inclusion in *Sensation* at the Brooklyn Museum in 1999 prompted indignant demands for cancellation of the show and countercharges of censorship (see "Public Funding of Controversial Art," page 772).

DAVID HAMMONS Nurturing viewer introspection is the driving force behind the art of DAVID HAMMONS (b. 1943). In his *installations* (artworks creating an artistic environment in a room or gallery), he combines sharp social commentary with beguiling sensory elements to push viewers to confront racism in American society. He created *Public Enemy* (FIG. 25-45) for an exhibition at the Museum of Modern Art in New York in 1991. Hammons enticed viewers to interact with the installation by scattering fragrant autumn leaves on the floor and positioning helium-filled balloons throughout the gallery. The leaves crunched underfoot, and the dangling strings of the balloons gently brushed spectators walking around the installation. Once drawn into the environment, viewers encountered the central element in *Public Enemy*—large black-and-white photographs of a public monument depicting President Theodore Roosevelt (1858–1919) triumphantly seated on a horse, flanked by an African American man and a Native American man, both appearing in the role of servants. Around the edge of the installation, circling the photographs of the monument, were piles of sandbags with both real and toy guns propped on top, aimed at the statue. By selecting evocative found objects and presenting them in a dynamic manner that encouraged viewer interaction, Hammons attracted an audience and then revealed the racism embedded in received cultural heritage. In this way, he prompted reexamination of American values and cultural emblems.

JAUNE QUICK-TO-SEE SMITH Another contemporary artist who has explored the politics of identity is JAUNE QUICK-TO-SEE SMITH (b. 1940), a Native American artist descended from the Shoshone, the Salish, and the Cree tribes and raised on the Flatrock Reservation in Montana. Quick-to-See Smith's native heritage has always informed her art, and her concern about the invisibility of Native American artists has led her to organize exhibitions of their art. Yet she has acknowledged a wide range of influences, including "pictogram forms from Europe, the Amur [the river between Russia and China], the Americas; color from beadwork, parfleches [hide cases], the landscape; paint application from Cobra art, New York expressionism, primitive art; composition from Kandinsky, Klee or Byzantine art."[29] She has even compared her use of tribal images to that of the Abstract Expressionists.

Despite the myriad references and visual material in Quick-to-See Smith's art, her work displays coherence and power, and, like many other artists who have explored issues associated with identity, she

25-46 JAUNE QUICK-TO-SEE SMITH, *Trade* (*Gifts for Trading Land with White People*), 1992. Oil and mixed media on canvas, 5′ × 14′ 2″. Chrysler Museum of Art, Norfolk.

Quick-to-See Smith's mixed-media canvases are full of references to her Native American identity. Some of the elements refer to the controversy surrounding sports teams that have American Indian names.

1 ft.

challenges stereotypes and unacknowledged assumptions. *Trade* (*Gifts for Trading Land with White People*; FIG. 25-46) is a large-scale painting with collage elements and attached objects, reminiscent of a Rauschenberg combine (FIG. 25-22). The painting's central image, a canoe, appears in an expansive field painted in loose Abstract Expressionist fashion and covered with clippings from Native American newspapers. Above the painting, as if hung from a clothesline, is an array of objects. These include Native American artifacts, such as beaded belts and feather headdresses, and contemporary sports memorabilia from teams with American Indian–derived names—the Cleveland Indians, Atlanta Braves, and Washington Redskins. The inclusion of these contemporary objects immediately recalls the vocal opposition to these names and to acts such as the Braves' "tomahawk chop." Like Edwards, Quick-to-See Smith uses the past to comment on the present.

LEON GOLUB In his paintings, American artist LEON GOLUB (1922–2004) expressed a brutal vision of contemporary life through a sophisticated reading of the news media's raw data. His best-known work deals with violent events of recent decades—the narratives people have learned to extract from news photos of anonymous characters participating in atrocious street violence, terrorism, and torture. Paintings in Golub's *Assassins* and *Mercenaries* series suggest not specific stories but a condition of being. As the artist said,

> Through media we are under constant, invasive bombardment of images—from all over—and we often have to take evasive action to avoid discomforting recognitions. . . . The work [of art] should have an edge, veering between what is visually and cognitively acceptable and what might stretch these limits as we encounter or try to visualize the real products of the uses of power.[30]

Mercenaries IV (FIG. 25-47), a huge canvas, represents a mysterious tableau of five tough freelance military professionals willing to fight, for a price, for any political cause. The three clustering at the right side of the canvas react with tense physical gestures to something one of the two other mercenaries standing at the far left is saying. The dark uniforms and skin tones of the four black fighters flatten their figures and make them stand out against the searing dark red background. The slightly modulated background seems to push their forms forward up against the picture plane and becomes an echoing void in the space between the two groups. Golub painted the mercenaries so that the viewer's eye is level with the menacing figures' knees. He placed the men so close to the front plane of the

25-47 LEON GOLUB, *Mercenaries IV*, 1980. Acrylic on linen, 10′ × 19′ 2″. Courtesy Ronald Feldman Fine Arts. Art © Leon Golub/Licensed by VAGA, New York.

The violence of contemporary life is the subject of Golub's huge paintings. Here, five mercenaries loom over the viewer, instilling a feeling of peril. The rough textures reinforce the raw imagery.

1 ft.

When I put my hands on your body, on your flesh, I feel the history of that body. Not just the beginning of its forming in that distant lake but all the way beyond its ending. I feel the warmth and texture and simultaneously I see the flesh unwrap from the layers of fat and disappear. I see the fat disappear from the muscle. I see the muscle disappearing from around the organs and detaching itself from the bones. I see the organs gradually fade into transparency leaving a gleaming skeleton gleaming like ivory that slowly revolves until it becomes dust. I am consumed in the sense of your weight the way your flesh occupies momentary space the fullness of it beneath my palms. I am amazed at how perfectly your body fits to the curves of my hands. If I could attach our blood vessels so we could become each other I would. If I could attach our blood vessels in order to anchor you to the earth to this present time I would. If I could open up your body and slip up inside your skin and look out your eyes and forever have my lips fused with yours I would. It makes me weep to feel the history of you of your flesh beneath my hands in a time of so much loss. It makes me weep to feel the movement of your flesh beneath my palms as you twist and turn over to one side to create a series of gestures to reach up around my neck to draw me nearer. All these memories will be lost in time like a … [partly illegible]

25-48 David Wojnarowicz, *"When I put my hands on your body,"* 1990. Gelatin-silver print and silk-screened text on museum board, 2′ 2″ × 3′ 2″. Private collection.

In this disturbing yet eloquent print, Wojnarowicz overlaid typed commentary on a photograph of skeletal remains. He movingly communicated his feelings about watching a loved one die of AIDS.

1 ft.

work that the lower edge of the painting cuts off their feet, thereby trapping the viewer in the painting's compressed space. Golub emphasized both the scarred light tones of the white mercenary's skin and the weapons. Modeled with shadow and gleaming highlights, the guns contrast with the harshly scraped, flattened surfaces of the figures. The rawness of the canvas reinforces the rawness of the imagery. Golub often dissolved certain areas with solvent after applying pigment and scraped off applied paint with, among other tools, a meat cleaver. The feeling of peril confronts viewers mercilessly. They become one with all the victims caught in today's political battles.

DAVID WOJNAROWICZ   As a gay activist and as someone who had lost many friends to AIDS (acquired immune deficiency syndrome), David Wojnarowicz (1955–1992) created disturbing yet eloquent works about the tragedy of this disease. (Wojnarowicz himself died of AIDS.) In *"When I put my hands on your body"* (FIG. 25-48), he overlaid a photograph of a pile of skeletal remains with evenly spaced typed commentary that communicated his feelings about watching a loved one dying of AIDS. Wojnarowicz movingly described the effects of AIDS on the human body and soul. He juxtaposed text with imagery, which, like the works of Barbara Kruger (FIG. 25-36) and Lorna Simpson (FIG. 25-42), paralleled the use of both words and images in advertising. The public's familiarity with this format ensured greater receptivity to the artist's message.

KRZYSZTOF WODICZKO   When working in Canada in 1980, Polish-born artist Krzysztof Wodiczko (b. 1943) developed artworks involving outdoor slide images. He projected photographs on specific buildings to expose how civic buildings embody, legitimize, and perpetuate power. When Wodiczko moved to New York City in 1983, the pervasive homelessness troubled him, and he resolved to use his art to publicize this problem. In 1987 he produced *The Homeless Projection* (FIG. 25-49) as part of a New Year's celebration in Boston. The artist projected images of homeless people on all four sides of the Soldiers and Sailors Civil War Memorial on the Boston Common. In these photos, plastic bags filled with their few possessions flanked the people depicted. At the top of the monument, Wodiczko projected a local condominium construction site, which helped viewers make a connection between urban development and homelessness.

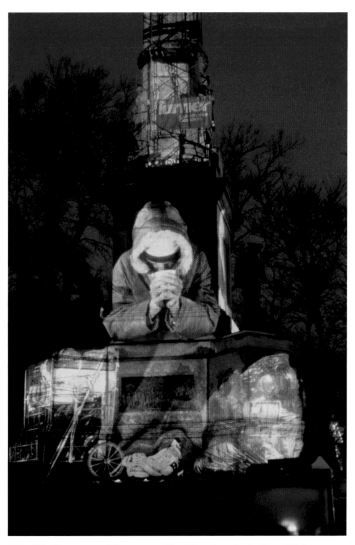

25-49 Krzysztof Wodiczko, *The Homeless Projection,* 1986. Outdoor slide projection at the Soldiers and Sailors Civil War Memorial, Boston.

To publicize their plight, Wodiczko projected on the walls of a monument on the Boston Common images of homeless people and their plastic bags filled with their few possessions.

25-50 MAGDALENA ABAKANOWICZ, *80 Backs,* 1976–1980. Burlap and resin, each 2′ 3″ high. Museum of Modern Art, Dallas.

Polish fiber artist Abakanowicz explored the stoic, everyday toughness of the human spirit in this group of nearly identical sculptures that serve as symbols of distinctive individuals lost in the crowd.

MAGDALENA ABAKANOWICZ The stoic, everyday toughness of the human spirit has been the subject of Polish fiber artist MAGDALENA ABAKANOWICZ (b. 1930). A leader in the recent exploration in sculpture of the expressive powers of weaving techniques, Abakanowicz gained fame with experimental freestanding pieces in both abstract and figural modes. For Abakanowicz, fiber materials are deeply symbolic:

> I see fiber as the basic element constructing the organic world on our planet, as the greatest mystery of our environment. It is from fiber that all living organisms are built—the tissues of plants and ourselves. . . . Fabric is our covering and our attire. Made with our hands, it is a record of our souls.[31]

To all of her work, Abakanowicz brought the experiences of her early life as a member of an aristocratic family disturbed by the dislocations of World War II and its aftermath. Initially attracted to weaving as a medium that would adapt well to the small studio space she had available, Abakanowicz gradually developed huge abstract hangings she called Abakans that suggest organic spaces as well as giant pieces of clothing. She returned to a smaller scale with works based on human forms—*Heads, Seated Figures,* and *Backs*—multiplying each type for exhibition in groups as symbols for the individual in society lost in the crowd yet retaining some distinctiveness. This impression is especially powerful in an installation of *80 Backs* (FIG. **25-50**). Abakanowicz made each piece by pressing layers of natural organic fibers into a plaster mold. Every sculpture depicts the slumping shoulders, back, and arms of a figure of indeterminate sex and rests legless directly on the floor. The repeated pose of the figures in *80 Backs* suggests meditation, submission, and anticipation. Although made from a single mold, the figures achieve a touch-

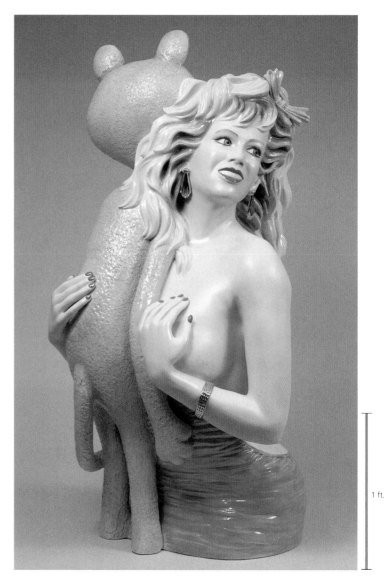

25-51 JEFF KOONS, *Pink Panther,* 1988. Porcelain, 3′ 5″ × 1′ 8½″ × 1′ 7″. Museum of Contemporary Art, Chicago (Gerald S. Elliot Collection).

In the 1980s Koons created sculptures that highlight everything wrong with contemporary American consumer culture. In this work, he intertwined a centerfold nude and a cartoon character.

ing sense of individuality because each assumed a slightly different posture as the material dried and because the artist imprinted a different pattern of fiber texture on each.

JEFF KOONS While many contemporary artists have pursued personally meaningful agendas in their art, others have addressed society-wide concerns, for example, postmodern commodity culture. American JEFF KOONS (b. 1955), who was a commodities broker before turning to art, first became prominent in the art world for a series of works in the early 1980s that involved exhibiting common purchased objects such as vacuum cleaners. Clearly following in the footsteps of artists such as Marcel Duchamp (FIG. **24-27**) and Andy Warhol (FIG. **25-24**), Koons made no attempt to manipulate or alter the objects. More recently, he has produced porcelain sculptures, such as *Pink Panther* (FIG. **25-51**), in which he continued his immersion in contemporary mass culture by intertwining a magazine centerfold nude with a famous cartoon character. Koons reinforced the trite and kitschy nature of this imagery by titling the exhibition of which this work was a part *The Banality Show.* Some art critics have argued that Koons and his work instruct viewers because both

25-52 Robert Arneson, *California Artist*, 1982. Glazed stoneware, 5′ 8¼″ × 2′ 3½″ × 1′ 8¼″. San Francisco Museum of Modern Art, San Francisco (gift of the Modern Art Council). Art © Estate of Robert Arneson/Licensed by VAGA, New York.

Underscoring the importance of art critics in the contemporary art world, Arneson produced this self-portrait incorporating all the stereotypes a *New York Times* critic attributed to California artists.

artist and work serve as the most visible symbols of everything that is wrong with contemporary American society. Whether or not this is true, Koons's prominence in the art world indicates that he, like Warhol before him, has developed an acute understanding of the dynamics of consumer culture.

ROBERT ARNESON During his career, ROBERT ARNESON (1930–1992) developed a body of work of predominantly figural ceramic sculpture, often satirical or amusing and sometimes biting. In 1981 the influential *New York Times* art critic Hilton Kramer (b. 1928) published a review of an exhibition that included a scathing assessment of the artist's work. Arneson, who spent his life in a small town north of San Francisco, created *California Artist* (FIG. 25-52) as a direct response to Kramer, particularly to the critic's derogatory comments on the provincialism of California art. This ceramic sculpture, a half-length self-portrait, incorporates all of the stereotypes Kramer perpetuated. The artist placed the top half of his likeness on a pedestal littered with beer bottles, cigarette butts, and marijuana plants. Arneson appears clad only in a denim jacket and sunglasses, looking very defiant with his arms crossed. Of course, by creating an artwork that responded directly to Kramer's comments, Arneson validated the importance of art critics in the contemporary art world.

MARK TANSEY This kind of interaction between artists and critics also underscores the self-consciousness on the part of contemporary artists about their place in the continuum of art history. For many postmodern artists, referencing the past is much more than incorporating elements from earlier works and styles in their own art. It involves a critique of or commentary on fundamental art historical premises. In short, their art is about making art.

In his humorous *A Short History of Modernist Painting* (FIG. 25-53), American artist MARK TANSEY (b. 1949) provides viewers with a tongue-in-cheek summary of the various approaches to painting artists have embraced over the years. Tansey presents a sequence of three images, each visualizing a way of looking at art. At the far left, a glass window encapsulates the Renaissance ideal of viewing art as though one were looking through a window. In the

25-53 MARK TANSEY, *A Short History of Modernist Painting*, 1982. Oil on canvas, three panels, each 4′ 10″ × 3′ 4″. Courtesy Gagosian Gallery, New York.

Tansey's tripartite history of painting includes the Renaissance window onto the world, the modernist insistence on a painting as a flat surface, and postmodern artists' reflections on their place in art history.

25-54 Hans Haacke, *MetroMobiltan*, 1985. Fiberglass construction, three banners, and photomural, 11′ 8″ × 20′ × 5′. Musée National d'Art Moderne, Centre Georges Pompidou, Paris.

MetroMobiltan focuses attention on the connections between political and economic conditions in South Africa and the conflicted politics of corporate patronage of art exhibitions.

1 ft.

center image, a man pushing his head against a solid wall represents the thesis central to much of modernist formalism—that the painting should be acknowledged as an object in its own right. In the image on the right, Tansey summarizes the postmodern approach to art with a chicken pondering its reflection in the mirror. The chicken's action reveals postmodern artists' reflections on their place in the art historical continuum.

HANS HAACKE   Along with a conscious reappraisal of the processes of art historical validation, postmodern artists have turned to assessing art institutions, such as museums and galleries, and their role in validating art. Many artists have also scrutinized the discriminatory policies and politics of these cultural institutions. German artist HANS HAACKE (b. 1936) has focused his attention on the politics of art museums and how acquisition and exhibition policies affect the public's understanding of art history. The specificity of his works, based on substantial research, makes them stinging indictments of the institutions whose practices he critiques. In *MetroMobiltan* (FIG. 25-54), Haacke illustrated the connection between the realm of art (more specifically, the Metropolitan Museum of Art in New York) and the "real" world of political and economic interests. *MetroMobiltan* is a large sculptural work that includes a photomural of a funeral for South African black people. This photomural serves as the backdrop for a banner for the 1980 Mobil Oil–sponsored Metropolitan Museum show *Treasures of Ancient Nigeria*. In 1980, Mobil was a principal U.S. investor in South Africa, and Haacke's work suggests that one of the driving forces behind Mobil's sponsorship of this exhibition was the fact that Nigeria was one of the richest oil-producing countries in Africa. In 1981 the public pressured Mobil's board of directors to stop providing oil to the white South African military and police. Printed on the blue banners hanging on either side of *Metro-Mobiltan* is the official corporate response refusing to comply with this demand. Haacke set the entire tableau in a fiberglass replica of the Metropolitan Museum's entablature. By bringing together these disparate visual and textual elements that make reference to the mu-

seum, Mobil Oil, and Africa, the artist forced viewers to think about the connections among multinational corporations, political and economic conditions in South Africa, and the conflicted politics of corporate patronage of art exhibitions, thereby undermining the public's view that cultural institutions are exempt from political and economic concerns.

ARCHITECTURE AND SITE-SPECIFIC ART

Some of the leading architects of the first half of the 20th century, most notably Frank Lloyd Wright (FIGS. 24-77 to 24-79), Le Corbusier (FIG. 24-75), and Ludwig Mies van der Rohe (FIG. 24-74), concluded their long and productive careers in the postwar period. At the same time, younger architects rose to international prominence, some working in the modernist idiom but others taking architectural design in new directions, including postmodernism and Deconstructivism. Still, one common denominator exists in the diversity of contemporary architectural design: the breaking down of national boundaries, with major architects pursuing projects on several continents (MAP 25-1), often simultaneously.

Modernism

In parallel with the progressive movement toward formal abstraction in painting and sculpture in the decades following World War II, modernist architects became increasingly concerned with a formalism that stressed simplicity. They articulated this in buildings that retained intriguing organic sculptural qualities, as well as in buildings that adhered to a more rigid geometry.

FRANK LLOYD WRIGHT   The last great building Frank Lloyd Wright designed was the Solomon R. Guggenheim Museum (FIG. 25-55), built in New York City between 1943 and 1959. Using rein-

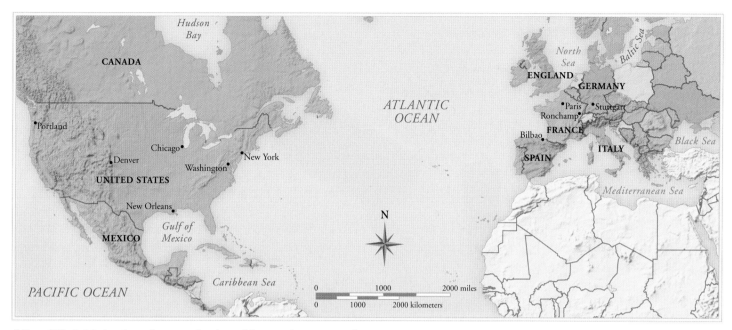

MAP 25-1 Modernist and postmodernist architecture in Europe and America.

forced concrete almost as a sculptor might use resilient clay, Wright, who often described his architecture as "organic," designed a structure inspired by the spiral of a snail's shell. Wright had introduced curves and circles into some of his plans in the 1930s, and, as the architectural historian Peter Blake noted, "The spiral was the next logical step; it is the circle brought into the third and fourth dimensions."[32] Inside the building (FIGS. 25-1 and 25-85), the shape of the shell expands toward the top, and a winding interior ramp spirals to

connect the gallery bays. A skylight strip embedded in the museum's outer wall provides illumination to the ramp, which visitors can stroll up (or down, if they first take an elevator to the top of the building), viewing the artworks displayed along the gently sloping pathway. Thick walls and the solid organic shape give the building, outside and inside, the sense of turning in on itself, and the long interior viewing area opening onto a 90-foot central well of space creates a sheltered environment, secure from the bustling city outside.

25-55 FRANK LLOYD WRIGHT, Solomon R. Guggenheim Museum, (looking northeast) New York, 1943–1959.

Using reinforced concrete almost as a sculptor might use resilient clay, Wright designed a snail shell–shaped museum with a winding interior ramp for the display of artworks along its gently inclined path (FIGS. 25-1 and 25-85).

25-56 Le Corbusier, Notre-Dame-du-Haut, Ronchamp, France, 1950–1955.

The organic forms of Le Corbusier's mountaintop chapel present a fusion of architecture and sculpture. The architect based the shapes on praying hands, a dove's wings, and a ship's prow.

LE CORBUSIER Compared with his pristine geometric design for Villa Savoye (FIG. 24-75), the organic forms of Le Corbusier's Notre-Dame-du-Haut (FIG. 25-56) come as a startling surprise. Completed in 1955 at Ronchamp, France, the chapel attests to the boundless creativity of this great architect. A fusion of architecture and sculpture, the small chapel, which replaced a building destroyed in World War II, occupies a pilgrimage site in the Vosges Mountains. The monumental impression of Notre-Dame-du-Haut seen from afar is somewhat deceptive. Although one massive exterior wall contains a pulpit facing a spacious outdoor area for large-scale open-air services on holy days, the interior (FIG. 25-57) holds at most 200 people. The intimate scale, stark and heavy walls, and mysterious illumination (jewel tones cast from the deeply recessed stained-glass windows) give this space an aura reminiscent of a sacred cave or a medieval monastery.

Notre-Dame-du-Haut's structure may look free-form to the untrained eye, but Le Corbusier based it, like the medieval cathedral, on an underlying mathematical system. The builders formed the fabric from a frame of steel and metal mesh, which they sprayed with concrete and painted white, except for two interior private chapel niches with colored walls and the roof, which Le Corbusier wished to have darken naturally with the passage of time. The roof appears to float freely above the sanctuary, intensifying the quality of mystery in the interior space. In reality, a series of nearly invisible blocks holds up the roof. The mystery of the roof's means of support recalls the reaction to Hagia Sophia's miraculously floating dome (FIG. 9-4) a millennium and a half before. Le Corbusier's preliminary sketches for the building indicate he linked the design with the shape of praying hands, with the wings of a dove (representing both peace and the Holy Spirit), and with the prow of a ship (a reminder that the Latin word used for the main gathering place in Christian churches is *nave,* meaning "ship"). The artist envisioned that in these powerful sculptural solids and voids, human beings could find new values—new interpretations of their sacred beliefs and of their natural environments.

EERO SAARINEN Dramatic, sweeping, curvilinear rooflines are characteristic features of the buildings designed by Finnish-born architect EERO SAARINEN (1910–1961). One of his signature buildings of the late 1950s is the former Trans World Airlines terminal (FIG. 25-58) at John F. Kennedy International Airport in New York, which Saarinen based on the theme of motion. The terminal consists of two immense concrete shells split down the middle and slightly rotated, giving the building a fluid curved outline that fits its corner site. The shells immediately suggest expansive wings and flight. Saarinen also designed everything on the interior, including the furniture, ventilation ducts, and signboards, with this same curvilinear vocabulary in mind.

25-57 Le Corbusier, interior of Notre-Dame-du-Haut, Ronchamp, France, 1950–1955.

Constructed of concrete sprayed on a frame of steel and metal mesh, the heavy walls of the Ronchamp chapel enclose an intimate and mysteriously lit interior that has the aura of a sacred cave.

25-58 EERO SAARINEN, Trans World Airlines terminal (terminal 5), John F. Kennedy International Airport, New York, 1956–1962.

Saarinen based the design for this airline terminal on the theme of motion. The concrete-and-glass building's dramatic, sweeping, curvilinear rooflines appropriately suggest expansive wings and flight.

JOERN UTZON Saarinen was responsible for selecting the Danish architect JOERN UTZON (b. 1918) to build the Sydney Opera House (FIG. 25-59) in Australia. Utzon's design is a bold composition of organic forms on a colossal scale. Utzon worked briefly with Frank Lloyd Wright at Taliesin (Wright's Wisconsin residence), and the style of the Sydney Opera House resonates distantly with the graceful curvature of Wright's Guggenheim Museum. Two clusters of immense concrete shells—the largest is 200 feet tall—rise from massive platforms and soar to delicate peaks. Recalling at first the ogival shapes of Gothic vaults, the shells also suggest both the buoyancy of seabird wings and the billowing sails of the tall ships that brought European settlers to Australia in the 18th and 19th centuries. These architectural metaphors are appropriate to the harbor surrounding Bennelong Point, whose bedrock foundations support the building. Utzon's matching of the structure with its site and atmosphere adds to the organic nature of the design.

Begun in 1959, completion of the opera house had to wait until 1972, primarily because Utzon's daring design required construc-

tion technology that had not yet been developed. Today the opera house is Sydney's defining symbol, a monument of civic pride that functions as the city's cultural center. In addition to the opera auditorium, the complex houses auxiliary halls and rooms for concerts, the performing arts, motion pictures, lectures, art exhibitions, and conventions.

MIES VAN DER ROHE Sculpturesque building design was not the only manifestation of postwar modernist architecture. From the mid-1950s through the 1970s, other architects created massive, sleek, and geometrically rigid buildings. They designed most of these structures following Bauhaus architect Mies van der Rohe's contention that "less is more." Many of these more "Minimalist" designs are powerful, heroic presences in the urban landscape that effectively symbolize the giant corporations that often inhabit them.

The "purest" example of these corporate skyscrapers is the mid-1950s rectilinear glass-and-bronze Seagram Building (FIG. 25-60) in Manhattan, designed by Mies van der Rohe and American architect

25-59 JOERN UTZON, Sydney Opera House, Sydney, Australia, 1959–1972.

The two soaring clusters of concrete shells of Utzon's opera house on an immense platform in Sydney's harbor suggest both the buoyancy of seabird wings and the billowing sails of tall ships.

25-60 Ludwig Mies van der Rohe and Philip Johnson, *Seagram Building*, New York, 1956–1958.

Massive, sleek, and geometrically rigid, this modernist skyscraper has a bronze and glass skin that masks its concrete and steel frame. The giant corporate tower appears to rise from the pavement on stilts.

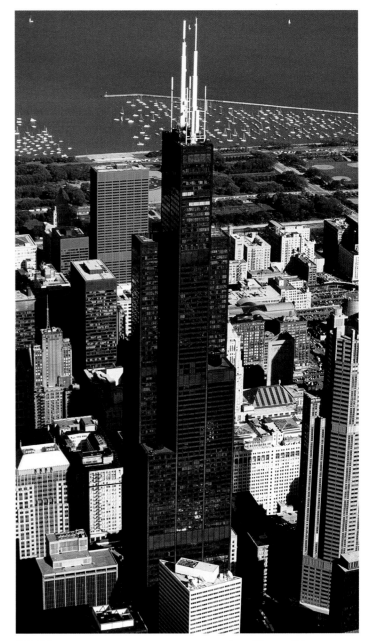

25-61 Skidmore, Owings and Merrill, *Sears Tower*, Chicago, 1974.

Consisting of nine black aluminum and smoked glass shafts soaring to 110 stories, the Sears Tower dominates Chicago's skyline. It was the tallest building in the world at the time of its erection.

Philip Johnson (FIG. 25-64). By this time, the concrete-steel-and-glass towers pioneered by Louis Sullivan (FIGS. 23-40 and 23-41) and carried further by Mies van der Rohe (FIG. 24-74) had become a familiar sight in cities all over the world. Appealing in its structural logic and clarity, the style, easily imitated, quickly became the norm for postwar commercial high-rise buildings. The architects of the Seagram Building (FIG. 25-60) deliberately designed it as a thin shaft, leaving the front quarter of its midtown site as an open pedestrian plaza. The tower appears to rise from the pavement on stilts. Glass walls even surround the recessed lobby. The building's recessed structural elements make it appear to have a glass skin, interrupted only by the thin strips of bronze anchoring the windows. The bronze metal and the amber glass windows give the tower a richness found in few of its neighbors. Mies van der Rohe and Johnson carefully planned every detail of the Seagram Building, inside and out, to create an elegant whole. They even designed the interior and exterior lighting to make the edifice an impressive sight both day and night.

SKIDMORE, OWINGS, AND MERRILL The architectural firm Skidmore, Owings, and Merrill (SOM), perhaps the purest proponent of Miesian-inspired structures, designed a number of these simple rectilinear glass-sheathed buildings, and SOM's success indicates the popularity of this building type. By 1970 the company employed more than a thousand architects and had offices in New York, Chicago, San Francisco, Portland, and Washington, D.C. In 1974 the firm completed the Sears Tower (FIG. 25-61), a mammoth corporate building in Chicago. Consisting of nine clustered shafts

soaring vertically, this 110-floor building houses more than 12,000 workers. Original plans called for 104 stories, but the architects acquiesced to Sears's insistence on making the building the tallest (measured to the structural top) in the world at the time. The tower's size, coupled with the black aluminum that sheathes it and the smoked glass, establish a dominant presence in a city of many corporate skyscrapers—exactly the image Sears executives wanted to project.

MAYA YING LIN Often classified as a work of Minimalist sculpture rather than architecture is the Vietnam Veterans Memorial (FIG. 25-62) in Washington, D.C., designed in 1981 by Maya Ying Lin (b. 1960) when she was only 21. The austere, simple memorial, a V-shaped wall constructed of polished black granite panels, begins at ground level at each end and gradually ascends to a height of 10 feet at the center of the V. Each wing is 246 feet long. Lin set the wall into the landscape, enhancing visitors' awareness of descent as they walk along the wall toward the center. The names of the Vietnam War's

Maya Lin's Vietnam Veterans Memorial

Maya Lin's design for the Vietnam Veterans Memorial (FIG. 25-62) is, like Minimalist sculptures (FIGS. 25-15 and 25-16), an unadorned geometric form. Yet the monument, despite its serene simplicity, actively engages viewers in a psychological dialogue, rather than standing mute. This dialogue gives visitors the opportunity to explore their feelings about the Vietnam War and perhaps arrive at some sense of closure.

The history of the Vietnam Veterans Memorial provides dramatic testimony to this monument's power. In 1981 a jury of architects, sculptors, and landscape architects selected Lin's design in a blind competition for a memorial to be placed in Constitution Gardens in Washington, D.C. Conceivably, the jury not only found her design compelling but also thought its simplicity would be the least likely to provoke controversy. But when the jury made its selection public, heated debate ensued. Even the wall's color came under attack. One veteran charged that black is "the universal color of shame, sorrow and degradation in all races, all societies worldwide."* But the sharpest protests concerned the form and siting of the monument. Because of the stark contrast between the massive white memorials (the Washington Monument and the Lincoln Memorial) bracketing Lin's sunken wall, some people saw her Minimalist design as minimizing the Vietnam War and, by extension, the efforts of those who fought in the conflict. Lin herself, however, described the wall as follows:

> The Vietnam Veterans Memorial is not an object inserted into the earth but a work formed from the act of cutting open the earth and polishing the earth's surface—dematerializing the stone to pure surface, creating an interface between the world of the light and the quieter world beyond the names.[†]

Due to the vocal opposition, a compromise was necessary to ensure the memorial's completion. The Commission of Fine Arts, the federal group overseeing the project, commissioned an additional memorial from artist Frederick Hart (1943–1999) in 1983. This larger-than-life-size realistic bronze sculpture of three soldiers, armed and in uniform, now stands approximately 120 feet from Lin's wall. Several years later, a group of nurses, organized as the Vietnam Women's Memorial Project, gained approval for a sculpture honoring women's service in the Vietnam War. The seven-foot-tall bronze statue by Glenna Goodacre (b. 1939) depicts three female figures, one cradling a wounded soldier in her arms. Unveiled in 1993, the work occupies a site about 300 feet south of the Lin memorial.

Whether celebrated or condemned, the Vietnam Veterans Memorial generates dramatic responses. Commonly, visitors react very emotionally, even those who know none of the soldiers named on the monument. The polished granite surface prompts individual soul-searching—viewers see themselves reflected among the names. Many visitors leave mementos at the foot of the wall in memory of loved ones they lost in the Vietnam War or make rubbings from the incised names. Arguably, much of this memorial's power derives from its Minimalist simplicity. Like Minimalist sculpture, it does not dictate response and therefore successfully encourages personal exploration.

* Elizabeth Hess, "A Tale of Two Memorials," *Art in America* 71, no. 4 (April 1983), 122.
[†] Excerpt from an unpublished 1995 lecture, quoted in Kristine Stiles and Peter Selz, *Theories and Documents of Contemporary Art: A Sourcebook of Artists' Writings* (Berkeley and Los Angeles: University of California Press, 1996), 525.

25-62 MAYA YING LIN, Vietnam Veterans Memorial (looking southwest), Washington, D.C., 1981–1983.

Like Minimalist sculpture, Lin's memorial to the veterans of Vietnam is a simple geometric form. Its inscribed polished walls actively engage the viewer in a psychological dialogue about the war.

57,939 casualties (and those still missing) incised on the memorial's walls, in the order of their deaths, contribute to the monument's dramatic effect.

When Lin designed this pristinely simple monument, she gave a great deal of thought to the purpose of war memorials. She concluded that a memorial

> should be honest about the reality of war and be for the people who gave their lives. . . . [I] didn't want a static object that people would just look at, but something they could relate to as on a journey, or passage, that would bring each to his own conclusions. . . . I wanted to work with the land and not dominate it. I had an impulse to cut open the earth . . . an initial violence that in time would heal. The grass would grow back, but the cut would remain.[33]

In light of the tragedy of the war, this unpretentious memorial's allusion to a wound and long-lasting scar contributes to its communicative ability (see "Maya Lin's Vietnam Veterans Memorial," page 783).

Postmodernism

The restrictiveness of modernist architecture and the impersonality and sterility of many modernist structures eventually led to a rejection of modernism's authority in architecture. Along with the apparent lack of responsiveness to the unique character of the cities and neighborhoods in which modernist architects erected their buildings, these reactions ushered in postmodernism, one of the most dramatic developments in later-20th-century architecture as in contemporary painting and sculpture. Postmodernism in architecture is also not a unified style. It is a widespread cultural phenomenon that is far more encompassing and accepting than the more rigid confines of modernist practice. In contrast to the simplicity of modernist architecture, the terms most often invoked to describe postmodern architecture are pluralism, complexity, and eclecticism. Whereas the modernist program was reductive, the postmodern vocabulary of the 1970s and 1980s was expansive and inclusive.

Among the first to explore this new direction in architecture were Jane Jacobs (1916–2006) and Robert Venturi (FIG. 25-66). In their influential books *The Death and Life of Great American Cities* (Jacobs, 1961) and *Complexity and Contradiction in Architecture* (Venturi, 1966), Jacobs and Venturi argued that the uniformity and anonymity of modernist architecture (in particular, the corporate skyscrapers dominating many urban skylines) were unsuited to human social interaction and that diversity was the great advantage of urban life. Postmodern architects accepted, indeed embraced, the messy and chaotic nature of urban life.

When designing these varied buildings, many postmodern architects consciously selected past architectural elements or references and juxtaposed them with contemporary elements or fashioned them of high-tech materials, thereby creating a dialogue between past and present. Postmodern architecture incorporates not only traditional architectural references but references to mass culture and popular imagery as well. This was precisely the "complexity and contradiction" Venturi referred to in the title of his book.

CHARLES MOORE A clear example of the eclecticism and the dialogue between traditional and contemporary elements found in postmodern architecture is the Piazza d'Italia (FIG. 25-63) by American architect CHARLES MOORE (1925–1993). Designed in the late 1970s in New Orleans, the Piazza d'Italia is an open plaza dedicated to the city's Italian-American community. Appropriately, Moore selected elements relating specifically to Italian history, dating all the way back to ancient Roman culture.

Backed up against a contemporary high-rise and set off from urban traffic patterns, the Piazza d'Italia can be reached on foot from three sides through gateways of varied design. The approaches lead to an open circular area partially formed by short segments of colonnades arranged in staggered concentric arcs, which direct the eye to the focal point of the composition—an *exedra*. This recessed area on a raised platform serves as a *rostrum* (speaker's platform) during the annual festivities of Saint Joseph's Day. Moore inlaid the piazza's pavement with a map of Italy centered on Sicily, from which the majority of the city's Italian families originated. From there, the map's Italian "boot" moves in the direction of the steps that ascend the rostrum and correspond to the Alps.

25-63 CHARLES MOORE, Piazza d'Italia, New Orleans, Louisiana, 1976–1980.

Moore's circular postmodern Italian plaza incorporates elements drawn from ancient Roman architecture with the instability of Mannerist designs and modern stainless-steel columns with neon collars.

Philip Johnson
on Postmodern Architecture

Philip Johnson, who died in 2005 at age 98, had a distinguished career that spanned almost the entire 20th century, during which he transformed himself from a modernist closely associated with Mies van der Rohe (FIG. 25-60) into one of the leading postmodernists, whose AT&T Building (FIG. 25-64) in New York City remains an early icon of postmodernism. The following remarks illustrate Johnson's thoughts about his early "Miesian" style and about the incorporation of various historical styles in postmodernist buildings.

> My eyes are set by the Miesian tradition . . . . The continuity with my Miesian approach also shows through in my classicism. . . . [But in] 1952, about the same time that my whole generation did, I became very restless. . . . In the last decade there has been such a violent switch that it is almost embarrassing. But it isn't a switch, so much as a centrifugal splintering of architecture, to a degree that I don't think has been seen in the past few hundred years. Perfectly responsible architects build, even in one year, buildings that you cannot believe are done by the same person.*

> Structural honesty seems to me one of the bugaboos that we should free ourselves from very quickly. The Greeks with their marble columns imitating wood, and covering up the roofs inside! The Gothic designers with their wooden roofs above to protect their delicate vaulting. And Michelangelo, the greatest architect in history, with his Mannerist column! There is only one absolute today and this is change. There are no rules, surely no certainties in any of the arts. There is only the feeling of a wonderful freedom, of endless possibilities to investigate, of endless past years of historically great buildings to enjoy.†

* Quoted in Paul Heyer, *Architects on Architecture: New Directions in America* (New York: Van Nostrand Reinhold, 1993), 285–286.
† Ibid., 279.

25-64 PHILIP JOHNSON and JOHN BURGEE (with SIMMONS ARCHITECTS), AT&T (now Sony) Building, New York, 1978–1984.

In a startling shift of style, modernist Johnson (FIG. 25-60) designed this postmodernist skyscraper with more granite than glass and with a variation on a classical pediment as the crowning motif.

The piazza's most immediate historical reference is to the Roman forum (FIGS. 7-12 and 7-43). However, its circular form alludes to the ideal geometric figure of the Renaissance (FIG. 17-22). The irregular placement of the concentrically arranged colonnade fragments inserts a note of instability into the design reminiscent of Mannerism (FIG. 17-54). Illusionistic devices, such as the continuation of the piazza's pavement design (apparently through a building and out into the street), are Baroque in character (FIG. 19-4). Moore incorporated all of the classical orders—most with whimsical modifications. Nevertheless, challenging the piazza's historical character are modern features, such as the stainless-steel columns and capitals, neon collars around the column necks, and neon lights that frame various parts of the exedra.

In sum, Moore designed the Piazza d'Italia as a complex conglomeration of symbolic, historical, and geographic allusions—some overt and others obscure. Although the piazza's specific purpose was to honor the Italian community of New Orleans, its more general purpose was to revitalize an urban area by becoming a focal point and an architectural setting for the social activities of neighborhood residents. Unfortunately, the piazza suffered extensive damage during Hurricane Katrina in 2005.

PHILIP JOHNSON Even architects instrumental in the proliferation of the modernist idiom embraced postmodernism. Early in his career, PHILIP JOHNSON (1906–2005), for example, had been a leading proponent of modernism and worked with Mies van der Rohe on the design of the Seagram Building (FIG. 25-60). Johnson had even served as the director of the Department of Architecture at New York's Museum of Modern Art, the bastion of modernism, from 1930 to 1934 and from 1946 to 1954. Yet he made one of the most startling shifts of style in 20th-century architecture, eventually moving away from the severe geometric formalism exemplified by the Seagram Building to a classicizing transformation of it in his AT&T (American Telephone and Telegraph) Building (FIG. 25-64)—now the Sony Building—in New York City. Architect JOHN BURGEE (b. 1933) codesigned it with assistance from the firm SIMMONS ARCHITECTS. This structure was influential in turning architectural taste and practice away from modernism and toward postmodernism—from organic "concrete sculpture" and the rigid "glass box" to elaborate shapes, motifs, and silhouettes freely adapted from historical styles (see "Philip Johnson on Postmodernist Architecture," above).

The 660-foot-high slab of the AT&T Building is mostly granite. Johnson reduced the window space to some 30 percent of the building, in contrast to modernist glass-sheathed skyscrapers. His design of its exterior elevation is classically tripartite, having an arcaded base and arched portal; a tall, shaftlike body segmented by slender *mullions* (vertical elements dividing a window); and a crowning pediment broken by an *orbiculum* (a disklike opening). The arrangement refers to the base, column, and entablature system of classical architecture (FIG. 5-14). More specifically, the pediment, indented by the circular space, resembles the crown of a typical 18th-century Chippendale high chest of drawers. It rises among the monotonously flat-topped glass towers of the New York skyline as an ironic rebuke to the rigid uniformity of modernist architecture.

MICHAEL GRAVES Philip Johnson at first endorsed, then disapproved of, a building that rode considerably farther on the wave of postmodernism than did his AT&T tower. The Portland Building (FIG. 25-65) by American architect MICHAEL GRAVES (b. 1934) reasserts the wall's horizontality against the verticality of the tall, fenestrated shaft. Graves favored the square's solidity and stability, making it the main body of his composition (echoed in the windows), which rests upon a wider base and carries a set-back penthouse crown. Narrow vertical windows tying together seven stories open two paired facades. These support capital-like large hoods on one pair of opposite facades and a frieze of stylized Baroque roundels tied by bands on the other pair. A huge painted keystone motif joins five upper levels on one facade pair, and painted surfaces further define the building's base, body, and penthouse levels.

The modernist purist surely would not welcome the ornamental wall, color painting, or symbolic reference. These features, taken together, raised an even greater storm of criticism than that which greeted the Sydney Opera House or the AT&T Building. Various critics denounced Graves's Portland Building as "an enlarged jukebox," an "oversized Christmas package," a "marzipan monstrosity," a "histrionic masquerade," and a kind of "pop surrealism." Yet others approvingly noted its classical references as constituting a "symbolic temple" and praised the building as a courageous architectural adventure. Whatever will be history's verdict, the Portland Building, like the AT&T tower, is an early marker of postmodernist innovation that borrowed from the lively, if more-or-less garish, language of pop culture. The night-lit dazzle of entertainment sites such as Las Vegas, and the carnival colors, costumes, and fantasy of theme park props, all lie behind the Portland Building design, which many critics regard as a vindication of architectural populism against the pretension of modernist elitism.

25-65 MICHAEL GRAVES, Portland Building, Portland, 1980.

In this early example of postmodern architecture, Graves reasserted the horizontality and solidity of the wall. He drew attention to the mural surfaces through polychromy and ornamental motifs.

ROBERT VENTURI As a coauthor of *Learning from Las Vegas* (1972), ROBERT VENTURI (b. 1925) codified these ideas about populism and postmodernism, and in his designs for houses he adapted historical as well as contemporary styles to suit his symbolic and expressive purpose. A fundamental axiom of modernism is that a building's form must arise directly and logically from its function and structure. Against this rule, Venturi asserted that the form should be separate from function and structure and that decorative and symbolic forms of everyday life should enwrap the structural core. Thus, for a Delaware residence (FIG. 25-66) designed in 1978 with JOHN RAUCH (b. 1930) and DENISE SCOTT BROWN (b. 1931), Venturi respected the countryside setting and its 18th-century history by recalling the stone-based barnlike, low-profile farm dwellings with their shingled roofs and double-hung multipaned windows. He fronted the house with an amusingly cut-out and asymmetrical parody of a Neoclassical portico.

25-66 ROBERT VENTURI, JOHN RAUCH, and DENISE SCOTT BROWN, house in eastern Delaware, 1978–1983.

Venturi asserted that form should be separate from function and structure. This rural home has the low profile of a farmhouse, but its facade is an asymmetrical parody of a Neoclassical portico.

25-67 RICHARD ROGERS and RENZO PIANO, Georges Pompidou National Center of Art and Culture (the "Beaubourg"), Paris, France, 1977.

The architects fully exposed the anatomy of this six-level building, as in the century-earlier Crystal Palace (FIG. 22-48), and color-coded the internal parts according to function, as in a factory.

with visitors since it opened. The flexible interior spaces and the colorful structural body provide a festive environment for the crowds flowing through the building and enjoying its art galleries, industrial design center, library, science and music centers, conference rooms, research and archival facilities, movie theaters, rest areas, and restaurant (which looks down and through the building to the terraces outside). The sloping plaza in front of the main entrance has become part of the local scene. Peddlers, street performers, Parisians, and tourists fill this square at almost all hours of the day and night. The kind of secular activity that once occurred in the open spaces in front of cathedral entrances now takes place next to a center for culture and popular entertainment.

ROGERS AND PIANO During their short-lived partnership, British architect RICHARD ROGERS (b. 1933) and Italian architect RENZO PIANO (b. 1937) used motifs and techniques from ordinary industrial buildings in their design for the Georges Pompidou National Center of Art and Culture in Paris, known popularly as the "Beaubourg" (FIG. 25-67). The architects fully exposed the anatomy of this six-level building, which is a kind of updated version of the Crystal Palace (FIG. 22-48), and made its "metabolism" visible. They color-coded pipes, ducts, tubes, and corridors according to function (red for the movement of people, green for water, blue for air-conditioning, and yellow for electricity), much as in a sophisticated factory.

Critics who deplore the Beaubourg's vernacular qualities disparagingly refer to the complex as a "cultural supermarket" and point out that its exposed entrails require excessive maintenance to protect them from the elements. Nevertheless, the building has been popular

Deconstructivism

In architecture, as in painting and sculpture, deconstruction as an analytical and design strategy emerged in the 1970s. Architectural *Deconstructivism* seeks to disorient the observer. To this end, Deconstructivist architects attempt to disrupt the conventional categories of architecture and to rupture the viewer's expectations based on them. Destabilization plays a major role in Deconstructivist architecture. Disorder, dissonance, imbalance, asymmetry, unconformity, and irregularity replace their opposites—order, consistency, balance, symmetry, regularity, and clarity, as well as harmony, continuity, and completeness. The haphazardly presented volumes, masses, planes, borders, lighting, locations, directions, spatial relations, as well as the disguised structural facts, challenge the viewer's assumptions about architectural form as it relates to function. According to Deconstructivist principles, the very absence of the stability of traditional categories of architecture in a structure announces a "deconstructed" building.

GÜNTER BEHNISCH Audacious in its dissolution of form, and well along on the path of deconstruction, is the Hysolar Institute (FIG. 25-68) at the University of Stuttgart, Germany. GÜNTER BEHNISCH (b. 1922)

25-68 GÜNTER BEHNISCH, Hysolar Institute, University of Stuttgart, Stuttgart, Germany, 1987.

The roof, walls, and windows of this Deconstructivist structure seem to explode, avoiding any suggestion of clear, stable masses and frustrating the observer's expectations of what a building should look like.

Architecture and Site-Specific Art   **787**

Frank Gehry on Architectural Design and Materials

Frank Gehry has been designing buildings since the 1950s, but it was only in the 1970s that he began to break away from the rectilinearity of modernist architecture and develop the dramatic sculptural style seen in buildings like the Guggenheim Museum (FIGS. 25-69 and 25-70) in Bilbao. In 1999 the Deconstructivist architect reflected on his career and his many projects in a book titled *Gehry Talks*.

> My early work was rectilinear because you take baby steps. I guess the work has become a kind of sculpture as architecture.... I'm a strict modernist in the sense of believing in purity, that you shouldn't decorate. And yet buildings need decoration, because they need scaling elements. They need to be human scale, in my opinion. They can't just be faceless things. That's how some modernism failed.*

25-69 FRANK GEHRY, **Guggenheim Bilbao Museo, Bilbao, Spain, 1997.**

Gehry's limestone-and-titanium Bilbao museum is an immensely dramatic building. Its disorder and seeming randomness of design epitomize Deconstructivist architectural principles.

They teach materials and methods in architecture school, as a separate course. I'm a craftsman.... It seems to me that when you're doing architecture, you're building something out of something. There are social issues, there's context, and then there's how do you make the enclosure and what do you make it with? ... I explored metal: how it dealt with the light .... It does beautiful things with light.... Flat was a fetish, and everybody was doing that. I found out that I could use metal if I didn't worry about it being flat; I could do it cheaper. It was intuitive. I just went with it. I liked it. Then when I saw it on the building, I loved it.... Bilbao ... [is] titanium.... [I] prefer titanium because it's stronger; it's an element, a pure element, and it doesn't oxidize. It stays the same forever. They give a hundred-year guarantee![†]

* Milton Friedman, ed., *Gehry Talks: Architecture + Process,* rev. ed. (New York: Universe, 2002), 47–48.

[†] Ibid., 44, 47.

designed it as part of a joint German–Saudi Arabian research project on the technology of solar energy. The architect intended to deny here the possibility of spatial enclosure altogether, and his apparently chaotic arrangement of the units defies easy analysis. The shapes of the Hysolar Institute's roof, walls, and windows seem to explode, avoiding any suggestion of clear, stable masses. Behnisch aggressively played with the whole concept of architecture and the viewer's relationship to it. The disordered architectural elements seem precarious and visually threaten to collapse, frustrating the observer's expectations of what a building should look like.

FRANK GEHRY The architect most closely identified with Deconstructivist architecture is the Canadian-born FRANK GEHRY (b. 1929). Trained in sculpture, and at different times a collaborator with Donald Judd (FIG. 25-16) and Claes Oldenburg (FIG. 25-26), Gehry works up his designs by constructing models and then cutting them up and arranging them until he has a satisfying composition. Among Gehry's most notable projects is the Guggenheim Museum (FIG. 25-69) in Bilbao, Spain. The immensely dramatic building appears as a mass of asymmetrical and imbalanced forms, and the irregularity of the main masses—whose profiles change dramatically with every shift of a visitor's position—suggests a collapsed or collapsing aggregate of units. The scaled limestone- and titanium-clad exterior lends a space-age character to the building and highlights further the unique cluster effect of the many forms (see "Frank Gehry on Architectural Design and Materials," above). A group of organic forms that Gehry refers to as a "metallic flower" tops the museum. In the center of the museum, an enormous glass-walled

25-70 FRANK GEHRY, atrium of Guggenheim Bilbao Museo, Bilbao, Spain, 1997.

The glass-walled atrium of the Guggenheim Bilbao Museum soars to 165 feet in height. The asymmetrical and imbalanced screens and vaults flow into one another, creating a sense of disequilibrium.

atrium (FIG. 25-70) soars to 165 feet in height, serving as the focal point for the three levels of galleries radiating from it. The seemingly weightless screens, vaults, and volumes of the interior float and flow into one another, guided only by light and dark cues. Overall, the Guggenheim in Bilbao is a profoundly compelling structure. Its disorder, its seeming randomness of design, and the disequilibrium it prompts in viewers epitomize Deconstructivist principles.

DANIEL LIBESKIND Deconstructivist architecture remains very much in vogue today. One of the leading practitioners is Polish-born DANIEL LIBESKIND (b. 1946), whose studio is in Berlin, Germany, but who has, like other successful contemporary architects, erected buildings in several countries, including the United States. Libeskind achieved instant international fame with his design for the reconstructed World Trade Center complex in New York City. More recently, his 146,000-square-foot expansion of the Denver Art Museum (FIG. 25-71) created a sensation when it opened to the public in October 2006. Libeskind has stated that he drew his inspiration for the design from the jagged peaks of Colorado's Rocky Mountains, and the stone-and-titanium structure, despite its kinship with Gehry's Bilbao museum (FIG. 25-69), presents a striking contrast with that building's swelling curves. Tilted walls, asymmetrical shapes, and surprising sequences of spaces engender a sense of disorientation in visitors to the galleries, which, appropriately, house the museum's collection of modern and contemporary art.

25-71 DANIEL LIBESKIND, Denver Art Museum, Denver, Colorado, 2006.

Inspired by the jagged peaks of the Rocky Mountains, Libeskind's expansion of the Denver Art Museum features tilted walls, asymmetrical shapes, and a disorienting sequence of spaces.

Environmental and Site-Specific Art

Like Maya Lin's Vietnam Veterans Memorial (FIG. 25-62), works of *Environmental Art,* sometimes called *earthworks,* exist at the intersection of architecture and sculpture. The Environmental Art movement emerged in the 1960s and included a wide range of artworks, most *site-specific* (created for only one location) and existing outdoors. Many artists associated with these sculptural projects also used natural or organic materials, including the land itself. It is no coincidence that this art form developed during a period of increased concern for the American environment. The ecology movement of the 1960s and 1970s aimed to publicize and combat escalating pollution, depletion of natural resources, and the dangers of toxic waste. The problems of public aesthetics (for example, litter, urban sprawl, and compromised scenic areas) were also at issue. Widespread concern about the environment led to the passage of the U.S. National Environmental Policy Act in 1969 and the creation of the federal Environmental Protection Agency. Environmental artists used their art to call attention to the landscape and, in so doing, were part of this national dialogue.

As an innovative art form that challenged traditional assumptions about art making and artistic models, Environmental Art clearly had an avant-garde, progressive dimension. But like Pop artists, Environmental artists insisted on moving art out of the rarefied atmosphere of museums and galleries and into the public sphere. Most encouraged spectator interaction with their works. Ironically, the remote locations of many earthworks have limited public access.

ROBERT SMITHSON A leading American Environmental artist was ROBERT SMITHSON (1938–1973), who used industrial construction equipment to manipulate vast quantities of earth and rock on isolated sites. One of Smithson's best-known projects is *Spiral Jetty* (FIG. 25-72), a mammoth 1,500-foot-long coil of black basalt, limestone rocks, and earth that extends out into the Great Salt Lake in Utah. As he was driving by the lake one day, Smithson came across some abandoned mining equipment, left there by a company that had tried and failed to extract oil from the site. Smithson saw this as a testament to the enduring power of nature and to humankind's inability to conquer it. He decided to create an artwork in the lake that ultimately became a monumental spiral curving out from the shoreline and running 1,500 linear feet into the water. Smithson insisted on designing his work in response to the location itself. He wanted to avoid the arrogance of an artist merely imposing an unrelated concept on the site. The spiral idea grew from Smithson's first impression of the location. Then, while researching the Great Salt Lake, Smithson discovered that the molecular structure of the salt crystals coating the rocks at the water's edge was spiral in form.

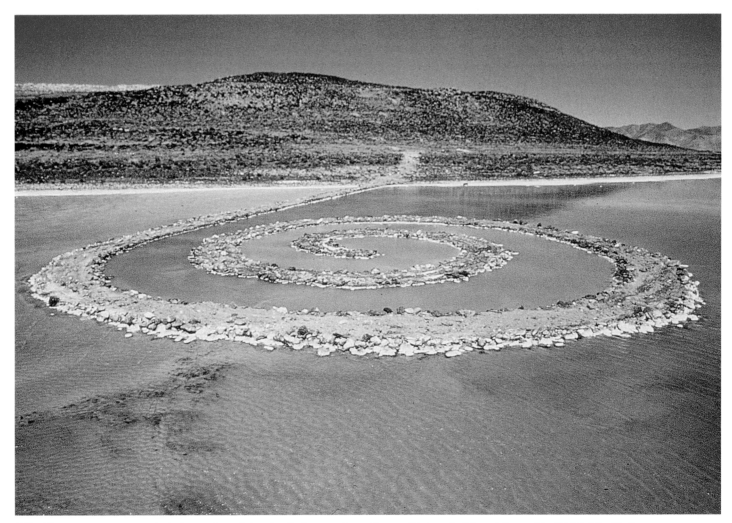

25-72 ROBERT SMITHSON, *Spiral Jetty,* Great Salt Lake, Utah, 1970. Art © Estate of Robert Smithson/Licensed by VAGA, New York.

Smithson used industrial equipment to create Environmental artworks by manipulating earth and rock. *Spiral Jetty* is a mammoth coil of black basalt, limestone, and earth extending into the Great Salt Lake.

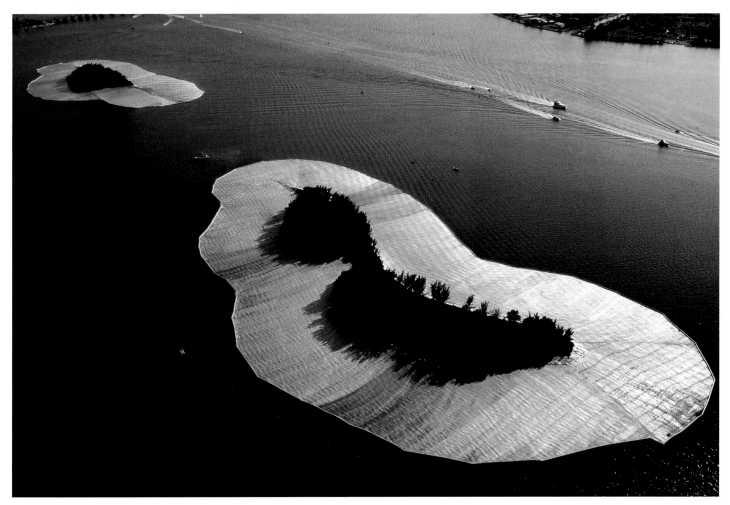

25-73 CHRISTO and JEANNE-CLAUDE, *Surrounded Islands 1980–83, Biscayne Bay, Miami, Florida,* 1980–1983.

Christo and Jeanne-Claude created this Environmental artwork by surrounding 11 small islands with 6.5 million square feet of pink fabric. Characteristically, the work existed for only two weeks.

As I looked at the site, it reverberated out to the horizons only to suggest an immobile cyclone while flickering light made the entire landscape appear to quake. A dormant earthquake spread into the fluttering stillness, into a spinning sensation without movement. The site was a rotary that enclosed itself in an immense roundness. From that gyrating space emerged the possibility of the Spiral Jetty.[34]

Smithson not only recorded *Spiral Jetty* in photographs but also filmed its construction in a movie that describes the forms and life of the whole site. The photographs and film have become increasingly important references, because fluctuations in the Great Salt Lake's water level often place *Spiral Jetty* underwater.

CHRISTO AND JEANNE-CLAUDE Like Smithson, CHRISTO and JEANNE-CLAUDE (both b. 1935) seek to intensify the viewer's awareness of the space and features of rural and urban sites. However, rather than physically alter the land itself, as Smithson often did, Christo and Jeanne-Claude prompt this awareness by temporarily modifying the landscape with cloth. Christo studied art in his native Bulgaria and in Vienna. After a move to Paris, he began to encase objects in clumsy wrappings, thereby appropriating bits of the real world into the mysterious world of the unopened package whose contents can be dimly seen in silhouette under the wrap.

Starting in 1961, Christo and Jeanne-Claude, husband and wife, began to collaborate on large-scale projects that normally deal with the environment itself. For example, in 1969 the couple wrapped a million square feet of Australian coast and in 1972 hung a vast curtain across a valley at Rifle Gap, Colorado. Their works of art require years of preparation and research and scores of meetings with local authorities and interested groups of local citizens. These temporary works are usually on view for only a few weeks.

Surrounded Islands 1980–83 (FIG. **25-73**), created in Biscayne Bay in Miami, Florida, for two weeks in May 1983, typifies Christo and Jeanne-Claude's work. For this project, they surrounded 11 small human-made islands in the bay (from a dredging project) with 6.5 million square feet of specially fabricated pink polypropylene floating fabric. This Environmental artwork required three years of preparation to obtain the necessary permits and to assemble the labor force and obtain the $3.2 million needed to complete the project. The artists raised the money by selling preparatory drawings, collages, models, and works they created in the 1950s and 1960s. Huge crowds watched as crews removed accumulated trash from the 11 islands (to assure maximum contrast between their dark colors, the pink of the cloth, and the blue of the bay) and then unfurled the fabric "cocoons" to form magical floating "skirts" around each tiny bit of land. Despite the brevity of its existence, *Surrounded Islands 1980–83* lives on in the host of photographs, films, and books documenting the project.

Richard Serra's *Tilted Arc*

When Richard Serra installed *Tilted Arc* (FIG. 25-74) in the plaza in front of the Javits Federal Building in New York City in 1981, much of the public immediately responded with hostile criticism. Prompting the chorus of complaints was the uncompromising presence of a Minimalist sculpture bisecting the plaza. Many argued that *Tilted Arc* was ugly, that it attracted graffiti, that it interfered with the view across the plaza, and that it prevented using the plaza for performances or concerts. Due to the sustained barrage of protests and petitions demanding the removal of *Tilted Arc,* the GSA held a series of public hearings. Afterward, the agency decided to remove the sculpture despite its prior approval of Serra's maquette. This, understandably, infuriated Serra, who had a legally binding contract acknowledging the site-specific nature of *Tilted Arc.* "To remove the work is to destroy the work," the artist stated.*

This episode raised intriguing issues about the nature of public art, including the public reception of experimental art, the artist's responsibilities and rights when executing public commissions, censorship in the arts, and the purpose of public art. If an artwork is on display in a public space outside the relatively private confines of a museum or gallery, do different guidelines apply? As one participant in the *Tilted Arc* saga asked, "Should an artist have the right to impose his values and taste on a public that now rejects his taste and values?"† One of the express functions of the historical avant-garde was to challenge convention by rejecting tradition and disrupting the complacency of the viewer. Will placing experimental art in a public place always cause controversy? From Serra's statements, it is clear he intended the sculpture to challenge the public.

Another issue *Tilted Arc* presented involved the rights of the artist, who in this case accused the GSA of censorship. Serra filed a lawsuit against the government for infringement of his First Amendment rights and insisted that "the artist's work must be uncensored, respected, and tolerated, although deemed abhorrent, or perceived as

25-74 RICHARD SERRA, *Tilted Arc,* Jacob K. Javits Federal Plaza, New York City, 1981.

Serra intended his Minimalist *Tilted Arc* to alter the character of an existing public space. He succeeded but unleashed a storm of protest that caused the government to remove the work.

challenging, or experienced as threatening."‡ Did removal of the work constitute censorship? A federal district court held that it did not.

Ultimately, who should decide what artworks are appropriate for the public arena? One artist argued, "we cannot have public art by plebiscite [popular vote]."§ But to avoid recurrences of the *Tilted Arc* controversy, the GSA changed its procedures and now solicits input from a wide range of civic and neighborhood groups before commissioning public artworks. Despite the removal of *Tilted Arc* (now languishing in storage), the sculpture maintains a powerful presence in all discussions of the aesthetics, politics, and dynamics of public art.

* Grace Glueck, "What Part Should the Public Play in Choosing Public Art?" *New York Times,* February 3, 1985, 27.
† Calvin Tomkins, "The Art World: *Tilted Arc,*" *New Yorker,* May 20, 1985, 98.
‡ Ibid., 98–99.
§ Ibid., 98.

RICHARD SERRA Other artists have created site-specific works that are not set in nature but in the built environment. Their purpose is to focus attention on art's role in public spaces. One work that sparked national discussion about public art was *Tilted Arc* (FIG. 25-74) by American artist RICHARD SERRA (b. 1939). The General Services Administration (GSA), the federal agency responsible for, among other tasks, overseeing the selection and installation of artworks for government buildings, commissioned *Tilted Arc.* This enormous 120-foot-long, 12-foot-high curved wall of Cor-Ten steel bisected the plaza in front of the Jacob K. Javits Federal Building in

lower Manhattan. Serra situated the sculpture in a way that significantly altered the space of the open plaza and the traffic flow across the square. He intended *Tilted Arc* to "dislocate or alter the decorative function of the plaza and actively bring people into the sculpture's context."[35]

By creating such a monumental presence in this large public space, Serra succeeded in forcing viewers to reconsider the plaza's physical space as a sculptural form—but only temporarily, because the public forced the sculpture to be removed (see "Richard Serra's *Tilted Arc,*" above).

PERFORMANCE AND CONCEPTUAL ART AND NEW MEDIA

Among the most significant developments in the art world after World War II has been the expansion of the range of works considered "art." Some of the new types of artworks are the result of the invention of new media, such as computers and video cameras. But the new art forms also reflect avant-garde artists' continued questioning of the status quo. For example, in keeping with the modernist critique of artistic principles, some artists, in a spirit reminiscent of Dada and Surrealism (see Chapter 24), developed the fourth dimension—time—as an integral element of their artwork. The term that art historians use to describe these temporal works is *Performance Art.*

Performance Art

Performance artists replace traditional stationary artworks with movements, gestures, and sounds carried out before an audience, whose members may or may not participate in the performance. Generally, documentary photographs taken contemporaneously are the only evidence remaining after these performances. The informal and spontaneous events Performance artists initially staged anticipated the rebellion and youthful exuberance of the 1960s and at first pushed art outside the confines of mainstream art institutions (museums and galleries). Performance Art also served as an antidote to the affectation of most traditional art objects and challenged art's function as a commodity. In the later 1960s, however, museums commissioned performances with increasing frequency, thereby neutralizing much of the subversiveness that characterized this new art form.

JOHN CAGE Many of the artists instrumental in the development of Performance Art were students or associates of the charismatic American teacher and composer John Cage (1912–1992). Cage encouraged his students at both the New School for Social Research in New York and Black Mountain College in North Carolina to link their art directly with life. He brought to music composition some of the ideas of Duchamp and of Eastern philosophy. Cage used methods such as chance to avoid the closed structures marking traditional music and, in his view, separating it from the unpredictable and multilayered qualities of daily existence. For example, the score for one of Cage's piano compositions instructs the performer to appear, sit down at the piano, raise the keyboard cover to mark the beginning of the piece, remain motionless at the instrument for 4 minutes and 33 seconds, and then close the keyboard cover, rise, and bow to signal the end of the work. The "music" would be the unplanned sounds and noises (such as coughs and whispers) emanating from the audience during the "performance."

ALLAN KAPROW One of Cage's students in the 1950s was Allan Kaprow (b. 1927). Schooled in art history as well as music composition, Kaprow sought to explore the intersection of art and life. He believed, for example, that Jackson Pollock's actions when producing a painting (FIG. 25-6) were more important than the finished painting. This led Kaprow to develop a type of event known as a *Happening.* He described a Happening as

> an assemblage of events performed or perceived in more than one time and place. Its material environments may be constructed, taken over directly from what is available, or altered slightly: just as its activities may be invented or commonplace. A Happening, unlike a stage play, may occur at a supermarket, driving along a highway, under a pile of rags, and in a friend's kitchen, either at once or se-

quentially. If sequentially, time may extend to more than a year. The Happening is performed according to plan but without rehearsal, audience, or repetition. It is art but seems closer to life.[36]

Happenings were often participatory. One Happening consisted of a constructed setting with partitions on which viewers wrote phrases, while another involved spectators walking on a pile of tires. One of Kaprow's first Happenings, titled *18 Happenings in Six Parts,* took place in 1959 at the Reuben Gallery in New York City. For the event, he divided the gallery space into three sections with translucent plastic sheets. Over the course of the 90-minute piece, performers, including Kaprow's artist friends, bounced balls, read from placards, extended their arms like wings, and played records as slides and lights flashed on and off in programmed sequences.

FLUXUS Other Cage students interested in the composer's search to find aesthetic potential in the nontraditional and commonplace formed the *Fluxus* group. Eventually expanding to include European and Japanese artists, this group's performances were more theatrical than Happenings. To distinguish their performances from Happenings, the artists associated with Fluxus coined the term *Events* to describe their work. Events focused on single actions, such as turning a light on and off or watching falling snow—what Fluxus artist La Monte Young (b. 1935) called "the theater of the single event."[37] The Events usually took place on a stage separating the performers from the audience but without costumes or added decor. Events were not spontaneous. They followed a compositional "score," which, given the restricted nature of these performances, was short.

KAZUO SHIRAGA Some artists produced works that involved both painting and performance. Gutai Bijutsu Kyokai (Concrete Art Association), a group of 18 Japanese artists in Osaka, expanded the action of painting into the realm of performance—in a sense, taking Jackson Pollock's painting methods into a public arena. Led by Jiro Yoshihara (1905–1972), Gutai, founded in 1954, devoted itself to art that combined Japanese traditional practices such as Zen with a renewed appreciation for materials. In the *Gutai Art Manifesto,* Yoshihara explained: "Gutai does not alter the material. Gutai imparts life to the material. . . . [T]he human spirit and the material shake hands with each other, but keep their distance."[38] Accordingly, Gutai works, for example, *Making a Work with His Own Body* (FIG. 25-75), by

25-75 KAZUO SHIRAGA, *Making a Work with His Own Body,* 1955. Mud.

The Performance artists of the Japanese Gutai Bijutsu Kyokai (Concrete Art Association) expanded action painting into the realm of performance. Shiraga used his body to "paint" with mud.

Carolee Schneemann on Painting, Performance Art, and Art History

Carolee Schneemann (FIG. 25-76), one of the pioneering Performance artists of the 1960s, also produced works in other media. In notes she wrote in 1962–1963, Schneemann contrasted her Performance works with more traditional art forms.

> Environments, happenings—concretions—are an extension of my painting-constructions which often have moving (motorized) sections. . . . [But, the] steady exploration and repeated viewing which the eye is required to make with my painting-constructions is reversed in the performance situation where the spectator is overwhelmed with changing recognitions, carried emotionally by a flux of evocative actions and led or held by the specified time sequence which marks the duration of a performance. In this way the audience is actually *visually* more *passive* than when confronting a . . . "still" work . . . . With paintings, constructions and sculptures the viewers are able to carry out repeated examinations of the work, to select and vary viewing positions (to walk with the eye), to touch surfaces and to freely indulge responses to areas of color and texture at their chosen speed.*

Readers of this book will also take special interest in Schneemann's 1975 essay entitled "Woman in the Year 2000," in which she envisioned what introductory art history courses would be like at the beginning of the 21st century:

> By the year 2000 [every] young woman will study Art Istory [sic] courses enriched by the inclusion, discovery, and re-evaluation of works by women artists: works (and lives) until recently buried away, willfully destroyed, [or] ignored.†

A comparison between this 13th edition of *Art through the Ages* and editions published in the 1960s and 1970s will immediately reveal the accuracy of Schneemann's prediction.

---

* Quoted in Bruce McPherson, ed., *More Than Meat Joy: Complete Performance Works and Selected Writings* (New Paltz, N.Y.: Documentext, 1979), 10–11.
† Ibid., 198.

25-76 CAROLEE SCHNEEMANN, *Meat Joy,* 1964. Performance at Judson Church, New York City.

In her performances, Schneemann transformed the nature of Performance art by introducing a feminist dimension through the use of her body (often nude) to challenge traditional gender roles.

KAZUO SHIRAGA (b. 1924), involved such actions as throwing paint balls at blank canvases or wallowing in mud as a means of shaping it. In *Making a Work,* Shiraga used his body to "paint" with mud. The Gutai group dissolved upon Yoshihara's death in 1972.

CAROLEE SCHNEEMANN Like Gutai, CAROLEE SCHNEEMANN (b. 1939) integrated painting and performance in her artworks (see "Carolee Schneemann on Painting, Performance Art, and Art History," above). Her self-described "kinetic theater" radically transformed the nature of Performance Art by introducing a feminist dimension through the use of her body (often nude) to challenge "the psychic territorial power lines by which women were admitted to the Art Stud Club."[39] In her 1964 performance *Meat Joy* (FIG. 25-76), Schneemann reveled in the taste, smell, and feel of raw sausages, chickens, and fish.

JOSEPH BEUYS The leftist politics of the Fluxus group in the early 1960s strongly influenced German artist JOSEPH BEUYS (1921–1986). Drawing on Happenings and Fluxus, Beuys created actions aimed at illuminating the condition of modern humanity. He wanted to make a new kind of sculptural object that would include "Thinking Forms: how we mould our thoughts or Spoken Forms: how we shape our thoughts into words or Social Sculpture: how we mould and shape the world in which we live."[40]

Beuys's commitment to artworks stimulating thought about art and life derived in part from his experiences as a pilot during World War II. After the enemy shot down his plane over the Crimea, nomadic Tatars nursed him back to health by swaddling his body in fat and felt to warm him. Fat and felt thus symbolized healing and regeneration to Beuys, and he incorporated these materials into many of his sculptures and actions, such as *How to Explain Pictures to a*

25-77 Joseph Beuys, *How to Explain Pictures to a Dead Hare,* 1965. Performance at the Schmela Gallery, Düsseldorf.

In this one-person event, Beuys coated his head with honey and gold leaf. Assuming the role of a shaman, he used stylized actions to evoke a sense of mystery and sacred ritual.

Dead Hare (FIG. **25-77**). This one-person event consisted of stylized actions evoking a sense of mystery and sacred ritual. Beuys appeared in a room hung with his drawings, cradling a dead hare to which he spoke softly. Beuys coated his head with honey covered with gold leaf, creating a shimmering mask. In this manner, he took on the role of the shaman, an individual with special spiritual powers. As a shaman, Beuys believed he was acting to help revolutionize human thought so that each human being could become a truly free and creative person.

JEAN TINGUELY The paradoxical notion of destruction as an act of creation surfaces in a number of kinetic artworks, most notably in the sculpture of JEAN TINGUELY (1925–1991). Trained as a painter in his native Switzerland, Tinguely gravitated to motion sculpture. In the 1950s, he made a series of *metamatics,* motor-driven devices that produced instant abstract paintings. He programmed these metamatics electronically to act with an antimechanical unpredictability when viewers inserted felt-tipped marking pens into a pincer and pressed a button to initiate the pen's motion across a small sheet of paper clipped to an "easel." Viewers could use different-colored markers in succession and could stop and start the device to achieve some degree of control over the final image. These operations created a series of small works resembling Abstract Expressionist paintings.

In 1960, Tinguely expanded the scale of his work with a kinetic piece designed to "perform" and then destroy itself in the sculpture garden of the Museum of Modern Art in New York City. He created *Homage to New York* (FIG. **25-78**) with the aid of engineer Billy Klüver (1927–2004), who helped him scrounge wheels and other moving objects from a dump near Manhattan. The completed structure, painted white for visibility against the dark night sky, included a player piano modified into a metamatic painting machine, a weather balloon that inflated during the performance, vials of colored smoke, and a host of gears, pulleys, wheels, and other found machine parts.

This work premiered (and instantly self-destructed) on March 17, 1960, with New York Governor Nelson Rockefeller, an array of distinguished guests, and three television crews in attendance. Once

25-78 Jean Tinguely, *Homage to New York,* 1960, just prior to its self-destruction in the garden of the Museum of Modern Art, New York.

Tinguely produced motor-driven devices programmed to make instant abstract paintings. To explore the notion of destruction as an act of creation, he designed this one to perform and then destroy itself.

Tinguely turned on the machine, smoke poured from its interior and the piano caught fire. Various parts of the machine broke off and rambled away, while one of the metamatics tried but failed to produce an abstract painting. Finally, Tinguely summoned a firefighter to extinguish the blaze and ensure the demise of *Homage to New York* with his ax. Like the artist's other kinetic sculptures, *Homage to New York* recalls the satiric Dadaist spirit and the droll import of Klee's *Twittering Machine* (FIG. 24-53). But Tinguely deliberately made the wacky behavior of *Homage to New York* more playful and more endearing. Having been given a freedom of eccentric behavior unprecedented in the mechanical world, Tinguely's creations often seemed to behave with the whimsical individuality of human actors.

Conceptual Art

The relentless challenges to artistic convention fundamental to the historical avant-garde reached a logical conclusion with *Conceptual Art* in the late 1960s. Conceptual artists asserted that the "artfulness" of art lay in the artist's idea rather than in its final expression. These artists regarded the idea, or concept, as the defining component of the artwork. Indeed, some Conceptual artists eliminated the object altogether.

JOSEPH KOSUTH American artist Joseph Kosuth (b. 1945) was a major proponent of Conceptual Art.

> Like everyone else I inherited the idea of art as a set of *formal* problems. So when I began to re-think my ideas of art, I had to re-think that thinking process . . . . [T]he radical shift was in changing the idea of art itself. . . . It meant you could have an art work which was that *idea* of an art work, and its formal components weren't important. I felt I had found a way to make art without formal components being confused for an expressionist composition. The expression was in the idea, not the form—the forms were only a device in the service of the idea.[41]

Kosuth's work operates at the intersection of language and vision, dealing with the relationship between the abstract and the concrete. For example, in *One and Three Chairs* (FIG. 25-79), Kosuth juxtaposed a real chair, a full-scale photograph of the chair, and an enlarged reproduction of a dictionary definition of the word "chair." By so doing, the Conceptual artist asked the viewer to ponder the notion of what constitutes "chairness."

BRUCE NAUMAN In the mid-1960s, Bruce Nauman (b. 1941) made his artistic presence known when he abandoned painting and turned to object-making. Since then, his work has been amazingly varied. In addition to sculptural pieces constructed from different materials, including rubber, fiberglass, and cardboard, he has also produced photographs, films, videos, books, and large room installations, as well as Performance Art. Nauman's work of the 1960s intersected with that of the Conceptual artists, especially in terms of the philosophical exploration that was the foundation of much of his art, and in his interest in language and wordplay. *The True Artist Helps the World by Revealing Mystic Truths* (FIG. 25-80) was the first of Nauman's many neon sculptures. He selected neon because he wanted to find a medium that would be identified with a non-artistic function. Determined to discover a way to connect objects with words, he used the method outlined in *Philosophical Investigations,* in which the Austrian philosopher Ludwig Wittgenstein (1889–1951) encouraged contradictory and nonsensical arguments. Nauman's neon sculpture spins out an emphatic assertion, but as Nauman explained, "It was kind of a test—like when you say something out loud to see if you believe it. . . . [I]t was on the one hand a totally silly idea and yet, on the other hand, I believed it."[42]

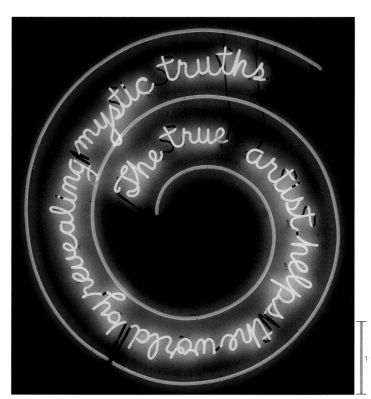

25-79 Joseph Kosuth, *One and Three Chairs,* 1965. Wooden folding chair, photographic copy of a chair, and photographic enlargement of a dictionary definition of a chair; chair, 2' 8$\frac{3}{8}$" × 1' 2$\frac{7}{8}$" × 1' 8$\frac{7}{8}$"; photo panel, 3' × 2' $\frac{1}{8}$"; text panel, 2' × 2' $\frac{1}{8}$". Museum of Modern Art, New York (Larry Aldrich Foundation Fund).

Conceptual artists regard the concept as an artwork's defining component. To portray "chairness," Kosuth juxtaposed a chair, a photograph of the chair, and a dictionary definition of "chair."

25-80 Bruce Nauman, *The True Artist Helps the World by Revealing Mystic Truths,* 1967. Neon with glass tubing suspension frame, 4' 11" × 4' 7" × 2". Private collection.

Nauman, like other Conceptual artists, explores his interest in language and wordplay in his art. He described this neon sculpture's emphatic assertion as "a totally silly idea," but one that he believed.

Other Conceptual artists pursued the notion that the idea is a work of art itself by creating works involving invisible materials, such as inert gases, radioactive isotopes, or radio waves. In each case, viewers must base their understanding of the artwork on what they know about the properties of these materials, rather than on any visible empirical data, and must depend on the artist's linguistic description of the work. Ultimately, the Conceptual artists challenged the very premises of artistic production, pushing art's boundaries to a point where no concrete definition of "art" is possible.

New Media

During the past half century, many avant-garde artists have eagerly embraced new technologies in their attempt to find fresh avenues of artistic expression. Among the most popular new media are video recording and computer graphics.

VIDEO Initially, only commercial television studios possessed video equipment, but in the 1960s, with the development of relatively inexpensive portable video recorders and of electronic devices allowing manipulation of recorded video material, artists began to explore in earnest the expressive possibilities of this new technology. In its basic form, video recording involves a special motion-picture camera that captures visible images and translates them into electronic data that can be displayed on a video monitor or television screen. Video pictures resemble photographs in the amount of detail they contain, but, like computer graphics, a video image consists of a series of points of light on a grid, giving the impression of soft focus. Viewers looking at television or video art are not aware of the monitor's surface. Instead, fulfilling the Renaissance ideal, they concentrate on the image and look through the glass surface, as through a window, into the "space" beyond. Video images combine the optical realism of photography with the sense that the subjects move in real time in a deep space "inside" the monitor.

NAM JUNE PAIK When video introduced the possibility of manipulating subjects in real time, artists such as Korean-born Nam June Paik (1932–2006) were eager to work with the medium. Inspired by the ideas of John Cage and after studying music performance, art history, and Eastern philosophy in Korea and Japan, Paik worked with electronic music in Germany in the late 1950s. In 1965, after relocating to New York City, Paik acquired the first inexpensive video recorder sold in Manhattan (the Sony Porta-Pak) and immediately recorded everything he saw out the window of his taxi on the return trip to his studio downtown. Experience acquired as artist-in-residence at television stations WGBH in Boston and WNET in New York allowed him to experiment with the most advanced broadcast video technology.

A grant permitted Paik to collaborate with the gifted Japanese engineer-inventor Shuya Abe in developing a video synthesizer. This instrument allows artists to manipulate and change the electronic video information in various ways, causing images or parts of images to stretch, shrink, change color, or break up. With the synthesizer, artists can also layer images, inset one image into another, or merge images from various cameras with those from video recorders to make a single visual kaleidoscopic "time-collage." This kind of compositional freedom permitted Paik to combine his interests in painting, music, Eastern philosophy, global politics for survival, humanized technology, and cybernetics. Paik called his video works "physical music" and said that his musical background enabled him to understand time better than could video artists trained in painting or sculpture.

Paik's best-known video work, *Global Groove* (FIG. 25-81), combines in quick succession fragmented sequences of female tap dancers, beat-generation poet Allen Ginsberg (1926–1997) reading his work, a performance by Fluxus artist and cellist Charlotte Moorman (1933–1991) using a man's back as her instrument, Pepsi commercials from Japanese television, Korean drummers, and a shot of the Living Theatre group performing a controversial piece called *Paradise Now.* Commissioned originally for broadcast over the United Nations satellite, the cascade of imagery in *Global Groove* gives viewers a glimpse of the rich worldwide television menu Paik predicted would be available in the future.

25-82 ADRIAN PIPER, *Cornered*, 1988. Mixed-media installation of variable size; video monitor, table, and birth certificates. Museum of Contemporary Art, Chicago.

In this installation, Piper, a light-skinned African American, appeared on a video monitor, "cornered" behind an overturned table, and made provocative comments about overt racism and more subtle bigotry.

ADRIAN PIPER One video artist committed to using her art to effect social change—in particular, to combat pervasive racism—is ADRIAN PIPER (b. 1948). Appropriately, her art, such as the installation *Cornered* (FIG. **25-82**), is provocative and confrontational. This piece included a video monitor placed behind an overturned table. Piper appeared on the video monitor, literally cornered behind the table, as she spoke to viewers. Her comments sprang from her experiences as a light-skinned African American woman and from her belief that although overt racism had diminished, subtle and equally damaging forms of bigotry were still rampant. "I'm black," she announces on the 16-minute videotape. "Now let's deal with this social fact and the fact of my stating it together. . . . If you feel that my letting people know that I'm not white is making an unnecessary fuss, you must feel that the right and proper course of action for me to take is to pass for white. Now this kind of thinking presupposes a belief that it's inherently better to be identified as white," she continues. The directness of Piper's art forces viewers to examine their own behaviors and values.

BILL VIOLA For much of his artistic career, BILL VIOLA (b. 1951) has also explored the capabilities of digitized imagery, producing many video installations and single-channel works. Often focused on sensory perception, the pieces not only heighten viewer awareness of the senses but also suggest an exploration into the spiritual realm. Viola, an American, spent years seriously studying Buddhist, Christian, Sufi, and Zen mysticism. Because he fervently believes in art's transformative power and in a spiritual view of human nature, Viola designs works encouraging spectator introspection. His recent video projects involve using techniques such as extreme slow motion, contrasts in scale, shifts in focus, mirrored reflections, staccato editing, and multiple or layered screens to achieve dramatic effects.

The power of Viola's work is evident in *The Crossing* (FIG. **25-83**), an installation piece involving two color video channels projected on 16-foot-high screens. The artist either shows the two projections on the front and back of the same screen or on two separate screens in the same installation. In these two companion videos, shown simultaneously on the two screens, a man surrounded

1 ft.

25-83 BILL VIOLA, *The Crossing*, 1996. Video/sound installation with two channels of color video projection onto screens 16′ high. Private collection.

Viola's video projects use extreme slow motion, contrasts in scale, shifts in focus, mirrored reflections, and staccato editing to create dramatic sensory experiences rooted in tangible reality.

in darkness appears, moving closer until he fills the screen. On one screen, drops of water fall from above onto the man's head, while on the other screen, a small fire breaks out at the man's feet. Over the next few minutes, the water and fire increase in intensity until the man disappears in a torrent of water on one screen (FIG. **25-83**) and flames consume the man on the other screen. The deafening roar of a raging fire and a torrential downpour accompany these visual images. Eventually, everything subsides and fades into darkness. This installation's elemental nature and its presentation in a dark space immerse viewers in a pure sensory experience very much rooted in tangible reality.

COMPUTER GRAPHICS Perhaps the most promising new medium for creating and manipulating illusionistic three-dimensional forms is computer graphics. This new medium uses light to make images and, like photography, can incorporate specially recorded camera images. Unlike video recording, computer graphic art allows artists to work with wholly invented forms, as painters can. Developed during the 1960s and 1970s, this technology opened up new possibilities for both abstract and figurative art. It involves electronic programs dividing the surface of the computer monitor's cathode-ray tube into a grid of tiny boxes called "picture elements," or *pixels*. Artists can electronically address pixels individually to create a design, much as knitting or weaving patterns have a grid matrix as a guide for making a design in fabric. Once created, parts of a com-

25-84 DAVID EM, *Nora*, 1979. Computer-generated color photograph, 1′ 5″ × 1′ 11″. Private collection.

Unlike video recording, computer graphic art allows the creation of wholly invented forms, as in painting. Em builds fantastic digital images of imaginary landscapes out of tiny boxes called pixels.

1 in.

puter graphic design can be changed quickly through an electronic program, allowing artists to revise or duplicate shapes in the design and to manipulate at will the color, texture, size, number, and position of any desired detail. Computer graphics pictures appear in luminous color on the cathode-ray tube. The effect suggests a view into a vast world existing inside the tube.

DAVID EM One of the best-known artists working in this electronic painting mode, DAVID EM (b. 1952) uses what he terms "computer imaging" to fashion fantastic imaginary landscapes. These have an eerily believable existence within the "window" of the computer monitor. When he was artist-in-residence at the California

Institute of Technology's Jet Propulsion Laboratory, Em created brilliantly colored scenes of alien worlds using the laboratory's advanced computer graphics equipment. He also had access to software programs developed to create computer graphics simulations of NASA's missions in outer space. Creating images with the computer gave Em great flexibility in manipulating simple geometric shapes—shrinking or enlarging them, stretching or reversing them, repeating them, adding texture to their surfaces, and creating the illusion of light and shadow. In images such as *Nora* (FIG. 25-84), Em created futuristic geometric versions of Surrealistic dreamscapes whose forms seem familiar and strange at the same time. The illusion of space in these works is immensely vivid and seductive. It almost seems possible to wander through the tubelike foreground "frame" and up the inclined foreground plane or to hop aboard the hovering globe at the lower left for a journey through the strange patterns and textures of this mysterious labyrinthine setting.

JENNY HOLZER Another contemporary artist who has harnessed new technology for artistic purposes is JENNY HOLZER (b. 1950), who created several series of artworks using electronic signs, most involving light-emitting diode (LED) technology. In 1989, Holzer did a major installation at the Guggenheim Museum in New York that included elements from her previous series and consisted of a large continuous LED display spiraling around the museum's interior ramp (FIG. 25-85). Holzer's installation focused specifically on text, and she invented sayings with an authoritative tone for her LED displays. Statements included "Protect me from what I want," "Abuse of power comes as no

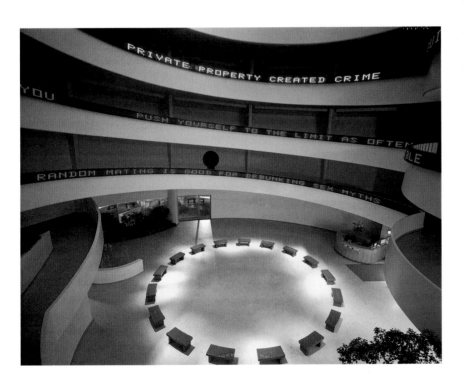

25-85 JENNY HOLZER, *Untitled* (selections from *Truisms, Inflammatory Essays, The Living Series, The Survival Series, Under a Rock, Laments,* and *Child Text*), 1989. Extended helical tricolor LED electronic display signboard, 16′ × 162′ × 6′. Solomon R. Guggenheim Museum, New York, December 1989–February 1990 (partial gift of the artist, 1989).

Holzer's 1989 installation consisted of electronic signs created using light-emitting diode (LED) technology. The continuous display of texts spiraled around the Guggenheim Museum's interior ramp.

25-86

TONY OURSLER,
Mansheshe, 1997.
Ceramic, glass, video
player, videocassette,
CPJ-200 video
projector, sound,
11″ × 7″ × 8″ each.
Private collection.

Video artist Oursler
projects his digital
images onto sculp-
tural objects, insin-
uating them into the
"real" world. Here,
he projected talking
heads onto egg-
shaped forms
suspended from
poles.

1 in.

surprise," and "Romantic love was invented to manipulate women." The statements, which people could read from a distance, were intentionally vague and, in some cases, contradictory.

TONY OURSLER While many artists present video and digital imagery to the audience on familiar flat screens, thus reproducing the format in which we most often come into contact with such images, TONY OURSLER (b. 1957) manipulates his images, projecting them onto sculptural objects. This has the effect of taking such images out of the digital world and insinuating them into the "real" world. Accompanied by sound tapes, Oursler's installations, such as *Mansheshe* (FIG. **25-86**), not only engage but often challenge the viewer. In this example, Oursler projected talking heads onto egg-shaped forms suspended from poles. Because the projected images of people look directly at the viewer, the statements they make about religious beliefs, sexual identity, and interpersonal relationships cannot be easily dismissed.

MATTHEW BARNEY One of the major trends in the art world of the opening decade of the 21st century is the relaxation of the traditional boundaries between and among artistic media. In fact, many artists today are creating vast and complex multimedia installations combining new and traditional media. One of these artists is MATTHEW BARNEY (b. 1967). The 2003 installation (FIG. **25-1**) of his epic *Cremaster* cycle (1994–2002) at the Solomon R. Guggenheim Museum in New York typifies the expansive scale of many contemporary works. A multimedia extravaganza involving drawings, photographs, sculptures, videos, films, and performances (presented in videos), the

Cremaster cycle is a lengthy narrative that takes place in a self-enclosed universe Barney created. The title of the work refers to the cremaster muscle, which controls testicular contractions in response to external stimuli. Barney uses the development of this muscle in the embryonic process of sexual differentiation as the conceptual springboard for the entire *Cremaster* project, in which he explores the notion of creation in expansive and complicated ways. The cycle's narrative, revealed in the five 35-mm feature-length films and the artworks, makes reference to, among other things, a musical revue in Boise, Idaho (Barney's hometown), the life cycle of bees, the execution of convicted murderer Gary Gilmore, the construction of the Chrysler Building (FIG. **24-76**), Celtic mythology, Masonic rituals, a motorcycle race, and a lyric opera set in late-19th-century Budapest. In the installation, Barney tied the artworks together conceptually by a five-channel video piece that is projected on screens hanging in the Guggenheim's rotunda. Immersion in Barney's constructed world is disorienting and overwhelming and has a force that competes with the immense scale and often frenzied pace of contemporary life.

No one knows what the next years and decades will bring, but given the expansive scope of postmodernism, it is likely that no single approach to or style of art will dominate. But new technologies will certainly continue to redefine what constitutes a "work of art." The universally expanding presence of computers, digital technology, and the Internet may well erode what few conceptual and geographical boundaries remain and make art and information about art available to virtually everyone, thereby creating a truly global artistic community.

EUROPE AND AMERICA
AFTER 1945

PAINTING AND SCULPTURE

▐ The art of the second half of the 20th century reflects cultural upheaval: the rejection of traditional values, the civil rights and feminist movements, and the new consumer society.

▐ The first major postwar avant-garde art movement was Abstract Expressionism, which championed an artwork's formal elements rather than its subject. Gestural abstractionists, such as Pollock and de Kooning, sought expressiveness through energetically applied pigment. Chromatic abstractionists, such as Rothko, struck emotional chords through large areas of pure color.

Pollock, *Lavender Mist*, 1950

▐ Post-Painterly Abstraction promoted a cool rationality in contrast to Abstract Expressionism's passion. Both hard-edge painters, such as Kelly and Stella, and color-field painters, such as Frankenthaler and Louis, pursued purity in art by emphasizing the flatness of pigment on canvas.

▐ Pop artists, such as Johns, Lichtenstein, and Warhol, turned away from abstraction to the representation of subjects grounded in popular culture—flags, comic strips, movie stars.

▐ Superrealists, such as Flack, Close, and Hanson—kindred spirits to Pop artists in many ways—created paintings and sculptures featuring scrupulous fidelity to optical fact.

▐ The leading sculptural movement was Minimalism. Tony Smith and Judd created artworks consisting of simple unadorned geometric shapes to underscore the "objecthood" of their sculptures.

Warhol, *Marilyn Diptych*, 1962

▐ Much of the art since 1970 addresses pressing social issues. Leading feminist artists include Chicago, whose *Dinner Party* honors important women throughout history and features crafts traditionally associated with women; Sherman and Kruger, who explored the "male gaze" in their art; and Mendieta and Wilke, whose bodies are their subjects.

▐ Other artists explored race, ethnicity, class, and sexual orientation. Ringgold and Simpson addressed issues important to African American women, Edwards civil rights themes, and Quick-to-See Smith Native American heritage. Wodiczko's art has documented the plight of the homeless. Wojnarowicz recorded the devastating effect of AIDS on the gay community.

Chicago, *The Dinner Party*, 1979

ARCHITECTURE AND SITE-SPECIFIC ART

▐ Some of the leading early-20th-century modernist architects were also active after 1945. Wright built the snail-shell Guggenheim Museum, Le Corbusier the sculpturesque Notre-Dame-du-Haut, and Mies van der Rohe the Minimalist Seagram skyscraper. Later modernists Saarinen and Utzon designed structures having dramatic curvilinear rooflines.

▐ In contrast to modernist architecture, postmodernist architecture is complex and eclectic and often incorporates references to historical styles. Among the best-known postmodern projects are Moore's Piazza d'Italia and Graves's Portland Building, both of which echo classical motifs.

▐ Deconstructivist architects seek to disorient the viewer with asymmetrical and irregular shapes. Among the most prominent practicing today are Gehry and Libeskind.

Gehry, Guggenheim Museum, Bilbao, 1997

▐ Site-specific art exists at the intersection of architecture and sculpture and is sometimes temporary in nature, as was Christo and Jeanne-Claude's *Surrounded Islands.*

PERFORMANCE AND CONCEPTUAL ART AND NEW MEDIA

▐ Among the most significant developments in the art world after World War II has been the expansion of the range of works considered "art."

▐ Performance artists, notably Schneemann and Beuys, replace traditional stationary artworks with movements and sounds carried out before an audience. Their Performance Art often addresses the same social and political issues that contemporary painters and sculptors explore.

Oursler, *Mansheshe*, 1997

▐ Conceptual artists, including Kosuth and Nauman, believe that the "artfulness" of art is in the artist's idea, not in the work resulting from the idea.

▐ Paik, Piper, Viola, and others have embraced video recording technology to produce artworks that combine images and sounds, sometimes viewed on small monitors, other times on huge screens.

▐ Em, Holzer, Oursler, and Barney have explored computer graphics and other new media, often in vast and complex museum installations.

NOTES

Chapter 21

1. Translated by Robert Goldwater and Marco Treves, eds., *Artists on Art,* 3d ed. (New York: Pantheon, 1958), 157.
2. Quoted in Thomas A. Bailey, *The American Pageant: A History of the Republic,* 2d ed. (Boston: Heath, 1961), 280.
3. Translated by Elfriede Heyer and Roger C. Norton, in Charles Harrison, Paul Wood, and Jason Gaiger, eds., *Art in Theory, 1648–1815: An Anthology of Changing Ideas* (Oxford: Blackwell, 2000), 451–453.

Chapter 22

1. Théophile Gautier, *Histoire de Romantisme* (Paris: Charpentier, 1874), 204.
2. Quoted in Helmut Borsch-Supan, *Caspar David Friedrich* (New York: Braziller, 1974), 7.
3. Translated by Jason Gaiger, in Charles Harrison, Paul Wood, and Jason Gaiger, eds., *Art in Theory, 1815–1900: An Anthology of Changing Ideas* (Oxford: Blackwell, 1998), 54.
4. Quoted by Brian Lukacher, in Stephen F. Eisenman, ed., *Nineteenth Century Art: A Critical History,* 2d ed. (New York: Thames & Hudson, 2002), 125.
5. Quoted in John W. McCoubrey, *American Art, 1700–1960: Sources and Documents* (Upper Saddle River, N.J.: Prentice Hall, 1965), 98.
6. Quoted in Thomas A. Bailey, *The American Pageant: A History of the Republic,* 2d ed. (Boston: Heath, 1961), 280.
7. Quoted in Linda Nochlin, *Realism and Tradition in Art, 1848–1900* (Upper Saddle River, N.J.: Prentice Hall, 1966), 42.
8. Quoted in George Heard Hamilton, *Manet and His Critics* (New Haven, Conn.: Yale University Press, 1954), 45.
9. Quoted in Eisenman, 286.
10. *New York Weekly Tribune,* September 30, 1865.
11. Quoted in Nikolai Cikovsky Jr. and Franklin Kelly, *Winslow Homer* (Washington, D.C.: National Gallery of Art, 1995), 26.
12. Quoted in Lloyd Goodrich, *Thomas Eakins, His Life and Work* (New York: Whitney Museum of American Art, 1933), 51–52.
13. Quoted in Nicholas Pevsner, *An Outline of European Architecture* (Baltimore: Penguin, 1960), 627.
14. Letter from Delaroche to François Arao, quoted in Helmut Gernsheim, *Creative Photography* (New York: Bonanza, 1962), 24.
15. Quoted in Naomi Rosenblum, *A World History of Photography* (New York: Abbeville, 1984), 69.
16. Quoted in Kenneth MacGowan, *Behind the Screen* (New York: Delta, 1965), 49.

Chapter 23

1. Clement Greenberg, "Modernist Painting," *Art and Literature,* no. 4 (Spring 1965): 193–194.
2. Quoted in Linda Nochlin, *Realism* (Harmondsworth: Penguin, 1971), 28.
3. Quoted in Linda Nochlin, *Impressionism and Post-Impressionism 1874–1904: Sources and Documents* (Englewood Cliffs, N.J.: Prentice Hall, 1966), 35.
4. Translated by Carola Hicks, in Charles Harrison, Paul Wood, and Jason Gaiger, eds., *Art in Theory, 1815–1900: An Anthology of Changing Ideas* (Oxford: Blackwell, 1998), 595.
5. Quoted in John McCoubrey, *American Art, 1700–1960: Sources and Documents* (Englewood Cliffs, N.J.: Prentice Hall, 1965), 184.
6. Quoted in Harrison et al., 835–836.
7. Quoted in Robert Goldwater and Marco Treves, eds., *Artists on Art, from the XIV to the XX Century* (New York: Pantheon, 1945), 322.
8. Ibid., 375.
9. Vincent van Gogh to Theo van Gogh, September 1888, in J. van Gogh–Bonger and V. W. van Gogh, eds., *The Complete Letters of Vincent van Gogh* (Greenwich, Conn.: New York Graphic Society, 1979), 3: 534.
10. Vincent van Gogh to Theo van Gogh, July 16, 1888, in W. H. Auden, ed., *Van Gogh: A Self-Portrait: Letters Revealing His Life as a Painter* (New York: Dutton, 1963), 299.

11. Quoted in Belinda Thompson, ed., *Gauguin by Himself* (Boston: Little, Brown, 1993), 270–271.
12. Quoted in Sam Hunter, John Jacobus, and Daniel Wheeler, *Modern Art,* 3d ed. (Upper Saddle River, N.J.: Prentice Hall, 2004), 28.
13. Cézanne to Émile Bernard, March 1904. Quoted in Goldwater and Treves, 363.
14. Cézanne to Émile Bernard, April 15, 1904, in ibid., 363.
15. Translated by Akane Kawakami, in Harrison et al., 1066.
16. Quoted in George Heard Hamilton, *Painting and Sculpture in Europe, 1880–1940,* 6th ed. (New Haven, Conn.: Yale University Press, 1993), 124.
17. Quoted in V. Frisch and J. T. Shipley, *Auguste Rodin* (New York: Stokes, 1939), 203.
18. Quoted in Eileen Boris, *Art and Labor: Ruskin, Morris, and the Craftsman Ideal in America* (Philadelphia: Temple University Press, 1986), 7.

Chapter 24

1. Quoted in John Elderfield, *The "Wild Beasts": Fauvism and Its Affinities* (New York: Museum of Modern Art, 1976), 29.
2. Translated by Charles Harrison and Paul Wood, eds., *Art in Theory, 1900–2000: An Anthology of Changing Ideas* (Oxford: Blackwell, 2003), 65.
3. Quoted in Frederick S. Levine, *The Apocalyptic Vision: The Art of Franz Marc as German Expressionism* (New York: Harper & Row, 1979), 57.
4. Quoted in Sam Hunter, John Jacobus, and Daniel Wheeler, *Modern Art,* rev. 3d ed. (Upper Saddle Hill, N.J.: Prentice Hall, 2004), 121.
5. Quoted in George Heard Hamilton, *Painting and Sculpture in Europe, 1880–1940,* 6th ed. (New Haven, Conn.: Yale University Press, 1993), 246.
6. Ibid., 238.
7. Quoted in Edward Fry, ed., *Cubism* (London: Thames & Hudson, 1966), 112–113.
8. Quoted in Michael Hoog, *R. Delaunay* (New York: Crown, 1976), 49.
9. Quoted in Françoise Gilot and Carlton Lake, *Life with Picasso* (New York: McGraw-Hill, 1964), 77.
10. Filippo Tommaso Marinetti, *The Foundation and Manifesto of Futurism* (Le Figaro, February 20, 1909). Translated by Joshua C. Taylor, in Herschel B. Chipp, *Theories of Modern Art: A Source Book by Artists and Critics* (Berkeley and Los Angeles: University of California Press, 1968), 284.
11. Ibid., 286.
12. Quoted in Robert Short, *Dada and Surrealism* (London: Octopus, 1980), 18.
13. Quoted in Robert Motherwell, ed., *The Dada Painters and Poets: An Anthology,* 2d ed. (Cambridge, Mass.: Belknap Press of Harvard University, 1989).
14. Hans Richter, *Dada: Art and Anti-Art* (London: Thames & Hudson, 1961), 64–65.
15. Ibid., 57.
16. Tristan Tzara, "Chronique Zurichoise," translated by Ralph Manheim, in Motherwell, *Dada Painters,* 236
17. Quoted in Arturo Schwarz, *The Complete Works of Marcel Duchamp* (London: Thames & Hudson, 1965), 466.
18. Quoted in Sam Hunter, *American Art of the 20th Century* (New York: Abrams, 1972), 30.
19. Ibid., 37.
20. Charles C. Eldredge, "The Arrival of European Modernism," *Art in America* 61 (July–August 1973), 35.
21. Quoted in Gail Stavitsky, "Reordering Reality: Precisionist Directions in American Art, 1915–1941," in Diana Murphy, ed., *Precisionism in America 1915–1941: Reordering Reality* (New York: Abrams, 1994), 12.
22. Quoted in Karen Tsujimoto, *Images of America: Precisionist Painting and Modern Photography* (Seattle: University of Washington Press, 1982), 70.
23. Dorothy Norman, *Alfred Stieglitz: An American Seer* (Millerton, N.Y.: Aperture, 1973), 9–10.
24. Ibid., 161.
25. Pablo Picasso, "Statement to Simone Téry," in Harrison and Wood, *Art in Theory, 1900–2000,* 649.

26. Quoted in Roland Penrose, *Picasso: His Life and Work*, rev. ed. (New York: Harper & Row, 1971), 311.

27. Quoted in Matthias Eberle, *World War I and the Weimar Artists: Dix, Grosz, Beckmann, Schlemmer* (New Haven, Conn.: Yale University Press, 1985), 54.

28. Ibid., 22.

29. Ibid., 42.

30. Quoted in William S. Rubin, *Dada, Surrealism, and Their Heritage* (New York: Museum of Modern Art, 1968), 64.

31. Quoted in Hamilton, *Painting and Sculpture*, 392.

32. Quoted in Richter, *Dada*, 155.

33. Ibid., 159.

34. Quoted in Rubin, *Dada, Surrealism*, 111.

35. Quoted in Hunter, Jacobus, and Wheeler, *Modern Art*, 179.

36. Quoted in William S. Rubin, *Miró in the Collection of the Museum of Modern Art* (New York: Museum of Modern Art, 1973), 32.

37. Translated by Norbert Guterman, quoted in Chipp, *Theories of Modern Art*, 182–186.

38. Translated by Howard Dearstyne, in Robert L. Herbert, *Modern Artists on Art*, 2d ed. (Mineola, N.Y.: Dover, 2000), 117.

39. Ibid., 124.

40. Translated by Herbert Read and Leslie Martin, quoted in Chipp, *Theories of Modern Art*, 325–330.

41. Translated by Nicholas Bullock, quoted in Harrison and Wood, *Art in Theory, 1900–2000*, 281.

42. Quoted in Kenneth Frampton, *Modern Architecture: A Critical History*, 3d ed. (New York: Thames & Hudson, 1992), 147.

43. Quoted in Michel Seuphor, *Piet Mondrian: Life and Work* (New York: Abrams, 1956), 117.

44. Piet Mondrian, *Plastic Art and Pure Plastic Art* (1937), quoted in Hamilton, *Painting and Sculpture*, 319.

45. Mondrian, quoted in Chipp, *Theories of Modern Art*, 349.

46. Ibid., 350.

47. Quoted in H. H. Arnason and Peter Kalb, *History of Modern Art*, 5th ed. (Upper Saddle River, N.J.: Prentice Hall, 2004), 154.

48. Quoted in Robert L. Herbert, *Modern Artists on Art*, 2d ed. (Mineola, N.Y.: Dover, 2000), 173.

49. Ibid., 177.

50. Quoted in Vivian Endicott Barnett, "Banned German Art: Reception and Institutional Support of Modern German Art in the United States, 1933–45," in Stephanie Barron, *Exiles and Emigrés: The Flight of European Artists from Hitler* (Los Angeles: Los Angeles County Museum of Art, 1997), 283.

51. Quoted in Milton Meltzer, *Dorothea Lange: A Photographer's Life* (New York: Farrar, Straus & Giroux, 1978), 133, 220.

52. Quoted in Frances K. Pohl, *Ben Shahn: New Deal Artist in a Cold War Climate, 1947–1954* (Austin: University of Texas Press, 1989), 159.

53. Quoted in Henry Louis Gates Jr., "New Negroes, Migration, and Cultural Exchange," in Elizabeth Hutton Turner, ed., *Jacob Lawrence: The Migration Series* (Washington, D.C.: Phillips Collection, 1993), 20.

54. Wanda M. Corn, *Grant Wood: The Regionalist Vision* (New Haven, Conn.: Yale University Press, 1983), 131.

55. Quoted in Matthew Baigell, *A Concise History of American Painting and Sculpture* (New York: Harper & Row, 1984), 264.

56. Quoted in Hans L. Jaffé, *De Stijl* (New York: Abrams, 1971), 185–188.

57. Piet Mondrian, *Dialogue on the New Plastic* (1919). Translated by Harry Holzman and Martin S. James, in Harrison and Wood, *Art in Theory, 1900–2000*, 285.

58. Walter Gropius, from *The Manifesto of the Bauhaus*, April 1919.

59. Ibid.

60. Ibid.

61. Quoted in John Willett, *Art and Politics in the Weimar Period: The New Sobriety, 1917–1933* (New York: Da Capo, 1978), 119.

62. Quoted in Wayne Craven, *American Art: History and Culture* (Madison, Wis.: Brown & Benchmark, 1994), 403.

63. Quoted in Vincent Scully Jr., *Frank Lloyd Wright* (New York: Braziller, 1960), 18.

64. Quoted in Edgar Kauffmann, ed., *Frank Lloyd Wright: An American Architect* (New York: Horizon, 1955), 205, 208.

65. Quoted in Philip Johnson, *Mies van der Rohe*, rev. ed. (New York: Museum of Modern Art, 1954), 200–201.

Chapter 25

1. Dawn Ades and Andrew Forge, *Francis Bacon* (London: Thames & Hudson, 1985), 8; and David Sylvester, *The Brutality of Fact: Interviews with Francis Bacon*, 3d ed. (London: Thames & Hudson, 1987), 182.

2. Clement Greenberg, "Toward a Newer Laocoon," *Partisan Review* 7, no. 4 (July–August 1940): 305.

3. Clement Greenberg, "Sculpture in Our Time," *Arts Magazine* 32, no. 9 (June 1956): 22.

4. Marcus Rothko and Adolph Gottlieb, quoted in Edward Alden Jewell, "The Realm of Art: A New Platform and Other Matters: 'Globalism' Pops into View," *New York Times*, June 13, 1943, 9.

5. Reprinted in Harold Rosenberg, *The Tradition of the New* (New York: Horizon, 1959), 25.

6. Quoted in Thomas Hess, *Barnett Newman* (New York: Walker and Company, 1969), 51.

7. Quoted in John P. O'Neill, ed., *Barnett Newman: Selected Writings and Interviews* (New York: Knopf, 1990), 108.

8. Rothko and Gottlieb, 9.

9. Quoted in Selden Rodman, *Conversations with Artists* (New York: Devin-Adair, 1957), 93–94.

10. Clement Greenberg, "Recentness of Sculpture," in Gregory Battcock, ed., *Minimal Art: A Critical Anthology* (New York: Dutton, 1968), 183–184.

11. Louise Nevelson, quoted in John Gordon, *Louise Nevelson* (New York: Praeger, 1967), 12.

12. Quoted in Deborah Wye, *Louise Bourgeois* (New York: Museum of Modern Art, 1982), 22.

13. Ibid., 25.

14. Quoted in Lucy Lippard, *Eva Hesse* (New York: New York University Press, 1976), 165.

15. Ibid., 56.

16. Quoted in Richard Francis, *Jasper Johns* (New York: Abbeville, 1984), 21.

17. Andy Warhol, *The Philosophy of Andy Warhol* (New York: Harcourt Brace Jovanovich, 1975), 100.

18. Quoted in Christine Lindey, *Superrealist Painting and Sculpture* (London: Orbis, 1980), 50.

19. Ibid., 130.

20. Fredric Jameson, "Postmodernism and Consumer Society," in Hal Foster, ed., *The Anti-Aesthetic: Essays on Postmodern Culture* (Port Townsend, Wash.: Bay, 1983), 113.

21. Quoted in Grace Glueck, "Susan Rothenberg: New Outlook for a Visionary Artist," *New York Times Magazine*, July 22, 1984, 20.

22. Quoted in *Walker Art Center: Painting and Sculpture from the Collection* (Minneapolis: Walker Art Center, 1990), 435.

23. Quoted in Susanna Torruella Leval, "Recapturing History: The (Un)official Story in Contemporary Latin American Art," *Art Journal* 51, no. 4 (Winter 1992): 74.

24. Ibid.

25. Hannah Wilke, "Visual Prejudice," in *Hannah Wilke: A Retrospective* (Columbia: University of Missouri Press, 1989), 141.

26. Quoted in Donald Hall, *Corporal Politics* (Cambridge: MIT List Visual Arts Center, 1993), 46.

27. Kobena Mercer, "Black Hair/Style Politics," in Russell Ferguson, Martha Gever, Trinh T. Minh-ha, and Cornel West, eds., *Out There: Marginalization and Contemporary Culture* (New York: New Museum of Contemporary Art, 1990), 248–249.

28. Ibid.

29. Jaune Quick-to-See Smith and Harmony Hammond, *Women of Sweetgrass: Cedar and Sage* (New York: American Indian Center, 1984), 97.

30. Quoted in Richard Marshall and Robert Mapplethorpe, *50 New York Artists* (San Francisco: Chronicle, 1986), 448–449.

31. Quoted in Mary Jane Jacob, *Magdalena Abakanowicz* (New York: Abbeville, 1982), 94.

32. Peter Blake, *Frank Lloyd Wright* (Harmondsworth: Penguin, 1960), 115.

33. Quoted in "Vietnam Memorial: America Remembers," *National Geographic* 167, no. 5 (May 1985): 557.

34. Quoted in Nancy Holt, ed., *The Writings of Robert Smithson* (New York: New York University Press, 1975), 111.

35. Quoted in Calvin Tomkins, "The Art World: *Tilted Arc*," *New Yorker*, May 20, 1985, 100.

36. Quoted in H. H. Arnason and Peter Kalb, *History of Modern Art*, 5th ed. (Upper Saddle River, N.J.: Prentice Hall, 2004), 489.

37. Quoted in Barbara Haskell, *Blam! The Explosion of Pop, Minimalism, and Performance 1958–1964* (New York: Whitney Museum of American Art, 1984), 53.

38. Jiro Yoshihara, "Gutai Art Manifesto" (1956), translated by Reiko Tomii, in Alexandra Munroe, *Japanese Art after 1945: Scream against the Sky* (New York: Abrams, 1994), 370.

39. Quoted in Bruce McPherson, ed., *More Than Meat Joy: Complete Performance Works and Selected Writings* (New Paltz, N.Y.: Documentext, 1979), 52.

40. Quoted in Caroline Tisdall, *Joseph Beuys* (New York: Thames & Hudson, 1979), 6.

41. Quoted in "Joseph Kosuth: Art as Idea as Idea," in Jeanne Siegel, ed., *Artwords: Discourse on the 60s and 70s* (Ann Arbor, Mich.: UMI Research Press, 1985), 221, 225.

42. Quoted in Brenda Richardson, *Bruce Nauman: Neons* (Baltimore: Baltimore Museum of Art, 1982), 20.

GLOSSARY

a secco—Italian, "dried." See *fresco.*

Abstract Expressionism—The first major American avant-garde movement, Abstract Expressionism emerged in New York City in the 1940s. The artists produced abstract paintings that expressed their state of mind and that they hoped would strike emotional chords in viewers. The movement developed along two lines: *gestural abstraction* and *chromatic abstraction.*

action painting—Also called *gestural abstraction.* The kind of *Abstract Expressionism* practiced by Jackson Pollock, in which the emphasis was on the creation process, the artist's gesture in making art. Pollock poured liquid paint in linear webs on his canvases, which he laid out on the floor, thereby physically surrounding himself in the painting during its creation.

additive light—Natural light, or sunlight, the sum of all the wavelengths of the visible *spectrum.* See also *subtractive light.*

additive sculpture—A kind of sculpture *technique* in which materials (for example, clay) are built up or "added" to create form.

aerial perspective—See *perspective.*

airbrush—A tool that uses compressed air to spray paint onto a surface.

aisle—The portion of a *basilica* flanking the *nave* and separated from it by a row of *columns* or *piers.*

alchemy—The medieval study of seemingly magical changes, especially chemical changes.

altarpiece—A panel, painted or sculpted, situated above and behind an altar. See also *retable.*

Analytic Cubism—The first phase of *Cubism,* developed jointly by Pablo Picasso and Georges Braque, in which the artists analyzed form from every possible vantage point to combine the various views into one pictorial whole.

anamorphic image—A distorted image that must be viewed by some special means (such as a mirror) to be recognized.

ancien régime—French, "old order." The term used to describe the political, social, and religious order in France before the Revolution at the end of the 18th century.

apse—A recess, usually semicircular, in the wall of a building, commonly found at the east end of a church.

arcade—A series of *arches* supported by *piers* or *columns.*

Arcadian (adj.)—In Renaissance and later art, depictions of an idyllic place of rural peace and simplicity. Derived from Arcadia, an ancient district of the central Peloponnesos in southern Greece.

arch—A curved structural member that spans an opening and is generally composed of wedge-shaped blocks (*voussoirs*) that transmit the downward pressure laterally. See also *thrust.*

armature—The crossed, or diagonal, *arches* that form the skeletal framework of a *Gothic rib vault.* In sculpture, the framework for a clay form.

arriccio—In *fresco* painting, the first layer of rough lime plaster applied to the wall.

Art Deco—Descended from *Art Nouveau,* this movement of the 1920s and 1930s sought to upgrade industrial design as a "fine art" and to work new materials into decorative patterns that could be either machined or handcrafted. Characterized by streamlined, elongated, and symmetrical design.

Art Nouveau—French, "new art." A late-19th- and early-20th-century art movement whose proponents tried to synthesize all the arts in an effort to create art based on natural forms that could be mass produced by technologies of the industrial age. The movement had other names in other countries: Jugendstil in Austria and Germany, Modernismo in Spain, and Floreale in Italy.

assemblage—An artwork constructed from already existing objects.

atmospheric perspective—See *perspective.*

atrium—The central reception room of a Roman house that is partly open to the sky. Also the open, *colonnaded* court in front of and attached to a Christian *basilica.*

attribute—(n.) The distinctive identifying aspect of a person, for example, an object held, an associated animal, or a mark on the body. (v.) To make an *attribution.*

attribution—Assignment of a work to a maker or makers.

automatism—In painting, the process of yielding oneself to instinctive motions of the hands after establishing a set of conditions (such as size of paper or medium) within which a work is to be created.

avant-garde—French, "advance guard" (in a platoon). Late-19th- and 20th-century artists who emphasized innovation and challenged established convention in their work. Also used as an adjective.

baldacchino—A canopy on *columns,* frequently built over an altar. The term derives from *baldacco.*

baldacco—Italian, "silk from Baghdad." See *baldacchino.*

baldric—A sashlike belt worn over one shoulder and across the chest to support a sword.

Baroque—The traditional blanket designation for European art from 1600 to 1750. The stylistic term *Baroque,* which describes art that features dramatic theatricality and elaborate ornamentation in contrast to the simplicity and orderly rationality of Renaissance art, is most appropriately applied to Italian art of this period. The term derives from *barroco.*

barrel vault—See *vault.*

barroco—Portuguese, "irregularly shaped pearl." See *Baroque.*

base—In ancient Greek architecture, the molded projecting lowest part of *Ionic* and *Corinthian* columns. (*Doric* columns do not have bases.)

basilica—In Roman architecture, a public building for legal and other civic proceedings, rectangular in plan with an entrance usually on a long side. In Christian architecture, a church somewhat resembling the Roman basilica, usually entered from one end and with an *apse* at the other.

bas-relief—See *relief.*

battlement—A low parapet at the top of a circuit wall in a fortification.

Bauhaus—A school of architecture in Germany in the 1920s under the aegis of Walter Gropius, who emphasized the unity of art, architecture, and design.

bay—The space between two columns, or one unit in the *nave arcade* of a church; also, the passageway in an *arcuated* gate.

Beaux-Arts—An architectural style of the late 19th and early 20th centuries in France. Based on ideas taught at the École des Beaux-Arts in Paris, the Beaux-Arts style incorporated classical principles, such as symmetry in design, and included extensive exterior ornamentation.

belvedere—Italian, "beautiful view." A building or other structure with a view of a landscape or seascape.

benday dots—Named after the newspaper printer Benjamin Day, the benday dot system involves the modulation of colors through the placement and size of colored dots.

bent-axis plan—A *plan* that incorporates two or more angular changes of direction, characteristic of Sumerian architecture.

Biomorphic Surrealism—See *Surrealism*.

Book of Hours—A Christian religious book for private devotion containing prayers to be read at specified times of the day.

bottega—An artist's studio-shop.

breakfast piece—A *still life* that includes bread and fruit.

breviary—A Christian religious book of selected daily prayers and Psalms.

bucranium (pl. **bucrania**)—Latin, "bovine skull." A common motif in classical architectural ornament.

buon fresco—See *fresco*.

burgher—A middle-class citizen.

burin—A pointed tool used for *engraving* or *incising*.

buttress—An exterior masonry structure that opposes the lateral *thrust* of an *arch* or a *vault*. A pier buttress is a solid mass of masonry. A flying buttress consists typically of an inclined member carried on an arch or a series of arches and a solid buttress to which it transmits lateral *thrust*.

caduceus—In ancient Greek mythology, a magical rod entwined with serpents, the attribute of Hermes (Roman, Mercury), the messenger of the gods.

calotype—From the Greek *kalos,* "beautiful." A photographic process in which a positive image is made by shining light through a negative image onto a sheet of sensitized paper.

camera lucida—Latin, "lighted room." A device in which a small lens projects the image of an object downward onto a sheet of paper.

camera obscura—Latin, "dark room." An ancestor of the modern camera in which a tiny pinhole, acting as a lens, projects an image on a screen, the wall of a room, or the ground-glass wall of a box; used by artists in the 17th, 18th, and early 19th centuries as an aid in drawing from nature.

campanile—A bell tower of a church, usually, but not always, freestanding.

canon—A rule, for example, of proportion. The ancient Greeks considered beauty to be a matter of "correct" proportion and sought a canon of proportion, for the human figure and for buildings. The fifth-century BCE sculptor Polykleitos wrote the *Canon,* a treatise incorporating his formula for the perfectly proportioned statue.

capital—The uppermost member of a *column,* serving as a transition from the *shaft* to the *lintel*. In classical architecture, the form of the capital varies with the *order*.

capriccio—Italian, "originality." One of several terms used in Italian *Renaissance* literature to praise the originality and talent of artists.

cartoon—In painting, a full-size preliminary drawing from which a painting is made.

carving—A *technique* of sculpture in which the artist cuts away material (for example, from a stone block) in order to create a *statue* or a *relief*.

cassone (pl. **cassoni**)—A carved chest, often painted or gilded, popular in Renaissance Italy for the storing of household clothing.

casting—A sculptural *technique* in which the artist pours liquid metal, plaster, clay or another material into a *mold*. When the material dries, the sculptor removes the cast piece from the mold.

cathedral—A bishop's church. The word derives from *cathedra,* referring to the bishop's chair.

cella—The chamber at the center of an ancient temple; in a classical temple, the room (Greek, *naos*) in which the *cult statue* usually stood.

central plan—See *plan*.

chancel arch—The arch separating the chancel (the *apse* or *choir*) or the *transept* from the *nave* of a basilica or church.

chapter house—The meeting hall in a *monastery*.

chartreuse—A Carthusian *monastery*.

chasing—The engraving or embossing of metal.

château (pl. **châteaux**)—French, "castle." A luxurious country residence for French royalty, developed from medieval castles.

chiaroscuro—In drawing or painting, the treatment and use of light and dark, especially the gradations of light that produce the effect of *modeling*.

chiaroscuro woodcut—A *woodcut* technique using two blocks of wood instead of one. The printmaker carves and inks one block in the usual way in order to produce a traditional black-and-white print. Then the artist cuts a second block consisting of broad highlights that can be inked in gray or color and printed over the first block's impression.

choir—The space reserved for the clergy and singers in the church, usually east of the *transept* but, in some instances, extending into the *nave*.

chromatic abstraction—A kind of *Abstract Expressionism* that focuses on the emotional resonance of color, as exemplified by the work of Barnett Newman and Mark Rothko.

chronology—In art history, the dating of art objects and buildings.

city-state—An independent, self-governing city.

Classical—The art and culture of ancient Greece between 480 and 323 BCE. Lowercase *classical* refers more generally to Greco-Roman art and culture.

clerestory—The *fenestrated* part of a building that rises above the roofs of the other parts. The oldest known clerestories are Egyptian. In Roman *basilicas* and medieval churches, clerestories are the windows that form the *nave*'s uppermost level below the timber ceiling or the *vaults*.

cloison—French, "partition." A cell made of metal wire or a narrow metal strip soldered edge-up to a metal base to hold *enamel,* semiprecious stones, pieces of colored glass, or glass paste fired to resemble sparkling jewels.

cloisonné—A decorative metalwork technique employing *cloisons;* also, decorative brickwork in later Byzantine architecture.

coffer—A sunken panel, often ornamental, in a *vault* or a ceiling.

collage—A composition made by combining on a flat surface various materials, such as newspaper, wallpaper, printed text and illustrations, photographs, and cloth.

colonnade—A series or row of *columns,* usually spanned by *lintels*.

color—The value, or tonality, of a color is the degree of its lightness or darkness. The intensity, or saturation, of a color is its purity, its brightness or dullness. See also *primary colors, secondary colors,* and *complementary colors*.

color-field painting—A variant of *Post-Painterly Abstraction* in which artists sought to reduce painting to its physical essence by pouring diluted paint onto unprimed canvas and letting these pigments soak into the fabric, as exemplified by the work of Helen Frankenthaler and Morris Louis.

colorito—Italian, "colored" or "painted." A term used to describe the application of paint. Characteristic of the work of 16th-century Venetian artists who emphasized the application of paint as an important element of the creative process. Central Italian artists, in contrast, largely emphasized *disegno*—the careful design preparation based on preliminary drawing.

colossal order—An architectural design in which the *columns* or *pilasters* are two or more stories tall. Also called a giant order.

column—A vertical, weight-carrying architectural member, circular in cross-*section* and consisting of a *base* (sometimes omitted), a *shaft,* and a *capital*.

combines—The name American artist Robert Rauschenberg gave to his *assemblages* of painted passages and sculptural elements.

complementary colors—Those pairs of colors, such as red and green, that together embrace the entire spectrum. The complement of one of the three *primary colors* is a mixture of the other two.

compline—The last prayer of the day in a *Book of Hours*.

compose—See *composition*.

Composite capital—A capital combining *Ionic* volutes and *Corinthian* acanthus leaves, first used by the ancient Romans.

composition—The way in which an artist organizes *forms* in an artwork, either by placing shapes on a flat surface or arranging forms in space.

Conceptual Art—An American avant-garde art movement of the 1960s whose premise was that the "artfulness" of art lay in the artist's idea rather than its final expression.

condottiere (pl. **condottieri**)—An Italian mercenary general.

confraternity—In Late Antiquity, an association of Christian families pooling funds to purchase property for burial. In late medieval Europe, an organization founded by laypersons who dedicated themselves to strict religious observances.

connoisseur—An expert in *attributing* artworks to one artist rather than another. More generally, an expert on artistic *style*.

Constructivism—An early-20th-century Russian art movement formulated by Naum Gabo, who built up his sculptures piece by piece in space instead of carving or *modeling* them. In this way the sculptor worked with "volume of mass" and "volume of space" as different materials.

contour line—In art, a continuous line defining the outer shape of an object.

contrapposto—The disposition of the human figure in which one part is turned in opposition to another part (usually hips and legs one way, shoulders and chest another), creating a counterpositioning of the body about its central axis. Sometimes called "weight shift" because the weight of the body tends to be thrown to one foot, creating tension on one side and relaxation on the other.

corbel—A projecting wall member used as a support for some element in the superstructure. Also, courses of stone or brick in which each course projects beyond the one beneath it. Two such walls, meeting at the topmost course, create a corbeled *arch* or corbeled *vault*.

Corinthian capital—A more ornate form than *Doric* or *Ionic;* it consists of a double row of acanthus leaves from which tendrils and flowers grow, wrapped around a bell-shaped *echinus*. Although this *capital* form is often cited as the distinguishing feature of the Corinthian *order,* no such order exists, in strict terms, but only this style of capital used in the *Ionic* order.

cornice—The projecting, crowning member of the *entablature* framing the *pediment;* also, any crowning projection.

corona civica—Latin, "civic crown." A Roman honorary wreath worn on the head.

course—In masonry construction, a horizontal row of stone blocks.

cross-hatching—See *hatching.*

crossing square—The area in a church formed by the intersection (*crossing*) of a *nave* and a *transept* of equal width, often used as a standard *module* of interior proportion.

cruciform—Cross-shaped.

Cubism—An early-20th-century art movement that rejected naturalistic depictions, preferring compositions of shapes and forms abstracted from the conventionally perceived world. See also *Analytic Cubism* and *Synthetic Cubism.*

cupola—An exterior architectural feature composed of a *drum* with a shallow cap; a *dome.*

cutaway—An architectural drawing that combines an exterior view with an interior view of part of a building.

Dada—An early-20th-century art movement prompted by a revulsion against the horror of World War I. Dada embraced political anarchy, the irrational, and the intuitive. A disdain for convention, often enlivened by humor or whimsy, is characteristic of the art the Dadaists produced.

daguerreotype—A photograph made by an early method on a plate of chemically treated metal; developed by Louis J. M. Daguerre.

De Stijl—Dutch, "the style." An early-20th-century art movement (and magazine), founded by Piet Mondrian and Theo van Doesburg, whose members promoted utopian ideals and developed a simplified geometric style.

deconstruction—An analytical strategy developed in the late 20th century according to which all cultural "constructs" (art, architecture, literature) are "texts." People can read these texts in a variety of ways, but they cannot arrive at fixed or uniform meanings. Any interpretation can be valid, and readings differ from time to time, place to place, and person to person. For those employing this approach, deconstruction means destabilizing established meanings and interpretations while encouraging subjectivity and individual differences.

Deconstructivism—An architectural style using *deconstruction* as an analytical strategy. Deconstructivist architects attempt to disorient the observer by disrupting the conventional categories of architecture. The haphazard presentation of volumes, masses, planes, lighting, and so forth challenges the viewer's assumptions about form as it relates to function.

Der Blaue Reiter—German, "the blue rider." An early-20th-century German *Expressionist* art movement founded by Vassily Kandinsky and Franz Marc. The artists selected the whimsical name because of their mutual interest in the color blue and horses.

Die Brücke—German, "the bridge." An early-20th-century German *Expressionist* art movement under the leadership of Ernst Ludwig Kirchner. The group thought of itself as the bridge between the old age and the new.

diptych—A two-paneled painting or *altarpiece;* also, an ancient Roman, Early Christian, or Byzantine hinged writing tablet, often of ivory and carved on the external sides.

disegno—Italian, "drawing" and "design." *Renaissance* artists considered drawing to be the external physical manifestation (*disegno esterno*) of an internal intellectual idea of design (*disegno interno*).

divisionism—See *pointillism.*

documentary evidence—In art history, the examination of written sources in order to determine the date of an artwork, the circumstances of its creation, or the identity of the artist(s) who made it.

dome—A hemispherical *vault;* theoretically, an *arch* rotated on its vertical axis. In *Mycenaean* architecture, domes are beehive-shaped.

donor portrait—A portrait of the individual(s) who commissioned (donated) a religious work, for example, an *altarpiece,* as evidence of devotion.

Doric—One of the two systems (or *orders*) invented in ancient Greece for articulating the three units of the elevation of a *classical* building—the platform, the *colonnade,* and the superstructure (*entablature*). The Doric order is characterized by, among other features, *capitals* with funnel-shaped *echinuses, columns* without *bases,* and a *frieze* of *triglyphs* and *metopes.* See also *Ionic.*

dressed masonry—Stone blocks shaped to the exact dimensions required, with smooth faces for a perfect fit.

drum—One of the stacked cylindrical stones that form the *shaft* of a *column.* Also, the cylindrical wall that supports a *dome.*

drypoint—An *engraving* in which the design, instead of being cut into the plate with a *burin,* is scratched into the surface with a hard steel "pencil." See also *etching, intaglio.*

earthworks—See *Environmental Art.*

echinus—The convex element of a *capital* directly below the *abacus.*

écorché—The representation of a nude body as if without skin.

edition—A set of impressions taken from a single print surface.

elevation—In architecture, a head-on view of an external or internal wall, showing its features and often other elements that would be visible beyond or before the wall.

empiricism—The search for knowledge based on observation and direct experience.

enamel—A decorative coating, usually colored, fused onto the surface of metal, glass, or ceramics.

encaustic—A painting *technique* in which pigment is mixed with melted wax and applied to the surface while the mixture is hot.

engaged column—A half-round *column* attached to a wall. See also *pilaster.*

engraving—The process of *incising* a design in hard material, often a metal plate (usually copper); also, the *print* or impression made from such a plate.

Enlightenment—The Western philosophy based on empirical evidence that dominated the 18th century. The Enlightenment was a new way of thinking critically about the world and about humankind, independently of religion, myth, or tradition.

entablature—The part of a building above the *columns* and below the roof. The entablature has three parts: *architrave, frieze,* and *pediment.*

Environmental Art—An American art form that emerged in the 1960s. Often using the land itself as their material, Environmental artists construct monuments of great scale and minimal form. Permanent or impermanent, these works transform some section of the environment, calling attention both to the land itself and to the hand of the artist. Sometimes referred to as earthworks.

escutcheon—An emblem bearing a coat of arms.

etching—A kind of *engraving* in which the design is *incised* in a layer of wax or varnish on a metal plate. The parts of the plate left exposed are then etched (slightly eaten away) by the acid in which the plate is immersed after incising. See also *drypoint, intaglio.*

Eucharist—In Christianity, the partaking of the bread and wine, which believers hold to be either Christ himself or symbolic of him.

Events—See *Fluxus.*

exedra—Recessed area, usually semicircular.

exemplum virtutis—Latin, "example or model of virtue."

Expressionism (adj. **Expressionist**)—Twentieth-century art that is the result of the artist's unique inner or personal vision and that often has an emotional dimension. Expressionism contrasts with art focused on visually describing the empirical world.

facade—Usually, the front of a building; also, the other sides when they are emphasized architecturally.

fantasia—Italian, "imagination." One of several terms used in Italian *Renaissance* literature to praise the originality and talent of artists.

fasces—A bundle of rods with an ax attached, representing an emblem of authority in ancient Rome.

Fauves—French, "wild beasts." See *Fauvism.*

Fauvism—An early-20th-century art movement led by Henri Matisse. For the Fauves, color became the formal element most responsible for pictorial coherence and the primary conveyor of meaning.

Favrile—A type of leaded stained glass patented by Louis Comfort Tiffany in the late 19th century.

femmages—The name American artist Miriam Schapiro gave to her sewn *collages,* assembled from fabrics, quilts, buttons, sequins, lace trim, and rickrack collected at antique shows and fairs.

femme savante—French, "learned woman." The term used to describe the cultured hostesses of *Rococo* salons.

fenestrated—Having windows.

fête galante—French, "amorous festival." A type of *Rococo* painting depicting the outdoor amusements of French upper-class society.

feudalism—The medieval political, social, and economic system held together by the relationship between landholding *liege lords* and the *vassals* who were granted tenure of a portion of their land and in turn swore allegiance to the liege lord.

fin-de-siècle—French, "end of the century." A period in Western cultural history from the end of the 19th century until just before World War I, when decadence and indulgence masked anxiety about an uncertain future.

finial—A crowning ornament.

fleur-de-lis—A three-petaled iris flower; the royal flower of France.

Floreale—See *Art Nouveau.*

florin—The denomination of gold coin of Renaissance Florence that became an international currency for trade.

Fluxus—A group of American, European, and Japanese artists of the 1960s who created *Performance Art.* Their performances, or Events, often focused on single actions, such as turning a light on and off or watching falling snow, and were more theatrical than *Happenings.*

flying buttress—See *buttress.*

fons vitae—Latin, "fountain of life." A symbolic fountain of everlasting life.

foreshortening—The use of *perspective* to represent in art the apparent visual contraction of an object that extends back in space at an angle to the perpendicular plane of sight.

form—In art, an object's shape and structure, either in two dimensions (for example, a figure painted on a surface) or in three dimensions (such as a statue).

formal analysis—The visual analysis of artistic *form.*

formalism—Strict adherence to, or dependence on, stylized shapes and methods of composition. An emphasis on an artwork's visual elements rather than its subject.

freestanding sculpture—See *sculpture in the round.*

fresco—Painting on lime plaster, either dry (dry fresco, or fresco secco) or wet (true, or buon, fresco). In the latter method, the pigments are mixed with water and become chemically bound to the freshly laid lime plaster. Also, a painting executed in either method.

fresco secco—See *fresco.*

frieze—The part of the *entablature* between the *architrave* and the *cornice;* also, any sculptured or painted band in a building. See *register.*

frottage—A *technique* in which the artist rubs a crayon or another medium across a sheet of paper placed over a surface having a strong textural pattern.

Futurism—An early-20th-century Italian art movement that championed war as a cleansing agent and that celebrated the speed and dynamism of modern technology.

genre—A style or category of art; also, a kind of painting that realistically depicts scenes from everyday life.

German Expressionism—An early-20th-century regional Expressionist movement.

gesso—Plaster mixed with a binding material, used as the base coat for paintings on wood panels.

gestural abstraction—Also known as *action painting.* A kind of abstract painting in which the gesture, or act of painting, is seen as the subject of art. Its most renowned proponent was Jackson Pollock. See also *Abstract Expressionism.*

giant order—See *colossal order.*

giornata (pl. **giornate**)—Italian, "day." The section of plaster that a *fresco* painter expects to complete in one session.

glaze—A vitreous coating applied to pottery to seal and decorate the surface; it may be colored, transparent, or opaque, and glossy or *matte.* In oil painting, a thin, transparent, or semitransparent layer applied over a color to alter it slightly.

gold leaf—Gold beaten into tissue-paper-thin sheets that then can be applied to surfaces.

Gothic—Originally a derogatory term named after the Goths, used to describe the history, culture, and art of western Europe in the 12th to 14th centuries. Typically divided into periods designated Early (1140–1194), High (1194–1300), and Late (1300–1500).

Grand Manner portraiture—A type of 18th-century portrait painting designed to communicate a person's grace and class through certain standardized conventions, such as the large scale of the figure relative to the canvas, the controlled pose, the landscape setting, and the low horizon line.

Greek cross—A cross with four arms of equal length.

grisaille—A monochrome painting done mainly in neutral grays to simulate sculpture.

guild—An association of merchants, craftspersons, or scholars in medieval and Renaissance Europe.

halberd—A combination spear and battle-ax.

Happenings—A term coined by American artist Allan Kaprow in the 1960s to describe loosely structured performances, whose creators were trying to suggest the aesthetic and dynamic qualities of everyday life; as actions, rather than objects, Happenings incorporate the fourth dimension (time).

hard-edge painting—A variant of *Post-Painterly Abstraction* that rigidly excluded all reference to gesture and incorporated smooth knife-edge geometric forms to express the notion that painting should be reduced to its visual components.

hatching—A series of closely spaced drawn or *engraved* parallel lines. Cross-hatching employs sets of lines placed at right angles.

hierarchy of scale—An artistic convention in which greater size indicates greater importance.

high relief—See *relief.*

horizon line—See *perspective.*

hôtel—French, "town house."

hue—The name of a *color.* See also *primary colors, secondary colors,* and *complementary colors.*

humanism—In the *Renaissance,* an emphasis on education and on expanding knowledge (especially of *classical* antiquity), the exploration of individual potential and a desire to excel, and a commitment to civic responsibility and moral duty.

icon—A portrait or image; especially in Byzantine churches, a panel with a painting of sacred personages that are objects of veneration. In the visual arts, a painting, a piece of sculpture, or even a building regarded as an object of veneration.

iconoclasm—The destruction of religious or sacred images. In Byzantium, the period from 726 to 843 when there was an imperial ban on such images. The destroyers of images were known as iconoclasts. Those who opposed such a ban were known as iconophiles.

iconoclast—See *iconoclasm.*

iconography—Greek, the "writing of images." The term refers both to the content, or subject, of an artwork and to the study of content in art. It also includes the study of the symbolic, often religious, meaning of objects, persons, or events depicted in works of art.

illuminated manuscript—A luxurious handmade book with painted illustrations and decorations.

illusionism (adj. **illusionistic**)—The representation of the three-dimensional world on a two-dimensional surface in a manner that creates the illusion that the person, object, or place represented is three-dimensional. See also *perspective.*

impasto—A layer of thickly applied pigment.

Impressionism—A late-19th-century art movement that sought to capture a fleeting moment, thereby conveying the illusiveness and impermanence of images and conditions.

incise—To cut into a surface with a sharp instrument; also, a method of decoration, especially on metal and pottery.

incubus—A demon believed in medieval times to prey, often sexually, on sleeping women.

indulgence—A religious pardon for a sin committed.

ingegno—Italian, "innate talent." One of several terms used in Italian *Renaissance* literature to praise the originality and talent of artists.

installation—An artwork that creates an artistic environment in a room or gallery.

intaglio—A graphic technique in which the design is *incised,* or scratched, on a metal plate, either manually (*engraving, drypoint*) or chemically (*etching*). The incised lines of the design take the ink, making this the reverse of the *woodcut* technique.

intensity—See *color.*

internal evidence—In art history, the examination of what an artwork represents (people, clothing, hairstyles, and so on) in order to determine its date. Also, the examination of the *style* of an artwork to identify the artist who created it.

International Style—A *style* of 14th- and 15th-century painting begun by Simone Martini, who adapted the French *Gothic* manner to Sienese art fused with influences from Northern Europe. This style appealed to the aristocracy because of its brilliant color, lavish costumes, intricate ornamentation, and themes involving splendid processions of knights and ladies. Also, a style of 20th-century architecture associated with Le Corbusier, whose elegance of design came to in-

fluence the look of modern office buildings and skyscrapers.

intonaco—In *fresco* painting, the last layer of smooth lime plaster applied to the wall; the painting layer.

invenzione—Italian, "invention." One of several terms used in Italian *Renaissance* literature to praise the originality and talent of artists.

Ionic—One of the two systems (or *orders*) invented in ancient Greece for articulating the three units of the elevation of a *classical* building: the platform, the *colonnade,* and the superstructure (*entablature*). The Ionic order is characterized by, among other features, *volutes, capitals, columns* with *bases,* and an uninterrupted *frieze.*

Japonisme—The French fascination with all things Japanese. Japonisme emerged in the second half of the 19th century.

Jugendstil—See *Art Nouveau.*

keystone—See *voussoir.*

lancet—In *Gothic* architecture, a tall narrow window ending in a *pointed arch.*

landscape—A picture showing natural scenery, without narrative content.

Landschaft—German, "landscape."

lateral section—See *section.*

line—The extension of a point along a path, made concrete in art by drawing on or chiseling into a *plane.*

linear perspective—See *perspective.*

lintel—A horizontal *beam* used to span an opening.

lithograph—See *lithography.*

lithography—A printmaking technique in which the artist uses an oil-based crayon to draw directly on a stone plate and then wipes water onto the stone. When ink is rolled onto the plate, it adheres only to the drawing. The print produced by this method is a lithograph.

local color—An object's true color in white light.

loggia—A gallery with an open *arcade* or a *colonnade* on one or both sides.

longitudinal plan—See *plan.*

lost-wax (cire perdue) process—A bronze-casting method in which a figure is modeled in wax and covered with clay; the whole is fired, melting away the wax (French, cire perdue) and hardening the clay, which then becomes a mold for molten metal.

low relief—See *relief.*

machicolated gallery—A gallery in a defensive tower with holes in the floor to allow stones or hot liquids to be dumped on enemies below.

magus (pl. **magi**)—One of the three wise men from the East who presented gifts to the infant Jesus.

maniera—Italian, "style" or "manner." See *Mannerism.*

maniera greca—Italian, "Greek manner." The Italo-Byzantine painting style of the 13th century.

Mannerism—A style of later *Renaissance* art that emphasized "artifice," often involving contrived imagery not derived directly from nature. Such artworks showed a self-conscious stylization involving complexity, caprice, fantasy, and polish. Mannerist architecture tended to flout the classical rules of order, stability, and symmetry, sometimes to the point of parody.

Mara—A spirit in Northern European mythology that was thought to torment and suffocate sleepers.

martyrium—A shrine to a Christian martyr *saint.*

mass—The bulk, density, and weight of matter in *space.*

Mass—The Catholic and Orthodox ritual in which believers understand that Christ's redeeming sacrifice on the cross is repeated when the priest consecrates the bread and wine in the *Eucharist.*

matins—The dawn prayer in a *Book of Hours*.

matte—In painting, pottery, and photography, a dull finish.

maulstick—A stick used to steady the hand while painting.

medium (pl. **media**)—The material (for example, marble, bronze, clay, *fresco*) in which an artist works; also, in painting, the vehicle (usually liquid) that carries the pigment.

memento mori—Latin, "reminder of death." In painting, a reminder of human mortality, usually represented by a skull.

mendicants—In medieval Europe, friars belonging to the Franciscan and Dominican orders, who renounced all worldly goods, lived by contributions of laypersons (the word *mendicant* means "beggar"), and devoted themselves to preaching, teaching, and doing good works.

metamatics—The name Swiss artist Jean Tinguely gave to the motor-driven devices he constructed to produce instant abstract paintings.

miniatures—Small individual Indian paintings intended to be held in the hand and viewed by one or two individuals at one time.

Minimalism—A predominantly sculptural American trend of the 1960s characterized by works featuring a severe reduction of form, often to single, homogeneous units.

mobile—A kind of sculpture, invented by Alexander Calder, combining nonobjective organic forms and motion in balanced structures hanging from rods, wires, and colored, organically shaped plates.

modeling—The shaping or fashioning of three-dimensional forms in a soft material, such as clay; also, the gradations of light and shade reflected from the surfaces of matter in space, or the illusion of such gradations produced by alterations of value in a drawing, painting, or print.

modernism—A movement in Western art that developed in the second half of the 19th century and sought to capture the images and sensibilities of the age. Modernist art goes beyond simply dealing with the present and involves the artist's critical examination of the premises of art itself.

Modernismo—See *Art Nouveau*.

modernist formalism—See *formalism*.

module (adj. **modular**)—A basic unit of which the dimensions of the major parts of a work are multiples. The principle is used in sculpture and other art forms, but it is most often employed in architecture, where the module may be the dimensions of an important part of a building, such as the diameter of a *column*.

mold—A hollow form for *casting*.

monastery—A group of buildings in which monks live together, set apart from the secular community of a town.

monastic order—An organization of monks living according to the same rules, for example, the Benedictine, Franciscan, and Dominican orders.

monochrome (adj. **monochromatic**)—One color.

mosaic—Patterns or pictures made by embedding small pieces (*tesserae*) of stone or glass in cement on surfaces such as walls and floors; also, the technique of making such works.

mullion—A vertical member that divides a window or that separates one window from another.

mural—A wall painting.

mystery play—A dramatic enactment of the holy mysteries of the Christian faith performed at church portals and in city squares.

mystic marriage—A spiritual marriage of a woman with Christ.

Nabis—Hebrew, "prophet." A group of *Symbolist* painters influenced by Paul Gauguin.

naturalism—The style of painted or sculptured representation based on close observation of the natural world that was at the core of the *classical* tradition.

Naturalistic Surrealism—See *Surrealism*.

nave—The central area of an ancient Roman *basilica* or of a church, demarcated from *aisles* by *piers* or *columns*.

nave arcade—In *basilica* architecture, the series of *arches* supported by *piers* or *columns* separating the *nave* from the *aisles*.

Neoclassicism—A style of art and architecture that emerged in the late 18th century as part of a general revival of interest in *classical* cultures. Neoclassical artists adopted themes and styles from ancient Greece and Rome.

Neo-Expressionism—An art movement that emerged in the 1970s and that reflects artists' interest in the expressive capability of art, seen earlier in *German Expressionism* and *Abstract Expressionism*.

Neo-Gothic—The revival of the *Gothic* style in architecture, especially in the 19th century.

Neoplasticism—The Dutch artist Piet Mondrian's theory of "pure plastic art," an ideal balance between the universal and the individual using an abstract formal vocabulary.

Neue Sachlichkeit—German, "new objectivity." An art movement that grew directly out of the World War I experiences of a group of German artists who sought to show the horrors of the war and its effects.

oculus (pl. **oculi**)—Latin, "eye." The round central opening of a *dome*. Also, a small round window in a *Gothic cathedral*.

odalisque—A woman in a Turkish harem.

ogee arch—An *arch* composed of two double-curving lines meeting at a point.

ogive (adj. **ogival**)—The diagonal *rib* of a *Gothic vault;* a pointed, or Gothic, *arch*.

oil painting—A painting technique using oil-based pigments that rose to prominence in Northern Europe in the 15th century and is now the standard medium for painting on canvas.

optical mixture—The visual effect of juxtaposed *complementary colors*.

orbiculum—A disklike opening.

order—In *classical* architecture, a style represented by a characteristic design of the *columns* and *entablature*. See also *superimposed orders*.

Orphism—A form of *Cubism* developed by the French painter Robert Delaunay in which color plays an important role.

orrery—A mechanical model of the solar system demonstrating how the planets revolve around the sun.

orthogonal—A line imagined to be behind and perpendicular to the picture plane; the orthogonals in a painting appear to recede toward a vanishing point on the horizon.

palette knife—A flat tool used to scrape paint off the *palette*. Artists sometimes also use the palette knife in place of a brush to apply paint directly to the canvas.

papier collé—French, "stuck paper." See *collage*.

parallel hatching—See *hatching*.

parapet—A low, protective wall along the edge of a balcony, roof, or bastion.

parchment—Lambskin prepared as a surface for painting or writing.

pastel—A powdery paste of pigment and gum used for making crayons; also, the pastel crayons themselves.

patron—The person or entity that pays an artist to produce individual artworks or employs an artist on a continuing basis.

pediment—In *classical* architecture, the triangular space (gable) at the end of a building, formed by the ends of the sloping roof above the *colonnade;* also, an ornamental feature having this shape.

pendentive—A concave, triangular section of a hemisphere, four of which provide the transition from a square area to the circular base of a covering *dome*. Although pendentives appear to be hanging (pendant) from the dome, they in fact support it.

Performance Art—An American avant-garde art trend of the 1960s that made time an integral element of art. It produced works in which movements, gestures, and sounds of persons communicating with an audience replace physical objects. Documentary photographs are generally the only evidence remaining after these events. See also *Happenings*.

period style—See *style*.

personal style—See *style*.

personification—An abstract idea represented in bodily form.

perspective (adj. **perspectival**)—A method of presenting an illusion of the three-dimensional world on a two-dimensional surface. In linear perspective, the most common type, all parallel lines or surface edges converge on one, two, or three vanishing points located with reference to the eye level of the viewer (the horizon line of the picture), and associated objects are rendered smaller the farther from the viewer they are intended to seem. Atmospheric, or aerial, perspective creates the illusion of distance by the greater diminution of color intensity, the shift in color toward an almost neutral blue, and the blurring of contours as the intended distance between eye and object increases.

philosophe—French, "thinker, philosopher." The term applied to French intellectuals of the Enlightenment.

photomontage—A composition made by pasting together pictures or parts of pictures, especially photographs. See also *collage*.

Photorealism—See *Superrealism*.

physical evidence—In art history, the examination of the materials used to produce an artwork in order to determine its date.

piazza—Italian, "plaza."

pier—A vertical, freestanding masonry support.

Pietà—A painted or sculpted representation of the Virgin Mary mourning over the body of the dead Christ.

pilaster—A flat, rectangular, vertical member projecting from a wall of which it forms a part. It usually has a *base* and a *capital* and is often *fluted*.

pinnacle—In *Gothic* churches, a sharply pointed ornament capping the *piers* or flying *buttresses;* also used on church *facades*.

Pittura Metafisica—Italian, "metaphysical painting." An early-20th-century Italian art movement led by Giorgio de Chirico, whose work conveys an eerie mood and visionary quality.

pixels—Shortened form of "picture elements." The tiny boxes that make up digital images displayed on a computer monitor.

plan—The horizontal arrangement of the parts of a building or of the buildings and streets of a city or town, or a drawing or diagram showing such an arrangement. In an axial plan, the parts of a building are organized longitudinally, or along a given axis; in a central plan, the parts of the structure are of equal or almost equal dimensions around the center.

plane—A flat surface.

Plateresque—A style of Spanish architecture characterized by elaborate decoration based on *Gothic*, Italian *Renaissance*, and Islamic sources; derived from the Spanish word *platero*, meaning "silversmith."

platero—See *Plateresque*.

plein air—An approach to painting much popular among the *Impressionists*, in which an artist sketches outdoors to achieve a quick impression of light, air, and color. The artist then takes the sketches to the studio for reworking into more finished works of art.

poesia—A term describing "poetic" art, notably Venetian *Renaissance* painting, which emphasizes the lyrical and sensual.

pointed arch—A narrow *arch* of pointed profile, in contrast to a semicircular arch.

pointillism—A system of painting devised by the 19th-century French painter Georges Seurat. The artist separates color into its component parts and then applies the component colors to the canvas in tiny dots (points). The image becomes comprehensible only from a distance, when the viewer's eyes optically blend the pigment dots. Sometimes referred to as divisionism.

polyptych—An *altarpiece* composed of more than three sections.

Pop Art—A term coined by British art critic Lawrence Alloway to refer to art, first appearing in the 1950s, that incorporated elements from consumer culture, the mass media, and popular culture, such as images from motion pictures and advertising.

portico—A roofed *colonnade;* also an entrance porch.

positivism—A Western philosophical model that promoted science as the mind's highest achievement.

Post-Impressionism—The term used to describe the stylistically heterogeneous work of the group of late-19th-century painters in France, including van Gogh, Gauguin, Seurat, and Cézanne, who more systematically examined the properties and expressive qualities of line, pattern, form, and color than the Impressionists did.

postmodernism—A reaction against *modernist formalism,* seen as elitist. Far more encompassing and accepting than the more rigid confines of modernist practice, postmodernism offers something for everyone by accommodating a wide range of *styles,* subjects, and formats, from traditional easel painting to *installation* and from abstraction to *illusionistic* scenes. Postmodern art often includes irony or reveals a self-conscious awareness on the part of the artist of art-making processes or the workings of the art world.

Post-Painterly Abstraction—An American art movement that emerged in the 1960s and was characterized by a cool, detached rationality emphasizing tighter pictorial control. See also *color-field painting* and *hard-edge painting*.

Poussiniste—A member of the French Royal Academy of Painting and Sculpture during the early 18th century who followed Nicolas Poussin in insisting that *form* was the most important element of painting. See also *Rubéniste*.

Precisionism—An American art movement of the 1920s and 1930s. The Precisionists concentrated on portraying man-made environments in a clear and concise manner to express the beauty of perfect and precise machine forms.

predella—The narrow ledge on which an *altarpiece* rests on an altar.

primary colors—Red, yellow, and blue—the *colors* from which all other colors may be derived.

primitivism—The incorporation in early-20th-century Western art of stylistic elements from the artifacts of Africa, Oceania, and the native peoples of the Americas.

print—An artwork on paper, usually produced in multiple impressions.

Productivism—An art movement that emerged in the Soviet Union after the Russian Revolution; its members believed that artists must direct art toward creating products for the new society.

proportion—The relationship in size of the parts of persons, buildings, or objects, often based on a *module*.

provenance—Origin or source; findspot.

psalter—A book containing the Psalms.

pulpit—A raised platform in a church on which a priest stands while leading the religious service.

punchwork—Tooled decorative work in *gold leaf*.

Purism—An early-20th-century art movement that embraced the "machine aesthetic" and sought purity of *form* in the clean functional lines of industrial machinery.

putto (pl. **putti**)—A cherubic young boy.

quadro riportato—A ceiling design in which painted scenes are arranged in panels that resemble framed pictures transferred to the surface of a shallow, curved *vault*.

quatrefoil—A shape or plan in which the parts assume the form of a cloverleaf.

quoins—The large, sometimes *rusticated,* usually slightly projecting stones that often form the corners of the exterior walls of masonry buildings.

Realism—A movement that emerged in mid-19th-century France. Realist artists represented the subject matter of everyday life (especially subjects that previously had been considered inappropriate for depiction) in a relatively naturalistic mode.

refectory—The dining hall of a Christian *monastery*.

regional style—See *style*.

Regionalism—A 20th-century American art movement that portrayed American rural life in a clearly readable, realist style. Major Regionalists include Grant Wood and Thomas Hart Benton.

register—One of a series of superimposed bands or *friezes* in a pictorial narrative, or the particular levels on which motifs are placed.

relief—In sculpture, figures projecting from a background of which they are part. The degree of relief is designated high, low (bas), or sunken. In the last, the artist cuts the design into the surface so that the highest projecting parts of the image are no higher than the surface itself. See also *repoussé*.

Renaissance—French, "rebirth." The term used to describe the history, culture, and art of 14th- through 16th-century western Europe during which artists consciously revived the *classical* style.

renovatio—Latin, "renewal." During the *Carolingian* period, Charlemagne sought to revive the culture of ancient Rome (renovatio imperi Romani).

retable—An architectural screen or wall above and behind an altar, usually containing painting, sculpture, carving, or other decorations. See also *altarpiece*.

revetment—In architecture, a wall covering or facing.

rib—A relatively slender, molded masonry *arch* that projects from a surface. In *Gothic* architecture, the ribs form the framework of the *vaulting*. A diagonal rib is one of the ribs that form the X of a *groin vault*. A transverse rib crosses the *nave* or *aisle* at a 90-degree angle.

rib vault—A *vault* in which the diagonal and transverse *ribs* compose a structural skeleton that partially supports the masonry *web* between them.

rocaille—See *Rococo*.

Rococo—A style, primarily of interior design, that appeared in France around 1700. Rococo interiors featured lavish decoration, including small sculptures, ornamental mirrors, easel paintings, *tapestries, reliefs,* wall paintings, and elegant furniture. The term Rococo derived from the French word *rocaille* ("pebble") and referred to the small stones and shells used to decorate grotto interiors.

Romanesque—"Roman-like." A term used to describe the history, culture, and art of medieval western Europe from ca. 1050 to ca. 1200.

Romanticism—A Western cultural phenomenon, beginning around 1750 and ending about 1850, that gave precedence to feeling and imagination over reason and thought. More narrowly, the art movement that flourished from about 1800 to 1840.

rose window—A circular *stained-glass* window.

rostrum—Speaker's platform.

rotunda—The circular area under a *dome;* also a domed round building.

roundel—See *tondo*.

Rubéniste—A member of the French Royal Academy of Painting and Sculpture during the early 18th century who followed Peter Paul Rubens in insisting that *color* was the most important element of painting. See also *Poussiniste*.

rusticate (n. **rustication**)—To give a rustic appearance by roughening the surfaces and beveling the edges of stone blocks to emphasize the joints between them. Rustication is a technique employed in ancient Roman architecture, and was also popular during the *Renaissance,* especially for stone *courses* at the ground-floor level.

sacra conversazione—Italian, "holy conversation." A style of *altarpiece* painting popular after the middle of the 15th century, in which *saints* from different epochs are joined in a unified space and seem to be conversing either with one another or with the audience.

sacra rappresentazione (pl. **sacre rappresentazioni**)—Italian, "holy representation." A more elaborate version of a *mystery play* performed for a lay audience by a *confraternity*.

saint—From the Latin word *sanctus,* meaning "made holy by God." Applied to persons who suffered and died for their Christian faith or who merited reverence for their Christian devotion while alive. In the Roman Catholic Church, a worthy deceased Catholic who is canonized by the pope.

Saint-Simonianism—An early-19th-century utopian movement that emphasized the education and enfranchisement of women.

sarcophagus (pl. **sarcophagi**)—Latin, "consumer of flesh." A coffin, usually of stone.

saturation—See *color*.

satyr—A Greek mythological follower of Dionysos having a man's upper body, a goat's hindquarters and horns, and a horse's ears and tail.

school—A chronological and stylistic classification of works of art with a stipulation of place.

scudi—Italian, "shields." A coin denomination in 17th-century Italy.

sculpture in the round—Freestanding figures, carved or modeled in three dimensions.

secondary colors—Orange, green, and purple, obtained by mixing pairs of *primary colors* (red, yellow, blue).

section—In architecture, a diagram or representation of a part of a structure or building along an imaginary plane that passes through it vertically. Drawings showing a theoretical slice across a structure's width are lateral sections. Those cutting through a building's length are longitudinal sections. See also *elevation* and *cutaway.*

sfumato—Italian, "smoky." A smokelike haziness that subtly softens outlines in painting; particularly applied to the paintings of Leonardo da Vinci and Correggio.

shaft—The tall, cylindrical part of a *column* between the *capital* and the *base.*

sibyl—A Greco-Roman mythological prophetess.

signoria—The governing body in the Republic of Florence.

silk-screen printing—An industrial printing *technique* that creates a sharp-edged image by pressing ink through a design on silk or a similar tightly woven porous fabric stretched tight on a frame.

silverpoint—A *stylus* made of silver, used in drawing in the 14th and 15th centuries because of the fine line it produced and the sharp point it maintained.

simultaneous contrasts—The phenomenon of juxtaposed colors affecting the eye's reception of each, as when a painter places dark green next to light green, making the former appear even darker and the latter even lighter. See also *successive contrasts.*

sinopia—A burnt-orange pigment used in *fresco* painting to transfer a *cartoon* to the *arriccio* before the artist paints the plaster.

site-specific art—Art created for a specific location. See also *Environmental Art.*

space—In art history, both the actual area an object occupies or a building encloses, and the *illusionistic* representation of space in painting and sculpture.

spectrum—The range or band of visible colors in natural light.

stained glass—In *Gothic* architecture, the colored glass used for windows.

stanza (pl. **stanze**)—Italian, "room."

statue—A three-dimensional sculpture.

stigmata—In Christian art, the wounds Christ received at his crucifixion that miraculously appear on the body of a *saint.*

still life—A picture depicting an arrangement of inanimate objects.

stretcher bar—One of a set of wooden bars used to stretch canvas to provide a taut surface for painting.

stringcourse—A raised horizontal *molding,* or band, in masonry. Its principal use is ornamental but it usually reflects interior structure.

style—A distinctive artistic manner. Period style is the characteristic style of a specific time. Regional style is the style of a particular geographical area. Personal style is an individual artist's unique manner.

stylistic evidence—In art history, the examination of the *style* of an artwork in order to determine its date or the identity of the artist.

stylobate—The uppermost course of the platform of a *classical* Greek temple, which supports the *columns.*

stylus—A needlelike tool used in *engraving* and *incising;* also, an ancient writing instrument used to inscribe clay or wax tablets.

subtractive light—The painter's light in art; the light reflected from pigments and objects. See also *additive light.*

subtractive sculpture—A kind of sculpture technique in which materials are taken away from the original mass; carving.

successive contrasts—The phenomenon of colored afterimages. When a person looks intently at a *color* (green, for example) and then shifts to a white area, the fatigued eye momentarily perceives the *complementary color* (red). See also *simultaneous contrasts.*

superimposed orders—*Orders* of architecture that are placed one above another in an *arcaded* or *colonnaded* building, usually in the following sequence: *Doric* (the first story), *Ionic,* and *Corinthian.* Superimposed orders are found in later Greek architecture and were used widely by Roman and *Renaissance* builders.

Superrealism—A *school* of painting and sculpture of the 1960s and 1970s that emphasized producing artworks based on scrupulous fidelity to optical fact. The Superrealist painters were also called Photorealists because many used photographs as sources for their imagery.

Suprematism—A type of art formulated by Kazimir Malevich to convey his belief that the supreme reality in the world is pure feeling, which attaches to no object and thus calls for new, nonobjective forms in art—shapes not related to objects in the visible world.

Surrealism—A successor to *Dada,* Surrealism incorporated the improvisational nature of its predecessor into its exploration of the ways to express in art the world of dreams and the unconscious. Biomorphic Surrealists, such as Joan Miró, produced largely abstract compositions. Naturalistic Surrealists, notably Salvador Dalí, presented recognizable scenes transformed into a dream or nightmare image.

symbol—An image that stands for another image or encapsulates an idea.

Symbolism—A late-19th-century movement based on the idea that the artist was not an imitator of nature but a creator who transformed the facts of nature into a symbol of the inner experience of that fact.

Synthetic Cubism—A later phase of *Cubism,* in which paintings and drawings were constructed from objects and shapes cut from paper or other materials to represent parts of a subject, in order to engage the viewer with pictorial issues, such as figuration, realism, and abstraction.

tapestry—A weaving technique in which the *weft* threads are packed densely over the *warp* threads so that the designs are woven directly into the fabric.

technique—The processes artists employ to create *form,* as well as the distinctive, personal ways in which they handle their materials and tools.

tempera—A *technique* of painting using pigment mixed with egg yolk, glue, or casein; also, the *medium* itself.

tenebrism—Painting in the "shadowy manner," using violent contrasts of light and dark, as in the work of Caravaggio. The term derives from *tenebroso.*

tenebroso—Italian, "shadowy." See *tenebrism.*

terracotta—Hard-baked clay, used for sculpture and as a building material. It may be *glazed* or painted.

tessera (pl. **tesserae**)—Greek, "cube." A tiny stone or piece of glass cut to the desired shape and size for use in forming a *mosaic.*

texture—The quality of a surface (rough, smooth, hard, soft, shiny, dull) as revealed by light. In represented texture, a painter depicts an object as having a certain texture even though the paint is the actual texture.

tholos (pl. **tholoi**)—A temple with a circular plan. Also, the burial chamber of a *tholos tomb.*

thrust—The outward force exerted by an *arch* or a *vault* that must be counterbalanced by a *buttress.*

tonality— See *color.*

tondo (pl. **tondi**)—A circular painting or *relief* sculpture.

tracery—Ornamental stonework for holding *stained glass* in place, characteristic of *Gothic* cathedrals. In plate tracery, the glass fills only the "punched holes" in the heavy ornamental stonework. In bar tracery, the stained-glass windows fill almost the entire opening, and the stonework is unobtrusive.

tramezzo—A screen placed across the *nave* of a church to separate the clergy from the lay audience.

transept—The part of a church with an axis that crosses the *nave* at a right angle.

transubstantiation—The transformation of the Eucharistic bread and wine into the body and blood of Christ.

trefoil—A cloverlike ornament or symbol with stylized leaves in groups of three.

triglyph—A triple projecting, grooved member of a *Doric frieze* that alternates with *metopes.*

triptych—A three-paneled painting, ivory plaque, or *altarpiece.* Also, a small, portable shrine with hinged wings used for private devotion.

triumphal arch—In Roman architecture, a freestanding *arch* commemorating an important event, such as a military victory or the opening of a new road.

trompe l'oeil—French, "fools the eye." A form of *illusionistic* painting that aims to deceive viewers into believing they are seeing real objects rather than a representation of those objects.

Tuscan column—The standard type of Etruscan *column.* It resembles ancient Greek *Doric* columns but is made of wood, is unfluted, and has a *base.* Also a popular motif in *Renaissance* and *Baroque* architecture.

tympanum (pl. **tympana**)—The space enclosed by a *lintel* and an *arch* over a doorway.

value—See *color.*

vanishing point—See *perspective.*

vanitas—Latin, "vanity." A term describing paintings (particularly 17th-century Dutch still lifes) that include references to death.

vault (adj. **vaulted**)—A masonry roof or ceiling constructed on the *arch* principle, or a concrete roof of the same shape. A barrel (or tunnel) vault, semicylindrical in cross-*section,* is in effect a deep arch or an uninterrupted series of arches, one behind the other, over an oblong space. A quadrant vault is a half-barrel vault. A groin (or cross) vault is formed at the point at which two barrel vaults intersect at right angles. In a ribbed vault, there is a framework of *ribs* or arches under the intersections of the vaulting sections. A sexpartite vault is one whose ribs divide the vault into six compartments. A fan vault is a vault characteristic of English *Perpendicular Gothic* architecture, in which radiating ribs form a fanlike pattern.

veduta (pl. **vedute**)—Italian, "scenic view."

vellum—Calfskin prepared as a surface for writing or painting.

vita—Italian, "life." Also, the title of a biography.

volume—The *space* that *mass* organizes, divides, or encloses.

volute—A spiral, scroll-like form characteristic of the ancient Greek *Ionic* and the Roman *Composite capital.*

voussoir—A wedge-shaped stone block used in the construction of a true *arch.* The central voussoir, which sets the arch, is called the keystone.

wainscoting—Paneling on the lower part of interior walls.

warp—The vertical threads of a loom or cloth.

weft—The horizontal threads of a loom or cloth.

weld—To join metal parts by heating, as in assembling the separate parts of a *statue* made by *casting*.

wet-plate photography—An early photographic process in which the photographic plate is exposed, developed, and fixed while wet.

woodcut—A wooden block on the surface of which those parts not intended to *print* are cut away to a slight depth, leaving the design raised; also, the printed impression made with such a block.

zoopraxiscope—A device invented by Eadweard Muybridge in the 19th century to project sequences of still photographic images; a predecessor of the modern motion-picture projector.

BIBLIOGRAPHY

This list of books is very selective but comprehensive enough to satisfy the reading interests of the beginning art history student and general reader. The resources listed range from works that are valuable primarily for their reproductions to those that are scholarly surveys of schools and periods or monographs on individual artists. The emphasis is on recent in-print books and on books likely to be found in college and municipal libraries. No entries for periodical articles appear, but the bibliography begins with a list of some of the major journals that publish art historical scholarship in English.

SELECTED PERIODICALS

African Arts
American Art
American Indian Art
American Journal of Archaeology
Antiquity
Archaeology
Archives of American Art
Archives of Asian Art
Ars Orientalis
Art Bulletin
Art History
Art in America
Art Journal
Artforum International
Burlington Magazine
Gesta
History of Photography
Journal of Roman Archaeology
Journal of the Society of Architectural Historians
Journal of the Warburg and Courtauld Institutes
Latin American Antiquity
Oxford Art Journal
Women's Art Journal

GENERAL STUDIES

Baxandall, Michael. *Patterns of Intention: On the Historical Explanation of Pictures.* New Haven, Conn.: Yale University Press, 1985.

Bindman, David, ed. *The Thames & Hudson Encyclopedia of British Art.* London: Thames & Hudson, 1988.

Boström, Antonia. *The Encyclopedia of Sculpture.* 3 vols. London: Routledge, 2003.

Broude, Norma, and Mary D. Garrard, eds. *The Expanding Discourse: Feminism and Art History.* New York: Harper Collins, 1992.

Bryson, Norman. *Vision and Painting: The Logic of the Gaze.* New Haven, Conn.: Yale University Press, 1983.

Bryson, Norman, Michael Ann Holly, and Keith Moxey. *Visual Theory: Painting and Interpretation.* New York: Cambridge University Press, 1991.

Büttner, Nils. *Landscape Painting: A History.* New York: Abbeville, 2006.

Chadwick, Whitney. *Women, Art, and Society.* 4th ed. New York: Thames & Hudson, 2007.

Cheetham, Mark A., Michael Ann Holly, and Keith Moxey, eds. *The Subjects of Art History: Historical Objects in Contemporary Perspective.* New York: Cambridge University Press, 1998.

Chilvers, Ian, and Harold Osborne, eds. *The Oxford Dictionary of Art.* 3d ed. New York: Oxford University Press, 2004.

Corbin, George A. *Native Arts of North America, Africa, and the South Pacific: An Introduction.* New York: Harper Collins, 1988.

Crouch, Dora P., and June G. Johnson. *Traditions in Architecture: Africa, America, Asia, and Oceania.* New York: Oxford University Press, 2000.

Curl, James Stevens. *Oxford Dictionary of Architecture and Landscape Architecture.* 2d ed. New York: Oxford University Press, 2006.

Encyclopedia of World Art. 17 vols. New York: McGraw-Hill, 1959–1987.

Fielding, Mantle. *Dictionary of American Painters, Sculptors, and Engravers.* 2d ed. Poughkeepsie, N.Y.: Apollo, 1986.

Fine, Sylvia Honig. *Women and Art: A History of Women Painters and Sculptors from the Renaissance to the 20th Century.* Rev. ed. Montclair, N.J.: Alanheld & Schram, 1978.

Fleming, John, Hugh Honour, and Nikolaus Pevsner. *The Penguin Dictionary of Architecture and Landscape Architecture.* 5th ed. New York: Penguin, 2000.

Frazier, Nancy. *The Penguin Concise Dictionary of Art History.* New York: Penguin, 2000.

Freedberg, David. *The Power of Images: Studies in the History and Theory of Response.* Chicago: University of Chicago Press, 1989.

Gaze, Delia., ed. *Dictionary of Women Artists.* 2 vols. London: Routledge, 1997.

Hall, James. *Illustrated Dictionary of Subjects and Symbols in Eastern and Western Art.* New York: Icon Editions, 1994.

Harris, Anne Sutherland, and Linda Nochlin. *Women Artists: 1550–1950.* Los Angeles: Los Angeles County Museum of Art; New York: Knopf, 1977.

Hauser, Arnold. *The Sociology of Art.* Chicago: University of Chicago Press, 1982.

Hults, Linda C. *The Print in the Western World: An Introductory History.* Madison: University of Wisconsin Press, 1996.

Kemp, Martin. *The Science of Art: Optical Themes in Western Art from Brunelleschi to Seurat.* New Haven, Conn.: Yale University Press, 1990.

Kostof, Spiro, and Gregory Castillo. *A History of Architecture: Settings and Rituals.* 2d ed. Oxford: Oxford University Press, 1995.

Kultermann, Udo. *The History of Art History.* New York: Abaris, 1993.

Lucie-Smith, Edward. *The Thames & Hudson Dictionary of Art Terms.* 2d ed. New York: Thames & Hudson, 2004.

Moffett, Marian, Michael Fazio, and Lawrence Wadehouse. *A World History of Architecture.* Boston: McGraw-Hill, 2004.

Murray, Peter, and Linda Murray. *A Dictionary of Art and Artists.* 7th ed. New York: Penguin, 1998.

Nelson, Robert S., and Richard Shiff, eds. *Critical Terms for Art History.* Chicago: University of Chicago Press, 1996.

Penny, Nicholas. *The Materials of Sculpture.* New Haven, Conn.: Yale University Press, 1993.

Pevsner, Nikolaus. *A History of Building Types.* London: Thames & Hudson, 1987. Reprint of 1979 ed.

———. *An Outline of European Architecture.* 8th ed. Baltimore: Penguin, 1974.

Pierce, James Smith. *From Abacus to Zeus: A Handbook of Art History.* 7th ed. Upper Saddle River, N.J.: Pearson Prentice Hall, 1998.

Placzek, Adolf K., ed. *Macmillan Encyclopedia of Architects.* 4 vols. New York: Macmillan, 1982.

Podro, Michael. *The Critical Historians of Art.* New Haven, Conn.: Yale University Press, 1982.

Pollock, Griselda. *Vision and Difference: Femininity, Feminism, and Histories of Art.* London: Routledge, 1988.

Preziosi, Donald, ed. *The Art of Art History: A Critical Anthology.* New York: Oxford University Press, 1998.

Read, Herbert. *The Thames & Hudson Dictionary of Art and Artists.* Rev. ed. New York: Thames & Hudson, 1994.

Reid, Jane D. *The Oxford Guide to Classical Mythology in the Arts 1300–1990s.* 2 vols. New York: Oxford University Press, 1993.

Roth, Leland M. *Understanding Architecture: Its Elements, History, and Meaning.* 2d ed. Boulder, Colo.: Westview, 2006.

Schama, Simon. *The Power of Art*. New York: Ecco, 2006.

Slatkin, Wendy. *Women Artists in History: From Antiquity to the 20th Century*. 4th ed. Upper Saddle River, N.J.: Prentice Hall, 2000.

Steer, John, and Antony White. *Atlas of Western Art History: Artists, Sites, and Monuments from Ancient Greece to the Modern Age*. New York: Facts on File, 1994.

Stratton, Arthur. *The Orders of Architecture: Greek, Roman, and Renaissance*. London: Studio, 1986.

Sutton, Ian. *Western Architecture: From Ancient Greece to the Present*. New York: Thames & Hudson, 1999.

Trachtenberg, Marvin, and Isabelle Hyman. *Architecture, from Prehistory to Post-Modernism*. 2d ed. Upper Saddle River, N.J.: Prentice Hall, 2003.

Turner, Jane, ed. *The Dictionary of Art*. 34 vols. New ed. New York: Oxford University Press, 2003.

Wittkower, Rudolf. *Sculpture Processes and Principles*. New York: Harper & Row, 1977.

Wren, Linnea H., and Janine M. Carter, eds. *Perspectives on Western Art: Source Documents and Readings from the Ancient Near East through the Middle Ages*. New York: Harper & Row, 1987.

RENAISSANCE ART, GENERAL

Adams, Laurie Schneider. *Italian Renaissance Art*. Boulder, Colo.: Westview, 2001.

Andrés, Glenn M., John M. Hunisak, and Richard Turner. *The Art of Florence*. 2 vols. New York: Abbeville, 1988.

Campbell, Gordon. *Renaissance Art and Architecture*. New York: Oxford University Press, 2005.

Campbell, Lorne. *Renaissance Portraits: European Portrait-Painting in the Fourteenth, Fifteenth, and Sixteenth Centuries*. New Haven, Conn.: Yale University Press, 1990.

Cole, Bruce. *Italian Art, 1250–1550: The Relation of Renaissance Art to Life and Society*. New York: Harper & Row, 1987.

———. *The Renaissance Artist at Work: From Pisano to Titian*. New York: Harper Collins, 1983.

Frommel, Christoph Luitpold. *The Architecture of the Italian Renaissance*. London: Thames & Hudson, 2007.

Hall, Marcia B. *Color and Meaning: Practice and Theory in Renaissance Painting*. Cambridge: Cambridge University Press, 1992.

Hartt, Frederick, and David G. Wilkins. *History of Italian Renaissance Art*. 6th ed. Upper Saddle River, N.J.: Prentice Hall, 2006.

Haskell, Francis, and Nicholas Penny. *Taste and the Antique: The Lure of Classical Sculpture 1500–1900*. New Haven, Conn.: Yale University Press, 1981.

Kent, F. W., and Patricia Simons, eds. *Patronage, Art, and Society in Renaissance Italy*. Canberra: Humanities Research Centre and Clarendon Press, 1987.

Levey, Michael. *Florence: A Portrait*. Cambridge, Mass.: Harvard University Press, 1998.

Lubbock, Jules. *Storytelling in Christian Art from Giotto to Donatello*. New Haven, Conn.: Yale University Press, 2006.

Paoletti, John T., and Gary M. Radke. *Art, Power, and Patronage in Renaissance Italy*. Upper Saddle River, N.J.: Prentice Hall, 2005.

Pope-Hennessy, John. *Introduction to Italian Sculpture*. 3d ed. 3 vols. New York: Phaidon, 1986.

Richardson, Carol M., Kim W. Woods, and Michael W. Franklin. *Renaissance Art Reconsidered: An Anthology of Primary Sources*. Oxford: Blackwell, 2007.

Smith, Jeffrey Chipps. *The Northern Renaissance*. New York: Phaidon, 2004.

Snyder, James, Larry Silver, and Henry Luttikhuizen. *Northern Renaissance Art: Painting, Sculpture, the Graphic Arts from 1350 to 1575*. Upper Saddle River, N.J.: Prentice Hall, 2005.

Thomson, David. *Renaissance Architecture: Critics, Patrons, and Luxury*. Manchester: Manchester University Press, 1993.

Wittkower, Rudolf. *Architectural Principles in the Age of Humanism*. 4th ed. London: Academy, 1988.

CHAPTER 21:
EUROPE AND AMERICA, 1700 TO 1800

Bermingham, Ann. *Landscape and Ideology: The English Rustic Tradition, 1740–1850*. Berkeley: University of California Press, 1986.

Boime, Albert. *Art in the Age of Revolution, 1750–1800*. Chicago: University of Chicago Press, 1987.

Braham, Allan. *The Architecture of the French Enlightenment*. Berkeley: University of California Press, 1980.

Brion, Marcel. *Art of the Romantic Era: Romanticism, Classicism, Realism*. New York: Praeger, 1966.

Conisbee, Philip. *Painting in Eighteenth-Century France*. Ithaca, N.Y.: Phaidon/Cornell University Press, 1981.

Crow, Thomas E. *Painters and Public Life in Eighteenth-Century Paris*. New Haven, Conn.: Yale University Press, 1985.

Gaunt, W. *The Great Century of British Painting: Hogarth to Turner*. New York: Phaidon, 1971.

Harrison, Charles, Paul Wood, and Jason Gaiger, eds. *Art in Theory, 1648–1815: An Anthology of Changing Ideas*. Oxford: Blackwell, 2000.

Herrmann, Luke. *British Landscape Painting of the Eighteenth Century*. New York: Oxford University Press, 1974.

Honour, Hugh. *Neo-Classicism*. Harmondsworth: Penguin, 1968.

Irwin, David. *Neoclassicism*. London: Phaidon, 1997.

Kalnein, Wend Graf, and Michael Levey. *Art and Architecture of the Eighteenth Century in France*. New York: Viking/Pelican, 1973.

Lee, Simon. *David*. London: Phaidon, 1999.

Levey, Michael. *Rococo to Revolution: Major Trends in Eighteenth-Century Painting*. London: Thames & Hudson, 1966.

Rosenblum, Robert. *Transformations in Late Eighteenth-Century Art*. Princeton, N.J.: Princeton University Press, 1970.

Roston, Murray. *Changing Perspectives in Literature and the Visual Arts, 1650–1820*. Princeton, N.J.: Princeton University Press, 1990.

Rykwert, Joseph. *The First Moderns: Architects of the Eighteenth Century*. Cambridge, Mass.: MIT Press, 1983.

Stillman, Damie. *English Neo-Classical Architecture*. 2 vols. London: Zwemmer, 1988.

Waterhouse, Ellis Kirkham. *Painting in Britain: 1530–1790*. 4th ed. New Haven, Conn.: Yale University Press, 1979.

Wilton, Andrew. *The Swagger Portrait: Grand Manner Portraiture in Britain from Van Dyck to Augustus John, 1630–1930*. London: Tate Gallery, 1992.

19TH AND 20TH CENTURIES, GENERAL

Arnason, H. H., and Peter Kalb. *History of Modern Art: Painting, Sculpture, Architecture, Photography*. 5th ed. Upper Saddle River, N.J.: Prentice Hall, 2004.

Ashton, Dore. *Twentieth-Century Artists on Art*. New York: Pantheon Books, 1985.

Brown, Milton, Sam Hunter, and John Jacobus. *American Art: Painting, Sculpture, Architecture, Decorative Arts, Photography*. New York: Abrams, 1979.

Burnham, Jack. *Beyond Modern Sculpture: The Effects of Science and Technology on the Sculpture of This Century*. New York: Braziller, 1968.

Chipp, Herschel B. *Theories of Modern Art*. Berkeley: University of California Press, 1968.

Chu, Petra ten-Doesschate. *Nineteenth-Century European Art*. 2d ed. Upper Saddle River, N.J.: Prentice Hall, 2006.

Coke, Van Deren. *The Painter and the Photograph from Delacroix to Warhol*. Rev. ed. Albuquerque: University of New Mexico Press, 1972.

Colquhoun, Alan. *Modern Architecture*. New York: Oxford University Press, 2002.

Craven, Wayne. *American Art: History and Culture*. Madison, Wis.: Brown & Benchmark, 1994.

Doss, Erika. *Twentieth-Century American Art*. New York: Oxford University Press, 2002.

Driskell, David C. *Two Centuries of Black American Art*. Los Angeles: Los Angeles County Museum of Art; New York: Knopf, 1976.

Eisenman, Stephen F., ed. *Nineteenth-Century Art: A Critical History*. 3d ed. New York: Thames & Hudson, 2007.

Elsen, Albert. *Origins of Modern Sculpture*. New York: Braziller, 1974.

Foster, Hal, Rosalind Krauss, Yve-Alain Bois, and Benjamin H. D. Buchloh. *Art since 1900: Modernism, Antimodernism, Postmodernism*. New York: Thames & Hudson, 2004.

Frampton, Kenneth. *Modern Architecture: A Critical History*. 3d ed. London: Thames & Hudson, 1992.

Frascina, Francis, and Charles Harrison, eds. *Modern Art and Modernism: A Critical Anthology*. New York: Harper & Row, 1982.

Giedion, Siegfried. *Space, Time, and Architecture: The Growth of a New Tradition*. 4th ed. Cambridge, Mass.: Harvard University Press, 1965.

Goldwater, Robert, and Marco Treves, eds. *Artists on Art*. 3d ed. New York: Pantheon, 1958.

Greenough, Sarah, Joel Snyder, David Travis, and Colin Westerbeck. *On the Art of Fixing a Shadow: One Hundred and Fifty Years of Photography*. Washington, D.C.: National Gallery of Art; Chicago: Art Institute of Chicago, 1989.

Hamilton, George H. *Painting and Sculpture in Europe, 1880–1940*. 6th ed. New Haven, Conn.: Yale University Press, 1993.

Harrison, Charles, and Paul Wood. *Art in Theory, 1900–2000: An Anthology of Changing Ideas*. Oxford: Blackwell, 2003.

Herbert, Robert L., ed. *Modern Artists on Art*. Upper Saddle River, N.J.: Prentice Hall, 1971.

Hertz, Richard, and Norman M. Klein, eds. *Twentieth-Century Art Theory: Urbanism, Politics, and Mass Culture*. Englewood Cliffs, N.J.: Prentice Hall, 1990.

Heyer, Paul. *Architects on Architecture: New Directions in America*. New York: Van Nostrand Reinhold, 1993.

Hills, Patricia. *Modern Art in the USA: Issues and Controversies of the 20th Century*. Upper Saddle River, N.J.: Prentice Hall, 2000.

Hitchcock, Henry-Russell. *Architecture: Nineteenth and Twentieth Centuries*. 4th ed. New Haven, Conn.: Yale University Press, 1977.

Hunter, Sam, John Jacobus, and Daniel Wheeler. *Modern Art: Painting, Sculpture, Architecture, Photography.* Rev. 3d ed. Upper Saddle River, N.J.: Prentice Hall, 2004.

Jencks, Charles. *Modern Movements in Architecture.* Garden City, N.Y.: Anchor; Doubleday, 1973.

Kaufmann, Edgar, Jr., ed. *The Rise of an American Architecture.* New York: Metropolitan Museum of Art; Praeger, 1970.

Krauss, Rosalind E. *The Originality of the Avant-Garde and Other Modernist Myths.* Cambridge, Mass.: MIT Press, 1985.

———. *Passages in Modern Sculpture.* Cambridge, Mass.: MIT Press, 1981.

Lewis, Samella S. *African American Art and Artists.* Rev. ed. Berkeley: University of California Press, 1994.

Licht, Fred. *Sculpture, Nineteenth and Twentieth Centuries.* Greenwich, Conn.: New York Graphic Society, 1967.

Marien, Mary Warner. *Photography: A Cultural History.* 2d ed. Upper Saddle River, N.J.: Prentice Hall, 2006.

Mason, Jerry, ed. *International Center of Photography Encyclopedia of Photography.* New York: Crown, 1984.

McCoubrey, John W. *American Art, 1700–1960: Sources and Documents.* Englewood Cliffs, N.J.: Prentice Hall, 1965.

Newhall, Beaumont. *The History of Photography.* New York: Museum of Modern Art, 1982.

Osborne, Harold. *The Oxford Companion to Twentieth-Century Art.* New York: Oxford University Press, 1981.

Pohl, Francis K. *Framing America: A Social History of American Art.* New York: Thames & Hudson, 2002.

Rose, Barbara. *American Art since 1900.* Rev. ed. New York: Praeger, 1975.

Rosenblum, Naomi. *A World History of Photography.* 3d ed. New York: Abbeville, 1997.

Rosenblum, Robert. *Modern Painting and the Northern Romantic Tradition: Friedrich to Rothko.* New York: Harper & Row, 1975.

Rosenblum, Robert, and Horst W. Janson. *19th-Century Art.* Rev. ed. Upper Saddle River, N.J.: Prentice Hall, 2005.

Ross, Stephen David, ed. *Art and Its Significance: An Anthology of Aesthetic Theory.* Albany: State University of New York Press, 1987.

Russell, John. *The Meanings of Modern Art.* New York: Museum of Modern Art; Thames & Hudson, 1981.

Scully, Vincent. *Modern Architecture.* Rev. ed. New York: Braziller, 1974.

Spalding, Francis. *British Art since 1900.* London: Thames & Hudson, 1986.

Spencer, Harold. *American Art: Readings from the Colonial Era to the Present.* New York: Scribner, 1980.

Steinberg, Leo. *Other Criteria: Confrontations with 20th-Century Art.* New York: Oxford University Press, 1972.

Szarkowski, John. *Photography until Now.* New York: Museum of Modern Art, 1989.

Upton, Dell. *Architecture in the United States.* Oxford: Oxford University Press, 1998.

Weaver, Mike. *The Art of Photography: 1839–1989.* New Haven, Conn.: Yale University Press, 1989.

Whiffen, Marcus, and Frederick Koeper. *American Architecture, 1607–1976.* Cambridge, Mass.: MIT Press, 1983.

Wilmerding, John. *American Art.* Harmondsworth: Penguin, 1976.

Wilson, Simon. *Holbein to Hockney: A History of British Art.* London: Tate Gallery & Bodley Head, 1979.

CHAPTER 22:
EUROPE AND AMERICA, 1800 TO 1870

Bergdoll, Barry. *European Architecture 1750–1890.* New York: Oxford University Press, 2000.

Boime, Albert. *The Academy and French Painting in the 19th Century.* London: Phaidon, 1971.

———. *Art in the Age of Bonapartism, 1800–1815.* Chicago: University of Chicago Press, 1990.

Brown, David Blayney. *Romanticism.* London: Phaidon, 2001.

Bryson, Norman. *Tradition and Desire: From David to Delacroix.* New York: Cambridge University Press, 1984.

Clark, T. J. *The Absolute Bourgeois: Artists and Politics in France, 1848–1851.* London: Thames & Hudson, 1973.

———. *Image of the People: Gustave Courbet and the 1848 Revolution.* London: Thames & Hudson, 1973.

———. *The Painting of Modern Life: Paris in the Art of Manet and His Followers.* Princeton, N.J.: Princeton University Press, 1984.

Clay, Jean. *Romanticism.* New York: Phaidon, 1981.

Eitner, Lorenz. *Neoclassicism and Romanticism, 1750–1850: An Anthology of Sources and Documents.* New York: Harper & Row, 1989.

Fried, Michael. *Courbet's Realism.* Chicago: University of Chicago Press, 1982.

———. *Manet's Modernism, or, The Face of Painting in the 1860s.* Chicago: University of Chicago Press, 1996.

Hilton, Timothy. *The Pre-Raphaelites.* New York: Oxford University Press, 1970.

Holt, Elizabeth Gilmore, ed. *From the Classicists to the Impressionists: A Documentary History of Art and Architecture in the Nineteenth Century.* Garden City, N.J.: Anchor Books; Doubleday, 1966.

Honour, Hugh. *Romanticism.* New York: Harper & Row, 1979.

Janson, Horst W. *19th-Century Sculpture.* New York: Abrams, 1985.

Krell, Alain. *Manet and the Painters of Contemporary Life.* London: Thames & Hudson, 1996.

Kroeber, Karl. *British Romantic Art.* Berkeley: University of California Press, 1986.

Mainardi, Patricia. *Art and Politics of the Second Empire: The Universal Expositions of 1855 and 1867.* New Haven, Conn.: Yale University Press, 1987.

———. *The End of the Salon: Art and the State in the Early Third Republic.* Cambridge: Cambridge University Press, 1993.

Middleton, Robin. *Architecture of the Nineteenth Century.* London: Phaidon, 2003.

Middleton, Robin, and David Watkin. *Neoclassical and 19th-Century Architecture.* 2 vols. New York: Electa/Rizzoli, 1987.

Needham, Gerald. *19th-Century Realist Art.* New York: Harper & Row, 1988.

Nochlin, Linda. *Realism and Tradition in Art, 1848–1900: Sources and Documents.* Upper Saddle River, N.J.: Prentice Hall, 1966.

Novak, Barbara. *American Painting of the Nineteenth Century: Realism and the American Experience.* New York: Harper & Row, 1979.

Novotny, Fritz. *Painting and Sculpture in Europe, 1780–1880.* 3d ed. New Haven, Conn.: Yale University Press, 1988.

Porterfield, Todd. *The Allure of Empire: Art in the Service of French Imperialism 1798–1836.* Princeton, N.J.: Princeton University Press, 1998.

Rosen, Charles, and Henri Zerner. *Romanticism and Realism: The Mythology of Nineteenth-Century Art.* New York: Viking, 1984.

Rubin, James Henry. *Courbet.* London: Phaidon, 1997.

Sloane, Joseph C. *French Painting between the Past and the Present: Artists, Critics, and Traditions from 1848 to 1870.* Princeton, N.J.: Princeton University Press, 1973.

Symmons, Sarah. *Goya.* London: Phaidon, 1998.

Taylor, Joshua, ed. *Nineteenth-Century Theories of Art.* Berkeley: University of California Press, 1987.

Vaughn, William. *German Romantic Painting.* New Haven, Conn.: Yale University Press, 1980.

Wolf, Bryan Jay. *Romantic Revision: Culture and Consciousness in Nineteenth-Century American Painting and Literature.* Chicago: University of Chicago Press, 1986.

Wood, Christopher. *The Pre-Raphaelites.* New York: Viking, 1981.

CHAPTER 23:
EUROPE AND AMERICA, 1870 TO 1900

Adams, Steven. *The Barbizon School and the Origins of Impressionism.* London: Phaidon, 1994.

Broude, Norma. *Impressionism: A Feminist Reading.* New York: Rizzoli, 1991.

Duncan, Alastair. *Art Nouveau.* New York: Thames & Hudson, 1994.

Escritt, Stephen. *Art Nouveau.* London: Phaidon, 2000.

Garb, Tamar. *Bodies of Modernity: Figure and Flesh in Fin-de-Siècle France.* New York: Thames & Hudson, 1998.

Gerdts, William H. *American Impressionism.* New York: Abbeville, 1984.

Herbert, Robert L. *Impressionism: Art, Leisure, and Parisian Society.* New Haven, Conn.: Yale University Press, 1988.

Jensen, Robert. *Marketing Modernism in Fin-de-Siècle Europe.* Princeton, N.J.: Princeton University Press, 1994.

Lewis, Mary Tompkins. *Cézanne.* London: Phaidon, 2000.

Nochlin, Linda. *Impressionism and Post-Impressionism, 1874–1904: Sources and Documents.* Upper Saddle River, N.J.: Prentice Hall, 1966.

Rachman, Carla. *Monet.* London: Phaidon, 1997.

Rapetti, Rodolphe. *Symbolism.* Paris: Flammarion, 2006.

Rubin, James H. *Impressionism.* London: Phaidon, 1999.

Schorske, Carl E. *Fin-de-Siècle Vienna: Politics and Culture.* New York: Knopf, 1980.

Shiff, Richard. *Cézanne and the End of Impressionism: A Study of the Theory, Technique, and Critical Evaluation of Modern Art.* Chicago: University of Chicago Press, 1984.

Silverman, Debora L. *Art Nouveau in Fin-de-Siècle France: Politics, Psychology, and Style.* Berkeley: University of California Press, 1989.

Smith, Paul. *Impressionism: Beneath the Surface.* New York: Abrams, 1995.

Sund, Judy. *Van Gogh.* London: Phaidon, 2002.

CHAPTER 24:
EUROPE AND AMERICA, 1900 TO 1945

Antliff, Mark. *Cultural Politics and the Parisian Avant-Garde.* Princeton, N.J.: Princeton University Press, 1993.

Antliff, Mark, and Patricia Leighten. *Cubism and Culture.* New York: Thames & Hudson, 2001.

Baigell, Matthew. *The American Scene: American Painting of the 1930s.* New York: Praeger, 1974.

Barr, Alfred H., Jr. *Cubism and Abstract Art: Painting, Sculpture, Constructions, Photography, Architecture, Industrial Arts, Theatre, Films, Posters, Typography.* Cambridge, Mass.: Belknap, 1986.

Barron, Stephanie. *Exiles and Emigrés: The Flight of European Artists from Hitler.* Los Angeles: Los Angeles County Museum of Art, 1997.

———, ed. *Degenerate Art: The Fate of the Avant-Garde in Nazi Germany.* Los Angeles: Los Angeles County Museum of Art, 1991.

Bayer, Herbert, Walter Gropius, and Ise Gropius. *Bauhaus, 1919–1928.* New York: Museum of Modern Art, 1975.

Bearden, Romare, and Harry Henderson. *A History of African-American Artists from 1792 to the Present.* New York: Pantheon, 1993.

Breton, André. *Surrealism and Painting.* New York: Harper & Row, 1972.

Brown, Milton. *Story of the Armory Show: The 1913 Exhibition That Changed American Art.* 2d ed. New York: Abbeville, 1988.

Campbell, Mary Schmidt, David C. Driskell, David Lewis Levering, and Deborah Willis Ryan. *Harlem Renaissance: Art of Black America.* New York: Studio Museum in Harlem; Abrams, 1987.

Cox, Neil. *Cubism.* London: Phaidon, 2000.

Curtis, Penelope. *Sculpture 1900–1945.* New York: Oxford University Press, 1999.

Curtis, William J. R. *Modern Architecture since 1900.* Upper Saddle River, N.J.: Prentice Hall, 1996.

Davidson, Abraham A. *Early American Modernist Painting, 1910–1935.* New York: Harper & Row, 1981.

Eberle, Matthias. *World War I and the Weimar Artists: Dix, Grosz, Beckmann, Schlemmer.* New Haven, Conn.: Yale University Press, 1985.

Edwards, Steve, and Paul Wood, eds. *Art of the Avant-Gardes.* New Haven, Conn.: Yale University Press, 2004.

Elderfield, John. *The "Wild Beasts": Fauvism and Its Affinities.* New York: Museum of Modern Art, 1976.

Fer, Briony, David Batchelor, and Paul Wood. *Realism, Rationalism, Surrealism: Art between the Wars.* New Haven, Conn.: Yale University Press, 1993.

Friedman, Mildred, ed. *De Stijl, 1917–1931: Visions of Utopia.* Minneapolis: Walker Art Center; New York: Abbeville, 1982.

Gale, Matthew. *Dada and Surrealism.* London: Phaidon, 1997.

Goldberg, Rose Lee. *Performance: Live Art 1909 to the Present.* New York: Abrams, 1979.

Golding, John. *Cubism: A History and an Analysis, 1907–1914.* Cambridge, Mass.: Belknap, 1988.

Gordon, Donald E. *Expressionism: Art and Idea.* New Haven, Conn.: Yale University Press, 1987.

Harrison, Charles, Francis Frascina, and Gil Perry. *Primitivism, Cubism, Abstraction: The Early Twentieth Century.* New Haven, Conn.: Yale University Press, 1993.

Herbert, James D. *Fauve Painting: The Making of Cultural Politics.* New Haven, Conn.: Yale University Press, 1992.

Hitchcock, Henry-Russell, and Philip Johnson. *The International Style.* New York: Norton, 1995.

Hurlburt, Laurance P. *The Mexican Muralists in the United States.* Albuquerque: University of New Mexico Press, 1989.

Jaffé, Hans L. C. *De Stijl, 1917–1931: The Dutch Contribution to Modern Art.* Cambridge, Mass.: Belknap, 1986.

Krauss, Rosalind. *The Originality of the Avant-Garde and Other Modernist Myths.* Cambridge, Mass.: MIT Press, 1986.

Kuspit, Donald. *The Cult of the Avant-Garde Artist.* Cambridge: Cambridge University Press, 1993.

Lloyd, Jill. *German Expressionism: Primitivism and Modernity.* New Haven, Conn.: Yale University Press, 1991.

Lodder, Christina. *Russian Constructivism.* New Haven, Conn.: Yale University Press, 1983.

Martin, Marianne W. *Futurist Art and Theory.* Oxford: Clarendon, 1968.

Motherwell, Robert, ed. *The Dada Painters and Poets: An Anthology.* 2d ed. Boston: Hall, 1981.

Rhodes, Colin. *Primitivism and Modern Art.* New York: Thames & Hudson, 1994.

Richter, Hans. *Dada: Art and Anti-Art.* London: Thames & Hudson, 1961.

Rosenblum, Robert. *Cubism and Twentieth-Century Art.* Rev. ed. New York: Abrams, 1984.

Rubin, William S. *Dada and Surrealist Art.* New York: Abrams, 1968.

———, ed. *Pablo Picasso: A Retrospective.* New York: Museum of Modern Art; Boston: New York Graphic Society, 1980.

———, ed. *"Primitivism" in 20th-Century Art: Affinity of the Tribal and the Modern.* 2 vols. New York: Museum of Modern Art, 1984.

Selz, Peter. *German Expressionist Painting.* Berkeley: University of California Press, 1974. Reprint of 1957 edition.

Silver, Kenneth E. *Esprit de Corps: The Art of the Parisian Avant-Garde and the First World War, 1914–1925.* Princeton, N.J.: Princeton University Press, 1989.

Smith, Terry. *Making the Modern: Industry, Art, and Design in America.* Chicago: University of Chicago Press, 1993.

Stott, William. *Documentary Expression and Thirties America.* New York: Oxford University Press, 1973.

Taylor, Joshua C. *Futurism.* New York: Museum of Modern Art, 1961.

Tisdall, Caroline, and Angelo Bozzolla. *Futurism.* New York: Oxford University Press, 1978.

Trachtenberg, Alan. *Reading American Photographs: Images as History—Mathew Brady to Walker Evans.* New York: Hill and Wang, 1989.

Tsujimoto, Karen. *Images of America: Precisionist Painting and Modern Photography.* Seattle: University of Washington Press, 1982.

Tucker, William. *Early Modern Sculpture.* New York: Oxford University Press, 1974.

Vogt, Paul. *Expressionism: German Painting, 1905–1920.* New York: Abrams, 1980.

Weiss, Jeffrey S. *The Popular Culture of Modern Art: Picasso, Duchamp, and Avant-Gardism.* New Haven, Conn.: Yale University Press, 1994.

Whitford, Frank. *Bauhaus.* New York: Thames & Hudson, 1984.

CHAPTER 25:
EUROPE AND AMERICA AFTER 1945

Alloway, Lawrence. *American Pop Art.* New York: Whitney Museum of American Art; Macmillan, 1974.

———. *Topics in American Art since 1945.* New York: Norton, 1975.

Anfam, David. *Abstract Expressionism.* New York: Thames & Hudson, 1990.

Archer, Michael. *Art since 1960.* New ed. New York: Thames & Hudson, 2002.

Ashton, Dore. *American Art since 1945.* New York: Oxford University Press, 1983.

———. *The New York School: A Cultural Reckoning.* Harmondsworth: Penguin, 1979.

Battcock, Gregory, ed. *Idea Art: A Critical Anthology.* New York: Dutton, 1973.

———. *Minimal Art: A Critical Anthology.* New York: Studio Vista, 1969.

———. *The New Art: A Critical Anthology.* New York: Dutton, 1973.

———. *New Artists Video: A Critical Anthology.* New York: Dutton, 1978.

Battcock, Gregory, and Robert Nickas, eds. *The Art of Performance: A Critical Anthology.* New York: Dutton, 1984.

Beardsley, John, and Jane Livingston. *Hispanic Art in the United States: Thirty Contemporary Painters and Sculptors.* Houston: Museum of Fine Arts; New York: Abbeville, 1987.

Beardsley, Richard. *Earthworks and Beyond: Contemporary Art in the Landscape.* New York: Abbeville, 1984.

Broude, Norma, and Mary D. Garrard. *The Power of Feminist Art: The American Movement of the 1970s, History and Impact.* New York: Abrams, 1994.

Bürger, Peter. *Theory of the Avant-Garde.* Minneapolis: University of Minnesota Press, 1984.

Causey, Andrew. *Sculpture since 1945.* New York: Oxford University Press, 1998.

Cockcroft, Eva, John Weber, and James Cockcroft. *Toward a People's Art.* New York: Dutton, 1977.

Cook, Peter. *New Spirit in Architecture.* New York: Rizzoli, 1990.

Crow, Thomas. *The Rise of the Sixties: American and European Art in the Era of Dissent.* New Haven, Conn.: Yale University Press, 2005.

Cummings, P. *Dictionary of Contemporary American Artists.* 6th ed. New York: St. Martin's, 1994.

Deepwell, K., ed. *New Feminist Art.* Manchester: Manchester University Press, 1994.

Ferguson, Russell, ed. *Discourses: Conversations in Postmodern Art and Culture.* Cambridge, Mass.: MIT Press, 1990.

Fineberg, Jonathan. *Art since 1940: Strategies of Being.* 2d ed. Upper Saddle River, N.J.: Prentice Hall, 2000.

Frascina, Francis, ed. *Pollock and After: The Critical Debate.* New York: Harper & Row, 1985.

Geldzahler, Henry. *New York Painting and Sculpture, 1940–1970.* New York: Dutton, 1969.

Ghirardo, Diane. *Architecture after Modernism.* New York: Thames & Hudson, 1996.

Godfrey, Tony. *Conceptual Art.* London: Phaidon, 1998.

Goldberg, Rose Lee. *Performance Art: From Futurism to the Present.* Rev. ed. New York: Abrams, 1988.

Goldhagen, Sarah Williams, and Réjean Legault. *Anxious Modernisms: Experimentation in Postwar Architectural Culture.* Cambridge, Mass.: MIT Press, 2002.

Goodman, Cynthia. *Digital Visions: Computers and Art.* New York: Abrams, 1987.

Goodyear, Frank H., Jr. *Contemporary American Realism since 1960.* Boston: New York Graphic Society, 1981.

Green, Jonathan. *American Photography: A Critical History 1945 to the Present.* New York: Abrams, 1984.

Greenberg, Clement. *Clement Greenberg: The Collected Essays and Criticism.* Edited by J. O'Brien. 4 vols. Chicago: University of Chicago Press, 1986–1993.

Grundberg, Andy. *Photography and Art: Interactions since 1945.* New York: Abbeville, 1987.

Guilbaut, Serge. *How New York Stole the Idea of Modern Art.* Chicago: University of Chicago Press, 1983.

Hays, K. Michael, and Carol Burns, eds. *Thinking the Present: Recent American Architecture.* New York: Princeton Architectural, 1990.

Henri, Adrian. *Total Art: Environments, Happenings, and Performance.* New York: Oxford University Press, 1974.

Hertz, Richard, ed. *Theories of Contemporary Art.* 2d ed. Upper Saddle River, N.J.: Prentice Hall, 1993.

Hoffman, Katherine. *Explorations: The Visual Arts since 1945.* New York: Harper Collins, 1991.

Hopkins, David. *After Modern Art, 1945–2000.* New York: Oxford University Press, 2000.

Hughes, Robert. *The Shock of the New.* New York: Knopf, 1981.

Hunter, Sam. *An American Renaissance: Painting and Sculpture since 1940.* New York: Abbeville, 1986.

Jacobs, Jane. *The Death and Life of Great American Cities.* New York: Random House, 1961.

Jacobus, John. *Twentieth-Century Architecture: The Middle Years, 1940–1964.* New York: Praeger, 1966.

Jencks, Charles. *The Language of Post-Modern Architecture.* 6th ed. New York: Rizzoli, 1991.

———. *What Is Post-Modernism?* 3d ed. London: Academy Editions, 1989.

Johnson, Ellen H., ed. *American Artists on Art from 1940 to 1980.* Boulder, Colo.: Westview, 1982.

Joselit, David. *American Art since 1945.* New York: Thames & Hudson, 2003.

Kaprow, Allan. *Assemblage, Environments, and Happenings.* New York: Abrams, 1966.

Kirby, Michael. *Happenings.* New York: Dutton, 1966.

Kramer, Hilton. *The Age of the Avant-Garde: An Art Chronicle of 1956–1972.* New York: Farrar, Straus & Giroux, 1973.

Leja, Michael. *Reframing Abstract Expressionism: Subjectivity and Painting in the 1940s.* New Haven, Conn.: Yale University Press, 1993.

Lippard, Lucy R. *Mixed Blessings: New Art in a Multicultural America.* New York: Pantheon, 1990.

———. *Pop Art.* New York: Praeger, 1966.

———, ed. *From the Center: Feminist Essays on Women's Art.* New York: Dutton, 1976.

———. *Six Years: The Dematerialization of the Art Object from 1966 to 1972.* New York: Praeger, 1973.

Lovejoy, Margot. *Postmodern Currents: Art and Artists in the Age of the Electronic Media.* Ann Arbor, Mich.: UMI Research Press, 1989.

Lucie-Smith, Edward. *Art Now.* Edison, N.J.: Wellfleet, 1989.

———. *Movements in Art since 1945.* New ed. New York: Thames & Hudson, 2001.

Mamiya, Christin J. *Pop Art and Consumer Culture: American Super Market.* Austin: University of Texas Press, 1992.

Marder, Tod A. *The Critical Edge: Controversy in Recent American Architecture.* New Brunswick, N.J.: Rutgers University Press, 1980.

———. *An International Survey of Recent Painting and Sculpture.* New York: Museum of Modern Art, 1984.

Meyer, Ursula. *Conceptual Art.* New York: Dutton, 1972.

Mitchell, William J. *The Reconfigured Eye: Visual Truth in the Post-Photographic Era.* Cambridge, Mass.: MIT Press, 1992.

Norris, Christopher, and Andrew Benjamin. *What Is Deconstruction?* New York: St. Martin's, 1988.

Perry, Gill, and Paul Wood. *Themes in Contemporary Art.* New Haven, Conn.: Yale University Press, 2004.

Polcari, Stephen. *Abstract Expressionism and the Modern Experience.* Cambridge: Cambridge University Press, 1991.

Popper, Frank. *Origins and Development of Kinetic Art.* Translated by Stephen Bann. Greenwich, Conn.: New York Graphic Society, 1968.

Price, Jonathan. *Video Visions: A Medium Discovers Itself.* New York: New American Library, 1977.

Reichardt, Jasia, ed. *Cybernetics, Art, and Ideas.* Greenwich, Conn.: New York Graphics Society, 1971.

Risatti, Howard, ed. *Postmodern Perspectives: Issues in Contemporary Art.* Upper Saddle River, N.J.: Prentice Hall, 1990.

Robbins, Corinne. *The Pluralist Era: American Art, 1968–1981.* New York: Harper & Row, 1984.

Rosen, Randy, and Catherine C. Brawer, eds. *Making Their Mark: Women Artists Move into the Mainstream, 1970–1985.* New York: Abbeville, 1989.

Rosenberg, Harold. *The Tradition of the New.* New York: Horizon, 1959.

Rush, Michael. *New Media in Art.* 2d ed. New York: Thames & Hudson, 2005.

Russell, John, and Suzi Gablik. *Pop Art Redefined.* New York: Praeger, 1969.

Sandford, Mariellen R., ed. *Happenings and Other Acts.* New York: Routledge, 1995.

Sandler, Irving. *Art of the Postmodern Era.* New York: Harper Collins, 1996.

———. *The Triumph of American Painting: A History of Abstract Expressionism.* New York: Praeger, 1970.

Sayre, Henry M. *The Object of Performance: The American Avant-Garde since 1970.* Chicago: University of Chicago Press, 1989.

Schneider, Ira, and Beryl Korot. *Video Art: An Anthology.* New York: Harcourt Brace Jovanovich, 1976.

Shapiro, David, and Cecile Shapiro. *Abstract Expressionism: A Critical Record.* New York: Cambridge University Press, 1990.

Smagula, Howard. *Currents: Contemporary Directions in the Visual Arts.* 2d ed. Upper Saddle River, N.J.: Prentice Hall, 1989.

Sonfist, Alan, ed. *Art in the Landscape: A Critical Anthology of Environmental Art.* New York: Dutton, 1983.

Sontag, Susan. *On Photography.* New York: Farrar, Straus & Giroux, 1973.

Stiles, Kristine, and Peter Selz. *Theories and Documents of Contemporary Art: A Sourcebook of Artists' Writings.* Berkeley and Los Angeles: University of California Press, 1996.

Taylor, Brendon. *Contemporary Art: Art since 1970.* Upper Saddle River, N.J.: Prentice Hall, 2005.

Tuchman, Maurice. *American Sculpture of the Sixties.* Los Angeles: Los Angeles County Museum of Art, 1967.

Venturi, Robert. *Complexity and Contradiction in Architecture.* New York: Museum of Modern Art, 1966.

Venturi, Robert, Denise Scott-Brown, and Steven Isehour. *Learning from Las Vegas.* Cambridge, Mass.: MIT Press, 1972.

Waldman, Diane. *Collage, Assemblage, and the Found Object.* New York: Abrams, 1992.

Wallis, Brian, ed. *Art after Modernism: Rethinking Representation.* New York: New Museum of Contemporary Art in association with David R. Godine, 1984.

Wheeler, Daniel. *Art since Mid-Century: 1945 to the Present.* Upper Saddle River, N.J.: Prentice Hall, 1991.

Wood, Paul. *Modernism in Dispute: Art since the Forties.* New Haven, Conn.: Yale University Press, 1993.

CREDITS

*The author and publisher are grateful to the proprietors and custodians of various works of art
for photographs of these works and permission to reproduce them in this book.
Sources not included in the captions are listed here.*

INDEX

Boldface names refer to artists. Page numbers in italics refer to illustrations.

Abakanowicz, Magdalena: work of, 776, *776*
Abbey in the Oak Forest (Friedrich), 626, *626*
Abstract Expressionism, 748–751, 753, 754–755, 757, 758, 761, 763, 764, 765, 773, 795, 801
Action painting, 749, 750
Adam, Robert: work of, 598, *598*, 599
Adams Memorial (Saint-Gaudens), 675, *675*
Adoration of the Magi, xiv
Adoration of the Shepherds, xiv
Advantages of Being a Woman Artist, The (Guerrilla Girls), 769, *769*
Aesculapius (Asklepios), xiii
African Negro Art (MoMA exhibit), 730
Agony in the Garden, xv
Aisle, xx
Alloway, Lawrence, 757
Altamira (Spain), 680
Amalienburg lodge (Cuvilliés), 584, *585*
Ambulatory, xx
"American Action Painters, The" article, 750
American Gothic (Wood), 733, *733*
American Realism, 651, 708
American Scene Painters, 733
American Sources of Modern Art (Aztec, Maya, Inca) (MoMA exhibit), 730
Among the Sierra Nevada Mountains, California (Bierstadt), 628, *629*
Amor (Eros, Cupid), xiii
Analytic Cubism, 697, 711
Anatomy of a Kimono (Schapiro), 767, *767*
Ancient Mexico (Rivera), 735–736, *735*

Ancient of Days (Blake), 617, *617*
Animal Locomotion (Muybridge), 650
Annunciation group (Reims Cathedral), *xiv*
Annunciation to Mary, xiv
Annunciation to the Shepherds, xiv
Annunciation to the Shepherds, medieval lectionary, *xiv*
Antiquities of Athens (Stuart and Revett), 603
Aphrodite (Venus), xiii
Aphrodite of Knidos (Praxiteles), *xiii*
Apollinaire, Guillaume, 694, 697
Apollo, xiii
Apotheosis of Homer (Ingres), *614,* 615
Apotheosis of the Pisani Family (Tiepolo), *588, 589*
Apse, xx
Arc de Triomphe, 625
Arch of Trajan, Benevento, *xix*
Arches, xviii, *xviii;* pointed, xx
Archipenko, Aleksandr, 728; work of, 700–701, *701*
Architectural design/materials, Gehry on, 788
Architecture of democracy, 741, 742, 743
Architrave, xvi
Ares (Mars), xiii
Armored Train (Severini), 704, *704*
Armory Show (1913), 684, 713, 721, 729, 743; described, 710–711; installation photo of, *710*
Arneson, Robert: work of, 777, *777*
Arp, Jean (Hans): work of, 705, *705*
Art and Progress, on Armory Show, 710
Art brut, 747, 748
Art Deco, 740, 741
Art history: public understanding of, 778; Schneemann on, 794

Art Institute of Chicago, Grosz and, 729
Art News, Lichtenstein in, 759
Art Nouveau, 674, 678–679, 680, 683; Arts and Crafts movement and, 678; Symbolism and, 673
Artemis (Diana), xiii
Arts, The: Zayas in, 700
Arts and Crafts movement, 661, 674, 679, 680, 683; Art Nouveau and, 678; Morris and, 689
Ascension, xv
Ascension of Christ, Rabbula Gospels, xv
Ash Can School, 709
Asklepios (Aesculapius), xiii
Assemblages, 758
At the Moulin Rouge (Toulouse-Lautrec), 663, *663*
AT&T (Sony) Building (Johnson, Burgee, with Simmons Architects), 785–786, *785*
Athena (Minerva), xiii
Athena Parthenos (Phidias), *xiii*
Athens: Parthenon, 635, 763
Automatism, 719, 723
Avant-garde, 687, 696, 708, 724, 743, 748, 757, 793, 801; introduction of, 684; MoMA and, 730; new media and, 797; painting, 709–714; public ridicule for, 721; rejection of, 733; sculpture, 709–714; the Steins and, 694
Aztecs, 736

Baalbek, 602
Bacchus (Dionysos), xiii
Bacon, Francis: work of, 747, *747*
Ball, Hugo, 705
Balla, Giacomo: work of, *702, 703*
Ballet Mécanique (Léger), 702
Ballet Rehearsal (Degas), *660,* 661
Baptism, xiv

Bar at the Folies-Bergère (Manet), 660, *660*
Barbizon School, Millet and, 632
Barcelona, Casa Milá, 680, *680*
Barcelona Academy of Fine Art, 694
Barlach, Ernst, 721; work of, 719, *719*
Barney, Matthew, 801; work of, *744,* 800
Baroque, 587, 616, 617, 644, 785
Barr, Alfred H., Jr., 729, 730
Barrel vault, xviii, *xviii*
Barry, Charles: work of, *642,* 643
Bartholdi, Frédéric Auguste: work of, 681
Base (column), xvi
Basilican churches, xx
Basket of Apples (Cézanne), 670, *670*
Bath, The (Cassatt), 662, *662*
Bather (Lipchitz), 700, *700*
Baths of Diocletian, *xix*
Baudelaire, Charles, 641, 654
Bauhaus, 738, 739, 740, 743, 781
Bay, The (Frankenthaler), 753, *753*
Bear Run, Kaufmann House, 742, *742,* 743
Beardsley, Aubrey: work of, 673, *673*
Beata Beatrix (Rossetti), 642, *642*
Beaux-Arts style, 644
Beckmann, Max, 721, 729; work of, 717–718, *717*
Behnisch, Günter: work of, 787–788, *787*
Bell, Clive, 694
Bellori, Giovanni Pietro, 599
Benevento, Arch of Trajan, *xix*
Benton, Thomas Hart: work of, 734, *734*
Betrayal and Arrest of Jesus, xv
Beuys, Joseph, 801; work of, 794–795, *795*
Bibliothèque Sainte-Geneviève (Labrouste), 644, *645,* 651

Bierstadt, Albert, 651; work of, 628–629, *629*

Big Self-Portrait (Close), 762, *762*

Bilbao, Guggenheim Bilbao Museo, 788, *788*

Biomorphic Surrealism, 719, 728, 743, 756

Bird in Space (Brancusi), 727, *727*, 730, 743

Black Mountain College, 793

Black Paintings (Goya), 620

Blake, Peter: on Guggenheim Museum, 779

Blake, William, 618; work of, 617, *617*

Blanc, Charles, 664

Blessed Art Thou among Women (Käsebier), 674–675, *675*

Bliss, Lillie P., 709, 730

Blue Period (Picasso), 694

Boccioni, Umberto: work of, 703–704, *703*

Boffrand, Germain: work of, 584, *584*

Bohr, Niels, 691

Bonheur, Marie-Rosalie (Rosa): work of, *634*, 635

Borghese, Camillo, 612

Borghese, Pauline, 612, 651

Bottle, Newspaper, Pipe, and Glass (Braque), 698, 699, *699*

Boucher, François, 589, 601, 607; work of, 588, *588*

Bouguereau, Adolphe-William, 636–637, *637*

Bourgeois, Louise: work of, 756, *756*

Boyle, Richard, 607; work of, 602–603, *603*

Brady, Matthew B., 649

Brancusi, Constantin, 728, 729, 730, 743; on abstract sculpture, 727; Armory Show and, 710; work of, 727, *727*

Braque, Georges, 694, 700; Armory Show and, 710; Cubism and, 697, 743; work of, 697, *697*, 698, 699

Breakfast Scene (Hogarth), 594, *594*

Breton, André, 719, 720, 723; Dada and, 704; Kahlo and, 736

Breuer, Marcel: work of, 738–739, *739*

Bride Stripped Bare by Her Bachelors, Even, The (The Large Glass) (Duchamp), 706–707, *706*

Brighton, Royal Pavilion, 643, *643*

British Museum, 598

British Royal Academy of Arts, 595, 599, 617, 655

Brown, Denise Scott: work of, 786, *786*

Brussels, van Eetvelde house, 679, *679*

Buddhism, 691, 798

Buffalo, Guaranty (Prudential) Building, 682, *682*

Buffon, Count de, 590

Burgee, John: work of, 785, *785*

Burgess, Frank Gelett: work of, *696*

Burghers of Calais (Rodin), 676–677, *677*

Burial at Ornans (Courbet), 630–632, *631*, 635

Burial of Atala (Girodet-Trioson), 614, *614*

Burke, Edmund, 616, 627

Byzantine architecture, xxi

Byzantine art, 773

Cabaret Voltaire, 705

Cadeau (Gift) (Ray), 711, *711*

Cage, John, 793, 797

Caillebotte, Gustave: work of, 657–658, *657*

Calais, siege of, 676, 683

Calder, Alexander, 704, 743; work of, 729–730, *730*

California Artist (Arneson), 777, *777*

California Institute of Technology, Em and, 799

California Institute of the Arts, 765

Calling of Matthew, xiv

Camera lucida, 647

Camera obscura, 597, 607, 646, 647

Camera Work (journal), 714

Cameron, Julia Margaret: work of, 649, *649*, 651

Campbell, Colin, 602

Campus Martius, 698

Canaletto, Antonio, 607; work of, 597, *597*

Canova, Antonio, 651; work of, 612, *612*

Canyon (Rauschenberg), 758–759, *758*

Capitals, xvi; Corinthian, 645

Caprichos, Los (Goya), 618, *618*, 651

Carlyle, Thomas, 649

Carpeaux, Jean-Baptiste: work of, 676, *676*

Carrà, Carlo, 703

Carrying of the Cross, xv

Carson, Pirie, Scott Building (Sullivan), 682, *682*

Casa Milá (Gaudí), 680, *680*

Cassatt, Mary, 694, 708; Impressionists and, 662; Japanese art and, 661; work of, 662, *662*

Cast-iron construction, 644, 651

Catherine the Great, 585

Cave painting, 680

cella, xvi

Cellini, Benvenuto, 589

Central-plan buildings, 644

Central-plan churches, xxi

Centro de Arte Reina Sofia, 716

Ceres (Demeter), xiii

Cézanne, Paul, 663, 682, 683, 694, 695, 697; work of, 668–670, *670*

Chacmools, 728

Chalgrin, Jean François Thérèse, 625

Champfleury, Jules-François-Félix Husson, 632

Champs de Mars or *The Red Tower* (Delaunay), 698, *698*

Chardin, Jean-Baptiste-Siméon, 607; Diderot on, 592; work of, 592, *592*

Charles IV, King, 618, 619

Charles X, King, 623

Charlottesville (Va.), Rotunda and Lawn, *604*, 605

Chartres Cathedral, *xx*

Chateaubriand, François René de, 614, 642

Chevreul, Michel Eugène, 625, 664

Chicago: Carson, Pirie, Scott Building, 682, *682;* Marshall Field wholesale store, 681, *681;* Robie House, 741–742, *741;* Sears Tower, 782, *782*

Chicago, Judy (Judy Cohen), 801; on *Dinner Party,* 766; work of, 765–766, *766*

Chiswick House (Boyle and Kent), 602–603, *603*, 604, 605, 607

Chopin, Frédéric, 622

Christ (Jesus): life of, xiv

Christianity, 685, 798

Christo, 801; work of, 791, *791*. *See also* **Jeanne-Claude**

Chromatic abstraction, 749, 801

Chronik der Brücke (Kirchner), 689

Chrysler Building (van Alen), 740, *741*, 800

Church, Frederic Edwin, 651; work of, 629–630, *629*

Church of the Holy Wisdom. *See* Hagia Sophia

Churches: medieval, design of, xx

City, The (Léger), *702*

Civil rights movement, 746, 771, 772, 801

Civil War (U.S.), 630; photographs of, 649, 650; Winslow Homer and, 638

Claesz, Pieter, 648

Clarkson, Thomas, 627

Classical art: Enlightenment and, 599

Classical order, xvi

Classicism: influence of, 613; revival of, 597

Cleansing of the Temple, xiv

Clerestory, xx

Clock Tower, 643

Clodion (Claude Michel): work of, 589, *589*

Close, Chuck, 801; on portrait painting/photography, 762; work of, 762, *762*

Coalbrookdale Bridge (Darby and Pritchard), 591, *591*, 607

Cohen, Judy. *See* Chicago, Judy

Cole, Thomas, 651; work of, 628, *628*

Collage, 698

Collage Arranged According to the Laws of Chance (Arp), 705, *705*

Colonial empires, map of, *686*

Colonialism, 696

Colonnade, xvi

Color: complementary, 664; local, 656; Matisse on, 688; mixing of, 656; primary, 664; psychological dimension of, 664; secondary, 656, 664; simultaneous contrasts of, 664; theory, 19th-century, 664; van Gogh on, 666

Color-field painting, 752–753

Column (Gabo), 725, *725*

Columns: Corinthian, 612, 644

Comic books and strips, 759, 801

Commission of Fine Arts: Vietnam memorial and, 783

Communist Manifesto, The (Marx and Engels), 653

Complexity and Contradictions in Architecture (Venturi), 784

Composition in Red, Blue, and Yellow (Mondrian), 726, *726*

Computer art, 793

Computer graphics, 797, 798–799, 801

Comte, Auguste, positivism and, 630

Conceptual Art, 793, 796–797, 801

Concerning the Spiritual in Art (Kandinsky), 691

Concrete construction, xviii

Constable, John, 627, 629, 651; work of, 626, *627*

Constantinople: Hagia Sophia, xxi, *xxi*, 780

Constitution Garden, 783

Constructivism, 724–726, 737, 743

Copley, John Singleton: work of, 596–597, *596*

Corinthian capital, xvi, *xvii*

Corneille, Pierre, 601
Cornelia Presenting Her Children as Her Treasures, or Mother of the Gracchi (Kauffmann), 599, *599*
Cornered (Piper), 798, *798*
Coronation of Napoleon (David), 611, *611*
Correspondence littéraire: Diderot in, 592, 593
Cosmic Cubism, 711
Courbet, Gustave, 635, 641, 648, 651, 654, 694; photography and, 647; on Realism, 631; rejection of, 655; work of, 630–632, *630*
Courier du dimanche: Courbet's letter in, 631
Cremaster cycle (Barney), *744,* 800
Crimean War, photographs of, 649
Cross vault, xviii
Crossing, xx
Crossing, The (Viola), 798, *798*
Crucifixion, xv
Crucifixion (Daphni), *xv*
Crystal Palace (Paxton), 591, 644–645, *645,* 651, 787
Cubi XIX (D. Smith), 754, *754*
Cubism, 684, 694–702, 710, 724, 726, 729, 743, 748, 753; Analytic, 697, 711; Cosmic, 711; Picasso on, 700; Synthetic, 698, 701–702, 711, 712, 713, 731
Cubism and Abstract Art (MoMA exhibition), 730
Cumul I (Bourgeois), 756, *756*
Cupid (Eros, Amor), xiii, 582, *588,* 589
Cupid a Captive (Boucher), *588*
Cut with the Kitchen Knife Dada through the Last Weimar Beer Belly Cultural Epoch of Germany (Höch), 707, *707*
Cuvilliés, François de: work of, 584, *585*
Cyclops, The (Redon), 672, *672*

Dada, 704–708, 716, 748, 756, 759, 793; pessimism of, 704, 724; Surrealism and, 719, 720
Dadaists, 707, 721, 724, 743; manifestos of, 704–705
Daguerre, Louis-Jacques-Mandé, 646, 651; work of, 647, *647*
Daguerreotypes, 646, 647–648
Dalí, Salvador, 719, 729; work of, 722, *722*
Dance, The (Derain), 689, *689*
Dante Alighieri, 615, 623, 642, 676
Darby, Abraham, III: work of, 591, *591*
Dark Ages, 616
Darwin, Charles, 649, 654

Darwinism, 653–654
Das Staatliche Bauhaus, 738
Daughters of Edward Darley Boit, The (Sargent), 639, *639*
Daumier, Honoré, *634,* 635, 648, 651, 732; photography and, 647; printmaking and, 633; work of, 633–634, *633, 646*
David, Jacques-Louis, 607, 618, 620, 624, 625; French Revolution and, 601; on Greek style/public art, 600; Napoleon and, 611, 651; Neoclassicism and, 613, 651; students of, 613–615; work of, 600–601, *600, 601,* 609, 611, *611*
David (Michelangelo), 754
Davies, Arthur B., 694, 710
Davis, Stuart: work of, 712, *712*
De Chirico, Giorgio: work of, 719–720, *720*
de Kooning, Willem, 759, 765, 801; work of, 750–751, *750*
De Stijl, 724–726, 738, 740, 743; defining, 737
De Stijl (magazine), 726
de Zayas, Marius, 700
Death: symbol of, 638
Death and Life of Great American Cities, The (Jacobs), 784
Death of General Wolfe (West), 596, *596*
Death of Marat (David), 601, *601*
Death of Sardanapalus (Delacroix), 622, *622,* 623, 651
Decline and Fall of the Roman Empire (Gibbon), 599
Deconstructivism, 763, 778, 787–789, 801
Decorative arts, 678–682, 683
Degas, Edgar, 650, 674; Impressionism and, 683; influence of, 663; Japanese art and, 661; photography and, 647, 648, 660; work of, 660–662, *660, 661*
Degenerate art, 721, 729
Déjeuner en fourrure, Le (Oppenheim), 722, *723*
Déjeuner sur l'Herbe, Le (Manet), 635–636, *635,* 655
Delacroix, Eugène, 608, 615, 626, 635, 648, 651, 668; in Morocco, 624; Nadar and, 649; photography and, 647; Romanticism and, 622; work of, 622–625, *622, 623, 624*
Delaroche, Paul, 647
Delaunay, Robert: work of, 697–698, *698*
Delaware residence (Venturi, Rauch, and Brown), 786, *786*

Delivery of the Keys to Peter, xiv
Demeter (Ceres), xiii
Demoiselles d'Avignon, Les (Picasso), 695–696, *695, 696,* 697, 730
Demuth, Charles, 743; work of, 713, *713*
Denver Art Museum (Libeskind), 789, *789*
Departure of the Volunteers of 1792 (Rude), 625, *625*
Deposition, xv
Der Blaue Reiter, 691, 692, 698, 711
Der Jugend, 678
Der Krieg (The War) (Dix), 718, *718*
Der Sturm, 687
Derain, André, 710; work of, 689, *689*
Derrida, Jacques, 763
Descartes, René, 589
Descent into Limbo, xv
Dessau, Shop Block, 738, *738*
Diana (Artemis), xiii
Diderot, Denis, 593; on Chardin/ Naturalism, 592; work of, 590
Die (Smith), *754,* 755
Die Brücke, 689, 690, 691, 702
Dinner Party, The (Chicago), 765–766, *766,* 801; Chicago on, 766
Diocletian, 598
Dionysos (Bacchus), xiii
Dispute in the Temple, xiv
Divisionism, 664
Dix, Otto, 721; work of, 718, *718*
Doge's Palace, 597
Domes: concrete, xviii; hemispherical, *xviii*
Doric order, xvi
Doric portico (Stuart), *603,* 607
Doubting of Thomas, xv
Douglas, Aaron, 732, 743; Cubism and, 712; work of, 712, *713*
Drum (of dome), xviii
Dubuffet, Jean: work of, 747–748, *747*
Duchamp, Marcel, 650, 711, 729, 758, 776, 793; Armory Show and, 710; Cubism/Futurism and, 684; Dada and, 705; the Steins and, 694; work of, *684,* 706–707, *706*
Dürer, Albrecht, 633
Dynamism of a Dog on a Leash (Balla), *702,* 703

Eakins, Thomas, 648, 651, 676, 732; work of, 638–639, *638*
Early Operation under Ether, Massachusetts General Hospital (Hawes and Southworth), 648, *648*

Early Renaissance, 641
Earthworks, 790
Easel painting: Pollock on, 749
Eastern philosophy, 793, 797
Echinus, xvi
École des Beaux-Arts, 644
Edwards, Melvin, 774, 801; work of, 771–772, *771*
Église du Dôme (Hardouin-Mansart), 602
Eiffel, Alexandre-Gustave: work of, *652,* 681
Eiffel Tower (Eiffel), 591, *652,* 681, 683, 698, 736
Eight, The, 708, 709–710
18 Happenings in Six Parts (Kaprow), 793
80 Backs (Abakanowicz), 776, *776*
Einstein, Albert, 691, 697
Eldana Abbey, 626
Em, David, 799; work of, 799, *799*
Emancipation Proclamation, 640, 641
Encyclopédie, Diderot and, 590, 592
Engaged half-columns, xvi
Engels, Friedrich, 632, 653
English Gothic, 642, 643
Enlightenment, 589–597, 601, 618, 622, 691; architecture, 602–606; classical art and, 599; Greece/ Rome and, 607; Neoclassicism and, 616; philosophy of, 589–591; Rationalism and, 630; rebellion against, 621; science of, 589–591; sculpture, 602–606
Entablature, xvi
Entartete Kunst exhibition, 721, *721*
Entombment, xv
Entry into Jerusalem, xv
Environmental Art movement, 790–792
Epic of American Civilization: Hispano-America (Orozco), *734,* 735
Epidauros: tholos at, xvi, *xvii*
Equitable Building, New York, 681
Ernst, Max, 709, 721, 729; work of, 720, *720*
Eros (Amor, Cupid), xiii
Etruscan Room (Adam), 598, *598,* 599
Etruscan tombs, 598
Eugène Delacroix (Nadar), *608,* 649
Europe, map of, *610*
Events (as art), Fluxus and, 793
Existentialism, 746, 747
Exposition des Arts Décoratifs et Industriels Modernes, 740
Exposition Universelle, 631, 641, 661, 696

Expressionism, 664, 680, 687, 692, 694; postwar, 746–748

Fallingwater. *See* Kaufmann House
Family of Charles IV (Goya), 618, *619*
Fantastic Art, Dada, Surrealism (MoMA exhibition), 730
Fate of the Animals (Marc), 692, *692*
Fauves and Fauvism, 665, 687, 689, 690, 697, 724, 743
Feminist art, 765–769, 772, 801
Feminist movement, 746, 770, 801
Femmages, 767
Fenton, Roger, 649
Ferdinand VII, King, 618, 620
Fin-de-siècle, 674
First Surrealist Manifesto, 719
Fit for Active Service (Grosz), *717*
Flack, Audrey, 801; work of, 761–762, *761*
Flag (Johns), 758, *758*
Flagellation, xv
Flight into Egypt, xiv
Floreale (Italian art style), 678
Florence, 597; Piazza della Signoria, 754
Flowers on Body (Mendieta), 768, *768*
Flutes, xvi
Fluxus group, 793, 794, 797
Flying buttresses, xx
Fontainebleau, 632
Forever Free (Lewis), 640–641, *640*
Formalism, 748, 755, 778
Foucault, Michel, 763
Fountain (Duchamp), 706, *706*
Fourth Style, 598
Fragonard, Jean-Honoré, 607; work of, *582,* 588–589
Franco, Francisco, 716
Frankenthaler, Helen, 801; on color-field painting, 753; Post-Painterly Abstraction and, 752; work of, 752–753, *753*
French Baroque, 584, 588, 607
French Realism, 630–637, 709
French Revolution, 590, 592, 600, 601, 609; Neoclassicism and, 598
French Rococo, 583, 584; painting, 586–589; sculpture, 586–589
French Romanticism, 618–625
French Royal Academy of Painting and Sculpture, 594, 655, 671; Fauves and, 687; salon of, 592, 593; Watteau and, 587
Freud, Sigmund, 671, 705, 719, 722
Friedrich, Caspar David, 651; work of, 626, *626*
Friend, The (Lehmbruck). *See Seated Youth*

Frieze, xvi
Fuller, Meta Warrick, 712
Fuseli, Henry, 618; work of, *616,* 617
Futurism, 684, 702–704, 724
Futurist Painting: Technical Manifesto, 703
Futurists, 698, 710, 711, 713, 743; sculpture and, 703–704, 726; World War I and, 704, 746

Gabo, Naum, 736; work of, 725, *725*
Gainsborough, Thomas, 607; work of, 594–595, *595*
Galatea, 672
Galerie des Glaces (Hardouin-Mansart and Le Brun), 584, *585*
Gardner, Alexander, 649
Gardner, Isabella Stewart, 709
Garnier, Charles: work of, 644, *644*
Gaudi, Antonio: work of, 680, *680*
Gauguin, Paul, 663, 672, 673, 679, 683, 687, 689, 692, 694; Japanese art and, 661; Symbolism and, 671; work of, 667–668, *667, 668*
Gauls, 642
Gehry, Frank, 801; on architectural design/materials, 788; work of, 788–789, *788*
Genghis Khan, 623
Genius of Christianity, The (Chateaubriand), 614, 642
George III, King, 595
George IV, King, 643
George Grosz: A Survey of His Art from 1918-1938 (exhibit), 729
George Washington (Greenough), 606, *606*
George Washington (Houdon), 605, *605*
Georges Pompidou National Center for Art and Culture ("Beaubourg") (Rogers and Piano), 787, *787*
Géricault, Théodore, 615, 625, 626, 635; work of, 620–621, *621*
German Expressionism, 665, 673, 689–693, 697, 698, 743, 763
Gérôme, Jean-Léon, 638
Gertrude Stein (Picasso), 694, *694*
Gestural abstraction, 749, 750, 765, 801
Giacometti, Alberto: work of, *746,* 747
Gibbon, Edward, 599
Giorgione da Castelfranco, 615
Girodet-Trioson, Anne-Louis, 615, 617, 651; work of, 614, *614*
Gizeh: Great Pyramids, of Khafre, Khufu, and Menkaure, *xi*
Glass skyscraper (Mies van der Rohe), 739

Gleaners, The (Millet), *632*
Global Groove (Paik), 797, *797*
Gods/goddesses: Greek/Roman, xiii
Goethe, Johann Wolfgang von, 623, 625
Golub, Leon: work of, 774–775, *774*
González, Julio: work of, 701, *701*
Goodacre, Glenna, 783
Gothic architecture, 642–643, 651
Gothic cathedrals, xx, *xx*
Government Services Administration (GSA), censorship and, 792
Goya y Lucentes, Francisco José de, 633, 651, 704, 732; work of, 618, *618, 619,* 620
Grand Canal, 597
Grand Manner portraiture, 595, 596, 605
Grand Tour, 603, 607; described, 597; Neoclassicism and, 598
Grande Odalisque (Ingres), 615, *615*
Grande Revue, La: Matisse in, 688
Graves, Michael, 801; work of, 786, *786*
Great Depression, 685, 686, 733, 740; art of, 730–731, 743
Great Exhibition, 645
Great Pyramids, Gizeh, *xi*
Greek cross, 602
Greek temples, xvi
Green Coca-Cola Bottles (Warhol), *760*
Green Dining Room (Morris), 678, *678*
Greenberg, Clement, 752, 754, 763; influence of, 748; on minimalism, 755–756; modernism and, 654; Post-Painterly Abstraction and, 751
Greenough, Horatio: work of, 606, *606*
Greuze, Jean-Baptiste, 599, 607; work of, 593, *593,* 595
Groin vault, xviii, *xviii*
Gropius, Walter, 739; Bauhaus and, 738, 743; work of, 738, *738*
Gros, Antoine-Jean, 615, 617, 620, 651; work of, 613, *613*
Gross Clinic, The (Eakins), 638–639, *638,* 648
Grosz, George, 721, 729; work of, 716–717, *717*
Grünewald, Matthias (Matthias Neithardt), 718
Guaranty (Prudential) Building (Sullivan), 682, *682*
Guernica (Picasso), 716, *716,* 729
Guerrilla Girls: work of, 769, *769*
Guggenheim Museum, Bilbao (Gehry), 788, *788;* atrium of, *788*

Guitar (Picasso), 699–700, *699*
Gutai Bijutsu Kyokai (Concrete Art Association), 793, 794

Haacke, Hans: work of, 778, *778*
Hades (Pluto), xiii
Hagia Sophia (Anthemius of Tralles and Isidorus of Miletus), 780
Hagia Sophia (Constantinople), xxi, *xxi*
Hall of Mirrors, 584, *585*
Hamilton, Richard: work of, 757–758, *757*
Hammons, David: work of, 773, *773*
Hang-Up (Hesse), 757, *757*
Hanson, Duane, 801; work of, 762–763, *763*
Happenings, 793, 794
Hardouin-Mansart, Jules, 584, 585, 602
Harlem Renaissance, 712, 732, 743
Harper's Weekly: Winslow Homer and, 638
Hart, Frederick, 783
Hartley, Marsden, 717; work of, 711–712, *711*
Harunobu, Suzuki, 660
Harvest of Death, Gettysburg, Pennsylvania, July 1863, A (O'Sullivan and Gardner), 649, *649*
Hatshepsut, Queen, 766
Hawes, Josiah Johnson, 651; work of, 648, *648*
Haywain (Constable), 626, *627*
Helena, Saint, 609
Hephaistos (Vulcan), xiii
Hepworth, Barbara, 729, 743, 756, 765; on abstract sculpture, 727; work of, 727–728, *728*
Hera (Juno), xiii
Herculaneum: excavation of, 598, 599, 607
Hermes (Mercury), xiii
Hermes and infant Dionysos (Praxiteles), *xiii*
Hesse, Eva: work of, 756–757, *757*
Hestia (Vesta), xiii
History of Ancient Art (Winckelmann), 599
Hitler, Adolf, 686, *721,* 729, 757; *Entartete Kunst* exhibition and, 721
Höch, Hannah: work of, 707–708, *707*
Hogarth, William, 599; work of, 594, *594*
Holbein, Hans, the Younger, 594

Holy Virgin Mary, The (Ofili), 772, *772*, 773

Holzer, Jenny, 801; work of, 799–800, *799*

Homage to New York (Tinguely), 795, *795*

Homeless Projection, The (Wodiczko), 775, *775*

Homer, Winslow, 650, 651; work of, 638, *638*

Hopeless (Lichtenstein), 759, *759*

Hopper, Edward, 743; work of, 731–732, *732*

Horse Fair, The (Bonheur), *634,* 635

Horse Galloping (Muybridge), 650, *650*

Horta, Victor: work of 847, *679*

Houdon, Jean-Antoine, 606, 638; work of, 605, *605*

Houses of Parliament (Barry and Pugin), *642,* 643

How to Explain Pictures to a Dead Hare (Beuys), 794–795, *795*

Hudson River School, 628, 629

Hue, in art, 664

Hysolar Institute (Behnisch), 787, *787,* 788

Iliad (Homer), 615

Illusionism, 589, 632; dimensions and, 755; expressionism and, 694, 748; moving away from, 635, 636; pictorial, 697; rejecting, 755

Impression: Sunrise (Monet), 654, *655,* 656

Impressionism, 624, 632, 635, 654–663, 664, 667, 668, 669, 670, 671, 673, 683, 687, 753; influence of, 676

Improvisation 28 (Kandinsky), 691, *691,* 692

Independent Group, origins of Pop Art and, 757, 758

Industrial materials, Judd on, 755

Industrial Revolution, impact of, 583, 590, 591, 607, 609, 626, 627, 643, 653

Ingres, Jean-Auguste-Dominique, 617; Neoclassicism and, 651; photography and, 647; work of, 614–615, *614, 615*

Insane Woman (Géricault), *621*

International Style, 739

Interpretation of Dreams, The (Freud), 671, 705

Ionic order, xvi

Isenheim Altarpiece (Grünewald), 718

Italian Baroque: architecture of, 586

Italian Renaissance, 607

Jack in the Pulpit No. 4 (O'Keeffe), 714

Jacob K. Javits Federal Building, 792, *792*

Jacobs, Jane, 784

Japanese art: influence of, 661

Japanese culture, 661

Japanese prints, influence of, 662, 663, 667, 668, 683

Japonisme, 661

Jeanne-Claude, 801; work of, 791, *791. See also* **Christo**

Jeanneret, Charles-Edouard. *See* Le Corbusier

Jefferson, Thomas, 589, 590, 607; work of, *604,* 605

Jefferson Medical College, 638–639

Jesus. *See* Christ

Johns, Jasper, 801; work of, 758, *758*

Johnson, Philip, on postmodern architecture, 785; work of, 782, *782,* 785–786, *785*

Jones, Inigo, 602

Judd, Donald, 788, 801; on sculpture/industrial materials, 755; work of, 755–756, *755*

Jugendstil, 678

Jung, Carl, 705, 719, 724, 749

Juno (Hera), xiii

Jupiter (Zeus), xiii, 671, *671,* 672, 759; statue of, 606

Jupiter and Semele (Moreau), 671, *671,* 672

Just What Is It That Makes Today's Homes So Different, So Appealing? (Hamilton), 757, *757,* 758

Kahlo, Frida, 743; work of, 736, *736*

Kandinsky, Vassily, 711, 721, 726, 749, 773; chair and, 738–739; work of, 691–692, *691,* 710

Kaprow, Allan: work of, 793

Käsebier, Gertrude: work of, 674–675, *675*

Kauffmann, Angelica, 607; work of, 599, *599*

Kaufmann House (Fallingwater) (Wright), 742, *742,* 743

Kelly, Ellsworth, 801; Post-Painterly Abstraction and, 752; work of, 752, *752*

Kent, William: work of, 602–603, *603*

Keystone, xviii

Kiefer, Anselm: work of, 765, *765*

Kinetic theater, 794

Kirchner, Ernst Ludwig, 721; Armory Show and, 710; work of, 689–690, *690*

Kiss, The (Klimt), 674, *674*

Kiyonaga, Torii: work of, 661, *661*

Klee, Paul, 721, 738, 773, 796; work of, 724, *724*

Klimt, Gustav: work of, 674, *674*

Klüver, Billy, 795

Kollwitz, Käthe: work of, 692, *693*

Koons, Jeff: work of, 776–777, *776*

Kosuth, Joseph, 801; work of, 796, *796*

Kronos, 620

Kruger, Barbara, 801; work of, 768, *768;* work of, 775

Kuhn, Walt: Armory Show and, 710

La Madeleine, Paris. *See* Madeleine, La

Labrouste, Henri, 651, 681; work of, 644, *645*

Ladies Luncheon Room (Mackintosh and Mackintosh), 678, *679*

Lamentation, xv

Landscape painting, 625–630; popularity of, 630

Lange, Dorothea, 743; work of, 731, *731*

Laocoön and his sons (Athanadoros, Hagesandros, and Polydoros of Rhodes), 676

Large Glass, The (Duchamp). *See Bride Stripped Bare by Her Bachelors, Even, The* (Duchamp)

Last Supper, xv; reinterpretation of, 766

Latrobe, Benjamin, 605

Lawrence, Jacob, 743; work of, 732–733, *733*

Le Brun, Charles, 584, 585

Le Corbusier, 701, 743, 778, 801; work of, 739–740, *740,* 780, *780*

Learning from Las Vegas (Venturi), 786

Lectionary of Henry II, xiv

LED technology. *See* Light-emitting diode technology

Léger, Fernand, 729; Purism and, 701–702; work of, 701–702, *702*

Lehmbruck, Wilhelm, 721; Armory Show and, 710; work of, 692–693, *693*

Leibl, Wilhelm: work of, 637, *637*

Lemoine, J. B.: work of, *584*

Lenin, Vladimir, 686

Leonardo da Vinci, 705

Lespinasse, Julie de: salons and, 585

Lewis, Edmonia: work of, 640–641, *640*

Liberty: personification of, 625

Liberty Leading the People (Delacroix), 623, *623*

Libeskind, Daniel, 801; work of, 789, *789*

Lichtenstein, Roy, 801; on Pop Art, 759; work of, 759, *759*

Light: response to, 664

Light-emitting diode (LED) technology, 799

Lin, Maya Ying, 790; work of, 782–784, *783*

Lincoln, Abraham, 638, 640, 641

Lincoln Memorial, 783

L'Indifférent (Watteau), *586,* 587, 589

Lipchitz, Jacques, 729; work of, 700, *700*

Lithography, 633, 651

Lives of the Great Greeks and Romans (Plutarch), 613

Living Theatre, 797

Livy, Titus, 601

Lobster Trap and Fish Tail (Calder), 730, *730*

London: Adelphi Terrace, 598; Chiswick House, 602–603, *603,* 604, 605, 607; Crystal Palace, 591, 644–645, *645,* 651, 787; Houses of Parliament, *642,* 643; Saint Paul's, 602

Lord Heathfield (Reynolds), 595, *595*

Lotus table lamp (Tiffany), *680*

Louis, Morris, 801; work of, 753, *753*

Louis XIV, King, 586; French culture and, 583, 584; portrait of, 587

Louis XV, King, 666; Rococo style and, 583, 585, 592

Lucky Strike (Davis), 712, *712*

Lynch Fragment series (Edwards), 771, 772

Mackintosh, Charles Rennie, 661; work of, 678, *679*

Mackintosh, Margaret Macdonald: work of, 678, *679*

Madeleine, La, Paris, 612, *612,* 651

Magritte, René, 719; work of, 722, *722*

Maison Carrée, 605, 612

Making a Work with His Own Body (Shiraga), 793–794, *793*

Male gaze, 767, 768, 801

Malevich, Kazimir, 736; Suprematism and, 724, 725; work of, 724–725, *725*

Man Pointing (Giacometti), 746, 747

Man Ray (Emmanuel Radnitsky), 743; work of, 711, *711*

Manet, Édouard, 637, 648, 651, 655, 658; Japanese art and, 661; work of, 635–636, *635, 636,* 660, *660*

Mannerism, 785; Italian, 589, 615

Mansheshe (Oursler), 800, *800*

Mapplethorpe, Robert, 772

Marat, John-Paul, 601

Marc, Franz, 691, 721, 763–764; work of, *692, 692*

Marilyn (Flack), 761–762, *761*

Marilyn Diptych (Warhol), 760, *760, 762*

Marinetti, Filippo Tommaso, 702, 703

Marquesas Islands, 668

Marriage à la Mode (Hogarth), 594, *594*

Mars (Ares), xiii

Marseillaise, La (Rude). *See Departure of the Volunteers of 1792*

Marshall Field wholesale store (Richardson), 681, *681*

Martinet, Achille-Louis: work of, *645*

Martyrdom, 596

Marxism, 653–654

Mary. *See* Virgin Mary

Mas o Menos (Stella), 752, *752*

Mass culture, Pop Art and, 757

Massacre of the Innocents, xiv

Matisse, Amélie, 687

Matisse, Henri, 694, 724, 743; Armory Show and, 710; on color, 688; Primitivism and, 696; work of, *687, 687, 688,* 689

Matronage, 709

Meat Joy (Schneemann), 794, *794*

Melancholy and Mystery of a Street (de Chirico), 719–720, *720*

Memoirs of Marmontel, 585

Mendieta, Ana, 801; work of, 768–769, *768*

Meninas, Las (Velázquez), 618, 619, 639

Mercenaries IV (Golub), 774–775, *774*

Mercer, Kobena, 771

Mercury (Hermes), xiii

Merz 19 (Schwitters), 708, *708,* 756

Metalwork, 668

Metaphysical painting, 719–721

Metopes, xvi

MetroMobiltan (Haacke), 778, *778*

Metropolitan Museum of Art (New York), 694, 778

Mexican Revolution, 734, 735

Michel, Claude. *See* Clodion

Middle Ages, 616, 641; art/architecture of, 643

Middlesex, Osterley Park House, 598, *598,* 599

Mies van der Rohe, Ludwig, 742, 778, 801; Johnson and, 785; work of, *739, 739,* 781–782, *782*

Migrant Mother, Nipomo Valley (Lange), 731, *731*

Migration of the Negro, The (Lawrence), 732, *733*

Milan, 597

Millais, John Everett, 642; work of, 641, *641*

Millet, Jean-François, 640; work of, 632–633, *632*

Minerva (Athena), xiii

Minimalism, 755–757, 761, 763, 781, 783, 792, 801

Miracles of Jesus, xiv

Miró, Joan, 719, 724, 730, 756; work of, 723, *723*

Mobiles, 729

Modernism, 654, 687, 710, 778–784, 786

Modernismo, 678

Modernist architecture, 784, 788, 801; map of, *779*

MoMA. *See* Museum of Modern Art

Mona Lisa (Leonardo): Duchamp and, 705

Mondrian, Piet, 729, 730, 737, 738; Cubism and, 726; work of, 726, *726*

Monet, Claude, 632, 661, 669, 682; Impressionism and, 683; work of, 654–657, *655, 656, 657*

Monroe, Marilyn, 760, 762

Mont Sainte-Victoire (Cézanne), 669, *669*

Monticello, Charlottesville, Va. (Jefferson), *604,* 605, 607

Monument to the Third International (Tatlin), 736–737, *737*

Moore, Charles, 801; work of, 784–785, *784*

Moore, Henry, 729, 743; on abstract sculpture, 727; work of, 728, *728*

Moorish-Spanish architecture, 680

Moreau, Gustave: Symbolism and, 683; work of, 671–672, *671*

Morisot, Berthe, 662; work of, 658–659, *658*

Morning of Liberty, The (Lewis). *See Forever Free*

Morris, William, 661; Arts and Crafts movement and, 689; work of, 678, *678*

Mosaics, 672

Mother of God, 674. *See also* Virgin Mary

Moulin de la Galette, Le (Renoir), 659, *659,* 664

Mount Olympus, 672

Mount Vesuvius, 598, 599

Mrs. Richard Brinsley Sheridan (Gainsborough), 594–595, *595*

Mukhina, Vera: work of, 729, *729*

Munch, Edvard, 690, 692; work of, 673, *673*

Mural painting: Pollock on, 749; Roman, 598

Musée Africain (Marseilles), 696

Musée du quai Branly (Paris), 696

Musée National des Arts d'Afrique et d'Océanie (Paris), 696

Museum für Völkerkunde (Berlin), 696

Museum of Modern Art (MoMA), 709, 729; avant-garde and, 730; commission by, 730; Hammons and, 773; Johnson and, 785; Picasso and, 716; Tinguely and, 795

Museums, 709; non-Western art collections of, 696

Mussolini, Benito, 605, 686

Muybridge, Eadweard, 639, 651, 676, 677; work of, 650, *650*

My Egypt (Demuth), 713, *713*

Nadar (Gaspar-Félix Tournachon), 646, 651; Delacroix and, 649; work of, *608,* 648–649

Nadar Raising Photography to the Height of Art (Daumier), *646*

Naples, 597

Napoleon at the Pesthouse at Jaffa (Gros), 613, *613,* 620

Napoleon Bonaparte, 618; Arc de Triomphe and, 625; art under, 609, 611–615, 651; classical tradition and, 642; David and, 611, 651; Neoclassicism and, 611, 651

Napoleon III, 655, 657

Napoleonic Empire, map of, *610*

Nash, John: work of, 643, *643*

National Endowment for the Arts (NEA), 772

National Socialist German Workers Party. *See* Nazi Party

Native American art, 773, 774

Nativity, xiv

Natoire, Charles-Joseph: work of, *584*

"Natural" art, 592–597

Natural History (Buffon), 590

Natural Surrealism, 719, 736, 743

Naturalism, 607; Diderot on, 592

Nauman, Bruce, 801; work of, 796–797, *796*

Nave, xx

Nave arcade, xx

Nazi Party, 685, 686, 716, 719, 729; Bauhaus and, 739; degenerate art and, 721

NEA. *See* National Endowment for the Arts

NEA Four, 772

Neithardt, Matthias. *See* Grünewald, Matthias

Neo-Expressionism, 763–765

Neoclassical portico, parody of, 786, *786*

Neoclassical style: architecture, 603, 604, 643; art, 597; painting, 599–601

Neoclassicism, 598–606, 607, 609, 618, 624, 651; Enlightenment and, 616; Grand Tour and, 598; popularity of, 613; Roman Empire and, 611; Romanticism and, 620; transition from, 616, 618

Neoplasticism, 726

Neptune (Poseidon), xiii

Neue Sachlichkeit, 716–719, 743

Neumann, Balthasar: work of, 586, *586*

Nevelson, Louise, 765; work of, 756, *756*

New media, 793, 797–800, 801

New School for Social Research, Cage and, 793

New York, Night (O'Keeffe), 714, *714*

New York City: AT&T (Sony) Building, 785–786, *785;* Chrysler Building, 740, *741,* 800; Equitable Building, 681; Museum of Modern Art, 730; New York Public Library, 135th Street, 732; School of Abstract Expressionism, 748, 750; Seagram Building, 781, *782,* 785, 801; Solomon R. Guggenheim Museum, 778–779, *779,* 781, 799, 800, 801; Trans World Airlines terminal, 780, *781*

New York Herald, on Armory Show, 710

New York Times, 777; on Armory Show, 710

New York World's Fair (1937), 716

Newman, Barnett, 753; work of, *750,* 751

Newton, Isaac, 590, 691; Enlightenment and, 589

Niépce, Joseph Nicéphore, 646

Nietzsche, Friedrich, 718, 720

Night (Beckmann), 717–718, *717*

Night Café (van Gogh), 665–666, *666*

Nighthawks (Hopper), 732, *732*

Nightmare, The (Fuseli), 616, *617*

Nigredo (Kiefer), 765, *765*

Nike, 703

Nike of Samothrace, 703
1948-C (Still), 754
Noah's Ark (Douglas), 712, *713*
Nocturne in Black and Gold (The Falling Rocket) (Whistler), *662, 663,* 678
Nolde, Emil, 721; work of, 690, *690*
Noli Me Tangere, xv
Nora (Em), 799, *799*
Notre-Dame, Paris, 611, 643
Notre-Dame-du-Haut (Le Corbusier), 740, 780, *780,* 801; interior of, *780*
Nude (Weston), 715, *715*
Nude Descending a Staircase (Duchamp), *684,* 710
Number 1, 1950 (Lavendar Mist) (Pollock), *748,* 749
No. 14 (Rothko), 751, *751*
No. 76 (Lawrence), 732, *733*
Nymphs and a Satyr (Bouguereau), *637*

Oath of the Horatii (David), 583, 600, *600,* 601, 607, 611, 613, 614
Oceania: art of, 690
Oculus, xviii
Odyssey (Homer), 615
Ofili, Chris: work of, 772, *772, 773*
Oil painting: French, 583
O'Keeffe, Georgia, 743, 765, 766; style of, 713–714, *714*
Old Masters, 654, 668
Oldenburg, Claes, 788; work of, 761, *761*
Olympia (Manet), 636, *636,* 637
On the Origin of the Species by Means of Natural Selection (Darwin), 654
One and Three Chairs (Kosuth), 796, *796*
Ophelia, Study no. 2 (Cameron), 649, *649*
Ophelia (Millais), 641, *641,* 642
Oppenheim, Meret: work of, 722–723, *723*
Orozco, José Clemente, 732, 733; work of, 734–735, *734*
Orpheus, 697
Orphism, 697, 698
Osterley Park House, Etruscan Room at, 598, *598,* 599
O'Sullivan, Timothy, 651; work of, 649–650, *649*
Oursler, Tony, 801; work of, 800, *800*
Oval Sculpture (No. 2) (Hepworth), 728, *728*
Oxbow, The (View from Mount Holyoke, Northampton,

Massachusetts, after a Thunderstorm) (Cole), 628, *628*

Pablo Picasso in his studio (Burgess), *696*
Paestum, 597; Temple of Hera II, xvi, *xvii*
Paik, Nam June, 801; work of, 797, *797*
Painting: American, 731–736; Schneemann on, 794
Painting (Bacon), 747, *747*
Painting (Miró), 723, *723*
Paleolithic art: cave painting, 680
Palladian architecture, 603
Palladio, Andrea, 602, 605
Panthéon, Paris (Sainte-Geneviève) (Soufflot), 602, *602,* 607
Pantheon, Rome, *xix;* Jefferson and, 604, 605
Paradise Now (Paik), 797
Paris: Arc de Triomphe, 625; Bibliothèque Sainte-Geneviève, 644, *645,* 651; Église du Dôme, 602; Eiffel Tower, 591, *652,* 681, 683, 698, 736; Georges Pompidou National Center for Art and Culture, 787, *787;* International Exposition, 716, 729; La Madeleine, 612, *612,* 651; Notre-Dame, 611, 643; Panthéon, 602, *602,* 607; Paris Opéra, 644, *644,* 660; Salon de la Princesse, 584, *584;* World's Fair, 655
Paris: A Rainy Day (Caillebotte), 657, *657,* 658
Paris Opéra (Garnier), 644, *644,* 660
Parthenon, 635, 763
Passion of Christ, xv
Passion of Sacco and Vanzetti, The (Shahn), 731
Pastoral Symphony (Giorgione and/or Titian), 635
Patronage: corporate, 778; politics of, 778. *See also* Matronage
Pauline Borghese as Venus (Canova), *612*
Pavilion of Realism, 631, 641, 655
Paxton, Joseph, 651, 681; work of, 644–645, *645*
Peacock Skirt (Beardsley), 673, *673*
Pediment, xvi
Pendentives, xxi
People's Commissariat for Enlightenment, 736
Performance Art, 793–796, 801; feminist, 772, 794; Schneemann on, 794
Peripteral temple, xvi
Perry, Cabot: on Monet, 656

Persistence of Memory, The (Dalí), 722, *722*
Phidias, 606, 615; work of, *xiii*
Philosopher Giving a Lecture at the Orrery, A (Wright of Derby), *590,* 591
Philosophes, 590
Philosophical Bordello (Picasso). *See Demoiselles d'Avignon* (Picasso)
Philosophical Enquiry into the Origins of Our Ideas of the Sublime and Beautiful, A (Burke), 616
Photography, 591, 608, 674, 714–715, 729–731; influence of, 663, 677, 683; invention of, 609, 647–650, 651, 743; portrait painting and, 762; wet-plate, 646
Photomontagists, 707
Photorealism, 761, 762
Piano, Renzo: work of, 787, *787*
Piazza della Signoria, 754
Piazza d'Italia (Moore), 784–785, *784,* 801
Picabia, Francis, 705, 713
Picasso, Pablo, 701, 722–723, 724, 729, 730, 767; Armory Show and, 710; Cubism and, 697, 700, 743; modernism and, 694; Primitivism and, 696; work of, 694–696, *694, 695, 698, 698, 699*–700, *699,* 716, *716*
"Picasso Speaks" (Zayas), quote from, 700
Pietà, 601, 692
Pietà (Michelangelo), 601
Pilgrimage to Cythera (Watteau), 583, 587–588, *587*
Pilgrimages, 597
Pink Panther (Koons), 776, *776*
Pioneer Days and Early Settlers (Benton), 734, *734*
Piper, Adrian, 801; work of, 798, *798*
Pisa, 597
Pisani family, 589
Piss Christ (Serrano), 772
Pissarro, Camille, 667, 668; work of, 658, *658*
Pittura Metafisica (Metaphysical Painting), 719, 720
Place du Théâtre Français, La (Pissarro), 658, *658*
Plutarch, 613
Pluto (Hades), xiii
Pointillism, 664, 665, 683
Poissy-sur-Seine, Villa Savoye, 740, *740,* 780
Political art, 770–778
Pollock, Jackson, *749,* 750, 756, 765, 793, 801; on easel/mural painting, 749; work of, *748,* 749

Polyphemos, 672
Pompadour, Madame de, 585, 588
Pompeii: excavation of, 598, 599, 607
Pop Art, 757–761, 763, 765, 786, 790, 801; British, 757; Lichtenstein on, 759
Portland Building (Graves), 786, *786,* 801
Portrait of a German Officer (Hartley), 711–712, *711,* 717
Portrait of Paul Revere (Copley), 596, *596*
Portraiture: photography and, 762
Portuguese, The (Braque), 697, *697*
Poseidon (Neptune), xiii
Post-and-lintel architecture, xviii
Post-Impressionism, 654, 663–670, 673, 679, 683, 687, 724; Japanese art and, 661
Post-Painterly Abstraction, 751–754, 757, 761, 801
Postmodern architecture, 784, 801; Johnson on, 785; map of, *779*
Postmodern painting, 763–778
Postmodern sculpture, 763–778
Postmodernism, 784–787, 800
Poussin, Nicolas, 587, 669
Pozzo, Fra Andrea, 589
Prairie house, 741, *741*
Praxiteles: work of, *xiii*
Pre-Raphaelite Brotherhood, 641–642, 649; Realism and, 641
Precisionism, 712–713, 714, 733, 743
Presentation in the Temple, xiv
Primitive art, 773
Primitivism, 694–702, 724
Printmaking, 633
Pritchard, Thomas F.: work of, 591, *591*
Productivism as art movement, 736
Pseudoperipteral temples, xvi
Public art: Jacques-Louis David on, 600
Public Enemy (Hammons), 773, *773*
Public funding of art, controversy over, 772
Pugin, A.W.N.: work of, *642,* 643
Pure Art, 735
Pure plastic art, 726, 743
Purism, 740; Synthetic Cubism and, 701–702
Puvis de Chavannes, Pierre: work of, *670,* 671
Pyramids: Egyptian, *xi*

Quetzalcoatl, 735
Quick-to-See Smith, Jaune, 801; work of, 773–774, *773*

RA. *See* Resettlement Administration

Rabbula Gospels, xv
Radnitzky, Emmanuel. *See* Man Ray
Raft of the Medusa (Géricault), 620, *621*
Raising of the Cross, xv
Raphael (Raffaello Santi), 615, 672, 756
Rationalism, Enlightenment and, 598, 630
Rauch, John: work of, 786, *786*
Rauschenberg, Robert, 774; work of, 758–759, *758*
Readymades, 706
Realism, 591, 616, 630–642, 651, 654, 667, 670, 676, 687, 694, 729, 763; American, 651, 708; Courbet on, 631; dismissal of, 671, 673, 683; French, 630–637, 709; Pre-Raphaelite Brotherhood and, 641; rise of, 609
Realistic Manifesto, The (Gabo and Pevsner), 725
Reclining Figure (Moore), 728, *728*
Red Blue Green (Kelly), 752, *752*
Red Room (Harmony in Red) (Matisse), 688, *688*, 689
Redon, Odilon, 683; work of, 672, *672*
Reflections on the Imitation of Greek Works in Painting and Sculpture (Winckelmann), 599
Regionalism, 733, 734
Rembrandt van Rijn, 633, 640, 759
Renaissance: style, 644
Renoir, Pierre-Auguste, 632, 661, 663, 694; Impressionism and, 683; on painting, 659; work of, 659, *659*
Resettlement Administration (RA), 731, 732
Resurrection, xv, 718
Revett, Nicholas: work of, 603
"Revolt against the City" essay (Wood), 733
Reynolds, Sir Joshua: work of, 595, *595*
Ribs, xx
Richardson, Henry Hobson, 683; work of, 681, *681*
Richter, Hans: on Dadaists, 705
Rietveld, Gerrit Thomas: work of, 737–738, *737*
Rifle Gap (Colorado), curtain at, 791
Rigaud, Hyacinthe, 587
Ringgold, Faith, 801; work of, 770–771, *770*
Riva degli Schiavoni, Venice (Canaletto), 597, *597*
Rivera, Diego, 743; work of, 735–736, *735*

Robert Mapplethorpe: The Perfect Moment (exhibition), 772
Robie House (Wright), 741–742, *741;* plan of, *741*
Rockefeller, Abby Aldrich, 709, 730
Rockefeller, Nelson, 795
Rococo, 582, 583–589, 592, 594, 598, 602, 616; architecture, 584, 586; art, 589, 607; feminine look of, 585; painting, 595; rebellion against, 601
Rodin, Auguste, 683, 693; on movement in art/photography, 677; work of, 676–677, *677*
Rogers, Richard: work of, 787, *787*
Roman architecture, xviii
Roman Empire: Neoclassicism and, 611
Roman Republic, 609
Roman temples, xvi
Romantic architecture, 642–645, 651
Romanticism, 606, 615, 616–630, 632; appeal of, 622; foreshadowing, 613; Neoclassicism and, 620; rise of, 609; roots of, 616–617, 651; transition to, 616, 618
Rome: Baths of Diocletian, *xix;* Pantheon, *xix,* 604, 605; Saint Peter's, 601, 602; Temple of Portunus, xvi, *xvii*
Ronchamp, Notre-Dame-du-Haut, 740, 780, *780,* 801
Rood, Ogden: on color theory, 664
Rosenberg, Harold: on action painting, 750
Rossetti, Dante Gabriel: work of, 641–642, *642*
Rothenberg, Susan: work of, 763–764, *764*
Rothko, Mark, 753, 801; on abstract expressionism, 748; work of, 751, *751*
Rotunda and Lawn, Monticello (Jefferson), *604,* 605
Rouen: Cathedral of, 656, 683
Rouen Cathedral: The Portal (in Sun) (Monet), 656, *656*
Rousseau, Henri, 683; work of, 672–673, *672*
Rousseau, Jean-Jacques, 590, 607, 625; Enlightenment and, 592, 616
Royal Pavilion at Brighton resort area (Nash), 643, *643*
Rubens, Peter Paul, 587, 594, 624
Rude, François: work of, 625, *625*
Rue Transnonain (Daumier), 633, *633*
Ruskin, John, 641, 663, 678
Russian Revolution, 685, 686, 725, 736

Saarinen, Eero, 781, 801; work of, 780, *781*
Sacred Grove (Puvis de Chavannes), 670, 671
Saint-Gaudens, Augustus: work of, 675, *675*
Saint-Lazare Train Station (Monet), 656–657, *657*
Saint Mark's, Venice, xxi, *xxi*
Saint Mary of Egypt among Sinners (Nolde), 690, *690*
Saint Paul's, London: dome of, 602
Saint Peter's, Rome, 601; dome of, 602
Saint-Sernin, *xix*
Salon d'Automne, 687
Salon de la Princesse (Boffrand), 584, *584*
Salon des Indépendants, 655
Salon des Refusés, 655
Salon of 1827, 615
Salon of 1848, Bonheur and, 635
Salon of 1874, 662
Salons, 585, 592, 593, 607, 655
Saltcellar of Francis I (Cellini), 589
Saraband (Louis), 753, *753*
Sardanapalus poem (Byron), 622, 623
Sargent, John Singer, 651, 708; work of, 639, *639*
Sartre, Jean-Paul, 746, 747
Saturation, of color, 664
Saturn Devouring One of His Children (Goya), 620, *620*
Satyr Crowning a Bacchanate (Clodion), *589*
Saying Grace (Chardin), 592, *592*
Schapiro, Miriam, 765; work of, 766–767, *767*
Schnabel, Julian: work of, 764–765, *764*
Schneemann, Carolee, 801; on painting/performance art/art history, 794; work of, 794, *794*
School of Athens (Raphael), 615
Schröder House (Rietveld), 737, *737*
Schwitters, Kurt, 711, 721, 756, 759; work of, 708, *708*
Science: art and, 691
Scream, The (Munch), 673, *673,* 690
Sculpture: abstract, 727; Donald Judd on, 755; industrial materials and, 755; outdoor, 754
Seagram Building (Mies van der Rohe and Johnson), 781, *782,* 785, 801
Sears Tower, 782, *782*
Seated Youth (Lehmbruck), 693, *693*
Self-Portrait (Vigée-Lebrun), 593–594, *593*

Senefelder, Alois: lithography and, 633
Sensation: Young British Artists from the Saatchi Collection (exhibition), 772, 773
Serra, Richard, 772; work of, 792, *792*
Serrano, Andres, 772
Seurat, Georges, 655, 663; pointillism and, 683; work of, 664–665, *665*
Severini, Gino, 703; work of, 704, *704*
Shahn, Ben, 743; work of, 731
Shchukin, Sergei, 694, 724
Sherman, Cindy, 768, 771, 801; work of, 767, *767*
Shiraga, Kazuo: work of, 793–794, *793*
Shop Block (Gropius), 738, *738*
Short History of Modernist Painting, A (Tansey), 777–778, *777*
Siena, 597
Silk: printing on, 758
Silueta (Silhouettes) (Mendieta), 768
Simmons Architects: work of, 785, *785*
Simpson, Lorna, 801; work of, 771, *771;* work of, 775
Site-specific art, 778–792, 801
Sixth Avenue and Thirtieth Street, New York City (Sloan), 708, 709
Skidmore, Owings, and Merrill (SOM): work of, 782, *782*
Skyscrapers, 681, 683, 714, 741, 782
Slave Ship, The (Slavers Throwing Overboard the Dead and Dying, Typhoon Coming On) (Turner), 627, *627,* 628
Sleep of Reason Produces Monsters, The (Goya), 618, *618*
Sleeping Gypsy (Rousseau), 672, *672,* 683
Sloan, John, 709–710; work of, *708*
Smith, David: work of, 754–755, *754*
Smith, Kiki: work of, 770, *770*
Smith, Tony, 801; work of, *754,* 755
Smithson, Robert: work of, 790–791, *790*
Social Contract (Rousseau), 616
Social History of the State of Missouri, A (Benton), 734
Société des Artistes Indépendants, 655
Sociopolitical art, 770–778
Solomon R. Guggenheim Museum (Wright), 778–779, *779,* 781, 801; Barney exhibit at, 800; Holzer exhibit at, 799
SOM. *See* Skidmore, Owings, and Merrill

Sony Building. *See* AT&T
S.O.S.-Starification Object Series (Wilke), 769, *769*
Soufflot, Jacques-Germain: work of, 602, *602*
Southworth, Albert Sands, 651; work of, 648, *648*
Spanish art styles: Romantic, 618–625
"Specific Objects" art essay (Judd), 755
Spiral Jetty (Smithson), 790–791, *790*
Stained-glass windows, xx; favrile, 680
Staircase (Horta), *679*
Starry Night (van Gogh), 666, *667*, 683, 730
Steerage, The (Stieglitz), 714, *715*
Stein, Gertrude and Leo, 694, *694*, 695
Stella, Frank, 801; work of, 752, *752*
Stereo Styles (Simpson), 771, *771*
Stieglitz, Alfred, 713, 714, 743; the Steins and, 694; work of, 714–715, *715*
Still, Clyfford: Post-Painterly Abstraction and, 754; work of, 754
Still Life in Studio (Daguerre), *647*, 648
Still-life painting, 592, 670, 683, 762
Still Life with Chair-Caning (Picasso), 698, *698*
Stone Breakers, The (Courbet), 630, *630*
Store, The (Oldenburg), 761, *761*
Street, Dresden (Kirchner), 690, *690*
Stuart, James, 607; work of, 603, *603*
Stuttgart, Hysolar Institute, 787, *787*, 788
Sullivan, Louis Henry, 683, 741, 782; work of, 681–682, *682*
Sunday on La Grande Jatte, A (Seurat), 655, 664, 665, *665*, 671
Supermarket Shopper (Hanson), 763, *763*
Superrealism, 761–763, 765, 801
Supper at Emmaus, xv
Suprematism, 724–726, 737, 743
Suprematist Composition: Airplane Flying (Malevich), 724, *725*
Surrealism, 719–724, 793; Biomorphic, 719, 728, 743, 756; Dada and, 719, 720; impact of, 721; Natural, 719, 736, 743; Pop, 786; psychic automatism of, 749
Surrounded Islands 1980-83 (Christo and Jeanne-Claude), 791, *791*, 801

Swing, The (Fragonard), *582*, 588–589
Sydney Opera House (Utzon), 781, *781*, 786
Symbolism, 638, 654, 670–675, 679, 683, 736; Art Nouveau and, 673; subjectivism of, 671
Synthetic Cubism, 698, 713, 731; influence of, 711, 712; Purism and, 701–702

Tahiti: Gauguin and, 668
Talbot, William Henry Fox, photographic process, 646, 647, 651
Tambo (Edwards), 771–772, *771*
Tanner, Henry Ossawa, 732; work of, 640, *640*
Tansey, Mark: work of, 777–778, *777*
Tapestries, 584
Tatlin, Vladimir, 725; work of, 736–737, *737*
Tattoo (Rothenberg), 764, *764*
Tattooing, 764, *764*
Temple of Hera II, Paestum, xvi, *xvii*
Temple of Portunus, xvi, *xvii*
Temples: Greco-Roman design, xvi
Thankful Poor, The (Tanner), 640, *640*
Third-Class Carriage (Daumier), *634*
Third of May, 1808 (Goya), 618, *619*, 620, 633, 704
Third Style, 598
This Is Tomorrow (exhibition), 758
Tholos, xvi
Three Marys at the Tomb, xv
Three Women in a Village Church (Leibl), 637, *637*
Tiepolo, Giambattista, 607; work of, *588*, 589
Tiffany, Louis Comfort: work of, 680, *680*
Tiffany Studios, 680
Tiger Hunt (Delacroix), 624–625, *624*
Tilted Arc (Serra), 772, 792, *792*
Tinguely, Jean: work of, 795–796, *795*
Titian (Tiziano Vecelli), 615
Toulouse: Saint-Sernin church, *xix*
Toulouse-Lautrec, Henri de: Japanese art and, 661; work of, 663–664, *663*
Tournachon, Gaspar-Félix. *See* Nadar
Trade (Gifts for Trading Land with White People) (Quick-to-See Smith), 774, *774*
Trans World Airlines terminal (Saarinen), 780, *781*

Transept, xx
Transfiguration of Christ, xiv
Treachery (or Perfidy) of Images, The (Magritte), 722, *722*
Treasures of Ancient Nigeria (exhibition), 778
Trials of Jesus, xv
Triptychs, xvi
Tropical Garden II (Nevelson), 756, *756*
True Artist Helps the World by Revealing Mystic Truths (Nauman), 796–797, *796*
Tub, The (Degas), 661–662, *661*
Tunnel vault, xviii
Turner, Joseph Mallord William, 597, 628, 651; work of, 626–627, *627*
Twilight in the Wilderness (Church), 629–630, *629*
Twittering Machine (Klee), 724, *724*, 796
Two Children Are Threatened by a Nightingale (Ernst), 720, *720*, 721
Two Fridas, The (Kahlo), 736, *736*
Two Women at the Bath (Kiyonaga), *661*

Ugolino and His Children (Carpeaux), 676, *676*
Unique Forms of Continuity in Space (Boccioni), 703, *703*
United States, map of, *584*
Untitled (Holzer), 799, *799*
Untitled (Judd), 755, *755*
Untitled (K. Smith), 770, *770*
Untitled (Your Gaze Hits the Side of My Face) (Kruger), 768, *768*
Untitled Film Stills (Sherman), 767, *767*
Urbanization, 653, 657
Utrecht, Schröder house (Rietveld), 737, *737*
Utzon, Joern, 801; work of, 781, *781*

Value, of color, 664
van Alen, William: work of, 740, *741*
van Doesburg, Theo, 726; on De Stijl, 737
Van Dyck, Anthony, 594
van Eesteren, Cor, 726
Van Eetvelde house, staircase for, 679, *679*
van Gogh, Vincent, 663, 679, 682, 683, 687, 689, 690, 730, 758; Japanese art and, 661; letters by, 665, 666; Symbolism and, 671; work of, 665–666, *666*, 667

Vanitas paintings, 648, 761
Vasari, Giorgio, 599
Vaults, xviii; Gothic, 781
Vecelli, Tiziano. *See* Titian
Veduta painting, 597, 607
Velázquez, Diego, 618, 619, 639
Venice: Doge's Palace, 597; Saint Mark's, xxi, *xxi*; Villa Rotonda, 602, 605
Venturi, Robert, 784; work of, 786, *786*
Venus, 651, 750
Venus (Aphrodite), xiii
Venus de Milo (Alexandros of Antioch-on-the-Meander), 612
Versailles, Palace at, 583, 584, 587, 602; Galerie des Glaces, 584, *585*; Hall of Mirrors, 584, *585*
Vesta (Hestia), xiii
Veteran in a New Field (Winslow Homer), 638, *638*, 650
Victory, portrayal in art, 615
Video images, 793, 797, 801
Vie Inquiète (Uneasy Life) (Dubuffet), 747, *747*
Vierzehnheiligen church (Neumann): interior of, *586*; plan of, 586, *586*
Vietnam Veterans Memorial (Lin), 782–784, *783*, 790
Vietnam Women's Memorial Project, 783
Vigée-Lebrun, Élisabeth Louise: work of, 593–594, *593*
Vignon, Pierre, 651; work of, 612, *612*
Villa at the Seaside (Morisot), 658, *659*
Villa Rotonda (Palladio), 602, 605
Villa Savoye (Le Corbusier), 740, *740*, 780
Village Bride (Greuze), 593, *593*
Viola, Bill, 801; work of, 798, *798*
Viollet-le-Duc, Eugène, 642–643
Vir Heroicus Sublimis (Newman), 750, 751
Virgin Mary: Annunciation and, 674; portrayal of, 773
Vision after the Sermon, or *Jacob Wrestling with the Angel* (Gauguin), 667–668, *667*
Visitation, xiv
Visitation group (Reims Cathedral), *xiv*
Vitruvius, 602
Voltaire (François Marie Arouet), 615, 622; Enlightenment and, 590, 592, 616
Volutes, xvi
Voussoirs, xviii
Vulcan (Hephaistos), xiii

Walk Home, The (Schnabel), *764,* 765

Walking Man (Rodin), 676, 677, *677*

War Monument (Barlach), 719, *719*

Warhol, Andy, 762, 776, 801; work of, 760–761, *760*

Washington, D.C.: Vietnam Veterans Memorial, 782–784, *783,* 790

Washington, George: statue of, 605, 638

"Wassily chair" (Breuer), 738–739, *739*

Watteau, Antoine, 589, 607; work of, 586–588, *586, 587*

West, Benjamin, 605, 607; work of, 595–596, *596*

Weston, Edward, 743; work of, 715, *715*

Wet-plate technology, 646, 649

"When I put my hands on your body" (Wojnarowicz), 775, *775*

Where Do We Come From? What Are We? Where Are We Going? (Gauguin), 668, *668*

Whistler, James Abbott McNeill, 678, 708; Japanese art and, 661; John Ruskin on, 663; work of, 662–663, *662*

Whitney Museum of American Art, New York, 709

Who's Afraid of Aunt Jemima? (Ringgold), 770, *770*

Wilke, Hannah, 801; work of, 769, *769*

Winckelmann, Johann Joachim: as art historian, 599

Wodiczko, Krzysztof, 775, 801; work of, 775, *775*

Wojnarowicz, David, 775, 801; work of, 775, *775*

Woman Combing Her Hair (Archipenko), 700, *701*

Woman Combing Her Hair (González), 701, *701*

Woman I (de Kooning), 750, *750*

"Woman in the Year 2000" essay (Schneemann), 794

Woman with Dead Child (Kollwitz), 692, *693*

Woman with the Hat (Matisse), 687, *687,* 694

Wood, Grant, 743; work of, 733, *733*

Worker and the Collective Farmworker, The (Mukhina), 729, *729*

World Trade Center: Libeskind and, 789

World War I, 644, 685, 689, 692, 693; Futurists and, 704, 746

World War II, 729, 742, 745, 747, 765; devastation of, 746, 748, 776; postwar art, 793, 801

Wright, Frank Lloyd, 737, 743, 781, 801; influence of, 742; work of, 741–742, *741, 742,* 778–779, *779*

Wright, Joseph (of Derby), 597; work of, *590,* 591

Yoshihara, Jiro. *See* Gutai Bijutsu Kyokai

Young, La Monte: Fluxus art and, 793

Zapotec culture, 736

Zeus (Jupiter), xiii, 671, 672, 759; statue of, *xiii,* 606